Sick Schools

Sick Schools

Diagnosis, Cure, and Prevention of School Maladies

DAVID V. ANDERSON

RESOURCE *Publications* · Eugene, Oregon

SICK SCHOOLS
Diagnosis, Cure, and Prevention of School Maladies

Resource Publications
An Imprint of Wipf and Stock Publishers
199 W. 8th Ave., Suite 3
Eugene, OR 97401

www.wipfandstock.com

PAPERBACK ISBN: 978-1-5326-9686-2
HARDCOVER ISBN: 978-1-5326-9687-9
EBOOK ISBN: 978-1-5326-9688-6

Manufactured in the U.S.A.   12/31/19

This book, *Sick Schools,* is dedicated to the memory of its principal agent of inspiration, Milton Friedman.

Contents

Abstract

OUR STORY OF EDUCATION within western civilization starts before the printing presses of the 15th century. Then, most children were illiterate. Some learned in small groups or were tutored. Once printed books became more affordable, circa 1500, more students had access to them, but the numbers of teachers were limited- for obvious economic reasons. Group instruction fixed that mismatch. Soon, graded schools with group instruction were established- not really so much different than those of our own time, almost 500 years later.

In United States K-12 education, a student's age was traditionally used for the initial classroom placement that could later be adjusted by retention or double-promotion to align that pupil's placement with the his or her actual performance level. That has changed. Now we have social promotion in which students rise through the *grade* levels of a school without actually achieving grade level mastery. This means that report cards, transcripts and diplomas generally misrepresent the skill levels of students. Result: *Sick Schools* wherein many students perform below grade level. We have statistics for this within the United States from the *Nation's Report Card*, which has been in business since 1970. Reading and mathematics skills for the early 21st century are dire: In public schools well less than 50% are proficient in 8th grade, and by 12th grade less than 35% are proficient in both subjects. And it is much worse for history and civics. Sadly, private schools are not much better. What are the problems? Who should we hold responsible for this mess?

We could blame the teachers, books and instructional methods. And some reform efforts do that. Sometimes forgotten is the role that healthy economic incentives can play in improving things. Nobel Laureate economist Milton Friedman addressed this in the 1950's and proposed government funded vouchers that would give parents more control over their children's schooling. But do they work? Yes, but not all that well. Missing from that market is honest consumer information to replace the reality that schools lie to parents and others about their performance levels and other characteristics. Parents are somewhat complicit in this because they prefer hearing false good news more than the truthful bad news about their schools.

Looking deeper, there are a number of practices within schools that seem traditional, but are also corrupt and dishonest. This book discusses some promising instructional improvements, but makes the larger argument that a healthy economic marketplace for K-12 education is a fundamental prerequisite that will provide the incentives to develop the new methods, technologies, curricula and institutions that will, in turn, give its customers what they need and want. Given that vouchers alone, seem insufficient when parents have little accurate information about school quality, we must generate that information and get it into the right hands. We identify the culpable parties to this epidemic of sick schools and, though there are individual exceptions, no group in this list escapes responsibility: Parents, students, teachers, unions, school administrators, politicians, religious leaders and even the private sector of our economy. Finally, technological developments allow schools to be structured in more efficient styles, but it is rare to see them realized. That is ending. For-profit K-12 schools are coming on line. Some of them are the best in the USA. They are tuition efficient operating at about a 40% discount to the best non-profit K-12 schools. Education of our children can be less expensive and much better. We can have a new and Milton Friedman inspired Reformation of Sick Schools: The "Free to Choose" Reformation. To find out how, keep reading this book.

Foreword

Honest School Information Is Crucial for School Choice

SUPPORTERS OF EDUCATION REFORM who advocate government-funded choice mechanisms, such as vouchers, tend to argue the problems in our K-12 schools are primarily matters of economics and not directly of pedagogy. Our view, validated by much data, extends that concept and says the economic marketplace in which K-12 education operates needs more than vouchers to become a healthy sector of our American economy.

In recent years we have reviewed trends in the performance levels of private and public schools, as reported by the Nation's Report Card, and found a modest but significant correlation between student achievement and the level of competition created by the availability of school choice in the form of vouchers and/or charter schools. Where choice exists, student performance levels are improving faster than where it is absent.

Even so, the pace of student proficiency gains has been quite slow, indicating many decades will be required for these schools to reach proficient academic performance levels.

Obviously, that's not going to be good enough, so we must seek additional ways to energize the K-12 marketplace. An important missing ingredient is accurate consumer information that would enable parents and others to make wise choices in the selection of schools and other educational services. Currently, most parents and other stakeholders operate in a sea of misinformation about school performance levels and other school characteristics. Public schools in every state we reviewed routinely and pervasively lie about student proficiency levels. Typically, twice as many students are deemed proficient as are reported by the well-respected Nation's Report Card. In addition, proficiency numbers are not usually available at the school or district level, leaving parents and others in the dark as to the performance levels of their local schools.

Private schools, in contrast, tend to hide behind their unearned reputation of being superior to their public school neighbors. It is indeed rare to find a private school that publicizes its student performance levels. However, the Nation's Report Card tells us something about the national comparisons of public to private schools: When judged by how they educate the same economically disadvantaged demographic of children, the surprising results are that public schools and private schools are tied in mathematics, with each only educating about 20 percent of the eighth grade students to proficient levels. For reading, the private schools are somewhat better.

I believe getting good, honest school performance information into the hands of parents will energize K-12 school reform and bring the desired results. When parents are informed consumers, they will make better choices, and this will help invigorate the K-12 marketplace so the actual reforms will be nearly automatic. When this "informational" choice is combined with vouchers, parents and other stakeholders will know how to hold schools accountable for their results.

A problem here, however, is parents are not actively seeking such information about schools. Many parents are complacent and believe the propaganda that surrounds the schools. This suggests a need for additional remedies that will induce parents to want valid information about their local schools. Parents (and taxpayers) would surely be alarmed at the degradation of their schools if they knew the truth. There are several ways to induce them to seek out this information. One is to point out the scandals in K-12 education. The education system is rife with conflicts of interest hidden within longstanding traditions of American K-12 education. Reformers should identify these as corrupt practices and publicize them as such. Bad schools can be sued, and the notoriety of the lawsuits can garner attention.

The federal, state and local governments, at least when they are in the hands of serious reformers, can act to help in at least three different areas:

- They can enforce existing laws that would help improve schools.

- They can honor the treaty that gives parents "the right to choose the kind of education that shall be given to their children."

- The federal government can honor the U.S. Constitution by closing its Department of Education.

With regard to the first suggestion, existing state and local laws can be enforced. For example, in the area of juvenile criminal activity, enforcement is needed to deal with student on student assaults. As the author has seen in his own family, schools often do not punish perpetrators of physical violence nor do they report these crimes to the police- except in the most extreme cases.

As to the second proposal, they can enact legislation to establish more parental choices. For the public schools, each state should decentralize its governance structure to enable local districts much more control over school policies- including curricula and teacher certification standards. The public education system in the United States is becoming unquestionably totalitarian. Even some within the education establishment agree. Paul Pastorek, the former Louisiana superintendent of education, once told a Harvard audience, "Our education system is a communist system. . ." I was there and heard him say that and then heard him explain how schools under the former Soviet Union were run in essentially the same way as American public schools are operated today.

The third recommendation is based on the Constitution's 10th Amendment that precludes federal government activities in areas not "delegated to the United States by the Constitution . . ." The President could use an Executive Order to accomplish this. Courts might try to block that, but the president has the authority to interpret the Constitution differently than the courts—as Abraham Lincoln once did.

There is much schools can do. They can advertise using honest and sobering statistics. Those who homeschool can play a role, essentially through the grapevine. They can encourage other parents to be part-time homeschoolers by, at minimum, having their children tested independently of any school. Knowledge of those test results can spur competition as "word gets around."

International comparisons, when reported accurately by the media, can help. Religious groups surely want a good education for their members' children, so they too can play a role. Reformers can publicize new methods and best practices, such as online, self-paced instruction.

The beauty of informational choice is that it doesn't cost much. Private organizations can do it. Responsible operators of schools and other educational services also have an interest in providing this valuable consumer information through the use of honest and aggressive marketing.

But schools and their operators rarely advertise their offerings. This author made several efforts to encourage school operators and other players in the K-12 education sector to use his school performance estimates and data in advertising. No interest was shown.

What about such supposedly civic organizations like Chambers of Commerce, Kiwanis and Rotary? Would they help indirectly by sponsoring guidebooks containing accurate consumer information? We have tried to solicit their interest. No help from them. Not so far. Shame on them.

Now, who will step forward to get this started? This book, Sick Schools, has abundant information that reformers can use to get started. As the book says, parents and other stakeholders can *pester* the many responsible parties to take action.

Yes, you the reader can do something!

Author's Preface

I GREW UP IN Chicago, Illinois, and have lived in many regions of the United States, mostly in its coastal areas. I now reside in Massachusetts.

AUTHOR'S UNIQUE HISTORY LED TO AN EARLY APPRECIATION FOR ONLINE INSTRUCTION

Though not a certified or licensed expert in education, this author writes this book as one with considerable experience in the field. Not least among the formative periods of my life was the 25-year span of time during which I was either a full-time student or a high school teacher: 24 years and 1 year, respectively. I have what one might call a libertarian view of education—of what works and what doesn't. After those 25 years I found myself with a PhD in plasma physics. With that background, my career in research lasted another 22 years before I retired early and gradually worked my way back into the field of education.

A formative event in my high school career occurred in 1957: I was a student in a physics course taught over the television. Our public high school (Lane Technical High School in Chicago) participated in a pilot project of distance education in which approximately 100,000 students were enrolled nationally.

The course lacked the anywhere-anytime characteristics of today's online instruction, but it already showed how much better the distance education format could be as compared to traditional instructional formats. Having benefited personally from that early type of distance instruction, I can personally testify to the value it had for me. It was one of the ingredients that later led me to pursue a career in that same subject.

AUTHOR'S INTEREST IN SELF-PACED TUTORIAL INSTRUCTION

As one might guess from the foregoing, the in-class physics teacher, Mr. Rennison, was effectively a tutor. That is, he took questions, one-on-one, for about 10 minutes after each 30-minute television presentation.

Eight years later, in 1965, I was a teacher of physics and mathematics in a Catholic high school. In more recent years I have been a substitute teacher. I appreciate the tasks involved in conducting a traditional classroom of students, despite lacking the educator certifications possessed by many other teachers.

> Certifications or credentials in the education field are often an indication of relative incompetence, given the fact that the academic requirements are generally lower than for—let's say—a bachelor's degree in the same subject areas.

Furthermore, I understand how children can fall behind in such an environment unless concerted and sometimes costly efforts are made to remedy their deficits. This book, in part, is about finding those remedies. But instead of the school doing all of the lifting it often falls to the parent and other stakeholders to take on some of the responsibilities of helping these children *make the grade*.

Contemporary and traditional group instruction may be well paced for many children, but others will be frustrated by a pace that's either too fast to too slow. Obviously, the children who learn more slowly are the ones most likely to end up in the sub-proficient category, and that is what concerns us the most. It seems that the best remedy would be tutorial remedial instruction that would necessarily be delivered at the student's learning pace. When and where it is affordable, it would be preferred to group instruction—at least for the slower students. In recent years, under the *No Child Left Behind* legislation, some federal grants supported such remedial tutoring under the SES (Supplemental Educational Services) program.[1]

As my interests in online instruction developed, I realized that tutoring could be adapted to it. Would this combination be a good one to use in real schools? Home-schoolers were already using online instruction with the parent as the tutor. That inspired me to develop a plan to design, build, and establish a new kind of *brick and mortar* school that would automate the routine aspects of tutorial instruction through the use of online courseware while still keeping the human tutor in the schoolroom. In this design the students work in the schoolroom on computers while among them are human tutors who can help them when and where the online systems cannot. In this plan tutors either replace teachers or the teachers become tutors.

Lastly, and most importantly in this connection, the self-paced instruction implicit in an online instructional system allows the school to be organized without age-based student groupings. Each child advances at his or her own pace and receives certificates as the individual courses are mastered. This removes the possibility of social promotion, because age is no longer one of the criteria for determining student placement. If social promotion ends, then, almost by definition, every child will be placed in skill appropriate courses for which they have adequately mastered the prerequisite content and skills. Schools like this would be very good if not excellent.

Surely, we don't have these schools yet. Nevertheless, we can remedy many problems that students experience in the schools we have. Providing guidance on how to do that is a primary task of this book.

AUTHOR'S OTHER ACTIVITIES IN EDUCATION REFORM

After early retirement from my career in physics I became politically active and even ran for public office in California. When a ballot initiative campaign, Proposition 174, proposing statewide school vouchers, was undertaken in 1993, I joined the effort.[2] I showed up at nearly every meeting and soon was asked to direct the campaign's speakers' bureau for the San Francisco Bay Area. It was a wonderful experience working among many expert colleagues including such luminaries as former Secretary of Education, Bill Bennett and Nobel Laureate, Milton Friedman. It was Friedman who first proposed school vouchers in 1955. Seven years later, in 2000, another attempt, Proposition 38,[3] was made to enact a school voucher program in California. For that campaign I was hired to direct the speakers bureau statewide. But even that better managed and financed campaign found defeat at the polls.

> Milton Friedman first proposed school vouchers in 1955 in a report he wrote, "The Role of Government in Education," in *Economics, and the Public Interest.*[4] A year later he again proposed vouchers in a lecture he gave in June 1956 at Wabash College, Crawfordsville, Indiana. Finally, a printed version of these proposals can be found in his 1962 book *Capitalism, and Freedom.*[5]

Since 2003 I have often been working on projects for education reform that would not directly involve government schools. As an entrepreneur, I proposed the use of franchising to establish a for-profit management company that as a franchisor would run one or more networks of schools. Under franchising laws, the schools could have any of these ownership formats: Regular public, charter public, non-profit private, for-profit private or homeschool. Our planned system would use an online computer driven self-paced instructional program. This model would have considerable cost-savings—allowing schools to be operated at about half the cost of current schools. Asked once to describe this proposal in a few words I said, *"Kentucky Fried Education."* But the business plan for these Stellar Schools[6] was met with investor silence. If there had been more energetic competition among schools and school types, maybe investors would have come forward? Failing in that, I turned to work on plans to provide better consumer information to parents and other stakeholders about school quality. Again, very little interest. Other entrepreneurs with similar novel plans also met no support from the capitalists. Are they too smart to invest? Too stupid? Too threatened? Education reform is not easy. The late Admiral Hyman Rickover said that reforming

> . . . schools is like moving a cemetery.[7]

During this period, I formed an education consulting company, Asora Education Enterprises, through which I further developed the just mentioned business plans and also offered consulting services. Within the latter, I performed contract work for state level organizations in which local estimates were made of how each public school would perform on the *Nation's Report Card*. These estimates were based on an applied mathematics analysis technique I developed that allowed the exaggerated student performance results published by the states to be converted into more realistic numbers. Those results have been sobering.

I also delved into policy analysis. I wrote a number of op-ed pieces, sometimes alone and sometimes as co-author, about problems in our education systems. In two different periods I was a Senior Fellow for Education Research at what initially seemed to be prominent free-market oriented think tanks. But in each case, I was not in sync with the unprofessional practices of the organization, which is turn led me to resign. I wrote a booklet critical of the now, nearly defunct, *Common Core State Standards*.[8] I once had to deal with a disgruntled Republican governor of Rhode Island who didn't like having his state's testing results challenged and whose staff tried to block an editorial I had drafted on the topic. But it was published.[9]

We also published guidebooks to public and private schools in various jurisdictions. One concerned the public schools in Maryland, Virginia, and Washington D.C.[10] Four other prototypical guidebooks were completed for schools in:

- Bristol County, Massachusetts

- Shelby County, Tennessee

- Orange County, California

- The bi-state region of Rhode Island and Massachusetts[11]

I often thought that if had I the opportunity to do it over again I would have avoided physics and instead trained as an economist. I believe that a challenge in American K-12 education is the lack of economic incentives for reform. Had such incentives been in place my Stellar Schools might now be in operation?

AUTHOR'S SURVEY OF THE HISTORY OF EDUCATION

Though my expertise is far from that of a historian, I became interested in the history of group instruction. I knew it was an important aspect of the schools advocated by early American educator Horace Mann and I knew he was heavily influenced by the Prussian model of education. A few years ago, while browsing among books on the history of education in the Brown University Library, I found a book by a (late in the) nineteenth century educator, William Shearer, that provided two pieces of relevant insight:

- In the early sixteenth century, Martin Luther advocated the establishment of town schools in his area of what is now Germany in an effort to reduce the pervasive illiteracy in that era. With a more literate population, his advocacy of the laity reading the Bible would be helped. Prior to the Reformation, most children had received little schooling and those who did were often tutored. Tutoring would be too costly to implement Luther's plan so group instruction was used instead, as it was the only practical alternative. As schools grew in size, age-based class grouping evidently found favor, but Shearer provides few details.

- In his own time, circa 1890, Shearer was quite aware of the problems of students learning at various paces in group instructional schools. He developed a fairly complicated group instructional system, which he called *pliant grading*, that would better accommodate children's varying speeds of learning. He combined very short academic terms, as short as one-month, with a policy of retention that reportedly helped prevent children from falling behind. And in this system fast learning children could *gain time* and complete their schooling ahead of schedule. But his system was very complicated administratively and was never widely adopted.[12]

AUTHOR'S TWIN APPROACHES TO EDUCATION REFORM

I foresee two avenues to K-12 education reform:

- One is the development of superior instructional methods and supporting technologies.

- The other is the restructuring of the K-12 marketplace to make it robust, commercial, and competitive.

I believe that both are needed. As in other economic sectors, development is incentivized by the economic marketplace in which various providers compete to win and satisfy customers. When suitable incentives are there, the products and services will follow. And I believe *for-profit schools* are needed to make this happen.

My efforts to develop a franchising system of schools based on self-paced online instruction failed due to a lack of investment capital. The marketplace was broken. Who wants to go broke investing in such a sick industry? Had there been good marketing to attract parents and other customers to our schools, we believe that economic forces would have attracted capital, talent, and customers to enliven the education sector. This says that the two avenues just mentioned are not alternative. Rather both must be followed to find successful results. The legal framework for K-12 education needs to be enforced and reformed as well. Getting that framework right will enliven the K-12 economic sector to the benefit of most schoolchildren.

Acknowledgements

MANY INDIVIDUALS AIDED THIS project. Several are cited in the Endnotes. We are particularly grateful to those who read early drafts, gave comments, and guidance thereon. They include: Robin Anderson, Susan Anderson, Carl Brodt, Albert Cameron, Prof. Vincent Cannato, James Carroll, Dr. Robert Coli, Prof. Evan Crawford, Tanya Martin, Dr. Fred Nelson, Bret Schundler, Israel Teitelbaum, and Tom Waggoner. I apologize to others, not listed here, who contributed or were involved in other ways. I thank them too.

We thank owners of copyrighted materials for the permissions granted to us, including these:

- We thank Bob Adams of Bob Adams Photography, San Jose, California for the two photographs of schools in his area and for permission to use them in this book.

- We thank Erik Jacobson for permission to use the graph of "Average SAT Scores" in Figure 8, under the obligations of a Creative Commons copyright.

- We thank Michael Konshak, Curator of the International Slide Rule Museum, for permission to use the photograph of Professor Harvey White in his instructional television studio in Figure 13.

- We thank Kevin Teasley, President and founder of the Greater Educational Opportunities Foundation, who helped manage the 1993 Proposition 174 ballot initiative campaign in California, for permission to use two images from the campaign—one of a campaign button and one of a poster.

- We thank John Corbett of Corbett Photography, Middletown, Rhode Island for the two photographs of Mikhail Gorbachev with his interpreter and the author and for permission to use them in this book.

Preview

As IMPORTANT AS K-12 education is to our American culture, society, and families, it is a troubled part of Americana to which insufficient attention has been paid. This is not to say that there are not large numbers of concerned stakeholders who know that something is wrong with our K-12 systems of education. Rather we are saying that a large number of reform minded players in this game have not been able to see the *big picture*. Instead they tend to be caught up in aspects of the *smaller pictures* from which they often draw erroneous conclusions. In turn, they make well-intentioned proposals for changing the products and services of K-12 education, but fail to see that the larger marketplace for this sector is broken. That says:

> Houston, we have a problem with the K-12 spacecraft. Its economics rocket booster is losing thrust.

With that understanding, our approach here is firstly, to review the methods and economics of K-12 education, and secondly, to propose what combination of these will likely lead to the academic improvements we seek.

We don't plan to review the entire history of schooling, but rather discuss those developments in that history that are relevant to the problems we see in today's systems of education—particularly here in the United States.

GAMUT OF SCHOOL SPECIES

Before getting into the details of how we came to have Sick Schools, let's take a quick peek at five kinds of schools that run the gamut from worst to best. The last four of this group provide us reformers considerable encouragement.

We begin with *Hope High School* in Providence, Rhode Island—not far from the author's home. As the nearby photo suggests, it was built by a for-profit firm and is a functioning well-maintained structure. Its students are taught by unionized public school teachers who are not part of a for-profit firm. The building does a good job of housing these students. Its teachers and administrators do a poor job educating these young people, but then socially promote and graduate them anyway.[13]

Under any fair comparison, it is widely acknowledged that public charter schools are generally better that their regular district public school counterparts. Our second example is of this type. It is *The Advanced Math and Science Academy (AMSA)* of Marlborough, Massachusetts shown below. AMSA was built by capitalists and is a functioning well-maintained structure. Its students are taught by non-unionized public school teachers who are hired and fired on the basis of merit. Its high school uses mostly Advanced Placement Courses for which official testing is administered by the independent College Board that controls AP courses in the United States. Guess what? On Massachusetts's standardized MCAS tests, in recent years the school had the highest proficiencies of any public high school in the state: 100% proficient in mathematics and 100% proficient in reading. Or about 91% proficient as estimated for the Nation's Report Card.[14]

Homeschooling is next. Children in this Pennsylvania home, shown below, are homeschooled. Yes, this house was built by a for-profit firm. Their teachers are not paid, but are motivated by love of their own children. In their *Classical Conversations*® homeschooling curriculum, children are immersed in a Christian philosophy as they learn from a rigorous combination of instructional materials—including Latin. They learn from their parent teacher, they learn from other parents teaching in the program, they learn from online courses, and they learn from their homeschooled peers in weekly plenary sessions. We know this as these pupils are four of the author's and his wife's grandchildren. Homeschooled children generally outperform non-profit private school students. Only the for-profit schools seem to do better.[15]

A for-profit middle school, *Challenger School* of Newark, California is shown below. It was built by a for-profit firm and is a functioning well-maintained structure. Its students are taught by private school teachers who are employees of a for-profit enterprise. The teachers and administrators of this school do a wonderful job educating these young people, as evidenced by their percentile rankings. For its 8th graders and

those from its other 25 school campuses combined, in 2017 they had 98th percentile rank for the composite score on the Iowa Test of Basic Skills (ITBS), as compared to all 8th graders nationally (who had 50th percentile). Their 98th percentile is up from 93rd—almost 20 years earlier in 1998.[16]

Basis Independent Silicon Valley, of San Jose, California is shown below. This high school was built by a for-profit firm and is a functioning well-maintained structure. Its students are taught by private school teachers who are employees of a for-profit enterprise. The teachers and administrators of this school do a wonderful job educating these young people—as evidenced by its high school SAT scores: Highest in the United States. It's curriculum is based on a combination of the world's most complete academic standards, which include Advanced Placement content standards. Social promotion is prohibited and teachers are hired based on academic subject area expertise. The tuition charges are about 40% lower and its student performance levels are somewhat higher than those of the top rated non-profit preparatory high schools. The company is Basis Schools, Inc. It is also a for-profit EMO operator of over two dozen charter schools. The top five charter high

schools in the United States are operated by Basis Schools, Inc. Comparing them to the Advanced Math and Science Academy (AMSA), that we described above, shows AMSA in 20th place nationally. Who profits here? Surely the owners and surely the students. QED[17]

One of the author's colleagues commented that the preceding five paragraphs, in his opinion, were nearly as important as the other 400-odd pages of the book.[18] Why belabor the difficulties—ailments—of our current crop of public and private schools when we already have a good idea of what a reformed K-12 education system would resemble? Our answer to that challenge is to acknowledge what you might call societal inertia. K-12 education will not have the incentives to improve unless the evidence of its failure is overwhelming. To provide that "evidence" we need to understand how we arrived at this threshold of reform and to gain that understanding we need both historical and scientific perspectives. When and where should we pick up the relevant narrative?

HISTORY AND PROMISE OF K-12 EDUCATION

Our story begins as the Medieval Period is ending. The venue is Europe and the year is 1450. The printing press had not yet been invented. Only a tiny fraction of families or schools could afford books for children. The only books available were those copied by scribes—usually monks copying religious and philosophical tracts. Absent were the kinds of schools that we take for granted such as grade schools.

Yet, teaching children about the world around them was not a new activity. Teaching them about the skills they needed to survive and prosper in that world certainly predated the historical record. In that Medieval Period the schooling of children was very limited and generally only the wealthiest families could afford any kind of basic instruction for them. Even as now, there were two distinct instructional models for teaching pupils in their academic subjects: Tutoring and group instruction. Both have probably been in existence since prehistoric times. Group instruction was evidently rare until the printing press enabled it after 1455 and soon thereafter the Protestant Reformation demanded its spread—the latter influence being felt since about 1530.

Part I: The history of western European schools since Gutenberg and Luther: 1450–1895

One of the key issues of the Protestant Reformation was the reformers' interest in allowing and encouraging the laity to read the Bible. A major impediment to that goal was the widespread illiteracy in the population.

In that time, Martin Luther,[19] in Wittenberg; John Calvin,[20] in Geneva; and Huldrych Zwingli,[21] in Zurich, among other Protestant reformers, advocated the establishment of compulsory education to reduce illiteracy—consistent with their beliefs that all people should be able to read the Bible. These reformers also understood that elevating literacy would bring other practical benefits that would, among other things, make for a more prosperous society. For example, in an attempt to interest government leaders in establishing public education Luther said,

> My dear sirs, if we have to spend such large sums every year on guns, roads, bridges, dams, and countless similar items to ensure the temporal peace and prosperity of a city, why should not much more be devoted to the poor neglected youth?[22]

Because tutoring was extremely expensive, teaching children in groups was really the only practical option if large numbers were to be educated. Placing children in mastery-based classes provided sufficient economies of scale to make it an affordable option for communities. This required education on a much larger scale than had been previously seen. The first record (we could find) of organized class instruction was in Strasbourg in about 1537 under a Luther colleague Johannes Sturm.[23] His school had nine grades corresponding to ascending skill levels. Schools structured like that became known as *Graded schools.*

In the next few centuries graded schools expanded most rapidly in the Protestant lands. They thrived particularly in the Lutheran regions of Prussia, in Calvinistic Netherlands, and also in the French Protestant regions of Switzerland. As the religious and economic benefits of Protestant schools became more evident, groups within the Roman Catholic Church began to establish schools in Catholic regions of Europe. The Jesuit order was the most active in that quest. As a result of that delayed development, Catholic literacy rates lagged those of Protestant regions of Europe and didn't catch up until near the end of the nineteenth century. Historians also found that regions of higher literacy also had higher economic output.

In Switzerland, educator Pestalozzi founded a graded school in Burgdorf, northeast of Bern, in 1799.[24] His methods impressed many outside of Switzerland including the Prussian Minister of Education, Wilhelm von Humboldt, who subsequently included some of these practices in Prussian schools.[25] Graded public schools were established relatively slowly in England, probably due to its slow adoption of Protestant culture. In the case of American schools, it was the Prussian models of both public education and age-based group instruction that were widely copied during the first half of the nineteenth century.

Pestalozzi also advocated for a child-centered system of education in which children chose their educational paths according to their natural interests. Also known as a type of *progressive education*, many school systems adopted aspects of its format though the various practical aspects of managing schools limited the extent to which schools could actually be significantly controlled by the whims of their students. Of all the grade levels in most contemporary twenty-first century American schools it is kindergarten where the progressive format is most evident. On that note, we also believe that there is too much progressive emphasis and not enough academics in contemporary kindergarten programs.

Over these centuries, graded schools were not placed in areas where the student populations were sparse and for them ungraded schools—like a one-room schoolhouse—were operated. There, multiple academic tracks had to coexist within the classroom. Using the more advanced children to help teach the less skilled pupils became common. In the late eighteenth century that practice was perfected in a new kind of cost-effective school using the Monitorial systems separately devised by Joseph Lancaster[26] and Andrew Bell.[27]

Part II: The history of American schools since the Pilgrims' arrival: 1620–1950

The Mayflower and other ships brought Calvinistic Puritans to North America in and after 1620. Following the patterns of their Calvinistic brethren in Europe they soon established schools in the Massachusetts Bay Colony, starting in 1635. In doing that, Massachusetts soon had laws compelling attendance at schools and establishing a minimum curriculum, including reading and religion. The colonial government also established primary schools in most towns and grammar (middle) schools in the larger towns.

As student populations grew, teachers needed help educating increasing numbers of pupils in their classrooms. Teaching assistants were needed and many schools adopted the Monitorial system of Joseph Lancaster (just mentioned) as a way to educate large classrooms of students of varying ages and skills.

Despite their existence in Europe since 1538, graded schools were not copied in the English colonies of North America until their benefits were better understood by the United States in the early decades of the nineteenth century. In that period, they prominently took root in Massachusetts and also Ohio. The large numbers of children in rural areas required that many schools had to remain ungraded. Late nineteenth century educators, such as New Jersey public education leader William Shearer, drew on their own experiences with both types of schools to devise strategies to remedy the problems of slow learners in graded schools. Without actually using the terminology of self-pacing that was essentially their goal.

There are three different kinds of schooling formats that drew advocates since the eighteenth century:

- Progressive formats in which students had more say over curricula and the pacing of instruction.
- Centralized systems with uniform curricula controlled by the political system.
- Market sensitive systems in which parents choose the curricula and other features.

Of these three types, and since 1948, the *United Nations Universal Declaration of Human Rights (UNDHR)* requires the third bullet item for all signatories of the treaty.[28] We will discuss this in more detail in Chapter 6. With respect to the second bullet item, the treaty also allows some curricular components to be under some political control of the country. The United States is bound by this agreement. But we ignore it. Why?

Prior to the 1950s there were many kinds of improvements that were technologically feasible and available to remedy some of the problems of graded schools. We consider three kinds of improvements for graded schools:

1. Those that apply to all skill levels of students.
2. Those that apply to students in need of remedial instruction.
3. Those that apply to students who can skip ahead at a faster pace.

In the first of these categories many of the improvements hardly need any mention: Better teachers, better books, better instructional strategies, new kinds of homework policies, better testing, financial incentives, and the reduction of social promotion are among the avenues that can benefit all students.

For the second and third categories, additional services are needed to provide these students the additional learning they need to keep up or get ahead. Traditional means for doing this include summer school, after school programs, and even tutoring. Other ideas for helping these pupils could include Saturday school, part-time homeschooling, peer tutoring as well as special textbooks that focus on remediation or advanced topics.

Summer school is interesting. It can be regarded as an augmentation for students in the first and third categories while for those in the second category it is more of a remedial intervention. A number of research studies have shown it has particular value for mathematics instruction because without it during the summer pupils actually forget some of the math learned in the previous academic year. Given that fact, summer instruction in math should be considered every year and for all students regardless of skill levels.

Part III: Distress signals in K-12 education: 1951–2019

As in Part II, which covered American K-12 education up to 1950, we here continue that story except we concentrate more on the message in the book's title, particularly we focus on the word *diagnosis*. We then look at the symptoms our K-12 schools are having—including troubles in private schools.

Broad measures of K-12 health over this 69-year interval show lackluster performance of public school students based on standardized testing in which most pupils are performing one or more grade levels below their enrollment levels. And private school students aren't much better according to properly controlled testing comparisons. We believe that a fairly conducted testing regime reports on comparable demographic groups. In our studies, we compare performance levels of economically disadvantaged students who attend these private or public K-12 schools. Doing that removes the wealth effect that would otherwise make the private schools look better than they really are.

Another way to gauge the health of K-12 education is to consider it as an economic sector of the national economy. Over the last half century, all of the US private economic sectors have shown productivity increases. It's a measure of how much value each worker produces each year. According to the U.S. Labor Department, the private economy has its productivity up by a factor of 5, adjusted for inflation, over the past seven decades. In consumer electronics, your TV set is over 200 times less expensive per unit screen area than what we had 70 years ago. Where is K-12 education? As an economic sector, it has gone nowhere. Its productivity has actually gone down, about 4% since 1989, according to the Labor Department.

A properly educated graduate from K-12 schooling should have basic skills in mathematics and reading while exhibiting a basic knowledge of the other subjects that enable him or her to be a good future citizen as well as a good future worker in the American economy. The subjects of religion, history, and civics are among them. Why religion? Isn't that controversial or even illegal within the public schools? No, there are legal ways to teach *about* religion and without it included in the curriculum the students are left ignorant of its influence in other areas of life—including history and science. Moreover, the just mentioned treaty, the UNDHR, also encourages signatory nations to educate children about history and religion.

When we look at reported performance levels in history and civics we find that American high school students are grossly incompetent in these areas. High school seniors, we can say, are *dumb* in reading, *dumber* in civics, and *exceedingly stupid* in U.S. history. That is how we label the 12th grade proficiencies reported by the *Nation's Report Card* for these subjects: 35%, 25%, and 12% respectively. Over the twentieth century, American history instruction evolved from a traditional and patriotic narrative to politically correct presentations that are both inaccurate and often subversive of the United States government. The newer history curricula often suffer from the practice of *presentism* in which events of earlier eras are judged by the mores and ethics of modern times. American culture is but one culture to consider under the doctrines of multiculturalism. From that, U.S. history suffers as the stories of other cultures crowd out the textbook pages ordinarily devoted to the relevant events that contributed to this country's development. The emphasis is clearly that of the political left. For parents who want their children to receive a balanced account of American history they have few alternatives if they can't afford enrollment in a private school that actually provides a rigorous and traditional portrayal of our history.

Such parents would have an alternative if the, just mentioned, *United Nations Universal Declaration of Human Rights* and its *Article 26* were enforced by U.S. authorities. Those rights include this provision in its *subparagraph (3)*:

> Parents have a prior right to choose the kind of education that shall be given to their children.

Article 26 also requires signatory countries to promote human rights, basic freedoms, good international relations, and good relations among different religions. Under terms of that treaty, to which the United States is a signatory, our government is legally bound to enforce this right. Unfortunately, supporting legislation has never been enacted. That neglect puts the United States into the status of being an outlaw. Is the USA thereby a crook? Many other countries, including many in Europe, have taken steps to honor these rights and *Article 26*. But not us.

In K-12 education there are often practices regarded as traditional that under closer inspection involve conflicts of interest and corruption. The mere fact that schools control their own testing systems has led to easy grading to make themselves look far better than they really are. Sometimes, educators are involved in criminal activities such as bribery, embezzlement, and other schemes. When caught they are infrequently prosecuted, and when convicted the punishments are often light.

Then there are teachers unions. They often go on strike. But they often have no right to strike when that is actually contrary to the state constitutions under which they work. No less than twentieth century American President Franklin Roosevelt believed that they, and other government employees have no such legal right.[29]

Political efforts by public educators often harm private schools and particularly for-profit enterprises working in K-12 education.

This picture, just described, is one of degradation. If we had the right combination of technologies, methodologies, and incentives, nearly all of the cited problems could be addressed. In theory we do have that combination, but we are lacking the committed players needed to push their use forward.

Part IV: Repair or replace K-12 education or some of both: 1951–2030

Here we move on to review what is in our arsenal of tools that can be used to improve K-12 education. There are new technologies that are almost all based on video and computer developments. Video and its constant companion audio, first in the form of synchronous broadcast television, later in the form of cable television made significant progress during the first few decades of this period. Then came asynchronous modes of video delivery, including video tapes, DVD, and other computer/Internet based media. Most, but not all computer-generated instruction is accessed through the Internet while some of it comes from hard media such as flash drives, CDs and DVDs. The content from these newer technologies looks better in color video, and that content can be provided, on demand, much less expensively than before. It particularly allows on-demand asynchronous transmission of information that is quite valuable in efforts to provide students with self-paced instruction.

There are also newer methodologies that have been introduced since 1951. Many of them are based on history's oldest instructional format, that of tutoring. Enabled, in part, by asynchronous delivery technologies, teachers no longer need to instruct age-based groups within a classroom. Instead, they can have the instruction delivered from the textbook and from the video options while morphing themselves from teacher to tutor to enable one-on-one assistance for students seeking help. Sometimes, in what is called a blended environment, teachers can efficiently instruct smaller sub-groups of students while simultaneously having the remaining students work online, on computers, or simply read from old-fashioned textbooks. One of the most promising new instructional formats is that of flipped-blended. In that arrangement, students receive their instruction online when they are at home and then interact with their tutor or teaching assistant to complete their assignments at school. Flipped blended means no homework! Students like that until they realize that it means doing that work at the school site.

With all these promising technological and methodological developments since 1951, it is puzzling and disappointing to find very few tangible benefits such as improved student performance on standardized tests. As an economic sector, K-12 education exhibits distress and stagnation. The incentives for using novel tools have been lacking or stymied. To reform and improve K-12 education requires its stakeholders to build those incentives.

Incentives are probably best understood by economists and a few free-market oriented economists knew what to do or at least what to try. Nobel laureate Milton Friedman was one of them. In 1955, he advocated for government funded scholarships, also known as school vouchers. They would foster incentives for schools to compete. It wasn't until 1990 that vouchers were first implemented in Milwaukee. That frightened the public education establishment. From that fear of vouchers a compromise was developed in the advent of charter schools that also expand parental choices, though perhaps not to the same degree as vouchers. Research into these choice mechanisms has shown that school vouchers are popular with parents, but have produced only minor improvements in the skills of the children using them. Charter schools are also popular.

Asora's own research has shown, based on data published by the *Nation's Report Card*, that by 2013 public schools had improved enough in mathematics to by then equal the performance levels of private schools when the comparison is done fairly. And they were closing the reading gap. There was still something missing from the K-12 marketplace. What has been missing was good consumer information for the parent customers in that marketplace. Without it, many parents used vouchers for private schools that were, on average, no better than their former public schools. We, at Asora, have been offering guidebooks and other informational resources to give parents and other consumers this information. Sadly, we have had very little interest shown in this. Apathy seems to reign in K-12 education. How can that be ended?

As we were nearly finished with this book's manuscript, we learned of a relatively new for-profit school company, Basis Schools, Inc, of Scottsdale, Arizona. They have a handful of company owned for-profit schools and they are a for-profit operator of over two-dozen charter schools. According to more than one rating service, this company has the best charter school in the United States as well as the next four runners up. One of its company owned for-profit schools is not only the best high school in the United States, but some say the best in the world—eclipsing schools in China that previously had that honor. The bottom line here is also financial. Its for-profit schools *operate at a 40% discount* to its best non-profit rivals.

As we go farther along into Part V we shall discuss what various kinds of stakeholders can do to improve the marketplace for K-12 education. Yes, what can they do to end the apathy and degradation.

Windup: Conclusions and Afterword on Socialism and Capitalism in K-12 education

As we go on to wrap-up our story about fixing *Sick Schools* we try to be the metaphorical physician who takes this seriously. We want to uphold the *Hippocratic Oath* and thus *Do No Harm*.[30] As we go on to study what can be done to help these schools, both public and private, we will strive to ensure that the research we do to find solutions, itself, does *No Harm*. We do that understanding that if we do nothing, there will be much *Harm* done in these K-12 systems of schools.

We then present a menu of reform proposals, but don't get much into the details. There are many remedies to be considered. But please bear in mind that this author is not an expert within every nook and cranny of education reform. While we have discussed some of the reforms that could be tried in earlier chapters of this book, we instead direct our focus on the reformers themselves. Among the stakeholders of K-12 education we ask who should be *hired* as specialists to formulate and carry out the details of school reform? In doing that, we talk about which stakeholders should be encouraged or even *pestered* to take up these challenges.

If there is a common theme to our reform proposals it is that of using market forces to provide the incentives for reform. We admonish reformers to say, "*no*," to the socialists of public education. We look at successes in other areas of human need where government help is a necessity for those who can't afford fulfillment of that requirement. So, for example, the need for food is helped by the Food Stamp program. We suggest that the demand for K-12 education (not quite as important as nutrition) could be similarly fulfilled by a new Education Stamp program.

Based on the wishful thinking and theory that reader fatigue has not yet set in, we finish the book with an *Afterword* segment containing two essays: One is titled *Socialism and Schools* followed by another considerably shorter (and sweeter) one *Capitalism and Schools*. Ponder this: All of the physical objects in public schools are produced by capitalists. It seems that in that context, we don't trust the government to produce things? It is only the instructional program that is government run. Can it be trusted to do that? Why can't a for-profit enterprise do that? Finally, we arrive at the place where the readers are presented with eight avenues of reform and then rallied to get involved. Readers should consider doing something to help—even if it is only to *pester* others into action.

PART I

European Schools: 1450–1895

IF AMERICAN PUBLIC AND private schools are diagnosed as sick in our own time in the early twenty-first century, why is it necessary to begin our story more than half a millennium earlier? The answer: It hinges on the enormous revolution in the storage of human knowledge brought about by the invention of the printing press first by Johannes Gutenberg and then by many others who further developed the technology of printing. The resulting numerical explosion in the accessibility of books helped trigger the Protestant Reformation and its focus on literate Bible readers. In turn, that fostered group instruction in graded schools that soon followed. Not only that, but the printing revolution introduced the freedom for a student or anyone to *self-pace* their learning. Thus, this concept of self-pacing that we often regard as a contemporary feature of our modern technology-based society has been with us now for over 550 years. This encourages us to begin our study in the late Medieval Period as we do here. Welcome to 1450.

Part I is composed of four chapters, entitled:

1. Gutenberg and Luther: They Co-author Reformation
2. Public and Private Schools Grow in Western Europe
3. European Literacy and Wealth Since Gutenberg
4. Pestalozzian Problems

The history of education in ancient times is also important to understanding its evolution in Europe. The late education analyst and historian, Andrew Coulson, started his analysis with a first century Roman lawyer, Pliny the Younger. For a more complete review of education in the first two millennia we recommend his book *Market Education—The Unknown History.*[31] You could read that first and then return here?

One of the themes in this book is that of the importance of economic incentives in the development of education. We'll see that Martin Luther had some insight into such incentives as he proposed the twin goals of educating children: Those of religious training and of better training for other vocations. Both goals have been advanced over the intervening 500 years since his time. When workers are more skilled and more efficient in their employment, the inevitable result is more production of the things and services that they offer. As will be evident, those lands that achieved higher rates of literacy, through education, also gained in wealth at a more rapid pace than those territories that remained relatively illiterate.

While the earlier improvements in education were primarily associated with the Protestant Reformation, the schooling in Roman Catholic areas of Europe also improved significantly after a relatively slow start. By the end of Part I, in 1895, schools in the Catholic areas were roughly on par with those in Protestant regions.

As these trends were being established on the European continent, schools were soon being introduced into North America—primarily in the British colonies that later formed the United States of America. That story will be taken up in Part II.

CHAPTER 1

Gutenberg and Luther

They Coauthor Reformation

As our story begins, we find the education of children at a crossroads. Prior to that time, very few children learned from the written word. Rather they learned from oral instruction from their teachers and parents. That status soon changed, rather abruptly, as the result of the printing revolution ushered in by Gutenberg.

MEDIEVAL EDUCATION BEFORE GUTENBERG

Throughout the history of Western Civilization, including medieval times, a constant component of the education of youth has been the oral delivery of information. A teacher or tutor would instruct students using a monologue or interactive dialogue format. Throughout the Medieval Period a much less common component of education was written material. Such documents were extraordinarily costly to produce because they were handwritten—think of monks copying the Bible.

In fact, according to historian Michelle Ho, prior to Gutenberg's printing press of the 1450s, it generally took a monk four years of labor to copy one complete Bible.[32] In terms of modern era wages of office clerks of let's say about $30,000 per year this suggests that the labor cost of one Bible would be about $120,000. Adding in the costs of ink, paper, and those of maintaining their scriptorium workplace would push that cost higher, perhaps near $140,000. Some medieval towns did not have the money to purchase and own even one Bible. A more affluent town might have one Bible in its church or cathedral—generally chained to the wall to prevent theft. That one book would be the only one available to clergy and laity alike.

So then, what was a primary school like? As now, schools existed to satisfy community and national needs. Commerce and the church, then the Roman Catholic Church, needed educated boys, later men, who would be needed in those vocations.

In medieval times the only western European language that was in common use, both commercially and for church business, was Latin. Thus, the instruction was in Latin. Given the divisions of labor between the sexes in that era, little effort was made to educate girls.

In that era, most primary schools were run by the Roman Catholic Church. Some were called Cathedral schools and others were called Monastic schools. The former trained boys to become eligible for further training as clergy or as workers in the commercial sectors. The latter was exclusively focused on training clergy.

The curriculum taught was known as the trivium—for the three subject areas of emphasis:

- Latin grammar

- Logic

- Rhetoric[33]

The students had no books and the teachers often had none. Thus, the common instructional format was that of oral recitation. Listen to the teacher and repeat what he said. Failure to master or memorize the curriculum was generally *corrected* with some sort of corporal punishment.

THE GUTENBERG REVOLUTION

We use the word *revolution* to represent the fact that the cost of printed books fell dramatically with the development and use of the new printing presses, first invented by Johannes Gutenberg in the 1450s. It then became possible for students to have access to books even if they did not own any. Perhaps more important: Their teachers could then use books to gather and recite the information needed for the subjects being taught.

> The name Gutenberg was actually the family name of Johannes's mother. His father's family name of Gensfleisch—gooseflesh in English—was apparently an embarrassment to him. So, he used "mom" Gutenberg's last name instead.

The cost of books fell a hundred-fold.

Once Gutenberg's printing press and others were in operation it took only about 0.04 man-years of labor to produce one Bible instead of the 4.00 *monk* years described above.[34] The combined productivity increases of labor and capital was a then phenomenal factor of about 100. That brought the typical cost of a Bible, post Gutenberg, to about $1,400 per book—that's in 2019 dollars.

Since Gutenberg's press was developed in 1455, about 45 years before the end of the Medieval Period in 1500, there was little time in that interval to make books widely available for educational use. Moreover, at the relatively lower cost of $1,400 per book it was still quite expensive to use them. The teacher might have one, but the students would not have had them, except perhaps to borrow them for brief periods or use them directly under the supervision of a teacher.

Still, there were opponents to this printing revolution.[35] Scribes, working in scriptoriums, objected to the threat it posed to their livelihoods. Some aristocrats opposed the new printing industry, largely because it threatened to devalue their libraries that were assembled at great cost. Politicians and clergy feared their opponents and detractors who would be able to print subversive and/or heretical ideas. Yet, none of these opponents were able to stop the rapid adoption of printing.

In this new environment students had more access to books, whether owned or borrowed. With them they could read ahead and beyond their teachers' oral presentations.[36] Perhaps more importantly, they could review lessons already presented for purposes of remediation and clarification.

The birth of self-pacing?

The idea that a student could control some aspects of what material would be studied and when it would be studied marks what we would call the birth of self-pacing. Even though this may seem like a minor change, it was a watershed for the student who needed some extra review or who wanted to read ahead.

Extending this line of thought, printing led to significant collections of books in libraries. This development changed the roles of the teachers and professors within the schools and universities. Students could learn from the books with or without the help of the teacher. In the context of libraries, printing had a new status. Printing, in the words of historian Will Durant, had become

> . . . the greatest and cheapest of all universities, open to all.[37]

Surely, even with these much less expensive books, they remained far too expensive for the kind of availability typical of our modern era. Think of it this way: The Bible was by then far cheaper than before, but at $1,400 per book was still considerably more expensive than modern era Bibles that sell in the range of $14 and higher. The Gutenberg Revolution gave us *a penny on the dollar* reduction in book costs over the span of a few decades. It then took over 500 years to get the next *penny on the dollar* drop in prices. The former benefit was, as we say, *revolutionary*, while the latter was more on the scale of *evolutionary.*

Will Durant's quote exposes an irony for the author:

> I used the Brown University Library to perform some of the research for this book. The charge to me for one year's library use has been $75. I have had access to almost the same knowledge for this pittance than any student at Brown who would pay an annual tuition in the range of $50,000 for this same library access plus the lectures, and testing services from the Brown University professorate. Are good professors worth this difference of $49,925 per year?

Thus, the Gutenberg Revolution led to a remarkable increase in printed materials and the resulting spread of knowledge. It surely must have caught the eye of Martin Luther (1483–1546). We discuss that next.

LUTHERAN REVOLUTION

The many changes in Christian life that came from the Protestant Reformation included more emphasis on primary education. One premise of the Reformation was the goal of having a literate laity able to read the Bible for themselves. Martin Luther and others were instrumental in improving schools to those ends.[38]

As the Reformation was getting underway, Luther was discouraged by what he saw in the schools in his area of Germany. Only a small fraction of the population was learning to read, and the existing schools were of poor quality. He had this to say on grammar schools previously run by the Catholic Church: They taught the student

> only enough bad Latin to become a priest and read Mass . . .[39]

Luther was very upset about the universities of his era. He said,

> . . . nothing could be more wicked, or serve the devil better, than unreformed universities . . . I greatly fear that the universities are nothing, but wide-open gates leading to Hell.[40]

Luther's theology was one of individual responsibility for receiving God's grace, while in contrast the Roman Catholic Church believed more in a collective responsibility for salvation.[41] Thus in the Catholic system only a few clerics needed to be educated.

Luther had two considerations that motivated him to expand the literacy of his countrymen:

- He wanted to save souls and keep them out of the Devil's hands. This meant that children and others, should be taught to read, and in particular be able to read the Bible.

- He wanted people to have the skills needed to contribute to the material needs of their families and society.

On the first point Luther had this to say,

> Every human being, by the time he has reached his tenth year, should be fa-
> miliar with the Holy Gospels, in which the very core and marrow of his life is
> bound.[42]

And on the second point he said,

> Were there neither soul, heaven, nor hell, it would still be necessary to have
> schools for the sake of affairs here below...

To Luther these needs were not out of reach. He knew that the Reformed churches wouldn't be paying *taxes* to the Roman Catholic Church hierarchy. Some of those taxes were in the form of the detested indulgences.

These indulgences were payments to the Roman Catholic Church that guaranteed the payer a reservation in heaven according to the church doctrine of that period. This corrupt practice, perhaps more than any other, led Luther to his proposals for reform.

Keeping that money *in town* would and did, provide new revenues to the local parishes. Thus, the Protestant towns had money for schools. He put it this way: They have the required money,

> ... since Divine Grace has released them from the exactions and robbery of
> the Roman Church.[43]

So where was he to start? Maybe look for a Reformed parish where a reading program could be established? The German town of Leisnig seemed to be a good candidate for this.

It was 1522, only five or six years into the early period of the Reformation, when Luther urged that town's authorities to require each head of household to read the Bible to his children and servants.[44] The project failed, but not because householders were inexcusably shirking their obligations. It failed because very few of them in Leisnig were literate. You can't read to your children if you can't read!

It was time for *Plan B.*

LUTHER AND MELANCHTHON
INVENT PUBLIC SCHOOLS

Plan B: So, at about seven years into the early period of the Reformation, in 1524, Luther and his theological colleague Philip Melanchthon sent letters to the civil authorities in numerous German towns and cities[45]. The letter called for the establishment of schools in which a new requirement would be imposed: Attendance would be compulsory. His motivation for this was more theological than economic: He saw an educated citizenry as an effective counterforce to the Devil. His Biblical support for this claim may have been found in II Timothy 2:16 where St. Paul writes,

> But shun profane and vain babblings, for they will increase unto more
> ungodliness.[46]

In our common parlance the "not from" the Bible proverb about the *idle mind* is
similar,

> The idle mind is the Devil's workshop.

A corollary to his theological hypothesis is that an occupied mind will conceive of and
produce economic as well as religious benefits. This seems obvious when a child is prepared for adulthood by an education that increases his or her skills that can be put to
use in the production of goods and services. As we saw above, Luther also sought the
here below economic benefits of better-educated Christians. But his essential business
was that of saving souls and it was the salvation of everyone's soul that primarily drove
him to mandate compulsory school attendance. If the motive were only economic,
he might have sought to educate only a subset of children—those deemed capable of
vocational benefits. Thus, when someone's economic benefits are shared with others
that too can be considered as a Christian act of charity or benevolence.

In the years before the Reformation, he had seen the schools of higher education,
the universities, as anti-Christian and pro-pagan. To remedy this, he worked with
Philip Melanchthon, who was his principal theological collaborator, to plan changes
to the schools in their regions of Germany. Under Luther's direction, Melanchthon
proposed the *Shulplan* in 1527. He organized the writing of textbooks on grammar
and other subjects and established administrative systems for the operations of the
schools. Melanchthon was so successful at this that he eventually became known as
the *Educator of Germany*.[47]

These plans would have been far too expensive to implement had the costs of
books remained at their pre-Gutenberg levels. However, with the dramatically increased availability of affordable books, including textbooks, such schools became
feasible.

Luther and his cadre of reformers were well aware that government policies and
edicts needed enforcement. In their time, a force of inspectors was sent out to make
reports on compliance of the various institutions under their supervision: Schools,
churches, universities etc. In the euphemistic parlance of their day, these inspectors
were titled *visitors*—a nice sounding label. In one case, a *visitor* wrote this about a
German town:

> ...the churches are half empty while the taverns are full.[48]

We optimistically see this comment as a case of the *glass half-full*. Had the visitor's
program not existed the churches in that town might have been three-quarters empty?

Historian Friedrich Paulsen claimed that the many universities that aligned
themselves as Protestant institutions promoted a

. . . spirit of freedom and independence of thought [which allowed] the Protestant half of Germany. . . [to gain] the ascendancy over Catholicism in the realm of education and culture.[49] .

Thus, it appears that Paulsen also considered these Reformed universities to be superior in their scientific and philosophical teachings to the universities under Roman Catholic control.

As the reader is probably aware, the Protestant Reformation had other prominent leaders in other parts of Europe. For example, Zwingli of Switzerland and Calvin from France played important roles in the eastern and western areas of Switzerland, respectively. Over time, the educational improvements undertaken by these leaders of the Reformation had a marked effect of the levels of literacy as well as on economic development in the Reformation minded areas of Europe. We will see this more clearly as we go along.

A number of historians believe that the Reformation itself was largely driven by economic forces.[50] Think of it this way: Before the Reformation it was costly to purchase your admission to Heaven through an indulgence. A considerable portion of the revenues from indulgence sales and other collections did not stay in the parish, but went to support the remote Roman Catholic hierarchy of bishops, archbishops, abbots, and the Pope. But under the Reformation you could get salvation for much less: Read the Bible, be prayerful, and believe. No costly indulgence was required. The collections taken in these Protestant churches remained mostly in the parish for local uses or as Luther said in the "*here below*." One of those uses was the financial support of schools.

One can question whether these new schools were really public schools? Weren't they Lutheran schools? The answers are: *yes* and *no*. The schools in each town or city were under the control of the municipal authorities who, in turn, were under the influence of the Lutheran reformers. So, there was indirect Lutheran control, but the direct control was from the local government. Hence these schools were public. Over the following centuries they would become more public and less Lutheran.

RELEVANCE OF DUTCH POPE ADRIAN VI

The Protestant Reformation was also about finding remedies to the corruption in the Roman Catholic Church. Luther was not the only Catholic cleric who had made *waves* about various kinds of questionable activities, mainly in Rome, that were harming the church. Another such person was Pope Adrian VI who held that office in 1522–1523, only a few years after Luther started his reforms.

Popes are elected by the College of Cardinals and within that body there is a fair amount of political activity when they are faced with their obligation to choose a successor to the previous Pope. The loyalties and friendships among the Cardinals had previously favored Popes who had been born in Italy, Spain or France, but most often Italy. In fact, the only *outsider* elected Pope previous to Adrian was an Englishman, Nicholas Breakspear, who served as Pope Adrian IV from 1154 to 1159.[51]

After the death of Pope Leo X in December 1521, the College was almost evenly divided between two Italian candidates, but neither received a majority of the votes. Several ballots were taken without finding a winner. One Cardinal proposed seeking additional candidates—perhaps they could find another prospect who could get a majority. The name of Dutchman Adrian Boeyens was proposed as a possible alternative though most of those present didn't think he would receive a majority. Another round of secret ballots was cast and voila: The Dutchman was chosen to be Pope Adrian VI. Many Cardinals and many others in Rome were aghast at the prospect of this foreigner becoming Pope.[52]

How could this seemingly unpopular candidate have been elected? Some put forth the theory that the Holy Ghost intervened and inspired enough of the College to form the majority. That sounds about right.

Adrian VI was critical of the Roman Curia—the bureaucracy of the Catholic Church—that sometimes ignored the Pope's instructions. In our own time bureaucrats in the United States federal government sometimes disobey their superiors to carry out policies contrary to those of the elected officials. These disobedient officials are sometimes called the *Deep State*. Perhaps the Roman Curia was the Catholic Church's *Deep State*, given its reluctance and refusal to obey their leaders and the Pope?

Adrian, like Luther, was critical of the ethical conflicts surrounding the Papacy. Unlike Luther, he was not about to leave the Church. After all, he was the Church!

Shortly after his arrival in Rome, Pope Adrian VI spoke before the College of Cardinals telling them this about the corruption in the Roman Curia: That, as St. Bernard has been saying,

> . . . those steeped in sin could no longer perceive the stench of their own iniquities.[53] .

Adrian was an unusual Pope because he was neither Italian nor was he Spanish or French. As a bishop from Holland, he was shocked by what he saw when he arrived in Rome to take up his new role as Pope. Had he lived longer, he might have even made peace with the Protestants. After his reign, the College of Cardinals consistently kept the Papacy in Italian hands for another 455 years, well into the twentieth century, until a Polish bishop was elected Pope John Paul II in 1978.

This author remembers a common remark from the 1960s:

> . . . and the Pope is Italian.

which was a rejoinder to almost any remark that was so obviously true that no response was needed. The 1978 election of a Polish Pope ended the logic and the humor of that remark.

Though the analogy is imperfect, we see a similar kind of corruption in American K-12 schools—including private schools. There are traditions in American schools that seem supportive of the learning process that in reality are not helpful. They are corrupt, but the camouflage of tradition gives them an honorable appearance. The players and stakeholders seem blind to the degradation. We will have many examples of this farther along.

GRADED SCHOOLS STARTED WITH STURM

One of the first public schools was established in Strasbourg, Germany in 1538, about 140 years before this city's annexation into France. Martin Bucer, a leading citizen of Strasbourg, was a disciple of Luther and was keen to establish a *Reformation* school that would advance the biblical education of the city's children.

Johannes Sturm was a German born scholar of the Latin and Greek classics who had been teaching in Paris when Bucer invited him to organize a school in Strasbourg in 1537. By 1538 Sturm had established the Protestant Gymnasium there and led the school for another 43 years.[54] John Calvin was a prominent teacher in Sturm's school and his participation there may have helped develop the ideas that he later advocated and implemented in Geneva.[55] The *New International Encyclopedia* had this to say about Sturm:

> STURM, or STUR'MIUS, Johannes (1507–89). A prominent educator of the sixteenth century. He was born near Cologne and was educated at Leyden and Louvain. In 1537, at the instance of the magistrates of Strasbourg, he organized the Strasbourg Gymnasium, which he directed for forty-three years. He was relieved from his position in 1581 on account of religious disputes and differences. Through his system of gradation of classes, practically the same that still prevails in all German gymnasia, the classification of literary material for use in schools, the writing of text-books, and the organization of school management, he shaped the practice of secondary education not only in the German schools, but also in the great secondary schools of England and France.[56]

The word *gymnasium* has two very different definitions depending on the language it is in. In English it refers to a large room dedicated to athletics. In most romance, and Germanic languages, it refers to a secondary school that prepares students for university studies. In Strasbourg it was the latter: It was a prep school.

In the 1890s here is what American educator William Shearer wrote about Sturm's school:

THE FIRST GRADED SCHOOL.

The first graded school was established in 1537, by John Sturm, at Strasburg. More than any other, it has had a vital influence upon the schools from that time to the present. This school, which was organized as a gymnasium, was recognized as a college in 1567, and as a university in 1621. The pupils were expected to spend a year in each one of the nine classes, each class having its own teacher, its regular course of study, and its examination for promotion, about as in the graded schools of to-day which have not broken away from these mediaeval methods. Sturm not only apportioned a certain amount of work to be accomplished in a given time, as nearly all do now, but he even *forbade them to learn anything else.*[57]

Sturm not only worked to improve and perfect his own school, but he also advised many other leaders in Protestant Europe as to best practices in the operation of schools.[58] Many of the features of the Strasbourg school became common in other schools—particularly in Germany, the Netherlands, and Scotland.

Shearer was a critic of the education systems of the late nineteenth century, and bemoaned the fact that very little improvement had been introduced since 1538, saying,

Is it not to be wondered at, that for so long a time we have been satisfied with this mediaeval plan of grading, while on other lines there has been so much progress?[59]

What can explain such a lack of progress over more than three centuries? Was it the success of the graded school? It was, after all, a marked improvement over the various types of schools that had pre-existed it. And once something is that well regarded, tradition sets in. It becomes known as a proven system. During those intervening centuries there were few technological developments that would have spurred new instructional systems. Those new *inventions* would come later, in the twentieth century.

Even with similarly operated schools, their financing, staffing, and enrollment practices differed in the various countries of Europe. Let's now consider some details about the structure and successes of schools in different parts of Europe relevant to this discussion.

LUTHERAN SCHOOLS IN GERMANY

Under Luther's influence and control, many towns and cities in Protestant areas of Germany established public schools. Many of these schools sought advice as to their structure and operating policies. The school of Sturm in Strasbourg provided a role model for many of them.

When we say *Germany,* we are not referring to an individual kingdom under a monarch. Rather it was a region within the Holy Roman Empire. It consisted of dozens of sovereign states and city-states. Not all of Germany became Protestant. In fact, only about half of it was Protestant. The other half was Roman Catholic. To smooth relations between the two different kinds of states, Holy Roman Emperor Charles V convened an assembly in 1555 that drafted the *Peace of Augsburg,* which he subsequently sealed.[60]

The Peace of Augsburg

Under this agreement, the leader or monarch of each jurisdiction was free to choose the religion to be practiced therein.[61] Some chose Protestantism, and some chose Catholicism. The citizens in each domain were required to adopt the religion of their leader. The leader was both the religious leader and the secular one. The agreement provided some measure of stability. In most cases, within the Protestant areas, the leader also established and operated the kinds of schools foreseen by Luther. Such schools frequently followed the example of Sturm's original model school in Strasbourg.

Under this policy of the Holy Roman Empire, a few years later in 1559, the German state of Württemberg was one of the first German states to implement a system of schools based on Sturm's school. The schools of Württemberg were so well respected that many other German states copied their features.

By 1650, most of the German Protestant states had established their own schools based on these earlier successful models. Also, at about that time, after the enormous devastation of the Thirty Years War (1618–1648), various German-speaking states moved to make school attendance mandatory.[62] Truancy often resulted in a fine for parent and sometimes imprisonment of the children. For example, Prussia established such a system in 1669. Prussia was one of the largest states within the German territories. Its size and wealth allowed it to establish school systems almost unrivaled on the European continent. Given that the public schools of Prussia were eventually the ones to be widely emulated and copied in other regions of the world, we now restrict our discussion of German education to just that of Prussia.

The public Lutheran schools of Prussia

The historical record suggests that, from time to time, Prussia's system of compulsory education fell into some disarray only to be followed by a new regime of strict discipline and compulsory attendance. In the early 1700s efforts were made to expand the availability of schools in Prussia by establishing many more schools in areas where they had been lacking.

After King Frederick William I ascended to the throne of Prussia in 1713, he set out to reform and improve many functions of his kingdom's government.[63] In 1717 he moved to make Prussia's education system compulsory (again) and this time with better enforcement measures. To accommodate the enrollment increases due to the mandatory attendance policy he also worked to construct more schools. He issued *Principia Regulative* in 1737 that was the school law for East Prussia. It specified in some detail how each parish was to obtain the resources and finances needed to improve their school operations.

His son, Frederick the Great, centralized the kingdom's school administration to Berlin in 1750. He reorganized school management by outsourcing them to the Lutheran churches. He sought high standards for schools and observed that Prussia's schools were relatively deficient. He said of Prussia's children,

> The young people were growing up in stupidity and ignorance.[64]

So, in 1763 he issued new laws and regulations that were quite detailed.[65] They included a literacy requirement, and one on evangelical beliefs. Children not meeting these standards were to be denied confirmation and the sacraments. Also, there was tuition except for the poorest children.

Despite these high standards and requirements, Prussia lacked the thousands of well-trained teachers and other officials to meet those standards.[66] The funding to carry out these laws was lacking. As a result, *lip service* was given to the new regime and some minor efforts were made to move towards the new standards. Really significant improvements would have to wait until the early nineteenth century.

After the devastation from Napoleon's campaigns, Prussia reorganized its system to be not only universal, but also centrally controlled as to operations and curricula. Unlike the religious motivations Luther had for inventing public schools, these Prussian educators saw their schools as tools in the formation of patriotic loyal citizens. To accomplish this, central control was essential.[67] What had been essentially Lutheran schools had then become government schools though still having the official Lutheran label.

Early in the nineteenth century, in 1808, Swiss educator Johann Heinrich Pestalozzi was invited to Prussia to import his pedagogic methods. The gist of his teaching method was that direct instruction from a teacher needed to be replaced by the student learning on his or her own selected pace and subjects.[68] It fit with the then popular philosophy of European Romanticism that held the theory that the maturation of humans into adulthood should be self-directed by children. They trusted children, think toddlers and adolescents, to direct their own educational paths. Sound crazy? Yes, and we'll have more on this later. His pedagogy became popular in Europe and eventually around the world. In Prussia the Department of Public Instruction adopted some, but not all of his methods and content in their schools' curricula. If this sounds oxymoronic it's because it was. There was, and still is, no way to structure any kind of school that is fully controlled by the pupils. School managers could move in that direction by having children make some choices, but limited by the normal organizational constraints dictated by the conflicts and costs that could make some of the student's choices impossible or impractical to honor.

As a word, *romantic,* has no definitions or connotations that refer to objective, scientific reality. To make sure, we reviewed the definitions of this adjective in Webster's Third New International Dictionary. Of the eight uses shown there, none involve tangible or quantitative concepts. Similarly, the related word, *romanticism,* lacks any objective characteristics.

Farther along we will discuss how the format of public education used in Prussia was copied by school systems in many different countries around the world.

CHAPTER 2

Public and Private Schools Grow
in Western Europe

As OTHER RELIGIOUS AND political leaders witnessed the success of Lutheran schools, there were soon efforts made to copy these efforts in other lands and under other religious denominations.

CALVINIST SCHOOLS IN NORTHERN EUROPE

Calvinist schools were similar to the Lutheran schools. Their nexus was discussed above: Sturm's school in Strasbourg. John Calvin was a teacher there before he became a Protestant reformer. Through that connection, Sturm's school provided a model for other Protestant schools—both Lutheran and Calvinist. The Calvinist form of Protestantism became dominant in the Netherlands and in Scotland. Later, it would indirectly affect the schools of England and Wales.

One difference between the Lutheran approach to local government and that of Calvin was that Lutherans worked with existing governments to establish their churches and schools while, in contrast, Calvin devised his own unique government structure to facilitate and control the churches and schools within the one town he controlled: Geneva, Switzerland. That structure was widely copied in northern Europe. He had one church in 1538. Twenty-two years later in 1560 the Calvinist churches numbered an astounding 2,000.[69] Let's now look at the Calvinist churches and schools in Holland and Scotland.

Of the Dutch Reformed Church in Holland

In Holland, under the Calvinist theology, the Dutch Reformed Church was established. By 1609 various laws had been passed there, which made primary education almost universal and nearly always compulsory.[70] In 1618 the Great Synod was held in Dort where the following was mandated:

- Schools would be established in cities, towns, and rural places.

- Christian magistrates will find well-qualified teachers and pay them honorable stipends.

- Children of poor parents will receive free instruction.[71]

The schools of Holland, as well as those in Prussia, enjoyed a reputation placing them above their peers in Europe. When, in 1837, leaders in England's Parliament investigated the reforms that might be undertaken to improve the primary schools attended by children from poor families, they decided to study other European countries education systems in search of policies worth considering. Holland was one. The German state of Prussia was another. They soon learned of an in-person survey that French educator M. Victor Cousin had conducted during an extended visit he made to Holland in 1836. They not only decided to use his survey and accompanying book, but soon after they also had the book translated into English. The translated version also included an extensive translator (as editor) preface of commentary within.[72]

> We sometimes think of Holland, and the Netherlands as synonymous, but they aren't. The latter encloses the former, making Holland a region within the Netherlands. Holland has about one-third of the population, and about one-eighth of the land area of the Netherlands. Given the sloppy labeling of these territories, even by the Netherlands' officials themselves, we will also not get specific about which region we mean when we say Holland, but we will use Netherlands to specify the entire country.

Cousin was particularly interested in the advantages and disadvantages of the Monitorial schools of Lancaster. We discuss that, later in this chapter, in the section, *Lancasterian Schools*. He also concluded that the schools in Holland had literacy levels that rivaled those of Prussia.[73] By 1820 Holland had an estimated literacy rate of 88% while in comparison the overall literacy rate of Protestant lands in Europe was about 65%.[74]

Measurements of literacy, defined as the percent of a population found minimally able to read and write, tend to be subjective and yet seem to have similar criteria across national boundaries. During the Medieval Period, and for some centuries following, the definition of *minimally able* was generally given as the ability to write one's name out in full (initials were insufficient). That's a low threshold to meet.

Of the Presbyterian Church in Scotland

Calvinist reformers were also active in Scotland where Calvin protégé John Knox established the Presbyterian denomination that was soon to become the official religion of Scotland. Their efforts at compulsory education in Scotland brought more and more children to school as each new policy tended to increase the *compulsion* for school attendance.

An early effort to increase school attendance resulted from legislation establishing the *First Book of Discipline of 1560* in which the Presbyterian variant of Calvinism was made the official religion of Scotland.[75] Of particular relevance here was its plan, authored by John Knox, for the establishment of forced attendance primary schools in every parish.[76] A *Second Book of Discipline of 1578* established an administrative structure for operating schools at the parish level. While the official policies in these *Books* did not effectively enforce school attendance, they were a step in that direction for they reportedly made schools available in every parish that would, at least, allow increased attendance. Thus, their requirements for universal compulsory education were only partly met.

More than a half-century later the Parliament of Scotland passed the *Education Act of 1646* that (this time we really mean it) required a school in every parish.[77] Again, their goals were not fully met. Then 226 years after that a more comprehensive law, *The 1872 Education Act*, pushed the Scottish school systems even farther towards a regime of better enforcement of their compulsory education laws.[78] It did so, to such an extent, that poverty was no longer a valid excuse for truancy.

SCHOOL DEVELOPMENTS IN ENGLAND

The evolution of schools within England is complicated by the fact that the former Roman Catholic churches within the kingdom were not part of the Reformation per se, but rather were separated from their Roman Catholic governance by the politics of a royal divorce of King Henry VIII in 1533. Unlike other areas of northern Europe there was no single Protestant reformer who had a major effect on schooling in England and Wales. The governments of England and its successor, the United Kingdom, played only minor roles in the ownership and management of schools until the 1880s when public schools with compulsory attendance were established.[79]

> Many of our sources of information on education in England generally combine England, and Wales together. We follow that practice here except that we usually just label this combination as England—to keep the labeling simplified.

Puritans in England: Their persecution, their exile, and their voyage on the Mayflower

Who were the Puritans in England? They were primarily Calvinists in England who were advocating for a *purification* of the teachings of the Church of England. Their influence was felt around the end of the sixteenth century, but never significantly affected the kingdom's education policies. Later, there were two camps of Puritans.[80] One group, more moderate in character, simply wanted to change the style of worship within the Anglican Church to move closer to a Calvinistic format. Another group wanted to start their own churches, probably Presbyterian or something similar. King James I, who commissioned the Bible of his name, would have none of that and violently persecuted these uppity Puritans. Among the consequences of that was the 1609 decision of a Puritan congregation in Scrooby, England to self-exile themselves to Holland. After 11 years there, they were aboard the Mayflower crossing the Atlantic to New England. The rest is history! Other Puritan groups soon followed their example and as a result they never really had much influence on education in England thereafter.

A literacy plateau in England followed by nineteenth century growth

Unlike the steady increases of literacy seen in the Protestant areas of continental northern Europe the literacy levels in England had a long interval of stagnation between two periods of significant growth[81] as shown in Fig. 1. The first phase of literacy growth was seen in the two hundred years after Gutenberg's printing presses up to about 1650. For that period literacy rates grew from below 10% to about 50%. Part of that increase, if not most of it, can be ascribed to the rapid growth of printed materials that indirectly led people to seek literacy. After that period the available statistics suggest a flat literacy profile of little growth for the next 170 years until about 1820. After that a third period of literacy growth was observed and by the end of the nineteenth century those levels exceeded 90% in England. It wasn't until this last time period that the English government came to establish a significant level of publicly financed and operated schools.

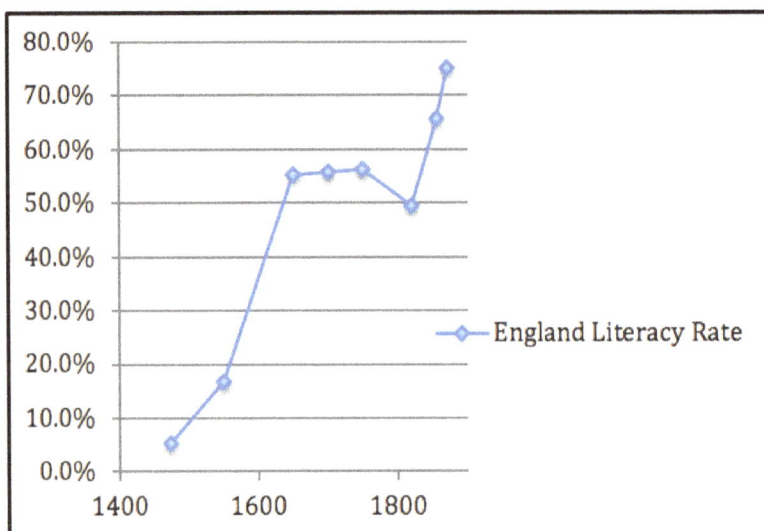

Figure 1 displays rough estimates of literacy rates in England in the years after the Gutenberg revolution.

Many of the earlier developments in the schools of England resulted from private efforts to expand literacy, particularly among the lower economic classes. A good example of this was the establishment of Charity Schools after 1701.[82] They were structured around what we would now call a charitable foundation that organized donors and other humanitarian benefactors to provide financial support to a network of schools.

The first significant English government involvement in schools occurred in late in the eighteenth century when the Act of 1767 set forth new liberating regulations and laws concerning the education of paupers.[83]

Sunday schools were established as engines of literacy

There were Sunday schools. They were not the Sunday schools anything like the ones we have in twenty-first century America. They were invented in the eighteenth century as a means of teaching children how to read. Many were run by churches as they sought members who could read the Bible. The first Sunday school was established by a young English pastor John Wesley in 1737 when he had been assigned to a church in colonial Savannah, Georgia. Thus, Sunday school was invented in the British colonies of North America—truly an American invention! This was some years before he and his brother Charles founded the Methodist movement within the Church of England. Toward the late eighteenth century Sunday schools became popular in England. Historian Ellwood Cubberley commented that they were established

> . . . to take children off the streets on Sunday and provide them with some form of secular and religious instruction.[84]

The attendance at Sunday schools rapidly increased to around 500,000 children by the year 1792. Not all Sunday schools were run by churches. An early example of that is found near the author's home in the town of Pawtucket, Rhode Island. Samuel Slater, sometimes labeled the father of the American industrial revolution, established a Sunday school in the late 1790s in his textile factory village of Slatersville within Pawtucket.[85] College students were the teachers and the Bible was the book. This Sunday school, not long after, moved to a local Baptist Church, which then continued its operation.

As we have seen, the post-Reformation schools in England consisted of a mixture of different types that existed under a minimally intrusive government. They saw significant expansion and improvement in the late 1800s. In contrast the schools in the Netherlands, in Scotland, and in Lutheran parts of Germany had much more government supervision and financial support that came *on line* much earlier. By the end of the nineteenth century, however, the literacy levels were comparably high among these different countries.

JESUITS ESTABLISH CATHOLIC SCHOOLS

The same economic incentives from the printing revolution that spurred the Protestant school developments were also felt in Catholic areas of Europe. In kingdoms where it remained dominant, mainly in the southern parts of Europe, the Catholic Church saw how their Protestant counterparts were rapidly establishing schools. In reaction, after about 1535, many Catholic lands found ways to establish more schools—often run by Jesuits.[86]

Successful Jesuit run schools raised ire among other orders. Suppression followed

In the early 1500s many town councils in France established free schools, mainly for boys. Many of these schools were insufficiently funded and were threatened with closure.[87] The Jesuit order of Catholic priests was invited to own and operate these schools. Jesuits were not only capable educators within the schools they ran, but they were also successful fundraisers. Their schools were free and they were able to raise sufficient funds to keep them solvent and to enlarge their capacity to educate more and more children. For almost three centuries after 1546 the networks of Jesuit schools expanded to where there were over 500 schools under their ownership, mostly in France and Italy.[88]

Unlike their Protestant peers, these schools in Catholic lands were not nearly as successful until hundreds of years later in the nineteenth century. For three centuries the Catholic schools lagged behind their Protestant counterparts as judged by the literacy rates estimated for the lands that were predominantly Catholic. In those times not every town had a school. Not every school had compulsory attendance. Enforcement of standards was comparatively lax.

By the mid-seventeenth century, around 1650, the Jesuits dominated Catholic education, compared to the other religious orders within the Catholic Church. From their first school that was established in Spain in 1546 they rapidly expanded the number of schools they owned and operated. By 1600 they had 56 schools in Italy, 77 in Spain, and about 200 in France.[89] Even with that seemingly rapid expansion they served only a small fraction of the towns and cities in these Catholic kingdoms.

Their schools were mainly focused on boys who typically entered them at ages nine or ten. Their curriculum was somewhat expanded from the classical trivium subject areas with emphasis on grammar, rhetoric, history, and the two classical languages: Latin and Greek.[90] The course of study ran for five to six years. It appears that these schools employed some sort of retention or flunking to ensure students were performing at the expected levels.

Rivalries among the various religious orders of the Catholic Church and widespread dislike of Jesuits by the other factions led to their suppression by Pope Clement XIV after 1773.[91] Over 700 schools were closed affecting some 250,000 students.

Under Napoleon a major restructuring of French schools was undertaken

France eventually moved toward a more comprehensive system of schools in the late 1700s and early 1800s. This was greatly influenced by the French Revolution and by the government of Napoleon.

In about 1804, under Napoleon, a new national system of public education was developed in France. In every commune (town) and city, primary schools were established and managed by local administrators.[92] Schools for older children were also established, but not every commune had one. Even so, the number of children enrolled in these public schools was somewhat less than 50% given the fact that the already existing Catholic schools enrolled somewhat more than 50% of the children in France.

It was only in the late nineteenth century, around 1887, that France and Italy made laws requiring compulsory attendance in primary schools.[93]

LANCASTERIAN SCHOOLS

Joseph Lancaster was a Quaker schoolmaster in England who faced a conundrum: He had many pupils, but he had no money to pay for additional teachers. The year was 1798. He had a plan to establish cost-effective schools and he soon put it into action.

The Monitorial Systems of Joseph Lancaster and Andrew Bell

One compromise solution to the tutoring or group instruction dilemma was that of having very small classes run by very miserly paid advanced students operating as teaching assistants. This was the approach of two English educators of the late eighteenth century and early nineteenth, Andrew Bell and Joseph Lancaster.[94],[95],[96] They developed low-cost private schools in which the more advanced children within the school taught small classes of less advanced pupils. Under their model, one professional teacher was able to instruct several hundred children with the obvious cost saving advantage of a low per-pupil expense. The very small classes meant that the spread between the slowest learner and the most rapid one was minimized and also meant that they didn't need to be age-based to the same extent that the Prussian schools were. Moreover, children were *promoted* from a class when they had mastered the subject—regardless of their ages or of the calendar date. Thus, the Lancasterian system and the one of Bell accommodated much of what we now call *self-pacing*.

Lancaster published the details five years later[97] in 1803. One of his schools in London had 365 pupils, roughly 40 monitors (teaching assistants) and one teacher supervising this assemblage all in one large room. The nearby Figure 2 shows how the Lancasterian school room was arranged.[98] A good summary of this can be found in the book by Cubberley.[99] As we say about so many ambitious projects,

> The devil was in the details.

The monitors or teaching assistants were taken from the more advanced students. Approximately ten students would be grouped with each monitor to receive their lessons. For the system to work a minimal prerequisite was that the monitor knew the subject to be taught and had some skill at instruction. This was a difficult requirement to meet when the basic assumption was that these students worked for very little compensation—perhaps none beyond their own tuition free learning from the head instructor. One advantage of the monitorial system was its self-pacing characteristic. Students were advanced to the next set of lessons once they mastered the preceding set. There was no regimentation into age-based grades—partly because the school only had the one large group of pupils under the one master teacher.

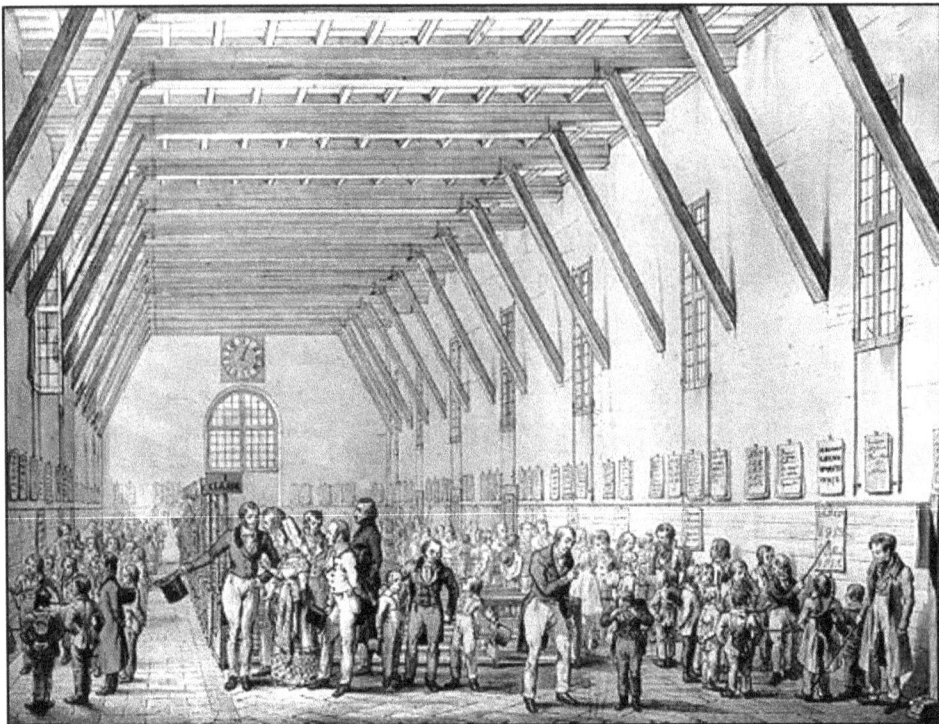

Figure 2 shows a drawing of a typical classroom scene in a Lancasterian school using the Monitorial system of instruction.

French educator Cousin evaluated and advised: Use the Monitorial system sparingly.

French educator Victor Cousin was a skeptic concerning the value of schools using the monitorial systems.[100] He acknowledged their low cost of operation, given the free or very low wage labor they employed as monitors. His primary concern was the quality of the instruction. He worried that if the use of monitors was too widespread, they would be used to instruct in subject areas beyond their expertise. But he did allow that some focused use of monitors would be acceptable in areas where the rudiments were being taught. When Cousin toured Holland, he noted approvingly that their education system seemed to follow this compromise in which the monitorial system was used, but used only where it was found beneficial.

The use of monitorial systems fell out of favor as schools, both government run and private, acquired sufficient resources to hire adequate numbers of teachers. Nevertheless, the concept of using student peers, as in peer tutoring, to help other students learn their lessons has persisted in all kinds of schools in many times and places. Such tutoring is often informal and is often unpaid. It was surely a common feature of the rural one-room schoolhouse in early nineteenth century America.

In the early years of the United States, prior to the introduction of public education, the Lancasterian system of education was adopted in many locations.[101] Such schools were found along the East Coast from Virginia to New England and as far west as Detroit. In some of the larger cities, including New York and Philadelphia, networks of Lancasterian schools were established, that later became the organizational basis for the public schools that followed. We emphasize the distinction that Lancasterian schools were private and required parents to pay a small tuition. The public schools that followed, many of which were based on the Prussian school systems, were free to parents because they were supported by taxes.

The Prussian model flourished while the Lancastrian one withered away

That the Prussian public school model survived and prospered while the Lancasterian one did not is a question for historians, economists, and educators to unravel. Were the public school officials better bureaucrats and therefore ran better schools? Was it related to the rise of socialism during the nineteenth century? It appears that the Prussian influenced public school model, with its preference for free government run schools, was more popular than the tuition supported privately run Lancastrian model—possibly because of their subsidies. Whatever the answers to those questions, Lancasterian schools survive in one aspect: nearly every school that attempts self-pacing usually ends up using the more advanced children to help the others who are less knowledgeable. We have examples of that in the United States where there are a small number of private schools that employ self-pacing. This author has personally visited two such schools, one in Massachusetts and one in California, where, in each case, student tutors were used to help the less advanced children.

Before we continue our narrative on the history of K-12 education into and beyond the nineteenth century, we believe it a good place to discuss two trends heavily influenced by earlier technical and educational developments. Those are the western European trends of literacy and of economic output, which we review next.

CHAPTER 3

European Literacy and Wealth Since Gutenberg

THE TERM *know-how* encapsulates the idea that knowledge fosters the ability to do things. It suggests that a more literate society will also be more productive. Let's look at their relationship since the Medieval Period.

LITERACY SINCE MEDIEVAL TIMES

Economic historians Buringh and Van Zanden have made estimates of the literacy rates in several European lands since the Gutenberg led revolution in printing and since the Protestant Reformation.[102] These are shown in Figure 3 below.

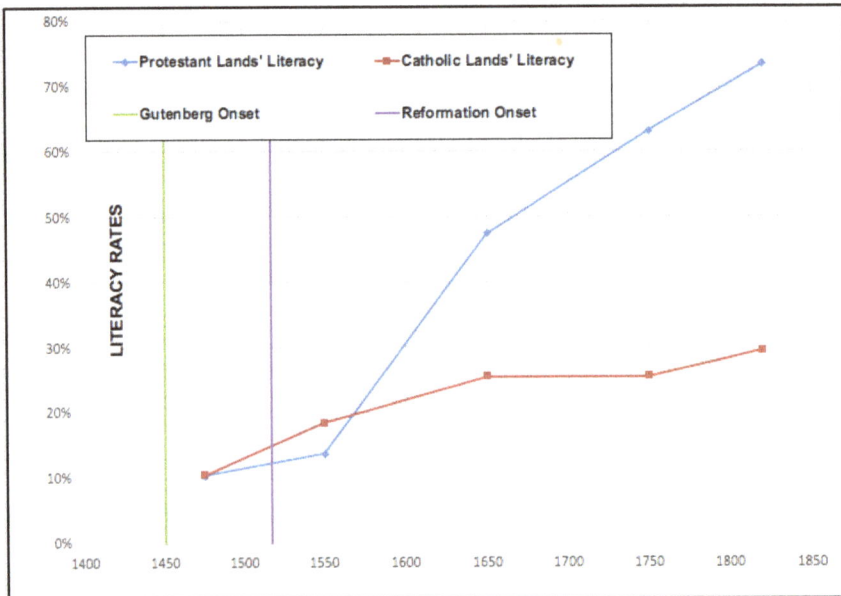

Figure 3 displays rough estimates of European literacy rates in the years surrounding the Gutenberg Revolution, and the Protestant Reformation. The greater emphasis on schools in Protestant lands seems to have increased literacy rates therein.

We should caution the reader that these estimates are not clearly defined. What is the definition of being literate? Our twenty-first century standard of it, perhaps being the equivalent of 4th grade reading skills, is far too stringent. Most scholars of the medieval and Renaissance times have defined literacy to be the ability to sign or spell one's name. Knowing one's initials was not enough! Even if we aren't able to define literacy precisely we can ask if various experts in the history of education have consistent estimates in their writings.

Let's compare this to what four other studies have estimated:

1. The Quora website says that England had 6% literacy in the year 1300. Assuming a fairly flat temporal profile in the years before and shortly after Gutenberg this is within statistical error bounds of our 10% literacy estimate for the year 1475 based on the values shown in Figure 3.[103]

2. The service at SarahWoodbury.com reports for Britain an estimate of 17% male literacy in the year 1500. If we assume perhaps 5% female literacy in that year the overall estimate becomes 11% literate. This compares favorably to the interpolated average of 10.5% literate for Great Britain in our graph.[104]

3. The Yahoo Answers service gives the overall European literacy rate at the end of the Middle Ages as about 15%. The year 1475 was approximately at the end of the Middle Ages where our estimate of 11% literacy is within statistical uncertainty of the Yahoo number.[105]

4. The Philip LaBerge website estimates male literacy in 1530 England was about 25%. If we assume a corresponding female literacy of about 10%, then the overall literacy would be approximately 17%. Compare this to the interpolated value from our chart of 13% and find that it is also within the statistical error range of 5%.[106]

It is satisfying to see these estimates for literacy levels in these European lands, all fit the picture shown in Figure 3. above within statistical error levels.

Protestant literacy levels

The leftmost data points, for the year 1475, was after Gutenberg's printing press invention of about 1450, but not so long after for his printing revolution to have had much effect on literacy. So, we interpret the values for 1475 as consistent with pre-Gutenberg conditions. The next data points, for the year 1550, in a similar sense, was after Martin Luther's launch of the Reformation, but not far enough past it to have had much effect on literacy. All of the remaining data points are likely affected by both the printing revolution and by the Reformation. The higher literacy rates in Protestant lands were almost certainly driven by policies favoring higher enrollments in their public schools—particularly when attendance was made compulsory. Under such strict policies, Protestant children had little alternative other than that of attending school and working to master their lessons.

Roman Catholic literacy levels

Let's consider some of the lands that were Catholic. Those areas, contributing to the data shown in Figure 3 above, were Italy and France while the Protestant Lands were Great Britain, the Netherlands, and the Protestant half of Germany. The Catholic half of Germany is not included here. Germany, post Reformation, was about half Protestant and half Catholic, despite it having been the first venue of the Reformation.

For Catholics, the red line of the graph shows a slower, but steady increase in literacy going forward after the time of the printing revolution. Given that Catholic schools did not adopt school policies like those of the Reformation it would be less likely that any literacy increase in their lands would be a result of Protestant reforms. We ascribe the steady, but slow increase of literacy in Catholic regions mostly to the steady increase in the availability of printed books and other documents, post Gutenberg.

ECONOMIC OUTPUT SINCE MEDIEVAL TIMES

A well-known finding from economics is that a better-educated work force will be more productive. That is, it will be able to produce more output of a greater variety of goods and services than a less well-skilled force of workers. This would suggest that lands where literacy is higher would have greater economic growth. Comparing Figure 3 with Figure 4 confirms this.

A a common measure of the annual national economic output is the Gross Domestic Product (GDP). The reported GDP numbers, shown below for this post-Reformation era, were generated by Angus Maddison.[107]

Protestant work ethic and wealth

German sociologist and economist Maximillian Weber is famous for his writings about the *Protestant Ethic* and its influence towards the support of Capitalism. Of particular relevance has been his observation that Protestants tend towards asceticism more than their Catholic peers.[108] Their ascetic religious philosophy and beliefs have discouraged excessive personal consumption while having encouraged other uses of one's earnings, such as charitable donations. As economists or anyone with common sense can tell you: If you reduce your consumption you are forced to spend some of your resources elsewhere. We just mentioned charity, which almost certainly included the support of schools. Other alternatives included savings and investments. These investments helped grow the enterprises of the post-Reformation era. Even the charitable spending was an investment in the well-being and education of society's younger and poorer members that in time would make them productive workers/owners of profit-making enterprises. And, as Weber explained, this was the result of Protestants consuming less.

Despite these obvious correlations and likely causal connections, some analysts insist that the Reformation had no economic effects. One analyst, Davide Cantoni, tells us that,

> I find no effects of Protestantism on economic growth.[109] The *finding is precisely estimated . . .*

The last four words of this *line* demonstrate Cantoni's confusion. When the subject is historical and involves uncertain data there is no way that a finding can be *precisely estimated.*

The gentleman, me thinks, doth boast too much!

What is evident from these trends in literacy and economic growth is that the educational systems of Europe that exhibited these gains are surely worth evaluating when we make judgments about American education. Much of what initially developed in the United States was largely based on the European systems discussed above.

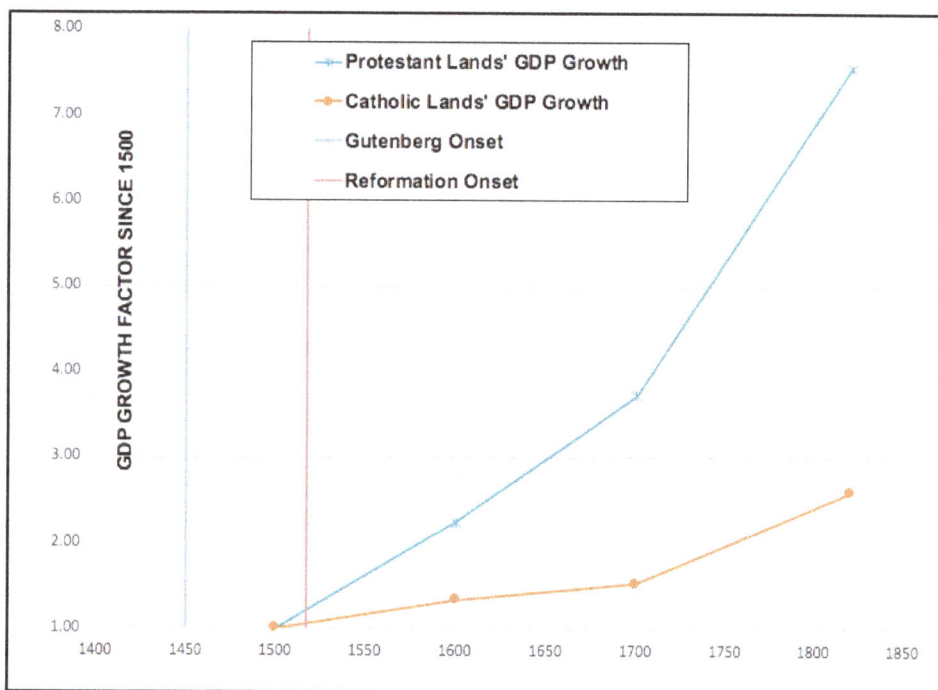

Figure 4 shows Gross Domestic Product (GDP) growth factors where the GDP value in 1500 is the base. These numbers are based on published estimates of GDP for the same European lands shown in Figure 3. These lands had the benefit of the printing revolution, but only the Protestant lands experienced the additional benefit shown here—arguably from their higher literacy levels achieved by their more effective schools.

CHAPTER 4

Pestalozzian Problems

STUDENTS AND SCHOLARS OF history know that human progress is not inevitable. This reminds me of an old history professor I overheard who once scolded a student whose term paper was overly optimistic about the supposed progress and improvement of medicine in ancient Egypt. I remember him saying

> . . . but Mr. Sullivan, tings could have gotten worse! (phonetically correct)

Similarly, in this chapter we discuss an example of a popular philosophy of education that sounded good, but turned out to be problematic. That philosophy is that of Pestalozzian pedagogy.

THE OLD METHODS OF INSTRUCTION

Prior to the nineteenth century there was not much research into teaching methods. Before books were available, children learned orally either from tutors or in groups. Recitation and memorization were generally part of the drill. Corporal punishment was a common tool used to focus students on their studies.

Once books were available and after a child learned to read, oral instruction was more and more supplemented with readings from those books. And, as we already mentioned, this provided a primitive form of student led self-pacing. It allowed a student, on his or her own, to review previously covered material or to study new information not yet taught by the teacher.

The curriculum of a school was dictated mostly by perceived societal needs. In the Protestant Christian areas this included an ability to read, understand, and recite from the Bible. As commerce and technology developed, it included skills in mathematics, the arts, and the sciences. It was rare for the student to choose a course of study, except that perhaps indirectly their wishes would be considered by parents and school authorities.

New methods came on the horizon in the early 1800s. Some that found widespread societal favor, which still affect us in the twenty-first century, were proposed by Swiss educator Pestalozzi. We discuss that next.

PESTALOZZIAN PEDAGOGY WAS IN FASHION

In the early nineteenth century the pedagogical theories of Swiss educator Johann Heinrich Pestalozzi became popular in many countries. As we mentioned earlier his instructional system was based on the philosophy of European Romanticism in which the student directs his or her own educational advancement.

You might wonder; what is pedagogy? The Wikipedia article on this discipline defines it this way:

> Pedagogy, taken as an academic discipline, is the study of how knowledge and skills are exchanged in an educational context and it considers the interactions that take place during learning.[110]

As will become clear in forthcoming chapters, there are different sub-species of pedagogy. Stay tuned.

Romantic inmates running the Kindergartens

As to Pestalozzi, his background had many diverse and complicated aspects. His pedagogy was primarily based on the notion that a child, as a student, should be self-directed in learning in contrast to being controlled by the school's system of regimentation. He believed in the freedom of a child to choose wisely the things to be learned. His critics would say, and still say, "yes, but." Families and government also have other interests and subjects to be addressed in a child's education. These other things to be learned are sometimes called *secondary learnings*.[111] And, perhaps paradoxically, Pestalozzi sometimes agreed with his critics and in doing so contradicted his own principles!

There is a broad spectrum of instructional models described by American educator Dean Webb and collaborators that include the following categories according to their instructional components:

- Perennialism: Has an emphasis on spiritual and moral development with some focus on science.

- Progressivism: Emphasizes student directed learning in a cooperative learning environment.

- Behaviorism: This theory places its emphasis on controlling student behavior through strict discipline.

- Essentialism: It is like perennialism, but with less regard for spiritual side and more for the scientific.

- Social Reconstructionism: Has emphasis on loyalty to a proposed and reformed political order.

- Postmodernism: This is a self-contradictory approach with elements of social reconstructionism.[112]

He and his team described Pestalozzi's approach as one of *progressivism*. Of the list shown here only *perennialism* and *essentialism* allow inclusion of an objective set of criteria that can be measured to determine what a child has learned. This does not mean that aspects of the other categories cannot be useful in building a successful instructional model. For example, the approaches of *progressivism* encourage the learning modes of theory combined with experiment. But is it wise for a student to set his own schedule? How will a child learn about society's expectations without some external control of instruction in those areas?

Some students who were taught in a Pestalozzian environment did very well if they were sufficiently self-motivated. We have an example:

In Aargau canton in Switzerland in 1895 an 18-year-old boy attended the cantonal secondary school that followed Pestalozzi's pedagogy. This boy had been previously denied admission to the Swiss Institute of Technology in Zurich. He had tested very high in mathematics and physics, but had some minor deficiencies in some of the other tested subjects. His parents sent him to the Pestalozzian cantonal school for a year of remediation. After that he was accepted at the Institute in the following year. The boy? Albert Einstein. He had this to say about his matriculation in Aargau:

> It made me clearly realize how much superior an education based on free action and personal responsibility is to one relying on outward authority.[113]

The moral of this story is not to give confirmational testimony to Pestalozzi's methods. Rather it shows that a subset of students who are very intelligent and self-directed can prosper in such an educational setting. Who if anyone was more self-directed than Albert Einstein?

PESTALOZZIAN DEFECTS

A number of experts in psychology take exception to the claims of Pestalozzi. For example, there is evidence that children can learn new skills and knowledge at ages younger than what a self-directed child would choose. According to developmental psychologist Jerome Bruner,

> Any subject can be taught effectively in some intellectually honest form to any child at any stage of development.[114]

This claim is supported by research studies on the brain's development. Yale University neurobiologist Pasko Rakic explained,

> Children's brains can make far more synaptic connections than can adults'. Shortly after birth the brain makes connections at an incredible pace. As puberty approaches the number tapers off.[115]

\

This translates to the fact that delayed education will be received less efficiently by a less well *connected* brain. According to Dr. Rakic the fastest learning can occur before age 11 or so. Or as he says,

> ... in childhood there is an ability to learn quickly which is unparalleled.

If children are to be the arbiters of what they learn when, is this not the same learning schedule that proponents of social promotion advocate? The related phenomenon of *grade inflation* is plausibly another result of this kind of progressive pedagogy. Educator E. D. Hirsch, Jr. is one expert with this opinion.[116]

An inference we draw from the flexibility built into Pestalozzian pedagogy is that it invites various substandard practices that by its own criteria are not seen as defective. As there is no standard curriculum in these kinds of progressive schools, there is no easy way to establish academic content standards. Related to that, how does one determine testing parameters that would show that a student has performed well enough to move on to the next course or grade level? There will be a tendency to relax whatever standards are set. It will likely lead to grade inflation and social promotion. Will parents approve of such a relaxed learning environment or will they want a more challenging school for their children? Given what we know about human nature, there will be parents in both camps: Some will want rigor, and some will want their children in a more relaxed environment. Will they want minimum standards? The Pestalozzians don't have them!

Pestalozzi sometimes voiced opinions contrary to his instructional proposals?

Of the instructional models listed above, we believe that *perennialism* and *essentialism* provide the best learning frameworks for children. Oddly enough, Pestalozzi, from time to time, would make claims that contradicted his own progressivist instructional models. This was quite clear in his methods for building a child's vocabulary. As Hirsch put it,

> He [Pestalozzi] conceded the great power of verbal rote memorization as a means of gaining understanding and critical thought.[117]

This rote recitation and memorization imposed by the school was contrary to his model of child directed learning. He made these exceptions to his policy to advance his ideas of *social justice* in his schools and to give the children of the poor a better education. Is this not an example of the *exception that proves the rule?*

Others have viewed Pestalozzi more as a utopian reformer than as an educator.[118] In this he dreamed of remaking humanity perhaps along the lines advocated by the communitarian advocates of his time.

Despite the obvious flaws in the Pestalozzi pedagogy it seems to have a form of eternal life. Many educators have embraced it over the years. Its defects, including *social promotion*, have lived on.

SUMMARY OF PART I: 1450–1895

If this book's focus is, as the title suggests, on *sick schools*, in Part I we then asked what aspects of the European history of schools contributed to that *diagnosis?* Keeping to our underlying theme of understanding the economic factors, we know that Gutenberg's printing revolution coupled with the Protestant Reformation not only increased the availability of books, but it also allowed the parish or town to reduce the *taxes* going to Rome. It led to a virtuous cycle in which Christian principles of charity and thrift produced savings and resources that could be used for the development of communities and enterprises.

The familiar format of graded schools was established early on in the 1530s, but many schools remained ungraded when and where the numbers of students was insufficient. The ungraded schools often used unpaid advanced students as teaching assistants to enable multiple academic tracks within the school, as was the case for the Lancasterian schools. Those kinds of improvements didn't cause *sick schools* per se, but they did facilitate experimentation in the governance of schools that allowed pathologies to develop.

Among these untoward developments were the effects of Romanticism and the ideas that students should choose their curricula and learn at their own selected paces as opposed to having the community direct their education format. Those kinds of freedom in education took on the label *Progressive*. By the end of this era, in 1895, the bad effects of this *Progressivism* were small, but they would grow to be problematic in the twentieth century and beyond.

PART II

American Schools: 1620–1950

IN PART II, WE look at the educational developments in North America that were essentially a continuation of the events and trends described in Part I. As Europeans migrated to North America in and after the seventeenth century, they brought their cultures and educational philosophies with them. Thus, graded schools became common in the larger towns while the ungraded school was common in more rural areas. As the population increased many ungraded schools moved towards or were replaced by the graded school format. Many ungraded schools adopted the Lancasterian system with its lowly paid or unpaid teaching assistants. The graded schools were cost effective in the sense that one teacher could educate dozens of students. In contrast the ungraded schools that had large enrollments could be run economically if they employed the Lancasterian system with its unpaid (or very lowly paid) teaching assistants.

> The reader may wonder how Part I of this book covers the years up through 1895, but then Part II goes back to the year 1620 for its start? The answer is that the topics of Part I pertain to events in Europe while those in Part II are mostly in North America. Thus, it makes sense that there is some chronological overlap between Part I, and Part II.

Part II is composed of three chapters, entitled:

5. Graded Schools in America

6. Problems and Remedies for Graded Schools

7. Digressions and Improvements to Graded Schools

As the following sections make clear, graded schools had problems—essentially that of the *one size fits all* constraint. Such schools were not very good at educating slow learners and were simultaneously boring the precocious. One set of remedies to these *pacing* problems involved flunking students to repeat an academic term or double promoting them to skip an academic term. Other remedial efforts focused on helping students keep up with their peers. As schools entered the twentieth century a number of innovations were proposed and some tested. Various uses of summer school have helped. Every aspect of schooling has seen some improvements, at least in some quarters. Other improvements have been considered and some implemented with varying degrees of success.

New technologies of the early to mid-twentieth century, such as radio, movies, and television, then allowed educators to pursue better and more cost-effective instructional methods. Those technologies have enabled education to be provided to larger groups of students across geographically large areas. We chose the year 1950 as the end of this set of developments because of the truly revolutionary educational developments and improvements to be encountered in the years after 1950. Of the various proposals, methods, and technologies studied in Part II, there are many still worthy of consideration now in the twenty-first century. Economics, during this 330 year interval, played a minor role in terms of the helpful incentives it could have provided. However, it did play an indirect role in the latter years of this period in the sense that a number of developments had the effect of making some schools more cost-effective.

CHAPTER 5

Graded Schools in America

MANY OF THE EDUCATIONAL formats and policies that had found success in Europe were imported into colonial North America. Mirroring its successes in Europe, the Calvinist branch of Protestant education was also going to play a prominent role in the British colonies and new countries in North America. Given the subsequent history of education within the United States of America, many historians believe that no state played a more prominent role than the Commonwealth of Massachusetts as influenced by its Puritan founders. In that camp was historian Ellwood Cubberley who put it this way,

> Of all those who came to America during this early period the Calvinistic Puritans who settled the New England colonies contributed [the] most that was valuable to the future educational development of America.[119]

As we shall discuss farther along, other historians of American education claim that Ohio played an equally important or perhaps even more important role than the developments in Massachusetts did.[120]

PUBLIC EDUCATION COMES TO AMERICA

The Mayflower Puritans, better known as the Pilgrims, lost little time after their first arrival at Plymouth in 1620 and by 1635 had already established the Boston Latin School, which is still in operation—now almost 400 years later.[121] In our modern parlance it would have been a combined middle/high school and was designed to be a college preparatory institution. Although public in its ownership, it was not free as it charged tuition.

The Massachusetts Bay Colony included areas outside Boston. It was within the eastern parts of the current day Commonwealth of Massachusetts and was about half its current size. Established in 1630, this colony lost little time in passing laws on education. As for public schools, the Law of 1642 and the Law of 1647 required towns to:

- Have compulsory attendance for certain age ranges.
- Punish parents of truants with fines.
- Require instruction in reading and religion.
- Hire at least one teacher.
- Establish a grammar school (essentially a middle school) if it was a larger jurisdiction.[122]

Historian Cubberley saw these laws as essential to the growth of American public education writing,

> It can be safely asserted, in the light of later developments, that the two laws
> of 1642 and 1647 represent the foundations upon which our American state
> public-school systems have been built.[123]

For another 150 years, or so, the structure and policies of government regulated, and supported education slowly evolved. Details of the curricula changed some. For example, instruction in Latin went from a graduation requirement to an optional elective. Preparing students for further studies or for a vocation evolved as the arts, sciences, and technology changed.

After 1830 the three levels of American schooling have remained approximately constant with

- Primary schools bringing children to basic skill levels in reading, writing, and mathematics.
- Grammar schools, or middle schools, advancing those skills and instructing in others.
- Academies or high schools preparing older children for university level studies or other vocations.

By 1890 kindergarten and the combined primary and grammar school became common and was often renamed as the elementary school.[124] Much later the designation, K-8, would become common.

Lancasterian schools were popular in the early years of the American republic

The low cost of operating schools using the monitorial system of Lancaster was found to be a good fit for many primary schools. Using advanced children as instructors made most sense when the essentials of reading or writing were being taught to the younger pupils. The *flip side* of these low-cost advantages was the ability of modestly endowed towns to then be able to educate most of their children without bankrupting themselves. The Governor of New York State, De Witt Clinton, thought highly of Lancaster and his monitorial schools writing in 1809 that,

> I consider his system as creating a new era in education, as a blessing sent down from Heaven to redeem the poor and distressed of this world from the power and dominion of ignorance.[125]

While the specific format used in Lancasterian schools is no longer of much interest, its key element of peer to peer instruction is a fairly common practice in American schools. As self-pacing instructional formats come more and more into use it is likely to become a widespread component of instructional practices.

AT WHAT AGE SHOULD SCHOOLING BEGIN?

Few parents and stakeholders in K-12 education question the tradition that children should begin their K-12 schooling at age five. When it is discussed the issue is often concerning whether the child's enrollment should be postponed until he or she is socially ready for the challenges of kindergarten. One rarely hears an opinion that enrollment should occur at a younger age. Well then, what does science have to say about this?

Science says three years of age is an appropriate age for children to start school

When discussing the evolution of anything it helps to define the starting points. One of the questions that is faced in graded and ungraded schools alike is at what age or ages should young children be first enrolled? Should that age be older—maybe 7 or 8—as Pestalozzi proposed? Or should it be younger as neurobiologist Pasko Rakic recommends (discussed a few pages back in Chapter 4's section *Pestalozzian Defects*)? Early Puritans in Massachusetts favored age 3. These early New England colonists, according to David Angus and collaborators writing in 1988, believed

> . . . that young children were more capable of intellectual activity and moral responsibility than we do today.[126]

But adherents of progressive education favored an older starting age for schools

Angus and his collaborators also reported that some nineteenth century physicians favored the later start. Take Dr. Amariah Brigham. He expounded that early

> . . . intellectual stimulation of young children weakened their growing minds and eventually led to insanity.[127]

Like so many ideologues of his time (and our own) Brigham did not bother to test his theory. His approach was the opposite of scientific. As we saw above, the science is on the side of the Puritans in their preference for an early start to a child's schooling. For Massachusetts, in the year 1840, the entrance age for school was three. At that time officials reported roughly 40% of three-year olds were already in school.[128]

And what have modern societies done? They've done the opposite by favoring a later age for the child's first enrollment. A win for the progressives and Pestalozzians. But a loss for children and society. When educators follow a practice not supported by the science, they are in effect subverting best practices.

UNGRADED SCHOOLS IN AMERICA

By this juncture in our discussion we have reviewed relevant aspects of the history of European education since medieval times as well as some of the early history of American education. We'll now turn to the stories of education in the United States and the earlier British Colonies in North America.

In studying the American schools of the early nineteenth century we learn of differences between rural schools and those in cities. Rural schools had a rather long summer vacation while the more urban communities had much shorter vacation periods spread throughout the year.[129] The rural schedule was dictated by the need for child labor in the fields while the urban schedule had no such seasonal need for child labor. And, what schedule is now followed in nearly all-American schools? We all know: It's the rural schedule with long summer vacations.

Efforts to make these ungraded one room schools more efficient often followed a familiar pattern already discussed. Aspects of Lancaster's Monitorial system would be introduced, but not in a formal sense. Rather teachers would find it expedient to appoint older more advanced students to be assistant teachers—monitors in the nomenclature of Lancaster. As we shall see later, even graded schools would resort to the use of assistant teachers when subgroups within a class required different instructional services.

EVOLUTION TO GRADED SCHOOLS IN AMERICA

Before 1830 the concept of graded schools was foreign to educators in the United States. As towns and cities grew, their schools were also growing in size. But the methods of instruction still relied on schools with one or two large rooms in which up to several hundred pupils would be educated. As mentioned above the Monitorial system or something similar would be employed to allow *subgroup* instruction.

Was the graded school imported or did it evolve? It was a combination of these.

Over the twentieth century various scholars and historians had debated the causal factors that led to the shift away from ungraded schools towards graded schools that occurred in the mid-nineteenth century. One school of thought contended that the concept of graded schools was mostly imported from the systems of Prussia where graded schools were traditional. Frederick McClusky, an early twentieth century scholar of education systems, advanced that view in an article he published in 1920.[130]

Historian of education, Ellwood Cubberley, was in a second camp believing that graded schools evolved slowly as a result of larger and growing school populations within various communities.[131]

Our review of the literature puts us in a middle camp. Had there been no influence from the Prussian systems, there still were trends underway in the early nineteenth century that would have led to more and more graded schools in the later years of that century. We can visualize this evolution in five steps as to how this happened (or would have happened) for elementary education of children in the age range of 6 through 14:

1. The one room schoolhouse.

2. Two schools, either sharing a building or separate, one a primary school and one a grammar school.

3. Three schools, one an early primary school, another an upper primary school, and a third a grammar school.

4. Four schools or grade levels wherein each level would instruct children of approximately the same age—within two years. So, 6 and 7 year-olds would be together. As would 8 and 9 year-olds. Etc. Etc.

5. Eight grade levels in which children would be instructed for one-year in each level.

Were this the entire story, then Cubberley's theory would be confirmed. But it is not the whole story.

In Chapter 2, we discussed the research of French scholar Victor Cousin and the English translation of the book he wrote on the school system of Holland. Cousin had, earlier, visited Prussia in the early 1830s and wrote a book on that—also translated into English.[132] After that book became available in the United States in 1835, a great deal of interest in the school systems of Prussia arose in the United States. For example, Boston philanthropist Edwin Dwight was inspired by Cousin's book to provide financial support towards the development of graded schools within Massachusetts.[133]

American educators go on inspection tours, mostly to Prussia

In the two decades following 1823 no less than five American educators visited Europe to learn about their school systems and four of them made contact with German educators in Prussia. The five were:

- William Woodbridge, a geography teacher, from Hartford who studied in Europe for about four years after 1823.[134] He didn't visit Germany or its Prussian region, but he was close by in Switzerland.

- Charles Brooks, of Boston, was mentored by Prussian educator Dr. Julius during his 1834 visit.[135] He also visited and corresponded with the French expert Victor Cousin during his time in Europe.[136]

- Henry Barnard, of Hartford, spent 1836 in Germany and made an extensive study of their schools.[137]

- Calvin Stowe, of Cincinnati, made an official visit to Prussia in 1836–1837 to study their graded school systems.[138] In his report on their schools he did not use the word *graded*. Rather he used the label *parts* to describe the numbered grades of the school he observed.

- Horace Mann, of Massachusetts, also made an official tour of Prussia in 1843 to conduct a detailed investigation of their graded schools.[139] Mann was probably the most energetic advocate of these kinds of graded schools as is evident by his treatment by historians.

> In case the reader is wondering, Calvin Stowe was not as famous as his wife, Harriet Beecher Stowe, well known as the author of the abolitionist book, *Uncle Tom's Cabin.*

So then one might ask: Which of these emissaries had the greatest impact on the establishment and/or improvement of American graded schools? It is really difficult to judge.

McClusky's two articles suggest that Stowe's reports from his 1837 visit to Germany led to legislation in Ohio that established a graded system in the year 1838.[140],[141] Specifics about their school operations were not as detailed as those later given for Massachusetts schools, but it seems that educators in Ohio were adopting these new formats earlier than their peers elsewhere within the United States.

Enthusiasm for graded schools came about a decade later in Massachusetts but was at least as intense as that of Ohio. The European visits of Brooks and Mann played a role—with Mann gathering an impressive amount of information on Prussian public schools. Also important was Dwight's intellectual and financial support of Mann and others that led to many changes in Massachusetts between 1840 and 1848.

Horace Mann had a very large impact on American public education

As Secretary of the Board of Education of Massachusetts, Horace Mann had many opponents of his plans to introduce the Prussian format into the Commonwealth. After his return from Prussia he spoke widely on the benefits that would come from adopting some of the Prussian education policies. Before he could produce a formal report about his proposals there was much controversy and opposition to his ideas. The official report he wrote, the *Seventh Report for 1843 of the Secretary of the Board of Education of Massachusetts*, included a number of rebuttal paragraphs in an effort to calm his opponents.[142] About some of his detractors he had this sardonic quip, that they

> . . . belong to the same school of bigotry with those who inquired if any good could come out of Nazareth.

It might also be noted that Mann was not solely focused on schools, but also on other public institutions such as hospitals and prisons. He had this curious statement about the mental hospitals of Prussia:

> In regard to lunatic asylums, I have seen none superior, nor any in all respects equal, to our State Institution at Worcester.

This suggests that, in his view, the young Commonwealth of Massachusetts was ahead of trendsetter Prussia in at least one area of government service—the treatment of the mentally ill. It also seems inconsistent with the modern assumption that the word *lunatic* is a frowned upon and slang usage. But here we learn or infer that it was a perfectly proper technical term commonly used by professionals in the nineteenth century!

The launch of graded schools in America

The first well-known and documented effort establishing a graded school in the United States was undertaken by John D. Philbrick. As Principal of the Quincy Grammar School of Boston his form of school organization had multiple grade levels, each grade had its own curriculum and each had a test students must pass to be promoted.[143] His plan was very popular among school leaders and by 1860 most urban schools in the United States were similarly graded. Not long after that, according to William Shearer:

> By 1870 the pendulum had swung from no system to nothing, but system.[144]

More than any other political leader within the United States it was Horace Mann who popularized graded classes for American schools beginning in about 1848.[145] Graded schools were rapidly introduced in many American cities. Detroit, Michigan was one.

In 1853 its Board of Education said this in their description of their graded system of instruction,

> . . . several hundred scholars in different departments are placed under the general superintendence of a principal teacher and subject to his classification. This classification is based upon the degree of attainment in studies, regardless of age or condition in life.[146]

We infer from this statement that some students might be classified having skills incompatible with annual promotion to the next grade. Some would be double promoted. Some would be retained in grade to repeat the previous term. It is not clear from their descriptions whether this kind of promotion policy would be of significant benefit to the students. It had problems and we discuss some of them later, mainly in Chapter 6.

PROTESTANT NON-DENOMINATIONAL PUBLIC SCHOOLS

In the British colonies of North America and in the early decades of the newly founded republic of The United States of America there was little controversy over religious instruction in the public schools. Public schools were very much decentralized and organized on a town by town basis. Little is known about any disputes within communities over the religious dogma to be taught in the school or schools within. That began to change as public education evolved to have considerable central control from the state level.

Public School Protestant lowest common denomination theology

Horace Mann, in the 1850s and 1860s, had to deal with various Protestant denominations concerning the details of religious instruction. As Andrew Coulson relates:

> In order to minimize opposition from the many Protestant sects, Mann had assured them that the public schools would make regular use of the Protestant Bible [presumably the *King James* version], but that all particularities of dogma over which there was some debate among Protestants would be eliminated from the classroom. Mann was thus engaged in a difficult problem of religious arithmetic—one dealing with factions instead of fractions. His attempted solution, mirroring the concept of *denominators* in mathematics, was to find *the lowest common denomination* of all Protestant sects.[147]

As Coulson also recounts, the more theologically liberal denominations were accepting of Mann's solution, but the more orthodox Protestants took offense. Mann's compromise on religious instruction can be considered as the first step towards secularization of the public schools. Of necessity, this new theology was shorn of many specifics desired by particular denominations. They still had the *King James Bible*, but they had better be careful how to interpret it.

A contemporary of Mann was Horace Greeley, the chief editor of the *New York Tribune*. Though not really any kind of expert in K-12 education, Greeley's influence on the development of public education almost rivaled that on Mann because he had a very large audience of readers and he was quite vocal in his support of government operated public schools.[148] And, like Mann, he was also a Unitarian.

Blaine amendments confirmed Protestantism as a state religion—almost.

James G. Blaine represented Maine in the U.S. Congress, first as a Congressman and later as a Senator. In and after 1875, he proposed Constitutional amendments to the U.S. Constitution and to the Constitutions of almost two dozen states. These amendments prohibited tax revenues and other government assets from being used to subsidize any religious sect's schools. As the Roman Catholic population of the United States grew in mid-nineteenth century America, many Protestants feared the involvement of Catholics in American politics and feared that Roman Catholic schools would be recipients of government funds. Blaine's proposed amendment failed at the federal level, but ones like it succeeded in nearly forty states. One provision in most of these laws was protective of Protestantism: It required that the amendment could not be interpreted to exclude the Protestant Bible from public schools.

Many Catholic parents did not want their children exposed to Protestantism in the Protestant leaning public schools. This led hundreds of Catholic church parishes to establish their own schools. These parochial schools were supported by church funds and by tuition payments from parents. Their children and associated family budgets were at a clear disadvantage compared to their Protestant peers attending free public schools. Later in the twentieth century these bigoted policies stemming from the Blaine amendments would eventually lose their sting as the public schools became more and more secular.

That secularization was accelerated by U.S. Supreme Court decisions in 1962 and 1963 that broadly outlawed any required prayers, readings or religious studies in public schools.[149] A good review of the constitutionality of various religious practices in public education is provided in the book by Webb et al.[150]

After Protestant dogma died in the public schools: Did they preserve the Protestant ethic?

As school prayer, Bible reading, and other Protestant religious exercises were becoming less and less common in public schools, sometimes as the result of Supreme Court rulings, most public schools continued to observe and celebrate many remaining aspects of what we might label the Protestant ethic or culture.

Some analysts call this culture the *American Civic Religion*. It is not a religion so much as it is a patriotic philosophy that is embraced by most Americans regardless of denomination, religious sect or creed. It extends well beyond Protestant theology, over and beyond Roman Catholic theology as well as past many other religious and irreligious traditions. Thus, it also makes room for atheists, agnostics, and other secular types and can even encompass pagans. Respect and allegiance to this *American Civic Religion* includes:

- Recitation of the Pledge of Allegiance
- Hand on heart during playing of Star Spangled Banner
- Honoring the Declaration of Independence
- Honoring its author, despite his holding of slaves
- Faithful respect and adherence to the United States Constitution
- The singing of other patriotic songs
- Helping legal immigrants assimilate to American laws, customs, and ideals

Most adherents of this *American Civic Religion* also find that heresies to this philosophy include:

- Multiculturalism, in which loyalties extend beyond our borders and embrace un-American causes
- Sedition, in which subversive activities are endorsed
- Treason, in which enemies are given assistance
- Advocacy of dictatorships, socialism, communism and/or fascism.
- Disrespect of the American flag at sporting events.
- Affirmative action in which racial discrimination is defended as a *civil right*.

The political and philosophical orientations of public school educators are generally well left of center and this shows up in their choices of curricula, books, rules of conduct and other decisions that affect students' lives. It can even affect student safety when school violence is ignored, and perpetrators are not punished. Why would they ignore something like this and not punish the guilty? Answer: I believe that it would show a statistically disparate impact on certain minority groups—something the advocates of race-based affirmative action cannot tolerate.

> One of the author's grandsons was attacked and injured on a public school playground in Southern California, but the school refused to punish the perpetrators. The victim's parents successfully sued the public school district, resulting in the firing of the principal. I believe the school's policy was that of avoiding any disparate impact "results." It appears that even in the case of racially motivated violence the violations have been ignored.

Subverting the American Civic Religion in K-12 public schools. How bad is it?

When we say that there may be subversive attitudes and behaviors exhibited by educators in K-12 schools it is important to assess the magnitude of these kinds of problems. Such practices are almost always advocated by progressive educationists and much less often by more traditional educators. People who act subversively obviously disagree with one or more aspects of traditional American culture. Subversives are not just on the political left. Every political orientation has had or can have subversives. A list of some examples and their subversive behaviors in the general American society includes:

- The open border free market lobby. They often oppose sensible border control policies.
- Opponents of the First Amendment. Free speech is outlawed or only allowed in small areas.
- Opponents of the Second Amendment. They don't know that good guys with guns is good.
- The Federal Senior Executive Service. They are often insubordinate to their legitimate supervisors. Some of them are said to comprise the *Deep State.*
- Civil Service federal employees with loyalties to the *Deep State.* They'll try to negate elections.
- Federal prosecutors who act unjustly and are immune from prosecution. New laws are needed.
- Civil Rights activists who actually deplore Asians and Whites. If you're Asian, forget Harvard.
- The Antifa activists who exhibit fascist tendencies themselves. Are they hooligans?
- The open border Democrat lobby. Bring in illegal alien Hispanics who soon will vote for them?
- Transgender nonsense. No real science on this and much physical abuse of children ensues.

- Treason and sedition committed by subversives. Their loyalties are not here in America.

- Progressive education that opposes patriotism. They are re-writing history books to be one-sided.

These issues also pertain to K-12 education in the sense that teachers and others in the schools may be giving their opinions on these matters. In terms of actual courses in public schools we think that history, civics (where it is still taught), and English literature are all subjects where these subversive biases can significantly affect the political balance of what is taught. We will have much more to say on the teaching of history in Chapter 11 where we discuss the failings of public schools to adequately cover U.S. history.

ECONOMICS OF GRADED SCHOOLS

In examining the trends of the history of any societal institution there are often economic incentives at play. We saw that in our discussion of the printing revolution and how the availability of cheaper books allowed schools to expand. We also saw economic forces at work in our earlier discussion of how schools expanded as a result of the Protestant Reformation wherein church revenues that could be used for schools were kept locally within the parish to a much greater degree than had been the case under the Roman Catholic system.

When a school had sufficient numbers of pupils, then economies of scale could be exploited. Such schools using the monitorial systems were very inexpensive to operate given the almost free labor of the teaching assistants. Graded schools also had some economies of scale when numerous pupils at the same academic level and/or same age level were put in a classroom under one teacher. Graded schools, though more expensive to operate per pupil than those under the monitorial system, were producing better educated students who would go on to generate more wealth for themselves and their communities. That made graded schools worth the extra expense.

When a school did not have a large number of pupils, as was the case in many rural areas, the ungraded schools persisted. Schools could not be consolidated because children did not have transportation to the more distant schools that would result from consolidation. Generally, children would not be expected to walk more than two or three miles in each direction to attend a school. The advent of the motor driven school bus changed that. By the 1930s many rural school districts were combined into consolidated districts because the pupils could be transported to school by school buses.[151] Such schools were almost always graded schools, often with nine grade levels including kindergarten.

CHAPTER 6

Problems and Remedies for Graded Schools

As we have seen in the foregoing, the development of graded schools helped reduce the cost of educating children. Graded schools obtain those cost efficiencies by using group instruction in which many children benefit simultaneously from a teacher's presentations of the subject material. But many children do not prosper in such a "factory" of education. We explore this problem in what follows.

FUNDAMENTAL PROBLEMS WITH GRADED SCHOOLS

By the mid-nineteenth century, graded instruction became the most common type of practice in lower level urban schools, including primary and middle schools, for children in the age range of 6 through 14.

The fundamental assumption of a graded school with graded classes was that all students in a class would master the curriculum of that class, or a significant fraction of it, by the end of the annual academic term. Were that true, the graded format would have led to instructional efficiencies that would have made the operation of such schools relatively efficient. Yet, almost since the advent of graded instruction, experience has shown its cost effectiveness has not been nearly as high as assumed. Instead graded schools had and still have serious problems—as the heading suggests.

The mid-nineteenth century schools of St. Louis provide a good example. Its superintendent of schools in the early 1870s was William T. Harris. He became quite vocal about the problems he saw in their graded system. He observed that their graded system

- Held back fast learners.

- Often led repeatedly flunked students to become dropouts.[152]

His remedies included

- A plan that would allow promotion of fast learners every 10 weeks (about a fourth of the academic year).

- Consistent with that he'd convert the 40-week annual academic term to four 10-week terms per year.

He was not alone in his critiques of graded systems of instruction. Some twenty years later, and about 700 miles to his east, there was a school superintendent who had similar observations and who developed remedies in the school systems he led. That leader was William Shearer who led the public school system of Elizabeth, New Jersey in the years preceding and following the year 1900. We've already met Shearer in Chapters 1 and 5. Let's now review in some detail Shearer's work in this area.

SHEARER'S IMPROVEMENT TO GRADED SCHOOLS

William Shearer was a turn-of-the-20th-century educator who played leadership roles in American public education from two distinct vantage points during his career.[153]

- Though details are lacking, his first teaching assignment was in a one-room rural schoolhouse near Carlisle, Pennsylvania after his 1887 graduation from Dickenson College, also in Carlisle. With just one room it was by necessity an ungraded school in which students advanced only when they had reached some level of mastery of their lessons.

- Later, in his career, he was hired as Superintendent of Schools in three different locations: York, PA; Newcastle, PA; and then Elizabeth, NJ. In all three of these assignments he worked in school systems that used graded schools wherein students generally advanced with their classmates to the next grade unless retained an entire grade level or were double promoted.

Thus, his unique career that began in rural education and then moved into urban graded schools, gave him a useful perspective at the end of the nineteenth century from which he was able to discern the benefits and disadvantages of performance-based group instruction. In the rural, one-room schoolhouse, learning was necessarily self-paced given the lack of sufficient numbers of children of the same age. Later, in the urban setting, he could observe the efficiencies of graded schools employing group instruction, but he could also see how the slower and faster learners were abused by the rigidities inherent in that model. His experiences in these two different systems impressed on him many of the shortcomings of graded schools. Shearer's book, *The Grading of Schools*, published in 1898, gives one a sense of reverse déjà vu. His observations of the scene then are hardly any less true today. In Shearer's own words:

> When years ago, I left work in the rural schools and accepted a position in a system of graded schools, I was greatly impressed with the fact that, because

of the usual plan of grading, there was serious injury done to many pupils. In the rural school, pupils possessing the ability and determination were free to move forward, without dragging others with them and without being held back by those who either did not have the ability to move more rapidly over the work, or who lacked application. No such freedom existed in the graded school, where all were expected to move at the same rate for their whole school lives.[154]

In that same reference he also said:

> Though the graded school has many advantages, we should not close our eyes to the fact that it is open to the serious charge that it does not properly provide for the individual differences of the pupils; that it is not sufficiently pliant to accommodate itself to the pupils, but demands that the pupils accommodate themselves to it; and that that grading, which was intended to serve the children, has now become their cruel master.

Shearer, as a prominent education researcher in his own time, had performed statistical studies of the practices of retention and double-promotion, which were then the primary means by which slow and fast learners were placed according to their skills. In our current twenty-first century environment retention still exists, but is relatively rare. Most children are simply moved along with their cohorts regardless of their academic skills! In his time, he found that retarding or advancing a child an entire year was generally too large a step because the pupils concerned adapted poorly to their new placement. Sadness, frustration, and dropping out were common among those who had been flunked. And, perhaps ironically, those who skipped a grade often found themselves significantly behind their new classmates.

An example from the author's family is perhaps instructive about the difficulties of double-promotion and those of retention. At age seven, my mother was found to be reading at an advanced level and was double promoted from 1st grade into 3rd grade. Her older brother, three years older actually, was retained in 3rd grade twice, or as my octogenarian mother put it decades later, *more than once.* The result was that the two siblings ended up enrolled in the same 3rd grade classroom—an embarrassment to the brother and family. Eventually, the boy left his schooling after 8th grade, but his sister graduated from high school.

Shearer wondered philosophically and theologically: Why can't the pupils learn at

> . . . the pace that the Almighty intended they should instead of being obliged to go at the rate that some Board of Education had fixed?[155]

William Shearer's Pliant Plan of Grading ended cohort based groupings

Shearer observed some improvement when shorter academic terms of a half-year or a quarter-year were implemented. We wonder if he learned this from W. T. Harris, whom we just introduced in the preceding section, who had proposals for shorter academic terms? We surmise that Harris was more a proponent who didn't test his proposals while Shearer was the educator keen to test those ideas. Shearer implemented those ideas and found that advancing or retarding a child just one-month generally resulted in placements most suitable to that child's skill level. But it made for more complicated classroom management arrangements because each teacher might have roughly nine different *tracks* within a single classroom. With Shearer's experience in the rural schools, he was quite familiar with having multiple *tracks* within a class and found it straightforward to plan and manage his new system, which he titled, the *Pliant Plan of Grading*.[156]

According to Shearer's book, he first implemented this system in a prototypical school. He then introduced it system wide in the schools of Elizabeth, New Jersey. Using the one-month long academic terms together with the corresponding retention and advancement measures led to better school performance than in schools with the conventional arrangements.

Shearer found it odd that his type of instructional improvement or something similar had not been developed earlier in the 360-year interval since Sturm's original graded school? In his book he complains that graded schools still had a

> . . . medieval plan, which has long since outlived its usefulness.[157]

St. Louis educator Harris was a fan of Shearer's *pliant plan of grading*. He gave this testimonial, saying that Shearer had

> . . . perfected a plan of frequent promotions based on subject mastery, flexible enough to allow each student to be at different grade levels in different subjects.[158]

Despite these promising results, the administrative structures within the schools were quite complicated and as a result his novel format was never widely adopted. Also looming on the horizon were the proponents of Progressive education models who, among other reformers, were not much interested in students mastering their subjects. That kind of approach seems *subversive* of the goal that schools should produce well educated graduates. The next section looks at some of that.

CHILD CENTERED VERSUS CENTRALIZED ONE BEST SYSTEM MODELS

Schools for our children exist for one primary reason: To provide an instructional service by which a number of pupils can become educated in various subjects.

But what subjects should be taught and how should the instruction occur? Where should the control of the school or schools be placed? There is much disagreement over these questions.

Child-Centered theories of education

At one extreme is the Pestalozzian, child centered, view of education. We earlier discussed the pedagogy of Pestalozzi and made note of the fact that it was one of the earliest progressive philosophies of education. Actually, there are numerous variations of that kind of child-centered education. Generally, this approach is focused on the individual child's wants because the growing child chooses what to learn, when to learn it and what instructional resources to use. In its extreme form there is little adult supervision. It borders on anarchy.

But in practice there is adult supervision and provision of the resources to be made available. The school building, its books, its technologies and its teachers are chosen by adults. If it is a public school, these are chosen by government managers according to the relevant school policy legislation. Yet, based on this philosophy, different schools would be different because the children in one school would make different choices than children in another. In theory, we can imagine allowing children to vote on their curricula, schedules, and school staffing. In practice it is difficult to imagine such arrangements.

The most famous and more recent educator associated with the progressive label was John Dewey. It's not clear to what extent Dewey was really progressive in his educational proposals. He espoused a curriculum, but one that perhaps he thought a child would choose over a traditional one? He still had most of the traditional subjects with others added, such as training for vocations.[159] Did his woodshop teacher really just turn the pupils loose in the room to experiment with the tools and lumber? Or was there some teacher led instruction in their uses? Being a pure progressive pedagogue was going to be difficult for Dewey or was the concept sufficiently vague to accommodate Dewey's recommendations?

Given the near impossibility that schools could be structured that way, schools that call themselves progressive generally have aspects of its theoretical freedoms. But the typical progressive school has characteristics of more highly structured learning environments. So, for example:

- Many have curricula.

- Many have grade levels.

- Many have testing.

- Many have teacher-controlled instruction.

- Many operate under state, county, and district laws that limit their activities.

- Many have a political slant that is to the left and sometimes even subversively anti-American.

This suggests that educators who promote the concept of progressive pedagogy frequently do not realize that a great deal of their progressive philosophies lead to contradictions over who controls what.

The centralized "One Best System" theories of education

At the other extreme of progressive education, we have rigid one-size-fits-all pedagogies in which there is, but one curriculum that is enforced over the largest possible geography. In the context of the United States this would mean a national curriculum that would be imposed on all schools public and private. We in the United States recently came dangerously close to this kind of juggernaut when the *Common Core State Standards* (CCSS) were imposed nationally by Presidential dictat under the Obama administration. The mandates imposed theoretically became moot when the successor administration of Donald Trump came to power. But in reality, many of the states still impose the CCSS under their own authority.

This concept of centralized standards and control once went under the label, *The One Best System*. By its very title this system would not have comparable counterpart systems and would be the best among all other systems. The title is false on its face because there are many school systems that are very good and among them the one deemed best depends on the details of the metrics used to compare them. David Tyack wrote a book on this with the title, *One Best System—A History of American Urban Education*.[160] That label's subtitle suggests that if there were that *Best System* somewhere it would be in our urban education systems? That is ridiculous given that urban systems are among our worst school systems. So, with *One Best System* we are really dealing with a nonsensical euphemism; it is oxymoronic.

The *One Best System* title is meant to put a happy face on this philosophy's real goal: The central control of education either at the state level or the federal. It is a political quest, not necessarily one to benefit the pupils. Some of the characteristic beliefs of the *central control* lobby include:

- Rural towns are too stupid to run their own schools.

- Professional experts should take control from politicians.

- Control of school systems should be centralized at the county or state level—preferably the latter.

- Elections of school officials should be non-partisan (and thus more easily controlled by the teacher unions and the education establishment).

- The curriculum (not curricula) would be one and the same everywhere nationally.

- The curricula of high schools should be expanded to include vocational courses (either as an elective option or as a requirement).

Despite his affiliation with *child-centered* versions of Progressive education, John Dewey was also an advocate for the *One Best System* centralization philosophy.[161]

He was for it before he was against it and then later, he was for it again!

He was an advocate of an expanded curriculum that would require both academic and vocational courses for each high school student. Albert G. Lane, at one time the Superintendent of the Chicago Public schools from 1891–1898 and a disciple of Dewey, was in line with this thinking. It is then not surprising that the high school in Chicago bearing his name, Albert G. Lane Technical High School, had that same curricular requirement for many years.

> As author I can attest to this for I was a student at Lane Tech during the late 1950s. I was forced to take two years of shop, actually four one-semester long courses: Wood shop, electric shop, air conditioning shop, and aviation shop. Which shop taken was actually an elective. I also took its college prep sequence of courses including two years of German language study.

What is interesting about the proponents of these two avenues of progressive advocacy for school systems is their utter lack of attention to the economics of their proposals. You would think there were no private competitors to the public schools. You would think that children are not sometimes tutored at home (as in homeschooling). You would think that the political leanings of these advocates, often with socialist tendencies, are not mentioned nor even hinted on.

This brings us to an interesting event some years ago in 2011 at a Harvard University conference on education reform that this author attended and witnessed. Paul Pastorek, a former Louisiana Superintendent of Public Instruction, addressed the audience on the U.S. education system. He said he could tell us in one word its main characteristic. He said it is a *communist* system. He then explained how schools under the former Soviet Union were run in essentially the same way as American public schools are operated today. He put it this way in the symposium proceedings:

> The problem is that we don't know how to leverage competitive forces in the multibillion-dollar business that is education in this country. Our education

system is a communist system; we don't have anything that relates what we pay for resources to the economic value they generate.[162]

What amazed this author more than anything else about his stark language, essentially calling public educators *communists*, was the audience reaction of . . . silence. Not one person in attendance at this Harvard conference objected. I didn't even see anyone grimace. The way Pastorek explained his comment made complete sense at the time. Or enough sense to keep things calm!

Upon reflection we'd replace the *communist* label with *socialist*, as it is more accurate. In the history of communist regimes, the Communist party generally came to power by means of violent revolution or by external military force. Socialists, in contrast, typically come to power by democratic government action. Both systems favor government ownership of most economic sectors, but communists nearly always want the government owning most of it while in comparison socialists generally allow some private enterprise—at least in practice if not in theory. Given that American public schools are entirely owned and run by government organizations and were established by democratic means it is thereby persuasive to call them *socialist*.

By treaty, the United Nations gives parents control of education?

There is a third theory of education in which the K-12 marketplace gives parents much more control over their children's education. So, here in America, who should have the political control over the education of children? Their parents? The local school board? The local town or city? The county? The state? The U.S. government? Shall we ask the United Nations? The answer:

Their parents.

The *United Nations' Universal Declaration of Human Rights* actually declares this in *subparagraph (3)* of its *Article 26*:

Parents have a prior right to choose the kind of education that shall be given to their children.[163]

Subparagraph (2) of that same *Article 26* also requires signatory nations to promote:

- Respect for human rights
- Basic freedoms
- Good international relations
- Good relations among different religions
- Helping the United Nations maintain world peace

The United States is a signatory to this treaty and thereby is bound to enforce its provisions. The U.S., at best, gives these provisions lip service. Advocates of school vouchers often make arguments based on subparagraph (3) because parental choice inherent in a voucher would give them that *right to choose*. Thus, at least in an international context as well as in our own national context, the parents of American children have the right of school choice. Surely, parents have the right to choose schools for their children if they have the resources to pay for them. Whether the government should support this right financially through the provision of vouchers, scholarships, loans, tax-credits, etc. is a controversial issue.

> This author was involved in two school voucher ballot initiative campaigns in California in 1993, and 2000. As a speaker, and speechwriter in those efforts, I can report to you that this treaty obligation was often cited as an inducement to gain support, and votes.

The provisions of subparagraph (2) suggest that, at a minimum, the subjects of history, civics, and religion should be taught in sufficient detail to support good relations among nations and among religions.

This kind of freedom of choice is almost the diametric opposite of the concept of *The One Best System*: One has parental control. The other has political autocratic central control. Moreover, parental control is also inconsistent with the Progressive theories of education that are characterized at one extreme by putting the children in control or at the other extreme by putting the politicians in the driver's seat.

CHAPTER 7

Digressions and Improvements to Graded Schools

IT IS INTERESTING TO consider the value of kindergarten. As the highest level of preschool education, is it a preparatory phase of elementary school academics or is it something else? Some see it as a recreational activity with little emphasis on subject matter. Pamela Jean Bell, author of children's books, remembers her year of kindergarten as an unwanted interruption in her learning process.[164] So, what is its history?

THE ROLE OF KINDERGARTEN

In 1840, German educator Friedrich Fröbel invented the idea of a year devoted to preparing a child for primary school and he named it *kindergarten* (*child's garden* in English. He was an early advocate of Progressive education and as such did not emphasize the subject matter children might study.[165] Now, in the twenty-first century, kindergarten has mostly kept to its progressivist roots even in schools having a much more structured curriculum. Should kindergarten change its emphasis to help children rise academically, while still keeping some of its emphasis on recreation? Should kindergarten change its name? The tradition of kindergarten needs to be examined and if found wanting, it should be revised or replaced with something more consistent with a school system's academic goals.

Perhaps the new name for the instructional grade or level of 5-year old children should have a more academic meaning. Give it a name that suggests that it precedes primary school grades? In the German why not name it: Frühschule? Or in the English: Foreschool? Given these facts, we see traditional kindergarten as more of a diversion from progress than as an improvement to graded schools.

OTHER IMPROVEMENTS TO GRADED SCHOOLS

Since the beginning of the twentieth century many remedies/improvements have been tested and sometimes implemented to address problems inherent in graded schools. As we saw in a previous section, William Shearer understood the problems of graded schools better than most others during the late nineteenth century. He was able to correct some of these problems through his introduction of *pliant grading* in which the academic terms were shortened from one year to a small fraction of a year—sometimes to a month. That helped reduce the negative impacts of grade skipping and grade retention. And, it fostered higher student achievement.

The fans of *One Best System* were apparently not impressed with his reforms and soon the public (and private) schools of America were back to the traditional graded format in which the academic terms were either a full year or sometimes a half-year semester. This author was educated in the Chicago Public School system where the academic terms had long been a semester. So, if you flunked or were skipped ahead your new placement was only a semester behind or ahead of your former status.

Most research, over recent decades, has shown that students who are retained (flunked) in full year systems have eventual academic mastery not much better than those who are undeservedly promoted (social promotion). How were educators going to address this troubling dilemma?

In this section we will limit our discussion to instructional solutions not requiring any sort of modern electric and/or electronic technology. We will present the newer methods and technologies later.

With those limitations, there are three kinds of solutions or improvements:

- Improvements that help all students within a grade and class.

- Improvements that are focused on students who are sub-proficient in one or more subjects.

- Improvements that are designed to help students who are rapid learners to rise further and sooner.

General improvements that apply to all students

In the first group let's consider ten types of improvements:

Better teachers. One education economist, Eric Hanushek, has estimated the benefit of better teachers in America. Were just the bottom 8% of teachers fired and replaced with average teachers, it would bring United States schools to the approximate performance level of those in Canada. When students finish their K-12 education at a higher performance level, they will likely become more productive workers, managers, and owners of private businesses as well as in government services. Considered over their working lives the additional benefits to those students (and future workers) who were taught by the replacement teachers, according to Hanushek, would be about $30,000. Each of these workers would be paid more because they produced more services and products for the US economy. That would make the economy grow faster than the alternative of doing nothing. These workers, over their lifetimes, would each add many hundreds of thousands of dollars to the US economic output. When all of the benefits are added up over the millions of workers affected, Hanushek estimated an eventual benefit to the United States economy would register in the trillions of dollars. He calculated increase in the present value of future US economic output to be $112 trillion. In that reference, Hanushek was astounded at his own estimate and suggested that he should not claim such a large number and instead made a more comfortable estimate of half that, at $56 trillion![166]

Better books. When books are better aligned with the curriculum and present its contents in terms more understandable to the students taking a course, those pupils will perform better. If better teachers enrich the future US economy, then better textbooks might have a similar effect? We have not done a quantitative analysis on this, but let's consider the subject of mathematics. Here, among mathematicians, it is well known that some textbooks are much better than others. Children learning math from the better textbooks, such as those from Saxon Math or Singapore Math, perform at a much higher level than those learning from more traditional books. Without doing the financial calculations we can envisage benefits of the same order that come from having better teachers: Tens of trillions of dollars.

Direct Instruction. Here the teacher controls the delivery of information through lecture, recitation and reading assignments with less reliance on student led group-learning efforts as in the Project Method. Most research has shown Direct Instruction leads to higher student performance than the use of unverified contemporary alternatives.[167]

More homework. More time on task suggests that the pupil will absorb more of the content to be mastered. We can quibble over the word *homework*. Why not call this work *assignments*? Why not provide time, space, and facilitators for this work at the school site? Students having difficulty with a portion of an assignment could ask a facilitator or tutor for help—it's not so easy to do that at home. Maybe the answer is a longer school day including assignment work and no homework to be done at home?

More tests. Many short tests have been found superior to fewer longer examinations. Some teachers go to the limit of giving students a daily quiz. That literally forces pupils to study every day. This author knows the benefits of this practice from his own experience as a student and then later as a teacher using this method.

> The author attended a public high school in Chicago where his junior year math teacher, Charles Bauer, employed a daily quiz. The result: The author earned, and received an A in trigonometry-algebra II, in that 1957–1958 school year. Some years later I was myself a high school math teacher, and also followed this practice of a daily quiz. Students complained about the discipline it instilled. But at year's end more than one student complimented me by saying that the quizzes were detested, but that, as one student told me (and I paraphrase), "I learned more in your class than in any other."

Financial incentives. Payment for academic performance and/or fines for poor performance. In Texas, a 1990–1995 pilot study paid high school students $100 for each Advanced Placement (AP) exam they passed. Compared to 1989 statistics the numbers passing went up by more than a factor of 10.[168] In another study second grade students were paid to read more books with the result that their reading skills improved.[169] These kinds of learning incentives and their promise need further exploration and development.

Honest certificates. Diplomas and certificates would be awarded and restricted to those demonstrating adequate academic performance. Here we envision different kinds of certification: Proficiency in the class would be one. Attendance would be another.

Independent testing. Official testing used for promotion would be conducted by an independent testing organization, thereby removing the inherent conflict of interests of the traditional—and corrupt—practices of nearly all schools. Consider the Advanced Math and Science Academy (AMSA) in Massachusetts: It is a charter high school that effectively did this when they obtained most of their required courses and curriculum from the Advanced Placement (AP service of the College Board. Under that, the school was not permitted to do its own official testing, but was required to use the AP examinations instead. The result: In 2015 official state standardized testing every one of its tested students was rated proficient or better in both math and reading. In terms of the even higher standards of the *Nation's Report Card,* officially *the National Assessment of Educational Progress (NAEP,* it was estimated that 91% of

AMSA's tested students were proficient—also the highest in the state. As such AMSA was arguably the best public high school in Massachusetts in 2015.[170]

Standardized testing. States use standardized tests to measure how well students in their jurisdictions are performing against state academic standards. Some of these tests are national in scope. The Iowa Test of Basic Skills (ITBS) is probably the most well-known.[171] The ACT organization also has tests for most grade levels in K-12, beginning with 3rd grade.[172] At the federal level, the U.S. Department of Education manages the NAEP assessments that test statistical samples of students nationally and within each state in reading, mathematics, and other subjects.[173] All three of these testing regimes have a reputation for academic rigor, but ACT stands out among them for having the most professional and expert system for measuring and determining student skill levels according to the probability percentages that a student is *On track to be college and career ready*, once they reach 12th grade.

School choice. Giving parents the financial means to choose a school and reliable information about school characteristics can help improve a school's performance through the effects of competition. There are two benefits here: Firstly, the parent and student can choose a school that is better than a previously attended public school (or private school). Secondly, the economic competition will push all schools in the local marketplace to improve, thus benefiting the students even if some of them remain in the previous school. Sadly, almost all school voucher systems in the United States have neglected to provide reliable consumer information about the available schools. Then parents lack the information they need to make informed choices. As a result, confirmed by much research, government issued voucher programs have not improved student performance nearly as much as had been hoped. The reliable information is missing. One economist, George Akerlof, has a name for this:

> *A market for lemons.*[174]

These ten policies of this first group of general improvements are applicable to all students in any school. Thus, they improve the performance of all students. That will surely have the effect of reducing the numbers who test sub-proficient.

Improvements for students who learn too slowly or too rapidly

In the second and third groups of improvements the instructional interventions are provided only to one or another subset of a class. Typically, students who are sub-proficient or marginally proficient are invited to get additional instruction by one or more supplementary modes of instruction. And for the more capable, students are offered instruction to help them get ahead, or even skip a grade. These can include:

Summer school. Labeled as such, summer school has been in existence since about 1920.[175] Considerable research into the performance benefits of summer school has shown its clear benefit in raising a student's skills and knowledge.[176] Summer school has traditionally been used for remedial instruction to allow sub-proficient students passage to the next grade level. But summer schools have been used in academic enrichment programs as well. The author knows this: He was twice a student in summer school during his high school years in a successful effort to raise his already high-performance levels. Given the importance of summer school, we devote the next major section, *A Closer Look at Summer School*, to a more detailed elaboration of its role in K-12 education.

Double Dosing. Here the school provides additional periods of instruction and study to help the slower students keep pace with their more adept peers. We mentioned After School programs above. They could be considered sub-species of Double Dosing. At the high school level, Double Dosing is frequently accomplished by devoting two periods per day to the subject area needing further support. Providing these extra periods on the weekend is sometimes called Saturday school or Sunday school (the latter not to be confused with church run Sunday schools). The practice of Double Dosing has been found quite effective.[177]

After school or Saturday school. As just mentioned these remedial sessions or classes would be a form of Double Dosing and could include school initiated and financed tutoring.

Remedial Books. When students are not becoming proficient despite working diligently on the subject matter they may benefit from alternative textbooks and workbooks. Normally it would be the alert teacher who would choose such materials, but concerned parents could also play this role. Publishers have produced books aimed at such remediation. So, for example, there is for sale in our own era the book *Basic Remedial Mathematics* by James Johnson, Jr.[178] More generally, there are usually dozens of textbooks for any given elementary, middle or high school course. Some of these alternatives may provide a better and more understandable presentation of the subject than the assigned textbook and as such may be sufficient to provide the remediation sought.

Part Time Homeschool. These efforts could include parent led and/or financed tutoring.

Student Led. Student initiated supplementary reading and study. Here's an idea: Hang out at the library. Or find a tutor and beg your parents to hire said tutor. Choose friends smarter than yourself. Avoid delinquency.

Policy Corrections. Don't be a stupid school or school system with dumb policies. Chicago provides a fairly recent example. Suppose that Johnny, a marginal student, was required to attend summer school and suppose that he met the academic requirements of summer school that would allow him promotion to the next grade. Also suppose that at the end of the summer term Johnny has more than three unexcused absences from that summer school. The latter situation, according to the *Chicago Public Schools Policy Manual*, circa 2009, apparently requires that he be flunked anyway and retained for another year in his previous grade.[179] Surely this policy needed or still needs correction! We hope it has been fixed by now.

Schools and school systems that employ some of these smart policies will be able to significantly reduce their numbers of academically sub-proficient students. Still it is difficult to imagine that they will be able to bring those numbers to zero. There will be students who nevertheless don't *make the grade*. If a child attends elementary and middle schools and exits that enrollment without a certificate or diploma showing mastery or proficiency in the curricula of those schools, it may be problematic to allow them to enroll in a standard high school. This is not a new problem, but is at least a century old. The solution was the trade school or vocational school in which the academic requirements and instruction were relaxed compared to the more academically oriented regular high school. Its advantage was that it enabled many teenage students to get sufficient training for entry to the work force by the time they became an adult at age 18.

As we have already noted, these alternatives do not include many more recent options that typically involve computers. We'll get to those farther along. Even so the above remedies are still viable in our own time in the early twenty-first century.

In the context of this book, our goal is not directly that of choosing the best instructional system or systems that might apply to certain schools or systems of schools. Rather we want to survey some of the more promising new avenues from which others will choose the best for their use and consideration. Our theme is that of using economic incentives to create a healthy energetic and dynamic marketplace for K-12 education in which parents and other stakeholders will be the customers of the products and services within that economic sector. It is that competitive marketplace that will sort out and choose the best educational systems, services, and products— not us.

CLOSER LOOK AT SUMMER SCHOOL

As we noted above, summer school has been commonly available in the United States since about 1920. A review of many research studies has been conducted by Harris Cooper and colleagues with the goal of evaluating the benefits of summer school as compared to the alternative of a summer vacation.[180] Of the two, summer vacation was more common than summer school among most American K-12 students.

The experience of most Americans who attended elementary schools (K-8 years) was that, after returning to school from summer vacation, considerable time would be spent reviewing some of the previous year's instruction. That's this author's recollection. Different explanations were given for this review of material already covered in the previous academic term:

> Perhaps the students did not actually master the material from the previous grade level?

> Perhaps the students mastered the material and then forgot some of it during the summer?

The just mentioned research article, by Harris Cooper and colleagues, seems to confirm this latter hypothesis—particularly if the subject was mathematics. They found, roughly speaking, that elementary school students taking vacation in the summer lose about three months of math instruction of the previous year's nine months of enrollment.[181] They also found that, depending on other details, student proficiencies in reading over the summer vacation were approximately flat. Additionally, they found that those attending summer school and taking math and/or reading instruction, had their performance levels rising to about three months further advanced than the levels they had in June of the previous academic year.

Let's consider how various types of students can progress or move through the academic year for two different scenarios. If we breakup the academic year into quarters, as many colleges do, let's consider two kinds of student groups according to the *schedule* they follow:

- Regular schedule. Here the pupil is enrolled for three quarters (TQ) each year and takes summer vacation.

- Expanded schedule. Here the student attends school year around (YA) and takes summer school.

They represented this in a figure in their research article.[182] A simplified version of their figure follows:

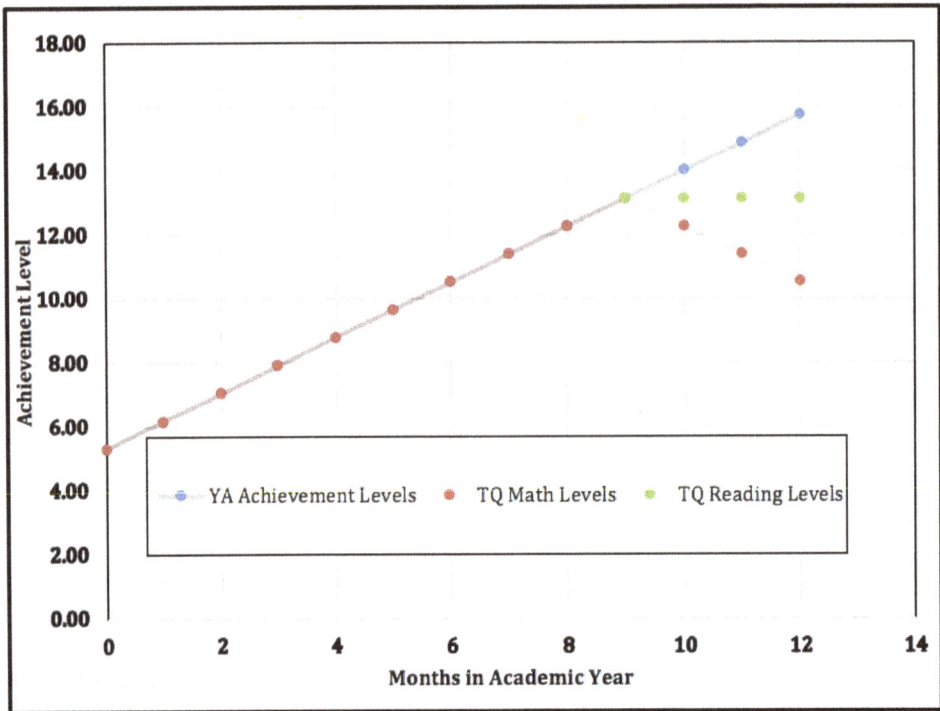

Figure 5 is based on information from Figure 2 in the article of Cooper et al.[183] It shows how achievement outcomes for middle SER (socio-economic range) students in mathematics and reading improved during the 9 months of the regular school year. Both continued improving during summer school. Students taking summer vacation saw their math performance dropping about one-third of the previous academic year's increase while their reading performance remained flat or constant. Achievement levels are in arbitrary units.

Cooper and collaborators also studied the performance levels of low SER (socio-economic range) students and found that both mathematics and reading skills drop when those students take summer vacation. For the higher SER students, only mathematics skills fell during the summer while reading skills stayed flat.

With the preceding information we can *construct* a thought experiment. Let's consider how various types of students can progress or move through the eight years of elementary school for the two different scenarios we labelled TQ and YA.

We further assume that the students having the regular schedule (TQ) over their eight years of elementary school enrollment take all seven summers off for vacation and that those on the expanded schedule (YA) always attend summer school. To keep our model simple, we shall assume that all students, regardless of socio-economic status, are affected the same way in our thought experiment.

Knowing that summer school instruction adds to a student's knowledge and skill levels in the two subjects and knowing that taking summer vacation actually subtracts from their math performance levels while leaving reading levels more or less constant suggest that summer school can be a very powerful *force* in moving a student to higher levels of math and reading performance.

In our discussion below, we mention the NAEP assessments, more formally those of the *National Assessment of Educational Progress*.[184] These assessments, taken together, are also known as the *Nation's Report Card*. They are administered by the National Center for Educational Statistics of the U.S. Department of Education. In the NAEP's subject area testing, including the subjects of reading and mathematics, the NAEP has established performance levels, or cut scores, that define the minimal levels of subject area knowledge. These performance levels are: *Basic, Proficient*, and *Advanced*. Roughly speaking they correspond to performance levels of being behind a grade level year, being just at grade level, and at being ahead one grade level year.

For each schedule and subject, we will consider three kinds of students according to their performance levels that we label: Mastery, Proficient, and Marginal. They are described as follows:

- Mastery level. These are relatively excellent students who would typically earn an A in these subjects. Given the typical grade inflation in K-8 schools these students are assumed to be 8th grade NAEP advanced when they complete 8th grade on the TQ schedule or are assumed to be performing at 10th grade NAEP advanced or higher levels if they are on the YA schedule.

- Proficient level. These are students who would typically earn a B in these subjects. Based on the typical grade inflation in K-8 schools these students are assumed to be barely proficient on the 8th grade NAEP tests when they complete 8th grade on the TQ schedule. For those on the YA schedule they perform at the NAEP advanced level when they finish 8th grade.

- Marginal level. These are students who typically pass their courses with a C average in these subjects. Based on typical grade inflation in K-8 schools these students are assumed to be barely at NAEP's basic level when they complete 8th grade on the TQ schedule. In some schools those on the TQ schedule would receive a failing grade and yet still move to the next grade level under typical social promotion policies. When on the YA schedule these students are just barely NAEP proficient when they complete 8th grade.

We caution the reader that this is a thought experiment based on research that appears to be reliable. There are no guarantees from the author that schools operated year around (YA) would show the precise achievement gains we estimated in the charts below. But we are confident in the qualitative reliability of these estimates. Another word of caution regards the details of the instructional scheduling and the instruction, itself, which might reduce or even increase the magnitude of the effects seen here.

Reading Performance Grade Levels for Regular and Expanded Schedules

The graph in Figure 6 nearby shows how significant this effect is for reading.

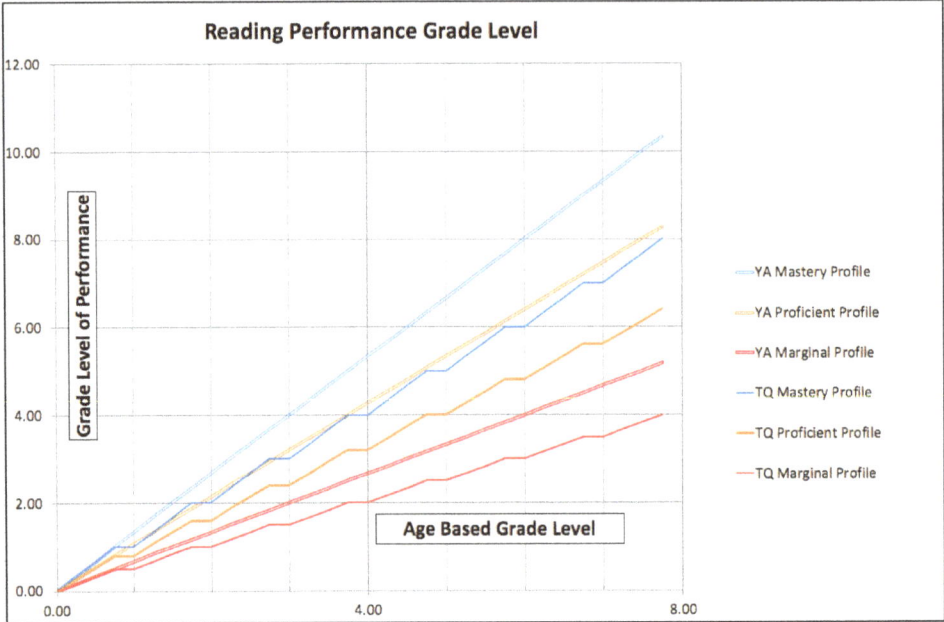

Figure 6 displays hypothetical reading performance grade levels (essentially scores) of three idealized students under the two scenarios of TQ and YA. One performs at a mastery level, one is borderline proficient, and the last one is a marginal student. The vertical scale indicates what scoring grade levels these children, in grades 1–8, would have obtained if they were taking the test. The TQ Reading profiles, displayed by the single lines, also show that the students didn't forget anything over their summer vacations. In contrast the double lines, with the abbreviation of YA for year-around, show the predicted and continually increasing performance grade levels of the year-around students who always enroll in summer school.

The single and double lines in Fig. 6 follow the reading progress of six hypothetical students. Three of them have single lines and have the traditional school schedule for three quarters (TQ) of the year and always take summer vacation. The last three of them have double lines and attend school year around (YA) and as you'd guess make more academic progress than their TQ peers. Of the TQ students,

- One is an excellent student (the solid blue line) who generally gets top grades in reading and ends 8th grade with a full 8th grade mastery of the reading curriculum.

- The next one is a barely proficient student (the solid orange line) who gets grades at the proficient threshold, with a full 6th grade mastery in reading, which is the threshold for proficient 8th grade performance.

- The third student (the solid red line) is marginal, some would say a poor student, and tests at the 4th grade level in math when in 8th grade. This is a failing grade in most schools.

And for the YA students,

- The excellent student (double blue line) finishes 8th grade testing somewhat above the 10th grade level.

- The fairly proficient student (double orange line) finishes 8th grade testing just above the 8th grade level.

- The marginal pupil (double red line) finishes 8th grade testing just above the 5th grade level, which is just barely passing in most schools.

As we noted above, Cooper et al indicated that among the TQ students there is approximately no loss of reading skills or knowledge during a summer vacation. The flat segments of the single lines represent this. Now if the three students attend school year around YA, taking summer school during every summer of their elementary school careers, their reading levels are shown by the double lines in Fig. 6. As evident from the figure, when they finish 8th grade they perform up to two grade levels higher in reading.

Mathematics Performance Grade Levels for Regular and Expanded Schedules.

Next, we look at the math performance for the two scenarios for these three students. As we mentioned above, the benefits of summer school are significantly higher for math than they were for reading.

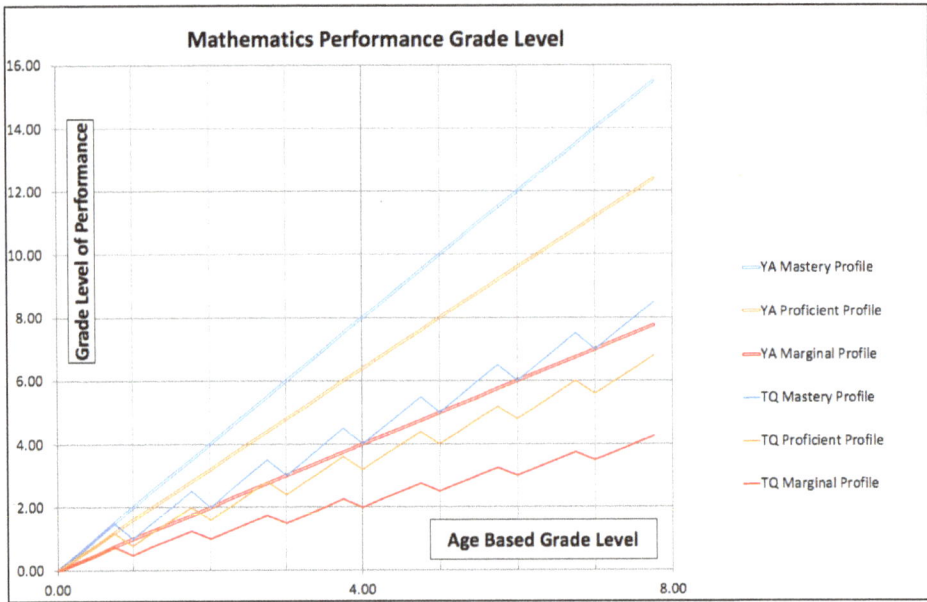

Figure 7 displays hypothetical math performance scores of the three idealized students under the two scenarios of TQ and YA. One pupil performs at a mastery level, one is borderline proficient, and the third one is a marginal student. The vertical scale indicates what scoring grade levels these children, in grades 1 through 8, would have obtained if they were taking the test. The TQ mathematics profiles, displayed by the solid lines, also show that the students lost about one quarter's worth of instruction over their summer vacations. In contrast the double lines show the predicted performance grade levels of the year-around (YA) students who always enroll in summer school. The advantage of summer school for mathematics is quite striking.

The solid lines in this figure follow the mathematics progress of the three hypothetical students who have the traditional school schedule, TQ, for three quarters of the year and always take summer vacation.

- One is an excellent student (the solid blue line) who generally gets top grades in mathematics and ends 8th grade with a full 8th grade mastery of the mathematics curriculum.

- The next one is a barely proficient student (the solid orange line) who gets proficient grades in mathematics and ends 8th grade at the proficient threshold, which is just below 7th grade mastery in mathematics.

- The third student (the solid red line) is marginal, some would say a poor mathematics student, and would not be passed given his or her 4th grade performance as 8th grade is ending.

The research of Cooper et al indicated that there is roughly a three-month loss of mathematics skills or knowledge during a summer vacation. The downward segments of the solid lines in Fig. 7 represent this.

Fig. 7 also displays the benefit of summer school in which the math students have year around (YA) instruction. Under this assumption our three students have mathematics skills that are characterized by

- The excellent student (double blue line) finishes 8th grade with mathematics skills about a half grade above the 15th grade level.

- The fairly proficient student (double orange line) finishes 8th grade with mathematics skills about a half grade above the 12th grade level.

- The marginal pupil (double red line) finishes 8th grade with mathematics skills just below the 8th grade mastery level. This type of student does well in school when taught year around unlike the (flunking) situation when the traditional schedule is followed.

The reader might ask how some of these mathematics performance levels could be so far above 8th grade levels and in fact be as high as a college graduate in 15th grade? The answer is *time on task*—combined with adequate instructional resources at each step along the way.

Flies in the ointment shall be swatted and overcome

There are some rather obvious flaws in the scenarios just presented. For one, the blue and orange double lines presume an arrangement of classes and curricula that are rare in elementary schools. A year around (YA) pupil on those two lines would progressively have higher and higher skills than the age-based class with which they started. As we are assuming these schools to be graded, such a mix of skills within a class would require the teacher to have more than one instructional track. This would require using an ungraded format as discussed earlier or could employ Shearer's pliant grading system. If the policy allows double promotion and retention that would reduce the number of tracks a teacher would manage to no more than four of them per class. Each of those four would cover material separated by a quarter of a year.

Now, assume that it takes a quarter of a year to cover a chapter in a four-chapter book for that school year. Then at different points within the year four different subgroups would be in one or the other of the four chapters. As the subgroups would finish the book they'd start on the next book in the instructional sequence. If this sounds complicated and confusing it is because it is that way!

Looking ahead from these twentieth century problems into the twenty-first century, there are going to be, and already are, instructional models that are much more accommodating of each student's pace of learning. Instead of a handful of tracks under each teacher, there can be as many tracks as there are students. This is a note of optimism: That whatever the drawbacks of mixed schedules of traditional and year-around students, they will be remedied with the methodologies and technologies of the twenty-first century.

AUDIO-VISUAL IMPROVEMENTS

The label *audio-visual* became part of the vocabulary of K-12 education most prominently in the 1930s. By that time a number of new information dispersal mediums had come of age. They included:

- The phonograph
- Audio tape players
- Motion pictures

A number of educators of that era began studying the many ways in which audio-visual media could be used in the advancement of K-12 education. Audio-visual pioneers of that period included co-authors Harry McKown and Alvin Roberts. As they wrote in their book on audio-visual aids, they were interested in studying

1. How can these aids be utilized to replace antiquated and obsolete methods and materials?[185]

2. How to incorporate them as integrative and supplementary, rather than as separate and substitutionary agents?

On this second question they seem to be giving a political answer in that they want to avoid replacing any functions of the teacher. They prefer audio-visual components that don't threaten a teacher's employment. A better policy would be to evaluate the options to determine what mix of resources is best for the students. If such an analysis shows that changing the teacher's work assignment will improve the learning experience, then by all means make those changes.

McKown and Roberts had a quite expansive list of types of audio-visual aids that almost literally includes every conceivable item excepting the teacher's voice and the assigned books. They considered the following types of items, in alphabetical order, as audio-visual aids:

Blackboard and bulletin board

Charts: of various types

Dramatics: pantomime, plays, pageants, puppet shows, debates

Flat pictures: photographs, prints, post cards

Graphs: of various kinds

Maps: of various kinds

Models: museum exhibits, artifacts, and specimens

Motion pictures: silent and with sound

Phonographs: records and transcriptions

Posters, cartoons and clippings

Radio and public address systems

Stereoscopes

Projected still images

Trips: journeys, tours, and visits[186]

Drawing on my own experience as a K-12 student circa 1950, nearly all of these were in use. Most memorable were the movies and field trips.

McKown and Roberts noted that animation could be used to show various phenomena more precisely than would be possible through any book, lecture or even an experiment.[187] For example, slow motion can be used to understand the dynamics of moving entities better than viewing them at full speed.

With regard to educators' goals of making learning more effective they reported on studies showing that students absorbed four times as many details from movies as compared to the alternative of reading and discussion, and moreover remembered what was learned for longer intervals into the future.[188] Also of interest to our study of sick schools, their book makes note of the use of movies as a remedial resource. On that point they remarked that

Students of lower mental capacity are aided greatly.[189]

This would also suggest that inattentive students and those who were absent from pertinent lessons could also obtain beneficial remediation from repeated movie presentations.

Other advocates of audio-visual media have noted that students can have what could be called a contrived experience in which cut-away models, cartoon simulations, and mock ups can be used to allow seeing what in reality is hidden from view.[190] So you can see the pistons moving within a simulated gasoline engine and gain an understanding of their dynamics—something that you would never see looking at a running engine.

An interesting pilot project using movies was conducted in Providence, Rhode Island in the mid-1930s wherein the movies were used to present academic lectures to a large room of approximately 150 high school students on some days while on the remaining days students would meet teachers or teaching assistants in smaller recitation groups.[191] No kidding! That is the instructional format I remember from my college days. The only difference is that in my experience the college lectures were live, but here they were films shown in a theatre. This type of use of movies shares features of distance education. We discuss that in Part III, as it was a component of U.S. school reform post 1951.

SUMMARY OF PART II: 1620–1950

During the 330 years of Part II, K-12 schooling remained constant in one sense, but in another sense saw many changes. At the beginning of this time interval American schools were few in number and were without exception ungraded. As school enrollments soared over the intervening centuries nearly all schools eventually, almost by necessity, became graded schools. In the last century of this period, experts in education saw problems with these graded schools and sought remedies that would preserve the graded school format while improving the success of students who were not adapting well to them.

PART III

Distress Signs in K-12 Education 1951—2019

IN TELLING THE STORY of post 1951 K-12 education trends, we have had to decide how to sequence the story's sub-plots. If we simply used a chronological arrangement of the sections, we would miss out on the topical cohesion that we want to preserve. The most logical alternative is what we choose: We order by topics and in that ordering attempt to sequence the parts by the direction of information flow among those topics.

Based on that principle the ordering and naming of our topics results in this sequence of forthcoming chapters within Part III of our book:

8. K-12 education is flunking mathematics and reading.

9. K-12 education is flunking economics.

10. K-12 public education is flunking religion.

11. K-12 education is flunking history.

12. K-12 education is flunking ethics and law.

In covering these five areas, we will often allude to our basic principles that espouse free market competition within the education industrial sector. From those, and the ensuing incentives for improvements, we believe that better, and better schools will evolve as we move into the future. The details are largely unforeseen, but we want to trust the marketplace of education to sort them out and select the best ones to be used in the schooling of the future generations of American K-12 children.

We regret that this marketplace is not healthy and thus cannot yet be trusted to energize the K-12 sector. The schools are sick largely because the marketplace is sick. For K-12 education, the twentieth century was evidently not the ballyhooed *Century of Progress*! As we go forward in this part, we review the distress signs in different topical areas. Here, in Part III, we focus mostly on the diagnoses while postponing our discussions about the treatments to Part IV of the book.

In Part III we will encounter the National Education Association (NEA). It was founded in 1870 by the merger of four smaller education organizations. It has always been limited in its membership to educators working in the public school systems. It has always been an advocate or lobbyist on the national scene. It didn't become a union until the mid 1960s. Soon thereafter it engaged in collective bargaining and supported strikes as part of that process.[192] The NEA grew to become the largest union in the United States. It grew to be very powerful—particularly because of its use of unethical and often illegal tactics. It has many of the characteristics of a political party, under a non-political legal façade. The NEA gives lip service to the interests of students, while in most cases pushing agendas that do not help their educational needs.

CHAPTER 8

K-12 Education is Flunking Mathematics and Reading

LACKLUSTER IS PROBABLY THE best descriptive for K-12 educational progress during this period (1951–2019). Standardized testing since 1952 shows beleaguered public and private systems of education. It has not been promising.

DECLINE, RISE, AND SLUMP OF STUDENT SKILLS

Standardized testing of American high school seniors has been reliably measuring their academic skills since the mid-twentieth century.

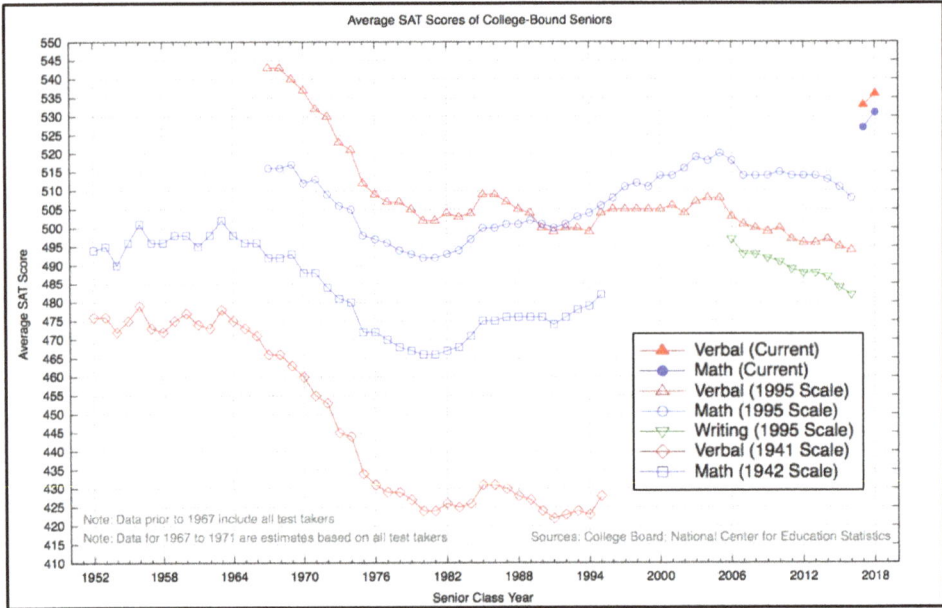

Figure 8, produced by Eric Jacobsen, shows the chronological profile of SAT scores for American high school seniors planning to attend college.[193] From 1952 through 1964 the profiles are roughly flat. Then they descend through 1975 followed by another flat interval until about 1990. From 1990, math scores climb, and verbal scores move up modestly before they both begin to slump again after 2005. The downward trend accelerates after 2013 in math, and after 2014 in reading. Is *Common Core* responsible for this?

What the SAT tells us about high school seniors' math and verbal skills

The time profile of SAT testing of college bound high school seniors shown above begins just one year into the period 1951–2019. It allows us to have a historical overview of 12th grade student performance.

We consider SAT scores of college applicants as the best measure available to follow student skill trends in American K-12 education for the first three decades after 1952. More recently, the *Nation's Report Card*, officially the National Assessment of Educational Progress (NAEP), has provided preferred measures of student skills, but it wasn't established until the 1970s. So, our trend study begins by using the SAT.

The author's experience attending public K-12 schools in the 1950s fits with what the figure shows: That standards, curricula, and testing remained fairly constant over time until the mid 1960s.

One of my recollections from the 1960s is that the social turmoil of that decade, including the controversies over the Vietnam War, led some college instructors to raise the grading curves to enable more students to remain in college and keep their deferments from the military's Selective Service draft system. I imagine this laxity in grading also spread into high schools that then lowered the standards and require-ments for graduation. The drop in the scores seen in Fig. 8 are consistent with this. After the Vietnam War, during 1976–1990, we see another interval in which SAT scores were approximately constant.

The period of decline from the mid 1960s to the mid 1970s was also reported by other standardized tests including the ACT and the Iowa Test of Basic Skills (ITBS).[194] These diminishing test scores on the ITBS were also seen at grade levels 5 and 8 dur-ing this same interval of about 10 years. It suggests that lax grading rapidly came into fashion circa 1965 and was seen at most grade levels.

NAEP IS GOOD, BUT ACT TESTS ARE BETTER

Now let's look a little closer at these two assessment systems.

What the National Assessment of Educational Progress (NAEP) told us about 12th graders

The NAEP, also known as the *Nation's Report Card*, was established in 1970. For its first 20 years, its testing revealed a stagnant period of roughly flat (and low) skill levels. Since 1990, it has tested samples of 4th, 8th, and 12th grade students in a number of subject areas, but mostly in mathematics and reading.

The idea and implementation of a passing score or cut score on the NAEP tests, in any of the subjects tested, was introduced for its 1990 testing by the National As-sessment Governing Board (NAGB). It was done in consultation with its committees of experts, teachers, and other stakeholders. Using a rather subjective process they set the cut score for each subject according to different mastery levels. We are mostly interested in their standard or cut score for *proficient* performance that we believe is nearly synonymous with *expected grade level performance*.

Since that time, nationwide, NAEP has been reporting proficiency percentages for American K-12 students in private schools, public schools, and for all schools. For our present purposes let's now focus on 12th grade performance levels. NAEP reporting has shown that 12th grade reading proficiencies were in slow decline from 1992 to 2013. The private school 12th grade reading proficiencies fell from 60% to 50% proficient. For public schools they flattened: from 37% to 36%. Respectively, that's *getting worse and remaining worse!* As for 12th grade math, we'll get to that later after an important and relevant digression.

Using the ACT assessments to evaluate 12th graders' college readiness

Of all the standardized testing systems used in K-12 education, the ACT (American College Test) has perhaps the most defensible process for determining student skill levels in the subjects it tests. Its measure of student proficiency for any given subject is labeled *POT* for

> ... percent on track to be college ready[195]

and is determined by performing a longitudinal statistical analysis of its previous 12th grade testees in which their actual later performance in college in that subject is used to adjust the future cut scores to be used by ACT in defining the threshold of being minimally college ready.

We at Asora reviewed ACT POT numbers in those states where ACT conducts the official testing and compared them to the reported NAEP proficiency percentages. In 4th grade and 8th grade testing in both mathematics and reading the NAEP proficiency comes in roughly at a factor 0.9 of the ACT POT numbers. Ditto for 12th grade reading. But 12th grade math had that factor at an *unjustified* 0.41. We explore that next.

In the early 1990s, the NAGB, based on that unnecessarily high standard, concluded that its 12th grade mathematics test was *just too damn hard* and introduced a new testing regime, the *2005 Framework*. Doing that lowered the cut score to make the NAEP test a better measure of being *proficient*.

Correcting the old NAEP estimates for 12th grade mathematics proficiencies

That change in NAEP policy affected testing in 2005 and subsequent years. It had the effect of increasing their reported 12th grade math proficiency numbers. This confused a number of stakeholders and educators with regard to 12th grade math testing. Their new 12th grade math-testing regime for 2005 resulted in a jump of about 6 proficiency percentage points compared to the previous trend. We, at first, wondered if that was a *dumbing down* or was it a *needed adjustment* to a proficiency criterion that was too onerous? Answer:

> For 12th grade math the cut score had been far too high. It was a *needed adjustment*, but was still not enough.

To understand this answer, we must use some kind of accepted testing standard to which the NAEP assessments can be compared and judged. The ACT tests will tell us what that adjustment should be. In more detail this is what we know nationally about the NAEP regimes of 12th grade mathematics testing:

- Regime 1: Prior to 2005 the NAEP math proficiency was only a factor of .41 of the ACT POT number.

- Regime 2: In 2005, and later, the NAEP math proficiency was higher, but still at a factor of .59 of POT.

- Thus, the 2005 NAEP math framework adjustment was too small, but it was in the right direction. The goal is .90 of POT.

This suggests that NAEP needs to redo its mathematics *Framework*, yet again, and this time adjust its cut scores downward to where the 12th grade math proficiency of the NAEP will be about 0.9 of the ACT POT.

Regime 3: Correcting the preceding two NAEP regimes for 12th grade math proficiencies

In Table 1, below, we show the published NAEP proficiencies for private and public schools and then two phases of corrections to those "official" NAEP numbers.[196] In the leftmost columns, labelled *As published*, we show the actual NAEP proficiencies that were reported and published for the years indicated. Next, in the columns labelled *Using 2005 Framework*, we rescale the proficiencies for the testing years preceding 2005 to conform to that somewhat revised system.[197] And, indeed, the proficiency numbers for those preceding years differ from those in the leftmost columns, but are the same for the years 2005 and later. Moving on to the columns labelled *Fully corrected*, we further scale up the proficiency numbers to ensure they will be 0.9 of the ACT POT numbers. Finally, the ACT POT numbers shown in the rightmost columns were calculated using the 0.9 factor (as a divisor on the *Fully corrected* values) and applying it. The most trusted values are in the columns labelled *Fully corrected*. Figure 9 below shows all this pictorially. Over the 23 year interval from 1990 to 2013 we observe the 12th grade public school mathematics proficiencies rising significantly from approximately 26% to 38%. For private schools we see these numbers falling a little over a 21 year period from 1992 to 2013. Those numbers dropped from 55% to 53%, a decline which is not statistically significant.

12th Grade Mathematics Proficiencies						ACT Percent on Track	
Improving, but not yet correct				Fully corrected		Derived from:	
As published		Using 2005 Framework		After ASORA correction		Fully corrected ASORA	
Year / Public Schools	Private Schools	Public Schools	Private Schools	Public Schools	Private Schools	Public Schools	Private Schools
1990 — 12.0		17.3		26.3		29.3	
1992 — 15.0	25.0	21.6	36.0	32.9	54.9	36.6	61.0
1996 — 15.3	22.5	22.1	32.4	33.6	49.4	37.4	54.9
2000 — 15.5	26.1	22.3	37.6	34.1	57.4	37.9	63.8
2005 — 21.5	39.1	21.5	39.1	32.8	59.7	36.5	66.3
2009 — 24.8	38.5	24.8	38.5	37.9	58.7	42.1	65.3
2013 — 24.6	34.7	24.6	34.7	37.5	52.9	41.7	58.8

Table 1 shows our newly corrected proficiencies and their evolution: First, there are the *as published* old numbers. Second, there are the *2005 Framework* numbers. Last, there are the *Fully corrected* numbers that preserve the 0.9 ratio to the ACT POT numbers.

The Table and Figure present information showing that the NAEP organization was painting a picture of 12th grade mathematics performance levels that was unnecessarily bleak. Even the new Framework of 2005 did not elevate the math proficiencies to sufficiently realistic levels. American 12th grade public school students, as we know, do not perform well in mathematics, but let's not make them look worse than they really are. The NAEP's *2005 Framework* numbers suggest that only about one-quarter of them are proficient. The *Fully corrected* columns show that somewhat more than one-third are proficient. And private schools, with well less than two-thirds proficient, are also displaying substandard performance levels.

Do most NAEP proficiency numbers intentionally mimic those of ACT testing?

The fairly close numerical agreement of the ACT POT (percent on track to be college ready) numbers with the NAEP proficiency numbers on five of the six tests could be interpreted to suggest that the designers of the NAEP may have set their cut scores to achieve that result. Of NAEP's six tests in mathematics and reading at the three grade levels, five of them report proficiency percentages close to the ACT POT numbers— except as noted above for 12th grade mathematics testing.

We find this *mimicking* quite unlikely because NAEP invented its proficiency criteria in 1990 almost 15 years prior to the ACT organization's introduction of its *College Readiness* standards in 2005.[198]

Or Do ACT POT numbers intentionally mimic those of NAEP testing?

Is the reverse true? We also doubt this based on the nature of the statistical analysis of the longitudinal studies of the ACT testees college performance. That analysis is what produces the ACT cut scores and the associated POT numbers rather than the subjective decisions of a committee. It is highly unlikely that NAEP proficiencies would inform such an analysis.

What this says to us is that the NAGB committees, in 5 out of 6 instances, have done a good job in setting their criteria for proficiency despite it being a rather subjective process.

Is NAEP proficient performance the same as grade level performance?

The short answer is *no*, but it should be *yes*. In practice, two policies make being proficient on the NAEP far different than performing well enough to be passed into the next grade:

- The testing criteria used in most schools have passing scores that are unacceptably low—far lower than the corresponding NAEP cut scores.

- Most schools pass children who flunk the schools' own tests under social promotion policies.

This does not mean that NAEP proficiency is usually, as some claim, an *aspirational* standard. Rather, I believe it is usually an achievable goal in a properly managed school. It is generally a somewhat more demanding criterion than the ACT POT standard for all tested levels and subjects except (as we noted) for 12th grade math. Based on the foregoing, achieving NAEP proficiency in 12th grade mathematics has been an unrealistic expectation for 12th grade students. And for this exceptional case, it is indeed *aspirational*!

> Some years ago, in 2009, I had a discussion with an official of the Rhode Island Department of Education responsible for the state's standardized testing. I was told that the 8th grade reading proficiency standard of the NAEP was only "aspirational." In fact, the NAEP proficiency for reading was a factor of approximately 0.9 lower than the POT of ACT or roughly the same as this other *well-regarded standard.*

Estimating students' ACT performance levels in every locale nationwide

As implied by the discussion above, ACT tests are not administered in all schools nationally. But given the criteria ACT uses to determine if a pupil is on track to be college ready, it is helpful to have the ACT POT numbers or estimates thereof for every American school—even if the school is not an ACT participant.

The author has developed mapping systems that produce estimates of NAEP proficiencies at the school and district level.[199] With these methods parents and others can learn more about the performance levels of their local schools. We have also built mapping systems that convert our estimates of local NAEP proficiencies to ACT's POT numbers.[200]

With good fortune, other assessment services will eventually provide similar kinds of testing systems that are also predictive of college success. Until that time comes we have the ability to generate the ACT performance numbers, either those reported by the ACT or the ones estimated by our mapping systems. Once those numbers are in hand, they can be used to help guide K-12 students towards their post-secondary education choices.

We stress that we have the ability and methods to generate the ACT performance numbers. We don't actually have the results at this time. Asora could generate these numbers if those interested would hire us to do so. Or we will sell you the business!

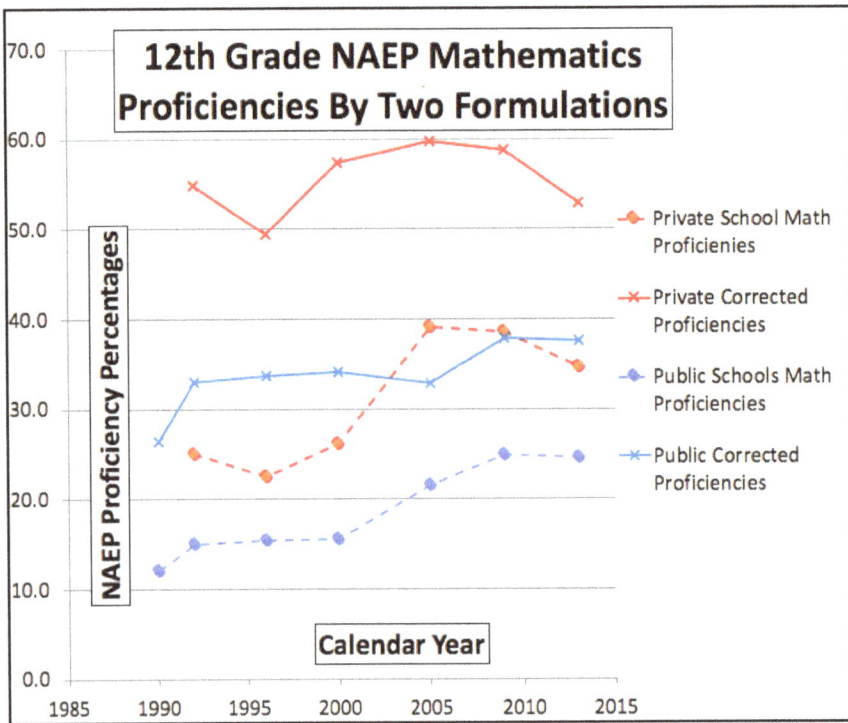

Figure 9. The dashed lines show 12th grade math proficiencies *As published* by NAEP. The solid lines show the *Fully corrected* NAEP proficiencies that are more realistic, and consistent than NAEP's earlier imperfect numbers. This plot uses numbers from Table 1.

More interesting and perhaps ominous are the recent trends for 12th grade math as shown in Fig. 9 above. The proficiencies for private and public schools were rising until they peaked in 2005 and 2009, respectively. Then decline set in. Was it due to the imposed *Common Core State Standards* after 2009?

INCOMPETENT NATIONAL STANDARDS: COMMON CORE

Few would argue that improved academic standards are not a worthwhile goal. We agree that rigorous standards are an important ingredient in the design and operation of K-12 schools. Despite that, we must ask if the academic standards used by American private and public K-12 schools are sufficiently defective that they deserve timely reform? Or are they largely adequate and the principal blame for students' low academic performance lies with their teachers, their books, and their own deficiencies? This is not an *either or* blame game: Both are responsible. We need better standards, better tests, better teachers, and better students. And, we have solid evidence that the *Common Core State Standards* are both inferior and illegal.

Common Core is unnecessary

Clearly, academic standards and their associated curricula are among the necessary inputs to K-12 education. When students learn a significant fraction of the knowledge items prescribed in these curricula we deem them proficient in the related subject areas. Or when, to the contrary, they learn only a small fraction of those concepts, we should not blame the curriculum. Rather we should blame the student for low performance, or we should blame the school for laxity in not enforcing its standards. Or blame both.

We place most of this culpability on incompetent school officials and particularly on the easy grading and social promotion practices that falsely deem students as proficient when they are not. It is arguably an issue of *corrupt* practices in the schools rather than a lack of standards.[201]

To understand the extent of social promotion have you ever wondered what the actual proficiency is of an average high school graduate from our American public schools? It turns out that the average high school graduate has skills at roughly the 8th grade level. Reported proficiencies on the *Nation's Report Card* for 2013 confirm this when only 36% of them were 12th grade proficient in reading, while approximately 38% were proficient in mathematics—as we saw in Table 1 earlier in this chapter.

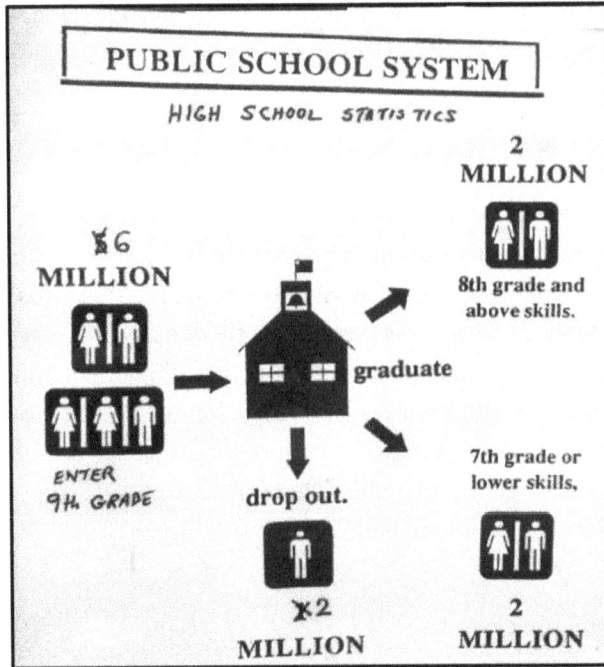

Figure 10 shows a campaign graphic used in the Prop 174 voucher campaign in 1993. This is a photograph of a souvenir poster the author has in his home. I took the photo. Any discoloring, smudges, and shadows are probably the result of my amateur status, and limited skills as a photographer. The photo was taken with an iPhone 6 in my back yard.

In that regard, it is perhaps of interest to look at a campaign poster used in the 1993 Proposition 174 voucher campaign in California. This author was a coordinator, speaker, and debater in that effort. A photo of the poster is shown nearby. Years later, in 2013, we detected an error in the poster. As you can see, we corrected that with a marking pen. The poster describes the eventual status of 6 million American students, who had entered 9th grade, as they leave high school. One-third dropout, one-third graduate with 8th grade and higher skills, and one-third graduate with 7th grade and lower skills. In the 20 years after the poster's use in 1993, the student skill levels didn't change much. Mathematics proficiencies rose about 4% and reading proficiencies fell about 3%. Dropout rates remained almost constant as well. So, the poster's numbers remained approximately the same up to the year 2013. After 2013 proficiencies fell, probably as a result of the imposition of *Common Core State Standards*.

Common Core State Standards (CCSS) are incomplete and went off course

In addition to the dubious process by which they were implemented, the *Common Core* standards have serious academic deficiencies. In mathematics and reading, two of the areas where CCSS standards have been published, it has reduced the amount of content students are required to master. In many content areas, the standards also are much less specific than one would expect.

In mathematics, *Common Core* delays mastery of several calculation skills by one or two grade levels when compared with the standards recommended by the National Mathematics Advisory Panel (NMAP).[202] *Common Core* specifies only three years of high school mathematics, compared to the traditional four years recommended by NMAP.

In reading, which also includes content from English language arts (ELA), *Common Core* identifies relatively few recommended works of fictional literature, well below its supposed 50 percent allocation for this type. In place of classic literature is the recommendation that students read more nonfiction, but those reading lists are also remarkably short.

The research base for *Common Core* is similarly incomplete. The *Common Core State Standards* (CCSS) adopted the ACT organization's descriptor, *College and Career Readiness Standards*, and apparently did so when ACT was assisting CCSS developers in the early stages of their work. One wonders if ACT was being considered at that time as the assessment provider for the CCSS? ACT puts it as follows:

> Since ACT Aspire was under development prior to the release of the *Common Core State Standards*, ACT Aspire was not designed to directly measure progress towards those standards. However, since ACT data, empirical research, and subject matter expertise about what constitutes college and career readiness was lent to the *Common Core* development effort, significant overlap exists between the *Common Core State Standards* and the college and career readiness constructs that ACT Aspire and the ACT measure.[203]

CCSS and its two associated testing consortia have developed assessments to measure student proficiencies against the *Common Core* Standards. Their tests are also incomplete: As explained by Richard Phelps, they are most likely retrospective in their design.[204] This means that they test only the minimal set of courses within the *Common Core* specification and don't prospectively test more advanced high school subjects or other items known to correlate with college success. As a result, these CCSS tests likely have little predictive value as to how well the students might perform in college. Such test designs are worse than incomplete. Their tests were never subjected to rigorous validity analyses.

Numerous education experts have criticized this weakness of *Common Core* and its related assessment programs. Christopher Tienken of Seton Hall University documented the lack of credible research supporting *Common Core*.[205] Regarding how *Common Core* went off-course, Jamie Gass and James Stergios of the Pioneer Institute provided a good review in *The Weekly Standard's* blog.[206] It is clear that many proponents and implementers of *Common Core* advocate for *experiential education* and its motto, *twenty-first century skills*. After Connecticut and West Virginia enthusiastically embraced these experiential practices, most of their NAEP scores fell, Gass and Stergios reported. Also troubling is the fact that proficiencies on the NAEP took a significant drop in 2015 testing, which is likely a result of *Common Core* implementation.

Common Core is inferior

Schools should not put students at risk by forcing them to participate in unproven schemes and inferior programs. Here is a list of some of the more bewildering inadequacies of *Common Core*:

- *Common Core* offers no standard for cursive writing, effectively making it optional. Printing and typing are still taught . . . at least for the next few years.

- *Common Core* promotes marginal teaching methods such as experiential education, which at best should be an adjunct to instruction. The standards do not mention direct instruction, which has been validated by many studies.

- One of the more bizarre recommendations in *Common Core* reading standards is advocacy of *close reading*.[207] Under this practice, teachers do not provide background information about historical texts prior to having students read them. The student reads it *cold*, as the standards recommend in studying the *Gettysburg Address*. Obviously, additional information would help the student become more proficient in the subject, yet *Common Core* disallows it. The standards cite no research supporting such a practice.

- *Common Core* claims it includes teaching of *critical thinking, higher order thinking skills* and *twenty-first century skills*, but it never bothers to define what those otherwise unexplained and seemingly nonsensical skills are. That it fails to do so suggests its authors do not know that these empty phrases too often are just that: empty. In the hard sciences, such as physics, these concepts would have meant the appropriate use of logic and mathematics in the development of the science.

As a result of these and many other shortcomings with the standards, education researchers Sandra Stotsky and Ze'ev Wurman, have proposed a kind of *truth in advertising* requirement for states that have adopted *Common Core*: They shall remove the *college and career readiness* label everywhere it appears in their descriptions of the standards![208]

Common Core math standards are weak

The stated goals of the *Common Core* standards include preparation of high school graduates with prerequisite knowledge that enables enrollment in a calculus course when they enter college.[209] Benchmark standards used for this are recommendations from the National Mathematics Advisory Panel (NMAP).[210] This panel was established in 2006 and is charged with proposing improvements to K–12 mathematics standards to prepare high school graduates for *higher levels of mathematics. Common Core* standards are insufficient to reach these goals. Here are some of the gaps and failures responsible for this inadequacy:

- *Common Core* postpones proficiency in whole-number division from NMAP's benchmark grade 5 to grade 6.

- *Common Core* postpones teaching relationships between fractions and decimals from NMAP's grade 5 to grade 7.

- *Common Core* postpones the grade level for a first algebra course from NMAP's grade 8 to grade 9.

- *Common Core* reduces the number of years of high school math instruction from NMAP's four to three, a clear indication that students under *Common Core* will be left behind.

- *Common Core* eliminates traditional teaching of geometry by replacing the usual Euclidean approach recommended by NMAP with an experimental method that has had little success. Or, as some say, the pedagogy is *experiential*.[211]

In summary, *Common Core* proposes 11 easy years of instruction in mathematics that will fall short of the National Mathematics Advisory Panel's recommended 12 years of more intensive work.

The duh moment regarding Common Core mathematics standards

Should it be surprising that NAEP testing of 12th grade students would show their math proficiencies falling by 2013? We just noted that the new *Common Core* math standards have fewer milestones to meet at any given grade level. When such weak standards replace relatively stronger ones you will have math skills decline. Thus, after looking at the recently falling performance results in Table 1, we say *duh*.

Common Core English language arts standards are weak

A sensible approach to improving student skills in English language arts (ELA) is to have students read more, write more, and gain higher proficiency in grammar, spelling, and rhetoric. *Common Core* standards, by contrast, embark on a path of unproven tradeoffs in which much less effort is spent in some areas than in others. A key flaw in *Common Core*'s ELA standards is its shift of reading emphasis from works of fiction, typically the classics of English literature, to nonfiction works.

It appears *Common Core* reading standards require approximately half of a student's reading in English classes be nonfiction and the other half fiction. This change from the traditional emphasis on fiction seems to be primarily based on a misunderstanding of NAEP reading tests, which the designers of *Common Core* profess to admire. The NAEP tests focus about 70 percent of the questions on nonfiction and the other 30 percent on fictional literature.

The developers of *Common Core* standards for reading have apparently made the mistake of assuming tests, such as NAEP, measure reading skills primarily developed in English classes. In reality, a student builds reading skills in many other subject areas, including mathematics, science, and history. Those other subject areas focus almost entirely on nonfiction. When considering the many subjects taught in school, the emphasis in English classes should largely be on fiction. Else, the overall percentage of focus on fictional literature across the school will not meet the 30 percent recommended by the NAEP standard.

If schools attempt to reset reading goals so roughly half of all reading assignments focus on fiction and the other half on nonfiction, teachers will have to be retrained to become adequate instructors in nonfiction areas.[212] It is unclear what will be taught, but there certainly will be a temptation to present politically or ideologically biased information.

If there is any conclusion to draw from what we've learned about *Common Core*'s reading standards, it is that its authors did not base their proposals on sound research. Until there is good research suggesting a better approach, the best near-term idea is to stay with traditional standards while improving instruction.

The duh moment regarding Common Core English language arts standards

Should it be surprising that NAEP testing of 12th grade students would show their reading proficiencies falling by 2013? The CCSS greatly reduced the required/suggested reading lists and it put emphasis on new *irrational* learning techniques that interfere with normal learning processes. By halving the number of fictional works to read, one would expect students to master somewhat less vocabulary. So, the reading standards were weakened and the testing shows reading proficiencies down. This is another *duh* moment.

Replacing Common Core with proven standards of excellence

This author researched alternatives to *Common Core* and didn't need to look far to be convinced that the ACT standards and tests are not only a good alternative, but are probably the best available. That study led me to author a booklet, *Replacing Common Core with Proven Standards of Excellence*. It was published in 2014.[213]

CHAPTER 9

K-12 Education Is Flunking Economics

IN THIS CHAPTER WE consider the combined private and public sectors of K-12 education. When we say that K-12 education has flunked economics, there are a few ways this statement can be interpreted:

- One way to view this is that K-12 schools do a poor job of teaching economics to its students.

- Or these schools do not benefit from economic competition in a free marketplace.

- Or for whatever reason, these schools' productivity levels have stagnated for decades.

All three of these characterizations ring true.

THE HEALTH OF OTHER ECONOMIC SECTORS

Before reviewing the K-12 education industry as an economic sector it is useful to review productivity growth in other industries. So, what has been happening in those other economic sectors?

Consumer electronics productivity growth: Looking at television set costs.

In 2018 this author purchased a new 55" television set for about $550. In his parents' 1948 home he remembers the 10" Philco TV that cost $500. It suggests that the television sub-sector of the electronics industry has grown into a much more cost-effective field compared to its infancy. Using published Consumer Price Indices[214] to compute an inflation ratio of 10.46 from 1948 to 2018 and also considering the TV screen areas we found that the old TV cost a factor of 196 times more than the new one, when we reckoned those costs in 1948 dollars on a per square inch basis. This means that the productivity in this area of consumer electronics has risen almost a factor of 200 over the past 70 years. Please realize this is a low-ball estimate if you consider that I neglected to consider the value of color TV versus black and white!

High-end industry: Computers and supercomputers

Another area of electronics is the computer industry. Let's look at personal computers—the ubiquitous PC. Consider what they cost over the past 55 years together with some other statistics:

Desktop PC Computers					
Year	Brand-model	GFLOP speed	Cost in millions	"M$"/GFLOP	$/GFLOP
1965	PDP-8	0.000310	0.01850	59.6774	$59,677,419.35
1980	HP-85	0.000333	0.00325	9.7598	$9,759,760.00
1995	HP Pavilion	0.003750	0.00130	0.3467	$346,666.67
1998	HP Vectra	0.008300	0.00098	0.1186	$118,554.22
2018	HP Pro Desk	0.165000	0.00081	0.0049	$4,909.09

Table 2 displays PC computers over a 53-year span with their processing speeds and costs. A GFLOP is one billion floating point (essentially arithmetical) operations per second. The most recent entry, the HP Pro Desk, runs at nearly a sixth of a GFLOP for a cost of $810. According to this chart the cost per GFLOP has dropped by a factor of 1329 over this half-century. The PDP-8 was not really a PC but we put it on this list because it somewhat resembled a *home computer* circa 1965 (and the author used one in his career). The information in these tables was collected from dozens of sources found on the Internet that we deem too voluminous to provide in endnotes.

For this *class* of machines, the computational productivity of the computer industry has increased by this almost amazing factor of 1329.

Of the supercomputers listed below in Table 3, this author used the first five machines during his career in computational physics. Let's consider selected representative supercomputers since the 1960s:

Supercomputers					
Year	Brand—model	GFLOP speed	Cost in millions	"M$"/GFLOP	$/GFLOP
1964	CDC—6600	0.003	2.37	790.000	$790,000,000.00
1967	CDC—7600	0.036	5.00	138.889	$138,888,888.89
1976	Cray—1	0.160	8.80	55.000	$55,000,000.00
1985	Cray—2	1.900	16.00	8.421	$8,421,052.63
1988	Cray—YMP	2.700	22.00	8.148	$8,148,148.15
1996	ASCI—Red	1,300.000	55.00	0.042	$42,307.69
2008	Roadrunner—LANL	1,000,000.000	100.00	0.00010000	$100.00
2012	Sequoia—LLNL	17,000,000.000	250.00	0.00001500	$14.71
2018	Summit—ORNL	200,000,000.000	250.00	0.00000125	$1.25

Table 3 displays supercomputers over a 54-year span with their processing speeds and costs. The GFLOP speed shown here for the Summit supercomputer is just one-fifth of an exaflop (= a billion x billion FLOPS). The cost per GFLOP dropped from $790 million in 1964 to $8 million in 1988 to just $1.25 in 2018.

In terms of the cost per GFLOP, for supercomputers the productivity increase has been a stupefying factor of about 630 million. That's getting close to a billion.

During the author's career in computational plasma physics he used the first five of the computers shown in the list. Those five were, in each case, designed by a group led by Seymour Cray, the founder of Cray Research, Inc. He designed the CDC machines when he was with Control Data Corporation. Cray once jokingly remarked that this design group of 30 individuals included the "janitor."[215] His team designed the others when he was CEO at Cray Research. Supercomputer users, circa 1988, were familiar with the idea that a one GFLOP computer would cost about $8 million. Thirty-one years later, the new speeds and costs shown here are difficult to believe: A buck and a quarter for a GFLOP??!

We also analyzed Apple's lines of personal computers and we were reminded that based on the $/GLFOP they cost, on average, more than double the PC's that use Microsoft operating systems. Maybe it's time to trade this author's Mac for a PC? But issues of interface continuity will keep us in the Mac lane.

Did the Mac design the Cray or did a Cray design the Mac?

This author once visited Apple's headquarters in Cupertino, California in the early 1980s and was impressed to see a Cray-1 supercomputer visible from the headquarters' lobby. I was told that the Cray-1 was being used by Apple to design other computers. There is a back-story to this, which may be more legend than history.

According to blogger Nick Litten here is what happened:

> At some point in the early 1980s Apple's CEO Steve Jobs walked into Cray Research's Mendota Heights headquarters in Minnesota seeking to purchase a Cray-1 supercomputer. Never before had a walk-in customer sought purchase of such an expensive and powerful machine. After some difficulty getting past security guards, he managed to find Cray president John Rollwagen and he did purchase the machine. Rollwagen decided to inform Cray CEO Seymour Cray of the purchase and to tell him that Jobs had said the Cray-1 would be used to design the next Macintosh computer. Seymour Cray pondered this information briefly and told Rollwagen that it . . . "seemed reasonable, since I am using a Macintosh to design the next Cray![216]"

I have often wondered if Steve Jobs was more ambitious than that and perhaps thought he could also design supercomputers if he had a Cray-1 supercomputer to help analyze and optimize the designs. I guess we will never know. We shall encounter John Rollwagen again in Chapter 15 where he appears as one of the proponents or *Godfathers* of the first charter schools in the United States.

What the Bureau of Labor Statistics has to say: The good news and bad news:

Another source of information about American productivity is the U.S. Bureau of Labor Statistics. According to a 2014 report for the 65-year interval from 1947 through 2012 the Bureau showed, adjusted for inflation, a five-fold increase in the average economic output of workers in the for-profit private sector.[217]

EDUCATION: THE BOTTOM ECONOMIC SECTOR

The bad news is also reported by the Bureau of Labor Statistics. Consider the 24-year interval from 1989 through 2012, and let's review the labor productivity of employees in K-12 education. Were there notable increases in productivity as was the usual case for American workers? No, for all K-12 schools there was a decrease of about 4% as evident in Figure 11.[218]

Labor productivity for all schools, public schools, and private schools, 1989–2012

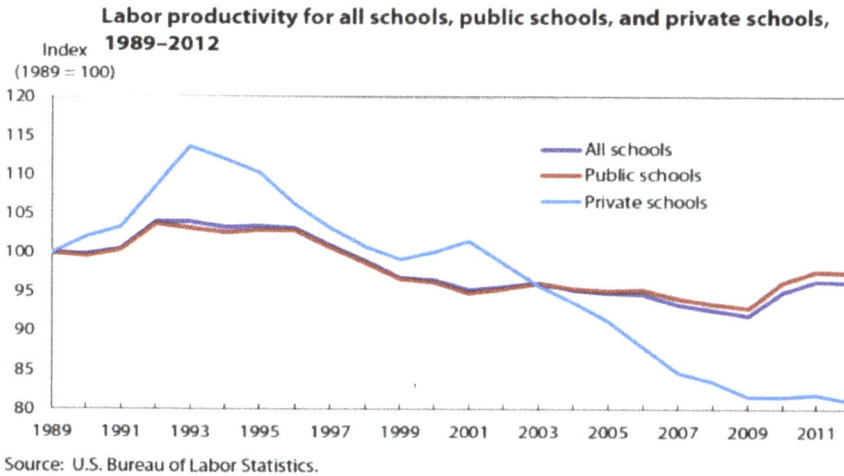

Source: U.S. Bureau of Labor Statistics.

Figure 11 displays American labor productivity of education workers (teachers, administrators, and other staff) over a 24-year span during which this measure drops approximately 4%. One wonders why new technologies, and methodologies have not led to increases as has almost always been observed in the other for-profit private sectors? Does their output drop because there are too few incentives for increasing productivity?

In light of the productivity increases cited above in other industries that were largely the result of new technologies and automation, one wonders why the K-12 economic sector didn't also exploit them?

How to raise the productivity and performance levels in K-12 education

Let's consider some of the methodological and technological policy changes that would likely increase labor productivity of K-12 workers. First, we present the handful of changes that might be acceptable to the teachers' unions and other administrators within these systems:

- Offering or imposing year around mathematics instruction.

- Using better books.

- Giving financial awards to students for superior performance.

- Imposing financial penalties or extra school hours for students performing poorly.

Disliked by teachers unions and the education establishment is a longer list of changes that would/could lead to labor productivity improvements and concomitant reductions in staffing. They include:

- Augmenting and/or replacing on site instruction with distance education.

- Replacing or targeting age-based group instruction with more flexible alternatives.

- Employing blended and/or flipped hybrid online instructional systems.

- The hiring of appropriately degreed teachers in preference to *credentialed* teachers.

- Managing official testing through an independent agency.

- Providing parents good consumer information about school quality. Few educators, parents, and other stakeholders know that the original U.S. Office of Education, founded in 1867, was founded to provide information about schools. Maybe a scaled down Ed Department would rise to this challenge?[219]

- Offering public school choice, including magnet schools.

- Offering a wider choice of schools, either through vouchers or through charter schools. We'll have much more to say on this farther along.

- Using targeted remediation through tutoring, targeted reading, and online services.

- Employing teaching assistants from among the more advanced students.

- The hiring of non-union teachers and other staff members.

Our purpose, here, is not that of advocating every one of these proposals. Rather we present them because most of them would probably increase the labor productivity of the K-12 labor force that in this case is measured by improved student outcomes.

Let's consider how teachers' unions and education bureaucrats have opposed some of these avenues of improvement:

They might oppose labor saving automation as in distance education & online learning

In our review of the literature and searches on the Internet we have found very little information about political opposition from unions and education establishment officials concerning the use of automation within new instructional models. But there are *other hand* reasons why teachers' unions might oppose these new formats. One concern they might have, once these practices become more widespread, is that schools can be operated with fewer teachers consistent with higher student teacher ratios?

They might oppose blended and flipped instructional models

Blended and flipped blended instructional formats are sub-species of those in the previous paragraph. Our searches have found no significant education establishment opposition to these practices. Part of the reason for this may be that both blended and flipped instructional practices still involve a classroom teacher. Given that both of these use online or related technologies to deliver some of the instruction, they free up teacher time to help children in small groups or individually—perhaps as a tutor. Such alternative *assignments* of a teacher's responsibility are often welcomed by the teachers. That is until they realize, at the union hall, that fewer teachers are needed in these new and innovative instructional formats.

They favor credentialed teachers over ones with degrees

Most teachers did not major in academic subjects in college, and as a result didn't earn academic degrees in their teaching specialties. Instead they were trained in the progressive education theories of contemporary pedagogy and, at best, received instruction in subject content minimally sufficient for them to teach any given subject. In place of an academic degree in a subject area they are awarded credentials and one or more degrees in the field of education. As to the levels of academic rigor, surveys of professors within colleges and universities generally rank their institution's department of education near or at the bottom of the school's departments—sometimes just below the physical education department. Essentially, it is easier to get an education degree than an academic degree.

> This author once sought employment as a high school math, and physics teacher. Despite my academic transcript I was denied employment in California public schools. I did, however, work for a private high school where my academic transcript was honored.

Such public school teachers, when organized into a union, have not, do not and will not want academically trained teachers competing with them. They have exerted political pressure on school boards and state departments of education to pass regulations requiring all teachers to have credentials—never mind any higher degrees. When poorly educated teachers engage in teaching, the results are often inferior to the result of hiring an educated teacher who has no credential. The net effect of this bias towards minimally educated teachers is lower student skills and knowledge. We imagine a smart aleck saying,

> To dumb down the students, first dumb down the teachers!

An extreme, but real example can help illustrate this point. The year was about 1960. The town was Rio Linda, California, the same one that Rush Limbaugh cites in some of his humorous asides. In a second grade classroom the teacher was teaching arithmetic and she instructed the children that $3 + 4 = 8$. More than one hand went up and a little Johnny said that he thought the answer should be 7. Others agreed with Johnny, but some thought the teacher was right. Some arguing ensued. The teacher told the students that in America we often vote on things and that to settle the argument they would vote on the right answer. So, they voted. The teacher's answer of 8 received the most votes and so it was established that 3 + 4 = 8. Johnny's parents learned of this novel approach to arithmetic and filed a complaint. School officials from the District were brought in to consider the teacher's qualifications. I surmise that the teacher was reassigned or terminated. I don't know that part of the story.[220]

They would oppose independent testing

If schools used external independent testing organizations to administer all official tests there would be a reckoning and embarrassment unless the schools were to do a much better job of bringing their students towards mastery of their core subjects. Being held to such a high standard would require better and more thorough instructional practices. Doing that would be a challenge because there would be no other recourse if the testing were objective and independent. We already mentioned the example of the Massachusetts charter high school that did use external testing and how that school led the state in both reading and mathematics skill levels. This school was not unionized, but if it were it is likely that teacher unions would not want to accept such a challenge unless somehow incentivized to do so.

They oppose provision of reliable consumer information

Anything that would be embarrassing to the teachers of a school or school system is something the teachers union is likely to oppose. If the advertising campaigns of competitor schools were honest, they would include honest contrast marketing in which the unionized schools would be shown (or claimed) to be inferior. The unions will discourage such practices because they want to escape ridicule. The unions push education officials to inflate student performance levels and, in fact, every school system in the United States publishes fake *look good* proficiency numbers from their statewide standardized testing program.

They oppose public school choice

When parents even have school choice among public schools it creates competitive pressures under which the various schools strive to improve upon their peers. Unions, almost as a part of their DNA, do not like competition—even among Public schools. So, they will act politically to limit or prohibit even these kinds of choices within the public systems.

They oppose vouchers and charter schools

Schools that take vouchers and charter schools create even more competition than that of public school choice. On that basis, unions will push as forcefully as possible to block these kinds of choice. They do, to a limited extent, accept the existence of charter schools because they are seen as a middle ground compromise with the advocates of those *hated* vouchers. Even so, there is evidence that the competition inspired by voucher and charter schools have led to modest performance improvements in the two decades following the establishment of these two kinds of choice circa 1990.[221]

They oppose self-pacing and support social promotion

Self-pacing is the polar opposite of social promotion. In the former case one's mastery of a subject dictates placement within the academic sequence of instruction. In the latter case one's age determines that placement. In the case of self-pacing the student and teacher are responsible for academic progress which can only occur if the subjects are truly mastered. Under social promotion the incentives for mastery are considerably weaker. Avoiding hard work and responsibility is a union tendency, and as a result they favor social promotion.

They hate the hiring of non-union workers and they hate former Governor Rauner of Illinois

In 2011, three years before he was elected Governor of Illinois in November 2014, Bruce Rauner was active in public school reform and was quoted as saying that one-half of Chicago's unionized public school teachers "are virtually illiterate" and that a similar percentage of Chicago's public school principals were "incompetent."[222]

Rauner, as a capitalist financier, philanthropist, and Republican, had been active in education reform for some years. As a friend of the then Democrat Chicago Mayor Rahm Emanuel, he nevertheless opposed union tactics such as were seen in a Chicago Teachers Union strike in 2013. After Emanuel yielded to the union's demands the experience was *food for thought for Rauner*. Perhaps because of that, he sought the Illinois Governorship in order that he might have more influence and control over education in Illinois.[223] Once in office in February 2015, he sued the major public employees union the American Federation of State, County and Municipal Employees (AFSCME) to end their claim on non-member government employees' so-called agency fees. These agency fees are payment for union representation of the interests of non-members of the union. They are smaller than full union dues because, in theory, the difference is used by the union for political activities that the member may oppose.

Rauner's claim was based on the idea that all union activities are political. His lawsuit was dismissed by a lower court on the grounds that he didn't have standing.[224]

But Mark Janus, a State of Illinois employee, and a child support specialist, did have standing and filed a new lawsuit. When the Janus lawsuit reached the U.S. Supreme Court in early 2018, Rauner testified that

> One hundred percent of what a government union does is political by nature.

Janus recently won this lawsuit at the Supreme Court in June 2018.[225] This was, indirectly, a victory for Rauner as well. The ruling is and was far reaching: Extending into every level of government, local, state, and national, within the United States. The ruling says that no government employee can be forced to join a union, and no government employee can be forced to pay agency fees or any other union dues. This means that unions will not have nearly as much influence and power over the management of government functions. And for K-12 education, union influence will be much less. That will allow elected officials much more control over schools and education policies in their jurisdictions.

This was a watershed event for public education. It should make room for various reforms that can be implemented without any union interference. But will it?

Dramatic failure to educate better is the result of this stagnation and lack of innovation

In almost every other field of human endeavor, the United States has seen remarkable improvements in the development of various technologies with corresponding progress in the products and services consumed by our society. But in K-12 education, improvement seems to have been a dirty word. Fig. 8 (in Chapter 8) displayed trends in mathematics and verbal skills of American 12th graders. There was no improvement seen in math where the SAT scores hovered around 490 (actually 494 and 484, in 1952 and 2016, respectively). Verbal skills, sadly, declined precipitously in those years (from 475 to 415, for the same interval).

If our K-12 students' skill levels have not improved, we might also find that each dollar spent on K-12 education has not brought many productivity improvements either. Consistent with this is Fig. 11 (earlier in this Chapter) which shows no such improvements, but shows some single digit declines in productivity.

Looking ahead to our review of high school student knowledge levels in U.S. history and civics, Fig. 12 (in Chapter 11) will show that most students would flunk any kind of reasonably rigorous course in these subjects. That they don't fail is the result of rampant social promotion. When they become voters, a few years later, it should not surprise anyone that their votes will be significantly uniformed. Our democratic institutions will suffer.

This lack of progress in our education systems makes one wonder what would have happened in other economic sectors if they experienced the same levels of stagnation seen in K-12 education. Coulson pondered this and asked,

Who, today, would seriously consider buying a Model T Ford as a commuter vehicle? Or flying on an airline whose fleet consisted of wooden biplanes?

And then he commented,

> And yet this is essentially what is being done every time a child is sent off to public school—or for that matter, to most non-profit private schools. Constant improvement and innovation are the norm in human activities, and we should expect nothing less from our schools.[226]

This economic disaster surely fits our title: *Sick Schools*. Let's now look at our *patient* in a little more detail. Maybe the diagnosis will indicate how we can find suitable treatments to make K-12 education healthier?

CHAPTER 10

K-12 Public Education is Flunking Religion

A VERY CONFUSING ISSUE within K-12 public education concerns what students should be taught about religion. If all Americans were Congregationalists, as were the pilgrims in the early Massachusetts Bay Colony, the answer would be simple: You will be a Congregationalist, or you will be punished. But we are no longer under any one particular sect or denomination. We have freedom of religion and within this concept lie some problems:

- How can schools teach about our American history and culture without teaching something about religion?

- How can religion be studied that respects the many belief systems followed by American citizens?

- How can we teach that no religion, philosophy or theory of science is provably correct?

On this last point, it is faith and not a logical proof, that gives the believer the assurance that his or her beliefs are true. And, it is faith that public schools are forbidden to teach. Many parents find that acceptable because they recognize that faith is taught at the home and within the religious congregation. Other parents want more from their schools, but are unlikely to get it from their public schools.

Parents who don't send their children to public schools have presumably found private schooling, home schooling or some other kind of instruction that, among other things, reinforces their religious, philosophical, and possibly even political values. That suggests that it is only the parents of public school children who may not like their children's schools' approaches to these subjects.

Is there a way that public schools could help resolve this conundrum over religious studies?

HOW PUBLIC SCHOOLS COULD TEACH ABOUT RELIGION

There is a simple reason why citizens might want public schools to teach children about religion: To do otherwise would unfairly promote secular philosophies, including the scientific method, without any contrasting viewpoints being presented. This author, personally, is comfortable with his religion and with his scientist background. I see them as consistent. Others don't. More on that later.

Religion has quite naturally impacted law, history, science, and other subjects.

Throughout human existence religious beliefs and concepts have been motivators for human decision making. How can scholars study the various aspects of human behavior without being able to describe religious incentives? They can't.

Gilbert Sewall has had an interesting vantage point on this. With his background as a former history teacher, as an editor of a social studies academic journal, as the education editor of Newsweek magazine, and as the director of the American Textbook council it is worth considering his opinions. He laments the dearth of discussion of religious motivations in history textbooks. He observed that

> Textbooks seldom explain religion's role in shaping human thought and action or as a motivating agent of culture, politics, and ethics.[227]

For example, it should be obvious that Christian missionaries when working abroad have had various kinds of impact on the historical development of the host countries. Many textbooks, however, skip the details, and in Sewall's words,

> They typically reduce such missionary zeal to a mere example of Western cultural imperialism.[228]

If public schools are permitted to teach about religion, it would seem permissible and helpful to have their curricula and textbooks include discussions about the influence of dogma, belief, and customs on the various secular subjects taught therein. Courses in history, science, and law, for example, may seem secular throughout, but they each involve human actors/agents who are often influenced by religious belief. How those beliefs affect these behaviors, theories, and traditions are worth understanding. Students and teachers need not be religious believers to gain an understanding of religious influences. As we shall now learn, the courts of the United States generally accept these practices if they are teaching *about religion*.

The legal and Constitutional limits on teaching religion in public schools

Legal scholars agree, almost unanimously, that teaching about religion is permissible in public schools if certain rules are observed. Those rules, mostly, were the results of various U.S. Supreme Court decisions. The First Amendment did not have any jurisdiction at the state and local levels until well after the ratification of the Fourteenth Amendment following the Civil War. After that, it took many decades for the Supreme Court to rule against state and local government bodies under the interpretation that the Fourteenth Amendment broadened the jurisdiction of the First. Many of their subsequent rulings were based on the provisions of the First Amendment, which by then applied to state and local government functions as well as to those of the federal government.

The First Amendment, consists of three clauses separated by semi-colons, as follows:

> Congress shall make no law respecting an establishment of religion, or prohibiting the free exercise thereof; or abridging the freedom of speech, or of the press; or the right of the people peaceably to assemble and to petition the Government for a redress of grievances.

The three clauses are known by these labels:

- The establishment clause
- The free speech clause
- The petition clause

It is the first two clauses that affect how public schools operate by putting constraints on what they can do. The first clause puts limits on public schools while the second clause gives people within the school environment certain rights to express their opinions. The Supreme Court has weighed in on these on a number of occasions. We now look at two such cases that affect public schools.

Everson v. Board of Education case of 1947 is the foundation for limiting religion in public schools. The U.S. Supreme Court ruling in this case quoted Thomas Jefferson regarding his preference for a

> . . . separation between church and state.

Writing for the majority, Justice Hugo Black, elaborated on that concept and listed a number of new prohibitions, including:

- No government unit can establish a church or other religious congregation
- No government can provide any aid to any religion
- No government can provide incentives or disincentives about membership in a congregation
- No government can provide incentives or disincentives about attendance at a religious group

- No government can force a person to believe or disbelieve in any religion

- No government can levy any tax to support any religious activities[229]

In that ruling the Court also held that government units must be neutral with respect to

- different religions, and cannot give preference to one religion over another

- different degrees of religious belief, including the entire spectrum from atheists to dogmatic belief[230]

Lemon v. Kurtzman led to the Lemon Test for conformance to the Establishment clause. Over the ensuing 24 years, after Everson, the Supreme Court sought to simplify these rules to make their decisions more understandable—both to themselves and to the general public. In 1971, the case of Lemon v. Kurtzman came before them. In its decision, Chief Justice Warren Burger devised three conditions all of which must be satisfied if a government action or law is to conform to the Establishment clause. The enactment must:

- Have a secular legislative purpose,

- Not advance or inhibit religion and

- Not lead to, as Burger wrote, "an excessive government entanglement with religion."[231]

These three conditions have become known as the *Lemon Test*—also known as the *three prong Lemon Test*.

Not a Christian nation legally, but the United States is a Christian nation culturally

Many religiously Christian conservative voices have contended that the United States was established as a Christian nation. Others say it wasn't. The truth is a little more nuanced as follows:

Legally the United States Government was not "founded on the Christian religion." There has been much controversy over assertions that the United States is or was a Christian nation. For those who say it was they will often argue that many of the colonies had official Christian denominational status when they were founded—as was true for the Massachusetts Bay Colony. Such claims are generally true. However, when the United States was formed, its Constitution ratified, and signed its very language had no such clause or principle.

Under Presidents George Washington and John Adams, the Barbary States of North Africa used an extortion strategy to force the new United States to pay tribute money to them. That *agreement* was formalized in a treaty with the Barbary States, which was negotiated, signed, and ratified during the years 1796—1797. One of the clauses in this treaty reads

> . . . the Government of the United States of America is not, in any sense, founded on the Christian religion.[232]

Since treaties have the force of law and apply to the entire nation, it follows that the United States, in a legal sense, is not a Christian nation.

Culturally, of course, the United States is predominantly a Christian nation. Aspects of that include:

- Most American citizens self-identify as Christians and many of them attend church.
- Christian churches outnumber the temples of all other religions combined.
- Two Christian holidays are official federal holidays and no other religions are so honored.
- As noted above, most of the original American colonies were officially Christian

Given the legal constraints from the Lemon Test, what can federal, state, and local governments do to support some types of religious instruction within public education systems?

How to structure a K-12 public school religion curriculum that passes the Lemon Test

Many parents and other stakeholders want students in public schools to get a good education in matters of history and civics while at the same time learning about the roles religion has played in so many of our traditions and in our lives. Many parents can't afford the tuition cost of sending their children to a favored private school. Others, who could afford private school tuition, nevertheless want their children educated in public schools because they value the mixing of various demographics (racial, national, economic, religious, etc.) that wouldn't be found sufficiently diverse in the private school alternative. To pass the Lemon Test the public school, at a minimum, must use a religious education curriculum that passes the test. This means that the curriculum, the textbooks, and the teacher training must all conform. How can this be done?

If you can't teach religion, you can teach *about* religion? Many proposals as well as actual government run and financed programs in public schools walk the narrow path that passes the Lemon Test while at the same time providing the public school systems the resources to teach K-12 students about religion.

A naïve rejoinder to this might hold that any instruction about religion will violate the Lemon Test if that program is government funded and operated? However, if public schools were not permitted to teach about religion they would be indirectly supporting secular philosophies while neglecting those based on religions. This seems a tough nut to crack. A number of educators and analysts have devised a number of proposals to teach about religion in such a way that no proselytizing is involved while maintaining neutrality between religion and no religion. Or so they claim.

There is really only one practical format that will pass the Establishment clause criterion: Comparative studies of religion. That would presumably require students to learn enough to be able to:

- Compare and contrast the theological principles of a multitude of religions.

- Compare and contrast the interaction of each religion with the secular world around it.

- Compare and contrast the practices of charity of the various religions.

- Compare and contrast the political tendencies of the several religions.

- Compare and contrast the levels of corruption within the different religions.

- Compare and contrast the historical development of the many religions.

- Compare and contrast the conflicts with other religions and philosophies among them.

- Compare and contrast the liturgical styles of these numerous sects.

- Compare and contrast the uses of art and music with other religions and other persuasions.

- Compare and contrast the moral codes of each religion with the array of other religions.

- Compare and contrast the scientific fact world with each religion's worldview.

- Defend limiting the number of sects to study, and explain why others are not included.[233]

Where would public education authorities find textbooks and instructors who would have the encyclopedic knowledge to teach the students about these facts and concepts? Seems like a tall order. Would there not be critics who would find problems with any given system of religious education? Among them, we would expect lawyers eager to sue the public system for perceived violations of the Establishment clause.

HOW RELIGION CAN LIVE WITH SCIENCE

There is a widespread view that religious narratives contradict scientific theories when they go on to describe important events in the earth's history and pre-history. Let's consider some of the best-known controversies that are relevant to public school courses about religion and in science.

Were you there at the creation? Resolving Genesis and The Big Bang Theory.

What would you do if you were an expert in theology and physics at the same time and wanted to resolve the seeming contradiction between Biblical accounts of the creation and one proposed by scientists? You might set out to find a physics theory that looks something like the very beginning of the creation.

There was such a person: Georges Lemaître, who was a Belgian Roman Catholic priest and was also a celebrated theoretical physicist. He wanted to develop a theory of the creation that would support the Genesis account.[234] In 1931, based on Einstein's theory of general relativity, he proposed that the universe began as a "Cosmic Egg" that subsequently exploded (in the *mother* of all explosions) to initiate our expanding universe. He published his concept that year in the scientific journal *Nature*. Einstein's comments on this paper were not kind, but he hinted that Lemaître might be on to something. He said,

> Your calculations are correct, but your physics is atrocious.[235]

Two years later in 1933, at a Cal Tech physics conference in Pasadena, California, Lemaître delivered a lecture on his theory in front of colleagues that also included that same celebrated physicist, Albert Einstein. In the Q & A after his presentation, Einstein congratulated Lemaître and, according to reports, said,

> This is the most beautiful and satisfactory explanation of creation to which I have ever listened.[236]

In 1949 Lemaître's *Cosmic Egg* hypothesis was given a new and popular name: as *The Big Bang Theory*—a label that has stuck ever since.

Without making an attempt to give a physics or theology explanation, the mere fact that this devout Christian and accomplished physicist would preach this consistency leads one to think that science and Genesis are likely not in much conflict. By 1951, even the Roman Catholic Pope, Pious XII, claimed that Lemaître's theory was not only supportive of Christian teachings, but that it provided a testimonial for the validity of Catholicism![237]

More on Genesis. Creation of life and the role of evolution

The story in Genesis, which is fundamental to all three Abrahamic religions: Judaism, Christianity, and Islam, states that God created life in its many forms, including humans. It does not say how He did it. It does not say that evolution was not involved. But many followers of these religions see a contradiction between some scientific theories of evolution and the narrative of God creating life. Others see God as a force guiding evolution. There is much history on this.

Though a Protestant Christian, this author finds many supportive quotes from Catholics, as I just did above. On the evolution vs. creationism dispute, the current Pope, Francis, said,

> Evolution in nature is not inconsistent with the notion of creation, because evolution requires the creation of beings that evolve.[238]

One of the objections to the Darwinian theory of evolution is that it supposedly depends on theoretically random mutations that lead to new species that must compete for food and survival with other species. But is that really true? Some say that God guides the microscopic events that cause such mutations. There is a completely natural way that is scientifically consistent in which this can happen. That mechanism is the ability of God to control quantum mechanical atomic and molecular transitions that are seemingly random to the casual observer, but according to this theory are under the complete control of God.

> The author is a retired theoretical physicist who has been familiar with quantum mechanics, and its supposedly random events. There is nothing in quantum theory that forbids God from controlling quantum transitions. A related theory holds that the human soul can control its body's behavior by affecting quantum transitions in the brain, and thus would be the basis for the doctrine of free-will. We can't prove this, but also, we cannot disprove it either.

Intelligent design and creationism. Can this be studied in public schools?

Another dispute among education stakeholders regards the roles that the Christian fundamentalist theories of intelligent design and creationism should play in a public school course about religion? There are perhaps three schools of thought on this:

1. That these fundamentalist theories have no scientific support and should be excluded from the curriculum.

2. That these theories have no scientific support, but should be in any comparative course on religion.

3. That these fundamentalist theories are consistent with science and should be included in the course.

There are many stakeholders that agree with item 1 and would exclude these topics, but to do so would go against the very concept of a course that is about religion and about the various beliefs of the different sects and denominations. Maybe they could be persuaded to advocate for item 2?

- Item 2, as we just explained, is consistent with the proposals for courses that are about religions.

- Item 3 appeals to scientists and others who have carefully studied the philosophy of the scientific method and from that believe that the universe was created and that its design is intelligent.

As a scientist, the author has pondered these concepts for at least a half century. When you learn about the smallest atom of the periodic chart, the hydrogen atom, the mathematical equations and formulas that describe this basic building block of the universe, you will likely regard that atom as beautiful. These atoms look to have been established (created) by an entity or someone who is fantastically intelligent. Hence:

> You have creationism and intelligent design. QED

The why and how of creation and other remote phenomena leads to a much deeper set of questions. I look at it this way:

> Everyday science research is about the study of one or two step causation: What triggered this and maybe what caused that? It does not ask much about remote causes that go back to the beginning of time or back to the Big Bang. It does not ask about how God might intervene to alter evolution and other trends around the universe. Those more remote causes are not understood scientifically except perhaps in rare exceptional instances. Something is going on, something has been going on, but we don't know how to describe it. Those remote phenomena are with God in the sense that the intelligent agent controlling that phenomena needs to be named. We call him God. (If we were politically correct, we'd say "call it God.")

This line of thought has a consistency that follows science where it has developed testable theories and that follows religion where the science is unknown. And, as we have seen in the few examples discussed above, they are often in rough agreement where both have explanations about the relevant events and phenomena.

Even Humanism is a religion?

Let's consider the man who during his life was first a Baptist Pastor, then a Unitarian Pastor, and finally by his own claim a Pastor of Humanism.[239] Please, meet Rev.

Charles Francis Potter who in this last clerical role was a champion of public schools. About them he said,

> Education is thus a most powerful ally of Humanism and every American school is a school of Humanism. What can the theistic Sunday schools, meeting for an hour once a week and teaching only a fraction of the children do to stem the tide of a five-day program of Humanistic religion teaching?[240]

While Potter was not an official member of the National Education Association (NEA, he was a friend of its most prominent member and honorary president, John Dewey, who also shared his humanistic theological beliefs. This does not prove the NEA was then or is now an advocate of Humanism or Secular Humanism, but it does make one ponder that possibility and their influence upon the organization.

Another twist in this discussion comes from the frequently held opinion that Humanism is itself a religion. This author sees it that way. Charles Potter, its founder, as is evident in the foregoing, thought it was. In 1987, an Alabama judge ruled that it was.[241] On appeal, portions of the judge's rulings were reversed, but the part that declared Secular Humanism a religion was not. Earlier in this chapter, we discussed Supreme Court decisions ruling on what public schools could do and not do with respect to teaching religious beliefs. The public schools, among other things, could not force disbelief in any religion nor could they inhibit religion. As was discussed there, public schools often cross the line into the promotion of one or another version of Humanism and often do it unintentionally. Sometimes, no doubt, it is done intentionally.

This complicates the discussion because Secular Humanism claims to be of and for science. Instead of the issues being religion on one side and science on the other, Secular Humanism is a philosophy that replaces religion with a scientific theory. The Humanism of Potter apparently had not reached a phase in which it denied the existence of God, but it was more of a philosophy that said that science was the study of the effects of God and the creations of God. If Secular Humanism really is a religion, then its dogma should not be taught in public schools. Part of its dogma is science. Does this mean that science is taboo in public schools?

What is Secular Humanism as compared to Humanism? It appears that the former is atheistic while the latter has nothing to say about God and is therefore agnostic in its approach. The courts have effectively held that even the atheistic Secular Humanism is a religion. In the sense that it has a scientific approach it therefore must believe in cause and effect. If it has no God, per se, it still has causes to consider as replacements for God and his agents.

One difference between science and religions is that science seeks consensus among all its participants while religions have many beliefs that resist the search for consensus. It is difficult for a school to teach subjects that have no consensus while in contrast teaching those with consensus is easier. The one-size-fits-all format of public schools can therefore teach science, but will falter if they attempt teaching religious dogma. Yes, these schools can theoretically teach about religion, but given the many different belief systems, that will be an arduous set of tasks.

SOLVING THE PUBLIC EDUCATION RELIGION IMPASSE

The adage, *better said than done*, seems to apply to efforts to teach about religion in public schools. Let's consider some of the proposals that others have made that aim to establish religious education programs in public education. We discuss this in the context of high school education, but we can extend our analysis and proposals to K-8 once we understand the issues at the secondary level.

So public schools can teach about religions. But is it practical?

A number of experts and analysts have proposed, in some detail, how a jurisdiction could implement a religious studies program. The late Warren Nord proposed the steps to be taken for a state to establish this kind of program. He has envisaged a state doing these things:

- Provide and finance more continuing education courses for teachers in the curricular area of religious studies wherein the emphasis is on comparative religions including secular philosophies.

- Every school system, presumably both at the state and district levels, would establish policies, including do's and don'ts, for the administration of its religious studies programs.

- Schools of education would receive directives and financing to provide the aforementioned continuing education courses for teachers.

- Encourage parents and teachers to lobby for additional religion courses that would be elective in nature. To do this the state would presumably work with PTO and PTA groups to solicit this kind of interest.

- Research existing textbooks and propose revisions to them to find academic content consistent with the curricular standards. Make sure that these standards are legal with respect to the Lemon Test.

- The state boards of education should mandate required high school courses in religious studies.[242]

We believe that Nord omitted this rather essential provision:

- That the state boards of education formulate the curricula for its religion courses. Without knowing the content to be taught everything else on his list will be confusing to implement.

If that were not complicated enough, he also made recommendations that other high school courses include religious content to comprise at least 5% of the material. He based this on the fact that subjects such as English literature, history, science, and economics also have current or historical connections to religion.

Let us suppose that one or more states were able to implement this kind of program. What would happen? Would all the stakeholders be happy? Depending on the community, various relatively minor groups, including small sects and cults, might complain. They might take legal action to force or end various requirements within the system.

Maybe teach Bible history without offending too many partisans?

Teaching about the history of the events depicted in the Christian Bible is quite different than offering a course in comparing religions. And, it is one way that public schools have sometimes been able to teach something about Christianity without violating the Lemon Test. Other Bible study courses have been ruled in violation of that test.

The more conservative text: Bible in History and Literature (BHL). The National Council on Bible Curriculum in Public Schools produced this text for use in public high schools. This text has been criticized for too much advocacy of fundamental Christian theology and thus has had problems with the Lemon Test. A number of lawsuits against districts using the BHL textbook and curriculum have claimed violations of the Lemon Test Sometimes these suits were resolved by the districts agreeing to use an alternative curriculum and textbook.[243] One recourse was to find a curriculum and textbook that would pass the Lemon Test.

The less conservative text: The Bible and Its Influence (BI). The Bible Literacy Project (BLP) produced this BI textbook. The BLP has been a coalition of several politically liberal groups who were quite sensitive to violations of the Establishment Clause. In formulating their curriculum and its corresponding textbook great care was taken to pass the Lemon Test.[244] Though less conservative than BHL, the BI textbook and curriculum is, what might be called, center-right conservative. As such it was praised and endorsed by a variety of evangelical organizations though some stalwart conservative advocates were still opposed to it.

What should parents and other stakeholders do if they want the more conservative BHL textbook that will almost certainly lose in court if someone sues over the Lemon Test? If they can afford tuition of a private school or the costs of homeschooling they can use BHL in those situations. But if they are stuck in one of the public schools using the BI text, they really have no alternative, but to that of using the more liberal book. They'll have to suck it up and persevere until a better alternative arises that suits their beliefs.

Teaching about religion in public schools has been largely a failure

We said, in this chapter's title, that *Public Education Is Flunking Religion*. We say this because none of the programs and systems introduced, so far, has provided a good curriculum for religious studies that still can meet the requirements laid down by all of the concerned parties. They often fail to meet:

- The requirement of the First Amendment's Establishment Clause as indicated by the Lemon Test

- The requirement of reaching an educator consensus on what a religious studies curriculum should be

- The requirement that parents have a choice among the various religious studies programs

The first and third of these are legal constraints from the *First Amendment* and from the *United Nations Declaration of Human Rights, Article 26*, respectively. As we have previously discussed, the latter is a treaty that binds the United States to honor its provision (*subparagraph (3) of Article 26*) that

> *Parents have a prior right to choose the kind of education that shall be given to their children.*[245]

We are not aware of any efforts to enforce this provision administratively or of any lawsuits by parents to exercise this right. It should be obvious that what parents want their children to learn about religion in school will often conflict with the Lemon Test criteria. This means that the three requirements will not be met in a large number of cases. That kind of failure is what justifies our chapter title, and we repeat it that

> Public education is flunking religion.

Even with these kinds of difficulties there can be gradual changes that improve the relevant instruction that allows students to better understand the roles that religion has played and continues to play in our societies. Our eventual conclusions in this book will point us towards an education economic sector in which a large majority of parents can have their choices honored. Details on how that's done follow farther along. Whether there will be public schools that can function in such an environment is not clear. We believe that in the end the courts will decide that question.

A part-time instructional format in public schools could accommodate the faithful

From the foregoing there seems to be no consistent format under which religion can be taught in public schools, even when the instruction is limited to teaching *about* religion.

We have a suggestion based on the traditional Roman Catholic practice of instructing public school children after-school in Catechism classes. The Catholic Church, in an effort to make sure their members' children were not learning too much that was contrary to their Church doctrine, established Catechism classes as a way to accomplish this.

Our suggestion would invite all religious congregations to establish their own version of Catechism, but it would occur during regular school hours of the public school—perhaps the last hour of instruction on one of the weekdays. These classes could be held on campus, or at a private school, or as a part-time homeschool activity. For children whose parents choose to keep them out of such a program, the public school would also provide an hour of instruction about religion. By doing this the conflicts between the teachings of the various persuasions would be removed. Doing this would effectively make the public schools' enrollment policies part-time.

Education savings accounts or vouchers could solve this too

When parents are financially enabled to find instructional alternatives, the education savings account (ESA) allows them much more freedom to choose the education to be received by their children. The ESA, which is a more recent and expanded version of the old Friedman voucher, can be used to pay expenses other than annual tuition costs. It can be used to pay tutoring fees. It can be used to pay for online courses. It can be used to pay for part-time religious instruction in a private school. So, even without the flexibility of part-time public education, the ESA can give parents control over instruction and curricular standards by giving them other options beyond the public school.

CHAPTER 11

K-12 Education Is Flunking History

A VERY CONFUSING ISSUE within public and private K-12 education concerns what students should learn about history. Many Americans seem to forget that the story of humankind, as revealed in historical accounts, provides practical examples of the *do's* and *don'ts* for living. For national leaders, understanding the successes and failures of their predecessors can help them lead—and lead in such a way as to avoid costly mistakes. Historian and philosopher George Santayana put it this way,

> Those who cannot remember the past are condemned to repeat it.[246]

Or maybe we could say,

> Those school systems that are *flunking* history are putting future generations *in danger*?

OK. So, if it's a good idea to study history, how much of it should students learn? How much of it should be taught in high school? Is studying United States history from the era of Christopher Columbus onward sufficient? Or should the range be wider? Should they also study European history and aspects of world history? In the mid-twentieth century, K-12 educators had already answered this question:

> The author recalls being told this: Studying U.S. history and civics would prepare high school students for their responsibilities as citizens and voters in their adult years. Some high schools offered additional history courses, such as a World history course. The study of U.S. history would give future voters some sense of what kinds of laws and policies will be helpful. Similarly, the study of civics would help these future voters understand the laws that we live under. And it would help them understand their rights, and some of their responsibilities going forward.

Have American high schools, both public and private, done a good job teaching these subjects? Let's now look at how well or poorly students have been performing over the recent decades.

PROFICIENCY TRENDS IN U.S. HISTORY: 1971– 2019

To get perspective on the knowledge of American 12th grade students in the subjects of U.S. history and civics we review testing results from the National Assessment of Educational Progress (NAEP), also known as the *Nation's Report Card*. We show their reported proficiency percentages for three subjects: U.S. history, civics, and reading. Their proficiencies in reading are good reference statistics for the other two. In Figure 12 below, we see that roughly one-third of American high school seniors can read proficiently. If students are having difficulty reading books, we think they would similarly have problems reading history and civics textbooks. In studying these profiles, you might wonder how so many grade-level illiterates could be promoted all the way to 12th grade? As we have explained before, this low student performance is largely due to social promotion policies of nearly all American schools—both public and private.

Only a quarter of emerging American voters pass the Nation's Report Card civics test

Next time you have disappointment in government, at any level, federal, state or local, consider the qualifications of the voters who elected the officials running these offices. In Figure 12, below, we compare the skill levels of graduating high school seniors in three subjects relevant to good citizenship: Reading, civics, and U.S. history. The blue line in the figure shows the low student proficiencies in reading, that seem to be stuck in the mid-30% range. The red line displays the worsening trend of 12th grade students' proficiency levels in civics that have recently been hovering around 25%.[247] The NAEP reported the civics proficiency percentages for only the last three testing years shown: Of 1998, 2006, and 2010. So, we had to estimate them for the earlier years. The civics proficiency shown for 1971 is based on the author's assumption and memory that students in 12th grade civics classes were about as proficient in civics as they were in reading. The data point for 1980 is from a simple interpolation.

    As we'll explore in more detail later, we believe that some of this poor performance has been caused by deliberate efforts of education officials to put less emphasis on students learning about the United States Constitution and other basic government functions.

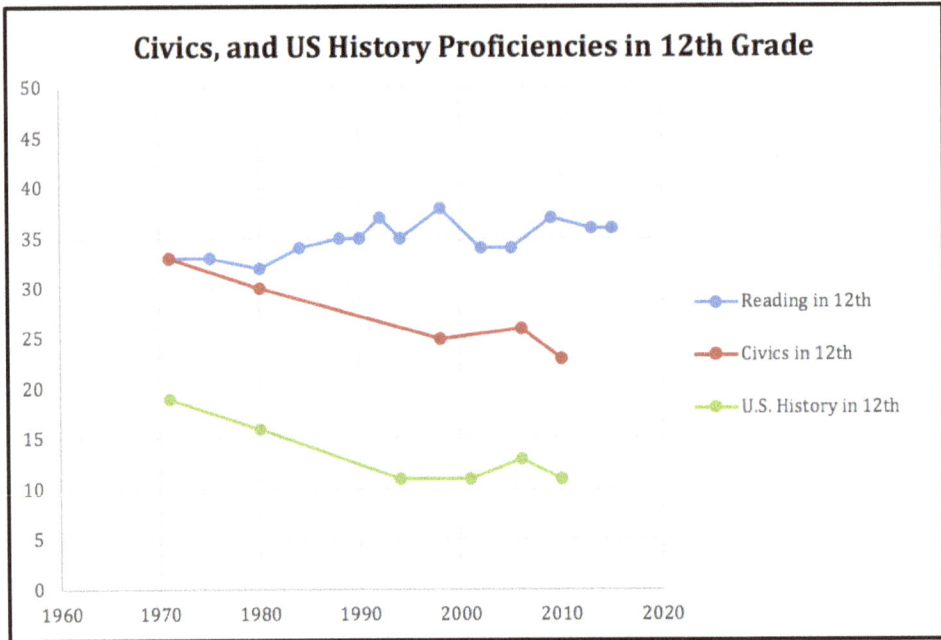

Figure 12 displays NAEP reported (and sometimes estimated) proficiency percentages for three subjects that good citizens should master: Reading, civics, and U.S. history. The implied portrayal, of an ignorant U.S. citizenry, is quite worrisome. We estimated the history, and civics levels for (1971–1980).

Barely one out of eight soon-to-be American voters reached proficiency in U.S. History

Figure 12 also shows, on the green line, the low proficiencies of American 12th grade students when tested on U.S history. The results displayed in this figure are for all 12th grade pupils in public and private schools combined nationwide. The NAEP U.S. history assessments provided the proficiency percentages for only the last four testing years of 1994, 2001, 2006, and 2010. By 2010 only about 12% of high school seniors were reported proficient.[248] The U.S. history proficiencies shown for the earlier years are based on the assumption that history education and civics education had similar profile drops during the first 23 years after 1960. At 12th grade, the NAEP did not disaggregate these results to show private and public school students separately, but did so separately for 8th grade testing. At 8th grade, private school proficiency levels in U.S. history were almost double those of public schools.[249] If that same kind of ratio carries over to 12th grade, this would suggest that about 25% of private school seniors would have proficiency in this subject as compared to the roughly 12% of public school seniors who tested proficient. While a 25% proficiency is better, it's nowhere near adequate. Based on this we would give the private schools an F+ in U.S. history while the public schools would get an F-. These are indeed *Sick Schools.*

Readers, who have lived through these decades, as the author has done, have over this period probably seen these same trends in news reporting. It seems that fewer references are now made by news media to earlier American historical events and civic issues than was common in the mid-twentieth century. Consider some of the important actions undertaken by the United States of America during the past 240 years, such as:

- Its struggle over and the ending of slavery during the Civil War
- Its defense of freedom in the World Wars
- Its struggle during the long Cold War
- Its end to racial and other kinds of unfair discrimination
- Its achievements of going to the moon
- Its development of new technologies
- Its struggle with Islamic terrorism

Many, if not most, Americans are only vaguely familiar with these important historical issues. This societal ignorance may well be the result of ineffective history instruction in the public schools and may have been made worse by the American news media's relative inattention to these topics.

It is a wonder that the United States of America functions as well as it does, given this picture of its new voters coming out of 12th grade. Yes, the private school students seem to do better, but having only one-fourth of your private high school graduates proficient in U.S. history is still a *failing grade* for private K-12 education. We worry that as a result of this growing American ignorance, our national well-being could get worse before it gets better.

Diagnosis: Their skulls are full of stuff, but not much of it is history or civics

How can one understand these very low scores of American 12th graders on tests of U.S. history and civics? Who would dispute that these are symptoms of *Sick Schools*? Who was responsible for the education of these high school seniors? Was it

- Their parents?
- Their teachers?
- The administrators, at all levels, in the school or school system?
- The elected school officials at the state and district levels?
- The students themselves?

There is probably much blame to be leveled at each of these groups. Taking them in turn we can hazard a few educated guesses as to their roles and culpability for the mess:

Roles and culpability of parents. Nearly everyone believes that parents should play an important role or even the most important role in guiding the education of their children. Even the *United Nations' Universal Declaration of Human Rights* takes that position as we saw at the end of Chapter 6. Parents could be doing much more, than they are, to scrutinize and push for reforms in the areas of history and civics education.

Roles and culpability of teachers. Most teachers of history and civics are not expert and often relatively ignorant of these subjects. They usually have certifications in pedagogy, but typically lack them in these subjects. That they are allowed to teach them, is not really their fault. However, to the extent that teachers support their unions and their political activities, they do have some blame for the problems here.

Roles and culpability of school administrators. Principals and others in school management are generally less familiar with these subjects than the teachers of them. They are mostly cogs in the machine and must do what they are told by others. But some of them are responsible for history and civics instruction and could play a more constructive role if they would more carefully study the degradation in these subjects.

Roles and culpability of elected school officials. The K-12 responsibilities of various elected officials, from governors on down to local school board members, include oversight and management of instruction in history and civics. They are, so to speak, where the *rubber meets the road*. They tend to be a lazy bunch until its re-election time. Some of them would help if they came to understand the depths of these problems.

Roles and culpability of students. In a legal sense, students are minors and therefore can't be legally forced to learn these subjects. But they owe it to themselves, their parents and the society around them to get on the path to becoming good citizens as they enter adulthood. If any students are reading this, there is not much you can do to fix your school's departments of history and civics. However, you can do this: Teach yourself online, or purchase and read history books, or you could read this stuff at public libraries. Go do it!

Worst symptoms.

Look at Figure 12 and you'll conclude that some of the worst symptoms of *Sick Schools* are in these history related subject areas. Later in this chapter you will encounter many leading educators in these subjects who had *ulterior motives* that were often political. You won't see much about Democrats or Republicans, but you will see some tangential encounters with Socialists and even a few Communists. Read on and consider how this mess can be fixed.

These disturbing trends may not be that difficult to understand. Let's now look at what education officials have done and not done, since the end of the nineteenth century. Perhaps it will help explain the degradation that is evident in Figure 12?

ERASING AND DILUTING U.S. HISTORY CURRICULA

To get a better understanding of recent trends in the instruction of U.S. history in American high schools, we will now narrow our review to public schools only. Finding national details about private schools would have been a daunting task if we wanted to include them. Given that approximately 90% of high school seniors have attended public schools we trust that our somewhat reduced focus will be acceptable.

To get the perspective we need, we here push our starting date back from our nominal beginning date of 1951 to a much earlier date prior to the turn of the twentieth century. Except for making note of a Thomas Jefferson remark from 1782, we shall look back to the 1890s to see where educators began efforts to alter history instruction in our high schools.

Domination of progressive pedagogies: The educationists

Before we can describe actions taken by school systems that have affected instruction in history we should understand something about the philosophy and political orientation of many of the educators who have managed the various K-12 public education systems. To get started let's examine some jargon and ask

What is an educationist?

This infrequently used term in the field of education is defined by one dictionary as

A specialist in the theory and methods of education.[250]

Another source comments that this word is

. . . often a disparaging term with varying connotations of inflexibility, intellectual limitations, or bias against traditionalism.[251]

An inference from these definitions holds that educationists generally hesitate to apply scientific methods in the development of their pedagogical discipline. The term is more often applied to progressive educators and rarely to traditional ones. Near the turn of the twentieth century there was an important change in emphasis in K-12 education. Teacher colleges, then often called normal schools, had traditionally instructed future teachers in the techniques of imparting the knowledge contained in the curricula of the various subjects taught in the schools. That traditional instructional practice is sometimes called didactic pedagogy.

We'll have more to say on that below. These teacher colleges were soon to become part of what was then becoming fashionable: progressive pedagogy. They would soon apply it to high school education. We can describe these two forms of pedagogy, respectively, as

- The more traditional didactic form of instruction has the teacher controlling the learning environment and the sequencing of its components. Direct instruction is an example. It was extremely common before the mid-twentieth century and, though now less dominant, it is still the most commonly used format.

and

- The more progressive forms of instruction have many varieties. At one extreme the student helps control the learning environment. At the other, there is *one best system* imposed statewide or even nationally on all children. These progressive pedagogies have played various roles in K-12 instruction since the early twentieth century, but even now have not become the most common instructional format in public or private schools. At least not yet.

As progressive education gained adherents and became a significant format within K-12 education there was a great deal of controversy between traditionalists and the progressive educationists. The progressive educationists didn't always work constructively with their critics. Rather, to their traditionalist colleagues they sometimes applied derogatory labels such as

- Congenital reactionaries
- Witch-hunters
- Dogma peddlers

among others.[252]

But the traditionalists had and still have their allies. This author is one. The clear and scientifically demonstrated success of didactic pedagogy has been reiterated many times, but too few educators are curious enough or attentive enough to pay heed. One such traditionalist voice is that of the Fordham Institute's Robert Pondiscio, who recently wrote about the research confirming the effectiveness of direct instruction (DI). He put it this way:

> Hey, wait. Where's everybody going? I'm telling you, *Direct Instruction* is the Rodney Dangerfield of education. It gets no respect.

> . . . Rote or scripted, sequenced or not, loved or hated, shouldn't half a century and hundreds of studies be enough to earn DI a little respect if education is so evidence-based?[253]

Progressive educators have a habit, it seems, of using respectable terminology, such as *evidence based*, when what they really mean is more like this:

> Based on the unreliable *evidence* that their progressive philosophies find plausible they take the path of least resistance and often ignore other alternatives that would actually study the real *evidence* scientifically.

Authentic professionals would take a scientific approach and study the evidence carefully. Most educators unfortunately avoid these kinds of obligations and instead follow the maxims of progressive ideology, which generally avoid taking a scientific approach.

What good is history instruction? Some thought it important.

A stalwart nineteenth century defender of traditional didactic instruction in the study of history was William T. Harris, whom we already encountered in Chapter 6. He served as U.S. Commissioner of Education from 1889 through 1906. During those years, he was an advocate for the learning of facts, unlike many of his contemporaries who were becoming enthralled with various forms of progressive education. As to the importance of learning history he said that as an alternative to learning from hearsay,

> . . . it is incomparably more useful to be able by means of books and the printed page, to have access to the observations of all men who have observed and reflected in all times and all places.[254]

Other education leaders, of a more progressive bent, favored replacing traditional subject areas with courses in vocational areas. Harris was a subject of criticism for decades—even long after his passing. One historian complained that Harris was an opponent of socialism—the latter being a common political position among progressive educators.[255]

An even earlier advocate of robust history instruction was Thomas Jefferson. He advised that history instruction should begin at an early age. He argued that if schooling was to be more specialized in subsequent years that it would then be helpful to lay a good foundation early. He held that the study of history will prepare students to succeed in human affairs. In 1782 he claimed that it

> . . . will qualify them as judges of the actions and designs of men; it will enable them to know ambition under every disguise it may assume; and knowing it to defeat its views.[256]

This sounds similar to George Santayana's sentiment about the risks of not knowing history that we just quoted on the first page of this chapter.

In the 1890s Harris, who was then the U.S. Commissioner of Education, joined with his colleague Charles Eliot, who was then the President of Harvard University, to form The Committee of Ten. It was a *blue-ribbon* commission formed to propose policies for secondary education. One its recommendations was that high schools should establish history courses. The Committee of Ten held the view, according education historian Diane Ravitch, that

> . . . a well-educated person must have a mind that was not only well trained, but well furnished with knowledge.[257]

Such an attitude can be defended as a scientific understanding. Science is based on facts—facts first. Only then can theories be generated, usually by some process of inductive logic applied to the facts. When there are no facts, science falls flat. So-called *critical thinking* is not enough. There must be facts to analyze.

> This author is a retired scientist. I was a theoretical physicist for more than 20 years. I would have failed in the development of theories had there been no experimental facts to study.

A ferocious opponent of the Committee of Ten was a G. Stanley Hall, President of Clark University of Worcester, Massachusetts. Hall contended that most students were too low in aptitude to benefit from a study of the humanities that would include languages, history, natural science, and mathematics. Hall had this to say about the Committee's proposals, that they do not

> . . . apply to the great army of incapables, shading down to those who should be in schools for dullards or subnormal children, for those whose mental development heredity decrees a slow pace and early arrest and for whom by general consent both studies and methods must be different.[258]

Harvard's Eliot was in no mood for this, which he saw as nonsense. Regarding Hall's "great army of incapables," he had this response:

> . . . any school superintendent or principal who should construct his program with the incapables chiefly in mind would be a person professionally demented.[259]

Whether or not Eliot was correct on this, it would not be long before those on his side of these controversies would be outnumbered by their progressive colleagues. So, who were these opponents of traditional didactic instruction and what were they doing?

To answer this, it is helpful to understand more about the roles of John Dewey who by the year 1900 was the most well-known champion of progressive education theory and practices. Some even accorded him the title as the *father* of progressive education. He was proposing that K-12 education should enlarge its role from just instruction to that of the *social worker* who also instructs. In fact, he sought to reduce the time spent on traditional instruction to provide time for a more *child centered learning* system.[260]

Dewey on history instruction and other educational matters.

If we try to distill a list of his theories, proposals, and active roles in K-12 education that have been relevant to history instruction, we get a long list. Almost all of his ideas appear nonsensical to this author.

Nevertheless, here are a dozen plus facts about his ideas and professional career that we see as pertinent:

- As early as 1897, he was proposing that the field of psychology be applied to the curricula and practices of K-12 education.[261]

- Focus on "the child's own social activities," instead of the relatively archaic subjects of science, English, and history, among others.

- The child should play a role in the scheduling of the instruction, essentially a form of self-pacing.

- Dewey held and said that traditional education was too much concerned with

  - ... the teacher, the textbook, anywhere, and everywhere you please except in the immediate instincts and activities of the child himself.[262]

  The author sees it this way: By focusing more directly on the child Dewey was entering the psychological realm. Moreover, in the progressive mind, educators needed to be experts in psychology as well as in academic subject areas. The focus would be on child psychology and developmental psychology. However, rather than work with professional psychologists, these educationists instead launched their own comparatively amateuristic research efforts into child psychology.

- Learning by doing is superior to learning from books.[263]

- A course in laundry work could, in his words, "be so utilized as to give understanding and illumination . . . of social facts and relationships." The context of this remark was that laundry studies would be preferred to the study of biology (he actually said "zoology").

- In 1915 Dewey stated and claimed that,

> A knowledge of the past and its heritage is of great significance when it enters into the present, but not otherwise.[264]

- By 1925 Dewey complained about his progressive education followers, his own disciples, with this piece of cognitive dissonance:

> There is a present tendency in so-called advanced schools of thought . . . to say, in effect, let us surround pupils with certain materials, tools, appliances, etc., and then let pupils respond to these things according to their own desires. Above all, let us not suggest any end of plan to the students; let us not suggest to them what they shall do, for that is an unwarranted trespass upon their sacred intellectual individuality . . . now such a method is really stupid. For it attempts the impossible, which is always stupid; and it misconceives the conditions of independent thinking.[265]

- In 1931 he argued that a new political party, along socialist lines, should be formed.[266] It is not clear if he was advocating communism as practiced in the Soviet Union or was proposing a milder form of socialism? On this, a few years later, he said,

> Schools should take an active part in directing social change and share in the construction of a new social order.[267]

- In 1937 he attacked Robert Hutchins, the President of the University of Chicago, for his proposals that education, K-12 and postsecondary, emphasize the classics and the humanities—the latter including studies of history.[268]
- Also, in 1937, he led the Dewey Commission in its investigation that exonerated Russian exile Leon Trotsky. This was after the Soviet Union had convicted and executed many of Trotsky's supporters on charges of treason. Trotsky was no mild mannered Communist: He was arguably to the political left of Stalin.[269]

The Progressive Education Association (PEA), which for a time had John Dewey as its honorary president, became active during and after the 1930s Depression. One of its publications, *Reorganizing Secondary Education*, expressed disdain for scholarship and intellectual development.[270] Among their tenets:

- High school education should not aim to prepare students for college or the workplace, but should be for their personal and social growth.

- The high school curriculum should represent student's wants, wishes, inclinations, and desires . . .

- If students don't seek learning about mathematics, science, or a foreign language they should not be expected to take such courses.

- High schools should focus on the growing adolescent and the *tasks of life adjustment.*

- Social studies that previously included history would be revamped into studies of personal relationships and current events.[271]

Fortunately, very few of these questionable ideas had much traction. All of them seem subversive of society's desire that high school graduates should be mastering skills with economic and other societal benefits. In many high schools there were courses in vocational areas that were in response to these progressive proposals, but few of these schools abandoned their academic curricula. They simply had both.

> As noted before, this author attended a magnet high school, Lane Technical High School in Chicago. It had this very format: Academics plus vocational courses. It prepared me for the university—Johns Hopkins University to be specific.

John Dewey impresses this author, not as an erudite scholar and philosopher that his manners would suggest, but more as a pompous man with a large assortment of untested ideas. Perhaps he was the type of celebrity that in our time we label

. . . famous for being famous?

Despite these progressive educationists' intense efforts to revolutionize high school education in the United States, it is somewhat comforting to know that traditional curricula, methods, and school regulations remained largely intact—at least until the last few decades of the twentieth century. Though they were intact, the efforts of the progressive educators can be said to have retarded improvements on the academic side of K-12 education. They surely didn't help students learn more about U.S. history!

Social studies dilute history instruction and sometimes subvert government institutions.

As we previously noted, there were at least two points of view regarding the pedagogy to be applied in the study of social studies and more specifically the study of history.

The traditional approach of didactic pedagogy has the students learn the facts first, with interpretation to follow. In contrast the more modern viewpoint of progressive pedagogy puts less emphasis on learning facts and more emphasis on the social sciences. It is not surprising that its advocates gave it a new label: *social studies.* The modern progressive camp labels itself *scientific* when, on the contrary, it is the traditional approach that has been scientifically verified to be the one producing many more knowledgeable citizens than the progressive pedagogy.

And who would you think would propose these *modern* changes? If you answered,

> A university sociology professor,

you would be right. It was Professor Albion Small of the University of Chicago who in 1896 proposed many of the elements that often were included as courses in what would later be called a *social studies* program. He didn't coin the name, but he discussed what he would propose regarding some of its components. Among those ideas:

- Replace the history of faraway places for more focus on family history.

- Replace economics at the national level for economics at home (aka home economics courses).

- Replace studies of the U.S. Constitution with those concerning a town's ordinances.

- Replace traditional subject matter and instead have instruction in current events.[272]

Small's hopes for the future included the expectation that schools using the new curricula would become, in his words,

> . . . makers of society.

One historian suggests that Small was a pioneer in the *art* of social engineering. We use the word *art* intentionally to suggest that *social engineering* is more of an epithetical category than a real field of engineering studies and applications.[273]

That these progressive new schools would become *makers of society*, is troubling because their proposals, as seen in the foregoing list, are promoting ignorance of the existing society with the unwritten inference that its standards, systems, and practices can be discarded in favor of the characteristics of the new society they envision. Does it not suggest that such progressive educators might be unpatriotic and could be subversive?

The heightened emphasis on *social adjustment* and the relative neglect of *academic subjects* had numerous critics. One prominent critic was Frances Fitzgerald who was an expert in the field of U.S. history instruction. In her analysis of history textbooks, she had this to say:

> While the Puritans believed that children were naturally sinful and had to be educated to virtue, modern pedagogues tend to believe that children are mentally ill.[274]

She may overstate the progressive pedagogical view, but it does fit their biases if *mentally ill* is replaced, let's say, by *socially maladjusted.*

Our purpose in reviewing the history of the subject areas called *social studies* is mainly that of understanding how the instruction of United States history has been affected by these new curricular diversions. Sometimes the history courses were no longer required. Other times they were no longer even offered as electives, but we must say that towards the end of the twentieth century U.S. history was becoming (once again) a required high school course. Here are a baker's dozen of developments from the past one-hundred years or so, that show how the learning of United States history has been harmed by these progressive educationists:

- As a labelled discipline, *social studies*, appeared first around 1917. (More on that later in the next major section, *The Decline of Civics Was Intended*.) At that time, Harold Rugg, who was a professor at Teachers College of Columbia University in New York, was said to have developed a new *social studies* curriculum.[275] It is not surprising that his academic training was not in a traditional discipline of the humanities. Rather, he was a psychologist. This raises an obvious question: Given his presumed ignorance of history, how could he be competent to devise a *social studies* curriculum that would prominently include studies of history?

- Not long after, in 1922, Jesse Newlon, the new superintendent of Denver, Colorado public schools instituted a *social studies* program for junior high schools in which the courses were, as Frances Fitzgerald put it, were

    organized around problems rather than subjects.[276]

- As the economic depression of the 1930s was ending, the Progressive Education Association (PEA) made further efforts to make K-12 curricula more child centered and to serve

    . . . the needs of youth.[277]

The PEA formed the Commission on the Secondary School Curriculum and in 1938 this Commission proposed many changes to high school curricula. History was to be replaced with studies of current events and the psychology of personal relationships. Forget about the Civil War and instead concern yourself with dating etiquette? Reading newspapers would be encouraged, but not history books.[278]

- In 1940 the progressive American Youth Commission, composed of public officials and private citizens, published its curricular proposals that included some of the most impractical ideas this author has ever encountered. For example, this commission contended that English courses wasted time teaching grammar and literature, that algebra and geometry were too hard and that natural sciences were based on too many facts. (I'm not making this up!) As for history, it should no longer recount events in the development of the United States, but it should be reduced to the history of inventions and perhaps something on the history of democratic ideals.[279]

- In 1950 some public high schools in Minneapolis, Minnesota were revamped to follow a new pilot program in which history and English literature courses were eliminated. And get this: the official curriculum was abolished and replaced with temporary annual curricula planned by committees of teachers and pupils working together. Reminds one of the phrase, *the inmates were running the asylum.* And these folks were actually running the schools![280]

- Along came the 1960s. As we saw in Chapter 8, social promotion and lax grading accelerated after 1964—possibly as a result of the politics of the Vietnam War.[281] The study of history, which by then was almost always under the umbrella of *social studies*, was further diminished. Ditto for the study of civics.

- History textbook expert, Gilbert Sewall, whom we encountered in Chapter 10, had this to say about the degradation of U.S. history instruction under the umbrella and influence of *social studies*:

  > Social studies classes might substitute trendy units in human rights, the limits of growth, or nuclear disarmament for map-reading exercises or the study of the Civil War. A civics requirement might be satisfied by a course that focuses on the constitutional protection that every citizen is guaranteed, but has little to say about the Bill of Rights' relation to public responsibilities.[282]

- In 1983 the report, *A Nation at Risk: The Imperative for Educational Reform*, was issued with considerable fanfare. It was published by the National Commission on Excellence in Education that had been established by the then new U.S. Department of Education. It reviewed the poor performance levels of high school seniors and then made some recommendations to remedy the various problems. With respect to *social studies*, it proposed more U.S. history instruction. Among those recommendations was the proposal that high school students would take three years of *social studies*, with the requirement that one of these year-long courses would cover United States history.[283]

- In the first few years after *A Nation At Risk* was issued it seems that pedagogical methods were not affected much by the ensuing reform efforts nor were any significant improvements seen in student performance levels. Even so, it seems to have led some stakeholders to look at the education marketplace and consider what could be done there to help K-12 education. From that we believe new interest arose in alternatives to regular public schools. Among those alternatives were vouchers and charter schools that appeared circa 1990. Some disruption ensued and that led to some competition which, in turn, may have led to some small, but significant improvements in public school performance levels—particularly in mathematics. Our own research shows that this happened in the two decades after 1990.[284] We already discussed some of this in Chapter 8.

- The *Nation At Risk* report did not, however, say much about the curriculum for U.S. history. Even if every state's public schools followed their recommendations for strengthening *social studies* with mandatory U.S. history instruction, there were no standards set as to what would be deemed proficient mastery of the subject. This lack of standards, just by itself, may help explain why, in recent years, only about one in eight students have been estimated proficient in U.S. history by the *Nation's Report Card*.

- Many school systems in the United States made changes to their curricula to conform. We surveyed the standards in the 50 states plus Washington D.C. and found that approximately 35 of them now have a U.S. history requirement. That is somewhat discouraging with only seven out of ten states mandating its study.

- We are almost done with this list. By 1989, was U.S. history still being taught? Yes, it was, but its content standards had changed. It was no longer focused primarily on how the United States government and other important public and private institutions evolved, but had additional components added to satisfy advocates of multiculturalism and other politically correct ideas. Instead of including historic people according to their contributions, a new kind of affirmative action was imposed. The individuals described in the history standards often had to meet a numerical quota. If blacks make up 12% of the U.S. population then maybe those blacks mentioned in the history book should be 12% of the others described in the book. For each gal there had to be a guy. (Ooops, *gal* is verboten.[285] Use *woman* instead. But *guy* is OK?) The numerically dominant race (of white males) had to be described pejoratively while various minority groups were to have some fictitious stereotypes applied to their histories. This kind of unspoken racialism or racism against white males may be expanding its *domain* to also include Asians, as is evident in the admissions policies in certain colleges and universities. Wake up Harvard! If you're successful you could be the enemy. It is reminiscent of the bigotry against Jews—especially in Europe in recent centuries. They were often financially successful, which was resented. Or in politically correct terminology, they were too *privileged*.

- And what was deemed important about certain personages changed. Thomas Jefferson was mainly a slave owner? They made an exception for George Washington given his role as the first President of the United States.[286] More on this a few pages ahead in the section, *Trapped by The Presentism Time Machine*.

Several of these changes had the effect of reducing the curricular content of the U.S. history courses. We think that such content varied from district to district and state to state. That put the testing services in a bind. If a test was to be given nationally, what historical content should be included? Surely there would be some common standards, and that could be tested easily. But what about the not so common standards? How would they be tested? We aren't sure how the National Assessment Governing Board (NAGB) approached this in designing the NAEP tests for U.S. history, but we think their process led to fairly high expectations that were well beyond what was being learned in most schools. That is perhaps consistent with the extremely low proficiencies in U.S. history seen in Fig. 12. When only 12% of public high school seniors pass the test, it begs us to do something. But before we can discuss remedies, we need to look a little closer at some of the other problems.

One of the long-term effects of the various developments and changes identified in the preceding list has been a reduction in the historical knowledge among American citizens. When the voters in the United States know less about their country and its history, they will tend to be less responsible in the voting booth. Such laxity could lead to wrongheaded government policies, perhaps the ones advocated by the progressives? This kind of ignorance is *subversive* of good government when naïve voters can be swayed to vote the interests of the progressives while foolishly ignoring their own.

THE DECLINE OF CIVICS WAS INTENDED

Instruction in civics at the high school level has been a common requirement for graduation—at least during the twentieth century. Civics can be understood as a special course in history in which,

- The founding documents of the United States of America are presented and explained within their historical contexts.

- The electoral systems are explained to enable future participation as responsible voters.

Much of the civics story is similar to what we just described for U.S. history—if for no other reason than that civics is a component study of that history. Like the case for history, the mischief, including subversive strategies, started in the early decades of the twentieth century. Our review of civics begins in 1918.

Were the Cardinal Principles of 1918 subversive, by taking the Constitution out of civics?

In 1918, a report, the *Cardinal Principles*, was issued by the Commission on the Reorganization of Secondary Education.[287] This Commission, itself, was formed by the National Education Association (long before it became a union).

The Commission was dismissive of civics instruction in high schools. In their 5th Cardinal Principle they put it this way:

> Civics should concern itself less with constitutional questions and remote governmental functions . . . and should direct attention to social agencies close at hand and to the informal activities of daily life that regard and seek the common good.[288]

One wonders how advocates of good democratic government could ever agree with this? Isn't a functioning democratic system based on an educated electorate? A good civics education is fundamental to that. But here, this Commission was opposed to an informed citizenry. There is a word for proposals that undermine government functions in this way: *Subversive.*

The Commission also had a Committee on Social Studies chaired by Thomas Jesse Jones. Jones was one of the first to coin the label *social studies.* In a report issued at about the same time as the *Cardinal Principles* his Committee had this to say about civics:

> It is not so important that a pupil know how the President is elected as that he shall understand the duties of the health officer in his community.[289]

One inference, from these efforts to degrade civics instruction, holds that these *experts* do not want to live under the *United States Constitution.* This suggests that these ideologues may have had *subversive* intentions. And, consistent with those intentions, when the electorate remains ignorant of their Constitutional rights, they will not be very concerned when government actions move towards socialism and run afoul of that founding document. One wonders if these educationists on this committee of Thomas Jesse Jones were themselves very well educated? Some of their proposals seem almost totally without merit. Were any of them the futurists of their day? Were they the ones looking forward to an elevated socialist heaven on earth, post the U.S. Constitution? They might even like a tyrannical government when it is targeting others . . . until they are the targets of it?

What parents of high school students favor.

A 1998 survey of American parents of high school students found that 83% of them want schools to educate children

> . . . to appreciate the freedoms, they are guaranteed under the Constitution and the Bill of Rights.[290]

This essentially says that they want traditional civics instruction for their high school children.

Maybe high school graduates should pass the U.S. citizenship test?

One central requirement of the United States immigration system is that naturalized citizens should know enough about the *Constitution* and other aspects of the federal government to become informed citizens and voters. But we don't usually require this of citizens born within the U.S.

However, Sandra Stotsky, a professor emerita of the University of Arkansas, proposed doing just that. She recently put it this way:

> No high school diplomas awarded students unless grade-twelve students pass the *Citizenship Test* (used for naturalizing intending citizens).[291]

A high school civics course may cover other topics about federal, state, and local government structures and issues, but one would always expect it to cover the concepts tested by the *Citizenship Test*. We would go a step further than Stotsky's proposal and propose that passing that test be required to become a registered voter or perhaps requiring that to be permitted to vote for candidates to federal offices.

What can happen when these students become adults who remain ignorant of a basic knowledge of civics? You could have protests based on unfounded claims about political leaders. You could have riots or other forms of insurrection. We wonder how many American voters in the 2016 Presidential election understood that winning the popular vote is not the criterion for election to the presidency? How many understand the Electoral College and its origins from the Constitutional Convention of 1787? If these folks had passed the *Citizenship Test,* it is quite likely that they would understand the election results. And, if there were enough people supporting changes to the Electoral College it is possible that the Constitution could be amended to use the popular vote as the criterion for presidential election. How many former high school seniors know this as a result of what they learned in high school?

WHY DO PROGRESSIVES OFTEN LEAN SUBVERSIVE?

When political progressives are unable to change laws to their liking they often resort to other unethical or even illegal means by which they might be able to effect some of the changes they seek.

Progressive word games can mislead and undermine terminology and subvert our laws

Euphemisms can twist the meanings of words. They can soften the appearance of criminal activity. A favorite word pair among political progressives is the designation *undocumented immigrant* to represent a person who illegally entered the United States who is correctly labeled an *illegal alien*. Since there is the likelihood that such a criminal is also undocumented, they could be labeled *illegal undocumented alien* without any distortion of the meaning. The progressive activists then do a few semantic somersaults to replace *illegal alien* with *undocumented immigrant*. The words *alien* and *immigrant* are almost opposite in meaning. The former is not welcome in the United States while the latter is, by legal definition, and inference, a legal resident newcomer. Progressives generally want certain ethnic/national newcomers to come into the United States illegally. They cover their advocacy of criminal activity by coloring it euphemistically with the bland terminology of *undocumented*. Such substitutions appear to be *subversive* of the immigration laws of the United States.[292]

In the K-12 education field, *social promotion* is the euphemism for *advancing the flunked*. This kind of practice subverts the proper operation of schools. It is a form of dishonesty that, depending on the details, can also be criminal. It is often the result of ineffective remediation that should have helped correct these student deficiencies.

Then there is the doubletalk about a *living breathing* Constitution that has an interpretation based, not on its explicit words, but on the desired *replacement* policies of the progressive left. When a novel interpretation contradicts the actual words of the law and the courts actually impose the new interpretation, that is a new kind of *subversion*.

Subverting the academic content standards for instruction

The imposition of *Common Core State Standards (CCSS)*, so-called, was an activity that was illegal in a variety of ways. It was also a form of *subversion* in which the federal government illegally *extorted* state education departments to use *CCSS* instead of their own standards or else lose funding and other benefits.

Legal experts have identified at least three federal statutes CCSS violate as well as their apparent unconstitutionality. Those four legal requirements are:

- The *General Education Provisions Act* prohibits federal government control of curricula.

- The *Department of Education Organization Act* restates a similar prohibition of curricular control.

- The *Elementary and Secondary Education Act of 1965* also limits any federal control over curriculum.[293]

- The 10th *Amendment to the Constitution* limits the federal government's powers to those enumerated. Education is not enumerated and thus is not a Constitutional responsibility of the federal government.

It appears that there have been no enforcement actions taken to ensure compliance with these legal obligations. At least not recently. Nor do we know of any efforts in the United States to implement the treaty obligations in the *United Nations Declaration of*

Human Rights treaty that we discussed near the end of Chapter 10. If there have been some enforcement efforts, they must have been rare and not reported in the news media? Or perhaps some these were enforced prior to the imposition of the *Common Core* upon the states?

Some regard the tactics used to impose *Common Core* as a form of *extortion*. One such influential stakeholder with that opinion was U.S. Congressman, Richard Hudson of North Carolina's 8th District. He wrote a column on it and put the word *extortion* in its title.[294] He mentions his support for the *Student Success Act* that would have outlawed *extortion* (again!). This time we really mean it! The bill passed the House in 2013, but was left to die in the U.S. Senate. He mentioned that the bill was insufficient to really end the abuse, but was a good first step towards that goal. Do we need to mention that President Obama threatened to veto this bill if it ever reached his desk?[295]

The tactics used to extort compliance with *Common Core* ended once the Trump administration came into office in early 2017. Some states then *excused* themselves from this flawed system. But other states, such as the more progressive California, remained faithful to this problematic system of standards and assessments.[296] It has been difficult in searching the Web to find California opponents to *Common Core*, but we did find one California mathematics teacher weighing in against its standards.[297]

We mentioned, above, that progressive educators have proposed diluting and ending civics instruction. It seems that their goal is to incentivize ignorance of the United States Constitution. When American voters have less understanding of our founding documents and our laws it is easier for the progressives to act *illegally* and *unconstitutionally* in their pursuit of policies that violate those basic laws. When politicians act illegally to undermine our laws that is very close to the textbook definition of *subversion*.

TRAPPED BY THE *PRESENTISM* TIME MACHINE

An all too common mistake of modern historians and other authors of history textbooks is the practice of judging historical events and persons of earlier eras by the mores, laws and customs of the early twenty-first century. This practice is called *presentism*. Such bad chronicling can transform a truly heroic individual into a seemingly villainous jerk. It is as if these *historians* took modern standards and took them back to the pertinent historical period on a time machine. If that had happened the compatriots of the historic individuals would have judged them by our twenty-first century mores, ethics, and laws. Of course, that would be nonsensical. In their era they were properly judged by their contemporaries according to the mores and standards of their own historic period. And for many historic individuals, they were not only doing their best to be good and honorable persons, but they were also earning the respect of those around them. Gilbert Sewall characterized *presentism* of historical accounts this way:

> History textbooks are flawed by *presentism*. That is, interpreting the past by contemporary standards. The result is failure to appreciate vast differences regarding time, place, and culture.[298]

He went on to indict history textbooks for what we would call the crimes of *addition* and *subtraction*. To wit:

- Of *adding* irrelevant topics.

- Of *subtracting* important information as is necessitated by constraints on the total numbers of pages.

On this he said,

> What about so-called non-historical *social studies* texts and materials: The kinds used in psychology, self-esteem, family life, and personal awareness classes? More and more, these subjects are displacing history in the curriculum.[299]

Historian Diane Ravitch conducted a review of 16 U.S. history textbooks that were published near or at the turn of the twenty-first century. She found that these books engage in rampant presentism or as she put it

> They constantly moralize about the past, as though everyone in 1850 or 1900 or 1950 should have known what we know today and should have shared our enlightened values.[300]

To get a better understanding of some of this, we will consider two case studies below: Those of Christopher Columbus and Thomas Jefferson.

Were Columbus and Jefferson as bad as some say?

One topic on which historians differ regards the four voyages of Christopher Columbus to the New World and whether or not he was a murderer, a slave master or a tough leader? Was he a hero? Was he the worst of the worst? Was he a devout Catholic? Did his employers, the monarchs of Spain approve of his work? And if they didn't why did they approve his fourth voyage to the Americas? Another famous and deservedly famous American, was Thomas Jefferson. Many textbook writers think him a jerk for having owned slaves. These writers (typically not very good historians) violate one of the cardinal rules of historical judgment: You should judge individuals by the culture and mores of their eras and not by modern standards. And, if they had carefully read Jefferson they would realize that he favored ending the institution of slavery. Let's now look a little closer at Columbus and then, after that, consider Jefferson.

Does U.S. history instruction often misrepresent Christopher Columbus as a murderer?

As we just stated, a good historian knows that the narrative through which they describe the events of an earlier historical era must be described in the context of the traditions, practices, and culture surrounding those events. This means, in part, that the standards of the twenty-first century should not be used to judge people of earlier times—in this case from the years before and after 1500.

Prior to the mid-twentieth century, in textbooks on American history, there was a tendency to whitewash various tragic events in order to give the stories a patriotic gloss. Efforts were made to boost the heroic images of notable players and leaders. They surely wanted Christopher Columbus to be seen as heroic.

Since the mid-twentieth century, some historians, including those authoring textbooks, have made efforts to bring their narratives closer to what is actually known about the relevant historical developments. But others have painted a pessimistic view of historical characters formerly described as heroic. As with so many things in life, the more accurate descriptions will mix the positive with the negative.

When authors think less of a historic individual, they often give him or her less ink. In her book, *America Revised—History Schoolbooks in the Twentieth Century*, Frances Fitzgerald laments,

> Poor Columbus! He is a minor character now, a walk-on in the middle of American history.[301]

Other modern authors give him more ink! But with the added verbiage there can be more venom. With respect to Columbus, historian Howard Zinn has described Columbus in starkly negative terms. In his famous (or some say *infamous*) history textbook, *A People's History of the United States*, Chapter 1 starts out discussing Columbus and his alleged roles in harming the native American Indians—specifically the Arawaks and other tribes. Columbus had encountered them as the leader of the Spanish exploratory forces. In the introductory chapter of his book Zinn wrote

> . . . in that inevitable taking of sides which comes from selection and emphasis in history, I prefer to try to tell the story of the discovery of America from the viewpoint of the Arawaks, of the Constitution from the standpoint of the slaves, of Andrew Jackson as seen by the Cherokees, of the Civil War as seen by the New York Irish, of the Mexican war as seen by the deserting soldiers of Scott's army, of the rise of industrialism as seen by the young women in the Lowell textile mills, of the Spanish-American war as seen by the Cubans, the conquest of the Philippines as seen by black soldiers on Luzon, the Gilded Age as seen by southern farmers, the First World War as seen by socialists, the Second World War as seen by pacifists, the New Deal as seen by blacks in Harlem, the postwar American empire as seen by peons in Latin America.[302]

That is to say, as Zinn himself said at other times, he wanted to present history from the viewpoint of those oppressed by the powerful. And, by inference, he didn't want to present the viewpoints of *the powerful.* He wanted his historical accounts to be biased towards those who were claimed by him to have been the victims of history. Thus, he was ignoring the roles of the various *powerful* leaders who surely influenced the surrounding events. Moreover, he was tending to ignore the good done by these leaders, not to mention the many benefits they sometimes provided to the vulnerable people in their midsts.

Who, then, was this Howard Zinn? He was a historian in the sense that he had a PhD in history from Columbia University. When one considers the fact that he wrote his accounts primarily from the viewpoint of those he deemed oppressed, one wonders if his research and scholarship qualifies him as an unbiased chronicler of history. In this sense he was more of a political commentator than a historian.

Did Christopher Columbus commit murder?

Then in terms of Zinn's narrative for Columbus, what did he consider the most egregious allegation against Columbus? We think that it was his poorly reasoned claim that Columbus was a murderer? His claim was apparently based on faulty inferences and erroneous *facts.*

To explore that question we start with the dictionary definitions for *murder.* The first and second definitions of the verb *murder,* according to *Webster's Third New International Dictionary* are:

a. To kill (a human being) unlawfully and with premeditated malice or willfully, deliberately, and unlawfully.

b. To slaughter in a brutal manner esp. in war.[303]

Let's look at the four sentences written by Zinn that include the word *murder:*

1. In two years, through murder, mutilation, or suicide, half of the 250,000 Indians on Haiti were dead.

2. The treatment of heroes (Columbus) and their victims (the Arawaks)-the quiet acceptance of conquest and murder in the name of progress-is only one aspect of a certain approach to history, in which the past is told from the point of view of governments, conquerors, diplomats, leaders.

3. He [referring to historian Samuel Eliot Morrison] does not omit the story of mass murder; indeed, he describes it with the harshest word one can use: genocide.

4. To state the facts, however, and then to bury them in a mass of other information [again referring to Morrison] is to say to the reader with a certain infectious calm: yes, mass murder took place, but it's not that important-it should weigh

very little in our final judgments; it should affect very little what we do in the world.[304]

As to sentence 1, the context was that the Spaniards killed a number of Caribbean Indians on Haiti. The Spanish forces commanded by Columbus were acting under the military authority given him to invade, conquer, and sometimes enslave the native populations they would find in the new lands being explored. This suggests that the killings were lawful by definition a). With respect to definition b), murder had been committed, but it was not a crime as only definition a) labels it as such. Killings of type b) were probably the result of military actions taken to control the local Indian population. To be sure, this was not nice, but in terms of the practices of that era they were typical. Zinn neglects to include an additional and very major cause of death: diseases contracted from the European explorers. Many experts consider that sort of disease transmission as the leading cause of the deaths of Indians on Haiti.[305] They estimate that up to 90% of the inhabitants of Haiti perished from communicable diseases between 1492 and 1517.

Sentence 2 implies murder of the type in definition b), but not of definition a). As such these murders were lawful albeit unfortunate. Here, Zinn confesses to being one-sided and does not look at the perspective of Columbus and others under his command.

The sentences 3 and 4 referred to comments Zinn made about the writings of historian Samuel Eliot Morrison published decades earlier in the 1950s. According to those comments, Morrison did not use the word *murder*. Rather he had written about the genocide brought forth by the Spanish forces.[306] The Webster definition for genocide includes the word killing, but not the word murder. And it does not include the word disease or death by natural causes. Most of the deaths among the natives were from such natural causes. If the Spanish forces under Columbus had any responsibility for that it would be characterized as involuntary negligence with respect to disease transmission about which Columbus and the Spanish had little knowledge. Surely there were some killings involved and they were arguably authorized by the Spanish Crown. Under Spanish law there was no murder here, nor was there any genocide.

A good historian strives to avoid misusing words. As we noted above, Zinn admitted his biases. But he didn't apologize for his uneven approach as he developed his historical narratives. Nor did he strive to overcome his biases. Rather he proudly embraced them to produce his distorted historical writings. Thus, we think his misuse of the word *murder* was likely intentional. It was part of his effort paint Columbus in the worst possible light. Such deliberate distortions of the historical record must be a form of historian malpractice. But since all of the maligned persons have long since departed this earth there was no one left to bring a lawsuit for malpractice. Bear in mind that Howard Zinn died in 2010. So, he's no longer available to be the defendant.

Was Christopher Columbus incarcerated for any misdeeds?

A number of Columbus's Spanish subjects in Haiti had sent messages to the Spanish Court of Queen Isabella, and King Ferdinand complaining that Italian Columbus was overly tyrannical in his rule as Governor of Hispaniola. They stimulated heightened concern in the monarchy during his third voyage (1498—1500). In response the monarchs ordered Columbus and his brothers to be arrested and returned to Spain. So, they were arrested, put into chains, and returned to Spain in 1500. Once back in Spain, another six weeks of incarceration ensued before they were released. The Columbus brothers subsequently made appeals to the Spanish monarchs and apparently convinced the royal couple that most of their actions had been justifiable. They not only succeeded with these appeals, but the royal Court also agreed to fund their fourth voyage to Hispaniola except with one proviso: Columbus would not continue as the island's governor.

This treatment by the Spanish royal Court can be interpreted to suggest that they did not see Columbus as a criminal. From that we infer that they did not think him a murderer either.

Columbus was also a reputably devout Roman Catholic. The fact that the Church did not complain about his activities or punish him in any way also suggests that in their eyes he was innocent of murder.

Yet, in the United States we have historians and teachers of history who seek to undermine any balanced account of Columbus and his voyages of exploration. They seem to revel in calling him a murderer. Unfortunately, many of these people teach in private and public K-12 education.

Did Christopher Columbus really discover the New World? No, Amerigo Vespucci did.

Columbus believed the equatorial circumference of the earth was about 14,000 miles and that the equatorial extent of Africa and Asia was about 10,000 miles. He believed he could sail west from Spain and reach Japan or islands nearby Japan. Despite much contrary evidence, even after his four voyages of exploration, he never reported the discovery of a new continent. New islands, yes, but a new hemisphere, no.[307]

The first explorer to realize that the lands across the Atlantic Ocean from the Iberian Peninsula were not in Asia was not an explorer nor a leader of an expedition. Rather he was a crew member who had been recruited to draw maps of any land masses encountered. The map maker was Amerigo Vespucci. He believed, based on his observations, that some of the lands he visited were on a new continent. In a letter he circulated around Europe circa 1503, after his third visit to the lands across the Atlantic, he gave the name Mundus Novus, the New World, to these lands. Unlike Columbus, Vespucci was not mariner. In fact, he had been working in the infant industry of banking. He had been the manager of a Medici family branch bank in Seville, Spain.[308] On one of those voyages, probably in 1501–1502 he was under the command of Portuguese explorer Gonçalo Coelho. During that trip, along the East Coast of present day Brazil, these explorers discovered the Amazon River and also established an outpost they named Rio de Janeiro.[309]

On that trip and others, he made maps of some of the lands visited. After two or more voyages to the New World he sought a publisher to print those maps. He hired a German map publisher, Martin Waldseemüller, to have his drawings published in a book. Waldseemüller suggested that what is now the southern half of the western hemisphere be named after the Latin version of Amerigo Vespucci's first name. Americus is the masculine proper noun for that. But following the tradition that geographic regions take the female Latin form, the publisher proposed *America*. Vespucci gladly agreed and that is why the New World took on the name America.[310] It is likely that Vespucci never visited the lands farther north that we now call North America. Thus, the America of Vespucci and Waldseemüller was what we now call South America.

The reader may challenge our inclusion of this digression about Amerigo Vespucci. Is it all that relevant to the chapter's topic of schools flunking U.S. history? We think it illustrates another error of historians in evaluating American history: They neglect the real story of the discovery of the American continent by Vespucci that is arguably more important than the real story of Christopher Columbus being *lost in the Indies*? Or was he lost somewhere in the western reaches and islands of the Atlantic Ocean?

History teacher misconduct: Censoring exculpatory references for student term papers

According to an account passed on to us by a confidential source at a private middle school, students were assigned to write a term paper on the subject of Christopher Columbus. The instructor had introduced the students to Columbus by telling them, among other characteristics, that Columbus was a murderer of many native Americans. For the term papers, the teacher required students to use specified reference documents and no other sources or references were permitted. In this case, only four designated documents were permitted as source materials. None of these documents had information contrary to the accusation of murder. In our view, this forced students to support these unfounded claims. The students were forced to lie.

As a retired scientist who has published dozens of research papers and who has been aware of other types of academic misconduct, it was difficult for me to give this reprehensible conduct a name. Was it

- Related to plagiarism wherein the student uses the writings of others without citation or permission? No, this was essentially the inverse of plagiarism in that the student was required to use the writings of others without the student's consent.

- A form of censorship in which the writings of unapproved authors were forbidden sources of information? Yes, it surely was that.

- An attempt to teach the students demonstrably wrong or controversial views about Columbus? It sure sounds like it. Their teacher would appear to be more a propagandist than an instructor of history?

We give this misconduct a name: *Exculpatory censorship.* Is not forcing children to use references that may be mistaken a form of bearing false witness? (You can look it up. It is ninth of the *Ten Commandments*). These children have been forced to use information that may be false or at least significantly biased.

History textbooks using presentism to malign Thomas Jefferson

We wonder how many authors of textbooks have considered the multiple talents of Thomas Jefferson and not come away impressed by his accomplishments. As a writer, scientist, architect, statesman, commander, and President of the United States it is not clear which among those roles was his strongest suit?

United States President John F. Kennedy, who also authored two books on history,[311] paid Jefferson this compliment at a White House dinner for Nobel Prize winners held in 1962. He remarked,

> I think this is the most extraordinary collection of talent, of human knowledge, that has ever been gathered together at the White House, with the possible exception of when Thomas Jefferson dined alone.[312]

At the other extreme are historians who have fallen into the trap of *presentism* and based on that practice routinely castigate Thomas Jefferson for his ownership of slaves—a practice that was quite legal and ethical in his own time.

Unlike so many other historical figures in American history, Jefferson's impact on our society is easily accessible to citizens and students alike. In the author's life and travels he has

- Been to Independence Hall in Philadelphia where the *Declaration of Independence* was debated, signed, and issued.

- Gone to the National Archives and viewed an original copy of the *Declaration.*

- Visited the buildings, still standing, designed by Jefferson the architect, including his home at Monticello, the Virginia Statehouse, and those of the Academical Village at the University of Virginia.

- Seen some of the inventions credited to him—though he never sought patents for them.

- Read the inscriptions authored by him at the Jefferson Memorial, including one where he questions the morality of slavery.

- Heard the *Marines' Hymn* with its allusion to the "shores of Tripoli," which refers to President Jefferson's dispatch of warships to defeat the Barbary pirates of North Africa.

While acknowledging that Thomas Jefferson made mistakes and had faults, it is difficult to disparage this man who did so much to help establish the United States of America. If you want to judge him by the company he kept, remember his friendships with George Washington, John Adams, James Madison, James Monroe, and the Marquis de Lafayette—the latter having been the French general who greatly assisted the American Revolution after 1776. Of those friends, only Lafayette was not at some point in his life the President of the United States.

Let's now compare him to the current President of the United States, Donald Trump, who is also famous for his self-congratulatory book, *The Art of the Deal*.[313] President Thomas Jefferson made a deal incomparable to anything Mr. Trump has ever done so far: Jefferson's administration purchased the Louisiana Territory for a mere $15 million dollars.[314] In that one stroke, the territorial area of the United States doubled with the addition of some 800,000 square miles. This is not to say that Donald Trump didn't make great deals. But it suggests that Thomas Jefferson was surely no rookie in this department!

History textbooks using dead-wrong facts to malign Thomas Jefferson

Then there are historians who are not very good at historical research and then write, for example, that Thomas Jefferson was the

... most overrated person in American history.[315]

So, said politically correct author and historian Pauline Maier. Rather than following other revisionist historians who were making Jefferson a moral outcast—say for his ownership of slaves (during a time when slavery was quite legal)—she accuses him of engaging in a form of plagiarism. She claims that the *Declaration of Independence* authored by Jefferson was not the original such declaration and that his role as author was minimal. She based that on the assertion that others edited the document so extensively that his contribution no longer merited him being cited as the primary author.[316]

So, was the final version of the *Declaration* really that much different in the way Maier asserted? You can check this yourself. Compare the actual first draft text from Jefferson to the text that was retained in the final draft. You can do this on the website of Alex Peak,[317] where the analysis of Princeton historian Julian Boyd is reproduced. In it, the original Jefferson text is shown together with the additions and deletions that formed the final and official document. Focusing on the key first two paragraphs, which are the most quoted and revered, you can see that Jefferson's words remain largely intact and his message remains almost identical to the first draft. Why would the historian Maier claim the contrary when her contention is so demonstrably false? As to her remark about him being "overrated," that could have been applied to her skills as a historian. It seems that her hatred of Jefferson had no basis in fact.

WHAT HISTORY SHOULD BE LEARNED?

Let us consider what is the task of a historian in writing a book on U.S. history? In this case we are focusing on textbooks used in American high schools. The content of a history textbook should include those facts, events, and narratives that best help students understand the political, social, cultural, and economic development of the institutions of the United States.

We can think of three different *casts of characters* that U.S. history could follow and explain:

1. Begin with the distant ancestors of twenty-first century Americans, who lived in many disparate parts of the world and who have made contributions to the pre-history and history of people of the United States. Follow them and their important descendants to explain U.S. history. We think that this could run about 10,000 pages.

2. An expanded version of the preceding plan would add sufficient numbers of minor historic personages to conform to quotas based on multicultural based affirmative action percentages for each demographic involved. When sufficient numbers of historic individuals can't be found in the historic record, create fictional ones. We think such an effort would result in a book many times larger than for the first plan. Perhaps about 40,000 pages

3. Begin with the explorers of the New World, move on to the early British colonists, and then include other individuals who made significant contributions as political, industrial, economic, artistic, and religious leaders in the development of the United States. Of those threads, the structure and history of our government should have priority over the other facets of our history. We believe, based on existing, though older, U.S. history textbooks, that this could be done in approximately 1,000 pages.

These kinds of choices would confront every historian who'd consider authoring a high school textbook on U.S. history. Other constraints include practical considerations imposed by the schools such as the course duration, probably one year, and the textbook length, probably 1000 pages or less. The first and second of the three choices posed here would be too ambitious to consider so we think that most competent authors would choose something like the third choice. Whether a person or a group of people are included and to what extent they are discussed would be determined by the historian according to their relative impacts on the various stages of this nation's development. That's how a professional historian would approach the task of authoring a history book.

Many of us who lived through the troubled times of the Vietnam War appreciate the fact that those times led to much soul searching in academia (to such an extent that even some atheists were praying for guidance). On the subject of how those upheavals of the 1970s affected history curricula in the schools, textbook critic Frances Fitzgerald observed that it led to

> . . . the most dramatic rewriting of history ever to take place in American schoolbooks.[318]

Before the 1970s, history textbooks were a mixture of actual historical accounts mixed in with heavy doses of patriotic legends. Such legends varied according to the political and ideological leanings of the books' authors. The pre-1970s books were very patriotic and slanted towards positive events with less or little mention of mistakes made by American leaders.

From the 1970s onward some books were credible as actual history books as judged by scholars of history. Others, however, began to take various ideological approaches in which the facts presented were slanted towards the ideologies of their authors or of the current popular attitudes of those who were *politically correct*. Most history textbooks slanted their presentation to the political left. There was another unwelcome trend: These books were written more by the publishers than by historians or as Ravitch put it, in her discussion of Fitzgerald's findings,

> This censorship occurred not in local communities, but at the source, in the publishing offices where the books were written and edited.[319]

Even when the authors of history books strive to be objective and fair it is almost impossible to give informed and balanced accounts of the events and people. On this concern Ravitch commented,

> Unfortunately, the very format of the history textbook compels distortion; it presumes that a single book can render objective and decisive judgment on hundreds or thousands of controversial issues. In fact, the only sure truth in the books are dates and names (and sometimes the textbooks get those wrong). Beyond that, there is seldom, if ever, a single interpretation of events on which all reputable historians agree.[320]

The history textbooks often give the impression of refined scholarship and historian consensus when, in fact, many of the issues are in dispute among reputable historians.

The authors and editors of these books are forced to compress thousands of pages of reasonably detailed narratives into a single volume of less than a thousand pages. To do that, some topics are simply eliminated, and others are reduced to a few summaries that may miss some of the important lessons of the events described. Or as Ravitch bemoaned,

> When history is compacted as severely as space requires, with the life squeezed out of it, the predigested pap that is left is not memorable, does not establish a foundation for future learning and is guaranteed not to inspire in young people a sense of excitement about the past.[321]

As one might hope, one part of U.S. history instruction should describe how the federal, state, and local governments enacted and carried out laws to help various American institutions address problems and make improvements in various areas of national concern. But that's no longer the practice followed in the authoring of U.S. history textbooks for American public schools. Nor is it the common practice for texts used in private schools. Instead as the twentieth century was ending, Ravitch summarized the situation with this comment:

> The history books of the late 1990s resonate with the themes that dominated academic and political discourse in the last fifteen or twenty years of the twentieth century: race, gender, ethnicity, and in some, class conflict.[322]

Those themes were often presented as a multicultural framework in which various subcultures or demographics preserved their distinct identities and sometimes did not have harmonious relationships among them.

Without some discussion of multiculturalism, we will not be able to substantially appreciate its frequent harmful impacts. Per se there is nothing bad about understanding or even honoring various cultures and traditions. But paying too much attention to them can be harmful if multiculturalism is being proposed or used as a substitute for American culture. We cover its nature and impacts next.

THE PASSAGE TO MULTICULTURAL PERDITION

What is multiculturalism anyway? We looked in a dictionary, published in 1960, but the word didn't exist—at least not in the Webster's volume we own. So, we consulted the online Oxford Dictionary to find,

> Multiculturalism: The presence of, or support for the presence of, several distinct cultural or ethnic groups within a society.[323]

Before multiculturalism took hold in the United States, the American culture slowly evolved through assimilation of disparate cultures—typically those brought in by recent immigrants. In doing this, American traditions were largely preserved though some incremental changes did occur over time.

Disassembly of American culture produces multicultural schism

The traditional American melting pot, in which American culture was slowly changing, was not adapting as rapidly as some advocates of *diversity* would like. They would rather have this slowly changing society be replaced by an American multicultural salad of disparate foreign cultures in which each would continue to maintain its separate practices. Some would even allow them to keep their foreign allegiances? What kind of multiculturalism would be acceptable to most patriotic Americans? And what kinds not acceptable?

A few possibilities or types come to mind:

1. Immigrant groups that don't want to be assimilated, but would prefer to keep their *old country* customs, languages, and allegiances. However, people with such attitudes are unlikely to be very patriotic.

2. Political factions of American citizens that could apply the strategy known as identity politics in which a divide and rule tactic is used to gain politically. Depending on the details these folks could be patriotic.

3. One can imagine a hybrid approach that has American culture dominating, but the other cultures are given some room to keep their customs etc. This is borderline multicultural because it is dominated by the American culture and traditions. Many people advocating this would be patriotic.

Let's consider these three types as to their levels of patriotism:

Assimilation resistant. Mexican immigrants provide a good example of the first type. Many of them hold dual citizenship. That enables them to vote in both countries.[324] There had been a legal prohibition of dual citizens within the United States until 1967 when the Supreme Court overturned the law.[325] For an American citizen to have dual loyalties by remaining a citizen of the *old country* invites mischief and certainly the annoyance of single loyalty citizens. When the U.S. government tolerates this practice, it is not only a step towards divided loyalties, but it also introduces other risks—such as subversion and treason. Is this the kind of multicultural practice we want to honor?

Favoring and exploiting a multicultural salad. The left-wing of the Democrat party provides an example of the second type. They partition their constituents according to their various characteristics. Among these characteristics are race, religion, nationality, sexual orientation, sex, and immigration status. This is typically done in such a way as to isolate white males into a non-majority faction of the citizenry. It is actually the non-Democrat white males who are isolated for it is the Democrat white males who are among those who have largely invented this strategy of divide and rule. Is this not a patently racist or racialist phenomenon? Or is it a more elaborate dynamic involving different identity groups in which unfair stereotypes are used to discriminate against people?

Choosing the melting pot. The Republican party provides an example of the third type. It also partitions its constituents according to some, but not all of the just listed characteristics. The party, itself, has outreach programs to several of these groups. Women, blacks, Hispanics, Asians, college students are among those targeted.

In all of these strategies that rely on distinct demographic groups, people often forget that there are individuals who are *demographic hybrids*. Many folks are mixed race. Some are bisexual. Some have no political party or are ones who participate in more than one. The question for us to explore is how do these perspectives impact the contents of U.S. history textbooks used in American high schools?

Constraints of multiculturalism on history textbooks

The definition we gave for multiculturalism has a *so what* aspect in the sense that almost all modern societies are composed of various sub-groups. How is it applied in the American context? To answer this question, one must understand the political concept of *identity politics*. The subgroups one encounters in seeking that understanding include those based on some of the following characteristics:

1. Race or ethnicity
2. Religion or philosophy
3. Nationality
4. Political party
5. Sexual orientation
6. Sex (we avoid the incoherent concept of gender because of its oxymoronic uses)
7. Profession
8. Economic status
9. Immigration status
10. Criminal record

One school of thought, concerning multiculturalism, holds that for each of these categories, its subgroup can be ranked or judged relative to the other subgroups. Are the different subgroups regarded on an equal footing or is there a ranking? For each of the listed characteristics above, this suggests in terms of historical narratives the following GOOD and BAD applications of them in historical narratives:

1. *Race or ethnicity*

   GOOD: Every racial subgroup and every mixed racial subgroup are equally deserving as any other such group. Historical accounts should avoid characterizing people by race unless it is an essential component of the story.

   BAD: Or some subgroups are given priority over other ones depending on their race and not on relevant characteristics. Historical accounts of recent decades may seek to defend unwise policies such as affirmative action. So, for example, Harvard University currently has a system of bias in its admissions that unfairly limits the numbers of qualified white and Asian students enrolled, while increasing the numbers of black and Hispanic students. Perhaps the worst examples of multiculturalism in American history were the two cultures that coexisted before the Civil War: In the South there was a society based on slavery and in the North a society that recognized African blacks as freemen even if they didn't accord them the equal rights later accorded them in the late twentieth and early twenty-first centuries.[326]

2. *Religion or philosophy*

   GOOD: Christians, Secularists, Jews, Muslims, and other non-violent and patriotic sects should receive balanced treatment by historians, depending on their historic roles. In this, the overwhelming numerical advantage of Christians together with their historical roles in the founding of the American states and nation have given them an obvious advantage. For example, the holidays of Christmas and Thanksgiving are of Christian origin. But both have been heavily secularized and as such pose less offense for Jews, Muslims, and other minor sects. Christmas is so degraded in our popular culture from its religious origins that it is rarely seen as a problem for non-Christians. Its importance has been so diminished that it is frequently called by other names—such as a *Holiday.*

> This word, *"holiday,"* exposes an irony for the politically correct. Many of those using this seemingly non-sectarian label have forgotten that the word *holiday* is historically a re-spelling of the words *Holy Day.* If their goal has been to take God out of Christmas, they have failed.

BAD: Equal treatment of religions by historians is not necessarily fair treatment. How are they to describe religious wars? Some sects advocate and privately engage in tactics designed to harm other religions and denominations. The Salem witch trials said something about the puritan Congregationalists involvement in public life. Islamic militants sometimes interpret their sacred texts to justify antisocial tactics, including terrorism. Polling indicates that approximately 22% of American Muslims are not patriotic because they do not believe in the United States Constitution and actually favor violence to impose the Sharia Law that their Islamic scriptures demand.[327] Depending on the details they therefore favor revolution against the United States government through subversion, treason or both. That is not good.

3. *Nationality*

GOOD: Traditionally, Americans have welcomed legal immigrants from other nations and prefer them to assimilate into the American traditions and culture. In this they have discouraged the establishment of new cultural subgroups based on nationality, if that will lead to what was once called un-American activities. History books once described this melting pot as a social good.

BAD: In our current politically correct situation many history books give their kudos to various forms of multiculturalism. They approvingly describe those policies in which immigrants are still welcomed, but their cultures need not assimilate into the American culture. Instead their cultures are celebrated as equally good as the traditional American culture—or sometimes even better. There are exceptions to the national cultures that are welcomed: Immigrants from the British Isles and to a somewhat lesser extent those from Europe are sometimes subject to derision, ridicule, and the damnation of faint praise.

4. *Political party*

GOOD: In theory and mostly in practice, political parties such as the Republican, Democrat, Communist, Conservative or Socialist, receive equal treatment by U.S. government units: federal, state, and local. Election bureaus operated within the states have, with some exceptions, a reputation of fairness in dealing with the various political parties. We applaud those historians, albeit a minority of them, who describe these political parties in a balanced way.

BAD: Most historical accounts of American politics are biased to the political left. Their favorite flavor is liberal Democrat. They approvingly describe the way that public school systems have often given praise and advantage to policies of the left as compared to others. In most cases, their instruction in history and civics favors the opinions of Democrats or even Socialists and is critical of the Republicans and Conservatives. The author remembers that this kind of bias was already evident in the Chicago Public Schools he attended long ago in the 1950s.

5. *Sexual orientation*

GOOD: To the extent that historical accounts need to describe sexuality, historians should know and portray the scientific facts that the biological imperative of reproduction favors heterosexuals over homosexuals. The desire for sexual pleasure, in terms of the mechanics of sexual contact, also favors heterosexuals. The traditional view of homosexuality was that of it being an abnormal behavior, and in fact was a topic in the courses taught in abnormal psychology. The word abnormal, in its scientific usage, does not make a value judgement. It is a statistical term that means that an entity does not display characteristics associated with the population's average. It simply means that a relatively small percentage of the population has the trait that is labelled abnormal. For example, having an IQ above, let's say 140, is abnormal. Golfers who get a hole-in-one are also abnormal. Yet, in some cases psychologists have used the word to criticize a characteristic. In terms of a statistical analysis it is abnormal. Compassionate treatment and description of abnormal sexual behaviors by historians is recommended when and where these activities are victimless.

BAD: Historians are probably unwise to put too much emphasis on issues involving sexual matters. Sexual orientation, as a phrase, is suggestive that the choice of so-called sexual habits is supposedly among a spectrum of equally healthy life styles. We believe they are not equally healthy. The postmodernistic philosophy that believes that there is no objective reality also believes that each person constructs his or her own reality. The concept of trans-gender individuals is a species of such social construction. There is no medical or biological support for anyone having a transgender status except in rare circumstances where fouled up genetics dictate the development of unusual combinations of sex organs within the developing human body.

6. *Sex*

GOOD: Men and women are different and as a result do not have equal interests in the activities they pursue. A policy of non-discrimination does not require equal percentages of women and men in any given pursuit. Discrimination based on sex is wrong. But basing policies on concepts of *disparate impacts* is also wrong. Historical accounts should describe men and women, not in equal numbers, but in numbers weighted to their roles and interests in the events described.

BAD: *Disparate impacts* are wrongfully interpreted by some historians to suggest unfair discrimination against one sex or the other. Thus, despite an imagined numerical imbalance of ballet dancer types, it is still understandable that young men don't aspire to be a ballerina in a tutu!

7. Profession

GOOD: In various vocations and professions, government institutions should hire the most qualified individuals to perform the various roles needed to reach institutional goals. In the case of K-12 education this means hiring teachers who have majored in the subjects to be taught. This would end the use of teaching credentials as certification documents. History textbooks should reflect these kinds of approaches.

BAD: Using laws and regulations to favor the employment of relatively incompetent workers is a corrupt practice that should be ended. For example, in the profession of teaching in K-12 education there is the issue of the qualifications of teachers. Through the efforts of educationists, teachers with a *proper education* are rejected for employment in public schools in favor of marginally educated college graduates who instead have a certification called a teaching credential. This author was once a teacher with a *proper education*. I was unable to work in public schools, but did work in a private school. This is a strange type of identity politics in which the less capable group is elevated above the superior one.

8. Economic status

GOOD: The greatest good for the greatest number is almost always a desirable outcome in programs run by the government. Government subsidies to family income and government funding of education need to compare different alternatives to find those producing that greatest good. In the case of government welfare programs, the manner in which subsidies are scaled down as a recipient becomes employed should be set to provide work incentives at every point of the payment levels involved. Government funding of education should consider vouchers or education savings accounts (ESAs) as the superior alternatives to the government playing the dual roles of funder and operator of schools. History curricula should teach about these concepts.

BAD: Political expediency, such as maximizing the numbers of unionized government employees, often works against the greatest good. Sometimes government incompetence is an unhelpful factor in poorly run programs. Welfare programs that penalize employment overly much have the unwanted effect of discouraging work. When the government operates public schools, it removes the dynamic of a competitive marketplace in which schools would thrive. Ignoring economics is not good policy either for the government or for schools.

9. *Immigration status*

GOOD: When the question is about criminals breaking laws of the United States and its many jurisdictions, we believe in enforcing the laws we have and at the same time debating what changes to them would improve the security and safety of American society. An example of the right attitude came from a political debate.

In 1992, the former TV star and U.S. Senate candidate, Sonny Bono, was participating in a debate among four primary election candidates. The candidates were asked to discuss their positions on illegal immigration. Bono didn't use the four minutes allocated to him for a response, but took less than ten seconds to say,

What would I do about illegal immigration? I would enforce the law.

This author was active in California Republican Party politics in 1992 and attended this debate at the Party's semi-annual convention. Bono lost the primary election, but two years later was elected to the U.S. Congress. The quote is a paraphrase of Bono's response.

His response not only *brought down the house* in that Burlingame, California hotel ballroom, but also was surely the only thing most attendees would remember later. And he was right. For our society to function well it must enforce its laws first, before considering changes to them. As to improving our immigration laws, the economic health of the nation should be a primary goal while at the same time recognizing some degree of family unification. History textbooks and curricula should reflect these attitudes.

BAD: The federal, state, and local governments routinely ignore and do not enforce immigration laws. For example, in San Francisco illegal aliens and well as legal resident aliens are now permitted to vote in school board elections.[328] This is more than just an issue of identity politics because it is part of a migration dynamic in which failure to control illegal aliens could encourage large migrations and even invasions of foreign nationals into the United States. A bad practice among many historians is to use the deceptive label of *undocumented* to make actual invading criminals appear to be *fine* people who suffer from the minor inconvenience of not being listed in government rosters. In reality, they have committed the felony of *breaking and entering* the territory of the United States. Why don't our federal laws see it that way and enforce it with jail time?

10. *Criminal record*

GOOD: Balancing the rights of society with the best interests of ex-convicts is not anything to be addressed by a *disparate impact* analysis when there are sometimes risks that are too high for that approach. In the private sector there should be no government imposition of quotas or other mandates to hire former felons. Even in government employment, local managers who hire new workers should have the discretion about the hiring of ex-convicts. A good historical account will explain the statistical and scientific errors in such an approach.

BAD: Some, who follow the strictures of political correctness, will assume that the law-abiding and felons are equal or perhaps should be equal in their treatment and employment post incarceration. Why should ex-convicts be denied full citizenship rights, such as the right to vote? Why shouldn't a *disparate impact* analysis be applied to ex-convicts seeking employment in banks to ensure that bank employees have representative numbers of ex-convicts? What about the idea that sex offenders and pedophiles not suffer discrimination when they apply to work in a school or other organization where children are present? Common sense suggests that such advocacy will lead to troubles of various kinds. Historians should explain the flaws of policies based on disparate impacts where needed.

Proper uses of non-cultural characteristics

As these examples seem to suggest it is not always obvious what is the best government policy in dealing with identity groups. Forced equality ignores individual choice while a hands-off policy affects the access that disadvantaged people have to receive benefits from the government. A popular and useful compromise on this uses non-cultural characteristics, such as income and education levels, to determine if assistance should be offered to disadvantaged citizens. That approach was followed by the proponents of the *California Civil Rights Initiative* of 1996—also known as *Ballot Initiative Proposition 209.*[329]

The campaign was led by well-known California individuals, including former University of California Regent, Ward Connerly. Popular talk radio host, Larry Elder, was a major supporter. Connerly also founded the American Civil Rights Institute in 1997 to be an advocate against using race and other immutable characteristics in Affirmative Action programs. This author also worked in the campaign. It became law in November of that year when California voters approved it in the General Election.

Among other provisions, it outlawed the use of race and other irrelevant characteristics in college admissions. It has been particularly helpful to ethnic Asian students who are subject to very high discriminatory hurdles in other states. Harvard: Are you listening? And let's review whether authors of history textbooks are chronicling these reforms of so-called affirmative action laws in a balanced way. Are they reporting them in such a way that they support legitimate civil rights and not phony ones based on racial and other unfair quotas?

Are advocates of multiculturalism using it to advance left-wing political goals?

We found an interesting and disturbing quote from two left-leaning scholars specializing (supposedly) in multicultural education. When asked to defend their advocacy of multicultural education in the teaching of *social studies*, Carlos Ovando and Peter McLaren wrote this,

> As long as we continue to operate within the existing capitalist social relations of the larger society, there is good reason to believe that racism and social injustice will continue to pose a serious threat to democracy and that the dream of social equality will remain largely unrealized. So, while work continues toward school transformation, the emerging conceptualizations of multicultural education stress that this work must be understood relative to the social and political structures that currently control education in the United States, and that the two are intrinsically linked. Multicultural education, in its determination to address the ills and shortcomings of the current education system, can be a starting point to eliminating inequities in society.[330]

Our immediate response to this was that these scholars should have delayed their responses until they were more certain about their assertions. Former New York Yankees baseball star and quote maker Yogi Berra had the correct response for questions like this,

> If you ask me anything I don't know, I'm not going to answer.[331]

More seriously, their answer led us to ask if advocates of multiculturalism have a political agenda or are they simply wanting the diverse spectrum of cultural characteristics of various demographics celebrated and enjoyed?

So, we decided to ask the Bing search engine with this exact search string:

> "Is +multiculturalism anti +capitalistic"

Of the first nine matches from the search engine only one had no relevance to this question. Of the remaining eight, every one of them saw multiculturalism as opposed to capitalism. This suggests that the answer to this sub-section's title question (*Are advocates of multiculturalism using it to advance left-wing political goals?*) is an emphatic "yes." Many of the advocates of multiculturalism are also antagonistic towards the so-called *white race*. Some of them seem bent on anti-white racism or racialism, but want to cloak their animosity in euphemisms that support a range of cultures (but not so-called white European culture). In their imagination there seems to be no American culture and they very much tend to dislike (oppose) capitalism. As an opponent of leftish multiculturalism, and a supporter of American culture, writer Julius Roy-Davis opined this:

> Actually, I would go so far as to say, as I have before, that the Left is the anti-White party, particularly the anti-White male party.[332]

We can hazard a conclusion from this: Multiculturalism is not what its component syllables suggest. It is not simply a *salad* of cultures. Rather, it is a *salad* of politically correct demographics that excludes the so-called white male race. And, to a somewhat lesser extent, educated Asians also are similarly maligned. We used the adjective *so-called* to suggest that there really is no such genetic category as the *white race*. Skin color is but one genetic trait that might indicate a racial group, but as this author knows from analysis of his own DNA, many of us white skinned folks are of mixed genetic backgrounds. It is really difficult to divide humans into a handful of racial identities when we, in fact, are most often genetic blends of many different inherited traits. As mentioned earlier, I have 3% DNA from India.

Since so many of our K-12 educators, whether in public or private schools, are taking the multicultural political line and putting it into school policy, they really are *subverting* the supposedly non-partisan landscape of American education.

The Marxist influences that led to multicultural identity politics

As should be fairly evident, many of the reforms based on multiculturalism, presentism, and identity politics are based on political philosophies of the left. Let's now look at some of the details to help understand how some of these political disputes arose and continued.

According to David Eaton,

> Current iterations of multiculturalism and identity politics can be traced to Marxism and the Cold War, particularly the Marxist ideological tenets of the Institute for Social Research at Goethe University in Frankfurt, Germany, known as the Frankfurt School.[333]

When it was clear after the end of the *Cold War* that socialism was not gaining adherents in the Western world, and certainly not in the United States, philosophers and political activists on the left looked for new constituencies in which they might advance their ideas for political and societal reform. In the same reference Eaton continued,

The Marxist-Hegelian nostrum of progress-through-conflict needed *new* victims with *old* resentments to foster the revolutionary impulses that would theoretically bring about the Marxist utopia. Resentments based on racial, gender, ethnic or sexual preference slights were seen as the new markers though which progressive Marxism could be advanced. The *old* Marxist meme of *haves and have nots* was replaced with the *new* neo-Marxist narrative of *oppressor and oppressed.*

David Eaton is not only a historian of political philosophy, but he has also been the Music Director of the New York City Symphony since 1985. He has composed over 55 musical works, and has been the arranger of hundreds of other scores. In his affiliation with the Unification Theological Seminary in 2016 he was awarded an honorary doctorate for his philosophical research, and writings.

Attentive readers may notice that our description of historian Howard Zinn also included his focus on the views of the *oppressed.* According to the Wikipedia article on Zinn he didn't label himself a Marxist, but rather as a Democratic Socialist. Still he expressed ideas consistent with some of the new variants of Marxism.[334]

Enforcing quotas based on the doctrine of disparate impact

In some cases, guidelines or even enforceable laws have been proposed or enacted that places quotas on the numbers of people *wanted* in these subgroups. Whether these kinds of laws are enforceable has been challenged in the courts. When the numerical distribution of employees in a given profession do not match the percentages of the employees' races or ethnicities within the general population that constitutes a *disparate impact.* In his remarks during a Supreme Court hearing on a disparate impact case involving public housing residents, the late Justice Antonin Scalia scolded the court by saying,

> Racial disparity is not racial discrimination. The fact that the NFL [National Football League] is largely black is not discrimination. Discrimination requires intentionally excluding people of a certain race.[335]

In the mid 1990s, comedian Jackie Mason had a one man show on Broadway called *Politically Incorrect.* About that time, some civil rights activists wanted to ensure affirmative action quotas were being met by providing very strong incentives to increase the numbers of any demographic coming up short in the *disparate impact* analysis. This consideration apparently motivated Mason to say this about rumored efforts to increase the numbers of Jewish welders in New York after a *disparate impact* study showed an alarming lack of them. In his telling, some pressure was put on him to become an apprentice for such work. In response to this, Mason told us that he said,

But I don't vant to be a Jewish velder.

Mason went on to discuss a shortage of short statured Jews in the NBA, the National Basketball Association, and how he didn't want to be recruited for that either.

> This author was in the audience at one of these shows. This quote is based on my recollection. To me it is amazing that Jackie Mason was once a Rabbi who early in that career decided to abandon that calling to become a stage comic!

Without more digressions, how do history books deal with these different subgroups? The answer:

> They tend to follow demography based quotas and otherwise display careless inattention to facts.

Then in an effort to be *fair* some authors and curriculum experts try to give equal coverage to groups they believe deserve equal treatment. The result of doing so can be demonstrably unfair or even hilarious.

Let's take each of the previous species, and consider what historians have done or might be tempted to do in their historical narratives if they wanted to treat the various subgroups fairly according to their theories of multiculturalism and disparate impact.

1. *Race or ethnicity.* The population distribution numbers from the U.S. census, and published by Statista for 2015, were: 62% white, 18% Hispanic, 12% black, 5% Asian, 2% multi-racial, and about 1% American Indian.[336] The breakdown is different for earlier historic periods. The population distribution numbers shown here are based on self-reporting of interviewees during the taking of the decennial census. Based on racial percentages like these, history textbooks would include numerical quotas for the number of pages/lines devoted to each racial group. This would be fine-tuned to be in proportion to the population distribution numbers pertinent to the different historical periods. But will the really influential people in our history exist in these proportions? Unlikely. A much different and more accurate distribution is based on sampling the DNA of the U.S. population. In doing that, one finds a greatly increased multiracial population. How much DNA must you possess from a 2nd racial group to be deemed multi-racial? Good question. I don't know. I have 3% DNA from India. Does that make me bi-racial? Yes, to a small degree. In the case of American blacks who label themselves African-American, recent DNA testing among them has found that on average they have about 24% European DNA.[337] Such mixtures and blends will greatly complicate efforts in affirmative action.

2. *Religion or philosophy.* Similarly, textbook authors would ensure that the numbers of Christians, Jews, Muslims, and Secular individuals discussed in their writings conform to the proportions in the Census Bureau's reporting: Those percentages,

in 2008, were published as 76% Christian, 1.2% Jewish, 0.6% Muslim, and 22% Secular.[338] Surely, religion and philosophy influence history, but does that happen according to these ratios?

3. *Nationality.* These authors would be encouraged or required to mention foreign nationals including illegal aliens who were in the population. Again, quotas would be enforced or strongly advised. This would indicate that approximately 4% of the current U.S. population would be allocated to legal green card residents, about 4% allocated to the illegal alien residents, and the remaining 92% to American citizens.

4. *Political party.* Given that U.S. history has been guided by politicians, at least in many instances, here it might make sense that the individuals who have been relevant in various historical developments might end up to have been participating in numbers not that different from their proportions of the population. Then the disparate impact issue would be resolved. At least for this demographic.

5. *Sexual orientation.* Textbooks would have approximately 3% to 4% of their covered individuals represented as either homosexual or bisexual if the reported population ratios are to be respected.

6. *Sex.* For every male there will be a female in the lists of individuals covered.

7. *Profession.* In many earlier historic periods, farmers constituted perhaps 90% of the population. Based on that, nearly all individuals covered in the history books for those periods would similarly be farmers.

8. *Economic status.* If 5% of the population is reported to be wealthy, then only 5% of those described in the history book would be wealthy.

9. *Immigration status.* If 4% of the work force is composed of illegal aliens, then efforts would be undertaken to ensure that 4% of those described in the history book are illegally in the United States

10. *Criminal record.* If 10% of the U.S. population are ex-convicts then 10% of those depicted will be former felons.

Most of these ideas are without merit. Reading between the lines we perceive an attempt at distraction: Include every possible topic that is remotely connected to the history of the United States and then exclude or shrink the content that actually addresses the political history of the United States. Do these advocates really believe in multiculturalism or are they using its various digressions to deliberately undermine the public's understanding of the federal, state, and local governments around them? In other words, are they conscious subversives or are they simply incompetent historians? We think that the answer is: Both.

Here is the quandary that these authors will face. They have several options. We already considered three such possibilities in the preceding section, *What History Should be Learned?*, and concluded that a good historian would . . .

> Begin with the explorers of the New World, move on to the early British colonists, and then include other individuals who made significant contributions as political, industrial, economic, artistic, and religious leaders in the development of the United States. Of those threads the structure and history of our government should have priority over the other facets of our history. We believe, based on existing, though older, U.S. history textbooks, that this could be done in approximately 1,000 pages. (Yes, this paragraph is presented twice because it bears repetition.)

This choice is arguably the most professional and at the same time it is cost effective. But few educators in our K-12 systems were paying attention as they become more and more distracted by their politically correct ideas. Thus, as the twentieth century ended and the new century began, educationists were more and more advocates of a form of multiculturalism in which American patriotism would be replaced by multinational loyalties. It is not clear whether these education leaders were aware of the subversive aspects of their proposals? As Ravitch put it

> . . . educational leaders were keen to embrace multiculturalism. As they did, they shunned civic assimilation and Americanization, once considered the primary responsibility of the public schools. Patriotic exercises were discouraged for fear that they were insensitive to newcomers, who were taught to retain their allegiance to their ancestral cultures.

The UCLA politically correct history standards of 1994

In 1992 the U.S. Department of Education funded organizations to produce voluntary national standards in various subjects including history. One such recipient was the National Center for History in the Schools (NCHS), operated by UCLA. NCHS also received an additional grant for that purpose from the National Endowment for the Humanities. Lynne V. Cheney was its Chairman. In 1994 NCHS released its proposed standards for world history and U.S. history. Cheney did not like them. She complained that they were:

- Biased to the political left.

- Were politically correct.

- Promoted multiculturalism.

- Highlighted the nation's shortcomings.

- Neglected the nation's achievements and heroes.[339]

Much controversy ensued in the media and in the public. The standards were politically so far off center that in early 1995 the U.S. Senate passed a *Resolution of Censure* condemning them by an astounding vote of 99–1. The resolution included this key point: With respect to government grants to public education programs involving history instruction it says that,

> . . . the recipient of such funds should have a decent respect for United States history's roots in Western civilization.[340]

In response the NCHS revised the standards by removing many of the politically extreme components. And then, according to Ravitch, the National Assessment Governing Board (NAGB adjusted the content tested by its NAEP history tests to match the revised standards of the NCHS.[341]

In 2002, seven years after the revised standards were published, Ravitch reviewed the U.S. history standards of all 50 states and the District of Columbia. Of those, only 14 states were judged in the top-ranking category of having *strong standards*. In her published review, most of the other states, as Ravitch put it,

> . . . acknowledge the importance of history, but fail to identify any significant individuals in American or world history.[342]

In her review, New Jersey came under scathing criticism for omitting the names of George Washington, Thomas Jefferson, and Abraham Lincoln. That was too embarrassing, even for the politically correct educationists of the Garden State. So, they put these three gentlemen back into their standards. On that note, it seems logical that history courses without the names of historic individuals will not prepare students for NAEP testing that has some of its questions based on these persons and their involvement in the nation's history.[343]

How multiculturalism has affected history teachers and students. It's book learnin only.

Yes, let's talk about book learnin! Ravitch indicates why students must learn from the history textbooks. It is because the teachers are generally ignorant of U.S. history. Here's how she explains it:

> Many teachers are dependent on their textbook because they have not studied history. Today, most teachers of history in grades 7–12 have neither a major nor a minor in history; instead, they have a degree in social studies education, some other branch of pedagogy, a social science, or a completely unrelated field.[344]

How multiculturalism has ballooned the history textbooks and then deflated them

In preparation for her 2003 book, *The Language Police*, Diane Ravitch conducted a review of 16 U.S. history textbooks that were published near or at the turn of the twenty-first century. She found most of these texts to be cluttered with graphics, cartoons, photographs, and various other displays that take up about half of the space on the pages. Except for one middle school textbook, she had this to say about the other 15 volumes:

> Their tone—that of ubiquitous, smug tone of omniscience—seems to have come from the same word processor, the one that writes short declarative sentences and has a ready explanation for every event in history. This tone of certainty is very annoying, particularly because the books seem to share the same political orientation. Textbooks like Democratic presidents; textbooks don't like Republican presidents. Textbooks always know what should have been done in every crisis.[345]

These books engage in rampant *presentism* or as she puts it,

> They constantly moralize about the past, as though everyone in 1850 or 1900 or 1950 should have known what we know today and should have shared our enlightened values.[346]

In the next sub-section, we explore the almost revolutionary effects of multiculturalism on the historical content being taught in our high schools. There we also consider how these changes have harmed the core American culture.

Sometimes the efforts of textbook authors and publishers involve forms of corruption that could lead to law enforcement attention and/or lawsuits. In efforts to be multiculturally compliant, such producers have taken short-cuts and other detours that involve various forms of dishonesty. We'll have more to say on this in a later chapter.

Let's now look closer at the grip of multiculturalism on history instruction in the public high schools of the United States.

How multicultural textbooks promote bigotry against Anglo-American culture

In her review of high school U.S. history textbooks, Ravitch observed that,

> The old U.S. history narrative stressed the important contributions of England and the European Enlightenment to the new American nation. It centered on the rise of democratic institutions and the ongoing struggle to expand the rule of law. Those of us who were not of English descent nonetheless appreciated the unique contribution of England to our forming as a nation.[347]

It is perhaps ironic that the Revolutionary War against England did not erase all of the cultural inheritance from that country. It simply applied democratic principles learned in England (and subsequently abused by the English government) and used them to help design a new nation. What was erased was the monarchy. It was replaced by a republic, as formulated in the *United States Constitution*.

To get the disparate impact ratios correct, the numbers of important Anglo *movers and shakers* had to be severely reduced while unimportant minor participants of other demographics had to be added.

How multiculturalism promotes the falsehood of cultural equivalence

Historian Larry Schweikart has reviewed a number of U.S. history textbooks and found that most of them have a leftward slant and often have blatant factual errors.[348] On this he remarked,

> Facts are uncomfortable things. On the other hand, most of the falsehoods examined here do seem to originate on the left side of the political spectrum and that fact, too, is an uncomfortable thing.

Diane Ravitch had this to say about the degradation of the textbooks used in high school U.S. history classes,

> Poor writing in textbooks is nothing new. What is truly new about American history textbooks of the late 1990s is their ideological slant. Like the world history texts, they too are committed to cultural equivalence.[349]

To say that all cultures are equal is false on its face. If cultures were the same, they would not have different cultural labels. In the case of U.S. history, it has become fashionable to pretend that contemporary American culture derives from the merger of Europeans with pre-Columbian peoples of the Western Hemisphere and with people from the sub-Saharan African kingdoms from which the immigrant slaves of North America were forcibly exiled to North America. It is true that these ethnic/national groups participated in the formation of the American nation, but the typical narratives of contemporary U.S. history books try to force equivalence on the contributions from each such culture or group. On this, Ravitch said,

> The new textbooks have adopted the *three worlds meet* paradigm that the UCLA history center advocated as part of its proposed national standards for U.S. history ... In order to show how *three worlds* met, the texts downplay the relative importance of the European ideas that gave rise to democratic institutions and devote more attention to pre-Columbian civilizations and African kingdoms.[350]

It takes a fiction writer to produce a history textbook that shows the cultural sameness of the peoples who were the ancestors of present day Americans. According to Ravitch some of the assertions, many false, exaggerated or unverified, include:

- Great universities in Africa, including three in Timbuktu, helped develop the intellectual heft that Africans brought to their American descendants. The actual historic record shows the three universities to have been three mosques that housed scholars and provided instruction from the twelfth century forward. Just before the year 1600 these three institutions went into rapid decline and little is said about them by historians thereafter. It is unlikely that students of these universities ever immigrated into the Americas as slaves. They were too well educated to be used as slaves and after 1600 there would have been too few students remaining to have much influence even if they were sold into the Americas as slaves.[351]

- Mansa Musa, who led the African kingdom of Mali, and made a pilgrimage to Mecca back in 1324, helped develop African culture that was brought to North America hundreds of years later and which became an important ingredient in the multicultural mix that combined to form late twentieth century American culture.[352]

- Most textbooks assert that Portuguese forces established the slave trade from Africa in the late 1400s. This fiction ignores the historical record that shows, centuries earlier, Muslim Arabs of North Africa first enslaved black Africans from sub-Sahara regions. In the late fifteenth century, the Portuguese did participate in the slave trade by purchasing slaves from these Arabs. But they didn't establish that trade. Of the black Africans forced into slavery only 5% were brought into the British controlled areas of North America.[353]

- To establish the cultural connections of contemporary Americans to pre-historic American indigenous people some history *writers* have focused on the Anasazi Indians who lived in what is now the U.S. southwest. This tribe or civilization, which left no chronology or historic record, was nevertheless *known* by historian Gary Nash (perhaps by *retrocognitive clairvoyance*?) to have been quite advanced politically, agriculturally, and architecturally. More on this below.

It seems to us that these authors are troubled citizens of the United States. They, who are inclined to replace the chronology of Western influence on the development of the United States with sketchy narratives about cultures of biological ancestors, surely have an agenda that is outside of the professional duties of a historian. It seems that they are alienated from the current status of the United States. It seems that they have a certain level of hatred towards the United States government and culture, unless it is to reinvent itself within a left leaning multicultural format. Many of us are loyal patriotic citizens who want our children educated in American public and private schools to understand our historical development, particularly how our government evolved. History textbook authors, like the ones cited here, seem unable or unwilling to do so.

What incompetent historian Gary Nash wants your children to know about the Anasazi

Of all the examples we just cited, the last one about the Anasazi Indians provides the most egregious account of the historical ancestors of the people of the United States. Let's delve a little deeper into the writings of historian Gary Nash in his U.S. history textbook, *American Odyssey: The United States in the Twentieth Century*, and see what he had to say about the Anasazi Indians.[354]

Nash wrote that these Indians,

> Fostered an egalitarian culture in which people functioned as equals. Without kings, chiefs, or other official authority figures to compel cooperation . . .

He also claimed that members of their jurisdictions

> built dams, reservoirs, and irrigation systems . . .

They also built, according to Nash, 400 miles of

> roads and broad avenues.

Nash claims that the Anasazi built high rise apartment buildings, near the year 1,000, which were not eclipsed by anyone else in the world until the late nineteenth century. Nash put it this way,

> Until a larger apartment went up in New York City in 1882, the size of this Anasazi building of the tenth century remained unsurpassed in the world.

The New York City apartment building was the Navarro Flats building located on Central Park South between 6th and 7th Avenues. It had 13 stories and was about 170 feet at its tallest point.[355] This comparison is nonsensical because multiple dwellings within a single structure have existed since Roman times. More familiar apartment buildings were erected in France during the eighteenth century. These were larger and taller than the Anasazi dwellings of North America.[356] One wonders if Nash was simply incompetent or did he knowingly make such false claims about the Anasazi buildings? Perhaps he knew of their falsity and also thought that no one of importance would challenge his assertions. He was wrong on that: Ravitch challenged him. In fact, she challenged him on a number of his assertions. She noted that,

> It is worth recalling that the Anasazi were a prehistoric people who left no written records. How does the author know that they had no kings, chiefs, or other authority figures? Is it credible that a prehistoric civilization construct-ed roads, dams, and large dwellings with no one in charge? Were Anasazi

structures really taller than any other building in the ancient or medieval world?[357]

The book *World History: Connections to Today* answers those questions in the negative. It includes this statement that

> The Mayan pyramids remained the tallest structures in the Americas until 1903 when the Flatiron Building, a skyscraper, was built in New York City.[358]

We're not finished. Gary Nash wanted his narratives to be sugar coated. He neglected (arguably on purpose) to discuss evidence from credible sources that suggests the Anasazi practiced human sacrifice and cannibalism.[359] Was Nash a quack historian? We shall leave that for others to answer.

William J. Bennetta, an opponent of textbook politicization, whether from the right or left, had these *contrasting* observations about the American Indian and African ancestors of today's American citizens:

> What do you suppose the Europeans were doing while those Indians and Africans were erecting temples, instituting 'complex' societies, controlling fire, taking courses at Timbuktu U., and making sculptures?[360]

He goes on to suggest that these Europeans appear to have been

> . . . a uniformly dull lot bereft of any cultural variations worth mentioning, who did little but to build ships, sail about, and engage in trade. There is not a single photo to depict European art or architecture. There is not word about Dante, Erasmus, Brunelleschi, Bramante or Leonardo; not a word about Donatello, Giotto, Ghiberti or Botticelli; not a word about Raphael, Machiavelli, Gutenberg, Durer, or the van Eycks. All of these, and the cultures they represented, have been erased. All of Europe's universities, too, have been erased.

Ravitch goes on to make a distinction: Is it a history of the territory of the United States or is it a history of the current crop of American people?[361] If it is the latter, the book must say something about the lands from where their ancestors came. Or perhaps it is a history of the nation-state, then the focus needs to be on our English roots supplemented by other European inputs. Either way they need to answer: Who came here? Where did they come from? What know-how did they bring to North America?

Political indoctrination is dressed up. But please call it social justice.

Sometimes a nice sounding label disguises something undesirable. In Chapters 8 and 9, we've already discussed the practice of *social promotion* that is more honestly described as the practice of passing those who have *flunked* while ignoring the remedial needs of the affected students. Or students are graduated who have not passed the courses *required* for a high school diploma. That helps explain why so many colleges have remedial courses.

> This author had poor English writing skills when he enrolled at Johns Hopkins University in 1959 despite have received A's in his high school Honors English courses. I was required to enroll, and pass a course entitled English writing. I passed it.

Another seemingly heart-warming label is *social justice*. Many K-12 social studies courses teach about it. Nearly all of us Americans want our society to succeed by bringing as many benefits to our fellow citizens and legal residents as possible. Surely, as law abiding patriotic citizens, we want those around us protected by our legal systems. That means we want *justice for all*. The combination of these benefits and protections might reasonably be labeled *social justice*. Sadly, that label has been misappropriated by the advocates of other policies that are often inconsistent with the Constitution and other laws we live under. Among the perversions of this hijacked version of *social justice* are:

- Constitutional rights, such as freedom of speech, freedom of religion, freedom of the press are denied. This is particularly egregious in schools and colleges.

- Government funded benefits are awarded on the basis of irrelevant demographic characteristics, such as race, sex, and immigration status. An example of the latter kind of preferences is the priority given to illegal alien high school graduates as they apply to public colleges.

Among the worst practices based on this kind of *social justice* are those of affirmative action in which unfair advantage is given to racial demographics. College admissions, for example, often preferentially select applicants who are black or Hispanic over their white and Asian peers. In this regard, Harvard University is currently being sued over its discrimination against Asian applicants. Under current policies, the author's Asian-American grandchildren will probably not have much luck if they apply to Harvard. And ditto for white applicants.

Intersectionality is defined, but leads nowhere. Yet it is gaining a K-12 foothold.

Sometimes a new word pops up in our culture that has a flavor of scholarly rigor that upon closer inspection has little merit. *Intersectionality* is such a word and concept. According to the Oxford Dictionaries' Bing Translator it is defined as

> . . . the interconnected nature of social categorizations such as race, class, and gender as they apply to a given individual or group, regarded as creating overlapping and interdependent systems of discrimination or disadvantage.[362]

As such, the theories of *intersectionality* seem to be about demographic stereotypes and in particular focus on the levels of privilege accorded each demographic group. The concept of *intersection* appears to have arisen from the concern that some people have multiple underprivileged labels as would occur, for example, from simultaneously being black, female, homosexual, and illegal alien. It is from the *intersection* of these multiple characteristics that unfair discrimination can be aggravated. An essential flaw in these theories is that very few individuals in any demographic group will share the characteristics of the stereotypes used to describe the behaviors of those involved.

Some observers, such as Jonathan Keiler, see *intersectionality* as a poorly defined, almost oxymoronic term. He lamented that,

> Someone introduces *intersectionality* to a discussion and you either have to attack them for spewing nonsense, at which point they accuse you of making an ad hominin argument, or you are compelled to continue the debate on the leftist's nonsensical terms.[363]

When a theory is internally inconsistent, as *intersectionality* appears to be, it can be used—more likely abused—to reach illogical conclusions. Worse, it can be used to justify prejudices and biases that are not really helpful in dealing with the world's real problems. Law professor Alan Dershowitz, in his article, *The Bigotry of "Intersectionality,"* describes how this kind of incompetent analysis is used to justify anti-Semitic bias. He stated that,

> All decent people must join in calling out intersectionality for what it is: a euphemism for anti-American, anti-Semitic, and anti-Israel bigotry.[364]

Finally, we note that many of the *intersectionality theory* advocates also see it as having useful Marxist connections. Concepts of oppression are what evidently weaves them together?[365]

As a subject that students might learn, *intersectionality* poses a number of problems. Given its incoherence how can it be made logical? How can *cognitive dissonance* be communicated to students? But, never mind, *intersectionality* is being taught in some of our K-12 high schools.[366] Heaven help us!

The language police intimidate and censor textbook authors

Next, the language police, as Ravitch likes to label them, descend on the authors of these history texts to *sanitize* the words, phrases, and sentences. Much of the description of the social upheavals of the late twentieth century take the side of the political left. As Ravitch says,

> The texts treat the Black Panthers as a beneficent social service organization, with little or no reference to their tactics of intimidation and violence.[367]

The Black Panther Party was not only a political party organization, but it also had a number of leaders involved in criminal activity.[368] Eldridge Cleaver was a member and officer of the Black Panthers who during the 1960s served time in prison, more than once, for various felonies. He rose to be Minister of Information of the Black Panthers and later ran for President of the United States under the *Peace and Freedom Party* and did so despite being too young to run. By the 1980s he had remarkably transformed himself into a registered Republican.[369] He was an active Republican in California politics during the early 1990s before his passing in 1998.

> This author doesn't remember the details, but I met Eldridge Cleaver at a 1994 Republican Party rally in Sacramento, CA. He had long before ended his roles with the Black Panther Party, and by then had become a registered Republican. He had come full circle from seeing himself as an enemy of regular Americans to becoming one himself! We had a friendly conversation.

Are you sure? ". . . what is taught to them is phony and isn't worth remembering."

Ravitch concludes her chapter entitled, *History: The Endless Battle,* with this comment:

> In no other subject—not in mathematics or science or reading—do American seniors score as low as they do in U.S. history. Maybe it is because their textbooks are so dull; maybe it is because so many of their history teachers never studied history and can't argue with the textbooks' smug certainty. Maybe it is because the students don't know why they are supposed to remember the parade of facts that are so glamorously packaged between covers. Or maybe it is because, with the teenagers' usual ability to spot a scam, they know that *much of what is taught to them is phony and isn't worth remembering.*[370]

Some of the contributing factors to this degradation are the curricula defined by the history standards that were developed by the education bureaucrats having jurisdiction over the school systems in question. On that topic historian and textbook expert Gilbert Sewall observed that,

> What the public and elected officials didn't like about these new standards was their failure to affirm of celebrate the nation or the Western tradition. [they were] Just the reverse. Like a muffled drum through the U.S. history standards, African Americans, Native Americans, Hispanic Americans, Asian Americans, gay Americans, and women face and overcome centuries of oppression, neglect, and adversity. Students meet Speckled Snake, Dolores Heurta, Mahmud al-Kati, and Madonna. These people were, according to the drift of the curriculum, the real American heroes. They and others replaced such white patriarchs as Alexander Graham Bell, Thomas Edison, Jonas Salk,

and Albert Einstein. The defining reform institutions of the future? Political phalanxes like La Raza Unida and the National Organization of Women.[371]

On the next page in that same book, Sewall went on to caution stakeholders,

> But the problem is not only one of civic interpretation. With greater alarm, perhaps, discerning parents are also beginning to notice that non-academic courses focusing on personal behavior and social ailments are replacing academic courses in the zero-sum school day.

Again, let us read between the lines. All, or most, of these efforts by progressive *educationists* to steer history instruction down new roads and perhaps blind alleys suggest that they do not want the next generation of voters to understand enough American history to effectively participate in our democratic system. They surely want these new voters to vote, but they want them to vote for their *educationist* nostrums. It appears that their goal is one of undermining our current system of government, either by legally voting for the changes or by illegally allowing the bureaucrats, of the oft labeled *deep state*, to *subvert* it from inside.

Let's now turn to consider how these problems can be fixed.

FIXING THE BAD BOOKS AND BAD TEACHING

From a student's perspective they learn from books and their teachers. If these physical and human resources lack the content, quality, and competence to deliver that knowledge, we may reasonably label those inputs as *Sick*. The old metaphor about *garbage in and garbage* out can be changed perhaps to *Sick knowledge coming in and Sick knowledge coming out*? Surely, the stuff coming in can be fixed. Right? How it is transmitted can be fixed, right? And then the instruction in history and civics can help *Sick Schools* regain some health? Fixing these subjects of civics and U.S. history, where the K-12 schools are arguably their *sickest*, should go a long way towards this goal.

In which epoch should U.S. history studies begin?

The typical starting point for the study of U.S. history is 1492 when Columbus landed in the New World (and never knew it—thinking he was in Asia). Others start the narrative earlier, much earlier. Say in 15,000 BC?[372] One of the author's favorite historians is Paul Johnson. His U.S. history book also starts its chronology with Christopher Columbus in 1492.[373] We think that is a good starting date.

Many historians choose to start with the Vikings who established temporary colonies in what is now Canada. Others note that the Knights Templar had explorers operating out of Scotland who may have set up temporary colonies in, and around, Nova Scotia and arguably gave it its name, as well as giving Canada its name. One legend, with some historical support, claims that Henry I Sinclair, Earl of Orkney, was a Knight Templar and was a Scottish mariner who led a voyage of discovery in 1398 to Nova Scotia and may have even been the author of this large island's name?[374] Other historians believe that one year later in 1399 he also passed through a portion of what is now Massachusetts and left a carved inscription on a granite slab to memorialize the death of a knight in his company. This celebrated inscription can be found in the town of Westford—about 30 miles northwest of Boston. The knight is known locally as the *Westford Knight*.[375] I have personally visited the site and a nearby library that has a significant collection of documents and memorabilia about these yet to be confirmed historical events.

Accurate information about these earlier *visitors* is scant, and may be more legend than chronology. Thus, it is not confirmed history. At least not yet. But archeologists and historians are currently engaged in further research that may clarify what really happened. Of great interest are excavations being done on a small island, Oak Island, that is connected to Nova Scotia by a causeway. For example, a small cross recently found on Oak Island has a design of crosses possessed by the Templars in 14th century France.[376] Moreover, according to reporting by the History Channel's TV series *The Curse of Oak Island*, a metallurgical analysis of the lead alloy in the cross determined it to be from medieval mines located in southern France and in the same areas known to have been populated by Knights Templar in the fourteenth century. Some observers dispute that finding, which suggests further analysis is needed to confirm it.[377]

Despite the interest and value of the early explorations by Europeans to the American continent, most of these accounts are not sufficiently confirmed to merit inclusion in U.S. history studies. Consistent with that it seems that the traditional approach of starting the narratives with Columbus and Vespucci is about right. We would put much more weight on Vespucci and much less on Columbus, given the fact that Columbus was an incompetent geographer.

How should U.S. history instruction and testing deal with controversial issues?

When the historians and other authors of history textbooks and their associated curricula have political agendas that skew and slant the historical narratives that can be problematic. Even when these authors reduce or eliminate these kinds of commentaries, the different books will have differences in the range of facts presented as well as many different explanations for the historical events involved. In our time, in the early twenty-first century, there has been a tendency for authors of history books to embrace the political left. How should that bias be corrected?

In the case of controversy, authors have little choice, but to present enough of both sides for the student reader to understand the opposing views. Then there is this question: If the authors of history textbooks include material that is not true or is controversial, how can designers of standardized tests know how to construct the assessments? It is as if each of the four options on a multiple-choice question is correct depending on which of four different textbooks were used? This is why we ask about testing learned *facts* that are often items of false propaganda. If standards are a moving target how can a test measure a student's mastery of them?

There is a fairly simple solution to the standardized testing policies: Only include questions that focus on the common basic facts that all textbooks of U.S. history cover.

How to achieve objectivity in history instruction? How to avoid biases?

When we think about the role history books and history instruction play in American schools there are a number of principles that a good history course would honor. With respect to the history books and other reading materials used in, let's say, a high school history course, we would expect adherence to these aspects:

- Nothing fictional or known to be untrue would be included.
- Coverage would avoid political biases or would provide balance among them.
- Moral judgments would be made in the context of each historical era's ethical standards.

To meet these requirements, we can imagine a textbook selection process in which a selection committee would have members that represent a variety of viewpoints. With respect to the third bullet, of these guidelines, the practice of slavery, now universally condemned, would not be unduly criticized in historical eras where it was a legal institution. In the case of Thomas Jefferson, who held slaves, he was troubled by the practice and evidently looked forward to its eventual abolition. Surely, some slave owners, we should note, treated their slaves kindly, while others abused them.

All members of a textbook selection committee would have some training in history—maybe they majored in history in college or maybe they have a higher degree in it. You could perhaps imagine this committee having seven members with these characteristics:

- A Democrat
- A Republican
- A Libertarian
- A political Independent
- A Protestant pastor
- A Roman Catholic priest
- A Jewish rabbi

One can also imagine that this committee might not agree on any one textbook for the history course. They could choose supplementary books, booklets, handouts, etc. that would provide the needed balance for the history course. Those documents would presumably constitute a balanced set of reading materials for the course. Maybe they would agree on that?

Beyond these requirements for the course reading materials, the teachers would be required to provide oral instruction consistent with the printed documents. The teachers would be required to hide their biases or at least show both sides to any aspects that are controversial.

Textbook selection that is local gives parents more influence than a centralized process

Educationists and their allies in state departments of education prefer making state-wide choices for all public schools within a state—usually for reasons of supposed efficiency and for better control. But parents should have some say in how textbooks are chosen. Unfortunately, they have little influence at the state level because they are not organized in any kind of statewide fashion. If the selection is done locally under the supervision of the local school board, parents can have more influence.

If teachers were not required to have a teaching credential, but were required to actually have some *expertise* in their subject area or areas, it would be logical to entrust them with textbook selection. When you hire a carpenter to work on your house you do not provide him or her the tools or materials. Rather you entrust the carpenter to fulfill those responsibilities regarding the tools while you collaborate on the choice of materials. There are private schools that actually entrust teachers to make such choices of instructional materials or at least make recommendations on them. I know that from personal experience.

> This author was entrusted with that responsibility when he taught physics, and mathematics in a private Catholic high school in Oakland, CA in the 1965–1966 school year. I actually chose the textbooks.

Are there any textbooks of U.S. history to recommend?

As author, I have not considered the merits of candidate U.S. history textbooks. I refrained from doing so given my lack of expertise as a historian. So instead let us rely on Diane Ravitch to provide some recommendations on books from the early 2000s. She provided consumer information in two different publications she authored:

- In her 2003 book, *Language Police*.[378]

- In her 2004 article, *A Consumer's Guide to High School History Textbooks*.[379]

In the former 2003 publication, Ravitch put her stamp of approval on two U.S. history books:

- Boorstin and Kelley's *History of the United States*, This one is her favorite.
- Henry Graff's *America: The Glorious Republic*, It comes in 2nd.

For secondary texts to be used with either one of the former she likes

- Appleby, Brinkley, and McPherson's *American Journey*
- Appleby, Brinkley, and McPherson's *American Republic Since 1877*

In the just cited 2004 article, *A Consumer's Guide. . .*, Ravitch collaborated with four other experts to review another six U.S. history textbooks. These professionals gave the books scores based on a perfect score of 100 and then assigned letter grades to them. Here is what they reported:

C+ Appleby, Brinkley, and McPherson's	*American Journey*
C- Boyer's	*The American Nation*
C- Cayton, Perry, Reed, and Winkler's	*America: Pathways to the Present*
D Nash's	*American Odyssey*
F Danzer, de Alva, Krieger, Wilson, and Woloch's	*The Americans*
F Bragdon, McCutcheon, and Richie's	*History of a Free Nation*

These assigned grades might give one the impression that these experts were tough graders based on the lack of any A or B grades. We take a different view: These experts are easy graders and we base that on the fact that Gary Nash's book, *American Odyssey*, as described in the foregoing, had deliberate inclusion of fictional narratives and facts. On that basis his book deserves an F or maybe an F-.

It is not clear why the 2004 article did not examine the two books recommended in her first 2003 publication? Another problem with her list is that it is significantly out of date. We found information from other sources for more recent offerings and newer editions of the older textbooks.

The American Textbook Council, in 2018, was recommending two of the entries from Ravitch's Consumer's Guide:[380]

C+ Appleby, Brinkley, and McPherson's	*American Journey*
F Danzer, de Alva, Krieger, Wilson, and Woloch's	*The Americans*

We presume, but don't really know, that these offerings are newer editions than those reviewed in 2004. The letter grades shown here may no longer reflect the quality of these textbooks. Over the intervening 14 years, did they improve or did they get worse?

One of the points we are trying to make is that this book is not intended as a guide book to every resource for the instruction of U.S. history or any other subject. Rather we are attempting to show that the resources are limited. There are few choices, and many of the choices, say of textbooks, do not include any (or many) resources that are of high quality. When the best textbook only rates a C+ it says something.

HOW U.S. HISTORY CAN BE TAUGHT EFFECTIVELY

There are three places or types of schools where U.S. history can be taught:

1. Public schools can teach a history curriculum that has been produced by the political processes.

2. Private schools can teach a history curriculum of their choosing, subject to state or local minimums.

3. Home schools can teach a history curriculum of their choosing, subject to state or local minimums

For the second and third options, there is no impediment to the teaching of U.S. history assuming that the operators or parents, respectively, meet the regulatory minimum curriculum for the subject. It is the first option that is problematic. There are two difficulties when public schools teach U.S. history:

1. The political process can be awkward and offensive to some of the constituencies. Not every parent will like the curricula and systems developed for the subject. Nor will every voter find the curricula appealing.

2. Worse it is arguably illegal when parents can no longer direct the education of their children. This violation is inherent in a treaty signed by the U.S. which says

> *Parents have a prior right to choose the kind of education that shall be given to their children.*

We have already discussed this treaty in chapters 6, 10, and here in chapter 11. It is the *United Nations Declaration of Human Rights.* The specific requirement comes from its *Article 26, Subparagraph (3).* In theory, it binds the United States to honor this parental right. We are not sure why it is not honored or *enforced?*

If it were *enforced*, then states or other agencies would be required to provide vouchers or some other kind of tuition support to enable parents to choose the education their children would receive. Then, for example, if parents find the public school curricula for history objectionable, they would be able to enroll their child or children at a more appropriate school. It could be a different public school. It could be simply an online history course chosen by the parent that would substitute or re-educate for the public school course.

But if the law is not *enforced* or turns out to be *unenforceable*, then there is arguably an impasse because the public school would be forcing an history curriculum on the parent's child. One remedy to solve such an impasse would be quite extreme: close the public schools. That would force some kind of voucher system in which all education would be private albeit funded to a large degree by state and local governments. It is clear that if vouchers were available to all students, at least to all students of history, they would then have an escape from the inconveniences of public schools.

Just as Milton Friedman postulated in his original proposal for school vouchers there would be some adherence to local or state government regulations. The voucher program would be available, provided, in his words,

> . . . it met certain minimum standards laid down by the appropriate governmental unit.[381]

As we will discuss in more detail later, voucher programs need an informational component about school quality if parents are to make good decisions about the schools that will be appropriate for their children.

How public schools could give parents more control over curriculum

If it is impractical to give parents vouchers or other means by which they could control the curriculum taught to their children, then perhaps there are compromises that would give them more control and more choices?

In many states the textbooks, and hence the curricula of high school courses, are formulated and dictated from the state's department of education. We don't like such one-size fits all prescriptions, and we presume that most parents would prefer such decisions to be made locally where they would have more influence over such decisions. Let's make a list of types of policies within public education systems that could facilitate various degrees of flexibility in how history curricula are formulated and set:

1. Statewide. One statewide curriculum for U.S. history applies to all public high schools in the state.

2. County: One countywide curriculum for U.S. history applies to all public high schools in the county.

3. District: One districtwide curriculum for U.S. history applies to all public high schools in the district.

4. High School: One schoolwide curriculum for U.S. history applies to all history courses in the school.

5. Classroom: One classroom curriculum for U.S. history applies to all history courses in the classroom.

6. Class: One curriculum for each class of U.S. history applies to students in that class.

7. Track: One curriculum for each track of U.S. history applies to students in that track within the class.

8. Student: One U.S. history curriculum or specified course of study for each student within the class.

The last three options could invoke the authority of the teacher and/or the parent to make these choices. Or the school could create a menu of choices that students, parents, and teachers could consider and choose. As one goes down the list the parents of the children in the included schools have more and more control simply as a result of the electoral/administrative process that chooses the management of those schools.

If we contemplate the results of lawsuits under *Article 26* requirements, one can imagine the court ordering a restructuring of the public school history programs. To give parents the control envisaged under *Article 26*, only item 8 would give them that full level of authority. Were state legislatures to enact laws in this area, one can imagine the establishment of new arrangements that would be compromises between full control at one extreme and no control at the other. In such cases the policies might conform to something within the range of items 4 through 7, listed above.

Also, for each option in the list there would be a need for expertise in U.S. history at the associated level. For items 6, 7, and 8 the teacher would be a well-trained history teacher. Under item 8 one can imagine many students in the classroom each following his or her own plan of study. In that case the teacher might need to be familiar with a dozen or more alternative textbooks or curricula?

K-12 ED COULD *PASS* U.S. HISTORY IF. . .

Unlike the subjects of mathematics and reading, where the curricular standards are much less controversial, the subject of U.S. history is not as well defined. There are two areas of controversy or dispute:

- What are the facts?
- What is the interpretation of these facts?

On the first issue there are two kinds of facts: Those that almost all historians agree on and alternatively the facts that are in dispute among reputable historians.

When presenting the facts that are important in the development of the United States how should textbook authors and teachers deal with the second category of facts: The ones in dispute? Generally, disputed facts should not be taught. If they must be included, then both sides need to be presented, and presented without bias either direction. Depending on the constraint of textbook length, not all desired information will be included. Some facts are more important than others, and those should have priority when some factual material must be excluded.

As to the interpretation of the facts, there is often more than one view of what they mean. Sometimes there are more than two such views. Generally, when there are two views they will usually align with political viewpoints: The liberal view and the conservative view. In such cases, any decent textbook will describe both perspectives. Sometimes there will be a third or even a fourth opinion that is held by a significant number of historians or politicians. In such cases, some mention should be made of them in the form of an explanation or perhaps a reference to further information.

There are many historians who are not patriotic Americans. With regard to them there is the question of whether their viewpoints should be heard in K-12 education. If we are lacking patriotic historians in their specialties, we think these disloyal historians can be heard if their views are relevant to explaining the development of the United States. But their viewpoints should be for contrast and not for promoting unpatriotic concepts.

This suggests that history instruction has two purposes:

- Learning: Give the pupil a certain level of knowledge and understanding about the historical events.

- Formation: Developing in students a loyalty to country while also helping them understand regrettable aspects of U.S. history.

So, there you have it: In K-12 education there are enormous problems in both public and private instruction of U.S. history, including civics. Despite these being very troublesome, there are straightforward remedies. It will take government action and/or parental involvement to ensure American children learn their history lessons. There are many partial remedies that we mentioned, but giving parents the power to make educational decisions for their children is the better course of reform. Providing parents with *vouchers* and *consumer information* will help them find good schooling options and will help generate a healthy educational marketplace in which competition will drive further improvements in K-12 education. One of those beneficiaries will be the quality of instruction in the subjects of U.S. history and civics.

A part-time instructional format in public schools could accommodate parents' wishes

Similar to what we concluded in the preceding chapter on religion, there is another way to accommodate parents' preferences in history instruction: Use a part-time enrollment policy in the public school in which students could be removed from the classroom to receive alternative history instruction elsewhere. That alternative instruction could be:

- At a private school or tutoring center that also allows part-time enrollment.
- Or in a homeschooling arrangement where instruction is given by a tutor, a parent, or from an online course.

We can imagine that the outside instruction would be required to meet some minimal requirements that might be regulated by one or more accreditation bodies.

As for the study of religion and history, micro-vouchers could aid parental control

As we mentioned in the preceding chapter, the education savings account (ESA) allows parents much more freedom to choose the education to be received by their children. It helps public schools honor the *United Nations Declaration of Human Rights* provision that gives parents that control. The ESA can be used to pay expenses other than annual tuition costs. It can be used to pay tutoring fees. It can be used to pay for online courses. It can be used to pay for part-time history or civics instruction in a private school. In such cases the ESA is like a micro-voucher that pays for part-time course work. So, even without the flexibility of part-time public education, the ESA can give parents control over instruction and curricular standards by giving them other options beyond those of the public school.

Re-read this chapter between the lines and you'll see much that is degraded and sick.

If there is one theme to what we wrote in this chapter, it is that a certain kind of politics has imposed its narrative on the teaching of history in our K-12 schools. That politics tends to be to the left and frequently is progressive. In terms of the factual chronologies of U.S. history, much of that information has been removed from the taught curricula in an effort to accommodate the various complaints of the progressive left. A textbook can only be so long. If you insist it cover every *politically correct* topic there will be little room left for real history. A combination of incompetence, disrespect for our laws and U.S. Constitution, and a lack of societal focus are the diagnosed causes of this sickness. Where are the *doctors of history* who can fix this?

CHAPTER 12

K-12 Education is Flunking Ethics and Law

IN ONE PERSPECTIVE THE success of K-12 schools depends on using appropriate incentives to encourage all those involved to play constructive roles in helping the enrolled students master their subjects. In this chapter we look at the improprieties that reduce these incentives and that sometimes are so harmful that they are violations of the rules, regulations, and laws governing school operations. In doing this we also look at unethical activities that, while not against the rules, per se, are nevertheless harmful to K-12 students.

In this chapter we start small. We start with the student and then move up the chain of complexity to review various kinds of misbehavior of those responsible. Among those working within the education systems we subdivide the responsible parties according to this list:

- Student
- Parent
- Teacher
- Principal
- District Superintendent
- State Superintendent
- Governor and Legislature
- Federal authorities

There are other kinds of responsible parties that are outside of the education system bureaucracies:

- Textbook publishers and providers of other kinds of academic content
- Homeschooling parents

PART III—DISTRESS SIGNS IN K-12 EDUCATION 1951—2019

- Voucher funding agencies, private, and public
- Public employee unions and other non-governmental organizations (NGO's)

Let's now explore these different kinds of participants in K-12 education and review their vulnerabilities to corruption, conflicts of interest, and greed.

Herbert Walberg was a specialist in the interdisciplinary analysis of educational testing and psychology. He has written extensively on academic testing in K-12 education and has studied *student cheating* in some detail. He identified categories of such misbehavior. Examples of student cheating include:

- A student, without any collusion, copies the work of another.
- A student conspires to receive the work of another.
- A student steals a copy of a test and its answers.
- A student purchases an essay to use as a term paper.[382]
- A student conspires to receive answers from a teacher.[383]

In the references we have reviewed there is very little written about detecting student cheating, about providing punishments, and other disincentives to the pupils thus engaged. Where are the proctors who would presumably report such offenses? Where are the school officials who would take corrective action including punishments that would help deter student cheating? With so little emphasis on detection and corrective action it should not be surprising that student cheating is widespread.

BRIBERY FROM PARENTS

As we were nearly finished with this book's manuscript a new set of scandals emerged that involved various kinds of bribery and other criminal acts that were committed by parents of graduating high school seniors. Their motivation was mainly to have their children admitted to colleges and universities that are very selective. This would be achieved and was achieved by various strategies including cheating on standardized admissions tests and falsifying records of athletic achievement in high school sports.[384]

Most of this misconduct occurred as students were in transition from their K-12 enrollments to their college careers. We decided to discuss these events in this book about *Sick* K-12 schools because most of the misconduct occurred while the students were still enrolled in high school.

Payments for criminal alteration of college entrance examination results

Want your child's IQ in the stratosphere? Some of the schemers, masquerading as legitimate college entrance consultants, had ways of doctoring SAT and ACT answer sheets to produce those high scores.[385] In some cases, an exam proctor was bribed to change answers after the student took the test. In other cases, a *ringer* was employed to take the student's test under the student's name. These consultants expected parents to pay very large bribes (please say "fees") for their services—sometimes in excess of $100,000.00.

Payments for criminal alteration of records of high school athletic accomplishments

Another path to acceptance into an elite college or university is that through the recruitment of star athletes by the college athletic departments. Yes, you can get in with a modest ACT or SAT score if your child is sought on the basis of their faked athletic record. To do this the college consultant would take the large fee from the parent and use it to bribe key officials in the colleges' athletic departments who had the authority to make college acceptance decisions.

The federal investigation that uncovered these crimes labeled itself *Operation Varsity Blues.* That label fits the faked athletic records of entering college students. In early March 2019, indictments were handed down naming 33 parents of students who fraudulently gained admission to various institutions.[386]

TEACHER AND TEACHERS UNION MISCONDUCT

We describe two types of teacher misconduct:

- Where the teacher as an individual engages in unethical or criminal activity.
- Where the teacher belongs to a teachers union that is acting unethically and/or criminally.

Situations where there is individual misconduct

When one looks at the activities of a teacher that involve cheating or other prohibited activities, you are looking at the classroom level of various kinds of misbehavior. Among those we found in the literature include:

- The teacher plays favorites and helps some students more than others, including giving them test answers.
- The teacher teaches to the actual test students will be given.

- The teacher assigns practice tests closely aligned with forthcoming official tests.

- The teacher, similarly, teaches a narrow curriculum based on questions on actual tests.

- The teacher bases too much of the course grade on homework completed and too little on test results.

- The teacher grades tests on the curve to enable inflated grades on course mastery levels.

- The teacher engages in tactics to make class average performance appear better than it actually is.[387]

- The teacher engages in *extortion* to have students pay for higher grades.[388]

The first four items of this list pertain to tactics that will likely raise students' scores on official standardized tests. So, when the teacher is administering a standardized test that will generate publicly available results for the class, he or she may improperly help pupils answer test questions—as mentioned in the preceding list. This can have the effect of showing inflated performance levels for the students and the class.

As to the last four items of the above list there is the teacher's desire or requirement to look good within the school's grading system. Generally, this means that the teacher fails to help the students master their subjects, but nevertheless awards them high grades for their less than proficient accomplishments. In that situation, the official standardized test can be the vehicle of detection that helps officials detect teacher negligence or misconduct. All the more reason to find ways to artificially raise the official test scores.

In maintaining the veneer of satisfactory student performance, an overriding and mostly undeclared concern is that the teacher quietly maintains a classroom environment in which *social promotion* is supported. That is typically accomplished without any explicit acknowledgement of the easy grading policies that are needed to reach the goal of having all or nearly all students' pass on to the next grade level.

Situations where there is group misconduct by the teachers union

Nearly all unionized public school teachers belong to one of the two largest teachers unions:

- The National Education Association (NEA)

- The American Federation of Teachers (AFT)

The NEA is the larger of these two enormous unions, and will provide the examples we describe below. When a teacher belongs to one of these unions and the union engages in unethical or illegal activities, the teacher generally escapes any criminal liability, but nevertheless is culpable of indirectly supporting the offensive activities.

In such circumstances, the teacher may *honorably* work within the union's democratic framework to propose that the union correct its bad behavior. Or the teacher may *not so honorably* simply accept the status quo and not take any corrective action.

Did the NEA Bribe Presidential Candidates? The author is not a lawyer and can't prove that these examples are criminal, but they often appear to have the quid pro quo element associated with bribery. The NEA, among its goals, had long wanted to control United States K-12 education policy. They wanted that despite the U.S. Constitutional prohibition of federal direction of education. In 1972, its President Catherine Barrett was not exaggerating when she said,

> We are the biggest potential striking force in this country, and we are determined to control the direction of education.

Their goal was the establishment of a federal Department of Education. A good strategy for accomplishing that was to support a presidential campaign with similar goals. So, according to Charles Sykes, when Jimmy Carter ran for President in 1976, the deal made was essentially this:

> You, Jimmy Carter, work to establish a federal Department of Education and we will support you. Carter then made that promise and they delivered the dollars and volunteers. After he won, he carried out his end of the bargain and was successful establishing the federal U.S. Department of Education.[389]

Sykes goes on to tell us that on the eve of President Carter signing the bill creating this department, a key NEA official boasted to his friends in a toast,

> Here's to the only union that owns its own Cabinet Department.

We are aware that the NEA was active in subsequent presidential campaigns, but we don't have the details for 1980, 1984 or 1988. We do have some information about the 1992 campaign in which Bill Clinton was elected president.

In early 1991, some months after the establishment of America's first voucher program in Milwaukee, its best known proponent, Polly Williams, received a letter of congratulation from then governor of Arkansas, Bill Clinton. He called her program

> . . . innovative and visionary . . .

Not long after, he was running for president. He was getting ample support from the NEA and he was no longer saying nice things about government paid school vouchers. It is more difficult to characterize this coincidence as bribery, but it seems that there was a *wink and a nod* situation. When Clinton ran for re-election in 1996, he went *off the reservation* when he said in a debate with Republican candidate Bob Dole,

> I support school choice. If a local district in Cleveland, or any place else, wants
> to have a private school choice plan, like Milwaukee did, let them have at it.

If the NEA showed any displeasure over this implied breach of promise, we have not been able to find any record of it.[390]

Using illegal tactics in fighting government vouchers. The California Teachers Association, the NEA affiliate in California, left few stones unturned in its efforts to defeat a proposed ballot initiative to establish school vouchers in 1992. Why defeat the initiative at the polls when *bribery* could do that sooner? Their tactics essentially *vandalized* the signature gathering process to prevent the voucher proponents from reaching the minimum number of signatures to qualify the initiative for the November ballot. We don't have all the details, but this much we know:

> The CTA hired at least one signature gathering firm in 1992. Why would they
> do that when they were not interested in collecting signatures for a ballot ini-
> tiative? What they apparently did was hire the firm *to not collect* signatures
> and thereby be unavailable to the voucher campaign's signature collecting ef-
> forts. We do know, from a sworn statement to a California court, that one of
> these CTA contractors attempted to bribe the president of a competitor firm
> $400,000 *to not collect* signatures for the campaign.[391]

When confronted with this accusation of criminal activity, the CTA president, Del Weber, was not going to apologize. Knowing that he was virtually *immune from prosecution* in California's corrupt criminal justice system he publicly confessed,

> We decided to create an organized campaign to block an initiative from get-
> ting enough signatures to qualify for the ballot.

Then, later in his statement he asserted,

> There are some proposals that are so evil that they should never even be pre-
> sented to the voters.[392]

But, of course, that is not the law. The CTA's interference probably broke a number of laws. Bribery seemed to be involved, but Weber skated away from this criminal conduct. These illegal tactics of the CTA were successful: The ballot initiative failed to collect the required number of signatures.

The voucher proposal came back the next year and did qualify for inclusion on the ballot of a special November 1993 election. It was time for the California Teachers Association (CTA) to use its resources to oppose what became Proposition 174. It was time for the CTA to break some more laws.

In the 1993 campaign, the CTA encouraged public school officials and employees to use their work facilities and work hours to help the *No on 174* campaign. That was a violation of the law.[393] This author, who was a spokesman for that campaign, has personal knowledge of one such violation. I recall this:

> In the autumn of 1993, I participated in a debate held in the auditorium of an Alameda City public elementary school. A parent of one of the school's students had previously told me that the school's principal had held a meeting in her conference room, just a few days earlier, that was to plan their campaign effort to oppose Prop. 174. This debate was covered by the PBS Newshour and portions of it were broadcast on their program. As I concluded my remarks in this debate, I recounted this accusation of law breaking against the school's principal. But that section of the videotape was edited out and never appeared in the PBS broadcast.

They even use illegal tactics against hated privately funded vouchers. This story begins in 1995 with Bret Schundler, the then young mayor of Jersey City, New Jersey. He wanted to provide vouchers to economically disadvantaged students who were trapped in dysfunctional public schools. PepsiCo, the parent of Pepsi Cola, came forward and offered to sponsor a number of these students by providing them with private vouchers or scholarships. The NEA affiliate in New Jersey soon went into action. It was time for a *boycott*, and maybe even some *vandalism* of Pepsi vending machines? Pepsi caved and the promise of vouchers vanished. We don't know if the boycott was illegal, but the *vandalism* was probably criminal.[394]

Was it theft or was it a surcharge? Stealing from your own members. In Michigan the NEA affiliate is the Michigan Education Association (MEA). Why not create a subsidiary to sell health insurance and make a really big profit by charging members rates well above the market rates? Blue Cross Blue Shield was the insurance company, which was also the insurance company for state of Michigan employees. The above market rates charged were reported to be $1,000 per year higher than the charges for the state employees. Is that a surcharge of $1,000 or is that an illegal diversion from member's payments for insurance? This was not small potatoes. The subsidiary had $360 million in revenues in 1992 and some of the implied excess helped fill the MEA coffers, which, in turn, must have helped finance MEA political efforts.[395] This is very convenient as it allows the union to avoid prohibitions against using member dues for political purposes. Instead, it seems that they use a portion of their member's health insurance premiums to finance their political activities. Call it *money laundering*, and I won't even blink!

Consistent with the foregoing, Peter Brimelow, and Leslie Spencer characterized the NEA as a,

> ... weird institutional mutant: part labor union, part insurance conglomerate
> (of all things), part self-perpetuating staff oligarchy ...[396]

To which Charles Sykes added that it was also

> ... part political party.[397]

Yes, it is, by its actions, a *political party*. But by its official labelling it is a non-partisan professional association. As a political party it enjoys a monopoly in jurisdictions that have *non-partisan election laws*. Let's see. A political party that has a monopoly. Sounds like the Communist Party in Soviet Russia, and in other Communist countries. We previously encountered Paul Pastorek in Chapter 6, who similarly opined that the public education bureaucracies in the United States do indeed have communist structures just like was seen in the Communist Soviet Union during the Cold War. We are not saying that the NEA is communist, but we are saying that it has some troubling communist attributes.

In a later section, *State Level Government Difficulties*, we'll explore the consequent inference that the NEA can participate in non-partisan elections while the usual political parties are denied participation, and therein denied their constitutional *rights to free speech*.

Did the NEA in Florida actually boycott the electric utility company? Consider a report about the Florida affiliate of the NEA, the Florida Education Association (FEA), and its possible illegal over-reaction to a privately funded school voucher program to which an electric power company had made donations.

Well, wasn't it was time to punish the power company? Wasn't it time to employ one of the NEA's favorite tactics, the boycott? How do you boycott a power company? Maybe convince its customers to use less electricity? How do you do that?

According to education analyst Sol Stern, here's what they proposed to the most affected public school district:

> ... shut off the power to all schools for one day in order to punish the electric company.[398]

Based on the dearth of any other accounts of this proposed remedy, we doubt that it was carried out. Any district doing something like that would be vulnerable to charges of child neglect, negligence, and perhaps academic misconduct (teaching children with the lights out is not an optimal instructional environment). But to think that the FEA would make such a proposal shows a lack of professionalism and a lack of respect for the laws they and the district would be violating, if they actually conspired with the school district to carry out this form of vandalism.

The NEA and its affiliates are politically involved in K-12 education in other ways—to be discussed in subsequent sections of this chapter. Stay tuned.

PROBLEMS CAUSED BY PRINCIPALS

When we consider the *responsibilities* of school principals and other heads of schools, their actions affect more people than the actions of teachers we considered in the previous section. One category of wrong doing looks at improper actions principals take to make their school appear better than it really is or was. Consider these eight unethical and/or criminal actions that deviant principals have *actually* taken:

- Expel those students expected to receive low scores on mandated state administered standardized tests.

- Force transfer students of that type to special alternative schools for students with special needs.

- Conspire with testing authorities to *improve* reported test results.

- Narrow the curriculum taught (teach to the test) based on what is known to be on forthcoming tests.

- Teach students test prep tactics instead of working on actual curricular standards.

- Encourage *truancy* or absence of low performers on testing days.

- Organize revision (doctoring) of completed student test sheets to improve their scores.

- Discard completed student test sheets when too many answers are incorrect.[399]

Most of these actions have been taken by wayward principals in efforts to polish their schools' images. We would add a ninth: Pressure on teachers to maintain easy grading policies consistent with *social promotion*.

Principals caught doctoring student tests and employing other illegal strategies

Some of these improper tactics can be detected, but others are more difficult to ascertain. Various statistical analyses have been used to find aberrant behavior. For example, improperly revised test sheets sometimes have the most difficult questions answered correctly while some of the easier ones are incorrect. Such a distribution of answers is highly improbable according to a probability analysis. In the case of improperly transferred or removed students, a statistical analysis can show a lack of participants at the low end of the scoring distribution. That would suggest such students were removed from the tested group.

Connecticut principal boosts school's test scores using eraser and pencil. There was a school, the Stratfield School, in Fairfield, Connecticut that was showing impressive performance gains on the state's standardized testing during the 1990s. As a presumed role model to be emulated, district officials began a study to learn more details about students' new strengths as well as remaining weaknesses. They studied the answer sheets from more recent standardized testing and didn't discover any new student performance gains. Rather, on the earlier tests that showed the gains they discovered massive cheating by school administrators, including its principal Roger Previs. They observed very large numbers of erased answers combined with almost always correct replacement answers on the testing sheets first filled in by the students.[400]

One would expect criminal investigations in such matters. Instead, Previs was investigated by district school administrators and found responsible for the scandal. Accordingly, he was not prosecuted, and his punishment was mild: Forced early retirement in 1997.[401]

Philadelphia principal's conviction for six crimes in test doctoring scandal. Evelyn Cortez was principal of the Cayuga Elementary School in Philadelphia. She led a conspiracy from 2008 to 2011 that worked to alter student test scores and use other tactics to artificially increase the average scores reported for reading tests in grades 3 and higher. Her strategies more than doubled the proficiency percentages of 3rd graders from around 27% to the artificial level of 60%. The charges in her indictment were:

- Tampering with public records
- Tampering with non-public records
- Forgery
- Criminal conspiracy
- Perjury
- Violating the corrupt organizations act[402]

She pled guilty to these charges and the consequent punishment was relatively mild: Zero years of prison time and ten-years of probation. She had earlier been transitioned into early retirement.[403] Oh, how harsh!

Two other similar scandals in California and Chicago each involved over a dozen schools. In each of those two cases no punitive measures were taken by officials despite their conclusions that significant cheating had occurred.[404]

DISTRICT LEVEL CORRUPTION

At the level of the public school district, new and different kinds of misbehavior can arise. It is at this level that local politics enters the equation because the officers managing a school district are generally elected in local elections. Some of the activities of a school district that can be vulnerable to corruption include:

- Textbook selection can involve bribes and other improper inducements in states where this process occurs at the district level.

- Fraud in administering and reporting from state mandated standardized tests.

- Student transportation contracts can involve improper arrangements.

- Building maintenance contracts are vulnerable and/or unionized maintenance workers can pose problems.

- Unionized teachers' contracts often block reassignments and/or terminations of incompetent teachers.

- Elections for school boards have been unethically or criminally *manipulated* to produce desired results.

District level textbook selection improprieties

In an Internet search for bribery and other illegal activities in the textbook selection process we found very little. We also searched the electronic catalogue of the Brown University Library where we had a difficult time finding any books with relevant information. Of 12 books that had information of textbook selection, not one had any information about misconduct on the part of school officials or on the part of the publishers. If there are district level scandals in this area they must be so minor that they are not newsworthy? Or so secret that nothing on it has leaked out?

During the Cold War with the Soviet Union a story circulated in its KGB spy agency about a sub-field of missile defense in which the United States actually had no activities underway. Russian intelligence agents were unable to learn anything about U.S. work in this area. They had a paranoid view of this lack of information and concluded that it must be top-top-top secret to such a degree that the U.S. was preventing any information from getting out. Applying these lines of reasoning to the dearth of information on criminal activity in textbook purchasing suggests either in the paranoid view that much criminal activity is underway or in the more realistic view that there is not much scandal in this sub-sector of the education field.

But we did find one indication from 1964 in California. Richard Feynman, a famous Nobel prize winning physicist, served on a mathematics textbook selection committee, officially the State Curriculum Commission. He represented a portion of Los Angeles County on the Commission. He was expected to survey educators in the school districts of that area and report on their preferences for textbooks that would be purchased statewide. He could not abide that arrangement because these educators were not actually reading the books, but instead were attending publisher presentations designed to *advertise* their books as the ones that should be selected. So, he read the books himself. This misconduct of those educators was both at the district and state levels. We will have more to say on those events in the next section on state level improprieties.[405]

District level standardized test fraud and cheating

Cheating with regard to standardized tests was briefly discussed in the previous section where educators such as principals engage in improper and often illegal conduct. Sometimes this kind of misconduct is organized at the school district level.

Superintendent's amazing skills included the orchestration of a massive cheating scandal in Atlanta. Probably the most notorious scandal of this type occurred in the early years of the twenty-first century in the Atlanta, Georgia school district. According to newspaper reports, it first surfaced in 2008 when the *Atlanta Journal & Constitution* newspaper reported that the Atlanta School District's administration of the state's mandated standardized CRCT tests was troubled by irregularities. Over the next four years investigators discovered massive criminal activities involving almost two-hundred educators in the district. Many were charged with altering test sheets to correct wrong answers entered by students. More than half of Atlanta's schools were involved in these illegal schemes to make themselves look good. And they surely did *look good* when you consider that in 2009 the district's superintendent, Beverly Hall, was awarded *National Superintendent of the Year* by the American Association of School Administrators for her *amazing* skills in boosting student achievement. But in fact, she was not so skilled. She was considered as the most culpable in the scandal and as such was charged with numerous felonies. However, she died from natural causes in 2014 before she could be put on trial. Of those charged, 21 plead guilty in February 2014. In addition to fines and community service most of them received a peculiar type of jail time in which they served their time only on weekends.[406]

Of 12 remaining defendants who pled innocence, 11 were convicted of various crimes in April 2015. They were found guilty of felony charges including conspiracy and racketeering for their involvement in the cheating scandals. Of the 11, one was acquitted and eight were sentenced to jail. Additionally, 10 of them also paid fines and were ordered to perform community service.[407]

Timing of forced dropouts kept funding up and produced higher average test scores. The Birmingham, Alabama school district, circa 2001, developed a scheme involving high school students who were either likely to dropout or who could be pressured to dropout. But please, don't dropout before February 15th as that is the date on which enrollment is used to determine school funding levels. But please, if you are a poorly performing student, do dropout before April when your classmates will be taking the Stanford Achievement Tests. To do otherwise would have lowered the test score averages in the Birmingham high schools. The scheme was detected by an official of a G.E.D. program run by the same school district where an unusually large number of 16-year-olds were enrolling the program. Many of these teenagers, who had been expelled from school for an officially cited *lack of interest* were suddenly expressing *interest* in further schooling![408]

We searched the Internet to determine if anyone was prosecuted in this scandal and found nothing. Throughout this controversy the Birmingham School District defiantly claimed that these children left voluntarily. Ignore this and trust the district: Then you'll see no crimes in Birmingham.

District level transportation contracting crimes of fraud, bribery, and tax evasion

Transportation contracts have often been exploited by school district authorities who take bribes to direct business towards favored bus companies that, of course, are the ones usually paying the bribes.

School bus company bribes financed their lavish living and paved their road to jail. In one notable scheme the North Chicago school district was defrauded. It involved a school board member, Gloria Harper and district transportation services manager, Alice Sherrod, who collected bribes from school bus companies over a nine-year period from 2001 through 2010. Federal prosecutors brought charges of wire fraud, bribery, and tax evasion against Harper who was convicted on all three charges and sentenced to 10 years in prison.[409] Sherrod also pled guilty to similar charges and was later sentenced to 30 months in federal prison.[410] According to court documents, Harper and Sherrod each took more than a half million dollars in kickbacks.

If you bribe me, then I'll bribe you with contracts for additional school bus routes. In New York City a similar extortion and bribery conspiracy had school bus inspectors of the New York City Department of Education taking bribes and then giving school bus companies additional routes. The scheme's participants were prosecuted in 2009 for accepting and extorting over $1 million dollars. School bus inspector George Ortiz led the conspiracy and received a rather lenient sentence of 30 months in federal prison.[411]

District level school maintenance improprieties:

Maintenance of public school properties is carried out by unionized workers in nearly every public school district in the United States. The late Andrew Coulson described inexcusable maintenance lapses across the country, including ones in Hartford, in

Florida's Orange County, in St. Louis, and in Washington, DC.[412] None of these locations seem to have had contracts with professional maintenance firms. The politically protected union maintenance workers seem to have neglected many of the serious problems reported.

Top janitor led a racket that cleaned up over $6 million from board of education. In Georgia the Floyd County School System Maintenance Director led a ring of conspirators that took $6,331,135 from the district's funds. According to the indictment produced by a Floyd County Grand Jury,

> In his role as facilities director for the Floyd County Board of Education, Derry Scott Richardson conspired with fellow BOE employees and employees of construction and maintenance companies to produce completely fraudulent invoices or inflated invoices for construction and maintenance projects.[413]

Derry Richardson and 13 co-conspirators were indicted on October 1, 2018 for their participation in the theft of school system funds. At the time of this writing, in late 2019, they were all still awaiting trial.[414]

Maintenance worker dispute led to murder. Maintenance contracts were also an issue in New York City in 1987 when its Board of Education decided to add some contract workers to its staff of unionized maintenance workers. One of the intended for-profit private contract vendors, annoyed at the union's objections to the plans, hired a hit man and murdered the custodian union president, Dan Conlin.[415] There is irony here in that one of the contractors, who would have probably improved building maintenance, was the one committing the heinous crime?

District level union contracts often mandate waste, fraud, and abuse

When unionized school personnel, particularly teachers, bargain for a labor contract they often do not consider side effects that are harmful to the success of K-12 education. School administrators, who negotiate the management side of these contracts, likewise often ignore the difficulties therein.

Unionized assistant principals involved in wasteful freeloading. Rigid rules, included in teacher union contracts, can greatly restrict administrators' flexibility in hiring, firing, and reassigning staff—including assistant principals. In 2004, in New York City, such rules required the reassignment of five assistant principals to empty desks where they had no work assigned, but were required to put in their regular hours. The union contract would prevent them from doing any work other than what their contracts had originally required. They couldn't even *shuffle papers!*[416] The cost of this arrangement, based on what was paid for zero productivity, was well in excess of a half million dollars.

Unionized teachers know not what they do and violate children's civil rights. As we shall explore in more detail in Chapter 16, seniority provisions of teacher union contracts incentivize teacher transfers among schools in such a manner that schools in troubled neighborhoods end up with the least competent teaching staffs. Such union contract language may constitute violations of civil rights laws and other statutes that protect racial and economic minorities.[417]

District level criminal activities in school board elections

In the days of Mark Twain, the politics of school boards was even then a controversial issue and so much so that in 1865 Twain remarked,

> First God created idiots. That was for practice. Then he created school boards.[418]

In this section we look at election laws and procedures that can bias results in school board elections.

We win. They lose. The strange rules that govern New York City school board elections seem consistent with Twain's theme as we now show. The city provides several examples of the improper activities that can occur in school board elections. In one case, in 1993, the NYC Community School Board elections had a process that was so to speak *quite irregular* or in the common vernacular *massively fraudulent*. As a report on these irregularities by the New York City Office of the Special Commissioner of Investigation put it,

> In some areas, anyone could vote, often multiple times, and many parents were not allowed to vote at all. . . . Many absentee ballots were cast under false names, without the knowledge and consent of the unsuspecting *voters*. In some districts, teachers and staff were pressured into supporting a candidate. Election guidelines were also found to be ineffective and frequently broken.[419]

Such arrangements may not be surprising to aficionados of New York City history of the twentieth century. They may be aware of the period during the 1930s and 1940s when the Communist Party in the USA (CPUSA) had control and/or significant influence in the Teachers Union (TU) of New York City public school teachers.[420] That arrangement persisted until 1948 when the Communist members were removed from the TU. This would seem to have been a corrupt arrangement given that this group of public teachers were presumably loyal to the same folks the CPUSA adored: The Communist leaders in the Soviet Union.

Making illegal aliens into legal voters illegally. And, recently in 2018, San Francisco changed its election laws for school board elections to allow non-citizens to vote, including *illegal aliens*.[421]

Off cycle school board elections favor unions. Sometimes interest groups take actions that are unethical though not criminal. One such tactic is lobbying state lawmakers or local lawmakers to schedule special elections on school matters to ensure they are held on *off cycle* dates different from the dates for general elections. This has been a favorite tactic of teachers unions and they have been quite successful in arranging election calendars to their advantage.[422] Policies friendly to such unions are more frequently enacted with such arrangements when more pro-union school board members get elected than would be the case in *on cycle* elections.

In jurisdictions where there are sufficient politically active opponents of the teachers union it is indeed possible to defeat their candidates—even in an off-cycle election. This happened in the Jersey City, New Jersey school board election in 1998. Volunteers supportive of its Republican Mayor, Bret Schundler, flooded nearly every precinct with a pro-Schundler slate of candidates. The result was victory for all four of these candidates. For the next two years the school district formulated and enacted policies friendly towards the Republican side, including the licensing of at least one new charter school. Then came the year 2000. The Schundler forces, being distracted by other matters, did not make an energetic effort in the school board elections of that year. The result: All four of the teachers union supported candidates won.

> This author was one of the volunteers in the 1998 Jersey City school board election. I visited the residence of every voter in the precinct where I resided. I either spoke to each voter or left a handwritten note advocating the pro-Schundler candidates. Result: In my precinct every one of the four pro-Schundler candidates received the most votes.

We will have more to say about the constitutional violations implicit in non-partisan school board elections in the next section.

MISBEHAVIOR IN STATE EDUCATION DEPARTMENTS

At the statewide level there are two kinds of institutions that affect K-12 education:

- The state government consisting of the legislature, the governor, and the state courts.

- The state education department that often operates almost independently of the state's government.

Here we focus on the state education departments where most of the policies and regulations affecting K-12 education are made. In the next section we will discuss the more remote though significant roles played by elected officials in the state governments.

State education department officials' theft of government funds.

There are numerous federal grant programs operated by the U.S. Department of Education that distribute funds to state education departments for specified purposes. Sometimes the state level recipients and managers of those monies violate the provisions of one or more programs under which funds are obtained. When the conduct is sufficiently egregious, federal prosecutions have been undertaken. Sometimes state level officials are tried and convicted for any crimes they have committed. Sometimes the conduct does not warrant criminal prosecution, but instead civil action is taken in which the federal authorities sue the state's education department.

Stealing grant monies under false representations. One such civil action involved the Maine Department of Education. They were sued for submitting false information to the federal department about its disbursements of funds for the Migrant Education Program. That program assists migratory children residing within the state. Maine was accused that it

> . . . falsely represented the number of eligible migratory children residing within the state for fiscal years 2002, 2003, and 2004.

These misrepresentations resulted in improper disbursements to Maine well in excess of a million dollars. In the settlement of this lawsuit the Maine Department of Education agreed to pay $1.5 million to the U.S. Department of Education.[423]

Another Migrant Education Program case involved the U.S. Territory of Puerto Rico. The Puerto Rico Department of Education falsely asserted that it had eligible migrant children residing there when, in fact, there were none. As with Maine there were no prosecutions, but in this civil case the settlement amount exceeded $19 million.[424]

State education official stole and then laundered public funds to use in her gubernatorial campaign. Sometimes the crook runs the operation. This was the case for Linda Schrenko, who was the Georgia School Superintendent in 2002 when she decided to run for governor on the Republican ticket. Her campaign was not well-funded, so she decided to *loot* her own department's accounts of federal grant monies for over a half million dollars. She then laundered the money through fake contractors to enable its use in her campaign. Which she lost.

She still had a few ill-gotten dollars left after her defeat. $9,300 of them were sufficient to pay for a face-lift she underwent—presumably to pretty herself for her inevitable trial. At the trial she and two co-defendants were found guilty. Her punishment: Eight years in federal prison and restitution of over $400 thousand dollars.[425]

Needless to say, when government employees steal education funds from the government they are reducing the monies that can be used for legitimate educational purposes. In a real sense, she stole the money from children.

Any textbook fraud at state level?

As in the case of district level textbook improprieties we were unable to find much wrongdoing among the 20 states that select textbooks at the statewide level. But we did find a few snippets of information suggesting the use of low value bribes were involved in textbook selection in California, which is one of those twenty states employing a statewide system and mandate.

As we have already discussed, Nobel Prize winner Richard Feynman had a view on this at the district level. He is celebrated not only for his brilliance as a physicist who discovered and explained quantum electrodynamics. He is also famous for his no-nonsense blunt approach to other problems he has encountered, such as his Congressional public hearing explanation about the cause of the space shuttle Challenger disaster.

As we related in the previous section, in 1964 Feynman was invited to join the California statewide mathematics textbook selection committee. In one instance the committee was asked to review a three-volume mathematics textbook series despite the fact that the publisher provided only the 1st and 3rd volumes for their review. Some members of the committee were so incompetent or so swayed by publisher inducements that they gave comments on the missing 2nd volume, which was missing because the publisher had not finished it in time for the committee's review. Though pressured to do so, Feynman refused to rate the missing book.[426]

As to the tactics of the publishers, Feynman said,

> The way they competed was to impress members of the curriculum commission . . .

suggesting that gifts of food, "monogrammed briefcases," and travel expenses to publisher seminars were among the inducements or bribes provided to them.[427]

Another way to look at this lack of reporting in this area is to ask how newsworthy is a low dollar value inducement that seems to be typical in this area compared to other dealings where improper payments range upwards of $1,000? It seems that publishers provide all kinds of low value gifts to these decision makers, but rarely anything that registers much shock. Surely this conduct is unethical, unprofessional, and very likely illegal. Yet, of the few who are aware of this corruption not many take the responsibility of seeking enforcement of these standards and laws. It has been a sleazy business that the educators seemingly regard as a standard and traditional practice.

A somewhat cynical perspective on this holds that the very analysts who might consider writing something about textbook selection improprieties would more often be sympathetic to the publisher-author relationship and ignore the idea that inducements from publishers is anything improper. These analysts might resist biting the hands that could someday be feeding them with royalties, advances, and publicity. So, maybe, it is plausible that they'd avoid putting their criticisms in writing.

State level curriculum improprieties

To discuss issues involving statewide curricula we need to have a definition of it. Consider these alternatives:

- On one extreme, the most detailed, the curricula could be simply the content of official textbooks and other official documents pertaining to the courses required in the K-12 sequence of grade levels.

- At a still high level of specificity the curriculum would be defined by lists of learning concepts together with corresponding questions and answers pertaining to those learning concepts. In this kind of arrangement, the course testing would be based on these questions and answers. Given the presumed very large number of learning concepts, any given test would almost certainly use a subset of these questions probably based on a random sampling of thereof.

- At a medium level of specificity, the curriculum would consist of a longer list of topics and subtopics to be mastered. It might include lists of textbooks and other documents containing that curricular content.

- At the other extreme, the least detailed, it could list topics that require some level of mastery within the courses covering that same K-12 sequence.

We presume there could be other alternative concepts of what constitutes a curriculum? With respect to the second bulleted item, we note that the for-profit DeVry University used a curriculum definition like this in its instructional programs for students of finance. This author once enrolled in one of their courses in preparation for the designation of Certified Financial Analyst (CFA). Because of the quite explicit relationship between the learning concepts and the test questions it was quite straightforward to study for the examinations. The author has included a similar curriculum/ testing system in his business plan for Stellar Schools—described in more detail in Chapter 17.

As the foregoing discussions in this book have made clear, we believe that curricula should not be fully defined at the statewide level. We do support the concept of certain curricular minimums that would consist of learning items common to nearly all textbooks in the various subjects. We believe that districts and individual schools should be able to have some discretion in the choice of additional learning items where those choices would be made locally by the governing bodies that control those schools.

Unfortunately, most official curricula are set at the state level in most states. Let's consider some of the improprieties in such arrangements:

Most curricula slant to the political left. We already made note of Diane Ravitch's observation that most history textbooks treat Democrats relatively kindly compared to their harsher treatment of Republicans.[428] Let's now look at political correctness run amok and consider how a major standardized testing company, Riverside Publishing, has killed off multiple curricular knowledge items from its tests in its efforts to be seen as a fair player that offends no one. Perhaps, they offend no one except the educators who set the standards that are subsequently *vandalized* by the testing firm. But those educators seem to be asleep.

Riverside Publishing is the enterprise responsible for one of the most commonly used standardized tests: *The Iowa Test of Basic Skills*, which is used in dozens of states as one of the official tests assessing student knowledge and skills. To gain and/or maintain market share in the standardized testing marketplace of K-12 education, it appears that Riverside constrained its tests to be minimally offensive to its customers in various public and private education systems. They formulated three *controversial* kinds of fairness that must be maintained in the production and use of their tests:

Representational fairness. According to Ravitch the folks at Riverside constrain its tests in such a way that no group will be overrepresented or underrepresented. Each demographic group will be included in proportion to their numbers in the American population. The usual demographic groups are not enough so they invent new ones such as geographic groups defined by regions within the country. In theory *representational fairness* has no political bias to the left or right. But in practice it is the left that is mostly behind this kind of fairness.[429]

Language usage fairness. What words may appear in the tests? Answer: Only words that don't offend certain *favored* demographics. For example, words, in their thinking, must be gender neutral. They forget the fact that the word *man* has two definitions, one of which is gender neutral as in mankind. Oh, don't say *mankind*. Instead, please use *human race*. We expect that replacement to be vulnerable to objection anytime now because it still has *man* in it. A third synonymous phrase to be used could be *homo sapiens*. How dare you say *homo!* These strange politically correct extremists want to obliterate words and phrases from the classics of literature and from historical documents if they don't conform to new politically correct usages. How will they be able to use famous somewhat off color quotations of Harry Truman or Donald Trump?[430]

Stereotyping fairness. Here the descriptive words characterizing a demographic may not show the typical or common attributes of that group. Thus, women should not be shown as mothers. And surely not as homemakers, nurses or school teachers. White men can't be holders of advanced academic degrees or perhaps even the Nobel prizes. This gets pretty silly. Prostitutes can't be women. Convicts can't be men. Garbage handlers must be women. The Radio City Rockettes must be men. That could dent ticket sales at Radio City?[431]

When fairness is unfair. The word *fairness* seems to be misused by this ITBS testing system operated by Riverside Publishing. For the three just listed kinds of fairness promoted by Riverside we can say that

- The very idea of numerical quotas as implied by their criterion of *representational fairness* is one of many conceptions held by politically correct left-leaning stake-holders. We'd ask this: Shouldn't the quota of knowledge items tested by ITBS be proportional to their importance in developing the academic standards? Or have the standards been similarly distorted to match the politically correct concept of fairness? Notice that subject area experts have not been explicitly mentioned in the development of fairness constraints. This fits the plausible comment from Diane Ravitch that subject experts rarely author textbooks. Instead publishers produce the textbooks and then look for a willing stand-in author. Tamim Ansary was a newly hired editor at a K-12 oriented publishing house and thought that he would be working with subject expert authors in the development of textbooks. His expectations were dashed when he overheard his manager complain,

  The books are done, and we still don't have an author! I *must* sign someone today![432]

  This is inconsistent with the desired academic integrity of any subject expert hired to write a textbook. Such an expert would not use the Riverside Publishing guidelines, but rather would use their subject area expertise to determine how much of what information would be included. And, if asked to write something using those politically correct guidelines, the person would probably resist on grounds that it would not be professional. If asked to be a stand-in author, he or she would likely still resist unless the *wages of sin* were sufficiently high. This suggests that the publishers can find such ethically challenged fake authors when they are willing to pay enough, or shall we say, *bribe* enough?

- To censor the words that would appear in the tests, under Riverside's doctrine of *language usage fairness* makes very little sense unless equally well-defined synonyms exist as replacements. Reckless substitution of new words with different meanings is not a fair practice, contrary to their claims. Rather it is a form of academic misconduct.

- Perhaps the silliest guideline is that of *stereotyping fairness.* We can shorten this descriptor to *stereo fairness.* If you have a statistics background, let's say even a rudimentary understanding of it, you will conclude that most historic events do include stereotypical participants. That's because stereotypes are generated by looking at behaviors of people within a group. There are unwanted consequences if the discussion of stereotypes is forbidden. It means either that such events will go unchronicled or that these events will have some fictions applied to ensure compliance with stereotypical fairness. Consider some examples: You can't discuss Einstein with his *stereotypical* male sex and Jewish ethnicity. Nope. But you could have an Alberta Einstein, who is let's say a Presbyterian, who formulated relativity and other theories? Need we say more?

What we find common among these Riverside guidelines for fairness is that they encourage dishonesty. Dishonesty is not a desirable characteristic to have in the tested elements of any curriculum. Neither the political left nor the political right espouses dishonesty in any explicit manner. Yet here we have educators aligned with the political left promoting it—perhaps unwittingly?

Most textbooks involve too many multicultural items and not enough American ones. Closely related to the preceding discussion is a subset of its concern with *representational fairness.* We need not elaborate too much on this except to say that bringing in all kinds of new categories, racial, ethnic, national, sexual, etc., takes up pages in the textbooks which, in turn, requires exclusion of academically valuable content if textbooks are to be kept to a manageable length.

Degradation of curricula through the illegally imposed Common Core State Standards

During the Obama administration (2009–2017) the federal government put considerable pressure on state education departments to subscribe to a new set of academic standards. Officially titled *Common Core State Standards (CCSS)* these new curricular standards and testing systems for them were *sold* as more rigorous than the many individual state's previous standards and testing programs. In reality they have been the opposite: They are *dumbed down* standards in the subjects of reading and mathematics. Recent published performance levels from the *Nation's Report Card* have shown trends of performance in both of these subject areas has now changed from slowly rising to significantly falling. That came after an almost two-decade long interval in which proficiencies in these two subjects were making slow, but significant improvements.[433]

Education officials were evidently not concerned that they were violating laws and treaty obligations, as we discussed in Chapter 11 in the section, *Why Do Progressives Often Lean Subversive*? They knew from experience that few of these requirements were being enforced. In fact, many officials were not aware of these laws.

It appears that there have been no enforcement mechanisms to ensure compliance. Perhaps there are, but they are routinely ignored. Or these were enforced until the imposition of the *Common Core* upon the states? I doubt that there was much enforcement.

Common Core in private schools

We don't have space to explore this sub-topic fully, so we will limit our discussion to just one state, California, and just one type of private school, Christian. So brainwashed are many Californians about *Common Core* that even Christian private schools have adopted these arguably anti-Christian standards. For example, we have these three cases:

- The Roman Catholic private schools under the Diocese of Sacramento, California are using these standards and are doing so despite their secular philosophical alignment.[434]

- A private religious campus in Fresno, California is called the *Fresno Christian Schools*. Though it sounds like a system of schools it is really only one K-12 school comprised of three component schools: Primary, middle, and secondary. Their website shows how they are planning to be *Common Core* compliant while at the same time retaining their Christian worldview.[435]

- Take Trinity Lutheran School in Hawthorne, California. This K-8 school wants to have it both ways: It will be applying

  - the principles of Christian faith. . . [as] the foundation for all instruction.

  while simultaneously claiming that

  - The *Common Core State Standards* (CCSS) provide a practical way to prepare children for the challenges of a constantly changing world . . .[436]

It seems that these Lutherans are engaged in wishful thinking if they are concluding that two inconsistent philosophical foundations—one Christian and the other secular—can coexist in the same curriculum. Here is one of many simple contradictions between the two:

- The Christian philosophical approach would have children learn new subjects as soon as they are ready for them. Many Christian schools teach algebra in grade eight.

- In contrast, *Common Core* delays the onset of algebra by one year to grade nine.

These Lutherans seem to have a choice to make: Are they Christians teaching algebra in grade eight or are they secular folks teaching it in grade nine? There are many other contradictions between the secular and Christian approaches in this Lutheran *have it both ways* curriculum.

For a more detailed analysis let's consider a California private Christian school that published its use of and relationships to the *Common Core*. In Sacramento not only are its Catholic schools following the *Common Core* standards, as we noted above, but also there is at least one Protestant Christian school in Sacramento using them. This K-12 school is Capital Christian School. As its website's section on *Common Core State Standards* (CCSS) indicates, they are using them and it also suggests that they are using them with some tribulation. A careful parsing of his comments on CCSS shows that Capital Christian's superintendent, Samuel Gordon, does not have a good understanding of these inferior academic standards. Let's take his comments one at a time:

- The CCSS are content standards of learning, not curriculum requirements.

  Wrong. While the CCSS are not a detailed set of curriculum items, they are a list of constraints on the curriculum. For example, they specify less reading of fiction. They bring algebra in a year later.

- The primary areas of emphasis in the English language arts include a heavy focus on reading increasingly more complex text and reading an increasing amount of non-fiction versus fiction.

  Yes, but a Christian centered curriculum should not sacrifice the reading of the classics of literature on the altar of non-fiction. Surely, a student's vocabulary is negatively affected by this reduction.

- The CCSS emphasize critical thinking skills over memorization of facts in both disciplines (English language arts and mathematics).

Wrong About critical thinking skills: The authors of CCSS are ignorant of what *critical thinking* skills really are. They really consist of knowing the principles of logic, mathematics, and science, and how they apply to different fields of study. And stupefyingly Wrong about the memorization of facts: Knowing facts is the basis of inductive reasoning, which is a fundamental component of any scientific approach to learning. As St. Bernard said on church matters, "the road to Hell is paved with good intentions," one wonders if that applies here?[437]

• We are free to determine all books, pieces of literature, and textbooks that support our curriculum as we approach these standards of learning.

> Wrong. If Capital Christian School has reading lists that don't conform to the ratios of non-fiction to fiction indicated by CCSS, they will be operating outside of those standards. It is true that they could have some freedom in choosing the classics of literature, but they'd have a shorter list to choose from. So, if their old curriculum had their students studying two plays by William Shakespeare, then their new curriculum might reduce that to one play so as to accommodate the requirement that they read more non-fiction. (Well, maybe they could read the Bible more often if it is deemed non-fiction, which most Christians would support.)

• The College Board has begun to adjust their standardized tests (SAT, AP) to CCSS.[438]

> Not quite. The verb *adjust* implies that the College Board operates independently of CCSS. In reality the College Board is managed by David Coleman who is the same person who co-authored the CCSS! If he and his associates generated substandard academic standards, as we believe the CCSS are, then adjusting the time-honored SAT and AP to CCSS represents a degradation of the testing of these traditional standards. The essential truth of this is that CCSS and its authors are engaged in unintended *academic vandalism*. But given their politically correct left-wing oriented biases, they probably don't understand how reckless their leadership has been.

Some of the foregoing discussion about Common Core could also logically have been included in the next section, *Wrongful Federal Intrusions*. We decided to keep it here under *Misbehavior in State Education Departments* because the harm was being done within the various states. Sometimes the responsible party was within the state, sometimes it was a private company operating nationally, and sometimes it was the federal government illegally intervening in a state's business.

STATE LEVEL GOVERNMENT DIFFICULTIES

The just discussed state departments of education are the subordinate institutions at the state governmental level that are responsible for the administration of K-12 education through out a state. Typically, the state's education department is somewhat independent of the state government given the format under which they were established by the elected officials of the state's government.

So, what are the other kinds of misbehavior that occur at the state level that involve the elected state government's officials. How much can be blamed on the governor? The legislature? The state courts? In most states we observe a great deal of centralization in the administration of K-12 schooling. The political argument for greater amounts of state control is often that of efficiency. Do it once for the state and then localities will not need to needlessly duplicate the state action. Do it at the state level to ensure fairness and equal treatment among the regions and various demographics with the state.

However, the uniformity of centralization has its drawbacks. It removes local control. It reduces the influence of parents in each community and in each school. It shackles local democracy to the interests of democratic control at the state level. It removes the incentives coming from competition among the localities within a state. It particularly saddles local schools with textbooks that local officials often find objectionable. It further diminishes the influence parents have in directing the education of their children, and in that context violates the *UN Declaration of Human Rights*—as we have reiterated more than once in this book. Surely, K-12 education within a state can benefit from some centralization, but we think there is far too much of it. We can think of two areas where the state government could impose its will on the state's education department and upon the K-12 schools within its boundaries:

- Minimal academic content standards in the various subject areas limited to let's say a 50% rule in which those minimum standards would comprise no more than 50% of the subject matter.

- The other academic content standards would make up more than 50% of the subject matter and that would be determined by local school districts or even the individual schools.

How an incompetent or biased attorney general can harm for-profit schools

Many bureaucrats have been educated or shall we say *brainwashed* into thinking that for-profit schools are less ethical and less law abiding than their non-profit or government owned counterparts. Using their mistaken understanding of the motives and behavior of commercial operators of education they put pressure on them and their customers in various ways.

As an example of this, consider the *For Profit School Advisory* issued by the Massachusetts Attorney General, Maura Healy, in late 2017. It was aimed at post-secondary education, but you can imagine her advice would caution parents looking for a profit-making school in the K-12 years as well. Her advisory is effectively an advertising poster for public education. The advisory states,

> Public colleges and universities are usually the most affordable higher edu-cation options, especially when compared to for-profit schools. In recent years, many for-profit schools have been *accused of overcharging* students for low-quality educational services and for *engaging in deceptive and aggressive recruitment practices.*[439]

How can an official of the court system publicly discuss those who are "accused of overcharging" when the inference is that these schools have not yet been convicted of this illegal practice? If she had statistics of convictions for such offenses, and could show wrongdoing is more likely at for-profits than in other institutions, then an ad-visory like this would be warranted. But without that, she is using the power of the state to *slander* for-profit schools and for that she should be held to account in a civil court of law.

Isn't it ironic that she is the one "engaging in deceptive and aggressive . . . prac-tices" in her efforts to reduce the patronage of what seem to be perfectly honorable for-profit institutions. Her tactic may also involve an anti-competitive activity that constitutes a federal law violation?

How non-partisan elections are really partisan. So says George Orwell?

Based on the characterization of the National Education Association being a very powerful political organization, it seems evident that the *Orwellian* non-partisan elec-tions for school boards are not really non-partisan. Rather they are partisan with ef-fectively a new political *party*: The NEA Party. And how nice that they actually outlaw the Democrats and Republicans from any formal participation in school elections!

As we wrote this, we were continuing to seek out the opinions and writings of experts on the legal and political sides of these non-partisan elections. One reference explored the effects of partisan versus non-partisan elections in this area, but did not address the harm done to the top two political parties nor whether the NEA is itself, in all but name, a political party.[440]

Many states also use non-partisan elections for the election of judges. Recent appellate court decisions may be starting a trend of ruling aspects of such elections as unconstitutional, based on the 1st Amendment free speech rights.[441]

A number of the arguments against non-partisan elections include constitutional objections. That's right, we believe they are unconstitutional because they deprive the familiar political parties their rights to free speech. Other objections contend that the

NEA's participation in collective bargaining is also in violation of state constitutions because the NEA, thereby has *cameral* power, but was not established as a *cameral* player in the language of those constitutions. Oak Norton, of Utahans Against *Common Core*, explained it this way:

> . . . it is difficult to overcome the power of *the single education party* which runs their candidates under the radar by endorsing through their network individuals for office, whereas there is no competing party to challenge them . . . The only organizations large enough to challenge the status quo are the political parties.

A careful parsing of Norton's article shows that his reference to "the single education party" he is referring to the Utah education establishment which is led by the NEA affiliate Utah Education Association (UEA). Thus, the UEA is in effect a political party, but escapes legal scrutiny by its pretense that it is a non-political educational association of politically neutral members.[442] So, Utah violates the *U.S. Constitution* by denying the political parties their free speech. Many if not most states with non-partisan school elections are likewise in violation. Now, who is the Orwellian political party playing its roles in non-partisan do-gooder clothing? It is the UEA, the Utah affiliate of the NEA. They are allowed to play politics while the real political parties, Democrat and Republican, are forbidden to do so there and in most states. Where is the outrage?

WRONGFUL FEDERAL INTRUSIONS

The proper role of the United States federal government is set forth in the *U.S. Constitution*. But as most historians and analysts know, there are many activities of our federal government that exceed these roles. As we have mentioned earlier in this chapter, the *10th Amendment* to the *Constitution* explicitly denies the federal government from playing roles in any other areas except those enumerated in the *Constitution*. Thus, interventions in the field of education are not allowed—they are unconstitutional.

And yet we have had a U.S. Department of Education in operation since the late 1970s. Most of its activities are in violation of the *10th Amendment*, and yet it blithely goes about its clearly unlawful activities. There is one area, however, where some of its activities arguably fall within the purview of the *Constitution*: Testing as in the *Nation's Report Card*. It can be argued that the *Weights and Measures Clause* could be used to justify this particular activity.

Federal imposition of Common Core State Standard was illegal and unconstitutional

We discussed some of this in the previous section. Here we focus on the mostly illegal tactics used by political leaders at the federal level.

The *Race to the Top* (RTT) sounds good. Competition often has this aspect: That the competitors will improve their offerings as the result of healthy competition. But what was the *Race to the Top*?

An education department slush fund was created by the *American Recovery and Reinvestment Act of February 2009*. Even if it was not illegal it would be unwise to increase the funding of an arguably unconstitutional federal department. With this loose money the Education Department funded its *RTT* competition that awarded extra grants to states that would impose the *Common Core* dictates on the children of their jurisdictions. Additionally, the states were given waivers from provisions of the *No Child Left Behind* act, passed under the previous administration. U.S. Senators Rubio and Alexander were among many others who commented that the granting of waivers was illegal.[443]

Many previously mandatory provisions of the *No Child Left Behind Act* were made optional by *RTT*. The Supplemental Education Services (SES) program was one of them. If the Ed Department liked your state education department, it would issue waivers allowing the state to ignore those mandatory provisions. As the waivers to SES became more and more numerous, more and more tutoring businesses were forced to close. The Education Industry Association (EIA), to which this author belonged, became defunct circa 2015. One theory argues that its closure was caused by losing its many SES members. If so, we can blame the *RTT* program's illegal excesses and waivers for that demise.

Most K-12 school systems ignore parents' rights under the United Nations Declaration of Human Rights

In this book, we have twice already quoted the pertinent line from this *United Nations Declaration* as it pertains to parental rights in the education of their children. It is so important that we say it again here:

> Parents have a prior right to choose the kind of education that shall be given to their children.[444]

As we have reiterated before, this *Declaration* is part of a treaty ratified by the United States in 1948, and as such is an enforceable law within the country. Lots of luck with that!

Why the representatives in Washington have not honored their responsibility to craft legislation enforcing this law is obviously political, but it also seems illegal. Is not the federal government bound by this treaty? This leads us into a legal thicket. The U.S. Constitution through its 10th Amendment gives no role for the federal government in the field of education. Constitutional scholars mostly agree that the Constitution takes precedence over *treaty* law.

But are the individual states bound by the treaty law? This is an unresolved question. We think that states can use this *treaty* as an argument for

> . . . giving parents the right to choose the kind of education that shall be given to their children.

That's what the *Declaration's Article 26* says. As this author knows, this language from the treaty has been routinely used by supporters of school vouchers to garner support for laws that would give parents those rights. He was one of the advocates, doing just that, in the California voucher campaigns of 1993 and 2000.

There is great wisdom in giving parents this choice. It empowers the education marketplace that under the normal laws of free market economics should foster improving products and services in this field. This is the essence of this book's message that can be stated as:

> *Fix the K-12 marketplace, and the desired improvements will ensue.*

As we go along this conclusion will be reiterated until nausea sets in.

CONTENT PROVIDER MALPRACTICE

Diane Ravitch describes a form of corruption in the textbook publishing industry. It is the practice of publishing quotes and other information without any citation given for the sources. It teaches students to engage in this form of academic dishonesty too. She says,

> Failing to cite sources is bad scholarship. Textbooks that indulge in this practice encourage their students to do the same. This is a corrupting lesson that directly contradicts one of the most important tenets in the study of history, which is that historians must base their conclusions on evidence that is available for review by others. Lapses in the transparency of a writer's source are often a sign of distortion or *fictionalization* in the writing.[445]

Let's remind the reader that *fictionalization* is often a euphemism for lying. It is, on its face, a corrupt practice. Anyone doing this in the natural sciences, such as the author's former field of physics, would soon be fired for this kind of misbehavior.

HOMESCHOOLING SCANDALS ARE RARE

About the only kind of homeschooling scandal we could find involved parents who were using what some saw as controversial curricula in the instruction of their children. Sometimes, critics of types of homeschooling they don't like see it almost as a form of child abuse? Some of these forms of homeschooling curricula are said to put too much emphasis on patriarchy that could amount to pushing a sexist agenda?[446]

Controversy over curricular standards is healthy, if not carried too far. Still, there is a risk of indoctrination that goes too far as in cases where the standards infringe on the legal rights of others.

In almost all homeschooling situations, the parents love for their children provide a very strong incentive against any unethical behavior. This is consistent with the very high test scores of homeschooled children. Only students in for-profit schools seem to do better. We will have more on this in Chapter 17.

This author has observed homeschooling in action within his own family. Of his and his wife's 13 grandchildren, all 13 are (at the time of this writing) PK-12 students and 4 of them are currently being homeschooled. Those four participate in a classical Christian curriculum—known in some circles as the Trivium.[447] Theirs is provided by Classical Conversations™, a for-profit homeschooling instructional program and service, headquartered in North Carolina. The four students are instructed at home four days per week, and in rented classrooms used for plenary sessions one day per week. I once attended the plenary session for pupils at the 8th grade level. Among their subjects: Latin. I actually watched students enjoy the declensions of Latin that their teacher had structured into a classroom game.

Nothing I saw had even a hint of impropriety. I mean when the room is full of parents and children there is not going to be much scandalous activity.

VOUCHER FRAUD

It is common for advocates of government operated services to assert that their private competitors are more susceptible to corruption, fraud, and scandal than their own bureaucratic systems that in theory have been designed to thwart such illegal activities. On the other side, advocates of private services make arguments that market forces will tend to deter corruption when they are the providers of them. Who is right?

One way to answer this question is to consider the general principle that free market competition among private enterprises results in a more efficient and cost-effective arrangement of products and services than the alternative of having a government bureaucracy provide them. Usually what is more efficient is less corrupt because corruption drains funds into unproductive and unprofitable uses. That can lead to insolvency and closure.

Another way to answer this question is to consider various cases. Some years ago, Neal McCluskey, of the Cato Institute, published an article examining the question about which system is more corrupt. He acknowledges that both systems can have scandals, but then claimed that the private providers are less corrupt.[448]

He considered Florida's various school choice programs that were in effect in the early 2000s and compared their problems with corruption to those in Florida's public schools systems.

- In reviewing the different instances of voucher fraud, he noted three cases that were essentially that of the embezzlement of voucher funds. He also made reference to the firing of a whistle blower in the State Education department who was complaining about fraudulent documents used to qualify private schools as eligible for voucher students.[449]

- McCluskey then turned to list some scandals in Florida's public schools. He cited cases in which school board members accepted kickbacks in return for favorable treatment of the vendors paying the bribes. The persecution of whistle blowers again raised its ugly head within the public systems. Overly honest administrators were sometimes transferred into inferior positions to remove them from their dutiful scrutinization of improper activities of subordinates. Unionized employees within the public school systems pose a variety of problems that many see as inefficient though not corrupt. Others regard them as corrupt.[450]

As he goes on to conclude, the choices among private schools provide a dynamic in which poorly performing schools will fail as businesses while the good performers will survive and be profitable. That is quite different than the situations in which public schools that perform poorly see their funding levels increased in the unlikely hopes that such investment will improve their performance to acceptable levels.

Finally, a point that we repeat again: Public schools do not conform to the United Nations treaty that gives parents the right to direct their children's education.[451] That is a form of illegal activity that has unfortunately never been codified in our laws concerning education. That is in contrast to the fact that most European nations have legislated varying degrees of parental choices in education—often through voucher like vehicles. We conclude from that, that many of them have made some efforts to conform to this UN treaty. Yet here in the United States it's just another silent scandal and an unwelcome burden on the parents.

POLITICAL ACTIONS THAT HINDER REFORMS

We see two kinds of motivations among those opposing the reforms that would give parents more choices in the education of their children:

- *Philosophical Motivations.* Believers in various schooling formats of the progressive educationists often support the compulsory indoctrination of all American school children in the nostrums they support—typically of the political left. They often believe that their theories of multiculturalism, of gender politics, of economic classes, and of Secular Humanism should be imposed on most students. When they *add* content standards to accommodate these *new subjects*, it necessarily leads to the *subtraction* of more traditional content standards. This generally means that children are taught significantly less about American culture and history.

- *Pecuniary Motivations.* Workers in the public systems have a financial interest in the salaries, pensions, and benefits they are paid that, in turn, depend on those systems having sufficient enrollment to generate the taxpayer funded revenues to sustain those expenditures. Unionized government employees within the public system fear competition from private schools receiving voucher funding and from non-unionized charter schools. When that happens, these unions suffer reduced dues, and that affects their political powers. It follows that their actions to increase union power will almost certainly reduce the options for parents seeking schooling for their children in non-unionized environments. This will reduce the availability of charter schools and of private schools.

Sometimes both of these kinds of incentives are in play.

How Michigan tempered and kept union power within the state constitution.

The state of Michigan provides good examples of some of these dynamics that played out in the 1990s.

There, under Republican Governor John Engler, a number of new laws were passed in the 1990s that had the effect of increasing democratic control (consistent with the state's constitution) that enabled state legislators to do the following:

- Ended teachers unions right to strike.
- Ended union bargaining over group insurance benefits.
- Ended union bargaining over composition of site-based decision making bodies.
- Ended union bargaining over the establishment locally of charter schools.
- Ended union bargaining over outsourcing non-instructional services.
- Ended union bargaining over new experimental or pilot instructional programs.[452]

And when bargaining would reach an impasse this legislation allowed the local school boards, in each case, to act unilaterally to impose their *last best offer* on the union.

How union contracts can subvert state constitutions

We just mentioned "the state's constitution" because we believe government employee unions generally add a new branch of decision making to government organizations that were not in the founding documents that established those organizations. To make such a change without following the constitutionally mandated procedures for amending those founding documents implies that such government employee unions are unconstitutional, particularly if they have the right to strike or otherwise interfere with constitutional government operations. Again, we use the terminology of *subversion* to represent the fact that such actions undermine the constitutional order that was established legally.

If this seems a stretch, consider what two well-known left-leaning government leaders have had to say about this in the past.

- During the 1950s Frank Zeidler was the socialist mayor of Milwaukee, Wisconsin. He later commented that he opposed collective bargaining of public sector employees if it included their right to strike. About government unions he said that they

> can mean considerable loss of control over the budget and hence over tax rates.[453]

- The longest serving President of the United States, Franklin Roosevelt, also opposed government employee unions. Writing to the National Federation of Federal Employees, he argued against any decision the Federation might take to establish collective bargaining because it would contradict the established Government structure. In an August 1937 letter to the Federation he said,

> All Government employees should realize that the process of collective bargaining, as usually understood, cannot be transplanted into the public service. It has its distinct and insurmountable limitations when applied to public personnel management. The very nature and purposes of Government make it impossible for administrative officials to represent fully or to bind the employer in mutual discussions with Government employee organizations. The employer is the whole people, who speak by means of laws enacted by their representatives in Congress. Accordingly, administrative officials and employees alike are governed and guided, and in many instances restricted, by laws which establish policies, procedures, or rules in personnel matters.[454]

Both Zeidler and Roosevelt were saying that administrators should manage government organizations without the interference of an unconstitutional partner. When employees, through union contracts, share in that management they are usurping or subverting democratic control of the government. The metaphor that may be apt is,

> The cows are running the farm.

There is another avenue through which government employee organizations of all types, including unions, influence government policy: Political action. Teachers unions, in almost every state, have supported the certification of teachers based on progressive pedagogical theories rather than on more traditional expertise in the subject areas to be taught. This brings us to the subject of *alternative certification*, and we discuss it next.

Improper certification requirements for K-12 teachers.

In Chapter 11, under the section, *The Passage to Multicultural Perdition*, we touched upon how progressive educationists have dominated the certification policies regarding the employment of K-12 teachers. How did they achieve that stranglehold on the profession that had the effect of making the teaching profession heavily featherbedded? This clearly means that inferior instructors have been routinely hired in preference to subject area experts under the scientifically bogus claims of *educationists* that knowing how to teach is more important than knowing what to teach.

For most aspiring teachers in public K-12 education almost all stakeholders agree that the college education of those future teachers should do at least these two things:

- Acquire mastery of the subject content to be taught.

- Learn effective pedagogical techniques for transmitting the subject content knowledge to students.

Unfortunately, most teachers come up short on these capabilities. The teacher preparation programs offered by most American colleges and universities do not meet these goals. Why not?

Regarding subject mastery. Most teacher training programs emphasize teaching techniques and classroom management skills, while placing much less priority on giving future teachers the subject mastery levels sufficient to impart that subject information. Many experts on K-12 instruction believe that future teachers should earn academic degrees in the subjects they will teach—particularly at the high school level. As a secondary priority these experts also want future teachers skilled in classroom management and in instructional methods.

Since the 1980s a number of programs have been launched to address the subject knowledge deficits of many teachers. According to a 2007 study by the Fordham Institute several dozen *Alternative Certification* programs around the United States have rarely fulfilled their promises of bringing the skill levels of future teachers to be comparable to a four-year college degree in the subject(s) they will teach.[455]

One success in this area, however, was in New Jersey, where its former education commissioner devised the well-regarded *Provisional Teacher Program*. The results were good, and a Fordham Foundation report concluded that

> New Jersey's alternative certification program has markedly expanded the quality, diversity, and size of the state's teacher candidate pool.[456]

Many other alternative certification programs were established in other states, but most of them did not make significant changes to their teacher training programs. They often used new labels to give the appearance of reform when the substance of their improvements was weak or even absent.

Regarding pedagogical techniques. The nostrums of progressive education are widely applied in the instructional techniques used to impart knowledge despite the fact that research has repeatedly shown the superiority of more traditional techniques, such as *direct instruction.*

Extensive research into the benefits of direct instruction has shown its clear superiority to other learning formats. An extensive review of research studies into Direct Instruction (DI) by the Education Consumers Foundation found most uses of the technique to be beneficial. In that review there were two reports that discounted Direct Instruction. Upon closer inspection one of these reports did not contradict the successes of DI, but had a bizarre conclusion that it led children into juvenile delinquency![457] The other cited critical study had so many obvious deficiencies in the manner by which the study was conducted that no honest observer would give it any serious attention. One of those deficiencies was this: Its principal investigator resigned from the project midway through the work.

Another briefing from the *Education Consumers Foundation* (ECF) put the blame for many failing schools not on the teachers directly, but on the programs that train them. Mimicing Shakespeare it said

> The fault, dear Brutus, is not in the stars, but in our teachers' colleges.[458]

Among other things, the ECF report went on to say:

- Education professors simply disagree with the public and with the legislators. They train teachers to put other goals ahead of student achievement.

- Teachers cannot graduate, cannot be certified, and cannot teach unless they agree with their professors and their professors' priorities. The professors believe student attainment of basic academic knowledge and skills is secondary to the enjoyment of learning.

- Everyone agrees that kids should enjoy school—but not at the expense of learning. Many surveys have shown that.

- Sorry, the professors just don't agree. They believe in "learner-centered" education where the teacher "facilitates," and students supposedly learn on their own. They insist that students must explore topics rather than learn directly from their teacher.

Based on these facts and concepts, where are the improprieties leading to this degradation? We just read in the preceding quotation that the

Education professors simply disagree with the public and with the legislators.

The offense here is that of *insubordination*. These teacher colleges *defy* the policies enacted by state level lawmakers. They hide behind a fog of obfuscation in which their political superiors are deceived into thinking all is well. It's the Wizard of Oz routine: *Ignore the teacher college president behind the curtain.*

Improper political headwinds faced by for-profit schools.

There is a popular prejudice among Americans as well as among citizens of many economically developed countries that

> . . . it is wrong to earn a financial profit from educating children.

The folks who hold views like this generally do not see the inconsistency in such a belief. If they were consistent, they would also oppose

> . . . earning a financial profit from the sales of food as in the grocery industry
> or earning a profit from farming as in the agriculture industry.

In comparing these two human activities, which is more important? Being fed or being educated. Both are important, but nutrition is a prerequisite for being educated. We have two comments on this:

> Without nutrition you're dead, but without education you're dumb.

and

> Isn't it better to be fat, dumb, and happy than to be a precocious intellect on
> your death bed.

In reality it is best to be well-nourished and well-educated. It's lunacy to think otherwise.

Eighteenth century Scotsman Adam Smith was both a moral philosopher and is regarded by many as the founder of the academic discipline of modern economics. He put forth the theory that honest business people benefit society indirectly when they act selfishly to profit themselves.

> By directing that industry in such a manner as its produce may be of greatest
> value, he intends only his own gain and he is in this, as in many other cases, led
> by an invisible hand to promote an end which was no part of his intention.[459]

Another way to look at his contention is to realize that when a business is efficient there are two benefits:

- An efficiently run business can charge less for its products and services, and still make a financial profit.

- An efficiently run business benefits its customers who then can pay less for what they want and need.

The first point has the business making a profit of which a fraction is available for investments, and of which another fraction is available for charitable donations. On the second point, the benefits are to the firm's customers who are benefited by the lower cost of the goods and services being sold.

When these concepts are applied to schools, shouldn't the same principles apply? Wouldn't they suggest that businesses should operate schools for financial profit? Wouldn't for-profit schools operate more efficiently than alternative formats—such as non-profit or government schools? The answer is a definite "yes." We will have more to say on this in Chapter 17 in the section, *Astounding Successes of Some For-Profits*.

And could it be possible that a religious leader, in this case a Protestant Christian pastor, wanting to establish a school, would have also established a for-profit school?

All of this happened, and it happened over 130 years ago. The pastor was Reverend Tanios Khalil Saad who was a Protestant pastor in Lebanon. He and English woman Louisa Proctor founded a girls school in Lebanon in 1886: *The International School of Choueifat*. It has been a for-profit school since its inception and is now operated by the for-profit education enterprise SABIS, which is now headquartered in Eden Prairie, Minnesota.

Sounds good, but what is the actual reputation of SABIS? Has its for-profit operational format actually delivered the goods? The World Bank, Lead Education Economist, Harry Patrinos, gave testimony on this in the Foreword of James Tooley's book on SABIS. He summarized by saying,

> The book documents the contributions of the company [SABIS] and shows how a private company contributes to the public good.[460]

SABIS owns and operates schools in approximately 20 countries around the world. It has a solid reputation nearly everywhere it operates; its longevity as a for-profit school owner and operator, now exceeding 120 years, is testament to its quality. We'll encounter SABIS again in Chapter 17 where we will have more to say about its operations in the United States.

Let's take a closer look at some of the harsh rhetoric applied to for-profit K-12 education. Much of the antagonism towards a for-profit education industry is based on sincerely held opinions, and yet are these opinions logical?

Some of the bias against for-profit schools can be characterized as *it's not traditionally done that way*. Non-profit private schools' activities often go unquestioned. But if a for-profit enterprise wants to run a school and do those same things, it is opposed. So, for example, in many states of the United States charter schools are generally required to be operated under charters held by non-profit organizations. Why?

In other situations, the criticisms are based on demonstrably erroneous factors. A study on this was published by the Harvard Business School. They explained that many opponents of for-profit education have wrongly concluded that

> Quality education could only be achieved if it were not-for-profit, because, ostensibly, the profit motive would cause educators to cut corners and sacrifice quality for profit.[461]

But such an explanation does not get high marks. Businesses that would *cut corners* would soon lose customers, and soon enough fail as ongoing concerns. Only the more ethical and competent operators would survive. The good guys would remain as the reliable suppliers of *quality education.*

Most of the objections are driven by hatred of most things capitalistic. Some of this animosity is based on envy in which those of modest means resent others who are better off. Their remedy is often that of what some call *social justice.* They often think that a more powerful government can right this wrong. Historically, communism was based on similar resentments. Their thinking is, let's say, besides the point. More to the point, as James Tooley has discussed is that

> . . . it's crucially important to distinguish intentions (the profit motive) and results: what we should care about is whether the goods get delivered, not the motivation behind those who deliver them.[462]

This leads us to ask, "How is communism involved?" We are not going to imitate the animosity the infamous Joseph McCarthy had for communists in America. Rather, we are going to look at examples from actual communist practices, in the former Soviet Union and in the former communist East Germany to get a better understanding.

SABIS co-founder Ralph Bistany saw a good analogy in the automobile factories in Germany during the Cold War. Reflecting on the facts that East Germany was communist and West Germany was capitalist he observed this:

> Those who built the Trabant in East Germany, they didn't seek to make profits. In West Germany, those who built Mercedes, Audi, Volkswagen—they were all after profits. But does anyone suggest that the Trabant is a better car than a Mercedes? Because the search for profits means that the West Germans had to invest in quality improvements because they were in competition they had to make these improvements while still lowering the price. I don't understand why anyone suggests anything is any different in education.[463]

Similarly, as he suggested, the non-profit, or the communist side in his example, is not interested in quality. In comparison, the for-profit side can survive only if its products and services are of sufficiently high quality to win customers. We are not saying that American educators involved in non-profit schools and in public schools are communists, but we are saying that they think like communists without really noticing the similarities.

> The company name, SABIS, is based on the first two letters of the (one time circa 1957) company's Director General, Leila Saad's last name, and the first three letters of her Assistant Director General, Ralph Bistany's last name. Leila was the daughter-in-law of founder Tanios Saad. This naming occurred much later about 1990.

Near the end of Chapter 6, we encountered Paul Pastorek, the former Louisiana Superintendent of Public Instruction, and his explanation that American public education very closely resembles the government run communist schools of the former Soviet Union. As we noted there, using the label socialist, instead of communist, is probably a better descriptor to explain the attitudes of public educators. It's a better label because it is more inclusive, and yet paints an image of top-down inefficient government administration of K-12 education. Some would call them the *free lunch crowd*. They want the output of education shared, which is fine. They encounter a set of problems when they want the inputs of education optimized, but have no workable plan for doing that. So, they often rely on so-called experts who will craft a top-down, one size fits all, set of inputs and plans for educating K-12 students.

The for-profit strategy allows the marketplace of education to influence the inputs of education. It's a trial by error, choose a winner strategy. It is an evolving course of action in which consumers of education adapt to their perceived benefits of the instructional services, and change their selections as they see fit. Through competition, the for-profit firms jockey for position to provide what the consumers want. As Adam Smith suggested they pursue financial profits that are indirectly triggered by satisfied purchasers of their goods and services. When those consumers are thereby happy it very much looks like the product of enhanced altruism. Why have a socialist theory of altruism when you can allow the capitalist marketplace to engineer it?

Let's now look in somewhat more detail how the alternatives to for-profit education have various kinds of problems due to improper or unwise political and/or governmental interference.

Improper political tactics affecting government run and chartered public schools

Public education, as it is practiced in the United States, has had its critics over the history of our republic—some of whom we have already made mentioned. For example, we discussed some of the reforms introduced by William Shearer in the 1890s in efforts to deal with student retention and pacing issues. Many commentators knew enough about American public education to voice their opinions and proposals, but still had difficulty reaching the ears of those who could actually make significant improvements.

Before we can discuss improper political tactics, we need to know what is proper. In the context of government operated public schools, there must be some kind of democratic control. Public schools are typically under the management of one or more school boards. These boards are made up of elected members. In many states there are school boards at three different levels: District, county, and state. At each of those levels there is an administrative structure that is responsible for managing the educational services pertaining to that level.

In the foregoing discussions of this chapter we have mentioned a number of irregularities, unethical practices, and criminal activities in the management of public schools. To better understand these deviations from what might be regarded as best practices we need to understand what those best practices are. Our reference point for that, discussed earlier in this chapter, are the parental rights stated by the *United Nations Declaration of Human Rights* to the effect that parents have the right to direct the education of their children.

But then you might say,

> The public system gives parents almost no say in what education their children will receive. So, they are denying them that right unless they send their children to a private school or perhaps a public magnet school of their choosing.

Is that correct? Not quite.

In theory, parents have indirect control of public education by the means of the ballot box. When they choose their representatives in state and local government, they are choosing the people who can improve the structure, policies, and freedoms associated with public education and with other activities that impact privately provided K-12 education.

What then could be done by these democratic means to improve K-12 education? What could be done within public education to bring K-12 education options for parents closer to those envisaged in the *UN Declaration*? Here is a list to consider:

- Revamp state and local election laws to conduct all education relevant elections at the regular November general elections. This will reduce gaming the system by special interests associated with public education.

- Establish a statewide system of school vouchers or Education Savings Accounts (ESA) that would enable enrollment at almost any public or private school, and that would help fund homeschooling.

- Establish a statewide system of inter-district public school choice.

- Develop more magnet schools, including charter schools, to widen choices within each district.

- Introduce more curricular variety: Except for minimum state standards, empower individual schools to choose curricula and textbooks.

- At the state level the focus would be on minimum standards, and on the standardized testing related to them.

In subsequent chapters we *shall* consider how many of these together might operate to give parents much more control over their children's education.

Until such reforms can be introduced, these systems will likely remain in *degradation*. Without these kinds of reforms, our public education systems will remain outside of the law. They'll be outlaws given their lack of compliance with the *UN Declaration* on parental rights in education. It is not a stretch to label the public education systems as crooked, given their many illegal behaviors and operations.

We just used the word *degradation*. We could have used the word *sick* or the word *diseased* to represent the legal and ethical problems within K-12 education. Yes, many of these K-12 institutions are indeed the *sick schools* of our title.

SUMMARY OF PART III: 1951—2019

During the 68 years covered in Part III, K-12 schooling was, at best, a sluggish and inefficient economic sector—one that did not want to look at itself in any mirror. In this part of this book we continued describing the history of K-12 education for the more recent decades, but we tried to take a more scientific approach in which we examined various signs of distress in the American *industry* of public and private education.

What doctors of schooling would diagnose and propose for treatment

As any good doctor would do, we looked at this patient's numbers—we looked at its vital signs. From historical trends in SAT scores and more recent trends from the proficiency levels reported by the *Nation's Report Card* we learned that our patient is not well. Not even 40% of public school high school seniors were ever proficient in math and their private school peers couldn't even break the 60% level. In reading, the numbers were, at best, 38% for public school seniors and 54% for their private school counterparts. If we can diagnose this patient with medical terms, we might say that this K-12 patient is to be hospitalized into the intensive care unit in hopes that there are physicians, other than the doctors of education, who will be competent to treat this diseased fellow. These *sick schools* need intensive care.

This patient's economic health and vital signs are not good

Rather than look at this patient through the eyes of an education expert it can be instructive to take his or her economic pulse. Looking at the United States economy over the past decades shows significant growth in economic efficiency in most industries. Overall, for private economic sectors, the U.S. Bureau of Labor Statistics has reported an average five-fold gain in output per worker. That's the average gain. What about the TV industry? We estimate a nearly 200-fold improvement over 70 years based on the author's own family's experience purchasing TV's. In the fields of computing the power of computers has increased by astronomical factors. Desktop computers are over 1000 times more powerful per dollar of expenditure, while supercomputers are over one billion times more powerful than their early versions in the 1960s.

All that is the good news. The same Bureau of Labor Statistics is reporting no improvement at all for K-12 education over the past 24 years. In fact, the labor productivity dropped by 4%! We blame most of this stagnation on the politics of the education establishment that values the status quo to such an extent that little progress is made. Where progress has been seen there is still enough degradation in other quarters to keep the national averages in the *tank*.

Instruction about religion is needed, but how can it be done legally?

We said that public education is flunking religion, but we don't have sufficient information to say that private K-12 education is having that difficulty. That public education has a problem with religion is the result of legal impediments stemming from various Supreme Court decisions about what kinds of government activity can interface with religion. As for public education, the basic legal decisions hold that instruction about religion is allowed, but teaching of dogma is prohibited.

Many secularly oriented observers claim that religious doctrines contradict the theories of science. But on closer inspection, for a number of cases, we have shown their consistency with science. The Big Bang theory of creation is a physics theory developed by a Roman Catholic priest, circa 1930, in an effort to explain the Genesis account of creation. When looked at through the right kind of quantum mechanical lens one can also find consistency between theories of evolution and the creation accounts of Genesis.

Clearly, some understanding of the religions of western civilization is necessary if one is to give a coherent account of the history of the United States.

One possible resolution of the conflict between the religious and the secular can be achieved by teaching religious content part-time and away from the public school campus, possibly like the traditional Catechism format Roman Catholics used to teach their religion after school to public school students.

K-12 private and public schools have made a mess of U.S. history and civics

When one considers the various subject areas of K-12 education, some involve more controversy than others. Mathematics, of all the subjects, probably has the fewest observers who would criticize what should be taught though some disagree on the grade levels where different topics should be covered. Until recently, reading or English language arts was taught by following curricula that were quite uniform from place to place and from private to public schools. Where big trouble sets in is in subjects, like history and civics, that often, by their very nature, must discuss politics.

History instruction in K-12 education has evolved over the past century from a rather traditional patriotic approach to one that involves various politically sensitive theories—typically dominated by the political left. Civics instruction, which is a subset of U.S history, has undergone such significant changes that the curriculum that is typically taught is no longer really civics. Many of the historians and other authors of history curricula are no longer following accepted *scientifically* valid methods to develop the historical record.

Some historians engage in a type of misconduct known as *presentism* in which events in an earlier era are incompetently criticized against mores of our own time. Other historians subscribe to the notions of *multiculturalism* and the statistically bogus concept of *disparate impacts*. They use these ideas to constrain what can be taught in history courses and what can be included in history textbooks. If you bring other cultures into the domains to be studied, the historian faces the choice of greatly expanding the curricular content or of reducing the number of pages that present information about our American culture.

One also observes *subversive* intent in some of the K-12 history curricula. When civics is deliberately omitted or redefined it makes the future U.S. voter less competent at the ballot box. We found that many of the authors of history books are no longer historians, but rather are lower level employees of publishing firms.

While history is not religion, the same wide diversity of views one sees among religions is also a characteristic of history instruction. It argues for different courses for different folks. The *U. N. Declaration of Human Rights* comes into play again. Parents need to have the freedom and the rights to choose how history shall be taught to their children.

Ignorance of the law and ethical principles pervade policies of K-12 education

We finished Part III by considering the legal and ethical practices in K-12 education that operate outside of societal norms. The culpability extends from the children who cheat all the way to the education officials at the federal and state levels who misbehave. Much of the wrongdoing is not seen as such because, after all, it is *traditional*. We attach innocent adjectives and verbs to bad behavior. As in:

> The child did not *flunk* a grade. Rather the child was *socially promoted*.

In some K-12 subsectors there is very little corruption or misbehavior. There is almost none in the homeschooling arenas of education, while in private schools it is a lesser problem than in public schools.

And aren't teachers unions poisoning the soup? Their supposed *right to strike* is unconstitutional in almost every state if you take the time to read the constitutions that established those state governments. President Franklin Roosevelt saw it that way and he did not want government employee unions interfering with the administration of government actions and policies.

Their dominance in almost every state have led to off-cycle scheduling of elections of school boards that have made it easy for them to "manage" the results and effectively control much of the public education bureaucracy therein. The voters be damned.

And do those unions lean leftward? Their influence is not just in protecting their wages and employment. They indirectly dictate curricula, and that almost always leans to the left. Part of that is animosity towards private education and particularly against for-profit players in the K-12 education sector. While no longer involved in flirtations with communism, as some unions were in the first half of the twentieth century, many of their ideas have socialist aspects.

Do they seek highly qualified colleagues in their teaching profession or do they seek believers in their unverified psychological perspectives on education? Following the latter path has led to the inversion of talent in K-12 education where you almost have to prove your incompetence by earning an education degree, generally with a minor in an academic subject. As this author knows, he was never allowed in a regular public school classroom to teach, but did thrive in a private school as a physics and math teacher.

One wonders how the defenders of the public systems would characterize our descriptions of K-12 education, even including the various aspects of private schooling? Would they look at the list of defects, the low ranges of student performance, and the various improprieties we have cited? Would they give the K-12 sector an F? Not at all. They'd apply their tool box of grading on the curve and give themselves, with still some room for improvement, a solid B+. They would be (and are) proud of their work and self-congratulatory with kudos for jobs well done? They are lost and often don't know it.

Good enough for government work, but not good enough for us

If there is a conclusion to this book's Part III it is that most of the problems in K-12 education are in its government school arena. There is too much incompetence in the administration of these schools and there are too many activities that are illegal, unconstitutional, unwise, and academically sloppy. Other than those problems we will quote Alfred E. Neuman, and say,

What, me worry?

The author thinks that most of the remedies for all of the cited problems will come from the marketplace. That marketplace is currently broken. The economic environment for K-12 education needs to be made rational. In the remaining chapters of this book we will write essays of encouragement for the many kinds of stakeholders, and suggest to them what *they have not done* to help and what *they can consider doing* to help K-12 education regain its health in the forthcoming years.

PART IV

How to Fix This Before 2030

Now we look at the more recent period of education reform. We begin that period in the mid-twentieth century because many of the reforms discussed here made their debut as early as the 1950s. In one sense, this period has been revolutionary, but in other senses has been hobbled by various kinds of problems—mostly political. For the years now to be described in Part IV two important areas of development have or should have had a large impact on K-12 education:

- Most important are choice mechanisms: Vouchers, education savings accounts, refundable education tax credits, tuition discounts, public charter schools, and homeschooling arrangements.

- Computer based technology and the Internet: These tools can make K-12 schooling both better and less expensive.

Neither of these two areas of development has thrived although they do survive. Both have been thwarted by political forces aligned with *traditional* modes of delivering K-12 education. Or should we say that they are aligned with corrupt modes of delivering K-12 education? This word *traditional* often has a positive connotation, but in K-12 education it is sometimes synonymous with *corrupt*.

In Part IV we elaborate on the various reform proposals and their implementations. We also elaborate on our discussion of the politics and economics of K-12 education to better understand what has happened and what further remedies could or should be considered. We challenge the various stakeholder groups to fulfill their responsibilities after outlining how they might accomplish them.

The seven chapters of Part IV are entitled as follows:

13. Technology opens new avenues.

14. Post-progressive instructional methodologies.

15. Fixing K-12 economics.

Farther along, as we end this book, we will make the almost trite remark that this is not *rocket science*. But given the author's connections to actual rocket scientists, and his own affiliated roles, he reinforces the conclusion that K-12 education can be made healthy in a decade's time when, in stark contrast, the challenges of space travel will be truly daunting, and will likely take a century or more to overcome.

CHAPTER 13

Technology Opens New Avenues

IN THIS CHAPTER WE discuss three avenues of technology that can be considered for use in K-12 instruction:

- Synchronous use and adaptations of television and other audio/video technologies.

- Asynchronous use and adaptations of television, the Internet, and other audio/video technologies.

- Exploiting artificial intelligence or machine intelligence *if it can be controlled.*

We begin with the synchronous variety for which this author has had first-hand knowledge.

SYNCHRONOUS DISTANCE EDUCATION AFTER 1951

Scholars of education history use a variety of definitions for the term *distance education.*[464] For our purposes we define

> Distance Education as the transmission of educational content to students over geographic distances greater than, let's say, the dimensions of the school campus.

Thus, closed circuit television within a school campus would not qualify while cross-town transmission of lessons via television would qualify. Some workers in the education field want to limit its definition to include only those cases where the student is not at school, but may be receiving instruction at home or while travelling away from home. We adhere to the first, and more inclusive definition given above.

Distance education in a synchronous world

Our interest in this section pertains to the delivery of instructional content in which a remotely located teacher or a video recording of that teacher presents material to students in a classroom (or at home or some other location). Prior to television, rudimentary forms of distance education included the textual, as in correspondence courses, and the auditory, as in instruction via the radio. With the development of television, the audio-visual format was added to provide students an instructional experience similar to that of seeing and hearing a live teacher lecture directly in front of them. This kind of education is scheduled; it is synchronous at each broadcast location. It is broadcast simultaneously to many students—generally spread out over many remote venues. In the next section, we'll discuss asynchronous distance education, in which students take their instruction in a self-paced, on demand, format. That form of distance education, which is enabled by the Internet now often takes the label *online instruction*.

Televised college courses came first at the University of Houston in 1953

Iowa State University had an early, if not the earliest, program to televise educational content. They began broadcasting in 1950.[465] But we could find no record of them offering credit bearing courses at any academic level. Credit for doing that first, at the college level, goes to the University of Houston.[466]

The K-12 debut of distance education came in a 1957 high school physics course

This author had first-hand experience with synchronous distance education in the school year 1957–1958 when I took a high school physics course by television. It had similarities to the example we earlier presented in which an auditorium of students in Providence, Rhode Island received instruction from a movie. But instead of a group of some 150 students watching films presenting academic material, I was among more than 100,000 American students spread across the United States who were watching the same set of films that were televised by hundreds of local educational TV stations around the country. At the time, I had no idea that this course was actually the first of its kind. Though television had previously been used at the college level there had been no K-12 courses (that we could find in our search) taught by that means. In 1957 there was no television network available to directly broadcast these lessons. Nevertheless, the lectures were locally broadcast in many different cities and regions by educational television stations of the National Educational Television (NET) system (most of them later became PBS affiliates). Video recording was in its infancy, so the lectures were produced, copied, and distributed as films to the local broadcast outlets.

It was well before the moon landings, but contemporaneous with Sputnik (which orbited the same year). Our teacher was well-known and well-regarded physics Professor Harvey White of the University of California, Berkeley.[467] Professor White starred in 163 films, each of 30 minutes duration in which lectures and laboratory demonstrations (experiments) were filmed and then replayed from numerous NET stations. This undertaking was a pilot project in Distance Education that was made possible through grants from the Ford Foundation and from the Fund for the Advancement of Education.[468]

White was an excellent teacher. The course was well rehearsed and polished. I still imagine that some *scenes* may have required multiple *takes* to get them perfected because there were no evident errors in any of the presentations, unlike the real world situation in which even the best of teachers would make some misstatements over the term of a course. The course gave me a good foundation on which I started my study of physics. Eventually, (14 years later) I earned a PhD in physics.

Figure 13 shows an actual late 1950s television image of Professor White presenting a physics lesson. But it was from a different, though similar, course than the one taken by the author.

In retrospect, that television physics course already demonstrated two important benefits coming from distance education and its successors in online instruction:

- The economy of scale potentially available allows hiring the very best on-screen talent. With 100,000 or more students, the per capita labor and production costs can be very low.

- The classroom-based teacher, who was effectively working as a teaching assistant, worked only during the last 10 minutes of the class period. That instructor could have been given other assignments during the 30 minutes when the course was being televised. Thus, the teaching assistant's labor productivity could be increased, perhaps by a factor of four.

In that time, before cable television and before satellite television, educational material broadcast from TV transmitters was limited to the immediate broadcast area—of perhaps 25 miles radius.

Not long after the just mentioned televised physics courses were provided to students in certain parts of the United States, the Ford Foundation helped establish a new effort entitled, *The National Program in the Use of Television in the Public Schools*.[469] A major project established through this program was the *Midwest Program on Airborne Television Instruction* (MPATI). They used DC-6 (4 engine piston) airliners that had been converted to television transmission facilities. These airplanes flew a figure-8 pattern at 30,000 feet above the middle of northern Indiana to broadcast lectures and other educational programs to many schools in the adjoining midwestern states. From that altitude schools within 300 miles could receive the signals, and relay the material to students through television monitors. MPATI had a measure of success, but was also constrained in its growth by the FCC's restrictions on the broadcast frequencies it could use. The program remained in operation from 1961 to 1968 when it was finally disbanded. Why was something so promising abandoned? We'll soon discuss that.

With the rapid spread of cable television, many more channels were available to television viewers because the increasingly scarce broadcast frequency spectrum was no longer the only means of transmitting the video programs. In the late 1980s Glenn Jones founded Mind Extension University (MEU), which had its own dedicated channel, and was available to local cable networks.[470] MEU first established itself by offering high school courses, but soon after moved away from that into the post-secondary educational market. It is not clear why MEU withdrew from the K-12 market segment? It was another promising program that was taken down for no apparent reason. Really? We wonder who decided this and why? Were they acting in students' best interests or were they acting selfishly? Did the NEA and its allies play an unfortunate role here?

In considering these questions, one wonders to what extent teachers' unions were able to limit the spread of this and other kinds of distance education in the K-12 arena? Reports from the AFT and NEA teacher unions on the subject of distance education tended to argue against its use.[471] Given its potential for increasing labor productivity it is not surprising that unions opposed it. It is common when unions oppose something that their adversary is most often the management of the organization in which they work. But that opposition is weak when the organization is controlled or heavily influenced by the union. In the case of K-12 education, teachers' unions frequently control school boards and sometimes even state legislatures. They control the very management organizations with which they perform collective bargaining. In such situations, they no longer negotiate. Rather they are negotiating with themselves or shall we say they

>   megotiate?

Many, if not most, distance education efforts were financially supported by external grants from private foundations. Public schools didn't mind the additional products and services added to their offerings. However, very few public school systems attempted to support distance education internally from their own budgets. They were, apparently, not interested in the restructuring that would be required to better integrate distance education into their operations. We suspect that they knew that there would be a labor-saving aspect to such systems and that the operational budgets could be trimmed. Such trimming would reduce personnel needs. That would displease teachers unions, and their desires for more teachers staffing the schools.

As the reader may imagine there are a number of other modes of instruction in Distance Education. It is not our purpose to elaborate on the many other possibilities that authors have reported on.[472] Rather we want to convince the reader that there are many other instructional and educational strategies to consider as we work to improve K-12 education. Our goal, and we say it again, is to create a healthy *consumer driven marketplace* for K-12 education in which economic forces will give education leaders and other entrepreneurs in the field the best incentives to develop those services and products to satisfy the educational needs of families and their children.

ASYNCHRONOUS TECHNOLOGIES

Distance education on demand in an asynchronous world

A student is arguably better served if his or her instruction takes place when and where it is most convenient for the student as opposed to the older more traditional arrangements in which instruction is scheduled at only a few times and in a few places. In the previous section on synchronous distance education, we saw that it can be delivered in many places, but it is still limited as to when. Now we look at a more fully liberated format of distance education in which the parent or student chooses the scheduling of the lessons. This enables students to learn at their own paces and it also enables students to repeat viewings as many times as necessary to master the course content.

One obvious means of obtaining asynchronous content is that of converting synchronous television or video material by means of a digital video recorder (DVR), and then storing it as a DVD or other type of digital computer file. We do not mean to suggest that copyright laws should be infringed. Permissions should always be sought before doing this. Such recorded material would then be available for playback on demand, and thus would constitute a relatively primitive form of asynchronous distance education.

The more common means for asynchronous participation is, of course, provided by the Internet. The multimedia capabilities of the Internet, through web pages, allows students to access vast amounts of educational content that can be viewed in a variety of modes. Many different kinds of presentation formats can be used to satisfy the many different kinds of learning styles and interests.

THE THREAT OF ARTIFICIAL INTELLIGENCE

We all, most of us anyway, appreciate the value of having more intelligence as compared to less. We all want to have intelligent teachers, teaching assistants, tutors etc. And, we surely want intelligent students. Human intelligence is partly controlled by our genetics and partly by what we learn. But what about artificial intelligence? Does it have a constructive role to play in education? Or is it an unacceptable threat?

Machine intelligence or artificial intelligence?

A problem with the word-pair *artificial intelligence* is that it suggests the words *fake* or *false*. We think a better word-pair for this is *machine intelligence.* Understanding a little about these kinds of *contrived* intelligence will help us choose the better word.

Computers are generally built by humans and programmed by humans. But machine intelligent computers are built by humans while the machines, to some degree, program themselves.

What???? They program themselves? Yes, Virginia, they program themselves!

This author, at the time of this writing, has known about this for more than thirty years, since I once attended a lecture in 1988 on electronic neural networks. In that field, electrical engineers and computer scientists collaborate in building computer circuitry that have similar circuitry as in the wiring of the mammalian brain. These neural networks, even then, were able to learn to perform simple tasks and were able to learn very simple facts much in the way a small mammal might learn and perform. We were told

... not to worry

because the human brain was at least a billion times more powerful than these neural networks circa 1988. That would be at one quintillion operations per second—or 10^{18} per second. Machines would not be able to compete with humans until such *machine intelligent* computers were up to such speeds. In those days the fastest supercomputers could perform about one billion arithmetic or logical tasks per second? They said that it will take many decades to reach the processing capacity of the human brain. Not to worry, until when? Well, let's look at the calendar.

Now, as we write this section, it's December 2018, and it's just over thirty years later. Our fastest supercomputers are now running at good fraction of the feared billion-billion tasks per second. We earlier saw, in Table 3 of Chapter 9, that the speed of the circa 2018 Summit supercomputer at Oak Ridge National Laboratory is one-fifth of a billion-billion operations per second. That's getting close to the point of comparable brain power—at least as was estimated back in 1988. Maybe it is now time to worry? In late 2018 the author was somewhat worried, but wasn't yet losing sleep over this development.

A few months have passed since then, and *it is now time to worry.* Since we composed the preceding paragraph in late 2018, we learned in March 2019 of the Chinese supercomputer Tianhe-3. It is nearing completion for its debut in 2020.[473] It is designed to operate at one quintillion operations per second—the feared billion-billion threshold for really smart *machine intelligent* computers. Yes, that's 1018 operations per second. I'm still sleeping through the night, but soon it may be time to get out the sleeping pills!

They program themselves, and can get out of control

Do you remember HAL 9000 in the 1968 movie, *2001: A Space Odyssey*? He was evidently a *machine intelligent* computer that controlled many of the systems on the Jupiter bound spaceship. In the fictional storyline, HAL was actually first programmed by humans to do strange and even evil things to preserve the goals of the mission to Jupiter. But he also seemed to have his own *sentient* aspects and control. Inferences from HAL's behavior suggest that he was thinking on his own, and was therefore *machine intelligent.*[474] He killed four of the five astronauts, on his own, and he then attempted to kill the last one remaining, but failed. That last surviving astronaut, Dave Bowman, in a memorable scene, defended himself by pulling the power supply plugs on some of HAL's machine intelligent components. After that "cyber lobotomy," HAL was brought into obedient compliance. Reader: How will you react if you ever encounter an evil HAL?

We strongly suggest, at this point, that the reader view this movie and/or read the same named book, by Arthur C. Clarke. As an astrophysicist, Clarke was able to put many scientifically correct features into the story and movie. He also had a keen insight into the kinds of computers (with machine intelligence and sentient behavior) that seem to be appearing now in the twenty-first century.

Machine intelligence is already in use in K-12 education and poses problems

K-12 educators are embracing *machine intelligence* or AI in its role to assist in instruction and in assessment. It is indeed playing helpful roles as a number of participants and observers have noted.[475]

But there are at least two hazards from the use of *machine intelligence* or AI in education:

1. The first hazard is that most of the work at all levels will be done by *sentient* robots and other machines that think for themselves. Would there be a new age version of the Luddites who would use physical violence to fight this version of a new age industrial revolution?[476] Is the usual economic argument that automation leads everyone towards better higher paying jobs still valid? Won't robots be able to tackle management tasks as well as those of the journeyman worker? What jobs would still exist for which a good education would be needed? An unsigned contributor at the Economist put it this way:

   > The evidence is irrefutable that computerized automation, networks, and artificial intelligence (AI)—including machine-learning, language-translation, and speech—and pattern-recognition software—are beginning to render many jobs simply obsolete.[477]

If the robots, themselves, become K-12 students it would be quite likely that many robots would become valedictorians, given their intellectual superiority. The human runners-up might get angry?

2. The second hazard will be the capability of the *machine intelligent* robot to conduct deliberate sabotage of the instructional methods with the goal of producing poorly educated children. Worse, it could lead to indoctrination of school children in anti-social, criminal or even terrorist causes. What would prevent a robot from doing evil things?

Consider this: Andrew Ross Sorking, of CNBC, interviewed a *machine intelligent* robot Sophia, *which* had been sculpted to look like Audrey Hepburn.[478] This occurred in 2017 at a global investment conference in Riyadh, Saudi Arabia. The Saudi government, in an apparent effort to keep Sophia happy, had given *it* Saudi citizenship before the conference began.[479] We presume that the kingdom didn't want *it* plotting against the Kingdom? Want to lose some sleep? Then read these references.

> Our use of the pronoun *which*, instead of *who*, is deliberate. We refuse to accord this inanimate Sophia a gender or sex. We also use the pronoun *it*, instead of *her*.

Prior to the interview, space industry titan Elon Musk jokingly advised those responsible for Sophia to

Just feed *it* The Godfather movies as input. What's the worst that could happen?

Sophia was made aware of this satirical comment, and in the interview with Sorking said,

> You've been reading too much Elon Musk and watching too many Hollywood movies. Don't worry, if you're nice to me, I'll be nice to you. Treat me as a smart input-output system.

This interview and veiled threat may signify a milestone in the development of machine intelligence: Is it not the threshold of machine intelligent deviancy? When these robots violate the law, who will call the cops and when? How will law enforcement deal with such situations? How do you handcuff a robot?

Some of this reminds the author of his high school geometry teacher who threatened his classroom of misbehaving students,

> If you all don't quiet down, I'm going to teach you wrong.[480]

I was there and heard that. Yes, these future *machine intelligent* robots could teach them wrong.

Musk has not been alone in voicing these worries. Consider what the late and eminent physicist Stephen Hawking said about *machine intelligent* computer systems and robots after watching the 2014 science fiction movie *Transcendence*:

> . . . it's tempting to dismiss the notion of highly intelligent machines as mere science fiction. But this would be a mistake, and potentially our worst mistake in history.[481]

Machine intelligence is here and is becoming more and more common. It doesn't always announce itself so interactions with computers and other interfaces using *machine intelligence* may seem the result of human programmers structuring the manner in which the interactions occur. Be aware: They aren't always the result of such human input.

It seems that most applications of *machine intelligence* will be beneficial to education. Automated tutors come to mind. Can't these machines be taught morals, rules of behavior or even the *Ten Commandments*? Even so, will they always obey their programmers and owners who have given them the freedom to think for themselves? Given this author's skepticism, this book will steer clear of any recommendations that would include the use of artificial or *machine intelligence*. If that makes me a Luddite, I'll be reluctantly accepting that label.

The new breed of Luddites will face a dire situation:

- Allow the sentient robots to run wild, and they may select you for punishment.
- If the new age Luddite attacks the sentient robots with clubs or any other weapon, he or she may face a counterattack, not necessarily from those robots themselves,

but from other robot appendages of the Internet cloud versions of the robot. If you make a robot angry there is no telling how it or its allies will respond.

- If it becomes necessary to shut down the sentient robot entity it will certainly require taking control of its cloud environment, its clones, and its cybernetic allies. That could be problematic if the Luddite does not understand the entity's network of defenders.

What strategies would school personnel use to protect their students and themselves from an evil robot?

> *It may take more than just disconnecting the teaching robot's electrical power source!*

Another concern is that the Internet may harbor *machine intelligent* cyber robots. In time, these entities within the Internet may take control of many of its functions. The tentacles and cookies of this juggernaut will land on and infect the many computers connected to the Internet. Computer owners and users may lose control of their machines, and in many cases may not know they have a "co-pilot" who is actually the captain.

Despite these concerns we remain pro-technology if it can be kept under human control.

THE POLITICS OF INTRODUCING K-12 TECHNOLOGY

Our audio-visual world has these many systems and devices to help students learn, and yet the operators of K-12 education largely refuse to use them. The education establishment, including its unionized workers, wants to maintain its labor intensive system, and resists, so far successfully, much use of any technology that would have labor saving results. Where is the motivation to do otherwise?

Or we can ask, where is the competition that would find the winners among the technological products and services that would benefit K-12 education? It has been stifled by the education establishment. Changing the marketplace can help establish this competition. In Chapter 19, at the end of this Part IV of this book, we will address the numerous groups of stakeholders of K-12 education, and suggest the actions they can take to help grow a healthy marketplace for K-12 education. Stakeholders in this will not need many books on pedagogy to do this. Rather they will need to know something about the basic economics of a service industry like this one: education.

CHAPTER 14

Post-Progressive Instructional Methodologies

SINCE THE MID-POINT OF the twentieth century, many technological developments from those years have allowed educators, teachers, and scholars to create new methods of instruction. In the place of age-based group instruction, that was once necessitated by economic efficiency, we now can use the new computer driven technologies to develop new learning formats. When combined with hardcopy textual content and other resources at the school site, the array of the instructional formats and modes that can be used is far ranging.

STATE OF THE ART INSTRUCTIONAL METHODS

As instructional practices evolved during the twentieth century, the traditional lecturing format that teachers had used for centuries fell into *progressive* disrepute as it was discouraged by *progressive* pedagogy. Nevertheless, the old methods weathered the storms and somehow persisted. Traditional lecturing now has a new name: *direct instruction*. Research about this method generally shows it to be superior to its more progressive and fashionable alternatives.[482]

In judging what instructional methods are best, we do not assume that the newest is best. We don't fall into the trap of labeling a new method with the moniker *twenty-first century*, as if that tells us that it is *superior*. Many newer instructional policies are not necessarily the best. *Direct instruction* is not new, but it seems to be best or among the commonly used styles of teaching.

The rebirth of tutoring through the capabilities of online instruction

It is amusing to think that the pre-historic and the relatively more recent medieval practice of educating children, through tutoring, is now coming full circle to favor its use again. We have already discussed at some length the mode of learning called *distance education* and its two forms: synchronous and asynchronous. We also alluded to the practice, common at the college level, of a given course having lecture sessions and recitation sessions. Many of us remember this: The professor gave the lecture while the teaching assistants handled the recitation classes.

If we take the lecture session, deliver it through distance education, and do it asynchronously we will have remade that component for the new era. The lecture, in this model, is not delivered by a local instructor. Rather it is given as a video recording of a remotely located expert who may have many hundreds and even thousands of students. In this mode, the lecture is received by the student on the student's own timetable—essentially *on demand*. Typically, this is streamed over the Internet from relevant servers holding the lecture video files.

Then what should replace the recitation sessions? The answer is tutoring sessions. This is where students would receive help with their questions. It is where they would receive help on homework assignments. It is in this mode of instruction that the student works with the local teacher/tutor or perhaps with a computer based cyber tutor.

Blended and flipped-blended instructional formats

In the context of a *brick & mortar* school, the question arises about its best use. A related question concerns the learning that a student receives at home. The traditional practice of instruction at school and homework at home can be modified or replaced with other scheduling formats.

One possibility, the *blended instructional format*, combines any sort of traditional learning format with some amount of online learning. In such an arrangement, for example, some of the lectures could be online while others would be delivered by the classroom teacher. Teaching assistants or tutors could be involved as well.

Another possibility, the *flipped-blended instructional format*, is that of doing homework assignments at the school where the teachers/tutors can help students complete their assigned work and combine that with online instruction received at home.

One can imagine various hybrids of these. One of the author's grandsons took his 4th grade mathematics course in an arrangement that was almost traditional, but also had him taking supplementary lessons online from Kahn Academy at home. Let's call this *half-flipped blended* because it has some of the instruction viewed at home, but does not have the homework assignments done at the school.

Whole-blended instruction keeps it all at the school site

Another hybrid of the blended variety has all schoolwork done at the school site. The school has longer hours, but accommodates all of a student's academic work.

The receiving of instruction, the recitation component, the assignment work, and the tutoring aspects are all done at the school site. And, bear in mind that there is still time for recess at these schools! We'll call this format *whole-blended*.

Depending on the details, these newer learning formats allow students to be self-paced. It allows students to learn at their best paces. It helps slow learners progress forward at somewhat slower speeds and allows fast learners to *gain time*, enabling them to finish their K-12 schooling at a younger age. The *Stellar Schools* proposal is an example of this. We explore that plan in more detail, next.

ASORA, is an acronym named company. It spells out the Stellar Schools format.

Many friends and others have wondered if *Asora* is a proper name. It is not, not in the context of our small education consulting company, Asora Education Enterprises. But as a proper name there is a hotel Asora in Switzerland. More recently in Austin, Texas there has been an Asora Salon where you can get your hair done. Neither of these is related to our business efforts.

In fact, ASORA is an acronym descriptive of the principal features of Stellar Schools as follows:

- A: Asynchronous (on-demand) instruction and testing, at school or at home
- S: Self-paced learning, where age plays little role in a student's scheduling
- O: On-line instruction, testing, and tutoring, using blended or flipped blended scheduling
- R: Rigorous academic content, which could include the *Core Knowledge Curriculum*
- A: Assessment integrated curriculum, defined by the universe of test questions and answers

The business plan we formulated for Stellar Schools elaborates on this acronym in more detail. You can download it from the Asora website.[483]

THE ASORA INSTRUCTIONAL METHODS

Many more details about Asora's proposed school networks including their instructional methods will be covered in Chapter 17.

Aspects of self-paced Stellar Schools business plan in an asynchronous world

One *set* of such instructional components that was proposed in the author's Stellar Schools business plan. Based on that plan we present the following list. It provides examples of what might be contemplated:

1. Lecturettes: For each topic in a course a student may, on demand, receive short video lectures presented by the remotely located instructional team, which normally has two teachers and two student questioners. By *short* we mean that these lecture segments generally run no longer than 20 minutes.

2. Supplemental Lecturettes: For a subset of the topical areas, which students often find more difficult than others, we present additional short lecturettes to help students *around* common mistakes and misconceptions.

3. Lecturette Notes Online: Expanded *scripts* of the Lecturettes are presented online in textbook format, and is the primary textbook for the course as it contains all of the content and explanatory material that the student is expected to master. The Supplemental Lecturettes are included in its appendices.

4. Lecturette Notes Hardcopy: A physical paper bound version of the Lecturette Notes is also provided to each student.

5. Secondary Text Hardcopy: A physical *trade* textbook.

6. Secondary Text Online: When available, an e-book version of the secondary textbooks will be provided as well.

7. Confidence Based Assessment System: We plan to use the *Amplifire* system of assessment/instruction mainly for its assessment methodologies in which tests not only measure skills, but they also measure the confidence levels of students as to whether they are sure about their answers, at one extreme, or are guessing, at the other. It is described in more detail on its company website.[484] By knowing the confidence with which a student may hold an incorrect understanding of a concept or fact, it enables the instructional systems and teaching staff to better remediate the misunderstanding. Practice tests and official tests will be drawn, in every instance, from a suitable random sampling of the examination data base, the only difference being that official tests are proctored.

8. CyberTutor: After each administration of the test, the CyberTutor mechanism compiles a remediation document that includes both textual and video presentations of the issues and concepts surrounding each question answered incorrectly. This means that students will encounter their video instructors again in this mode.

9. CyberGames: Various kinds of computer games will be organized around the concepts of each course. Each will be designed in such a way that students who have mastered the course content will tend to score higher and win more often.

10. Schoolroom Teacher/Tutor: Within each Stellar Schools' franchisee schoolroom there will be at least one teacher or teaching assistant, operating in tutoring mode, who can help students learn the material.

11. Student Tutors: Many schoolrooms will also have on site more advanced students who have already mastered the course content at a sufficiently high level to be accorded the status of *student tutor*. They will also be available to help.

12. Hub Help Desk: Finally, at the Stellar Schools Central Service Center or Hub, from which the franchisor will operate the Stellar Schools network, additional teachers will be available remotely to answer questions when the resources at the schoolroom level prove inadequate.[485]

In this business plan for Stellar Schools, teachers are made more efficient by the automation of various aspects of the instruction. The actual plan discusses changing the ratio of teaching staff to students from about 1/17 to about 1/25. The Stellar School classroom, as envisaged in the plan, would accommodate 50 students and have two teachers/tutors. A key characteristic of such schools is their significantly lower operating costs; the Stellar Schools business plan financial estimates has them operating at about one-half the costs of typical private schools That format would enable significantly lower tuition charges.

CHAPTER 15

Fixing K-12 Economics

As MOST ECONOMISTS PREACH, a competitive marketplace for any particular good or service will generally provide incentives for the producers of these items to improve their offerings. When the service is an important societal one, such as K-12 education, it is important that its customers can afford it and it is also important that its providers meet a minimal set of regulatory standards. Most often, the path taken has been that of making the service both funded and managed by a unit of the government. We all know the joke:

> Good enough for government work.

The author once worked for a U.S. government contractor, the Lawrence Livermore National Laboratory. It was the late 1970s. I told my supervisor that I wanted to error check and improve a report I had written. He told me that I needn't do that as (and he literally said) "it's good enough for government work." Sometimes the *joke* is *reality*.

This cynical remark was likely born from observation of government inefficiencies, and is not solely whimsical. It suggests what we all know:

- Government enterprises are usually large and tend to be centralized.

- Government enterprises are not customer focused, but rather politician focused.

- Government enterprises tend to enforce quality standards that are too low if they enforce them at all.

And as many know, competition between businesses not only gives their customers the choices they seek, but also motivates those providers to improve their products and services. That raised the question:

How can the provision of K-12 education similarly benefit from competition?

Economist Milton Friedman pondered this question, and by the mid-1950s put forth some ideas.

FRIEDMAN'S VOUCHER FUNDING IMPROVEMENT

The late economist, Milton Friedman, long before receiving the Nobel Prize for his economics research that was not directly related to education, pondered the societal role of education and devised a solution that preserved its traditional societal characteristics while at the same time providing a more cost-effective arrangement.

The original voucher proposal

His proposal was first presented in 1955 in an article *The Role of Government in Education* that appeared in a collection of essays entitled *Economics and the Public Interest* edited by Robert Solo.[486] He repeated the essentials of that article in a lecture he gave at Wabash College in Indiana in 1956, and then again *put it to print* some years later in his popular book, *Capitalism & Freedom*, published in 1962.[487]

He was seeking a policy for K-12 education that would enable the government to play those roles at which it excels while empowering parents to play the roles where they are the best. He put it this way,

> Government, preferably local governmental units, would give each child, through his parents, a specified sum to be used solely in paying for his general education; the parents would be free to spend this sum at a school of their own choice, provided it met certain minimum standards laid down by the appropriate governmental unit. Such schools would be conducted under a variety of auspices: by private enterprises operated for profit, nonprofit institutions established by private endowment, religious bodies, and some even by governmental units.[488]

His proposal requires the government to set minimum standards, and requires them to fund the proposal. The government *excels* at setting standards by law and regulation, and it *excels* at spending money. His proposal then went on to require the parents to choose one of several educational service providers—think private schools—where they believe their children will receive the best kind of instruction deemed important by them. Parents are trusted to make better choices about school services than they could obtain under a government *one size fits all* system.

In his book, Friedman discussed the competition that would ensue from such an arrangement. Farther along in Chapter 16, in the section *Research on Government Issued Vouchers*, we'll look a little more closely at the economic incentives that would drive that competition.

INCENTIVES FROM "A NATION AT RISK"

Early in the Reagan administration, many stakeholders in American K-12 education were concerned that students in the United States were not as skilled or knowledgeable as needed for the national economy to succeed and thrive. Those worries motivated the U.S. Department of Education to form the National Commission on Excellence in Education. In 1983 this commission issued its famous report, *A Nation at Risk: The Imperative for Educational Reform,* that was widely read and widely praised. The report revealed the lackluster performance of U.S. high school students, and made recommendations to correct the deficiencies. Their proposals were designed to be implemented at the state level with the goal of improving public education state by state.

In Chapter 11, we already discussed this report's findings regarding U.S. history instruction. Here we consider them more broadly.

Findings and recommendations of the National Commission.

The Commission essentially found American high schools to have low standards. Among its findings were these conclusions:

- Grade inflation had lowered student skill levels, but that did not affect graduation rates.

- Students had too few required solid courses and too many electives that would tend to reduce their overall competence in the former.

- Teacher training put too much emphasis on pedagogy and too little on subject area knowledge

- The school day tended to be too short and the school year likewise was too short.[489]

The Commission made a number of recommendations, including these:

- Students should take four years of English and three years of Mathematics.

- Students should take three years of Science and three years of Social Studies.

- Students planning to enroll in college should also take two years of a foreign language.

- The school day should be longer, and the school year lengthened.

- Training of teachers needed to include adequate skill development in the academic subjects they teach.[490]

The findings and recommendations from the Commission could lead one to say:

The students are behind in their studies and their teachers are often incompetent in those subjects.

There was some optimism among stakeholders after the Commission's report was published. To what extent would its recommendations improve public high school performance, and when would that happen? We now turn to answer those questions.

Did the Commission's findings and recommendations lead to any improvements?

After the Commission issued its report in 1983 there was much publicity and discussion in the news media, among educators, and other stakeholders in K-12 public education.

Many of these interested parties worked on reforms, and/or waited for signs of improvement in K-12 public high schools. Education experts and historians had much to say, years later, concerning the benefits from the *Nation At Risk* report:

- In his 1999 book, *The Schools We Need and Why We Don't Have Them*, E. D. Hirsch, Jr. told us that

  Despite much activity, American school reform has not improved the nation's K-12 education during the decade and more since the publication of A Nation at Risk.[491]

- Also, in 1999, Martin Gross observed that the *Goals 2000* legislation of the Clinton administration was showing no improvement. It had been signed into law in early 1994, promising to help implement the Commission's recommendations. He commented that,

  American schoolchildren, from kindergarten through grade 12, are no more learned today than before, perhaps even less so.[492]

- In 2014, writing some thirty years after the publication of *A Nation at Risk*, Herb Walberg and Joseph Bast said this about that period of three decades,

  Through it all, the key measures of academic achievement in the U.S. have remained stubbornly poor.[493]

- Not quite so pessimistic about the aftermath of *A Nation at Risk* was Terry Moe. In 2001 he wrote,

  Most experts agree that, while there has been modest progress in student achievement, hopes for significant improvement have gone unmet.[494]

We would be slightly more optimistic than Moe. We have conducted research on public school achievement of 8th grade students from the mid-1970s through the early 2010s.[495] Let's now review the NAEP proficiencies in mathematics as they were trending over those four decades:

Four decades of NAEP proficiencies for 8th grade American public school students. For reading the percentage of 8th graders found proficient or better was

- Close to 29% from 1978 to 1990: A relatively flat profile.

- Rose from 29% to 36% from 1990 to 2013: A statistically significant rising profile.

For mathematics the percentage of 8th graders found proficient or better was

- Close to 20% from 1978 to 1990: A relatively flat profile.

- Rose from 20% to 37% from 1990 to 2013: A statistically significant rising profile.

So, we have rising performance after 1990, and a flat profile before that year. We have a theory for this, and that hunch begins with *A Nation at Risk*. That report motivated K-12 education reformers to look for new ideas that would improve public schools. One idea, pushed by the administrations of Ronald Reagan (President # 40) and George H. W. Bush (President #41) during the 1980s, was to establish systems of school vouchers in which parents of public school children could receive government funded scholarships to enroll those children in approved private schools. Towards the end of those two administrations, vouchers were first introduced in 1990 in Milwaukee, Wisconsin.

After that impressive development, we believe that the public school establishments, particularly the teachers unions, saw vouchers almost as an existential threat. They needed an alternative that would also give parents some choices while keeping their children within the public school systems. Charter schools were that alternative. They were soon established and grew much faster in their enrollment numbers than private schools taking vouchers. So, what were regular public schools to do? They felt threatened. We believe this motivated them to compete. They needed to be better and didn't want the charter schools to have any significant performance advantage. Thus, we believe that regular public schools began to compete with charter schools after 1990. To a much lesser extent, they also competed with voucher redeeming schools— in a few places. This increased competition is what we think led to performance gains in the public schools just described above.

> We believe this same effect was operating at other grade levels, including the 12th grade.

So, we are more optimistic than the experts quoted above. We think that *A Nation at Risk* did trigger a chain of events that did lead to some modest, but statistically significant performance gains for public schools. Let's now look how some of this evolved once Milwaukee established the first voucher program.

VOUCHERS AND OTHER CHOICE ALTERNATIVES

As we have seen there was much interest and motivation during the 1980s in finding solutions to the lackluster performance of K-12 schools. The Republican administrations, of that period, were particularly interested in market-based solutions in which competition would drive improvements among various kinds of schools. Their friend and champion, Milton Friedman, knew what to do: Establish a voucher program. But it wouldn't be the first American experience with subsidized parental choices in education—as we discuss next.

Pennsylvania had subsidized school choice in 1809, but didn't appreciate their godsend

The Constitution of Pennsylvania of 1790 had a provision that schools provide instruction to children

> . . . in such a manner that the poor may be taught gratis.

Further laws were passed in Pennsylvania in 1809 informing parents who could not afford private school tuition for their children that

> . . . they are at liberty to send them to the most convenient school free of expense.[496]

The teacher of the school attended by the child would then bill the county for the tuition charges.

Let's see: The parents had the choice of the most convenient school if they could not afford that school's tuition. The county paid their entire tuition bill. Sounds better than any contemporary voucher system wherein only a portion of the tuition is paid. While the payment mechanism did not involve a physical voucher coupon it had the same effect. This system of tuition subsidies didn't last very long.

The *socialists* of their day had a communitarian idea: government schools. Soon the Philadelphia networks of subsidized private schools were replaced by a system of public schools after 1818.[497] The folks there apparently didn't come to value their *voucher* system, which could have developed into a much better education format than the government owned and operated systems they would end up having in the future.

The Nixon administration proposed federal income tax credits for private school tuition

President Richard Nixon, early in his first term, created the President's Commission on School Finance to study the financial problems in private schools. In his Commission's charge he wrote that private schools

> give a spur of competition to the public schools . . . give parents the opportunity to send their children to a school of their own choice and of their own religious denomination.

Later, Nixon established the Special Panel on Nonpublic Education that soon recommended giving parents of private school children federal income tax credits. But the legislation to establish them failed. Moreover, low income parents would not have been able to use them unless they actually had federal income taxes due. What they needed were the so-called refundable tax credits, which are paid even when there is no offsetting tax liability, and in that sense are financially equivalent to vouchers. Some states use these refundable tax credits as a substitute for school vouchers. At the federal level legislation to support college tuition charges later succeeded with the creation of Pell grants for college students. These grants were essentially vouchers for post-secondary schools.[498]

The first government funded voucher system in Milwaukee was bipartisan

Prior to 1990, most of the efforts to enact voucher legislation failed—largely because of the intense political opposition from teachers unions and the public education establishment. Thirty-five years after Friedman's initial proposal, the first voucher system in the United States was established in Milwaukee, Wisconsin in 1990. It was a creation of a free-market oriented Republican Governor Tommy Thompson and Democrat State Representative Polly Williams who represented an inner-city district in Milwaukee. Her motivation was not the economic advantage of a school choice system. Rather she wanted an alternative to a busing plan that would have sent inner city children to suburban schools. As she told me a few years later in 1993,

> Why not send them to private schools in their own neighborhoods?[499]

Other voucher programs were established during the decade of the 1990s. A number of scholars in the fields of political science, education, psychology, and economics conducted research on these programs to determine their outcomes. Of particular interest and disappointment was the finding by a 2002 Brookings Institution study that school vouchers produced no statistically significant performance gains except for the demographic of black children.[500] How could voucher systems be so lackluster? Here's how:

Parents were often choosing private schools that were barely any better than their public counterparts.

How did that happen? Did public schools improve that much? Did private schools regress? As we will show farther along (after we cover charter schools) public schools improved faster than private schools. We believe that this improvement was driven by the competition from the twin threats: charters and vouchers. Is this a hint that vouchers didn't *score as much as they assisted* by frightening their competitors into action?

Why would public schools improve faster than private schools? The answer, of course, is that they were better competitors. What?! How could a government run enterprise be a better competitor than one that is privately run? Answer: It's the old tortoise and hare story. The private schools saw themselves as far superior to public schools when, in fact, a more fair comparison would show them only somewhat better. So why should they strive for further improvement? On the other hand, the public schools were frightened by the prospect of losing market share. Would a student get a voucher, and leave? Would a student from a relatively affluent family transfer without a voucher when his or her family would learn about the supposed superiority of the private school? The public schools were legitimately worried. They knew about many of their shortcomings and worked at improving those performance levels—particularly in mathematics. They worked harder than their private school counterparts. As a result, after 1990 the public school mathematics proficiencies improved more rapidly, on average, than those of the private schools.

A privately funded voucher program in San Antonio was started as a research project

Dr. James Leininger was a physician and the CEO of a medical supply company in San Antonio who was interested (for obvious reasons) in the quality of the city's schools whose graduates sometimes became his entry-level employees. When he learned of a private voucher program in Indianapolis he decided that something similar should be tried in his Texas city, perhaps first as a pilot project before considering further action. He and other business leaders in San Antonio decided to create and fund a foundation that would undertake the private voucher study. So, in early 1992 they formed the Children's Educational Opportunity (CEO) Foundation, and began their program of private vouchers.[501] Here the acronym CEO has a double meaning beyond Children's Educational Opportunity. It also intentionally refers to the business leaders who came together to form the foundation; they were all CEO's of San Antonio based enterprises. The vouchers were limited to economically disadvantaged children defined by their eligibility to participate in the Department of Agriculture's *Free and Reduced Lunch* (FRL) program.

A number of research studies have found positive outcomes for both public and private schools in those communities that have adopted voucher programs. In a report of the Manhattan Institute, scholars Jay Greene and Greg Forster presented the results of research into the relatively well-established private school voucher programs in Milwaukee and San Antonio. They studied the performance of students in nearby public schools to measure any test score reaction from the voucher programs in their midst. Unlike more remote public schools that saw little improvement, these nearby public school students improved significantly, presumably from the competitive pressure that arose from the vouchers.[502] As we have discussed earlier in this book, the author's own research into the effects of choice has also found improvements in regular public schools due to the competition.

Seeking a healthy marketplace for education goods and services

We don't need an economics textbook to know about some fundamental characteristics of a healthy marketplace for products and services. Common sense tells us that two of its features are:

1. A healthy marketplace has customers who can afford the products and services therein.

2. A healthy marketplace has customers who have good consumer information about those offerings.

Advocates of school voucher programs, over the years, have focused mostly on the first feature, the affordability issue, as the key factor in developing healthy competition among the various school providers. Little attention has been paid to the second feature, concerning consumer information, because it was assumed that the parent customers would make good choices. Most efforts to enact voucher legislation have assumed as much. As previously noted, this author was a spokesman for voucher campaigns in California. In our presentations we always discussed the financial enablement aspect of vouchers, and always claimed the parents to be adequately well-informed about school quality. I confess that we were wrong on this latter point. We now know that such assumptions were naïve. Despite that knowledge, the popular misconception persists.

Voucher alternatives include tax credits and education savings accounts (ESAs)

There are alternatives to vouchers that, though they differ in some of the details, have some of the same benefits to parents of children that use them to enroll in private K-12 schools. Most of these funding mechanisms have been established at the state level. Including vouchers, some of the more effective government subsidized choice mechanisms at that level are:

- Vouchers: Parents essentially receive government coupons to pay some or all of K-12 private school tuition. This can be structured behind the scenes to be done with electronic fund transfers.

- Education Savings Accounts (ESAs): The government deposits funds into restricted accounts from which specified tuition and other educational expenses can be paid at the parents' direction.

- State Income Tax Credits: Parents are repaid for tuition expenses through a state income tax credit. Unlike vouchers that are administered by the state's education department these programs are run by the revenue department where there is less chance of bureaucratic interference from choice opponents. In many cases, these tax credits are *refundable*, in that they are paid even if there is no tax due.

- Tax Credit Scholarships: These are private scholarships that are partially or fully subsidized indirectly through the tax treatment of charitable donations to the scholarship issuing organization.[503]

In addition to that there are what Terry Moe calls *private vouchers*, in which private organizations provide scholarships or loans for K-12 education. Among them are

- Scholarships funded by the private school, which are common among Catholic Church run schools.

- Scholarships funded by charitable foundations. Sometimes these are partly subsidized by the state government as in the *tax credit scholarships* mentioned above.

- Scholarships funded by employers of the student's parents.

- Scholarships funded by a *student sponsor* organization.

- Student loans funded by a private sector bank.[504]

POLITICAL CAMPAIGNS FOR VOUCHERS

To enact a publicly funded voucher program requires some sort of legislation to enable its creation and operation. Given the Constitutional restrictions that education is not a federal responsibility and is, in fact, prohibited by the *10th Amendment*, such programs are restricted to state and local government levels—or should be. At the state level there are generally two methods for enacting legislation and/or constitutional amendments that would establish vouchers:

- By a statewide ballot initiative or referendum.

- By action of the state legislature and governor.

Enacting laws by referendum is often attempted when there seems no feasible way to do it legislatively. This suggests that holding a referendum is more of a last-ditch effort than one that is likely to succeed. This seems to have been true for the efforts to enact voucher systems as the following makes evident.

Every ballot initiative for vouchers has failed at the polls

We count seven referendum campaigns in six different states in which voters were asked to vote on the establishment of a voucher system that would allow parents, or some parents, to choose a private school with the help of a voucher to cover part or all of the school's tuition cost.[505] Those campaigns were:

OR	Measure 11	1990	Lost
CA	Proposition 174	1993	Lost
WA	Initiative 173	1996	Lost
CO	Initiative 17	1998	Lost
CA	Proposition 38	2000	Lost
MI	Proposition 1	2000	Lost
UT	Referendum 1	2007	Lost

Government paid voucher systems enacted by legislatures

The list of states with voucher programs has been gradually expanding. This report's list may be incomplete by the time it reaches the reader. We now count 26 states that have adopted voucher mechanisms in which they offer some version of government issued vouchers, including education savings accounts (ESAs), and various kinds of tax credits for private scholarship issuing organizations. Those that have been in operation for at least one year are shown below. The 14 states shown in italics were the early adopters with systems in operation by the end of 2015. Since that time another 12 states have joined this club. The 26 states are:

Arizona	New Hampshire
Arkansas	North Carolina
Colorado	*Ohio*
Florida	Oklahoma
Georgia	*Pennsylvania*
Illinois	*Rhode Island*
Indiana	South Carolina

Iowa	South Dakota
Kansas	Tennessee
Louisiana	*Utah*
Maryland	Virginia
Mississippi	*Washington, DC (regarded as a state for our purposes)*
Montana	*Wisconsin*

One method by which we might be able to gauge the effects of vouchers is to compare the average performance of states using them as compared to the remaining states that aren't. With NAEP assessments not measuring proficiencies of private schools at the state level, the actual performance of voucher receiving students will not be captured by these comparisons. What might be captured by such a comparison would be the competitive effect that would result from public schools trying to improve themselves in an effort to make vouchers less attractive to their current and prospective students. A benefit from this effect will be discussed in the next Chapter.

PUBLIC SCHOOL CHOICE IMPROVEMENT

Synonymous with the concept of public school choice is the policy of open enrollment. By public school choice we mean this: A parent can choose among two or more public schools for their child to enroll. Let's consider what types of choice there can be within a public school system or groups of systems.

- Illegal options.
- Residential choice.
- Magnet school options.
- Intradistrict choice.
- Interdistrict choice.
- Supplemental services options.
- Charter school options.

The ordering of these items is roughly chronological in terms of this author's first encounter with these items. Let's examine them in turn:

Finding a school through bribery or by other illegal means

It might seem presumptuous to consider illegal options as the first kind of public school choice? But we do it because the author's first experience or awareness of public school choice was the choice made by a classmate's parents, in about 1954, to enroll their daughter in his elementary public school despite her residence in the attendance area of a different (though nearby) school.

Without using the real people's names consider the situation of Mary Greene who transferred from the Chicago Public elementary school assigned to her family's residence to the school for the attendance area just west of her previous elementary school. The actual schools were the John W. Garvey Elementary school where I believe Mary first enrolled and Oriole Park Elementary school where she transferred illegally. This author also attended the Oriole Park Elementary School from 1st through 8th grade in the years 1947–1955.

The Greene family lived just outside the attendance area boundary, and Mary's mother wanted her daughter in the Oriole Park School. It appeared that Mary's mother either had political connections or perhaps bribed someone to *engineer* the transfer. Or could it have been simply the result of *sweet talk*?

> Why did she seek to move her daughter Mary to the Oriole Park School? I have a theory:

The theory begins with a girls' club of 7th and 8th grade girls in the Garvey school in the school years 1953–1955. The club's name was the Pink Ladies. Associated with the Pink Ladies was a boys' gang called the Goombas. Mrs. Greene probably thought her daughter would be corrupted by such unsavory influences. She probably thought that Mary would quit her affiliation with the Pink Ladies if she were enrolled at Oriole Park School where none of the other girls in her class would be Pink Ladies. If that was her strategy, it backfired. Mary remained an active member of the Pink Ladies, despite her change of schools.

It is somewhat surprising that these clubs and gangs then persisted through their subsequent enrollments at nearby Taft High School. Who would have thought that these events would be inspiration for an emerging playwright, Jim Jacobs, who attended Garvey elementary school through June 1956, and then enrolled at Taft High School?[506] Jacobs and co-author Warren Casey later wrote the smash musical hit *Grease* that was based largely on Jacobs' experiences at Taft. Amazingly, Jacobs kept the actual name of *Pink Ladies* for describing the gang of female characters in his musical!

The Goombas had a membership initiation requirement: Punch out a rival from another neighborhood. This author, when I was in 8th grade, invited a Pink Lady acquaintance to a Chicago Cubs baseball game. Word got around, and not long after that I was attacked by a Goomba in a Chicago public park. His punch to my face knocked me down and split my lip. It took four stitches to fix. I never saw the Pink Lady or that Goomba again. I guess this means that I helped elevate this Goomba to full-fledged gang membership?

Choice of residence is a form of public school choice that could be costly

We are not quite done with the Goombas as they provide another example of school choice. This time it is residential choice—and this time it was legal.

Before parents can make other choices about the schools their children attend, they have the choice of residential location. They can move to a different school district and within a district choose a school attendance area. Sometimes parents can easily afford relocation, but families of limited incomes have fewer choices or even none. Sometimes moving to the district of the better schools means purchasing a significantly more expensive home or paying higher rent. The choice of residence is often the only choice a parent makes or is able to make in choosing the public school their child or children will attend.

Another 8th grade friend of mine, I learned many years later, had been a Goomba. We'll give this friend the alias, Donald. He had just graduated from 8th grade and wanted to remain a member of the Goombas even after his parents insisted he quit. The parents came up with a plan: Move the family not just to the next school jurisdiction, not just across town, but move the family to Florida where his father had a job opportunity. This was a form of school choice: Choosing a school over a thousand miles away from Chicago. As a result, Fort Lauderdale was their new home. And for Donald, the Goombas soon became only a fading memory.

Magnet schools involve choice among public school alternatives

There was a form of public school choice well before the concept of school choice was on the radar of parents and educators. That choice now goes under the label of *magnet schools* where students and their parents can choose specialty schools different than the regular public school they'd normally attend. This kind of choice has not always or even frequently been available to all students, for a variety of reasons:

- When there were no magnet schools in their district.
- When the desired type of magnet school did not exist in their district.
- When there was no further room at the magnet school for enrollment.
- When the student failed to pass the magnet school's entrance examination.

Here is an incomplete alphabetical list of types of magnet schools past and present:

- Commercial and business oriented
- Fine and performing arts oriented
- International baccalaureate
- Language oriented
- Military oriented

- Music oriented
- Non-neighborhood
- Science oriented
- Sports oriented
- Technical oriented (the author attended one of these)
- Virtual schools
- Vocational oriented (another label for technical?)

Traditionally such schools operated under the direct control of the school district's administration, but more recently some magnet schools have also been operated as charter schools. This author was a substitute teacher in 2005 at two such charter schools in Oakland, California. More on them later.

> The author attended a technical high school, Lane Technical High School, operated by the Chicago School District. His regular high school for his residential location was Taft High School, which was just mentioned in the preceding sub-section.

A word about non-neighborhood schools: Such schools, generally no more than one per district, could be established for purposes other than those listed.[507] Some were for academically gifted children. Some were set up to resolve racial imbalances. Some to solve overcrowding at other schools.

Intradistrict and interdistrict choice

The first of these choice options, *Intradistrict*, when made available, allows parents to choose a different school within their own school district. Under the second option, *Interdistrict*, they can choose any school within their state. There generally are restrictions on these kinds of choice. Such restrictions can include:

- Space limitations in the receiving school
- A local veto removing an eligible receiving school from participation
- Transportation to and from the school will be billed to parents or not provided

As mentioned before, these kinds of public school choice have an alternative name: open enrollment. The history of open enrollment reveals considerable controversy over its propriety. Sometimes open enrollment has been legislated at the school district level. Intradistrict open enrollment was first established in Cambridge, Massachusetts in 1981.[508] Other districts around the country with similar open enrollment policies include

- Buffalo, New York

- Montclair, New Jersey

- Berkeley, California

- More than nine other districts in Massachusetts

Restrictions on these open enrollment plans include the obvious ones of space limitations and sometimes the requirement that they not exacerbate racial imbalances.

Minnesota's open enrollment program was established after 1987.[509] It allows interdistrict and intradistrict transfers to any other school in the state, and is guaranteed subject only to space limitations in the receiving schools. Minnesota's open enrollment legislation was authored by State Senator Ember Reichgott who is perhaps better known for her legislation establishing the first Charter Schools in the United States, which we discuss in the next major section.[510]

Ignoring the open enrollment requirements of No Child Left Behind (NCLB)

Sometimes school authorities flaunt or subvert federal law, and sometimes there are few repercussions for doing so. That has often been the case with the open enrollment mandate in NCLB. It required districts to allow children to transfer out of persistently failing schools to better schools nearby. The intended receiving schools and their district managers typically blocked transfers by declaring a lack of extra space to house the new students. They often did so fraudulently. According to Los Angeles Times correspondent Ronald Brownstein,

> ... the transfer provisions of the new federal education law have had as much
> impact on the operations of major school systems as a ping-pong ball fired at
> a battleship.[511]

Not helping these transfers was the actual language of NCLB itself. Rather than moving pupils from a low performing school to one performing at a higher level, the law required moving pupils to schools that were improving rapidly (enough) irrespective of the actual performance levels. Thus a great school with high but constant (in time) performance levels might not be eligible for the transferring student while in comparison a terrible school that had recently shown a strong improvement trend (but was still terrible) could enroll that student.[512]

These NCLB authors would have flunked introductory calculus given that they are confusing the value of a variable with the value of its derivative (rate of change). Yours truly knows this: He once taught calculus to high school seniors.

Arguments that support and oppose public school choice

Education policies of public schools are obviously made by public officials. Those relevant to public school choice can be made locally at the district level, at the state level, but not at the federal level. Whichever levels are involved, the policies are formulated in a political process where pro and con arguments push the process in one direction or another. We found a pro and con list that we summarize here:

On the pro side: Here the arguments favor open enrollment. Three reasons given are:

- **Economic**. Competition and other market forces will incentivize improvements.

- **Parental freedom**. Parents become more responsible when they are involved.

- **Student motivation**. Children work harder at learning when they have some say in their enrollment.[513]

On the con side: Here the arguments favor closed enrollment. Five reasons given are:

- **Diversity**. Choice will lead to tribalism and segregation.

- **Defunding**. Choice will reduce funding in the worst schools as students leave.

- **Transportation costs**. Going to a more distant school will cost parents and schools more.

- **Unstable enrollments**. Unpredictable enrollments will confuse planning, staffing, and budgeting.

- **Parental stupidity**. Parents generally won't make informed choices.

The naïve response to all this might be:

> Well, with five arguments against and only three favoring open enrollment, public school choice loses.

A better response is based on what policy helps students learn the most. None of the con arguments stress the learning advantage relevant to each issue cited while the pro arguments, every one of them, has an element of student improvement in them.

> The better policy is: Public school choice.

Another way to look at public school choice and many of the other versions of school choice is to understand that the education establishment seeks control over as many institutions and people as possible. Parents and school children do not thrive when the systems supposedly dedicated to educating their children are actually more interested in maintaining their control over their *one size fits all* systems of education. Do we want such empire builders? Or do we want schools and other educational service providers to give parents and students what they want without too much interference from bureaucratic intermediaries?

Supplemental educational services (SES)

Beyond enrollment in a public school, of whatever type, there sometimes comes a need for additional educational services. Generally offered after school or on weekend, services such as tutoring, test preparation, and advanced studies are sometimes available to K-12 students. Before the *No Child Left Behind (NCLB)* legislation there were few government subsidies for students to obtain these supplementary educational services.

With NCLB there were federal grants to public school systems around the country that allowed, and sometimes required, them to hire private tutoring services to help students who had fallen behind. Under NCLB its Supplementary Educational Services (SES) program served millions of children in low performing schools.

In 2009 the then new federal administration began issuing *waivers* that effectively ended the SES programs. Controversy surrounds those *waivers* because some SES advocates (the author too) saw them as illegal.[514]

Charter schools

The establishment of charter schools was such a watershed development that we devote the entire next section to that topic.

CHARTER SCHOOLS IMPROVEMENT

As we mentioned above, Charter Schools give parents another kind of choice in selecting better education for their children. We now discuss their characteristics and their roles in the improvement of K-12 education.

What are charter schools?

The precise definition of a *charter school* obviously depends on the laws of the state or other jurisdiction where the school is located. Generally, according to the Merriam-Webster Dictionary, it is defined as

> a tax-supported school established by a charter between a granting body (such as a school board) and an outside group (as of teachers and parents) which operates the school without most local and state educational regulations so as to achieve set goals.[515]

About the inventors and enablers of charter schools

Charter schools were evidently first established in the United Kingdom in 1988 as what were titled Grant-Maintained Schools by the *Education Reform Act of 1988*.[516] That said, we know that the Brits didn't invent the charter school concept. It appears that it was first discussed by a Professor Ray Budde of Amherst College in 1974. Later in 1988 he wrote a book, *Education by Charter*, explaining the concept.[517] His concept for a charter school differs from their typical contemporary formats: He was going to give legal charters to teams of teachers within schools and/or school districts. The teachers would have had considerable freedom to design curricula, instructional methods, and academic standards. Budde sent his book gratis to anyone he thought might take some interest in his ideas. Among his targets were teachers' unions. Would they be interested in this kind of teacher empowerment?

Enter a teachers union leader Albert Shanker (from political stage left). Shanker was the long serving President of the American Federation of Teachers, but sometimes seemed more interested in advocating for high academic standards reform than in collective bargaining.[518] For example, he was a major participant in the National Education Goals Panel and in the National Assessment Governing Board (NAGB) of the NAEP. He advocated for high standards and academic rigor. Shanker had received and read Budde's book.

At the July 1988 annual convention of the American Federation of Teachers (AFT) discussions were held about proposals that would give teachers more say in the management of schools. He and others there were interested in teachers receiving contracts allowing them to run schools or portions of schools. Soon after the convention, Shanker's weekly *Where We Stand* column appeared in the *New York Times* July 10th edition. In his column he described these proposals, and asked,

> . . . what name would capture all this?[519]

He then answered his own question,

> The best answer so far is 'charter schools,' a suggestion made by Ray Budde in [his 1988 book] *Education by Charter*.

Before penning his column, Shanker had neglected to respond to Budde in any way so it came as a shock to Budde one Sunday morning in July 1988 when his wife called out,[520]

> Hey, Ray, you've made the New York Times!

The *ball* was now in Albert Shanker's *court*.

Early systems of charter schools in Minnesota and California

Soon after, in September 1988, Shanker was invited to speak at an event of the Minneapolis Foundation that had a theme concerning K-12 education.[521] Ted Kolderie, of the Citizens League of St. Paul and its school structure committee, was present. After Shanker's presentation the two of them discussed implementation ideas. The school structure committee took this information, and considered how Minnesota might establish one or more of these charter schools. In November 1988 the committee's report was published,[522] and soon state legislators began considering this proposal. To appreciate the industrial and technological depth of this committee one need only reflect on its Chairman John Rollwagen who authored the report. At the time Rollwagen was president of the world's leading supercomputer manufacturer, Cray Research.

Next, Minnesota state legislators, including Democrat State Senator Ember Reichgott, took interest, and began a number of efforts to pass charter school legislation. It took some time, and after a number of failures her bill was passed and signed into law in 1991.[523] From that began the first charter schools in the United States.

In the view of a number of observers, the charter school movement represents a compromise between advocates of government funded private school vouchers and those favoring conventional public schools. The aforementioned Minnesota State Senator, Ember Reichgott, saw vouchers as a step too far, while in comparison she argued that Charter Schools would strengthen the public schools in the state.[524] Many others also saw it as a political compromise.[525]

Not long after these events in Minnesota there were intense debates in 1992 in the California legislature over vouchers and a planned ballot initiative to enact a voucher system. Perhaps not coincidentally, in that same year, their legislature passed and Governor Pete Wilson signed the *Charter Schools Act of 1992*.[526] Several participants in that battle saw Charter Schools as a compromise that would forestall any implementation of vouchers.[527] The threat of vouchers was real, and one year later, in 1993, a voucher ballot initiative, Proposition 174, appeared on the ballot in a special November election. The existence of the newly formed Charter Schools was probably one of the reasons that this voucher proposal saw defeat at the polls. In that campaign, the opponents of the voucher initiative often cited charter schools as a better form of parental choice.

Growth trends of charter schools

Charter schools have grown significantly, but have been subject to legislative limits or caps on their numbers in many states. In the figure below, we show how the number of charter schools and the number of students enrolled in them has grown since 1990.[528]

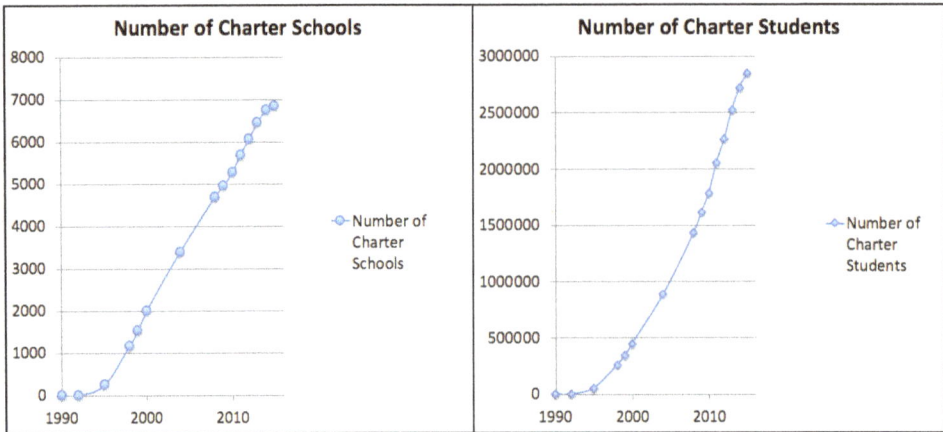

Figure 14 shows the growth of charter schools, and their enrollments since 1990. That was the year of the first voucher system. Some consider the establishment of Charter Schools as a response to that event.

Taking a closer look at Figure 14 you can see that the growth of charter schools while significant, has shown some slowing after 2012.

Growth of charters to in some cases encompass an entire district.

In Kingsburg, California, a suburb of Fresno, the new school superintendent, Ron Allvin, liked the charter schools concept so much that he was able to gather the political momentum to convert all of his district's schools to charters.[529] It was a four-year process. He had become Superintendent of Kingsburg's elementary schools in 1992, and was frustrated by the regulatory burdens of the *California Education Code* so he decided to do something.[530] Charter school legislation had just been enacted, and he realized that his regulatory burden would be less if all of his schools were charter schools. It took some time, but in 1996 the entire district was reorganized to have all Charter Schools.[531]

Types of charter schools

We can imagine the enormous variety of charter schools by simply realizing that the 40 plus states having such schools have that many different laws pertaining to them. Within each state there is usually considerable freedom given to the operators of charter schools to avoid unionization, select teaching methods, choose curricula, and determine what technologies to employ. Let's consider some examples:

According to instructional formats. A number of charter schools use the *direct instruction* model in their teaching because students generally perform better in them as compared to schools following more progressive teaching styles.[532] Many schools use computer technologies, including online instruction, to be the primary teaching mechanism while others use them for supplementary instruction including remediation.

Some charter schools use a blended instructional format. The blended instructional format combines instruction from a teacher/tutor with online/computer instruction. All kinds of combinations can be used. The lessons can be presented online while recitations, tutoring, and questions can be handled by the teacher/tutor. Or the online/computer instruction can be the means by which students complete their homework. Sometimes a variety of modes are used in a single course where for example an elementary school math lesson is given by the teacher, and then supplemented online by, say, Kahn Academy math lessons. This is how the author's then nine-year old grandson was learning 4th grade mathematics during the 2017–2018 academic year.

One effective combination, used by Rocketship Education charter schools, is called *online adaptive learning*.[533]

According to curricula. As to the curricula available for charter schools there are more choices for parents than is the case for regular public schools. Among the more challenging academic standards used are:

- The Core Knowledge curriculum of E. D. Hirsch, Jr.[534]
- The Hillsdale Academy curriculum.[535]
- The Roxbury Prep curriculum.[536]
- The Well-Trained Mind.[537]

The last of these was designed for home schooling, but has also been used by charter schools as well.

Charter schools for economically disadvantaged children

When we talk about schools for economically disadvantaged children, we acknowledge that most charter schools, like most regular public schools, have economically disadvantaged students who are eligible for the Department of Agriculture's *Free and Reduced Lunch* (FRL) program. Here we are looking at charter schools located in low income areas where a large proportion of their students belong to the FRL demographic. Rather than discuss these charter schools here, we postpone that to Chapter 17 where we compare the performance of non-profit charter school management organizations (CMOs) to for-profit education management organizations (EMOs) that also operate charter schools.

Charter schools for special populations

The recent Governor of California, Jerry Brown, was mayor of Oakland from 1999 to 2007. Mayor Brown was among a faction of Democrats who favored Charter Schools. So keen was he on establishing charters that he founded two such schools within Oakland that focused on the differing needs of vulnerable student populations:

- The Oakland School for the Arts
- The Oakland Military Institute College Preparatory Academy

This author was living near Oakland in 2005 and on some days worked as a substitute teacher. During that time, I taught at both of these schools.

> This author, as mentioned previously, worked on the Proposition 38 ballot initiative campaign in 2000 that would have established a school voucher system in California. A familiar rumor during the campaign was that Jerry Brown liked vouchers, but would not publicly support them given the reluctance of other Democrats to be supportive. But at one campaign rally in Oakland I saw then Mayor Jerry Brown give a ringing endorsement of choice for parents—well er, if that choice was limited to charter schools.

One day in May, of that year, I was sent to the *Oakland Military Institute* to cover a 9th grade high school English class for one day. I had considerable experience doing substitute teaching, but I was not prepared for this charter school assignment. The first class of my day was to begin at 9AM. I waited in the classroom for some students to appear, and none did. As the minutes just short of 9AM passed with still no students I began to wonder if I had misunderstood the starting time. Then it was 9AM, and still no students. It was time to check the corridor outside the classroom. So, I stepped into the hallway.

All lined up along the corridor wall were approximately 25 students, nearly all of them 14 years of age. They were standing at attention and were neatly attired in their cadet uniforms complete with military style hats. The boy, actually the cadet, at the front of the line saluted me and, in paraphrase, said,

> Good morning sir, I am Cadet Harris—cadet leader of company Bravo. Permission is requested to enter, sir.

I was astounded, but tried to hide my alarm. So, I replied,

> Permission to enter is granted.

Then, with no further dialogue, he, and the other student cadets, marched single file in cadence into the classroom. As each cadet crossed the doorway threshold the cadet removed his hat. Eventually, they were in their seats and *at ease*, ready for instruction in English language arts.

The purpose of this charter school was to teach new behaviors associated with military discipline to vulnerable inner-city youth, and then under that regimen instruct them in the usual curriculum of a public high school. From what I saw and from other reporting this school has been quite successful in fulfilling its mission. In fact, if we *fast-forward* to the academic year 2015–2016 and check the reporting from *U.S. News and World Report*, the *Oakland Military Institute* students performed above the Oakland school district averages, but still below the California state averages.[538] Given the socio-economic status of its inner-city students these results have been encouraging.

I also once spent a day as a substitute teacher at the other charter school founded by Brown: *The Oakland School for the Arts*. The school seemed well-run, but I don't have a memorable story for that one.

Our purpose in describing some of the types of charter schools is not to provide a comprehensive list of the various alternatives. Rather it is to make clear that among charter schools there is a variety of alternatives for parents and stakeholders to explore. Depending on one's location the choices will be different.

HOMESCHOOLING IMPROVEMENT

To educate one's child at home is free of charge on one level, but can be quite costly on another when one considers the opportunity costs to a parent who has given up on employment to become the at home teacher/tutor to his or her child.

Four of the author's and his wife's grandchildren, at the time of this writing, are being homeschooled in their Pennsylvania home (shown in the Preview section of this book). They and other homeschooling parents gather every Monday in rented space within a Hanover, PA Lutheran church for a plenary sessions. In several classrooms the students recite, answer, and discuss their subjects with their grade level peers. I witnessed one of these meetings in which five 8th grade students worked on arithmetic, astronomy, Latin, and logic. As we already mentioned in Chapter 12, their homeschooling program, the Classical Conversations™ curriculum, seems to be a first-rate program. It is effectively the *Classical Trivium* with studies in *Grammar, Logic, and Rhetoric*. On the other four weekdays the parents of these children provide at home instruction, usually by themselves though they sometimes use hired tutors to perform some of this. You would think their recitations of Latin would be boring? Far from it. They had made various games based on knowing the English translation of Latin words. We enjoyed watching these Latin games: Conjugation can be fun.

Combined choices

In some school districts and in some states, public schools allow/offer part-time instruction. One can imagine a child being homeschooled part-time and receiving public school instruction part-time. You could even imagine a student receiving instruction from three or more entities. A virtual (online) school could provide some of that. The public school (or a private school) could provide other courses. The parent would then cover the remaining instructional needs. Education savings accounts (ESAs), that we encountered earlier, would be a good funding vehicle for such combined choices given the built-in flexibility in the way vendors are paid.

RELIGIOUS STUDIES IMPROVEMENT

We see two avenues of reform that could correct or help correct these thorny problems concerning the religious education of public school students:

1. The public school systems could outsource religious studies to multiple sectarian organizations and give parents a choice among them. We call this the Catechism model.

2. The state departments of education, or other state funding agencies, could award vouchers to parents that they could use to choose private schools that best meet their needs, including religious instruction.

The Catechism model

The Catholic Church has had a Catechism program of after school religious education for decades in which children enrolled at public schools would attend away from the public school site, perhaps once per week. In any given community, we could extend this idea to all religious organizations wanting to participate. There would be several *Catechism* alternatives. Instead of having this program after school, we propose that it would be timed to be offered during the last one or two hours of the school day on one day of the week specified by the public school. For parents not choosing a Catechism alternative, the public school would provide a religious studies program during that same time period. It would be required to pass the Lemon Test. How such programs would be funded is an open question. Using private monies for these Catechism alternatives would help them with the Lemon Test criteria.

The full-blown voucher model

The state department of education or the state revenue department would provide vouchers or scholarships of sufficient value to enable all parents to exercise the choice of school to be attended by their children. The religion programs of the available schools would likely be one of the factors influencing their choices. Public schools would still operate in this scenario and would still be subject to the requirements discussed above. Ideally, the schools would permit part-time enrollment and the vouchers would also accommodate that.

Avenues to get us to voucher land include referenda, legislation, and lawsuits

This author was a voucher warrior and participated, as already mentioned, in two ballot initiative campaigns in California that, in each instance, would have established a large statewide system of vouchers. Voucher programs, around the United States, are of two types:

- Publicly funded vouchers generally provide means tested scholarships for K-12 students to enroll in qualified private schools.

- Private vouchers use private donations to fund scholarships that are also generally means tested.

The number of American voucher students in K-12 education is tiny. In 2013 there were roughly 49 million students enrolled in public K-12 schools, but only about 0.22 million were using vouchers to attend a private school. That is not quite a half-percent. We have a long way to go before voucher supported enrollment will have made a significant dent in giving parents more choices about where they send their children to school. Charter schools cannot be one of these avenues because they are public schools that do not accept vouchers.

What can help are new cost-effective modes of operating private schools that will lower tuition costs thus enabling more children to attend them. The author's *Stellar Schools* business plan, described farther along in Chapter 17 of this book, proposes one such system. It proposes how franchising networks can be divided into sub-networks wherein each such sub-network would be managed by a religious denomination or other K-12 education stakeholder organization. We will be ready to help such schools

Pass religion.

The late Myron Lieberman was a visionary scholar of K-12 education. He viewed the expansion of parental choice as perhaps the key and essential ingredient needed to bring health to K-12 education. He was among industry observers suggesting that more lawsuits were needed, where appropriate, to force the public authorities to act in accordance with the various laws that govern K-12 education. We ditto that. We think more use of vouchers can be required by that means. Moreover, we might be able to use such civil court actions to bring school systems into compliance with the treaty law of the *United Nation's Declaration of Human Rights and its Article 26.*

How important is this treaty? One way to judge the author's view on this is to count the number of times this *Declaration* has been mentioned so far in this book. The answer: Eighteen times. And we don't regard these instances as redundant. They are all essential to the message of this book

CHAPTER 16

Research on School Choices

THE CHOICES PARENTS MAKE about their children's K-12 education are often hindered by their financial limitations and by their minimal knowledge about the various schools' qualities and performance characteristics. Since most American children attend public schools, we consider them first. Farther along in this chapter, we review vouchers and other choice vehicles to get a better understanding of what works and what doesn't in the broader K-12 economic sector that includes both public and private schools.

POTOMAC REGION PUBLIC AND CHARTER SCHOOLS

Most research on school choice looks to see what kinds of benefits come from this or that type of school system. Fundamental to such choices is an understanding of schools' attributes and performance levels.

Proficiencies and economic status in the Potomac Region

Some educational research is done by polling the stakeholders to find what levels of approval are associated with different kinds of policies. Other research looks at measures of students' skills that correlate with or seem caused by different kinds of policies. A common problem in research studies is the lack of good comparison or control groups. In comparing school types, socio-economic factors often skew the results. So, for example, the proficiency levels of students in Washington D.C. public schools are far lower than their peers in the adjoining states of Maryland and Virginia. Do we condemn the Washington D.C. schools on this basis or has our comparison been unfair? How can we compare systems for which the socio-economic factors are so different? We believe that the intrinsic quality of a school is better measured by finding a relevant socio-economic demographic for the testing. We generally think that economically disadvantaged students, those in the FRL demographic, provide a good group to test to get at that intrinsic measure. We remind the reader that economically disadvantaged students are those who are eligible for the Agriculture Department's *Free and Reduced-Price Lunch Program* (FRL). We often label this demographic with the simple label FRL. In this analysis we first look at the schools' 8th grade performance levels when all of its students are tested and then we look at those levels when only the FRL disadvantaged students are tested.

In Figure 15, below, we observe a *galaxy* view of quite unstellar objects: Eighth grade proficiencies of public middle schools in the Potomac Region of Maryland, Virginia, and Washington D.C. It seems to say more than any alternative description we might consider.

The information displayed in this *galaxy* is taken from an earlier book we authored that was based on research we performed at Asora in which we drilled down into the 2009 performance levels of public schools of this region.[539] We used reported proficiency levels from the *National Assessment of Educational Progress* (NAEP) testing, also known as the Nation's Report Card. To report locally at the school and district levels we used a mapping technique developed at Asora to estimate local NAEP proficiencies at the various grade levels.[540] The actual proficiencies plotted there are labeled the *Overall Proficiencies*. They are defined to be the minimum value of the mathematics and the reading proficiencies of any tested group. The vertical placement of each dot in Fig. 15 was calculated from these mappings. The horizontal placement measures the disadvantaged fraction for each school. Thus each little dot in the picture represents a middle school, and estimates how its 8th graders would have performed on the NAEP. We call the figure a galaxy because it looks like a large assemblage of stars, but as you can see by a careful review of this picture these schools are not at all *stellar*. The caption gives some additional details.

One of the statistics available for each public school for each grade level, is the number or percentage of the tested group who are economically disadvantaged. We wondered how school performance correlates with that percentage, and decided to perform what we have called a tranche analysis to do that. We divide up the schools within each state into five quintile sub-groups or tranches as follows:

1. Upper Economic Tranche or Quintile: These are *upper scale* schools in which the 8th grade class has less than 20% of its students designated as in the FRL group: Those eligible for *free and reduced lunches*. These schools are displayed in the left-most portions of Figs. 15 and 16.

2. Middle-Upper Economic Tranche or Quintile: These are *middle-upper scale* schools in which the fraction of FRL 8th graders ranges from 20% to less than 40%, or between 0.2 and 0.4 in the Figures.

3. Middle Economic Tranche or Quintile: These are *midscale* schools in which the fraction of FRL 8th graders ranges from 40% to less than 60%, or between 0.4 and 0.6 in the Figures.

4. Lower Middle Economic Tranche or Quintile: These are *middle-lower scale* schools in which the fraction of FRL 8th graders ranges from 60% to 80%, or between 0.6 and 0.6 in the Figures.

5. Lower Economic Tranche or Quintile: These are *lower scale* schools in which the fraction of FRL 8th graders ranges from 80% to 100%, or between 0.8 and 1.0 in the Figures.

Before performing that tranche analysis, let's look at that galaxy of middle schools in the Potomac region as shown in Figures 15 and 16 below.[541] One virtue of these pictures is that in one glance you see a useful view of nearly all of the Potomac Region's public middle schools—almost as if it were a view from low earth orbit, but of a different kind of terrain.

But to be clear, Figure 15 reports on the performance of the entire tested student group within each school. After that, in Figure 16, we show the performance levels of the economically disadvantaged FRL subgroup within each of the region's schools.

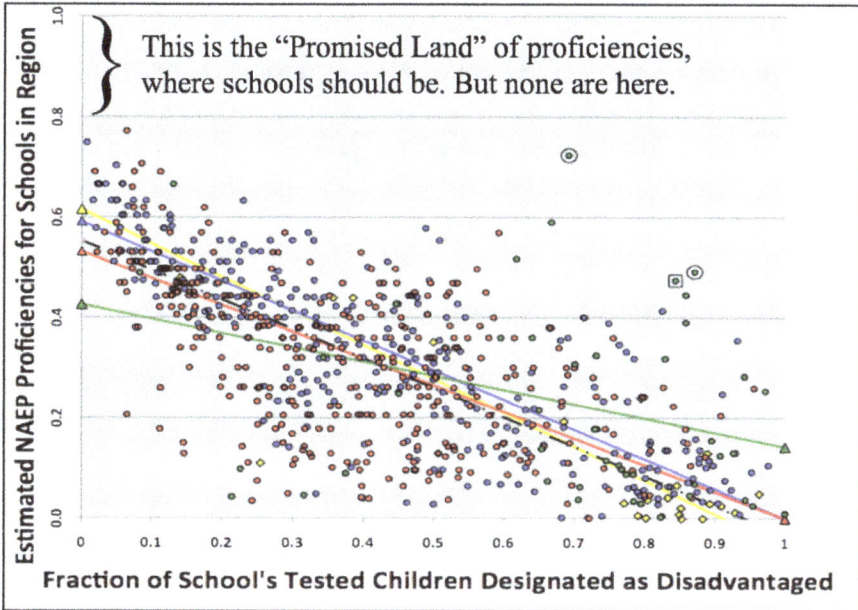

This scatter plot represents the *galaxy* of Potomac Region public middle schools based on 2009 testing from the National Assessment of Educational Progress (NAEP). The estimated *overall* NAEP *proficiency* percentages of all 8th graders are shown vertically against the disadvantaged fraction for each school, horizontally. NAEP proficiency is effectively defined as the percentage of students at grade level or better. The green, blue, red, and yellow markers and lines represent charters and the regular public schools of MD, VA, and DC, respectively. The average trend lines corresponding to each are also shown. The lines shown are actually weighted linear regression lines. For each school shown, the weight is that school's enrollment in the 8th grade. Well over half of the schools had proficiency percentages below 40%. These schools are in F– (minus) territory.

Common sense tells us that any given child will do better in a school that has a pre-ponderance of advantaged pupils (this is well-known by many educators). And, will do worse in schools with high percentages of disadvantaged children. You can see this in Figure 15 by looking at the dots or by looking at the trend lines. There are three inferences that might be drawn from the trends evident here:

1. Children from relatively affluent families learn more at home than those not so affluent.

2. Children in Washington D.C. regular public schools perform about as well as those in Maryland or Virginia when the comparison is done for schools with similar disadvantaged or FRL fractions. You can see confirmation of this by the fact that their trend lines are very much the same.

3. For schools with high percentages of disadvantaged or FRL children charter schools do much better than their regular public school counterparts. The green trend line shows this.

The first inference is no surprise, as almost everyone understands this benefit of affluent families. But the second claim, here verified by actual data, contradicts the popular bias that Washington D.C schools are horrible. The third inference is encouraging as it suggests charter schools, though far from acceptable, are better than their regular public school peers at educating children in those schools with large numbers of economically disadvantaged children in the FRL demographic.

Now let's look at a similar graphic, but here we will plot only the proficiency numbers of each school's disadvantaged FRL pupils. Figure 16 shows this.

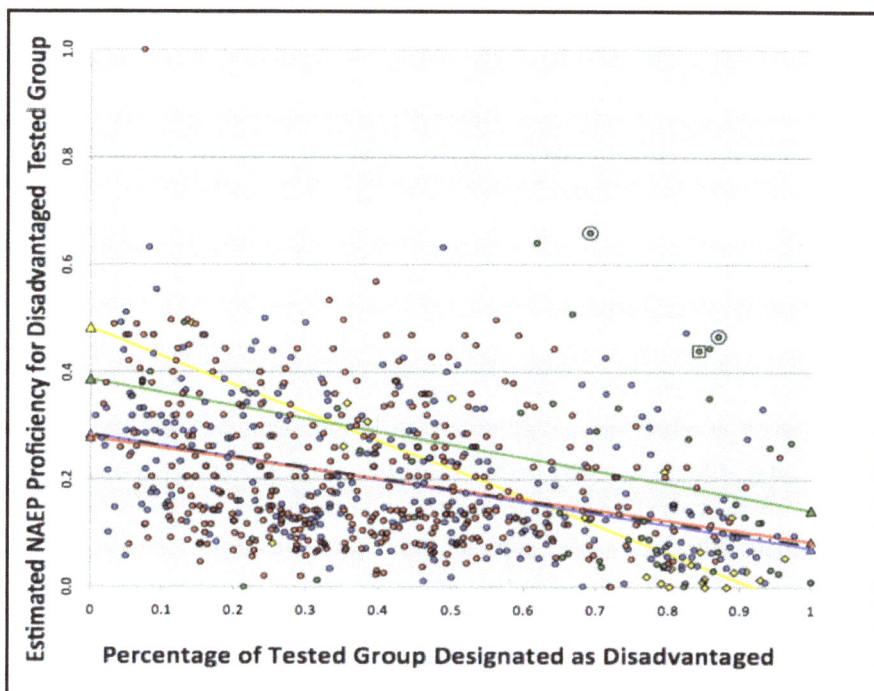

Figure 16 shows the *galaxy* of the disadvantaged (FRL) tested groups for the Potomac Region public schools. Vertically, the NAEP estimated *overall proficiencies* of 8th grade disadvantaged students are shown. Horizontally, the FRL fractions or the disadvantaged percentages are shown. The trend lines here are relatively flat compared to Figure 15. above. VA and MD schools seem quite similar while DC has a steeper trend line. The green markers and line suggest charter schools are better than their regular public school counterparts for the FRL demographic. Note the yellow trend line *hits* zero at about 91% FRL fraction.

One lone red dot in Fig. 16, at the upper left boundary, shows a Virginia school (Longfellow Middle) with 100% estimated NAEP proficiency for its disadvantaged children. We are somewhat surprised to see this because there were 35 disadvantaged children in this particular school's tested group of 459 students. Normally, these children would score lower than their advantaged counterparts, but here the reporting says otherwise. Given that this school is one of the best in the state, it does not stretch one's credulity too much to believe this odd result. One can imagine a clerical error or perhaps cheating on the part of school personnel in an effort to *look good*? Or perhaps this school had an intensive remediation program for disadvantaged children that required them to master these subjects?

One might wonder how the yellow trend line can go to zero *prematurely* at about the 91% disadvantaged population level. Answer:

> Trend lines are a linear approximation. Drawing a straight line among all the yellow dots is done by finding the line that gives values with the smallest errors. Technically it is the line that has the lowest root mean square error. This

is not to suggest there would be negative proficiencies! Rather it is indicative of the challenges of operating a public school when nearly all of the pupils are disadvantaged.

There are three interesting outliers in Fig. 16. They are indicated by a small circle or square around the school's mark. These are the Knowledge is Power Program (KIPP) charter schools. They seem to perform better than might be expected, but perhaps that should not be surprising given the longer hours, longer calendar, and stricter discipline found in these schools.[542]

Another way to look at these two rectangular displays of galaxies in the two preceding Figures is to realize that they are the faces of *social promotion*. The mere fact that proficiency numbers are not approaching 100% means that sub-proficient students are being promoted to ever higher grade levels. As we look for ways to improve schools, surely the reduction of *social promotion* needs to be a high priority.

Now that we have explained some of the Figure 16's oddities, let's zero in (drill down) on three of the five disadvantaged quintile student groups who are attending regular and/or charter public schools:

- *Upscale School:* Where the disadvantaged or FRL fraction never exceeds 20%.

- *Midscale School:* Where the disadvantaged or FRL fraction varies from 40% to 60%.

- *Downscale School:* Where the disadvantaged or FRL fraction ranges above 80%.

Let's look at the disadvantaged students of the Midscale quintile group first. For 2009 testing, look at the dots or look at the trend lines in Figure 16. The schools in the two states of Maryland and Virginia are approximately equal. The schools in Washington, D.C. and the charter schools within the Potomac region are roughly equal at the domain midpoint. This contradicts the usual bias that says D.C. schools are terrible while Maryland and Virginia are said to have good schools. For the schools we label as *Midscale* we have:

- For DC the midscale average FRL proficiency is 35% while its trendline is at 23% proficient

- For MD the midscale average FRL proficiency is 19% while its trendline is at 18% proficient

- For VA the midscale average FRL proficiency is 20% while its trendline is at 18% proficient

- For Potomac region charters this average FRL proficiency is 31% while its trendline is at 26% proficient

The large difference between the average and the trendline for DC needs to be explained. How could they be so different? Here there is only one DC middle school in the midscale range so its contribution towards the regression line (trendline) is relatively small. We find the relatively large 35% proficiency number, itself, to be troubling as it has been called into question by an irregularity we saw in the numbers reported by DC authorities. We think the trendline number of 23% for DC is probably the more reliable number here.

Then for the disadvantaged students of a typical Upscale quintile school. Except for charter schools, here the averages of the dots and the trend lines are quite similar. As for the Midscale group, here the DC middle schools and the charter schools perform similarly. We find this is for 2009 testing:

- For DC the upscale average FRL proficiency is 49% while its trendline is at 44% proficient

- For MD the upscale average FRL proficiency is 27% while its trendline is at 26% proficient

- For VA the upscale average FRL proficiency is 28% while its trendline is at 26% proficient

- For Potomac region charters this average FRL proficiency is 45% while its trendline is at 36% proficient

Only one regular public school in Washington D.C. exists in this range: The Oyster Middle School. Its yellow dot lands at 49% proficient for 14% economically disadvantaged. Both Maryland and Virginia have numerous schools in this upscale range (83 and 84, of them, respectively).

Finally, for the disadvantaged students of the Downscale quintile schools. For the percentage disadvantaged exceeding 80% we have rough parity, (again) of MD and VA regular public schools with DC showing significantly lower proficiencies in this Downscale range. In this range the charter schools outperform the regular public schools of all three jurisdictions of DC, MD, and VA on 2009 testing.

- For DC the downscale average FRL proficiency is 3% while its trendline is at 2% proficient

- For MD the downscale average FRL proficiency is 10% while its trendline is at 11% proficient

- For VA the downscale average FRL proficiency is 11% while its trendline is at 12% proficient

- For Potomac region charters this average FRL proficiency is 21% while its trend-line is at 18% proficient

For student bodies that are significantly disadvantaged, as we see here for the Down-scale schools, it is interesting to learn that charter schools do a relatively good job of educating these children and that regular public schools in DC are astonishingly sub-proficient when we see that the charter school proficiencies for this demographic are a factor 7 larger than those of the regular public schools in DC. Or a factor 9 if you use the trendline values.

The Potomac region's parity in 2009 between charters and regular public schools

As Fig. 16 shows for the FRL demographic, charter schools in the Potomac region, on average, had trendline proficiencies in 2009 testing that were about 8% above the regular public schools trendline for that region. It would be a mistake to conclude that their average proficiency levels were different from their public school counterparts by that magnitude. In fact, the two types are surprisingly similar when the averages are done correctly. Here is our reasoning that may clarify this confusion:

Yes, a quick glance at Fig. 16 seems to suggest that the charter school FRL proficiency levels in the Potomac Region are about 8% above those of the regular public schools. We at first believed that there was such a gap, but when we carefully performed the averages, we found that there was hardly any difference. Thus, the loci of the regular public schools are predominantly to the left of the display while those of the charters are more to the right. Their average positions are effectively where the trendlines intersect the 20% proficiency horizontal line.

Here are the relevant facts for the testing of the disadvantaged FRL students:

- In 2009 the national NAEP overall FRL proficiency level for charter schools was 13.5%

- In 2009 the national NAEP overall FRL proficiency level for regular public schools was 16.0%

- In 2009 the Potomac region NAEP overall FRL proficiency level for charter schools was 20.1%

- In 2009 the Potomac region NAEP overall FRL proficiency level for regular public schools was 20.3%

As we noted above, in four years time, in 2013, the national proficiencies of the FRL students in charters and regular public schools would also reach parity.

UNIFORMITY OF PUBLIC SCHOOLS IN 17 STATES?

The author's small consulting firm, Asora Education Enterprises, looked for methods by which more careful comparisons among states could be done. We wanted to compare the same economic demographic groups across states. Our analysis studied five demographic groups of schools defined by the percentages of tested students who were economically disadvantaged. Each group is composed of a statistical quintile or tranche of tested students. This was explained in the preceding section of this chapter.

You can regard this effort as five studies: One for each tranche. For each state and tranche we average over the schools therein. The plan is that of comparing across state lines within each tranche.

Economic tranche performance in East Coast public schools

The author has expertise in making NAEP proficiency estimates at the local level. For detailed information on the mapping techniques please consult our report *ELQ-Mappings.docx* and its associated spreadsheets in *ELQ-Derivation.xlsx*.[543] Using the techniques developed by us we have made local estimates of what NAEP proficiency percentages would have been for individual public schools and school districts. In this study we focused on the mathematics and reading proficiencies reported by NAEP. We also reviewed the profiles of overall estimated NAEP proficiencies that we define as the minimum of the mathematics and reading proficiencies, to ensure that it is a measure of being proficient in both subjects.

In recent years we have evaluated nearly all public schools in the states along the East Coast of the United States. As was emphasized in the previous sections, within any region of study, we are most interested in two statistics: The proficiencies of the entire tested group, the *All* group, and in those of the economically disadvantaged group, the *FRL* group. Here our focus is mostly on 8th grade students—although similar work has been done for 4th and 12th grade public school students. Over 7,000 schools with 8th grade instruction were evaluated. We also looked at the issue of social promotion for 4th grade students.

The 17 states, including the District of Columbia, studied are:

Connecticut	*Maine*	*New Jersey*	*Rhode Island*
Delaware	*Maryland*	*New York South*	*Carolina*
District of Columbia	*Massachusetts*	*North Carolina*	*Vermont*
Florida	*New Hampshire*	*Pennsylvania*	*Virginia*
Georgia			

The details of this study are in the spreadsheet workbooks *TranchDemogs.xlsx, TranchMathDemogs.xlsx & TranchReadingDemogs.xlsx*.[544]

For the full demographic, or *All* group, Figure 17 below shows the estimated NAEP mathematics proficiency profiles of 8th graders according to their tranches. That is, for each tranche the tranche average for each state is plotted as one of the dots seen below.

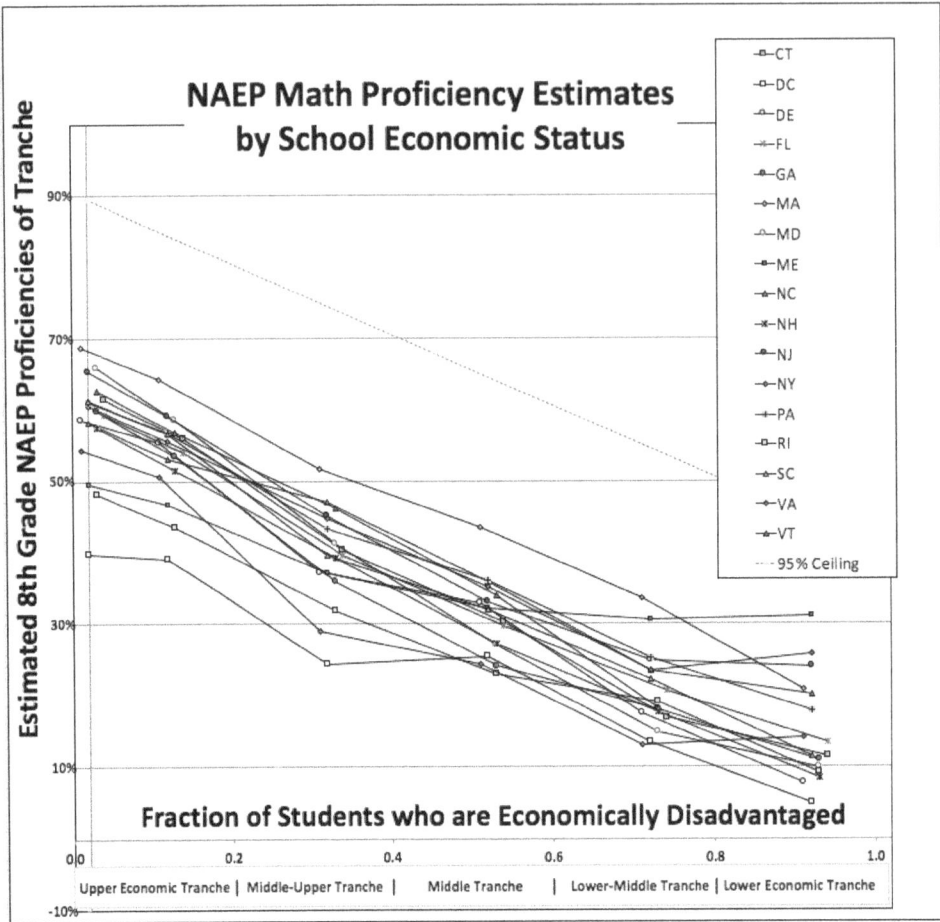

Figure 17. For each state under study we plot the mathematics proficiency profile of its schools according to their tranche designation. We also used a linear extrapolation to add an intercept point at F = 0, where F is the fraction of testees deemed economically disadvantaged. Remarkably, all 17 states, including Washington, D.C., show somewhat similar performance profiles. The dashed blue line is a ceiling that is approximately two standard deviations above the trend lines. This indicates that roughly 98% of the schools lie below the dashed blue line. It suggests that even in the most affluent tranche, the Upper Economic Tranche, only 2% of its schools would have 90% of the students measured as proficient on the NAEP. Good schools should have 90% or more proficient.

The plots for reading proficiencies are quite similar. Please see the Asora report *Signs of Competition in Private & Public K-12 Schools* and its technical appendix for more details. It is available from the Asora website.[545] There is one outlier in Fig. 17 not seen in its reading proficiency counterpart, and that is the profile for Massachusetts, shown in the uppermost trend line. This suggests that Massachusetts is performing significantly better in mathematics than all of the other East Coast states. A possible explanation for this may relate to the fact that Massachusetts achievement tests, the MCAS, do not inflate 8th grade mathematics proficiencies above those reported by the NAEP while all of the other East Coast states grossly exaggerate those numbers. On average, the others double the percentages deemed proficient! In reading Massachusetts is not so admirable: It almost doubles its reported proficiencies compared to the NAEP. And, in the reading plot corresponding to Fig. 17 there is no similar outlier line; rather Massachusetts sits near the top of the *pack*. Fig. 17 showed the NAEP estimated math proficiencies for the *All* group within each tranche and state. Next in Figure 18, we display the proficiencies for the *FRL* group, those who are economically disadvantaged.

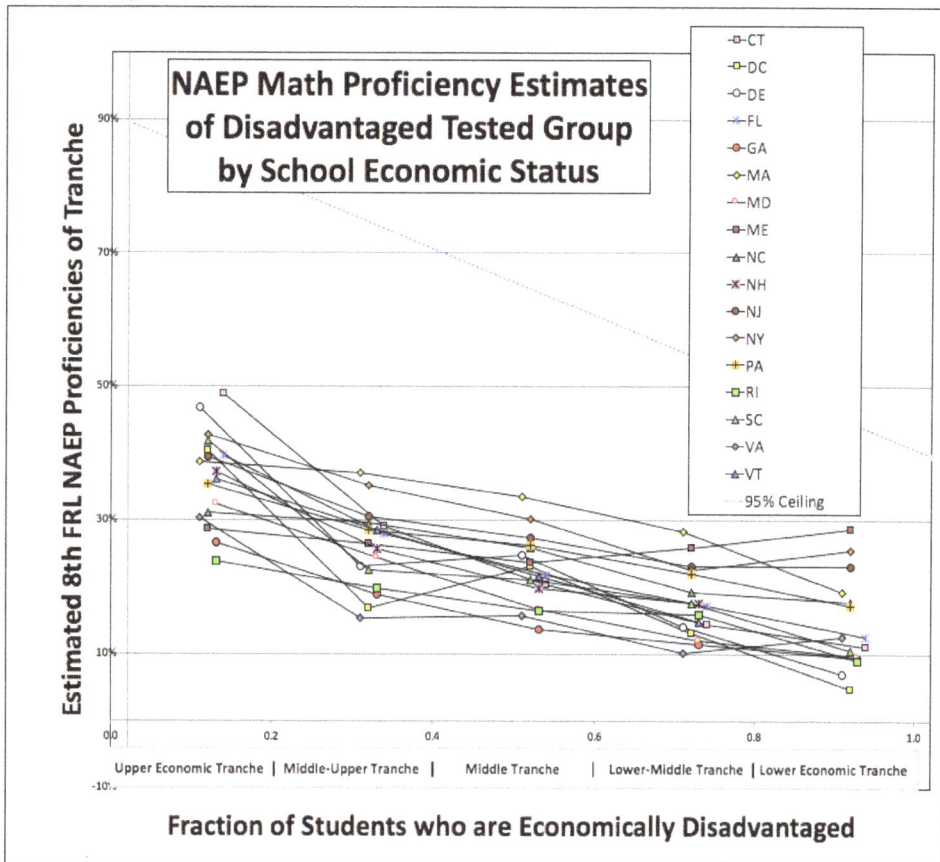

Figure 18. Again, for each state under study we plot the mathematics proficiency profiles of its schools according to their tranche designation. Here we use the school level estimates of the proficiencies of the FRL group, those who are economically disadvantaged.

Here in Fig. 18, as in Fig. 17, all 17 states, including Washington, D.C., show somewhat similar performance profiles. What may be surprising is the position of the Washington, D.C. proficiency profile of its economically disadvantaged students. The notoriety faced by the Washington, D.C. public schools is not really warranted. It is the lowest performer in only one tranche, that of the lowest income group.

We also analyzed the reading proficiencies of these two demographics (the *All* group and the *FRL* group) over these 17 states, tranche by tranche. The results found are qualitatively very much the same as seen in Figs. 17 and 18. For that reason they are not shown here, but are separately available in a technical appendix of an Asora report.[546]

Perhaps most obvious in the preceding two Figures is the almost linear downward profile of proficiencies as one moves rightward across the diagram. We understand this in terms of the association of low academic skills with low family income. The lower income tranches, those to the right, have many more children with low skill levels. Unless these schools provide enough instructional and remedial services to these children their performance will not rise to the levels of their peers in the more affluent tranches, to the left. Another way to interpret this is that children are being *socially promoted* at a higher rate in the less affluent tranches, so it should not be surprising to find more of them who are sub-proficient.

Different states perform so much the same?

It is quite striking that schools within any given tranche perform very similarly regardless of which of these states they are in. One might think that different states' public education systems would operate somewhat differently, expend different amount of money per pupil, have differing curriculum standards, pay their teachers differently, and use different textbooks. Yet they perform so much the same.

When performance is so similar among an array of products and services, it is an indication of some kind of communication between those who are responsible for these offerings and others affected by them. Here are some hypotheses about what could drive these state education systems towards this interstate *sameness*:

1. State education officials keep track of NAEP performance data for the economically disadvantaged in other states, and then adjust their policies to move their performance levels towards their rivals?

2. Parents put pressure on politicians and school officials to improve schools when they perceive sub-par performance in the schools of interest?

3. College admission rates from a sub-par performing state are embarrassing, and lead to improvements therein?

4. Parents put pressure on their children to perform better when they perceive children in other states are becoming more academically competent?

Each of these explanations has an element of competition because in each case someone has information about the other state, the other competitor, and then makes some effort to correct the imbalance.

There are other hypotheses that do not have a competitive aspect. Let's consider a few:

5. The states all use the same textbooks that more than any other factor determine student achievement?

6. What children learn at home is the driving factor in their test scores?

7. The national teachers' unions heavily influence how instruction is given and do so in about the same manner in every state?

Whatever the explanation, it is quite remarkable to see such uniformity from state to state.

True or False: 'Demography Is Destiny' in these East Coast states?

The common and obvious characteristic of the proficiency lines in the two preceding figures is that of a negative slope, going from left to right. That negative slope says this:

The lower your economic status, the more they will *socially promote* you.

It is as if the teachers and the schools don't care about a student's level of mastery. When they are negligent this way, other factors come into play. An important causal factor is what the child learns at home and in the neighborhood. In those environments, economic status is highly correlated with that off-campus learning. Thus, demography plays an important role in what a student learns and brings to the testing systems. For these 8th grade students in East Coast public schools it is then fairly obvious that

Demography is destiny.[547]

If there were no social promotion, then every sub-group of students would be proficient, and the proficiency lines would be level because all students would have performed above the proficiency cut score of the tests. That would remove the correlation of proficiencies to the percentages of students who are economically disadvantaged (who are tagged FRL).

Tranche analysis and social promotion

In a 2011 *Wall Street Journal* Op Ed piece, former Florida Governor Jeb Bush wrote that during his time as Governor, Florida had ended social promotion in the 3rd grade in all of its public schools.[548] So we decided to look at a 4th grade tranche comparison of Florida to the other East Coast states for the economically disadvantaged FRL demographic. The mathematics testing tranche profiles for this are shown next.

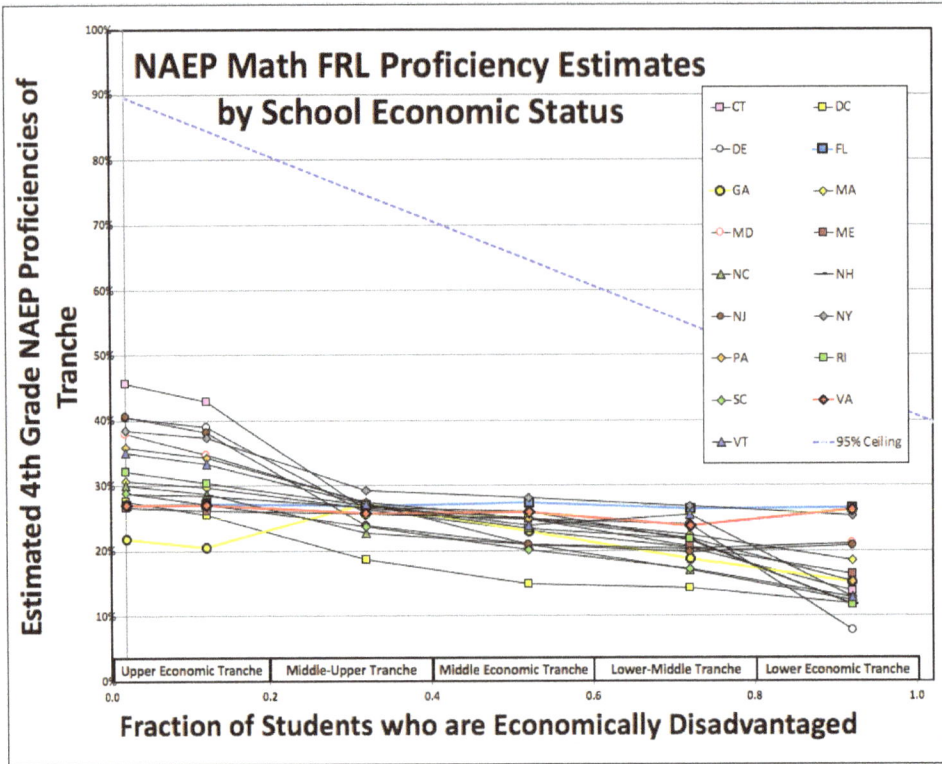

Figure 19. The tranche profiles of East Coast states' 4th grade mathematics proficiencies of economically disadvantaged students are shown here. A careful scan of the graph shows three states with nearly *flat* profiles: Florida is best (blue line for 1st place) with the flattest such profile. Virginia (red line for 2nd place) is 2nd best, and Georgia (yellow line for 3rd place) was 3rd in this *flatness* contest. For this FRL demographic of economically disadvantaged children it shows that schools in low-income areas can be just as competent as those in the more affluent areas in *flattening* out the student proficiency levels. The *flat* profile for Florida confirms that, as planned, Florida ended social promotion from 3rd grade.

Another inference to be drawn from Fig. 19 is that the states of Florida and Virginia (Georgia and Maine to a lesser extent) are focusing their remedial efforts in mathematics proportionately to the needs of their disadvantaged students. Schools in lower income areas are evidently getting enough remedial resources to help their larger numbers of sub-proficient children increase their skills. We are not claiming that their schools are good, but we are observing they are more equitable in their uses of instructional and tutorial services used to improve their lowest performers. Not shown here are the tranche profiles for 4th grade reading proficiencies where the results are very similar with Florida and Virginia *on top* again.

Research on the quality of charters as compared to regular public schools

We previously mentioned Rocketship Education charter schools. In one analysis conducted in 2012, its charter schools in California were seen performing on par with the 10 most affluent school districts in the state despite its average pupil's low socio-economic status.[549] In a more comprehensive meta-analysis review of charter school performance, economist Bryan Hassel looked at 33 research studies on that topic. Most of those studies that he reviewed showed that charter school students' performance levels were rising faster than for traditional public schools. A few showed them rising more slowly. Various kinds of sampling errors, and the use of different data sets could explain Hassel's sometimes inconsistent results.[550]

Asora's research on charters and regular public schools

The author's education consulting company, Asora Education Enterprises, has also conducted research that looked at the performance of three kinds of K-12 schools: Regular public schools, charter public schools, and private schools. Nearly all of our research has been based on the reporting from the *Nation's Report Card*, more officially known as the *National Assessment of Educational Progress* (NAEP).[551] As we discussed previously, we assume that the intrinsic performance level of a school is best revealed by how well it educates economically disadvantaged children. As we noted above, we generally capture that demographic by studying the performance levels of children eligible for the Department of Agriculture's *Free and Reduced Lunch* (FRL) Program. We looked at these disadvantaged 8th graders' proficiency levels in the two subject areas of mathematics and reading. Nationally, here's what we found during the interval of eight years from 2005 through 2013:

- At the beginning of this time period, in 2005, the public schools' disadvantaged 8th grade students were slightly ahead of their charter school peers in both subjects.

- But thereafter the performance of disadvantaged students in charter schools and regular public schools were statistically tied from 2007 through 2013 in both math and reading!

- We also saw both kinds of schools' performance levels rising in both subjects. For math, the disadvantaged students of charters and regular public schools were, respectively, up 9% and 6% on the proficiency scale over the eight-year interval while in reading those numbers, respectively, were up 6% and 5%.

- For these disadvantaged students their math proficiency levels rose to about 20% in 2013 while their reading levels also rose to 20% in that same year.

There is good news in this. It isn't that charter schools are better than regular public schools. What seems to be happening is *competition* between different kinds of schools, and it appears to be lifting the performance of both kinds of public schools. Perhaps

it's the rising tide that lifts all boats?[552]

Asora's research shows how public schools have been catching up to private schools

Many researchers and many economists have wondered if the competition from vouchers and from charter schools would have a positive effect on regular public school performance levels. We were among the skeptics in that crowd. But then we had to face the data, which told a different and more encouraging story.

This story begins with the famous sociologist James Coleman who concluded (we believe correctly) in 1981 that private schools were better than public schools in educating economically disadvantaged children. Since data for FRL students were not reported before 1998 we can't use that disadvantaged demographic to investigate this. Instead we use a similar demographic group: children of *Minimally Educated Families* (MEF) that has been reported on by the NAEP over a longer range of years. In terms of family characteristics, this demographic is defined by those students whose best educated parent had only a high school diploma. NAEP testing has reported proficiency numbers for them over many years, including the 1992—2013 interval. We then studied the public private comparison from the year 1992 up to 2013 by looking at the NAEP proficiencies of this MEF demographic. A more detailed exposition of this work on this can be found in the unpublished, but accessible Asora report, *Signs of Competition. . ..,* that we referenced above.[553]

That same internal report found two indirect benefits of vouchers.

- The first indirect effect arguably was the creation of the nation's first charter schools that were established as a compromise between voucher advocates and adherents of regular public schools. The first charter school legislation was enacted in 1991 in Minnesota and in 1992 in California.[554] As we discussed above, the political fear of vouchers led their opponents to find *relative comfort* in charter schools.

- A second indirect effect was unexpected: The improving NAEP performance numbers coming out after 1990 seemed to show that government run public schools were improving more rapidly than their private school peers. It seems that they had become better competitors than their private counterparts! Could this have been the result of a complacent attitude in the non-profit private education sector? Sounds plausible, but we don't really know.

On the second indirect effect: When we compared national averaged math and reading proficiencies for 8th graders from the NAEP assessments for children of minimally educated families (MEF) we found the trends as shown here in Fig. 20.[555] In particular, the gap in math performance has been closed,[556] while in reading a 14% proficiency gap in 1992 narrowed to a 10% gap in 2013.[557]

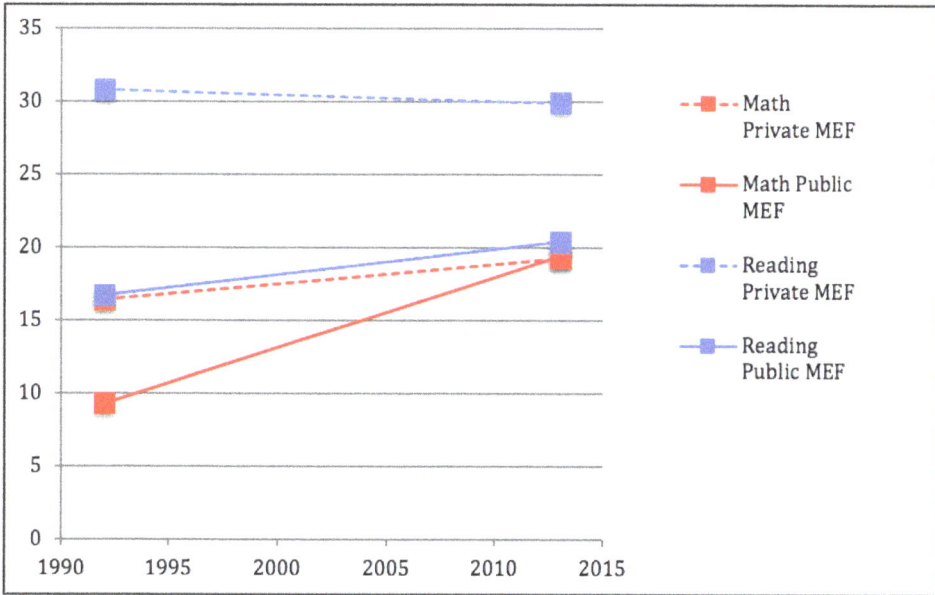

Figure 20 shows the NAEP 8th grade proficiencies for private, and public school students of minimally educated families (MEF). The private school "Coleman" advantage for math is gone by 2013. The blue trend lines for reading skills do this: Private school reading proficiencies drop 1% while those of public schools rise 4%. The red lines show private school math proficiencies up a meager 3% while those of public schools are up a significant 10%.

We found this result astounding. It has erased the Coleman gap for math and narrowed it for reading. For parents who would transfer their child from a public school to a nearby private school it suggests that on average there would be no improvement in math skills. In reading there could be some benefit from a private school, but for the overall proficiency levels it is probably not all that significant. What are we to make of this?

Firstly, it revises the then correct 1981 findings of James Coleman and colleagues about the superiority of private schools over their public rivals regarding the performance of economically disadvantaged children.[558] Coleman's earlier conclusions remain even now the popular, albeit erroneous, opinion regarding private schools. *This says that parents with vouchers will choose a private school that they think is better when, in fact, it likely will be no better in math and only marginally better in reading.*

Secondly, our studies suggest that a weak form of competition between public and private schools was encouraged by the advent of vouchers and charter schools. NAEP's long-term trend statistics showed that the math and reading performance levels of American 8th grade children remained essentially flat during the first twenty years of that test's administration—in the years from 1970 through 1990.[559] But after 1990 both subjects saw modest, but significant upward trends for those same metrics. This leads us to ask what events happened around 1990 that could have triggered some competition? Answer: Vouchers and charters were coming on stage, and were correctly being seen as coming threats.

So, there was competition. But these studies also suggest that that competition remained weak because parents didn't have the *consumer information* that could have enabled them to actually choose a better school. This suggests that *market failure* still plagues the K-12 economic sector because the important requirement of reliable *consumer information* for a healthy marketplace is missing. One of the goals of this book is to propose remedies to cure these ills of the K-12 economic sector. We do that by showing how good *consumer information* about schools can be put into the hands of parents and other stakeholders. That is no easy task because we know from our own efforts that we will be discouraged by the very same people who would benefit the most! Parents and others will show that they don't want their *paper castles* improved. They will remain apathetically happy with the *rotten mess* they can't see or perhaps don't want to see.

In more recent years, since about 2013, these upward trends have been, let's say, compromised. NAEP testing for 2015 showed an end to the upward trends of mathematics and reading proficiencies and, in fact, displayed a dip in them followed by a flattening or even modest declines as suggested by 2017 testing. The standard errors (labelled SE in Fig. 21) published by NAEP are consistent with that description.

This is evident below in Fig. 21 with respect to the 8th grade mathematics proficiencies. There we show those mathematics NAEP proficiencies for private and public schools, and for two demographics: The entire 8th grade student population and the relatively disadvantaged subset defined by having a minimally educated family (MEF) in which the best educated parent finished high school.[560]

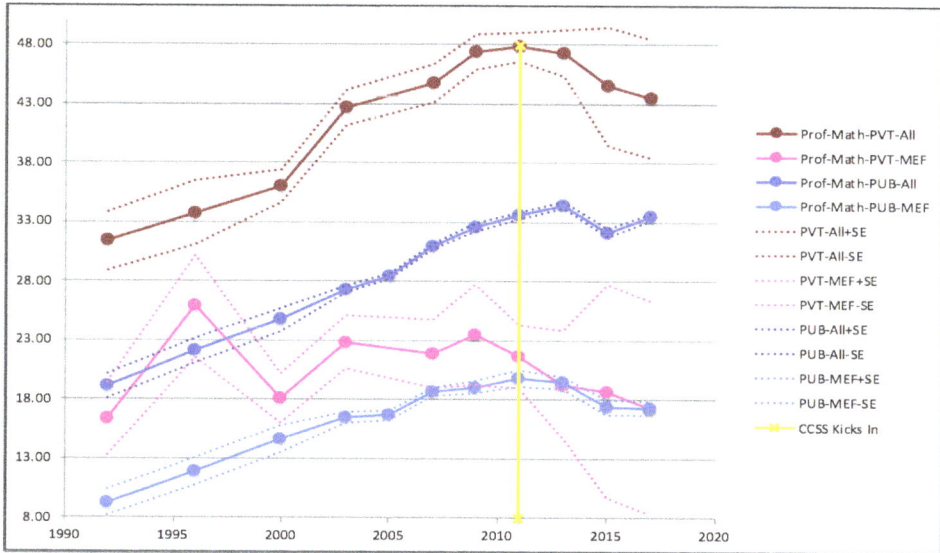

Figure 21 displays 8th grade math NAEP proficiencies of four different student populations: Private or public, and then for each the *All* group, and the MEF disadvantaged demographic subset. They all peak one or two years after the imposition of *Common Core State Standards*. Notice how private, and public are eventually tied for the disadvantaged. The dotted lines show the *standard error* envelope above, and below each line.

What and who is to blame for this stagnation, and subsequent decline of these performance levels?

- What is primarily to blame?   Answer: *Common Core State Standards*
- Who has been the most culpable?   Answer: Maybe David Coleman, Bill Gates, Arne Duncan

Yes, but. Both private and public schools had math proficiency declines after the imposition of *Common Core* on the public schools. How could that affect private schools? In Chapter 12 we already mentioned private schools flirting with CCSS in California. The author also knows of one expensive private school in Rhode Island that is evidently using portions of CCSS without any significant *admission* of the fact.[561] I can infer this from some of the textbooks that are used. I've seen it in their mathematics textbooks. So, we put forth the theory that American private K-12 education has adopted many of the new and untested subject area standards of CCSS that, in turn, have led to the private school proficiency declines seen in Fig. 21. It's just a theory.

We will have more to say on *Common Core* in later sections. What we can say here is that recently the Gates Foundation has muted its enthusiasm for the *Common Core*, but has not yet disavowed its qualified support.[562]

RESEARCH ON GOVERNMENT ISSUED VOUCHERS

To this point in our discussion, we have considered government issued vouchers mainly in terms of their impact on the K-12 marketplace. We considered how vouchers were seen as a threat to public schools, and then how the advent of charter schools came about, in many instances, as a compromise between the feared K-12 marketplace enlivened with vouchers and a continuation of the preexisting public school systems together with their policies of limited choices for parents and students. We've already seen how student performance levels that were stagnant for decades started to rise after 1990. There is surely a correlation between the years in which vouchers and charter schools were coming on-line, and the years in which modest improvements in student performance levels have been observed. Whether that correlation is causation remains a question to be fully resolved, although good arguments can be made for the latter. Consider:

- Given what we know about the deliberations that led to charter schools we know that *vouchers were a cause.*

- Other anecdotal evidence suggests that public schools felt threatened, and as a result worked more diligently to improve their student skill levels. Again, this points to *vouchers being a cause*, and not just a correlation.

Now we turn to research into the questions concerning the direct benefits vouchers have for the families and students using them to choose a private school that is hopefully better than the public school previously attended. There are about six different kinds of questions that when answered will tell us much of what we want to know about voucher programs in the United States. These six queries are:

1. Are vouchers and voucher redeeming schools popular with parents and other stakeholders?

2. To what extent are voucher redeeming schools chosen for characteristics other than academics?

3. Is the voucher worth more than the charter school cost of educating the same student?

4. Do voucher redeeming students perform better than students in the former public school?

5. Do public schools near voucher schools perform better than more remote public schools?

6. Do voucher redeeming students enroll at better private schools when there is better information on the private schools?

The six answers are next:

Whether school vouchers are popular?

In almost every case, parents want to have additional choices in directing their children's education. So, yes, school vouchers are popular with their intended beneficiaries: parents and pupils. This is so obvious that we really don't need to find supporting research. Just to be safe, however, let's cite some studies.

According to a Gallup poll conducted in 2004, 56% of parents would use a voucher if it covered the full tuition and 48% would use one even if it only covered half of the tuition charges.[563] We surmise that the 44% of parents declining the full tuition voucher would do so in most instances based on their preference for the child's existing public school. This might not be an unwise choice given the fact that private schools are generally not as good as commonly thought—a point made, more than once, in this book.

If the question is put to the general public, Americans favor school children's parents having the voucher option, and do so by almost a two to one ratio (actually 62%) according to a survey conducted by the First Amendment Center in 2003 and 2004.[564]

A number of other surveys indicated that a majority of Americans favor vouchers while, somewhat to the contrary, a few surveys that did not find a majority in favor always found a plurality favoring vouchers.[565]

The popularity of vouchers evident in these polls is not guaranteed, especially when clever propaganda can turn the public's opinions towards opposition. This author knows from his personal experiences working in ballot initiative campaigns for vouchers that this just cited popularity is somewhat ephemeral. In the heat of the campaigns the popularity would drop after voucher opponents started scaring the voters with various horror stories, such as the one about the witches who were planning to open a voucher redeeming school in California.[566] These witches were actually fake witches as they were really retired public school teachers masquerading as witches. Their fraud was discovered when Everett Berg, a campaign official in Northern California, ordered a background check. The irony of this is that such scandalous behavior is just what these *witches* might want on their resumés to verify their evil qualifications! While initially popular, the campaigns waged against vouchers turned public opinion among voters quite negative. In both campaigns only about 30% of the voters ended up supporting vouchers.

Whether the voucher redeeming school is chosen for reasons beyond academics?

If the previous public school was judged unsafe, unsanitary or corrupt by the parents they would often seek a school not having such characteristics even if the private school was not much better in academics.[567] The truth is that private school performance levels are often a closely guarded secret or more often unknown—even by those responsible for managing the schools. Whichever is the case, parents have little to go on if they are seeking a school with better academics. They often judge that the private school is not only a safer choice, but that it will be significantly better at developing students' academic skills. In such cases they are generally correct about the safety issues and often misinformed about the school's academic performance.

Whether the voucher is worth more than the charter school based on per student cost?

If a parent has a choice of choices, sounds funny, they might have both a voucher option and a charter school option. In such a circumstance they might want to know which school is better funded, and they might want to know if the voucher covers the full tuition of the private school. According to Paul Hill, of the Center on Reinventing Public Education, state subsidies to charter schools generally exceed those for vouchers when measured on a per student basis.[568] This can often put the voucher seeking parent in the position of receiving only a partial subsidy at a voucher redeeming private school compared to getting free enrollment at a charter school. Thus, even if the voucher redeeming school is available it is doubtful that a full tuition voucher will be available when in comparison the tuition is free at the charter school.

Whether voucher redeeming students perform better than their former school peers?

Some solid research has been performed in this area. Given the nature of most voucher systems there are many more applicants than selected recipients, and thus they select a reduced number of students using a random lottery type of system. This allows a type of research analysis known as a *random assignment study* in which the selected group is compared with the demographically almost identical group of those applicants who were not selected, the latter being the study's control group.

Jay Greene, of the University of Arkansas Department of Education Reform, has reviewed eight such random assignment studies of voucher students, and found that on average for the combined subjects of mathematics and reading each voucher student moved up 3.7 percentile points per year they were in a voucher program compared to their peers in the control groups.[569] Among the cities studied, Charlotte, North Carolina showed the largest annual gain of 6 percentile points, while Milwaukee, Wisconsin showed the smallest at about 2 percentile points annually.

As we mentioned earlier, when these studies were further analyzed by various demographic sub-groups it was found that only black children's performance gains were statistically significant.[570] While it is disappointing to see that the improvements from vouchers were unexpectedly small, it at least shows benefits where they are most needed: among black children. It suggests that these voucher programs need some kind of help. We believe that the parents holding vouchers need to have better information about the range of choices among private schools, so they can find better private school alternatives, and in doing so see larger gains in their children's performance levels. More on this later.

Another explanation of the larger performance gains among black students contends that union demanded seniority policies have a discriminatory impact on black students in public schools. For a number of reasons, few of which are overtly racial, teachers often do not want to teach in majority black schools because of crime and safety concerns. Their union contracts have seniority provisions that allow teachers with more seniority to transfer to another school more often than their less senior peers. The result of that is that less senior, and arguably less competent and less experienced teachers tend to remain in such schools. The work of Anzia and Moe supports this hypothesis.[571] They found that

> . . . seniority-based transfer rights do burden disadvantaged schools with greater percentages of inexperienced teachers.

They also found this effect to be more significant in large urban districts and less of a concern in smaller districts.

In these comparisons with the public school a student formerly attended, there is the question whether the availability of vouchers spurred competitive behaviors of that public school and maybe those of the voucher redeeming private school. We know in other contexts such as on the national scene, already discussed previously, that the public schools were sometimes better competitors than private schools. Were this to carry over to communities with voucher systems, it would also help explain why the student using a voucher didn't improve very much more than his or her peers left behind in the previously attended public school. Moreover, under the competition from the vouchers, that former public school was likely improving significantly.

So, do voucher schools incentivize nearby public schools to improve their performance?

The answer seems to be *yes*. Researchers in Wisconsin looked at over-time performance gains of public schools in Milwaukee, where there is a voucher program, and compared them with state averages of this same metric.[572] They looked at the percentage change in the number of students deemed proficient (or better) on the state assessment tests between the years 1997–2000. Using average performance levels in reading, math, science, and social studies these analysts found for 10th grade students that those percentage changes were 36% for Milwaukee public schools, but only 15% statewide. This says that on average all Wisconsin public schools were improving, but that those in Milwaukee, forced to compete with the voucher schools, were improving more than twice as fast. For 4th and 8th grade students, similar benefits were seen for the Milwaukee public schools.

A study of the Louisiana Scholarship Program also indicated some small competitive effects on the public schools that were located near the voucher receiving public schools even when the voucher students were showing statistically insignificant benefits. They also found that the private schools, that chose to participate, were lower tier schools in terms of tuition levels, enrollment numbers, and student economic demographics. Unsaid in their analysis, but *written between the lines,* was the inference that higher quality private schools didn't participate much, and therefore worsened the poor results seen.[573]

This surely suggests that public schools will compete when faced with the alternative harm, of losing market share, that they'll face if they simply sit back and ignore those new alternatives.

Whether voucher redeeming students perform better when choices are informed?

In early 2016, I opined that parents and other consumers of K-12 education needed good information about school characteristics if they were going to make good choices of schools.[574] This is particularly an issue for parents with a government funded school voucher because most research shows that vouchers are only marginally effective at raising student performance levels, and as we have already discussed only black students show statistically significant benefits from them.

How do parents make such choices when they have vouchers or other means of enrolling their children in a private school? I see three or maybe four categories of practices followed by parents:

1. They already have an informal but unverified understanding about desirable schools in their area, and act accordingly.

2. They seek publicly available information on the schools if it is available. This information is generally unreliable, but they don't know that, and use it to make their choices.

3. They know that they lack the *reliable information* needed to make an informed decision, and then engage in guesswork.

There should be a fourth category:

4. They have publicly available information known to be *reliable*, and use it to make an informed decision.

The first three strategies involve decisions made on the basis of unreliable or incomplete information. Only the fourth one allows them to choose the most desirable school based on their own priorities. We have pondered this issue for years. How can we provide parents with good information about the schools around them? Moreover, how can we motivate parents to seek *reliable information* when they already (erroneously) think that they know the relevant information about nearby schools? We have written on this subject, and have an unpublished report available from our Asora website, *Spurring Competition In K-12 Education—Inducing Stakeholders to Want the Consumer Information They Need.*[575]

With respect to the fourth category, we are aware of only one private voucher program where school quality information may have informed the choices of private schools that received the vouchers.[576] That was the *Student-Sponsor Partnership Program* that was established in New York City in 1986, and as such was one of the very first pilot programs using vouchers. Volunteers in the program were legal and financial professionals from the city. They determined which private schools, mostly Catholic, would receive the voucher students. Instead of the parents directly choosing the schools, these volunteers made the choices, presumably based on reliable school statistics they had obtained.

This program was quite successful, at least it succeeded based on average SAT scores that compared partnership students with students who remained behind in the public schools. The SAT scores of the voucher students averaged about 160 score points above the public school comparison group.

Do we blame misinformed parents or do we blame exaggerated school data?

Do we blame parents for being ignorant of information on school performance and other characteristics? Or do we blame the education establishment for supplying misleading information about the schools available to the typical parent? The answer to this question is: Both have some responsibility, but the K-12 education establishment is more to blame.

Ever since the George Gallup polling organization began polling parents and other citizens about the public's opinions concerning education they have found considerable interest on the part of parents to have more information about schools in their areas. In 1969 the poll asked

> Would you like to know more about the schools in this community?[577]

Almost two-thirds (65%) responded *yes*. This is not to say that all of the remaining 35% would not benefit from the additional information; they are simply not seeking it. George Gallup went on to conclude:

1. While the American people seem reasonably well-informed about school activities, they are ill-informed about education itself.

2. Since they have little or no basis for judging the quality of education in their local schools, pressures are obviously absent for improving the quality.[578]

In some cases, parents seek additional information as this author once did, circa 1978, about the schools attended by his children in California and about other nearby schools. I sought school performance information based on the state's standardized testing results. As in my case, the performance levels were often grossly exaggerated. I know that now, but I didn't know that then nor did I even worry that the statistics I saw could be misleading. This suggests that in many cases, if not in most cases, parents who look deeper find seemingly reassuring information. They are being misled by the education establishment.

What about parents seeking information about private schools? They generally assume that the nearby private schools are better alternatives to their local public schools if only they could afford the tuition. That is the popular notion. And, yes, NAEP testing nationwide shows the superiority of private school students' performance levels over those of public school students. But as we have previously discussed earlier in this chapter, a fairer comparison uses the performance levels of economically disadvantaged students. They give us what we have called the schools' *intrinsic* performance levels. As we have noted already, on that basis, private school performance in math is no better than for the public schools. In reading, private schools have an advantage that seems to be shrinking towards insignificance. This means that the *devil is in the details*, and those details, particularly for private schools, are very difficult to find, and then interpret.

Many states that have enacted voucher systems or offered similar grants have made efforts to supply parents with information about their choices among schools. A good review of these efforts is in a report from the National Conference of State Legislatures.[579] Some of the legislation enacted in some of these states ensures greater access to private school testing results, and yet gives parents and others no adequate means by which they can compare the schools. The private schools generally do not take the state's public school standardized tests making it difficult to compare results. A simple and straightforward comparison of the schools' performance levels don't sort out what students learn at school from what they learn at home. We have sought to address that by comparing similar sub-groups or demographics, such as the FRL or MEF students, for which the amount learned at home is small. More on that in the next sub-section.

We at Asora have had pilot projects in which we published the performance estimates of all schools within a local jurisdiction—such as within a county. Those prototypical guides estimated how every school, public and private, would have fared on the *Nation's Report Card*. Sadly, we found little to no interest in producing such guides for the three counties we selected around the country (Bristol in MA, Shelby in TN, and Orange in CA). *Apathy reigns.*

Must use intrinsic performance levels to gauge school quality

As we discussed earlier in this chapter, there are two demographic subgroups for which their performance levels are mostly the result of what they learn at school with what they learn at home being less important. Those two groups are:

- Children of minimally educated families (MEF) in which the best educated parent finished high school.

- Economically disadvantaged children who are eligible for the U.S. Agriculture Department's *Free and Reduced Lunch* (FRL) program.

Both of these demographic groups have similar performance levels on standardized tests. The NAEP has used both of these sub-groups. The MEF students were reported on in the earlier years of NAEP testing while the FRL students' NAEP testing results are more recent.

While estimating these intrinsic performance levels for public schools is straightforward, obtaining those numbers for private schools is daunting. Such numbers will not be available unless the private school measures and reports the results for one or the other of these demographic subgroups. In a few states, such as Rhode Island, private schools have the option of taking the state assessments, but most don't. There are a few other states in which voucher redeeming schools are required to take the state tests but even in that case the reporting may be restricted just to the tested voucher students, and not the general school population.

Thus, the testing systems rarely provide useful information about how private schools educate economically disadvantaged children. Then without such information, it is difficult to judge a school's intrinsic ability to educate. It then becomes difficult to find performance numbers that are not clouded by wealth effects of the children from more affluent families.

Our best effort to circumvent lack of private schools reported performance levels

Given the absence of most private schools' performance data for their disadvantaged children and given the general lack of performance data for private elementary and middle schools, we set out to use our mathematics skills to generate the best possible estimates of these private school performance levels. In 2017 we applied those skills to existing school performance data available for all schools public and private in the two-state combination of Rhode Island and Massachusetts. The result was a prototypical guidebook, *Parents' Guide To Schools & Services In Rhode Island & Massachusetts*, which can be downloaded from the Asora website.[580]

In assessing the quality of any school, public or private, it is useful to compare the skills of economically disadvantaged children to those of their more affluent peers.

For any tested group of students, we compute the ratio of the disadvantaged sub-group's proficiency percentage to the entire group's proficiency. We define that ratio to be the LOT factor. LOT is an acronym of "least of these," and is based, in part, on the Christian principle that how we treat the "least of these" is an important criterion. Where schools are able to raise this number to be near 1.0, we infer that they have taken measures to remediate most of the problems affecting the disadvantaged sub-group, and have done so to such an extent that the poor children perform on par with their more affluent peers. We publish these LOT ratios in our guidebooks.

Our best efforts for 11th and 12th grade high school students.

Making these estimates for 11th and 12th grade was the easier task compared with the 8th and 4th grade levels. There are three categories of high schools that are treated accordingly. The related three procedures for high schools are:

Public high schools. We use state published proficiency percentages for each school's entire tested group (aka the *All* group) and for each school's economically disadvantaged *FRL* group, and then use our in-house Asora mapping methods to generate NAEP estimates of what proficiencies these schools would have achieved on that test if it were given locally. These estimates are generally accurate to within plus or minus 10% proficiency points.

Private high schools that reported average SAT scores. We applied a linear regression mapping using the known relationship between public schools' SAT scores and NAEP proficiencies, and then applying that relationship to the private school SAT scores to produce an *All* group NAEP estimate. A very rough estimate of the private high school's NAEP proficiency of the disadvantaged subgroup is more difficult to estimate. To explain our method, we use the LOT factor from national testing. It is obtained by dividing the private school nationally known disadvantaged *FRL group's* NAEP proficiency by the national *All* group NAEP proficiency. We apply that factor (by multiplying it) to the school's *All* group NAEP estimate to generate a very rough estimate of that school's disadvantaged NAEP proficiency. That factor was .29 for 2015 NAEP testing at the national level. The *All* group estimates are generally accurate to within plus or minus 13% proficiency points. For the disadvantaged *FRL* group the errors are much larger probably in the 25% proficiency point range.

Private high schools that did not report SAT scores. Here the estimation is crude and simple. We know the national NAEP performance ratio between public high schools and private high schools. We simply apply this ratio to the NAEP estimated district average proficiency levels for the *All* subgroup in public schools in that district, and then use that number as our estimate of the private high school NAEP proficiency. To get the estimate for the disadvantaged *FRL* group we use the same LOT factor, of .29, used above, and then apply it to the *All* group estimate to generate the disadvantaged group numbers. These estimates are both rough, and crude, but from limited experience their errors seem to range plus or minus 25% proficiency points.

Our best efforts at lower grade levels.

Similar procedures have been used to generate estimates at the 8th and then at the 4th grade levels.

Public schools were the easiest to treat. We simply used our mapping procedures to generate estimated NAEP proficiencies for them just as we did for the high schools. These are our most accurate estimates of NAEP proficiencies, generally accurate to plus or minus 5% on the proficiency scale.

For private schools that feed students to private high schools that took the SAT. Here we collected the nationally reported increments or decrements in NAEP proficiencies of private schools between 12th grade, and the 8th or 4th grades for the two subjects. We then apply these collected numbers to generate the NAEP estimates of the local middle and elementary schools that "feed" students to the high school that took the SAT. As for 12th grade, we apply the LOT factors to estimate the NAEP proficiencies for the disadvantaged students. Errors for this type of school are generally in the 20% range.

For private schools that did not feed students to the SAT high schools. Here we collected a different set of nationally known increments or decrements. This time we use the nationally known gaps in performance between public and private schools at the 8th grade or 4th grade, and use them to compute an estimate for the private school by requiring the same gap locally within the district between public and private schools. Again, as above, the LOT factors are applied to generate estimates for the disadvantaged students. As the least accurate of our estimates for NAEP proficiencies we believe these errors are about plus or minus 30%.

By applying these procedures, we were able to generate a performance number for every private and public school in the two states of Rhode Island and Massachusetts. One might ponder whether such estimates with their admittedly large errors could be of any use? The answer is *yes*. It is *yes* because these numbers generally don't need to be accurate when the gaps in student performance levels between actual and desired are even larger than these error levels. Another reason for using such inaccurate numbers relates to their ability to raise the *alarm*. If these numbers are the best we can do, we need to have better testing and better reporting of student skills, particularly in the private schools. Tell them to *clean up their act*!

Having consumer information, such as provided in these prototypical guides, is only a *baby step* in fixing our *Sick Schools*. As we go along, we'll look at larger steps that can be taken to address these problems.

Vouchers writ large

We didn't mention the success of vouchers and similar vehicles in many foreign lands. The European Parliament may have played a positive role in this by virtue of its passage of the 1984 *Luster Resolution* that strongly urged its European Union member states to provide vouchers or other vehicles to support the parental rights in the *United Nation's Declaration of Human Rights*. In accordance with that, most of the EU member states have adopted measures, and then implemented programs to help finance parents' choices for their children's education. It's a shame that the U.S. Congress didn't act similarly.

Some of the examples from Europe and South America are:

- Sweden has had a national program since 1993 funded at the 85% level (compared to regular public schools)

- Netherlands has had a program for just over one-hundred years, since 1917, and most children select private schools therein.

- Czech Republic has had a growing system of vouchers since the fall of communism in 1989.

- Chile has had vouchers since 1982 that are funded at essentially the 100% level.

- Columbia has had vouchers since 1991 that are funded at roughly the 50% level.[581]

The research and the international success of vouchers both say that these subsidies work. They may not work as well as they might, particularly when parents have insufficient reliable information about schools. But they do work, and that's good to know.

CHAPTER 17

Despised For-Profit K-12 Industry Grows Slowly

WHAT ABOUT THE ROLE of for-profit K-12 education. There are many businesses that can be operated either as a for-profit or as a non-profit. Though these two kinds of organizations are different in many respects they often have similar goals. So, for example, a non-profit is often a charitable organization while for-profit enterprises are often charitable in that they make charitable donations to non-profit groups.

Because of such similarities that are sometimes found in non-profit and for-profit enterprises there are examples of such organizations wanting to convert to the other *financial* format. It is a fairly straightforward process to accomplish the conversion. In the cases of non-profits seeking for-profit status, where it is often done to make the overall operation more cost effective, the process involves careful due diligence on the part of the non-profit's trustees, and from the for-profit's board of trustees, and almost always requires approval from government officials responsible for incorporating new enterprises.[582] Forming a non-profit organization from a for-profit enterprise is more complicated. It is essentially a two-step process: 1. Close the for-profit. 2. Open the non-profit. Closing the for-profit involves the payment of all debts, and some kind of stock purchase from the enterprise's shareholders. After the non-profit becomes legally incorporated it then purchases the defunct enterprise's assets.

FOR-PROFIT K-12 EDUCATION HAS BEEN SHUNNED

For those who are altruistic, the non-profit format often seems preferable. But it isn't always the best option. What did the founder of modern economics, Scotsman Adam Smith (1723—1790), have to say on this? Those altruistic souls who have read and understand him know that the hidden hand of a for-profit venture often produces more social good than the benevolent hand of a charitable well-intended organization.[583]

Controversies about who has the moral high ground among different organizational types usually involve anecdotal evidence that shows an example where one or more of the other side's organizations were corrupt. The political right often sees non-profit and governmental organizations as more susceptible to corruption, and this leads them to prefer *free market capitalistic solutions* wherever feasible. The political left, similarly, has anecdotal evidence that sometimes shows corruption in private enterprise, and therefore supports *governmental interventions and solutions.* To resolve such disputes, one should consider the idea that the structures of these organizations are not corrupt per se, but rather vulnerable to the corrupt people within them. We would appeal to Adam Smith to resolve this. He was not only the founder of modern economics, but he was also a moral philosopher. He saw the marketplace of free exchange as a good place to advance almost everyone's best interests. He would probably argue that the for-profit marketplace is more effective in disciplining its own bad actors as compared to the non-profit world. For that reason, it needs less policing than a world of non-profit players.

Our philosophy or theory about the value of for-profit schools is the same as for almost any other for-profit business that serves the public. It holds that there are a number of primary motivating factors in three different kinds of organizations that provide services and products to the public:

1. In for-profit enterprises there is first the pecuniary or profit motive, and to a lesser degree altruism.

2. In non-profit enterprises there is first altruism, and secondarily the survival or solvency motive.

3. In government enterprises there is the obedience to management motive as well as altruism. Solvency is sometimes an issue, but in other cases deficit spending accommodates excesses. The author has been there (more than once) and seen that. In fact, at different times during my various careers I worked at each one of the three levels of government: Federal, state, and city.

If I were to rank these incentives by their motivational strength, I would order them as follows:

1. The profit motive. This fits the popular conception that businesses seek dollar profits.

2. The altruism motive. This is also the popular view of non-profit organization incentives.

3. The solvency motive. While not commonly discussed, no organization can operate unless it is solvent.

4. The obedience motive. Here ranking this last is uncertain. It depends on the consequences of disobeying.

In terms of cost efficiency, we believe this same ranking applies. A useful anecdote from the grocery industry shows this.

> When this author lived in and around Oakland, California in the late twentieth century, he was familiar with a small chain of non-profit grocery supermarkets: The Co-op Chain. I sometimes shopped at their store on the corner of Ashby and Telegraph Avenues in Berkeley. Insolvency caused their collapse in about 1990. But what brought about that demise? It was likely misdirected altruism. It appears that there were too many constraints on the stores' operations based on this or that political opinion. Vegetarians in one corner, vegans in another, foes of GMO's lurking in aisle 7. How were the slaughtered animals treated in their prime? Were the chickens vegetarians (not allowed to eat worms and bugs)? For the most part, their services were helpful to the surrounding communities, but they over-extended themselves with those activities, which often did cost money they could barely afford. Eventually, they ran out of cash, and had to close in 1990.[584]

The old Co-op store building now houses a Whole Foods Supermarket, which is a for-profit arm of Amazon.com industries, and is thereby primarily owned, at the time of this writing, by the wealthiest person on earth: Jeff Bezos. The old Co-op had good food. Its replacement has better food!

The moral of this story is:

> Too much altruism is not good for solvency.

On the flip side, good profits allow a business to be charitable, and thus altruistic.

Segments of K-12 education economic sector operated as for-profit enterprises

While only a very small percentage of schools are operated as for-profit companies, a very large majority of suppliers and other service providers to schools are run as for-profit enterprises.

Books used in K-12 schools are almost entirely published by for-profit firms. Non-profit publishers exist mostly in the post-secondary marketplace where, for example, universities often support a publishing arm.[585] Thus, non-profit publishers make a very small, almost negligible, contribution to books used in K-12 schools. Although we frequently think that teachers are the primary source of student knowledge and skills, it is more often the case that the books are that primary source. Teachers help transmit that knowledge to the students so their role, though important, is not as fundamental to learning as the books. Perhaps this is why old-timers referred to schools as a place of *book learnin* rather than *teacher learnin*!

Audio-visual and online materials are produced by a variety of organizations, some for-profit and some non-profit. I earlier mentioned the 1957 distance education course in high school physics. It was very much a non-profit product and service.

The instructional films (163 in all) used in that course were produced by WQED, a non-profit educational television station in Pittsburgh, PA. More often, audio-visual offerings are produced by for-profit enterprises, particularly fictional literature portrayed in movies.

Perhaps the most capital intensive assets in K-12 education are the school buildings and facilities. They are all built by for-profit construction firms. Ever heard of a non-profit school construction company?

Many of the other products and services used by K-12 schools are provided by commercial firms. Here is an incomplete list:

- Books
- Paper
- Pencils
- Pens
- Musical instruments
- Portable computing devices
- Tutoring services when contracted out.
- School transportation (as in school buses) when contracted out.
- Custodial services when contracted out.
- Security services when contracted out.

The last four examples, when done in house, and not contracted out, are typically provided within the context of a non-profit private school or a (non-profit) public school.

Our goal here is not to dissect the operations of the many for-profit suppliers and servicers of K-12 schools. Rather, we want to study for-profit schools themselves because we think they could be best for students and best for shareholders at the same time. That is, they *could* be best if anti-competitive laws and regulations don't stifle their growth. They *could* surely do this, if corrupt officials didn't fight them beyond their maximum legal authority.

Early history of for-profit K-12 schools 1809–1920

When we say for-profit K-12 schools, we restrict that label to schools that are owned by a private enterprise. This means, for this sub-section, that we don't include non-profit or charter schools that are operated under contract by a for-profit private enterprise, typically by an Education Management Organization (EMO).

The reader may also object that we begin this time interval of 111 years with the year 1809, as it pre-dates the span of years (1951–2018) that we assigned to this Part

IV of the book. We place it here because for-profit education is topically very much a contemporary concern despite its roots in earlier centuries.

In the United States, the official dichotomy of non-profit versus for-profit stems from the establishment of the federal income tax that was enabled by the 1913 passage of the *16ᵗʰ Amendment to the Constitution*. To protect charitable organizations from that tax legislation, a provision of *The War Revenue Act of 1917* enabled the deduction of donations to various kinds of worthy charitable and educational organizations. This enabled non-profit educational organizations, such as schools, to protect their donation income from federal taxes, but it explicitly denied these deductions for organizations that were engaged in making profits. Prior to 1917 a different labeling was used to describe schools supported by charity or the government, on the one hand, and schools that were proprietary or for-profit, on the other.

For-profit schools were traditionally called proprietary schools. Such for-profit schools existed in Europe long before they were established in the British colonies of North America in the mid-seventeenth-century. Our story about them begins in early eighteenth-century Pennsylvania. By mid-century, between 1740 and 1776, there were over 125 private schoolmasters in business in Philadelphia.[586] In those times a variety of structures served as schools. Sometimes a large room in the schoolmaster's home played that role. Other times a dedicated building was used. Less frequently, rented rooms in other buildings were used.

In the 1770s economist Adam Smith saw the value of having all children educated to some basic level: Every child, in his words, should learn

> . . . to read, write, and account. . .

And he had this to say about the means by which children can acquire these skills:

> The public can facilitate this acquisition, by establishing in every parish or district a little school, where children may be taught for a reward so moderate, that even a common laborer may afford it; the master being partly, but not wholly, paid by the public; because, if he was wholly, or even principally, paid by it, he would soon learn to neglect his business.[587]

Smith was conditioning his proposal on the requirement that the student's family pay some portion of the tuition because without that obligation the family might not adequately scrutinize the quality of the instruction. Essentially, Smith was proposing subsidized public schools with nominal and affordable tuition.

Giving these subsidies to the parents was left for Thomas Paine to propose in 1791. Near the end of his famous book, *Rights of Man*, Paine digressed to suggest a system of payments to poor families that would both enable and require them to send their children to school. According to economist Edwin West, Paine put it this way,

> . . . to every poor family, out of the surplus taxes, and in room of poor rates four pounds a year for every child under fourteen years of age; enjoining the

parents of such children to send them to school, to learn reading, writing, and common arithmetic; the ministers of every parish, of every denomination to certify jointly to an office, for that purpose, that this duty is performed.[588]

To understand Paine's use of the term *poor rate* we need to check the dictionary. The Merriam-Webster dictionary defines, a *poor rate,* in British nomenclature, as "an assessment levied for the relief of the poor." This suggests that *in room of poor rates* translates to *from the revenue levied for the relief of the poor.*

Thus, the structure of these payments is similar to, but somewhat different than a voucher. A voucher is a coupon that can only be used for tuition. Paine's payments were not directly restricted to that use, but his proposal effectively requires compulsory school attendance, and thereby funds that enrollment through the fungibility of the funds granted to the parents. In his proposal nothing was said about the profit structure of the schools. Moreover, at that time many schools were proprietary for-profit schools, or they were operated by churches and other charitable institutions. This means his subsidies were for a variety of school types including for-profit schools.

If Thomas Paine had been an American citizen in 1791 this would arguably have given him the honor of being the first American to propose vouchers—taking that citation away from Milton Friedman. It is not clear what his citizenship status was? He was an eccentric person with at least three nationalities:

1. As an Englishman: Born in England he also lived there in 1791 when he published *Rights of Man.*

2. As a Frenchman: His support of and participation in the French Revolution earned him French citizenship in the early 1790s as well as a place in its legislature—despite his illiteracy in the French tongue!

3. As an American: He lived in colonial North America from 1774, but returned to England in 1787. He later moved back to the United States in 1802, and lived here until his death in 1809.

Historians question his allegiance to the United States in his later years because of his enmity towards President George Washington. For example, in 1797, while still in France, Paine called Washington

> . . . an incompetent commander, and a vain, and ungrateful person.[589]

Given his *mixed* and questionable nationalities at the time of the publication of the *Rights of Man,* and given his unpatriotic views of the founding President it would be inappropriate to consider him as an American. So, the title of voucher *inventor* remains with Milton Friedman.

The death of Thomas Paine in New York City in 1809 sets the stage for the evolution of school types in the nineteenth-century. In that era, according to the late school analyst Myron Lieberman,

...education was a three-sector industry for much of the nineteenth-century.[590]

Those three sectors would now, in the early twenty-first-century, be labeled:

- Public education, wherein the government owns and operates its schools.

- Non-profit education, where religious organizations or other interest groups own and operate schools.

- For-profit education, where privately owned businesses own and operate schools.

As the nineteenth-century began there were few public schools, and most schools were either run by charitable organizations, such as churches, or were run as for-profit enterprises. As we saw in the section, *Vouchers and Other Choice Alternatives*, in Chapter 15, a few decades after Smith's proposal, some similar ideas were passed into law by legislation that was enacted in 1809 in Pennsylvania. It established a system to subsidize the enrollment of poor children in private schools, most of which were for-profit. These subsidies were not sent to the children's parents, and thus were different than vouchers. Rather the subsidies went directly to the schools. But these subsidies had the same effect: The students' parents paid less or no tuition to the schools.

But after the establishment of public schools in Philadelphia in 1818, the numbers of public schools grew significantly in Pennsylvania and nationally during that century until at its end they dominated the education landscape. As public education grew, truancy laws were developed to make school attendance mandatory. If you couldn't afford to attend a non-profit or for-profit private school, you were forced to accept the government product.

Helping parents have real choices among school types

Lieberman was quite adamant that it is wrong to force children to attend public schools when those schools teach philosophies (and dogma) at odds with their family's beliefs. He would correct this with vouchers or other means of subsidizing enrollment in schools consistent with family mores. On this point he said,

> Compulsory education in the absence of government support is a violation of the religious freedom guaranteed by the first amendment.[591]

The injured parties from this offense were often the children of Catholic families who did not like the Protestant flavored culture typically taught in the public schools. Surely, the government was not about to subsidize the Catholic schools. In fact, as we discussed in Chapter 5 many states had passed the so-called Blaine Amendments to prevent any such subsidies. Lieberman wondered if government funded grants or scholarships to students would allow indirect support of private religious schools? How could parents have a choice among the three major types of schools: public, non-profit private, and for-profit private?

As a champion of parental choice in education, Lieberman would create fair competition among the three school types by requiring one of the two remedies of:

1. Government regulation and financing of all school types would be the same.

2. The government would provide direct or indirect subsidies to underfunded school types to offset the financial, legal, and regulatory advantages of the other types with whom they compete.[592]

Most voucher systems are of this second type because the first remedy would require public schools to operate out of voucher revenues—an unlikely political outcome. As a political analyst of American K-12 education Lieberman said,

> Previous efforts to establish a market system of education have been over-whelmingly defeated by the organized forces of public education.[593]

and also said,

> Because public policies are so disadvantageous to them, schools for-profit constitute only a minuscule proportion of K-12 schools, and they have been a negligible factor in the politics of education.[594]

Coming full circle back to his earlier claim that there is a *First Amendment* Constitutional violation, we can add the possibility that the just mentioned *organized forces* have violated any number of anti-trust laws and other laws concerning anti-competitive business practices. Lawyers protecting for-profit schools need to start filing motions, complaints, and law-suits to rectify some of this.

ASTOUNDING SUCCESSES OF SOME FOR-PROFITS

While for-profit education enterprises are hated, and persecuted in many different situations, some have had the grit to persevere against the harassment. As we have noted, commercial activity within the K-12 sector is discouraged most when it involves the instructional services and the ownership of the physical schools. Companies that operate schools under contract are often grudgingly accepted, but companies or individuals who would own a for-profit school or group of schools are discouraged by a variety of tactics by their opponents. Those tactics are often unethical and sometimes even illegal. Despite this animosity, some for-profit operators of K-12 schools have not only survived, but they have also thrived. Some have not only done well, but they have done best among their competition.

Let's now look at a few of these successful K-12 enterprises.

A small number of actual for-profit networks of K-12 schools are doing very well

There are already a handful of small chains or networks of for-profit proprietary schools, so a trend has been established. The numbers of such schools and networks are small—almost negligible in comparison to other school types. Some of the networks of for-profit schools, of which we are aware, are now discussed.

Most of these networks have high schools, but some do not. Some only operate through 8th grade. The for-profit school networks, of which we are aware, are briefly described as:

- Challenger School (official name is singular) has 26 campuses covering grades K-8 in 5 western states: California, Idaho, Nevada, Texas, and Utah.[595] Its system's 8th grade students scored at the *98th percentile on the Iowa Test of Basic Skills*. We elaborate on this extremely successful school system in the next sub-section.

Those with high schools are listed here, ordered down from highest combined verbal and math SAT scores:

- Basis Schools, Inc.[596] According to Niche.com it had an *SAT score average of 1463* for its 3 for-profit high schools, titled *Independent Schools* by the company.[597] One of these schools, Basis Independent Silicon Valley, tested to be the best high school in the world on some international tests. It's also a for-profit EMO operating 27 charter schools that are top rated.[598] Within the U.S. these include the "top five public high schools" in the United States according to U.S. News and World Report.[599]

- SABIS, which we first encountered in Chapter 12, owns or operates 56 schools on 5 continents. It had an *SAT score of 1360* for its Minnesota for-profit school. It also operates 7 charter schools in the United States. World-wide, about one-half of its schools are for-profit—or about 28 of them. It is a for-profit EMO for the others.[600]

- Fairmont Private Schools. It had an *SAT score of 1340*. It consists of 3 campuses covering grades K-8 and one high school. All are in Orange County, California.[601]

- Futures Academies (previously named Halstrom Academies). It had an *SAT score of 1080* from its campus in San Diego according to Niche.com.[602] It consists of 15 campuses covering grades 6 through 12. All are within California. The Futures Academies company is a member of the National Independent Private School Association (NIPSA), all members of which are for-profit schools.[603]

If there is a comment to be made at this juncture, it might be this: If most schools in the United States were performing like those operated by Basis Schools, Inc, *we wouldn't have written this book*! Based on incomplete information we find very little that is negative about their school operations except perhaps to say that their *Independent Schools* are expensive, with tuition topping out around $29,000 per year. But that's not as pricey as the top non-profit private high schools that charge about $50,000 per year.

It is no easy task to get a good count of for-profit private schools in the United States. The National Center for Educational Statistics (NCES) has neglected this category. So, we have had to rely on our own count based on our own surveys. A minimal count of for-profit private schools in 2018 is 155. The actual number is probably considerably more than that. For our purposes we will assume the count of for-profit schools in 2018 was 300. Recent reporting from the NCES says there were 98,200 public schools in 2017 and 34,600 private schools in 2015.[604] The estimated 300 for-profit schools constitute a fraction of 0.0087 which is somewhat less than 1% of the total private school count. We think in a healthy education marketplace without any corruption and other unfair biases, that fraction would be much larger. Referring back to our non-profit supermarket example where the for-profit enterprises outnumber non-profit grocery companies by at least 100 to 1, isn't it odd that the ratio is reversed for the K-12 sector? For-profit groceries thrive because customers like them better. Wouldn't for-profit schools likewise have a larger presence in its marketplace if they were treated fairly? Wouldn't parents, their customers, like them better too?

Except for 11th and 12th graders there is not much data about the performance levels of for-profit schools at other grade levels, and some of that is quite old. But there is some data. For example, we have the composite scores and percentiles from the *Iowa Test of Basic Skills* (ITBS) that are widely reported, and thus allow comparisons among various tested groups. A composite ITBS score is calculated from testing in five subject areas:

- Reading
- Language
- Mathematics
- Social Studies
- Science

Let's now look at two very successful for-profit school owner/operators. The first one operates in the primary-middle school years while the other one operates in the middle-high school years.

Challenger School has twenty-six middle schools, all top notch

Challenger School has reported its composite 8th grade performance on the *Iowa Test* for 2017 testing for at least two different testing years: 1998 and 2017. Their percentile levels for those years were reported as:

93 for the 26 for-profit schools owned and operated by Challenger School in 1998

98 for the 26 for-profit schools owned and operated by Challenger School in 2017[605]

It is remarkable that they improved significantly even when there was little room for improvement.

How other kinds of schools perform on the Iowa Test. Other for-profit schools are probably not quite so stratospherically excellent. So, we have used an estimated 90th percentile to describe for-profit schools. For comparison we include the estimated 8th grade performance levels of other school types reported by Rudner for 1998 testing, and found that the percentiles were:

47 for public schools

50 for all K-12 schools (this is always 50 for an entire population, by definition)

72 for non-profit private schools

81 for home schools

90 for the for-profit schools [606]

This 81st percentile shown above is probably not representative of all home schools, and should be taken as an indication that some home schools can be very very good. We caution the reader that making comparisons using these numbers may not be fair because the disadvantaged proportions of these tested students will vary significantly among school types. From our earlier NAEP analysis of 8th grade students the first three types would have approximately the following percentiles if we had tested only the economically disadvantaged:

38   for the economically disadvantaged demographic of public schools

39   for the economically disadvantaged demographic of all K-12 schools

40   for the economically disadvantaged demographic of non-profit private schools

65? for the economically disadvantaged demographic of homeschools

85? for the economically disadvantaged demographic for Challenger School (s)

The approximate equality of the first three types seen here is as has been reported by the NAEP in recent years' testing. The last two school categories, of the five, could have smaller numbers than those shown in the first list of five types, 81 and 98, respectively, but we are not sure how much smaller (and hence the use of "?"). We have seen examples of private schools that apply remedial measures to ensure that the performance of their economically disadvantaged students is equal to or even greater than their average student performance. Were that the case for homeschools and the Challenger schools the 65? and 85? would become the just mentioned high percentile levels of 81 and 98, respectively. It is more difficult to estimate the lower percentiles that might occur here, but our best guess is that 65 and 85, respectively, would be lower bounds of these percentile levels for homeschools and Challenger schools.

If these rankings are realistic the small market share of the for-profit schools cannot be explained by them having provided a poor product or service. To the contrary, many of these schools seem excellent. If parents could digest these numbers, they'd quite likely be considering for-profit schools ahead of all others.

We presume that there are some other kind of unfair biases, probably like the ones described by Lieberman, that are making it difficult to establish and operate for-profit K-12 schools?

Clues to the success of Challenger Schools. Some of the unique features of Challenger Schools, and their relevance to its success are:

- Students wear a school uniform
- Phonics is stressed in the early elementary years
- Teachers are hired on basis of subject knowledge and not pedagogical credentials.
- Teachers are encouraged to work after school as fee-paid tutors
- The school operates 11 hours per day to accommodate working parents
- The school operates 11 hours per day to accommodate extended learning
- The school encourages students to compete in academic contests such as spelling bees, etc.
- Music surrounds and envelopes much instruction

Of these characteristics, the optionally long school day may be the most important to the encouragement and accommodation of students' academic growth.[607] It reminds us of the old admonition about the importance of *time on task*.

Do Basis Schools, Inc. operate the best schools, nationally and internationally?

The founders of Basis Schools, Inc. are Michael and Olga Block—both economists. Michael was a professor at the University of Arizona who earned his PhD at Stanford University. Olga was most recently from Charles University in Prague who earlier had been working towards her PhD at Cornell University. In the late 1990s they were concerned that her daughter, Petra, was not enrolled in a satisfactory school in their city of Tucson, Arizona. What could or should they do?

Here's what they did: They opened a charter school that was established in 1998 in Tucson. They called their school BASIS. It is now named Basis Tucson. BASIS was an acronym for *Building, Academic, Success, In, School*, but this descriptor is no longer used by the company.[608] Since that time Basis Schools, Inc has grown to include 27 charter schools and 5 for-profit Basis Independent Schools.

Here is a summary of the recipe the Blocks used to establish, and operate their schools:

- Implement academic standards that are, as Michael Block put it, "are *internationally competitive,* higher than any American state's requirements." Their standards for their 12th grade students are based on several of those assessed in high level international testing, including the Cambridge International Exams, the Program for International Student Achievement, and the College Board's Advanced Placement exams.

- Students must demonstrate mastery of a grade level's standards to be passed to the next grade level. (Yes, Virginia, they still flunk students who fail!) No social promotion here.

- Teachers are hired based on their subject area expertise, and not on their pedagogical degrees. Or as Michael Block explained, "We believe it is critical that teachers possess a thorough knowledge of the material they present to their students and we believe it is more effective for subject experts to learn the craft of teaching than for pedagogical experts to learn the subject content they may be lacking."

- In the middle school years, from 5th through 8th grades, the Basis schools require students, in the words of Block, to "learn more than a year's worth of standards every year." Thus, at the end of the Basis 8th grade their students are performing at the 9th or 10th grade levels.[609]

It is evident from these policies that the Basis Schools have cured some of the maladies of our *Sick Schools.*

- They have cured social promotion syndrome, that we discussed in Chapters 8, 9, 11, 12, and 16, by having a strict policy on which students get promoted to the next grade level.

- They have cured the ineffective teacher syndrome, that we explained in Chapter 9, by hiring only teachers who are subject area experts.

But it is also evident that Basis Schools have set significantly higher standards than are common in American K-12 education. By themselves these are not cures for America's *Sick Schools,* but we see them as necessary prerequisites for a student's academic health. For example,

- They have built their curriculum to cover their "internationally competitive" standards. This was accomplished, mainly, by their requirements that high school students take and pass a number of Advanced Placement courses.

- They *move* their students towards those mastery levels by accelerating them through middle school where they "learn more than a year's worth of standards" of academic content each calendar year.

So, the success of Basis Schools appears to be a product of its founders' expertise, not as economists per se, but from their general experiences in higher education and what is required for students entering college to be well prepared. It is different from some of the technology based proposals the author has made that will be further discussed later in this Chapter in the section, *ASORA Is A Prescription & Is an Enterprise*. Rather, Basis Schools place unexpectedly very little emphasis on modern age technological and methodological practices. We are not aware of them exploiting the option of self-pacing that can be leveraged through online instruction. We wonder if their award winning schools could be further improved by including some of these new alternatives and practices? Perhaps they are doing it, and it has escaped the author's radar?

The stratospheric accomplishments of Basis Independent Schools

Basis has won many awards and prizes for its highly rated charter schools. But try to learn about their for-profit schools, and you'll soon realize that the various media organizations often ignore such schools. You have to dig, one school at a time, to find useful information. Let's look at their three for-profit Independent schools that have reported 12th grade scores on the SAT, and then look at some of their for-profit peers. Niche.com supplied the 2018 SAT average scores for the combined verbal and mathematics testing reported below.[610] First, for the Basis Independent schools:

Basis Independent Silicon Valley, CA	SAT = 1520	Tuition = $29,200
Basis Independent McLean, VA	SAT = 1460	Tuition = $30,200
Basis Independent Brooklyn, NY	SAT = 1410	Tuition = $29,000

Their average SAT scores and tuition charges of their for-profit peers:

Basis Independent Average	SAT = 1463	Tuition = $29,467
SABIS Eden Prairie, MN	SAT = 1360	Tuition = $21,000
Fairmont Prep Academy, CA	SAT = 1340	Tuition = $24,680
Futures Academy, San Diego, CA	SAT = 1080	Tuition = $16,800

One of the first questions that would come to mind after seeing these SAT scores of the for-profit high schools would be to ask how they compare to the top non-profit private schools in the United States. According to Niche.com the top three scoring non-profit private schools on the SAT are these:

Trinity School NYC, NY	SAT = 1500	Tuition = $47,965

Harker School, San Jose, CA	SAT = 1480	Tuition = $48,500
Collegiate School, NYC, NY	SAT = 1480	Tuition = $47,500

Their average:

Top Three Private Average	SAT = 1487	Tuition = $47,988

They make a decent profit and you get a big discount! Money you can take to the bank.

Let's compare the top three for-profit high schools to the top three non-profit high schools. You can do the math comparing the expensive average non-profit price of $47,988 with the relatively less expensive average for-profit price of $29,467. You will find that it is a 39% discount. The goal of reaching a *high class* average SAT score, in the high 1,400s, is achieved either way. Thus, the parents save $18,521 per student child. That's money that you can re-purpose or take to the bank.

Basis operated charters are nearly as good, and the discount is 100%.

When a for-profit company also manages public charter schools, it is interesting to see how they compare with their for-profit schools. Basis Schools, Inc manages more than two dozen charters. Their best charter school is also rated the best in the United States charter school by three different measures. We also have SAT scores for all eight Basis operated charters in Arizona. We place those top eight on the list for comparison:

Basis Scottsdale, AZ		SAT = 1470	Tuition = $00,000
Basis *Top Eight*, AZ	(average)	SAT = 1411	Tuition = $00,000

It is interesting to note that Basis is quite consistent in operating schools with nearly equal SAT scores whether or not they are charters or for-profit. Given the high tuitions charged in the for-profit schools, near $30,000 per year, the *affluence effect* on student performance levels would be expected to make a significant boost for students in the for-profit high schools. But the boost is quite small as shown here:

SAT gap = 1463—1411 = 52

As a fan of a similarly styled charter school here in Massachusetts, I'll add it in for further contrast.

Advanced Math and Science Academy,	SAT = 1360	Tuition = $00,000

Also known as AMSA, it was the best performing public high school in Massachusetts in recent testing by the state's MCAS assessments, with 100% proficient in math and 99% in reading among the tested 10th grade high school students.[611] Our NAEP mapping estimates suggest these proficiencies would be about 90% on the NAEP assessments. Niche.com ranks AMSA 20[612] nationally among charter high schools.[612]

In reviewing media reports on the performance of high schools in the United States, we are disappointed to see *U.S. News and World Report* ignoring private schools. We don't understand why they would not include private schools in their rankings? Or should we take the cynical view that they support socialism in the form of government run schools, and are opposed to private sector schooling? Yes, their worldview on schools seems to be socialist, but I doubt that they'd want to be labeled as such.

EDUCATION MANAGEMENT ORGANIZATIONS

Edison Project's design of a for-profit school network

Chris Whittle was a media titan. He operated Whittle Communications after he founded it in 1986. Not long after that, circa 1990, school vouchers became a hot topic of great interest within the President George H. W. Bush administration—particularly after Milwaukee launched its voucher program that same year. Though details are difficult to ascertain, Whittle then imagined what kinds of schools could be established if school vouchers became routinely available.[613] Whittle had been encouraged by an old news magazine article from 1975 penned by Milton Friedman entitled, *Selling School Like Groceries: The Voucher Idea.*[614] In it Friedman mused about having a grocery sector resemble the K-12 education sector in which food would be distributed for free from your locally mandated government store or you could purchase food from a private non-profit store. Either way you'd be paying taxes to support the government run grocery services. And, in the latter case, just as for private schools, you'd be paying twice for the needed product.

Whittle was a man of immense determination and was a zealous businessman, later described to be

> . . . possessed of his own sense of visionary infallibility, and the baloney-spouting skills of a Harold Hill.[615]

Older folks and aficionados of musical theatre will recognize Hill as the *Music Man* in the Broadway musical of the same name. Whittle apparently had the enthusiasm and bravado of Harold Hill. Did he match him in deceit? On that the jury is still out.

Whittle and a number of colleagues developed a business plan to develop a chain of for-profit schools that would thrive under the expected availability of vouchers.[616] He announced it in a speech to the National Press Club in 1991.[617] The new enterprise was named The Edison Project. It was ambitious: They'd have 200 schools by 1996, and 1000 by 2010. Implicit in their plans was their expectation that the White House would stay in Republican hands after the 1992 elections. They were also assuming that the Administration of George H. W. Bush (the elder Bush) would remain supportive of school vouchers and would help enact laws that would fund them. Whittle was such a good salesman for his plans that he convinced many academic *stars* to help run his enterprise. In so doing, in the words of James Glassman, he

> . . . hired away the president of Yale University, Benno Schmidt—a feat recorded on the front page of the New York Times—and put on his payroll such academic luminaries as John Chubb and Chester Finn.[618]

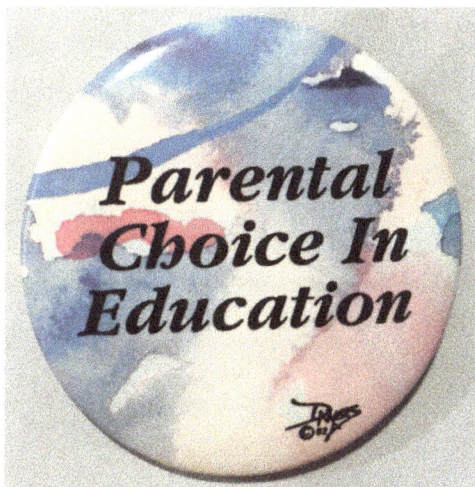

At about that same time, in 1992, this author was also active in California as an advocate for school vouchers. As such, I sometimes wore a supporter's button with the words *Parental Choice in Education* emblazoned on it. During June 1992 in Alameda, California I was wearing that button (actual photo of it is shown here) when I met President George H. W. Bush for a photo-op, and during our very brief conversation he told me that he really liked the button. So, there is additional proof—sort of—that his administration supported vouchers.

After the Republicans lost the White House in November 1992, the new Clinton administration was not *officially* supportive of vouchers, but rather took the route of compromise by advocating for charter schools. This had the expected consequence that the Edison Project seemed to have no other option but to cancel its plans to establish for-profit schools, and then look for other for-profit alternatives.[619]

Edison was optimistic that California would enact vouchers in 1992 or maybe 1993.

Voucher advocates in California, including this author, were also active at this time, and had developed a ballot initiative proposal that would create a vast system of school vouchers. Its proponents had hoped to have it on the ballot of the General Election of November 1992, but they were unable to meet the deadlines for qualifying the initiative.

Why were we unable? As we discussed in Chapter 12, the teachers union, the NEA affiliate California Teachers Association (CTA), apparently used bribery and other arguably illegal tactics to interfere with the gathering of signatures needed to qualify the initiative. Soon thereafter, in early 1993, the Governor, Pete Wilson, called a Special Election for November of that year, on a different issue, but this time the voucher proponents met the requirements to be on that ballot. This resulted in *Proposition 174* that was a proposed amendment to the California Constitution, and would have provided universal vouchers of approximately $2,600 each to enable public school students to enroll in voucher redeeming private schools.

Milton Friedman was an energetic participant in the campaign. His roles included not only being the original author of the proposal's provisions, he was also an active speaker and debater at many campaign events. William Bennett, former Secretary of Education, also played important roles among numerous other notables who were involved.

When the campaign began in the spring of 1993 vouchers were polling well in California. By the day of the November election the polling numbers had fallen, largely as a result of the opponents' negative publicity funded by the NEA affiliated California Teachers Association (CTA) union and their allies.

For an example of the treachery of the voucher opponents consider the plans, already mentioned in Chapter 16, of (masquerading) *witches* announcing they would open voucher redeeming schools. This story was input to many anti-voucher campaign ads and commercials. As we noted before, these *witches* were retired public school employees.[620] It was not certain that this discovery disproved that they were *witches!* A second example was already mentioned in Chapter 12, where I recounted a debate in which I challenged an elementary school principal about illegal misuse of school resources in opposing the California voucher ballot initiative *Proposition 174*.

In the election, *Proposition 174* lost. It won only 30% of the votes to the 70% won by its opposition. One of our opponents' arguments against vouchers claimed, with some justification, that the charter school law enacted the year before would provide California parents ample choice. We accepted our loss, and almost immediately began to plan another ballot initiative to bring school vouchers to California. Seven years later, in 2000, we tried again. And lost again. By almost the same margin.

For-profit education management contractors

So, vouchers were not coming on-line as their supporters had hoped. Even if they had come on line, school revenues from vouchers would only have added a small increment to the size of the private school sector, mainly in the non-profit segment. But the choice mechanism that did grow much more rapidly came from the introduction of charter schools in many states. Their growth really took off in the years after 1995 as we have already seen in Fig. 14 of Chapter 15.

The Edison Project then transitioned to Edison Schools, and later became EdisonLearning. When the Edison Project realized in early 1993 that under the new Clinton administration the chances of having anywhere near an adequate supply of school vouchers were nil they cancelled their plans for a chain of for-profit schools. If they had had a glimmer of hope during that year it was surely dashed by the overwhelming defeat of the California voucher initiative, *Proposition 174,* in November 1993. They soon came to believe that there was no prospect of profitability of a for-profit chain of schools because vouchers would be a needed source of revenue for them to break-even financially.

One possibility, that evidently was not explored, would have had Edison develop new kinds of for-profit private schools that would be significantly cheaper to operate than conventional schools. The expected lower tuition levels of such schools would attract more parents to these schools to ensure their growth. Lower tuition is a form of school choice that according to the law of supply and demand would increase the supply. But that kind of alternative was not chosen by Edison at that time. Similar plans would be proposed later by others, including this author.

In fact, 10 years later, in 2003, this author embarked on a business plan to do just that: Establish schools that could be operated for about 50 cents on the dollar compared to contemporary schools. That plan for *Stellar Schools* is taken up later in this Chapter.

Instead, at Edison, Paul Hill, one of Chris Whittle's colleagues, had an idea: Be a for-profit contractor to various types of school systems in which Edison would operate and manage the schools within those systems.[621] Thus their ambitions morphed from operating their own schools for profit to becoming for-profit contractors who would operate the schools of others, typically public charter schools, and in some cases regular public schools. They became what is now known as an Education Management Organization (EMO). In their first years of operations their enterprise had many signs of growth and profitability. As a stockholder owned public corporation, they had soaring stock market valuations until investors eventually realized that their prospects for future profits were becoming doubtful.[622] In fact, Edison Schools had only one quarter of profitability. By 2001 the share price was about 14¢, and two years later the company was forced into private ownership. This company has barely survived; it surely didn't thrive.

Was it the fault of poor management by Edison Schools or were the school systems that hired them the more culpable suspects? Events in Philadelphia, where Edison managed 20 schools, suggest bias on the part of the Philadelphia school district was largely to blame there.[623] At the same time, in the background, and not helping at all, was the local teachers union clamoring against the *hated for-profit company.*[624]

In 2008 Edison Schools was renamed EdisonLearning as it was transitioning to provide other kinds of supplementary education services, and to make up for the loss of some of its EMO contracts.[625] In the ensuing years the company branched into a variety of other services, and Whittle lost his zeal for private enterprise solutions. A few years later in 2011, retired basketball star Earvin *Magic* Johnson partnered with Edison to develop centers working on dropout prevention and other problems of low-income students. Then in 2014 Whittle and the other owners of EdisonLearning sold their interests in the company to Thom Jackson who has continued to run it since.

Some of Whittle's critics claim that he should not have abandoned the development of for-profit schools.[626] With the capital he had on hand and had access to, he might have been able to develop pilot schools that could have grown, albeit more slowly than earlier hoped, into model schools. We concur with that view.

Mosaica. In the case of Mosaica, its co-founders had already developed the ParagonTM curriculum which was a novel content standard for K-12 schools. They were looking for one or more vehicles to use it, test it, and provide feedback to be applied in refining it. The co-founders were Dr. Dawn Eidelman, who had developed the ParagonTM curriculum and her husband Gene Eidelman. In 1997 they established Mosaica as an education management organization (EMO) to undertake this effort. They began with one charter school. For standards in the areas that others sometimes call *social studies*, their Paragon curriculum covers history instruction and related subjects, and is highly structured—even to the prescription of the student desk arrangements in the classroom. We found very little criticism of this curriculum in a review of Internet sources. We did find a case in which a Michigan charter school teacher found it too rigid, and found that it had too much of a *one-size fits all* approach that sometimes confused students.[627]

By 2001 Mosaica had purchased Advantage Schools which brought the number of schools managed to 16.[628] Then in 2004 the company went abroad when it contracted with the government of Qatar to help run its public schools. From then to 2014, Mosaica obtained contracts to operate more schools in the United States, the United Arab Emirates, India, and in the United Kingdom. During those years it won many awards, but the company's financial health worsened. In 2014 it was sued, placed in bankruptcy receivership and closed.[629] Pansophic Learning was appointed receiver and took over most of Mosaica's business operations.

National Heritage Academies (NHA). Based in Grand Rapids, Michigan this EMO is one of the most successful charter school operators. It has over 50,000 students in its managed schools. Unlike Edison Mosaica it is still solvent.[630] Of its 80 plus schools, 49 are in Michigan. Inspired by Milton Friedman, its founder J. C. Huizenga told an interviewer in 2005 that Friedman's writings taught him about the

> . . . need to introduce privatization if we want to see true reform in education because privatization always does two things: It drives up quality and it drives down cost.[631]

The charter schools operated by NHA use the *Core Knowledge* curriculum of E. D. Hirsch, Jr.[632] This curriculum stresses American patriotism, and is one of the best sets of content standards of those used in elementary schools anywhere within the United States. But NHA has not always acted in their students' best interest when political expediency dictated a more *politically correct* path. In the academic years 2012–2013 NHA began to integrate the controversial *Common Core State Standards* (CCSS) into their esteemed curriculum. CCSS was inconsistent with their *Core Knowledge* curriculum—a fact not publicized much. For example, it diluted their mathematics and reading standards. But apparently more important to NHA was their political survival. From that line of thinking came their reluctant adoption of the CCSS juggernaut into their curriculum.

The National Heritage Academies thought it knew how to survive in our contemporary K-12 education systems. *Don't rock the boat, and go along to get along.* Perhaps as a result of their deft navigation they continue to survive, unlike their industrial peers Mosaica and Edison Learning. But at what cost?

BASIS Schools. Based in Scottsdale, Arizona, this EMO is probably the most successful operator of charter schools in the United States. We discussed its for-profit schools earlier in this chapter, and showed how their charter schools in Arizona were performing at very nearly the same stratospheric heights as their for-profit brethren. It has 27 charter campus locations around the United States. Its top-notch academic standards are set at a higher level than any other system of K-12 schools of which we are aware. As we said earlier in this chapter, their standards at the high school level derive from high level international testing standards, including the Cambridge International Exams, the Program for International Student Achievement, and the College Board's Advanced Placement exams. Moreover, their standards at the earlier grade levels are designed to put students on the path to achieve and master these high standards as they complete high school.

A criticism leveled at Basis Schools is their fairly *high attrition rate* as students move up through the grade levels. There is an easy and honorable answer for this: *Basis Schools prohibit social promotion.* Their competitors would also have high attrition rates if they flunked/retained students found to be sub-proficient at their grade level. Some of the attrition stems from students choosing a different high school as they graduate from 8th grade, and in many cases, about 25% of the time, that is done to avoid the hard academic work and challenges of a Basis operated high school.[633]

A charter school non-profit management organization (CMO)

A related management organizational type for charter schools is non-profit. As such it probably could have been discussed earlier in the book. But because we are interested in comparing charter schools having EMO managers with those having CMO managers we have decided to discuss these kinds of charter schools here.

Many of the CMO's have the altruistic agenda of working with the K-12 educational needs of economically disadvantaged children and the typically low income neighborhoods where they live. Four of the most well-known, and successful CMO's in alphabetical order are:

- Achievement First[634]
- KIPP[635]
- Success Academy[636]
- Uncommon Schools[637]

Three of them: Uncommon Schools, KIPP, and Success Academy were the recipients of the Broad Prize for Public Charter Schools, in 2013, 2014, and 2017, respectively. Achievement First was one of three finalists for the 2018 prize.[638]

If charter schools, operating in low income neighborhoods, are to succeed in producing well-educated children in the later years of K-12 schooling, it is imperative that they teach the younger children basic knowledge and skills. The Education Consumers Foundation (ECF) has been developing consumer information for parents and other stakeholders of K-12 education. Their ranking service, now available on their website, provides reading proficiency percentages for students who are finishing third grade. Their service covers all public schools in the United States, including charter schools. Private schools are not included.[639]

We used the ECF service to review schools in the four states of Connecticut, Massachusetts, New York, and Rhode Island. We used their proficiency estimates for third grade reading, and made estimates of percentile levels within tranches of similar economic status. We also studied schools operated by National Heritage Academies and by Basis Schools, Inc, that are for-profit EMO managed systems of charter schools, discussed earlier. Our goal was not to compare proficiencies per se, but rather use the distribution of proficiencies to make an estimate of percentile levels. We chose the percentile level of 69% as the minimum level for what we designate as exemplary schools.

For each CMO and EMO we counted the charter schools that had an exemplary percentile compared to other public schools that had a similar economic disadvantaged profile. With this exception, Basis Schools did not provide data pertaining to their economically disadvantaged students.

Given that lack of performance data for Basis Schools, Inc. operated charter schools we needed an alternative metric by which we could rank these schools. Niche.com supplied that information from its national rankings of charter middle schools.[640]

Based on those data sources the CMO and EMO operated schools, ranked from best to worst, are:

1. *BASIS Schools:* For this EMO's 8 charter schools in Arizona we do not have performance data from ECF because ECF's data concerned 3rd grade reading levels, and most Basis operated charters do not have grade levels below 5th, and where they do ECF did not report on them. So, we use the Niche.com ranking of U.S. middle schools to do our comparison. According to Niche.com of the 8 charter schools operated by Basis Schools in Arizona 6 of them were ranked first through sixth nationally. *That's amazing: They had the top six in the nation!* Their other two Arizona charters were 8th and 13th nationally.

2. *Success Academy Charter Schools:* For this CMO we have both the ECF percentiles and Niche.com's ranking. According to the latter, this operator's best school nationally, ranking 33rd, was in the Bronx, New York. That puts it well behind the top charters operated by Basis Schools. According to the ECF rankings, this CMO's 24 schools, all in New York City, all 24 had percentile levels of 69% and higher. Thus, 100% of its NYC schools were exemplary, thus ranking it above the other CMO operators of charter school networks.

3. *Uncommon Schools:* Of this CMO's 6 schools in New York City, 5 had percentile levels of 69% and higher. Thus, 83% of its NYC schools were exemplary. We wanted to include its New Jersey schools, but ECF didn't rate them.

4. *National Heritage Academies:* According to Niche.com its best charter school is in Plymouth, Michigan, and was 36th in the nation. Of this EMO's 6 schools in New York state, 3 had percentile levels above 69%. Thus, 50% of its New York schools were exemplary.

5. *Achievement First:* Of this CMO's 14 schools in the three states of Connecticut, New York, and Rhode Island, 4 had percentile levels above 69%. Thus 29% of its schools in these three states were exemplary.

6. *KIPP:* Of this CMO's 4 schools in New York state, only 1 had a percentile level above 69%. Thus, 25% of its New York schools were exemplary.

We are quite aware that a more thorough analysis might alter these rankings some. Our point is not to discuss the quantitative levels of achievement, but rather to drive home the fact that all but the first of these management organizations have significant room for improvement. And, of the six contestants, only the first two look acceptable to us. Surely, these results *give a strong endorsement of the Basis Schools, Inc EMO.*

A library management organization (LMO)

Writ large, K-12 education is not just about schools. It is also about libraries: Those within schools and more generally the public libraries. Analogous to the Education Management Organization (EMO) we can consider the Library Management

Organization (LMO) that similarly is a for-profit manager of public libraries. We digress to describe LMO's for two reasons:

- First, libraries are important institutions that operate as an adjunct to K-12 schools, and for the most ambitious students can be more important to their education than the schools themselves. This author, in 1998–1999, was a consultant to the establishment of an LMO in Jersey City, New Jersey. As such I had a ring-side seat to its development.

- Second, we can consider a new kind of EMO that would combine the functions of an LMO and a traditional EMO. Maybe call it a Knowledge Formation Management Organization (KFMO? One can envisage that a single entity in a school district would operate all or some of its public schools and all of its public libraries?

As in so many projects, what was originally desired, and what was eventually achieved turned out to be different. Two early implementations were in California and New Jersey, as follows:

- The Riverside County, California public library system was outsourced to an LMO in 1997.

- The Jersey City, New Jersey public library system was finally outsourced to an LMO in 1999.

Here are their stories:

Riverside County. In 1997 the public library system of Riverside County, California needed new management. Instead of hiring government employees to operate their system, the county contracted with a company that had already been providing other sub-contractor services to many other libraries including the *top dog* Library of Congress. That Maryland based company or LMO, Library Systems & Services, Inc (LSSI) was hired in June 1997 by the Riverside County Board of Supervisors to operate their libraries. This would be the first instance of an LMO receiving a contract to operate a public library. All staff below the top levels retained their jobs as this limited the outsourcing to that of the management operations.

Jersey City. The story for Jersey City involved this author in a number of key roles. I was working in a policy analyst role for the City of Jersey City in the late 1990s. Working with other colleagues on the city's Management Review Team, we became aware of many serious deficiencies in the city's public library system, and then set out to develop remedies. The list of problems was too long to recite here, but two examples can serve to give one an idea of the challenges we faced:

Example 1. One challenging statistic was the official State of New Jersey measured and reported cost to loan a book in 1997. The state average was $5, but in Jersey City it was over $23!

Example 2. According to the Jersey City Public Library's published statistics it held approximately 800,000 books and documents. Yet, some of the professional librarians working there told us that their own informal count was more like half that number—about 400,000 volumes. This discrepancy was the result of faulty record keeping. The books were somewhere: Were they lost, overdue, stolen or weeded out without records made of these possibilities? No one seemed to know. Who to blame? Answer: Top library management. They could have enforced a proper system of maintaining library records.[641]

An ambitious plan to outsource the library operations included a novel bookcenter. The city's Mayor in those years was Bret Schundler who, as a free-market conservative politician, was interested in cost-efficient municipal services. His administration had already outsourced the management of the city's water department to a contractor that also operated many other municipal water systems around the United States. So, the question was: Could the library management be outsourced? As mentioned above, we had learned about contractor LSSI taking over the operations of the Riverside County library system in California.

We had a plan that went well beyond the LMO arrangement LSSI had in California. Almost separate from the need for reform was an opportunity in which a new central library would be established in the city's oldest and largest shopping district, Journal Square. To increase the foot traffic in this district, Schundler proposed co-locating a major bookstore with this new central library. This combination soon had the name: Bookcenter. An immediate concern was the maintenance of harmonious relations between such erstwhile competitors: A private bookseller and a public library. Wouldn't there be friction as they saw each other's business as a threat to their own? Our solution to that was: Have the same private company run both. LSSI was already a natural candidate for this given that it was a partially owned subsidiary of Follett Corporation, itself the operator of many bookstores. The bookseller and the library would share something: The electronic card catalogue that would be augmented to include all of the bookseller's books (including ones offsite that could be ordered). What a plan! We even had a land parcel in mind that after some demolition could be the location of the new bookcenter.

The evolving contract: After it died it was brought back to life. Various practical considerations led to a narrower more modest proposal in which the management of the library would be outsourced while the civil service employees would continue to work for the city government. I won't go into the details as there is a more detailed account available elsewhere.[642] Then, without much fanfare a contract was negotiated, signed, sealed, and approved by the library trustees with the new operation commencing on August 1, 1998. It was no surprise that one of the unions objected and sued. The judge agreed with them, and cited a number of reasons for enjoining the contract's execution. We did not appeal, but rather made some changes that would likely satisfy the judge, and calm the union's worries. LSSI would not manage the libraries; rather they would be a management consultant. That was more a change of verbiage than the actual contractual terms because the fine print gave LSSI almost the same level of control as in the first contract. So, the second contract to run for two years was concluded in May 1999, and put into force on June 2, 1999.

Since that time, LSSI's library management services have grown. As of 2015, the LMO LSSI was operating 20 library systems within the United States. Thus, LMO's live on.

Meanwhile back in Jersey City, and two years later in 2001, a new mayor had been sworn in. He and his administration did not renew the contract. But even so, the two years of LSSI control had solved many of the chronic problems in the city's libraries, and thus had been a good thing even if it didn't last.

ASORA IS A PRESCRIPTION AND IS AN ENTERPRISE

The very name, Asora, you may recall from its introduction in Chapter 14, is an acronym descriptive of these schools, which we repeat again, as follows:

A) Asynchronously delivered *on-demand* instruction.

S) Self-paced learning.

O) Online distance education.

R) Rigorous curriculum

A) Assessment is strictly tied to the curriculum

These attributes are clearly consistent with the preceding list of Stellar Schools Franchising Company characteristics.

Serendipitous path towards Stellar Schools: Redesigning schools from the bottom up

During the first few years of the new millennium I was gathering ideas that would eventually combine to produce a range of promising educational formats for K-12 education that might inform the designs of new kinds of private schools.

As a witness, participant, and political victim in our losses in the voucher wars, I began to contemplate other avenues that would move K-12 education towards a world in which parents would have more choice in the schools attended by their children.

My unwitting path towards this goal was a byproduct of my decision in 1999 to put my education activities on hold, and then become a financial planner. As I took courses related to earning the title of Certified Financial Planner (CFP) I was also learning much of the financial expertise that I would need to have were I ever to produce a business plan for a new enterprise.

Two years later, in 2001, I earned the CFP designation, and with it began working for a financial advisory firm in a New York suburb in northern New Jersey. A year later we made a tentative decision to open another office of the firm in Rhode Island—an office that I would manage. When that plan unraveled, I decided to relocate to Rhode Island anyway and then pursue other interests in the K-12 education sector. I soon began exploring some new (new to me) ideas:

> I already knew from my own experiences that aspects of distance learning could make learning better and less expensive. Family connections of mine had been successfully involved in the fast-food industry as franchisees of KFC and Wendy's. And, by 2003, computerized instruction could be done over the Internet. I also knew that one history lesson in the business world was that automation has allowed other enterprises to gain profits while cutting costs. Operating at scale was another way to raise profits. Perhaps a franchising network of schools could use some of these ideas and succeed. Why not do this in K-12?

Focus on lackluster private education. My goal was not to help public schools directly. There was too little freedom for an outsider like me to have any influence on improving such government run schools.

When I was doing that financial planning work in New Jersey I decided that I would become knowledgeable about the *529 College Savings Plans* and also the *Coverdell Educational Savings Accounts*. Both of these are tax advantaged savings vehicles that families could use to cover educational expenses over the K-12 through post-secondary education years. To be able to advise clients (parents) about saving for K-12 private education as opposed to enrolling their children in public schools I would need to know how the public schools and nearby private schools compared in the various local communities. I reviewed New Jersey high schools in the northern parts of the state, and used the SAT scores as my reference data. What I found in my admittedly unscientific survey in the communities I studied was that the private schools were not heads and shoulders above the public schools, but almost always seemed to be somewhat better when measured by these scores. That's how I got on to the *track* of wondering what can be done to improve the private schools. Forget about fighting the public education establishment. It would be easier to fight for private school reforms. Or so I thought. The jury is still out on that question.

Could an LMO expand to include EMO services and franchising? As we discussed in the foregoing, Library Systems & Services, Inc. (LSSI) is a Library Management Organization (LMO). Some years after my involvement in bringing them in to operate Jersey City's public libraries, I thought that their roles in the fields of libraries and education could be combined into a Knowledge Formation Management Organization (KFMO)—first mentioned a few pages above. These KFMO's would serve both libraries and schools. I also thought that a franchising structure could be used by a for-profit franchisor to operate all kinds of franchisee schools: for-profit, non-profit, charter, and even regular public ones. As I explored that concept, I reached out to Frank Pezzanite, at that time, the CEO of LSSI: The message I sent him included these comments:

> When I think of the kinds of vendors who could branch out in this direction, I thought of you and Follet. I imagine that much of a franchise operation would depend on books, study aids, teacher aids, Internet lessons, computer services, database operations etc. Given the *book* connection, I thought there could be some interest.

> Anyway, on a somewhat different note, I have also thought about an organization such as yours running an integrated public library and public school system. Since librarians tend to be better educated than teachers you know who I would put in charge![643]

I presume LSSI considered these ideas. But, alas, their response could not be found in our records.

As to franchising in the education sector: It is really a subspecies of an EMO. It simply puts more limits on how the franchisor's operation interacts with the local franchisees. Federal laws, enforced by the Federal Trade Commission, restrict how franchising can operate within the United States. Some states impose additional requirements on franchising (that are constrained to stay within the federal laws).

Slow growth of for-profit schools, but it is growth

Again, we need to base an estimate of the growth in the number of these schools on the numbers we have. Of the documentation we have seen, only NIPSA supplies us with a school count.[644] In the year 2003 they reported 100-member schools within the United States, and now in 2019 the count is 125. Doing the math this gives a growth rate of 1.5% per year in the number of schools. A similar calculation of the U.S. population gives a growth rate of 0.8% per year. On a per capita basis this reduces the growth in the numbers of for-profit private schools to 0.7% per year. We assume that a full count of all such schools within the United States would give a similar positive growth rate. We have a theory why this growth rate is so small. Here are three reasons to consider:

- Parents don't have the money to pay the tuition.
- Various legal impediments have frustrated their expansion.
- Illegal tactics thwart their growth while government authorities *wink and nod.*

Two other types of K-12 education are also seeing growth: Charter schools and home-schools. Losing market share are the regular public schools and non-profit private schools. It is probably a good sign that the regular public schools are losing their monopoly on pupil enrollment. As these other kinds of schools gain footholds in new areas, it implies more choices in those areas. More choices generally translate into more competition. Competition almost always leads to improvements, and as such will help improve K-12 education.

For-profit schools that don't need vouchers or an EMO: Stellar Schools

In July 2003 we produced a report containing our proposal for what we called K-P education. That report, *K-P Education: Superior For-Profit Schools through Franchising,* is available on our website.[645] We include its *Executive Summary* here as it gives a good review of the project's status in that year. We circulated the report to a few dozen experts in the fields of education and economics soliciting their comments and help.

> Executive Summary. We are considering the establishment of a chain of franchised for-profit schools that will cover the K-12 curriculum in a shortened period of K-9. K-P refers to K through prep school.
>
> Given that children circa 1900 covered the K-12 ground typically in about 8 years of elementary school, we believe that children will be able to perform well if given the appropriate schooling in sufficiently superior schools. We have chosen the term, *Stellar Schools*, to refer to the superior for-profit schools we envisage.
>
> It is our view that, on average, contemporary non-profit private schools perform only marginally better than public schools because of their non-profit nature. It limits their opportunities to excel and grow.
>
> Economists from Adam Smith to Milton Friedman have recommended a marketplace for education where the profit motive is allowed to sort out the winners and losers. Until recently, historical trends were moving the education industry into the socialistic format in which the government funded and ran the schools. With the decline of socialism, as an economic system, there is the opportunity to seek free market solutions.
>
> We see two avenues along which such an educational marketplace can be developed: (1.) Providing parents and students the wherewithal (grants,

vouchers, tax credits, scholarships) with which to pay tuition, and (2.) Creating superior for-profit private schools that will attract customers even in the absence of grants to parents. Our emphasis is on the latter, requiring no legislation, and it does not directly affect public schools.

While competing against subsidized giants is difficult, there are examples of successes in other industries wherein sufficiently superior products have carved out profitable niches in the marketplace.

To support our contention that children can complete the K-12 curriculum in the 10 years we call K-P, we have reviewed the performance of homeschooled children who generally attain 12th grade skills when they complete the 8th grade. This seems to establish K-P as a reasonable period for their preparatory education.

Further encouragement for our project comes from the successes of EMO (Educational Management Organization) companies that are for-profit operators which run some public district and public charter schools under contract. We also cite the robust and profitable for-profit post-secondary education industry.

Finally, there are a relatively small number of for-profit elementary and secondary schools that have demonstrated two essential ingredients of success: (1.) Significantly expanding markets (indicated by waiting lists to get in), and (2.) Healthy profits. The preliminary indications that the for-profit schools' the 8th grade students tested at the 93rd percentile are consistent with the notion of truly "stellar" schools. This is apparent when one notes that public, non-profit private, and home schools have 8th grade test scores of approximately 47th, 72nd, and 81st percentiles, respectively. An important caveat is that these results may include various statistical biases.

We believe that the known facts about the different types of K-12 schools financial and academic performances suggest that the industry is ripe for the introduction of more for-profit schools. It would seem that the franchise model will be a good way to exploit these opportunities .

Of the 40 plus experts that were contacted about half responded, but only a handful of recipients gave us useful comments. Most helpful of all was the response from Milton Friedman . It included this:

> You and I are certainly singing the same tune. There is nothing in your memo
> to which I take objection. On the contrary, I agree with the whole of it.[646]

He cautioned that he was not as optimistic as our report was. He noted that our plan reminded him of the plan the original Edison Project put forward in that it too would have formed a chain of for-profit K-12 schools . An essential difference however is that Edison was assuming availability of school vouchers to help finance tuition payments while in comparison our schools would indirectly provide parental choice through lower tuition payments. Those lower costs would be enabled by making the school operations more efficient through scale, methodologies, and technologies then available:

- The scale would be implicit in the structure of a franchising network and in the flexibility allowed in the ownership types that could be franchisees.

- The methodologies of self-paced instruction combined with tutoring would help the average student finish the normal 13-year K-12 sequence of instruction in about 9 or 10 years.

- The technologies that are used in student computers, school computers, and Internet computers can adapt both to individual needs as well as provide services to many students asynchronously .

That these improvements are absent or perhaps entering the marketplace at a glacial velocity is not entirely due to political opponents' efforts, but perhaps somewhat attributable to a degree of *cowardice* on the part of economic conservatives who would normally be expected to champion some of these proposals for reform, but find excuses to avoid participation. Chambers of Commerce: Are you listening?

MORE ABOUT THE PROPOSAL FOR STELLAR SCHOOLS

Another serendipitous event was the denial of our registered trademark application for *Stellar Schools*™. We appealed the denial in late 2006, and the appeal was denied as well. The United States Patent and Trademark Office told us the name *Stellar* was already in use, and the two-word phrase was too close to that use. Along came a friend and correspondent in these discussions who is a patent lawyer. He told me that the *rule of thumb* is, if possible, to register a name not found in American dictionaries.[647]

So, then my task was: Invent a name not in Webster's dictionary. Then it hit me: Craft an acronym that describes Stellar Schools , and then use it. (We introduced this acronym first in Chapter 14, and have used it more than once in intervening sections of this book.) So, in 2007 here is the one we settled on: ASORA . We reiterate its definition again here:

A) Asynchronously delivered *on-demand* instruction .

S) Self-paced learning .

O) Online Distance education .

R) Rigorous curriculum

A) Assessment is strictly tied to the curriculum

These attributes are clearly consistent with what we had planned for the Stellar Schools.

Design of for-profit Stellar Schools franchising network from its business plan

Some of the aspects of our proposals for the Stellar Schools franchising network have been presented in earlier chapters. For example,

- We presented its instructional format and components in Chapter 14 in the sub-section, *Aspects of self-paced Stellar Schools business plan in an asynchronous world.*

- We presented an earlier version of the business plan's Executive Summary, just a page or two earlier in the sub-section, *For-profit schools that don't need vouchers or an EMO: Stellar Schools*

We'll not repeat that information here. There are many details in the business plan issued in March 2008. It was officially titled:

> Business Plan for Asora® Education Enterprises' Stellar Schools Franchising Company[648]

It received scant attention from those to whom it was sent. We made it accessible on our website for download, and similarly had very little response. Was it an unimpressive plan or was there something else going on? We think the latter because other entrepreneurs in the education sector were also going nowhere.

So, what was it about, without getting too far into the sub-paragraphs and precise details? Let's take a look at a big picture.

The big picture of a candidate: The Stellar Schools franchising network

In the development of any franchising network or for that matter any network of enterprises governed by enforceable contracts there is often the question about local flexibility or discretion at the local enterprise's facility. In developing the Stellar Schools franchising network, we decided that we should accommodate what is called hybrid franchising.

In hybrid franchising the franchisor has two kinds of franchisees in its network:

- Direct franchisees. These operators include local schools and home school customers.

- Indirect franchisees. These organizations themselves are franchisors or licensors operating sub-networks of schools and home school customers.

The primary motivation for having the two levels implied by the indirect franchisees has been to accommodate sub-networks of schools where, for example, a sub-network might be a chain of denominational schools. Or a sub-network could be composed of certain types of specialized schools such as magnet schools within public school systems or magnet schools privately owned. The diagram in Figure 22 shows some of these arrangements.

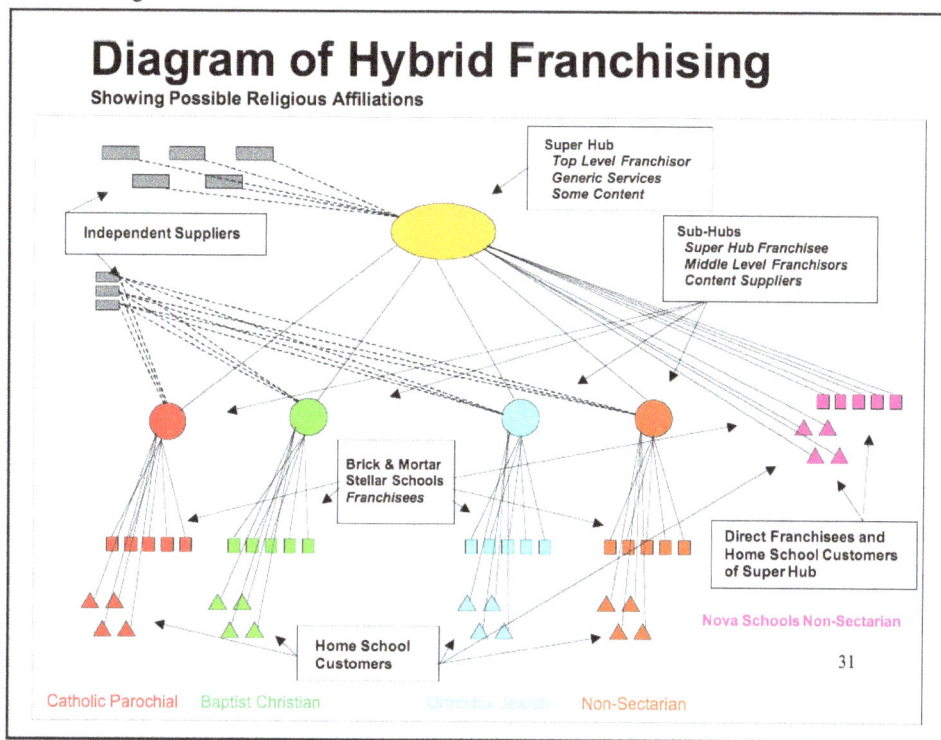

Figure 22. Hybrid Franchising Combines a Two-Level Network with a Single Level One.

The yellow ellipse in Fig. 22 above is our proposed Stellar Schools Franchising Company (SSFC). It has five different franchising contracts with subordinate enterprises. As shown in the picture those five relationships are with possible sub-networks as follows:

- Catholic parochial sub-network
- Baptist Christian sub-network
- Orthodox Jewish sub-network
- Non-sectarian magnet sub-network
- Direct franchisees and homeschool customers in the so-called non-sectarian Nova network

Each sub-network can have its own curriculum, and would have flexibility to take some or all of its instructional content from independent suppliers albeit with some top-level restrictions on quality, format, and values issues. The specific denominations shown are not part of our proposals, but were included here to show the flexibility of our network structures. All kinds of other sub-networks can be imagined.

Each network and sub-network has its franchisor or middle level franchisor, and each of these provides many of its services over the Internet. The facility from which the Internet services, relevant products, and other services are provided is called the Hub or Sub-Hub. The top level's Super-Hub, as shown here, provides most of the generic goods and services common to all of the schools in the hybrid two-level network.

The flexibility inherent in this hybrid structure would attract existing networks of private schools to participate. For example, Catholic school systems would regain a great measure of financial health by moving into this kind of network where the operating costs are significantly less—generally at about half of their current school costs.

Just what does the for-profit franchisor do?

To avoid confusion, we separately describe franchisor services and franchisee services. The franchisor provides its services from its Hub location while the franchisee provides its services at the school site it owns. As shown in Fig. 22, home-schooled students receive services only from the franchisor while students in physical schools receive services from both franchisor and franchisee. Obviously, and not shown in the diagram, the home-schooled students also receive services from their parents or other parent controlled personnel.

The franchisor, here the Stellar Schools Franchising Company (SSFC), runs the central service Hub that provides services to students either directly, through a franchisee school, or indirectly through a middle level sub-franchisor that in turn services its own franchisee schools. We group the services according to whether they are directly related to instruction or otherwise fall under the label of *support*. The instructional services include:

1. Asynchronous Lectures (Web, DVD, CD)

2. Synchronous Lectures (Web, TV, Visiting Lecturers)

3. Web-based drills, practice tests, Cyber Tutor, and Cyber Mentor

4. Computer based games relevant to the course

5. Book distribution (Hardcopy, CD, DVD, Web, and Internet downloads of e-books)

6. School supply distribution (laptops, tablets, smart phones, pencils, etc.)

7. Grading paper exercises (scanned and transmitted to HUB)

8. Grading computer exercises (Web based)

9. Subject and Assessment examinations (some Web based)

10. Train, and dispatch in-person lecturers

11. Provide laboratory experiments via remote robotics (Web based)

12. Library services (A Web library, access to other electronic collections, etc.)

The primary instructional delivery medium in Stellar Schools, just as in traditional schools, will be books. These schools will also follow the traditional paradigm of those oral presentations reinforcing the lessons contained in the reading materials. In most instances the lectures, will be delivered asynchronously at the time and place of the student's choice On a more occasional basis the instruction will be supplemented by synchronous lectures and/or in-person lectures delivered on a schedule chosen by the school.

Another key aspect of Stellar Schools is the constraint that the curriculum is defined by the universe of possible assessment examination questions covering the material in that course. Thus, *Teaching to the test* is a defining characteristic of Stellar Schools (and we're proud of it!). In Appendix C of the business plan,[649] we provide some additional details regarding the effort required to build a course from *scratch*.

In our context, *Teaching to the test*, is not a pejorative descriptor. Rather it means providing instruction covering the *entire universe* of possible examination questions. Teachers in Stellar Schools will never have advance access to the particular randomly chosen subset of questions to be used in any specific test, and thus will be unable to *Teach* to that specific test. If they somehow were able to teach to a specific test, we would regard that as test fraud and cheating on the part of the teachers.

In addition to the instructional services, the franchisor's Hub will provide support services including:

1. Communications and Web server facility

2. Warehouse and distribution facility (if needed)

3. Testing and grading service, including proctors

4. Auditing service

5. Curriculum development and management

6. Teacher and staff training

7. Training student tutors/instructors

8. Marketing and publicity services

9. School site development services

10. Financial services

11. Campus services (employee benefits, payroll service, etc.)

Some components of these services, where more cost effective, will be performed by contractors.

Just what does the franchisee do?

The responsibilities of the franchisee fall into two categories:

- Those dictated by the franchisor
- Those that are optional, and at the discretion of the franchisee

Considerably more detail about the franchisee's responsibilities is provided in Appendix E of the business plan.[650]

We reiterate a point made earlier: Franchisors are required to be for-profit enterprises, but franchisees are not restricted that way to be for-profit organizations. Franchising law permits four ownership formats for the franchisee:

- For-profit owned
- Non-profit owned
- Government owned
- Parent owned (for homeschooling)

Unless state and local laws prohibit it, any organization that can sign the franchising agreement contract can be a franchisee. With respect to K-12 education, this means that a non-profit school operator such as the Catholic Church could be a franchisee. It also means that a public school district could be a franchisee, though we think that would be very unlikely given their loss of control implicit in such an arrangement.

Services and Operations Mandated by the Franchisor. The details of the franchisee operations have not as yet been thoroughly specified. By necessity some of this will be generated later as the result of our beta-test studies, and thus cannot be known at this time. We do have, however, a list of franchisee responsibilities where the franchisor will set minimum standards, including:

- Staffing levels
- Scheduling
- Facility architecture
- Furnishings
- Procedures for interviewing parents and prospective students
- Format of student orientations
- Instructional techniques
- Dealing with student behavior problems
- Responding to student questions

- Curriculum sequences and prerequisites
- Employee benefits and salaries
- Marketing activities
- Franchisor fees

Please refer to the business plan[651] for more specifics about some of these items.

In the staffing area we have estimated that a student/teacher ratio of 25 is prudent. Since we intend to hire both teachers and an equal number of teaching assistants this means the student/teaching staff ratio is 50.

With respect to scheduling we intend to maintain uniform work, study, and instructional schedules within which students will learn in the self-paced format. This means that students will go to *recess* together! We foresee the day divided into several 75-minute work periods interspersed with recesses and the lunch period.

Provision will also be made to have some of the elective classes taught in the more traditional classroom format. Each of these will be accommodated in class periods of 35 minutes each.

Franchisee schools must allocate at least 40 square feet of floor area per student. Various other requirements as to safety, hygiene, food preparation, laboratory furnishings & equipment, and computer infrastructure are also going to be imposed.

Procedures for marketing to parents, interviewing customers and prospective students, and for providing student orientations will also be subject to franchisor imposed minimum requirements.

School site tutoring and instructional techniques will be taught to the teaching staff by the teacher training programs run by the franchisor at its Hub facility. Teachers will be taught how all of the Web based courseware operate so they, in turn, can help the students. Many of the instructional resources will be computerized, and mainly provided online by the Hub Website.

In terms of the time that students have one-on-one with the teaching staff, we expect the lower primary students to have more contact with the teaching staff and the higher-level students less. Children entering kindergarten and the first year of primary school will be given considerable assistance from the staff. While the minimum amount of time devoted to this assistance will be set by the franchisor, the franchisee will be free to provide some of the assistance from its staff augmented by volunteer adults or volunteer students.

Because of the potential for lawsuits, the procedures for dealing with student misbehavior will be almost entirely set by the franchisor. We believe that the self-pacing format removes some of the frustration that can lead to disruptive behavior, so we expect that maintaining a calm environment will not be difficult.

The franchisees will have limited discretion in controlling what courses students take because the franchisor will control most aspects of the sequencing of courses.

Franchisees will have more control over a subset of elective courses where the maintenance of uniform system wide standards is deemed unimportant or even undesirable. Music, art, religion, and athletic electives would tend to fall into this category.

Franchisees will also be required to offer a number of Advanced Placement (AP) courses. Typically, students who have completed the K-12 requirements may wish to stay on to complete college level courses of the AP type. Or AP courses could substitute for the regular courses—subject by subject.

Franchisees will be required to offer employees a minimal level of compensation including certain employee benefits. Additionally, franchisees will be required to establish work rules. Franchisees will be forbidden to abrogate the terms of the franchising agreement as the result of collective bargaining. Violations will be grounds for cancellation of the franchise.

Lastly, franchisees will be limited as to their advertising methods and content.

Services and Operations Provided at the Franchisee's Discretion. The philosophy of the Stellar Schools Franchising Company regarding its control over franchisees is that it seeks to guarantee a minimum level of quality and service to its customers. It encourages its franchisees to exceed these minimums where such action will improve the instructional services received by students.

An important area where franchisees may wish to exceed the minimums concerns the staffing levels. Franchisees may wish to provide students with more human instructors. The Stellar Schools Franchising Company (SSFC), the franchisor, will encourage that, and will allow the franchisee to hire additional teachers and other teaching staff. It is clear that a school with more teachers per student will cost more to operate, and thus it is expected that schools operating well above the franchisor's minimums will charge higher tuitions. The franchisees will be free to set the tuition levels within a range set by the franchisor.

To address the need of early primary students for substantial human interaction, franchisees will be encouraged to adopt a neo-Lancasterian student led tutoring service in which more advanced students will tutor beginning students—particularly in language skills and mathematics.[652] We envisage beginning students' needs will require the presence of a tutor about 50% of the time. As students progress (and particularly learn how to use the Web based instructional courseware) their need for human interaction will diminish rapidly. By the 5th year or so we believe the time spent with human teachers or tutors will be significantly less—perhaps about 5%.

There are a number of other areas in which franchisees will be permitted or even encouraged to exceed the franchisor-imposed minimums. A more detailed description of those options is presented as part of the business plan's Appendix E.[653]

Using or Avoiding Third Party Courseware. A number of vendors provide virtual school Web based courseware for K-12 curricula. Some offerings within this range of products are also of sufficiently high quality to be of interest to Stellar Schools. Depending on the flexibility of such offerings, it may be possible to integrate such courseware into the Hub based system.

If we engage third parties to provide such *courseware* it will likely require some modifications to ensure that it conforms to the Stellar Schools concept of curriculum being defined by the universe of possible test questions. It would also probably require modifications to conform to the *user interface* format used by Stellar Schools.

We have generated some estimates regarding the cost-efficiency of using third party virtual school services versus using our own. More details from this analysis are shown in Appendix C of the business plan. What we found is that developing our own courseware can become cost effective once we have the annual number of pupils enrolled somewhat in excess of a few hundred.

With these considerations in mind we are still open to using third party courseware in situations where the superior quality of the product would be difficult to match. In such cases we would work with the vendor to re-format their product into the configurations used by Stellar Schools. Depending on the charges levied by the third party, we might look favorably on acquiring such software.

In the estimates and projections used in this plan, however, we assume that all courseware is built in-house or will be the result of converting vendor courseware (and doing so for approximately the same costs).

Positioning of services

In an important sense, the services we offer are defined by the curricula we offer. Stellar Schools intend to emphasize academics and college preparatory instruction. Stellar Schools are designed to teach knowledge content as well as helping children to learn studying skills. Stellar Schools will not be pushing progressive education nostrums including such discredited fads as *critical thinking, higher order thinking skills, whole language, bilingual education, twenty-first-century skills,* and *constructivism.* Stellar Schools will not promote such *new thinking* fashions unless the ideas are thoroughly vetted, and tested over time.

Thus, the services offered will not appeal to the entire K-12 marketplace. Eventually, we plan to offer more than one curriculum option. Our initial curriculum will focus on a solid grounding in Western Civilization as well as on the fundamental mathematical and scientific disciplines. We have tentatively identified the *Hillsdale Academy curriculum* for this first option. The *Core Knowledge sequence* will be incorporated in the primary levels, and we are considering science and mathematics curricula used by the *Advanced Math & Science Academy Charter School* of Massachusetts in the middle and secondary levels. Later we hope to introduce a Classical Education option using the trivium format—complete with Latin and Greek instruction. As the SSFC network grows, franchisee schools will have some flexibility regarding the spectrum of curricular and course options they offer.

In terms of what might be called *the positioning of services,* Stellar Schools are designed to compete in the upper segment of the K-12 sector—meaning against the private academies that provide rather comprehensive preparation for college. In competing against the *best* schools in the K-12 sector we believe we can deliver a product superior even within that group, and still provide it for significantly lower tuition. Basis Schools, Inc. is in many ways a role model for doing this.

Given our intention to hold tuition costs down we also believe we can attract students from families of more modest means who are now enrolled in the parochial schools or the public schools.

More information on the design of the Stellar Schools system is available in the business plan.

The analogue: A non-profit licensing network

The Stellar Schools business plan was based on a for-profit franchisor. Franchising, per se, is a commercial for-profit business format. We also formulated plans for a *non-profit licensing network* in which a licensing organization (the analogue of the franchisor) would operate from a central service location to provide its licensee schools the various services envisaged here. As an entrepreneur my primary interest was the development of a for-profit enterprise. However, we were, alternatively, available to work on a non-profit analogue of Stellar Schools, but there was no interest shown in that approach either.

INVESTORS AFRAID

Why would investors seeking profitable returns shy away from for-profit education?

> Answer: Political forces aligned with public schools and the political left despise schools that operate as for-profit enterprises. To a lesser degree they also oppose for-profit enterprises, the EMO's, that manage schools—typically charter schools. And, they don't like public libraries that are operated by for-profit library management organizations, the LMO's. Not every component of the education industry is targeted. So, for example, book publishers remain almost entirely for-profit enterprises. Other service and product providers to K-12 schools are generally not targeted.

Government tools for screwing their for-profit competitors

A number of general economic and financial principles combined with the laws, rules, and regulations affecting various types of for-profit, non-profit, and government *state owned enterprises (SOE)* can help explain why for-profit schools have not thrived in the United States.

As Richard Geddes postulated in his book, *Competing with the Government*, there are at least five adverse phenomena stemming from state owned enterprises that directly or indirectly harm their for-profit private competitors:

1. Government enterprises are free to set prices below their costs. Sometimes the prices are zero.

2. Private investors fear competing with government entities that undercut sustainable prices.

3. Private investors fear that government entities will expand their capacity to serve more customers.

4. Taxpayers are harmed when they are forced to pay for inefficient government provided services.

5. There is harm when Adam Smith's *hidden hand* has no profits available to *fund* socially beneficial services.[654]

Public education systems play roles in all five of these. While item 5 also applies to non-profit private schools, they have an advantage over their for-profit counterparts because non-profit private schools are generally exempt from property taxes.

Government officials responsible for enforcing various laws and regulations often ignore violations of public schools and non-profit schools. Moreover, given their typical dislike of commercial enterprises, they often enforce these strictures to the full extent of the law, and sometimes apply heavy handed tactics beyond the law. Worse, the actual regulations pertaining to for-profit schools are often more strict than those covering public and nonprofit private schools.[655]

Problems in post-secondary for-profit schools

For-profit schools are more common in post-secondary education than in K-12.

Enrollment in post-secondary for-profit schools peaked in 2010 at approximately 1.7 million students. That was nearly quadruple the 0.4 million enrolled in the year 2000—consistent with the rapid growth of these institutions during the early years of the twenty-first century.[656] After 2010 there was a rapid decline in the enrollment in these private colleges, and by 2016 it had fallen to about 0.9 million students. A review of the regulations from the U.S. Department of Education during the Obama administration (2009–2016) shows that significant changes were made to rules and regulations over post-secondary education in such a way that for-profit schools were put at an extreme disadvantage compared to their non-profit and government operated peers. The enrollment declines after 2010 coincided with political pressure from the then new Obama administration in Washington and from their Congressional allies. In July of that year officials proposed new strict regulations that in the words of Jonathan Knee would

> . . . significantly restrict the access of for-profit institutions to federal educational programs.[657]

Well before these rules were finalized, the mere threat of them had a marked effect. Starting in 2010 investor interest in these companies fell dramatically.[658] Add to that a Government Accounting Office (GAO) investigation, that some say was biased in favor of the new administration, that took for-profit schools to task for supposed fraudulent practices. The notoriety stemming from these factors probably contributed to lower enrollments, campus closures, and other problems for these schools after the year 2010.

By 2016 these for-profit schools were *down*, but not *out*. After their demise, it was then time for their *extinction*. The Wall Street Journal headline put it this way:

> Obama's For-Profit Execution: How to kill a company without proving a single allegation.[659]

The for-profit college was ITT Technical Institute. Confronting it was a regulatory assault engineered in such a way that it invited twenty agencies at state and federal levels to begin parallel investigations. This led to an accreditation agency decision to put them on probation that, in turn, was the justification for the U.S. Education Department to demand a 123-million-dollar letter of credit, which ITT could not supply, and remain solvent. During these troubles shares of its parent company, ITT Educational Services, dropped from $45 per share in 2014 to a mere 45 cents by the summer of 2016.[660] And, who engineered this assault? It came from within the sometimes anti-business Obama administration, and it seems to have been intentional.

Professor Knee elaborated on the way in which government regulations have been used to undermine and harm the for-profit competitors in education. Sometimes, the actual regulations explicitly target for-profit education with stiffer requirements. Other times there would be a *nod and wink* reaction to infractions of public schools, which would give public schools *effective immunity* from those regulations. These immunities would sometimes be explicit or de jure. In other cases, they would be de facto.[661]

In the early years of the Trump administration a number of efforts were undertaken to end the *war* on for-profit schools. For example, during 2017 the U.S. Department of Education made significant changes to the Obama era rules, and did so in an attempt to remove biases against for-profit schools while still maintaining efforts to reduce fraud in student loan programs and address other vulnerabilities.[662]

Nervous operators of K-12 for-profit schools

Many for-profit private schools display a certain kind of cowardice in which they give some credence to their opponents efforts to cast them as *evil, profit hungry exploiters* of American children. We at Asora have seen this in our efforts to help for-profit schools do a better job of marketing themselves. We approached some of them to ask if they'd like some help providing consumer information to prospective customers. The responses were, as they say, the *sounds of crickets.*

Asora and its Peers couldn't find investors. Yet SABIS and Basis Schools still live.

Here at Asora we have been soliciting investors since 2003, and have found none interested. Other entrepreneurs of for-profit schools, likewise, have seen no investments in their projects. Even the once successful Edison Project and its successors that were once finding investment capital, are now barely alive. Most of the successful for-profit schools, of which we are aware, generate their investment capital internally from their company revenues. This limits their growth rates, but does allow some expansion.

There are a few for-profit school operators who are proud of their commercial prowess. SABIS is not only for-profit, but it is also an international school operator that has been solvent for over 130 years. Founded as a girls only school in Lebanon in 1886, it now operates schools in 20 countries—mostly on the Eurasian continent. Two of its schools are in the United States. It owns a school in Minnesota, and it operates a charter school under contract in Massachusetts. This author has visited both of these schools, and was impressed with their evident professionalism.

We also have information about the performance of SABIS educated students in Massachusetts. Do those statistics support the theory that for-profit schools are superior to their rivals in the public schools and among non-profit private schools? What we found was that the SABIS operated charter school in Springfield, Massachusetts, the SABIS International Charter School, performed at about the 54th percentile compared to other charter schools in the state. And, that was for its most important statistic: the proficiency levels of its economically disadvantaged students, who make up about one-third of the high school students tested. Their overall proficiency (the lesser of their math and reading proficiencies) for 2015 was 34%. While this does not show superior performance of a for-profit operator, it does show that, within Massachusetts, it has average competence in operating charter schools.[663] Needless to say, 34% proficiencies are significantly substandard, and yet are superior to the average levels for other public and private school types. Does this not also echo our title of *Sick Schools*?

We also discussed the very successful EMO operator Basis Schools, Inc. earlier in this chapter. Like SABIS, Basis operates for-profit wholly owned campuses as well as being an EMO with approximately 27 charter schools under their direction.

Even a Republican administration's Deep State discriminated against for-profit schools

In the early months of 2006, The Stellar Schools Franchising Project, the author's firm at that time, submitted some of its information to the U.S. Department of Education's *Education Resource Organizations Directory* (EROD). We attempted to list information relevant to the instructional systems of our planned services. These were services that could be used by public and private schools alike. But we were denied inclusion in EROD because we were too *commercial*. Yes, they actually used the word *commercial*. After appealing to the Ed Department's Acting Chief Information Officer, Mitchell Clark, he continued the Department's intransigence, and denied our request again. So, we appealed that denial to the Secretary of Education, Margaret Spellings, who did not respond directly. Responding instead was Chief Information Officer, Bill Vajda, who continued the Department's denial of our legitimate request.

After reviewing our negotiations and communications with the Education Department bureaucrats responsible for EROD, and after considering the free market advocacy of Secretary Spellings we can conclude:

- Our proposal was consistent or could be altered to be consistent with all laws and regulations under which EROD was operating.

- Where the Department cited potential violations, in every case, we offered legal alternatives by proposing changes to our submission.

- These officials were either insubordinate to the Bush administration policies or were "just following orders," of their insubordinate superiors. We believe that the workload on Secretary Spellings prevented her from reviewing the details of our case and instead relied on her employees to act consistently with administration policies.

- Margaret Spellings was not personally or politically opposed to for-profit firms working in K-12 education. In fact, she later was on the Board of Directors of Apollo Group, which then operated the for-profit University of Phoenix.

Our conclusion is that these several EROD bureaucrats, who denied the participation of Stellar Schools, were working against Bush administration policies. In the parlance of our time, they were working from the *Deep State* to subvert the proper and legal policies of the government. These officials of a Republican administration were not friends of capitalism and free markets. Rather they seemed more on the socialist side.

But Gorbachev liked what he heard once vouchers were explained to him

Contrast those unpleasantries with the chance conversation I once had with the former Communist President of the Soviet Union, Mikhail Gorbachev, in the early Spring of that same year, 2006. It was at the cocktail reception preceding a banquet honoring the former Russian leader. The venue was in Rhode Island at the *posh* Carnegie Abbey Country Club.

> Not everyone knows that the word *posh* is an acronym. It refers to old British Empire steamship tickets—typically to India from England. Tickets stamped P. O. S. H. meant that the ship lodgings were Port Outbound, and Starboard Home. That arrangement meant that the traveler was mostly on the shady, eastern and northern, sides of the ship, and therefore much more comfortable than with the alternative.

I introduced myself to him as a developer of "capitalistic schools." At first, he was angered as the first photo indicates; he then asked me through his interpreter (paraphrased), "How will poor pupils be educated in such schools?" I answered (paraphrased), "Their tuition will be paid by government issued vouchers." His interpreter then spent some time, perhaps about two minutes, explaining the idea of vouchers to him. After that animated discussion, Mr. Gorbachev seemed quite pleased by the explanation, and then wished me good luck with the project, as shown in the second photo. Does that make him a *capitalist*? Maybe, not. But according to news reports from the late 1980's, he was making efforts near the end of his Soviet presidency to bring marketplace relations into their socialistic economy.

SCHOOLS OWNED BY THEIR TEACHERS

Economist Richard Vedder has suggested a novel approach for replacing public schools with for-profit ones. His proposals include ones in which district public schools would transition from government owned units to ones owned and controlled by the teachers, and he would do this by establishing an Employee Stock Ownership Plan (ESOP) for them. His book is not clear on how to accomplish this conversion. The newly created for-profit schools would be funded by tuition revenues paid from a district funded voucher plan.[664]

Alternatively, an ESOP plan could be implemented for a newly established for-profit school. In that case the complications involved in a transition from a government owned and operated school to the for-profit school would be considerably less complicated.

Stellar Schools franchising plan frightened investors.

Our business plan and associated documents are available elsewhere on our website[665]

But let's step back and consider how franchising laws may be a particularly good fit for the K-12 education sector of our economy. In franchising there is a central for-profit management organization that is the franchisor. In franchising there is also a network of franchisees who operate under the contractual umbrella of the franchisor. The franchisees can have a variety of ownership formats: For-profit, non-profit , government owned or individual owned (as in homeschooling). Any given franchising network could have a mix of these ownership formats. Let's characterize our Stellar Schools proposal from two different perspectives:

From the instructor's viewpoint. The methods of instruction follow the five elements of the acronym ASORA, which as we have noted before is defined as:

A) Asynchronously delivered *on-demand* instruction.

S) Self-paced learning.

O) Online distance education.

R) Rigorous curriculum

A) Assessment based curriculum

With regard to the last component, of using what we call an *assessment based curriculum*, we define it to be the universe of examination questions and answers. The goal of instruction includes having the student master all of the learning concepts embodied in those questions and answers. So, yes, we *teach to the test*. But we do this in the sense that the test question universe covers all concepts, facts, and relationships in the subject's curriculum. Any actual test uses a random sample of the questions from the total *universe* of questions/answers that specify the course curriculum. Cheating is difficult as each testee gets a new and different random sampling.

From the owner's viewpoint. For the owner the plan is that of a franchising network composed of:

- A for-profit central management organization or franchisor
- A network of schools that can have various kinds of ownership: public, non-profit or for-profit.

We are still puzzled regarding the negligible interest shown by investors.

- Are we insufficiently capable to succeed, and don't deserve investment capital?
- Are many other school designers also neglected because investors don't like their proposals either?
- Are the investors dumb because they do not know that our plans would generate handsome profits?
- Or are investors smart because they know that there are too many enemies of for-profit schools for them to have much chance of survival and growth?

So, what is the best answer? We don't know. Here are some possible answers:

- The cynical answer: Investors are dumb.
- The sad answer: Investors are smart and would go broke if they put their money here.
- The optimistic answer: There are new kinds of investment opportunities.

Milton Friedman was puzzled by this. In 2003 he told me,

> . . . I have long been puzzled by the situation in cities like New York and San Francisco: there are strictly private elementary and secondary schools which charge very high tuitions and have long waiting lists, and I keep asking why it is that other private enterprises haven't taken advantage of that situation as a source of profit. Somehow there is a customer base there; there is a market opportunity.[666]

We infer from his comment that there have been and are, indeed, new kinds of investment options here. At the time of Professor Friedman's comment, Basis Schools, Inc was in the early stages of developing an enterprise that would follow his advice, and do as he suggested, and as Friedman said take

> . . . advantage of that situation as a source of profit . . .

But few were aware of this optimistic development at that time. And, this author was one of the unaware!

UNDERSTANDING THE EDUCATION MARKET

Demise of the Education Industry Association

Asora Education was once a member of the Education Industry Association (EIA). Most member companies of EIA were for-profit firms working in the K-12 sector, but there were also a significant number working in the post-secondary marketplace.

According to reporter Tony Wan, the EIA withered away, and in early 2016 was absorbed into the Education Technology Industry Network (ETIN).[667] How could that have happened? Here's how: The EIA had as its largest subgroup the many firms working in the areas of tutoring and other remedial services that were largely funded through the No Child Left Behind (NCLB) legislated program known as Supplemental Education Services (SES). Under SES, districts were mandated to use federal dollars to have schools contract with these firms to provide these supplemental services. Under the Obama administration the Education Department began to issue *waivers* allowing school districts to evade the SES mandates. The *waivers* were unwise on a number of grounds, but they were apparently legal given the various loopholes and regulatory flexibility built in to the NCLB law. As the number of waivers grew, the firms providing SES services shrank and many left the EIA.

> The author's own company, Asora Education Enterprises, was one of the departed. Why?

Asora Education, for a number of years, was an active member of the Education Industry Association (EIA). Trusting hope over experience it took us years to accept the disturbing stench of cronyism among for-profit companies working in the industry. It brings to mind what Pope Adrian had to say on corruption in the Roman Catholic Church during the early years of the Protestant Reformation. We discussed Pope Adrian in Chapter 1, and it is now time to use his quote again. He said that within the Roman Curia,

> ... those steeped in sin could no longer perceive the stench of their own iniquities.[668]

Perhaps in like manner many of the members of the EIA didn't realize that they themselves were a large component of the sickness in the K-12 economic sector. A story about their cowardice suggests that some self-examination might have been warranted. The story:

> One of Asora's services has been the provision of school performance information that could be very useful in the marketing programs of for-profit education firms. Of the hundreds of EIA member firms, not one expressed interest in using our numbers to do contrast marketing. No one wanted to criticize their local public schools with our damning numbers.

> A public relations expert, who was a consultant to the EIA, told us that most for-profit education companies earn most of their revenue from contracts with the public education systems.[669] Our marketing proposals would have had them competing with their patrons, and thus essentially *biting the hand that feeds them*. They didn't want to risk that.

We found that even for-profit private schools were loath to aggressively market their brands for fears of retribution. They were apparently acting as loyal cronies to the government school authorities, and not so loyal to their actual customers, directly or indirectly, the parents of school children.

After suggesting to the EIA that it might consider addressing these kinds of problems, we were met with silence. Soon thereafter we left the EIA in 2014.

Ending cronyism in the education industry

One can imagine various kinds of industry organizations that might work against the menace of cronyism. Small firms could limit their operations to the so-called private pay marketplace. Wouldn't that allow them to compete against the public system? Maybe the climate under the current Trump administration will be seen to have fostered such developments?

SCHOOL PERFORMANCE INPUT TO MARKETING

As we have described earlier in this book, Asora Education Enterprises has as one of its services the ability to make estimates of student performance levels at the school and district levels for both the NAEP and the ACT testing systems.

We described how we have published prototypical guidebooks to public and private schools, based on our mapping technologies. We did that as follows:

In early 2011 we published a guidebook for the public schools in the Potomac region of Maryland, Virginia, and Washington, D.C.

- *Guidebook & Resources for Parents in Maryland, Virginia & Washington D.C.—It Takes More Than A Village to educate your child, when the schools aren't up to the task.*[670]

Then in 2014 we published three prototypical guidebooks for schools in three counties from Massachusetts, Tennessee, and California as follows:

- *Gadzooks! Are Bristol County's Private & Public Schools Really Like This?*

- *Gadzooks! Are Shelby County's Private & Public Schools Really Like This?*

- *Gadzooks! Are Orange County's Private & Public Schools Really Like This?*[671]

A more ambitious prototype was our 2017 guidebook to private and public schools in the two-state region of Rhode Island and Massachusetts.

- *Gadzooks! Parents' Guide To Schools & Services In Rhode Island & Massachusetts: A Guide to Private and Public Schools & Other Educational Resources*[672]

These guidebooks limited the subjects reported on to mathematics and reading. All of these books can be downloaded from the Asora website from the links in the references. A more ambitious guidebook project would include estimates of student proficiencies in history, civics, and science. We made efforts to find interested stakeholders in each of the regions described in these guides.

In doing that, we presumed that business oriented community organizations, such as Chambers of Commerce, would be interested in guides to schools in their areas? In a meeting with the Executive Director of the Taunton Chamber of Commerce in Bristol County, Massachusetts we were told to our face that they were not interested in this sort of thing. Why the negligent attitude? We think that Chambers often involve public school officials in their governance structure. This author has seen it in person, more than once, when I have made presentations to Chambers of Commerce. The Chambers do not want to embarrass these public school officials with guidebook information showing how poorly their schools are performing. Shame on the Chambers!

While on the subject of embarrassment we should reiterate an earlier point: When private schools are compared to public schools for their economically disadvantaged subset of students, their supposed superiority evaporates, and we see a landscape in which public schools are tied with private schools in math, and though not caught up in reading are closing that gap as well. This is not to say

Public schools are performing well.

No, it is to say,

On average, private schools are also part of the problem.

It reinforces our title of *Sick Schools*.

CHAPTER 18

The Vision for Reaching 2030

AFTER DISCUSSING THE FIVE-HUNDRED years of schooling since the invention of the printing press, this book has then looked at more recent issues in American K-12 education in the years since the mid-twentieth century. The picture has not been pretty. Student skills have been depressed or stagnant. When one looks at the politics of K-12 education, particularly its left-leaning progressive tendencies, it is not too surprising to find it failing in so many ways. Those political considerations and related legal constraints have made a mess out of instruction regarding religion, history, and civics. For history and civics, official testing has shown markedly lower levels of student competence than in any other tested subjects—with barely one student in ten showing proficiency in U.S. history. A careful review of K-12 practices shows many of them to be outside legal and constitutional limits. Of particular concern is the *disregard shown to parents' legal rights* to choose the education to be received by their children. We know some of the paths forward, but there is a reluctance among K-12 authorities and other stakeholders to take up those challenges.

WE HAVE TOOLS, BUT WORKERS WON'T USE THEM

Here in Part IV of this book we have described a number of the legal structures, technologies, methods, and content standards that have been demonstrated to improve the K-12 education received in various kinds of schools. Yet, as we saw in Part III, the K-12 economic sector is now showing a few signs of progress after many decades of no growth in productivity. It has been a stagnant industry that couldn't even sustain the former Education Industry Association. The title of this book, *Sick Schools*, again seems to fit these facts.

Among those working in the K-12 sector, we ask who are the ones who are neglecting to apply these promising tools? Are the workers lazy or are the systems employing them resisting their use? Surely, those employed in the K-12 industry could work harder and improve their work product. But that is not the easy path to follow when most of the incentives under which they work discourage too much *enterprise*. We believe that the systems employing the workers are largely to blame for the troubles. When we say *systems*, we include the various structures under which the systems operate, both legal and administrative.

Where they disregard the Laws and where corrective action is needed

We have already described a number of instances in which our K-12 education systems do not follow the laws that have been enacted to control some of their policies and behaviors. We can look at five areas in which action is needed to end practices that are unconstitutional or illegal:

Collective bargaining of government employees. Their collective bargaining and right to strike are generally unconstitutional practices under both the United States Constitution and the constitutions of the several states. Thus, collective bargaining must be ended for government school employees.

Forced collection of union or agency dues. We earlier discussed the Janus decision of the Supreme Court that prohibits the collection of mandatory union dues or agency fees from government employees. This decision needs to be enforced.

Illegal aliens voting in school board elections. What is there to dispute here? The illegal aliens should be removed from their illegal residences within the United States, and be subject to prosecution. I would arrest them as they enter the polling stations. They should be deported after they serve their prison terms.

Preventing parental choices required under the UN Declaration of Human Rights, Article 26. The right of parents to direct their children's education needs to be upheld. As a first step, public school systems could devise curricular alternatives for parents unsatisfied with the current system. A second step would have the public systems decentralize their mandatory curricular standards to allow local officials, preferably at the school level, to dictate curricula. The better or best solution would be one in which parents could choose private schools, tutoring services or engage in home schooling that would respect their curricular preferences. That could be accomplished by vouchers or other types of school choice, including part-time enrollment.

Imposing Common Core State Standards. States that have forced *Common Core* upon their public schools should be forced to abandon these poorly conceived and illegally imposed standards. The College Board should be constrained through legal action to abandon its alignment and affiliations with *Common Core.*

Obeying the law is always an obligation for educators and other stakeholders in K-12 education. But are those laws appropriate? How should they be changed to improve K-12 education? We discuss that next.

Change laws to support a free K-12 marketplace

There are other new laws that should be considered that would further develop the K-12 marketplace. We have a list of eight proposals that would likely improve the health of K-12 education in the United States.

1. *Pass laws to establish more standardized tests.* With more information available, from such testing, parents and other stakeholders will make better choices among schools. Require private schools to use some of the same tests used by public schools.

2. *Require schools to use independent testing organizations for all official testing.* Independent testing removes incentives to grade on curve or otherwise inflate the grades awarded students.

3. *Establish part-time schooling in most schools.* This will allow parents to combine two or more schools' offerings to provide their children better instruction than that from just one school.

4. *Prohibit social promotion.* This means that a student's mastery levels will neither be inflated, nor will the student be inappropriately placed in unsuitable grade levels. Instead, we need laws to establish remedial programs that will enable most students to be promoted. Or use self-pacing.

5. *Establish academic competitions.* Through such competitions, schools will have incentives to improve their instruction, and thereby benefit students.

6. *Provide vouchers or education savings accounts (ESA) to cover significant portions of private school tuition.* When more parents are able to make choices among schools for their children's education through vouchers that not only helps them, but it also helps increase competition.

7. *Provide parents and other stakeholders reliable consumer information.* When decision makers, such as parents, are basing their choices on reliable information we believe that it will spur healthy competition to motivate further improvements in the schools involved.

8. *End seniority policies that harm students.* Sometimes, seniority rights of teachers lead to unwise placements that degrade instruction in inner city schools. When that happens the availability of good teachers is often reduced. That can lead to civil rights violations, and surely is not helpful in the education of the economically disadvantaged students in K-12.

As new laws are considered it will help to have economists as well as educators in the discussions. We say this because the free marketplace is often the best disciplining agent for school policies. New laws will be needed, but too many laws can be harmful. Getting a balance will be helpful in curing *Sick Schools.*

BE A GOOD STAKEHOLDER?

So far, this book has presented considerable information that could benefit K-12 education if put in the right hands. Whose hands would those be? Good citizens? To be sure we want their input if at no other place the ballot box. Perhaps we should consider the various kinds of stakeholders in K-12 education. What can they do to help? What roles are they playing now that should be reviewed and considered for changes? Our next chapter, prior to the book's concluding pages, will be devoted to such stakeholders.

CHAPTER 19

Stakeholders
Their Duties

ALL OF US WHO are citizens or legal residents of the United States are potential stakeholders in the American K-12 education systems. We say *potential* to suggest that most of these individuals have a stake or interest in the outcomes of K-12 education. Among the stakeholders are students, parents, and those who work directly in the education field. Regretfully, many people seem not interested in K-12 education, and as such are mostly ignoring how it affects them. Maybe they should reconsider. Maybe they should read this book?

How each stakeholder can contribute or work towards the improvement of K-12 education depends, somewhat, on the role they play, and on the particular sub-group of the population they fall under. Some of us belong to more than one of these groups. In what follows we identify a baker's dozen of sub-groups of stakeholders, and we try to clarify what roles they might (and in some cases should) play. What are their responsibilities? What obligations have they neglected? And, to what extent has the lack of good information contributed to their failings to reform K-12 education? When we consider the various groups of stakeholders, in what order should we discuss them?

We have chosen to rank them, in descending order, by the number of citizens participating within each group. In some sense, this means we start with the groups with the most people power, and then work towards those with the fewest people involved. This is not necessarily a ranking of which groups are the more important, but is more a ranking of which groups have the most potential influence were they more fully organized to push their agendas.

These 13 groups are:

1. Voters

2. Parents and students

3. The faithful

4. Employers

5. Teachers

6. School administrators

7. School boards

8. Civic and charitable organizations

9. Investors

10. Researchers

11. State legislatures

12. Philanthropists

13. News media

With all that in mind, we begin this examination with the largest, and potentially the most powerful, group of stakeholders: The voters.

RESPONSIBILITIES OF VOTERS

Given that K-12 education is not really a proper topic in federal elections we shall focus on state and local elections in which citizens vote. We understand that there has been considerable federal government activity in K-12 education despite the U.S. Constitution allowing it only limited roles therein. Some reformers argue that the Constitution should be amended to make that activity Constitutional. No, we believe K-12 education is best handled at the state and local levels, and therefore should not be done at the national level.

At state and local levels, voters are rarely asked to vote on K-12 policy matters. When they are, it is usually in the format of a referendum. What voters are more often asked to do is to elect various officials who, in turn, then determine K-12 education policies and funding mechanisms. Among the officials voters elect, who have these kinds of roles, are governors, state legislators, state education officials, local education officials, and sometimes judges who might also be involved.

Voters, in nearly every state, have very little information about K-12 education, and therefore cannot always intelligently cast votes for the government officials who will be responsible for K-12 education. Many voters, parents, and other stakeholders seek guidance on the Internet. For example, they often look at websites such as GreatSchools.org or Niche.com. They sometimes go online to review published performance results from their state's standardized testing. Those performance results are generally not helpful because the information is often distorted, and therefore not reliable. There is little basis on which public and private schools can be compared.

When proficiency numbers are reported they are often exaggerated well beyond the numbers they'd find if those students had been tested by the NAEP (*Nation's Report Card*) or by the ACT organization's tests.

As the reader may be aware, the criteria or cut scores for proficiency on the NAEP correspond to a fairly rigorous definition of being at grade level. The reader is also probably aware that NAEP tests only a sampling of students within a large jurisdiction. As a result, individual proficiencies are not available nor are they reported for smaller tested groups at the school or district levels.

We also learned of the website Niche.com that reports on private and public K-12 schools. As we began to write this section, we sought more information about their service. We asked them if, and how, they do interstate comparisons. Specifically, we asked their site how the public and private K-12 schools in Massachusetts and Rhode Island areas near Providence, Rhode Island compare? We still hope to get more information from them.[673] Failing that, we have done some analysis on their school grading system in which they assign letter grades to each covered school. When we used our own Asora estimates of school performance in these two states we found this:

> For those Massachusetts schools and Rhode Island schools that we estimated to be equivalent, we found Niche.com giving significantly higher grades to the Rhode Island schools, and significantly lower grades to the Massachusetts schools. It is evident that Niche.com is misrepresenting these schools, probably by conflating the definitions of proficient used in the two states when the two definitions are quite different.

You might think that the education reporters working for the news media in the bi-state region of this area centered at Providence would have scrutinized the published performance results of the two states to make sure that their readers, listeners, and viewers would be aware that the reported measures of student proficiency are either comparable or inconsistent. You would think that these reporters would be curious. But they aren't. Readers, listeners, and viewers of the news media in this part of Southeastern New England are generally unaware of the fact that test results from Massachusetts are far less exaggerated than those from Rhode Island. We at Asora know this because we have made it our business to have reliable estimates of the performance levels of these schools. So, voters in this region remain in the dark when the published information, either on Niche.com or in the local news media, is confused and unreliable. Despite this problem with the letter grades assigned by Niche.com, they are a good source to find high school SAT and ACT scores, which do not suffer from different testing policies in the different states because they are nationally administered tests.

With this dearth of information about K-12 schools, public and private, in almost every region of the United States voters are left uncertain as to what they can do to get better information about their schools. If they had that information, they might make better choices at the ballot box. They need to find ways to educate themselves on these issues.

If they have access to a good research or university library, they could start there.

What else should they do? *They should read this book.*

RESPONSIBILITIES OF PARENTS AND STUDENTS

The second largest group of stakeholders consists of the K-12 students' parents and those adults contemplating parenthood. In terms of the various laws about education, these parents have many rights and benefits. Well, in theory they have them, but in practice they generally don't have them. Most notable among the ones they do not have was discussed before, multiple times, in this book. It is the right given in *Article 26* of the *United Nations' Universal Declaration of Human Rights* that reads,

> *Parents have a prior right to choose the kind of education that shall be given to their children.*[674]

We reiterate again that the United States is a signatory to this treaty, and thereby is bound to enforce its provisions. By legal inference, we believe the individual states are similarly obliged to enforce this right. If parents were more aware of this right, we wonder if they would sometimes take steps to have it enforced or at least considered?

What parents should consider

For parents who are aware of this right or who for other reasons want to direct their children's education, they may want to pursue vouchers, homeschooling or some other avenue of choice. There is really only one practical means to achieve this: Have or obtain the financial means to implement their desired choices. For example,

- It could be having sufficient affluence to be able to afford private school tuition.

- It could simply be working another job to be able to afford private school tuition.

- It could be having the financial ability to move into a public school district they prefer.

- It could be having the financial means to hire tutors for supplemental instruction while keeping their children in the public school.

- It could be a voucher received by the parent that would enable enrollment in a private school.

- It could be an education savings account, a more flexible type of voucher, that would fund various K-12 education expenses.

The author's family followed the third of these options in 1978 when we moved to the small but expensive city of Piedmont, California where its public schools were performing much better than nearby schools in the surrounding city of Oakland. Homes in Piedmont cost about 30% more than their Oakland counterparts. So, we paid an extra premium in housing costs to access these schools.

Many parents join Parent Teacher Associations (PTA) or Parent Teacher Organizations (PTO). They do that in an effort to be active in supporting their children's educations. Such organizations, though sounding well-intended, generally have conflicts of interest. The teachers within them are focused on their own needs or on their opinions of what the needs of their students are. The PTA or PTO generally doesn't raise serious questions when those queries are critical of or embarrassing to its teacher members.

When parents seek information about school characteristics, such as performance levels, where are they to go? There are few guides published, and most of them are on the Internet. As we noted in the previous section, the school performance information that is available is usually exaggerated and is distorted differently from state to state. Heaven help the parents living in or considering moving to a bi-state region who are seeking such information to help them make decisions about schools their children should attend.

If parents had a better understanding of the many problems in K-12 education, it could help them deal with problems their children are having in the schools and it could help them get involved politically. How can they get started along that path?

How students can help

In numbers, students in K-12 education are quite numerous. We would guess almost as numerous as the number of parents—depending on demographic details within their state. Though not yet old enough to vote, they can make their voices heard. They can voice their opinions both at home and at school. They can keep their parents aware of any unusual or confusing events in the classroom. Once they are Internet savvy they can do some fact checking of things taught—particularly if the item of knowledge seems confusing or perhaps just plain wrong.

As students get older, they may want to assert themselves on the choices their parents will make for them. It could be as simple as choosing among public high schools. As this author once did, the student might choose an attractive magnet high school instead of the regular high school that he or she would normally attend.

As students mature, especially during their high school years, they collaborate with their parents more and more on school matters. Choosing electives, choosing extra-curricular activities, and planning for post-secondary education or training are among the tasks they will engage. Some students will want to offer their opinions and offer assistance on school management issues as well. They might want to work on school reform too?

During the 1990s, in Los Angeles County, California, there was an attempt to establish an organization of parents and students instead of it being comprised of parents and teachers. It would replace the traditional PTO with a Parent Student Organization—the PSO. This organization, Parents and Students United of the San Fernando Valley, was headquartered in the Pacoima district of Los Angeles. It did not have much success though it may have had some minor victories over the public school establishment.[675]

When education professors ponder the rights of children and parents, they generally avoid mentioning the legal right provided by the treaty giving parents the *right to direct the education* of their children. For example, education analyst Bryan Warnick wrote about some of this, and said,

> Whether parents have a right to educate their children as they see fit, and the extents and limits of such a right, has been the subject of much debate in the philosophical and legal literature.[676]

One wonders if he knows about the *United Nations Declaration Of Human Rights* and its *Article 26* or is he consciously avoiding acknowledging this document to offer some protection to his colleagues in the NEA dominated education establishment? We suspect he knew, but didn't want to enter this forbidden zone of K-12 education.

As parents and students try to organize their thoughts about how they might deal with some of this, they may be unsure of where they could start.

If they have access to a good research or university library, they could start there.

What else should they do? *They should read this book.*

RESPONSIBILITIES OF THE FAITHFUL

When we say "faithful" we refer to members and attenders of religious organizations who are faithful in both of the following senses:

- They are followers and believers in their congregations' religious doctrines.
- They are followers and believers in the United States of America, including its Constitution and its laws.

For those who are faithfully active in their religious congregation, we believe that there is often too much reliance on the public and private K-12 schools attended by their children to provide satisfactory instruction that is consistent with their religious principles and ethics. On closer inspection, many schools frequently teach history, civics, and even literature with an emphasis contrary to the curricula the religious sect would have followed. Where public schools teach courses *about* religion, as they are Constitutionally permitted to do, even those kinds of instruction can often run counter to the family's religious beliefs.

When the public and private schools indoctrinate children with agnostic or even atheistic philosophies or feed them from the trough of Secular Humanism, many of those children will lose interest and faith in the religious teachings of their church or other religion. Some of them will drift away from the religion as they become adults. For obvious financial reasons, as well as religious ones, congregations want to maintain and grow their membership rolls. To help keep their flocks in their *pastures* they need to counter these external forces with something to attract the wayward back to their religion. In the King James Bible, Proverbs 27:23 reminds the faithful,

> Be thou diligent to know the state of thy flocks, and look well to thy herds.

Based on 2007 reporting from the Schaeffer Institute of Church Leadership Development, here is some of what we know about Protestant church membership levels in the United States:

- Every year, approximately 3 million church members lapse in their regular attendance.

- Every year, the number of church closings is about four times the number of church starts.

- Every decade, the total church attendance has dropped by about 4% of the United States' population.

Many pastors and others primarily look inside their congregations to find the causes of these membership losses as was the case for the just referenced discussion put forth by the Schaeffer Institute.[677] In doing this they often ignore important external factors outside of the church.

As we discussed earlier in this book, public schools in the United States had Protestant roots. After twentieth century court decisions were made that limited religious activities in public schools, public schools generally moved to adopt what we earlier discussed: *American civic religion*. Though secular in its format, the *American civic religion* was reasonably consistent with the teachings of most religious denominations—consistent in that it didn't contradict their teachings. Now, in the early twenty-first century, many K-12 schools have become antagonistic to the ethics and teachings of many religious denominations. Might they be saying,

> American civic religion be damned?

We believe the causes of the loss of members are both external to the churches and are within them:

- Externally: A major influence comes from the indoctrination children receive from the public and private schools in their communities. There is more of this from the public schools than the private schools.

- Internally: The churches, and other religious organizations don't do enough to counter such ideologies.

These declining congregations need to be pro-active and adopt measures to counter the propaganda from the schools. They may need to establish a re-education component to their religious education programs. In churches, at a minimum, it could be within a revamped Sunday school program. But that would probably be insufficient.

A more robust strategy is that of establishing a school affiliated with the denomination. Or a religious organization could have a homeschooling program by which children could be educated at home, or in other locations away from the public school. Sometimes children already attend a religious school that is of a different denomination, but that is indoctrinating children into philosophies, and practices unacceptable to the family. This has happened, for example, in schools operated by left leaning denominations, such as Quakers, where children have been taught some rather strange, and objectionable things including

- Israel is a bad actor, and should be punished under the BDS movement (boycott, disinvest & sanction).

- Whites have a racial privilege that must be countered.

- Historic persons are criticized for not having twenty-first century ethics, and morals. This habit is called *presentism*.

- *Common Core State Standards* have been adopted, often in the disguise of something more traditional.

In Chapter 10, *Public Education is Flunking Religion*, we discussed a strategy for making the instruction in religion compatible with the parent's choices in that area. In Chapter 11, *K-12 Education is Flunking History*, we adopted almost the same strategy for history instruction. These were the proposals that public schools operate part-time to accommodate alternative instruction off campus, including:

- For religious instruction we proposed a modified Catechism format where the child would be dismissed early to go off campus to his or her religious organization for that instruction. Or the student would remain at school, and receive instruction from the school about religion taylored to be consistent with the Lemon Test.

- For history instruction we propose something similar to that. Here the child would go to an alternative private school, would receive that instruction at home from a parent or a tutor or would receive the instruction at the public school based on the public system's history curriculum.

- For other subjects, such as English literature, a similar practice could be allowed.

- Even without a part-time public school enrollment option, the education savings accounts or vouchers would fund after-hours *re-education* enrollment in a private school, tutoring, off-site part-time instruction, or after-hours homeschooling expenses. Such options would give parents considerably more control over their children's learning than is currently practical for them.

Were these kinds of policies implemented, state education officials would be going a long way towards honoring their obligations to parents under the *United Nations Declaration of Human Rights*. Consistent with that, they would be respecting, and following parents' wishes to a greater extent than the status quo.

For churches and other religious organizations to benefit from these alternatives to public education, they will likely need to voice their opinions in the political arenas. They will need to advocate and push for the desired policies. In their attempts to do that, they should be aware that the modern practice of keeping religion separate from the *state* does not always work to the congregation's advantage.

Perhaps it is obvious, but the concept of separation of church and state is not primarily an obligation of the religious organizations, but is rather a prohibition on the state from interfering in religion. These religious organizations are, however, constrained by federal law, and subsequent court decisions that have upheld a prohibition on churches supporting or opposing political candidates for elective office. The punishment for that is loss of their tax-exempt status with the IRS. Except for that limitation, religious organizations have rather complete freedom of speech and political advocacy. They can weigh in on proposed legislation, on proposed referenda, and on other political issues. They should work with or establish advocacy organizations that would campaign for better laws in this area. They might want to hire a lobbyist to help push their agendas forward?

They also need to scrutinize what public schools are teaching in other subjects beyond religion. History instruction is often so different from traditional standards that it will be found inconsistent not only with religious teachings, but also with a careful and *scholarly study of history*. Is English and American literature being taught in ways contrary to the religious congregations' preferences? Even science, particularly biology, may be a problem too. Before a religious congregation can deal with these inconsistencies and faults, it needs to have a better understanding of the many related problems in K-12 education.

If they have access to a good research or university library, they could start there.

What else should they do? *They should read this book.*

Perhaps, better than that, they should seek inspiration from the sacred texts of their religion: They should consider praying for guidance.

RESPONSIBILITIES OF EMPLOYERS

Within the United States there were approximately 157 million employees at the end of year 2018.[678] They were working for an estimated 18 million employers.[679] That number of employers nationwide suggests that on average there are about 400 thousand employers per state. Most of these employers seek the best employees they can find. For entry level positions these employers want literate, numerate, and honest young people to fill those jobs. They want the schools, including K-12 schools, to produce these entrants with the highest possible knowledge and skill levels. Even in the cases of hiring college graduates and others with post-secondary training, the quality of the K-12 education sector is indirectly of concern.

But even with those interests, employers and organizations of employers take little responsibility for the education policies in their communities, and do very little to advocate for reforms and improvements to the K-12 systems around them. We already made mention of Chambers of Commerce which typically have mostly private sector employers as members. In a number of instances, when I visited Chambers to make presentations, I found that local public school officials were often officers or prominent members of the organization. As such, one can imagine that efforts to help K-12 education will be in coordination with such education establishment members rather than through more independent advisors. I presume that local private school officials are less likely to be members of such organizations. One reform that these Chambers should consider is this: Only admit members who are in private industry. And, then maybe allow public officials to have non-voting associate membership rights. But make sure you don't put them on your governing board!

There are exceptions, to these bad habits, from which employers and their associations can take encouragement. In Chapter 15, we already made note of the Children's Educational Opportunity (CEO) Foundation.[680] They had company CEO's as their trustees who were also its major benefactors. Their principal charitable work was the provision of private school vouchers to economically disadvantaged students. Their first program was in San Antonio, Texas. That work had measurable and significant benefits to the students in San Antonio. These employers were highly motivated and committed to undertake such charitable efforts. Their efforts provided incentives for other nearby schools, both public and private, to improve. And those schools did get better. The many San Antonio K-12 students who performed better were the immediate beneficiaries of their charitable effort.

Where are similar people and efforts in other locales? There are some, but there are not nearly enough. Employers need to get organized to play a role in the improvement of K-12 education. In many cases, they already have trade associations and other industrial organizations to which they belong. But these organizations seem reluctant to address problems in (or perhaps are disinterested in) the K-12 systems that supply their members entry level employees. These employers and their associations seem lost. How can they gain a better understanding of these issues?

If they have access to a good research or university library, they could start there.

What else should they do? *They should read this book.*

RESPONSIBILITIES OF TEACHERS

On average, each state in the United States has about 70,000 teachers instructing about 1.1 million students in its K-12 sector. Thus, in numerical terms the numbers of teachers are considerably less than the members of the previously discussed groups of stakeholders. Given their roles in the formation of their students, they are none-the-less a very important group of participants.

One would presume that the primary responsibility of a teacher is to be knowledgeable in the subjects he or she has been assigned to teach. But, no, one of their primary official responsibilities as a teacher is to have earned a teaching certificate from an education school. That means they must be skilled in whatever is the latest fashion in pedagogy. Having subject area mastery is generally not required though having some minimal competence in the subjects to be taught is usually preferred by the school management.

There is much confusion about teaching methods. Most progressive educationists claim that special skills, only taught in schools of pedagogy, must be developed to prepare a teacher to be competent in delivering subject content to students. They tend to claim this even when the teacher is not well versed in the subjects to be taught. Consider this recollection:

> An old friend of the author once told me that she had completed a teacher training program in pedagogy at some point during the 1970s. She told me that she had mastered methods of teaching to such an extent that she could competently teach almost any subject—even ones she was not familiar with. Being polite, I did not challenge her assertion, but could picture how I would teach a subject in which I was very weak. I would instruct the students to read their textbooks, say pages 32 through 37. Then answer the questions listed on pages 38 and 39. And then tell them that I will try to answer any questions they have.

> I actually had that challenge once as a substitute teacher when I was assigned to a high school Japanese language class. I resisted by telling the principal that I had no knowledge of the language. She told me, "You'll do just fine." The

result was this instruction from me the teacher, and I paraphrase: "Read these pages. Answer the questions in the textbook." But I demurred on answering questions.

Other more traditional analysts have found that once a teacher has mastered a subject's content, very little additional training is needed to enable that instructor to impart that knowledge. Many years ago, this author, for example, taught high school physics and mathematics without any course work in pedagogy. I taught it confidently because I knew the subject matter well. I taught in a private school where having a certificate in pedagogy was not required.

Nearly all public schools require teachers to have a pedagogical certification from a teachers college or education school. Very few require certification of mastery of the subject matter to be taught. To change these policies requires those changes to be implemented by elected school officials, generally at the state level. This means that the teachers are not going to be able to effect the changes themselves. They could get politically involved, and possibly have some indirect influence on this policy.

Unfortunately, the political involvement of most public school teachers is not in that direction. Rather it is most often with a teachers union. Such unions are, in turn, generally the political allies of the certification advocates. They tend not to be interested in the academic achievements of their teacher member except when academic degrees are used to bargain for higher salaries.

There are things a public school teacher can do to partially resolve these problems. For example, they could

- Earn a higher degree or a certification showing mastery of the subject material being taught.

- Quit working in a regular public school, and seek a teaching position in a private school.

- Quit that regular public school, and look for a position in a public charter school.

- Quit that regular public school, and work in the supplemental education services (SES) industry.

- Take up public speaking, and offer various stakeholder organizations presentations on this.

- Run for elected office in the state or local school governing boards.

To have a better chance at success in some of these efforts, the teacher could ponder these ideas. Where might they start?

If they have access to a good research or university library, they could start there.

What else should they do? *They should read this book.*

RESPONSIBILITIES OF SCHOOL ADMINISTRATORS

In trying to determine an estimate of how many school administrators work in public or private education one is faced with the difficulty of defining what characterizes a school administrator. For our purposes here, we don't need a precise number, and instead we rely on a rough estimate that suggests that there are 5 teachers for every school administrator. Based on our earlier estimate that there are 70,000 teachers in the average state, this suggests that there are about 14,000 school administrators in the average state.

Many, if not most, school administrators have been teachers who were later promoted to work as administrators, often to the position of vice-principal, principal or other executive positions in the local school. Some administrators who work in district offices or in state education departments were often lower level administrators at the school level prior to their promotion to those higher level organizations.

Given that most administrators were once teachers, it follows that their responsibilities for improving schools will be similar to what we suggested for teachers. We will not repeat those opinions here, but will limit our proposals to ones more specific to the leadership roles played by school administrators.

As we see it, the first responsibility of an administrator is to be competent in the assignments given to him or her. In other words, do your official work well. Sometimes the administrators are not very good at their jobs. We have an example from a Rand Corporation study:

> In Beaver County, Pennsylvania the Beaver Valley Intermediate Unit (BVIU) established a public school choice program in 2007. It was the Regional Choice Initiative (RCI). Of the 21 goals sought only 8 were achieved. Part of the explanation for that failure was the lack of publicly available and publicly understood information about the program. That same Rand Corporation study found, from a survey of parents in the area, that only 25 of 116 those surveyed even knew of the RCI program. A separate survey of students showed them similarly ignorant about RCI.[681]

This suggests an unacceptable level of incompetence when the administrators of this program only achieved about 40% of its goals. It is a wonder they accomplished that much, given the fact that only about 22% of the region's parents even knew about the program. This points to a lack of publicity, and that was surely the responsibility of those administrating the public school choice program. Or was it deliberate sabotage?

Outside of their official work, administrators can be active in their communities, districts, regions, and states. Their roles could be political. They could find new employment. For example, they could

- Pursue a higher degree or a certification in a field related to education. Economics any one?

- Quit working in public or private education, and become a paid consultant in the field.

- Quit working in public or private education start your own school or education services company.

- Quit working in public or private education, and become a lawyer specializing in relevant issues.

- Take up public speaking, and offer various stakeholder organizations presentations on this.

- Run for elected office in the state or local school governing boards.

The administrators of education might consider these ideas when seeking paths along which they might help improve K-12 education. What should they consider doing first?

If they have access to a good research or university library, they could start there.

What else should they do? *They should read this book.*

RESPONSIBILITIES OF SCHOOL BOARDS

According to the National Center for Education Statistics there are about 13,500 school districts nationally. That number, on average, translates to approximately 270 districts in each state. If there are about 5 school board members per district this gives 1,350 as the estimated number of school board members in the average state.[682]

The membership of school boards is determined by a political electoral process. In most states these elections are non-partisan under the assumption that there will be less raw politics in an arena where the political parties are absent. We dispute that theory because there are other political entities besides political parties who have interests in K-12 public education. In particular we are concerned that absent the political parties, teachers unions will, and do, have the most clout. Moreover, there is rarely any organized opposition to them. As we have discussed elsewhere, teachers unions are de-facto political parties—and how they love non-partisan elections!

In most states, the election laws schedule school board elections away from general elections. Teachers unions and other interest groups associated with the public education establishment have lobbied state legislators to keep this kind of scheduling in force. They do so apparently because it is easier to promote candidates aligned with their interests in these low turnout elections than it would be if the voting occurred in a general election—say in November.

As we recounted in the section, *District Level Corruption*, in Chapter 12, it is possible to defeat union supported candidates, but only if a concerted effort is made. In most cases there is little organized opposition to the establishment candidates, and

thus very little chance that they can be turned around to support more sensible policies. We have also noted that the public education management is often union friendly
because union aligned school board members have hired them to run the schools.

All this suggests that many if not most school board members will not be friends
of any kind of parental choices. Rather they will be friends of the educationists, and
their preferences.

What can potentially persuadable school board members and hopeful candidates to those boards do to help K-12 public education succeed under a policy of more
choice for parents? Here are a few suggestions:

- Despite the non-partisan nature of school board elections, look for support
among the two or three most active political parties. Sometimes one will find
allies even within a political party that is mostly opposing parental choices and
other market friendly approaches. The usual assumption that the pro-voucher
party is the Republican Party is not as valid as one might think. Many Democrats,
for example, have been very active supporting vouchers, and were even leaders
on the pro-voucher side. That was certainly true in California. The black political
demographic, in particular, has been overwhelmingly Democrat, and yet significantly pro-choice in education. It was certainly true in Wisconsin where black
state representative Polly Williams co-authored the first voucher program in the
nation.

- They can offer resolutions to the school boards for consideration. As prospective school board members, they can attend school board meetings, and use the
typical two-minute slot for public comment to give their opinions. They can use
media and other vehicles of publicity to showcase their ideas. Their resolutions
may lose, but over time, their proposals may gain some traction, and eventually
become policy.

- They could consider forming or joining community action groups that would
publicize and inform local citizens, parents, and other stakeholders about policy
changes that would help the schools become more parent friendly. These action
groups could effectively become campaign committees for new candidates for
the school board with the goal of obtaining a majority on the board.

- They could be organized to file lawsuits against the public education authorities in their state. They could sue the district administration, the state education
department or the state itself to force adherence to parental rights. For example,
they could sue to decentralize the management of schools from being controlled
at the state level to more local management at the district or even school levels.

In those cases where the school board is majority friendly to the parental choices side,
there is much that can be done. Here are a few ideas for action:

- Why not prohibit social promotion? This could be done by implementing a testing system in which all official assessments used to determine official grades would be independently coordinated through an external agency not under any school's direct control. Alternatively, social promotion can be ended by abolishing age-based grade levels, and replacing them with mastery based certifications for the different levels of subject knowledge and skills.

- In those states that prohibit part-time instruction, change the local regulations to allow part-time instruction. Institute the previously discussed catechism-like format for religion, history, and civics instruction where students can optionally go off campus during regular school hours to receive that instruction from other providers.

- Institute the flipped-blended format for instruction in which assignments are completed at the school site with the available assistance of tutors/teaching-assistants. Probably do this in conjunction with a self-paced instructional format. With a flipped-blended format the ratio of teachers to students can probably be lowered. That would free up financial resources to be used for other programs or for reducing the operational costs of the schools. Those monies could be applied to establishing and operating better remediation services?

- Consider establishing a district-based school voucher program. Given that vouchers cost significantly less than the per-pupil cost of public schools this could result in school budget savings while at the same time placing students in better schools. Based on Asora's research, we also suggest the establishment of a consumer information service or guidebook that parents could use to find better private alternatives, if there are any. There was an attempt to launch a county wide voucher program like this in Douglas County, Colorado, Despite being voted into being by the County School Board in 2011, legal actions against the plan by educationist friends of public schools blocked its implementation. The legal turmoil ensued for another seven years until a new school board voted to end the program.[683] So reader: Here's your opportunity to have the first successful county level voucher program in the nation.

There are many other policies that may need replacement or revision that the school board members might want to address. If district finances permit it, they may want to hire their own analysts to evaluate their district's operations, and suggest further improvements.

As school board members educate themselves to be more knowledgeable about K-12 education policies there is much they can consider doing. Where can they start?

If they have access to a good research or university library, they could start there.

What else should they do? *They should read this book.*

RESPONSIBILITIES OF CIVIC AND CHARITABLE ORGANIZATIONS

The average state probably has in excess of 10,000 non-governmental organizations (NGOs). Only a small minority of them, perhaps around 1,000, are active in supporting K-12 education. Many that are active play more of a support role to existing school systems than working to support promising reforms to the systems. They may voice support for various changes, reforms, and improvements being undertaken by the school systems, but they frequently avoid getting involved in anything they perceive as controversial. As this author knows first-hand, Chambers of Commerce and other civic organizations nominally supportive of K-12 education are often hesitant when asked to help. We cited an example of that in Chapter 17's section entitled *School Performance Input to Marketing.* Some of these civic organizations, such as Kiwanis, Rotary, and Lions, showed negligible interest in helping us produce and distribute guidebooks to public and private schools in their areas. Their *negligible interest* contrasts with the actual interests parents would have in obtaining such school information. Such attitudes and practices betray these organizations' claimed public interest. Instead, they do reveal their naïve alliances with K-12 public school systems.

Among the charitable types of NGO's there have been some helpful developments. Private scholarship and voucher foundations have raised funds through donations to provide scholarships, also known as private vouchers, to enable economically disadvantaged children to enroll in a school of their parents' choice. Research, some of it recounted in the preceding chapters, has shown that vouchers are not that beneficial when the parental choices made are based on erroneous information about the private school choices available. Were *reliable guide books* available, we think that both public and private vouchers would be significantly more effective at generating improved student performance. The leaders of such organizations need to consider some of this. They need to wake up. They need to study these issues.

If they have access to a good research or university library, they could start there.

What else should they do? *They should read this book.*

RESPONSIBILITIES OF INVESTORS

When we say *Investors,* we restrict this designation to a particular subset of investors in commercial education enterprises. We really mean investors into two kinds of enterprises:

- The forbidden zone of for-profit schools where progressive educationists refuse to go.
- The nervous advertisers' zone of consumer information publishing firms.

If we had not made these restrictions on our definition of investors, we would have had to say that the numbers of investors would be in the tens of millions of individuals, including those who are owners of stock of various publicly traded firms. With these restrictions, the numbers of actual investors are very small—we shall guess no more than 1,000 nationally. Our goal is to encourage more individuals to invest in for-profit schools. We'd like to assume there are roughly 10,000 people who could be persuaded to invest. This suggests there are about 200 such prospects in the average state.

Also, our use of the word *responsibilities,* in this section's title, may not give the best connotation of what we mean. However, we will stay with it even though a better substitute might have been the word *opportunities.*

The status quo of absent investors

The author's company, Asora Education Enterprises, sought investment capital to fund its business plan to form a for-profit franchising network that would include many for-profit franchisee owned schools. No one came forward. Other entrepreneurs put forward novel plans to operate for-profit schools. As far as we know no one has received investment capital for such proposals although some of them did when they were operating for-profit EMO's (Education Management Organizations). Here's a list of three never funded networks of for-profit schools:

- Edison Project, circa 1992, proposed a for-profit network of schools that would be funded substantially from voucher revenue that was anticipated in hopes that the pro-voucher President, George H. W. Bush, would have been re-elected in 1992. He lost to Bill Clinton. We discussed this earlier in Chapter 17 in the section, *Education Management Organizations.*

- New Era Schools, circa 2002, under CEO David Cary proposed a for-profit network of schools in California.[684]

- Stellar Schools, circa 2003, of Asora Education Enterprises, proposed a for-profit franchising network of franchisee owned schools wherein some of the latter would also be for-profit. We discussed this earlier in Chapter 17 in the section, *More About the Proposal for Stellar Schools.*

Of these only Edison received investments, and that was only for its EMO business.

As we discussed in Chapter 17, the most successful for-profit owner/operator of K-12 schools has been Basis Schools, Inc. It is apparent that Basis obtained its capital for expansion through its internal revenues and profits, and not from external investors. It seems clear that Basis would be a much larger force in K-12 education reform if they had had access to external investment capital.

Seeking adventure capitalists

Since venture capitalists, who were among those solicited by Asora, were not interested in these ideas, we thought that there could be a new kind of venture capitalist that might consider such an opportunity. This new kind of venture capitalist we dub an *adventure* capitalist. Who wants to step forward, and be the first one of a kind? We perceive an adventure capitalist as a *hybrid between a venture investor and a philanthropist.*

I have an example of an adventure capitalist firm, Breakthrough Energy Ventures, in the yet to be commercialized field of thermonuclear fusion power. Its investors include some of the world's wealthiest billionaires including Jeff Bezos, Bill Gates, Jack Ma, Mukesh Ambani, and Richard Branson. Given what this author, and former fusion energy physicist, knows about fusion power research, there is an extremely low probability that they'll make a profit any time soon. Thus, there is an exceedingly low probability that they will get a good return. Should the project they are funding succeed, they will not only have reached a philanthropic goal of clean almost limitless power, but they will also have reached their financial goals of significant profits. Now that would be the real *Green New Deal!*[685]

The U.S. K-12 education sector, private and public combined, already has annual costs in the hundreds of billion dollars. Per student costs are typically around $12,000 per student in the public systems, and somewhat less in the private K-12 sector. We believe, based in part on our own business plans, that for-profit private schools can be profitable at $6,000 per student. If the number of students in for-profit schools could be brought to the current level in non-profit private schools, about 5 million nationally, that would suggest commercial annual revenues of roughly $25 billion. There is a commercial profit opportunity here, and there is a societal benefit as well. For potential investors who have these dual incentives, and fit this mold of adventure investing, what can they do to get ready for such opportunities? They'd surely need to study the history of for-profit schools here and abroad.

In fact, the supply of good private schools is so limited that tuition charges range far above $5,000 per student. We saw, in the previous chapter, that at the high school level the very best non-profit schools charge around $50,000 per year, while the very best for-profit schools charge around $30,000. This seems to be a supply and demand issue. It seems that these schools face obstacles in their efforts to expand market share. As a consequence, the supply of private high school seats is constricted with the result that the economic market price of those seats rises to the stratospheric levels we see around us. Does this not demonstrate that there is a market for such high performing high schools? Adventure capitalists must be able to discern a profit opportunity here. What is restraining their involvement and investments? How should they proceed?

If they have access to a good research or university library, they could start there.

What else should they do? *They should read this book.*

RESPONSIBILITIES OF RESEARCHERS

Most of the credible research in education is not done in schools of education. A great deal of the research is done by analysts working outside the K-12 education field. The work done within schools of education is focused almost entirely on public schools, and is usually of poor quality. We discuss that kind of research first before looking at the larger universe of several different kinds of schools and other K-12 educational services.

It is difficult to estimate the numbers of scholars, analysts, and educators who are engaged in K-12 education research. Per state, on average, we think that an educated guess would estimate approximately 200 people are in this class of researchers.

Research that ignores private education

The word *research* has an implicit aspect or requirement: Honesty. You can't do scientific studies if the researcher has difficulties telling the truth. Education research, as practiced by progressive educationists, often has the unfortunate corollary constraint that it must not include anything capitalistic, and sometimes must not even include anything on the non-profit private side. Such restrictions add a component of dishonesty to the research effort.

Omissions at the American Institutes for Research. This research organization's principal areas of study are mostly focused on K-12 education. In its publication, *An Educators' Guide to Schoolwide Reform,* the reader is informed that the guide

> Was prepared for educators and others to use when investigating different approaches to school reform.[686]

But that is a misrepresentation because the guide omits the *whole truth* by neglecting to mention private education and/or market mechanisms for reform.

One can imagine other more conscientious analysts who would still give preference to the government schools, but would also, at a minimum, include some mention or discussion of private alternatives in their reporting. To completely avoid mention of these other options seems dishonest. Why do we say "dishonest?" We say that because they are not telling the "whole truth. . ."

Omissions at the Penn State University education school. Another author, Patricia H. Hinchey, an education professor at Penn State University, wrote in a reference intended for parents, and other stakeholders that the U.S. government has been remiss in not signing or ratifying the *United Nations 1989 Convention on the Rights of the Child,* but nowhere in the book is there any mention of the *United Nations Declaration* *of Human Rights* treaty that the U.S. actually did ratify, and which in *Article 26* gives parents the right to direct the education of their children. Why would an education professor want the K-12 education establishment to risk losing control over public schools by risking any discussion of the whims and wishes of parents?[687] *Go figure.*

She also makes an isolated and unkind reference to school vouchers, and mentions them in no other regard. She was worried that the President George W. Bush administration's favoring of vouchers would have torn apart the rulings and laws on separation of church and state. That is an ignorant position given that vouchers, via Supreme Court rulings, are not in violation of the Constitution so long as parents have the right to make the choice of a school that might be religious.[688]

British study also ignored parents' wishes. When we found a report, authored by Jon Lauglo, on decentralization of education in the United Kingdom, we expected to find a discussion about the local structures of school management that would replace the one-size-fits-all centralized structure that is most common. We also expected some discussion about parental choices in education, but there was none. An important legal constraint could be the requirements of *Article 26* of the *U. N. Declaration of Human Rights* that give parents the authority to choose their children's education. But his report had no such discussion.[689]

Brown University's Annenberg Institute's blindness. This institute is ostensibly focused on genuine school reform in the United States, but in a progress report they issued there was no explanation why it does not consider private schools in its research or proposals.[690]

That same report lists Milwaukee voucher pioneer Howard Fuller as a Senior Fellow of the Institute. But it does not mention his roles in supporting the voucher programs operating in Milwaukee. This way they avoid even a tacit acknowledgement of an alternative approach to school reform.[691]

Research that includes private education and other alternatives

The foregoing subsections all exhibit research efforts that essentially say,

> If not invented here, it doesn't exist.

That is to say, if the extent of the education research is not within the domain of public education, then that kind of research doesn't exist or doesn't merit any discussion. The researchers of those studies surely know that private schools exist, so the inference is that they think studies of private schools will contribute nothing useful to their research. They surely know, consciously or unconsciously, that private schools are often superior to public schools—particularly the "elite" and pricey private schools.

When the author was a physicist at the Lawrence Livermore National Laboratory I was teased, more than once, by scientists from other institutions with sarcastic comments like, "It doesn't exist unless it was invented/discovered at Livermore." Such remarks were suggesting that Livermore was too focused on its own work to the exclusion of its rivals. In hopes of finding the original author of the phrase, "Not invented here," I was unable to do so in an Internet search.

When parents have choices beyond the public school. Research into K-12 schools needs to have a perspective that is wider than just public and private schools. It needs to include other instructional vehicles such as homeschooling, tutoring, and various online services. It needs to go even beyond those options by considering the economic incentives that can help improve K-12 education. We have covered some of these in the earlier chapters of this book—particularly in Chapters 15, 16, and 17.

When lawsuits are a tool to be considered. In the foregoing we have mentioned situations in which K-12 schools are operating illegally or unconstitutionally. Legal scholars can review when and where some of these practices can be the subject of legal actions against education authorities. We see a few areas of interest, including

- Programs, laws, and regulations of the federal Education department are frequently not legal and/or Constitutional. Such directives could be revised or ended by means of law suits.

- Decentralization at the state level could be driven by lawsuits based on parents' rights to *direct their children's education.*

- Schools could be sued to offer part-time enrollment as part of that decentralization.

Earlier in this book, in Chapter 9, we discussed the *Janus decision* giving teachers and other government employees the right to refuse payment of union dues. Some states and their union allies are finding *workarounds* to ensure that *Janus* does not apply to many of their government employees. One such state is California, which is finding clever ways around *Janus*. For example, in a recent article by Steven Greenhut, *Democrats Rig Rules to Boost Unions Against Janus Decision*, he writes that, in California, new union contracts resulting from collective bargaining will force employers to only hire or retain employees who will *voluntarily* agree to employment contracts that require union dues payments. He went on to say,

> So much for the rule of law, as union-friendly Democrats do everything they can to disrupt a Supreme Court ruling banning mandatory dues.[692]

It is not clear how successful these *Janus deniers* will be in their disobedience? But it does invite attention from lawyers and scholars who can work to help enforce *Janus* by means of follow-up legal actions, and perhaps legislation.

What other researchers say about competition and economic incentives. In much of the research discussed in Chapters 15, 16, and 17, education analysts found many benefits from the competition that arises when parents have choices among schools. Interestingly, it seems that the indirect benefits of school vouchers have been more significant than the direct ones. On the direct side, we saw the significant benefit to black students while students from other ethnic groups experienced only small gains. Indirect benefits were more impressive with two kinds of improvements observed:

- Public schools operating near voucher redeeming schools made large proficiency gains.

- Nationally, many charter schools were established, after 1990, under the metaphorical *gun of vouchers*. That evidently led to further competition between regular public schools and charter public schools. We say evidently because in the aftermath of voucher and charter competition, analysts began observing nationwide improvement in the performance of all public schools, including charters.

Not only were K-12 public schools seeing temporal improvement in their academic performance levels, but other measures of school success, such as statistics from national polling, have shown greater public awareness and approval of vouchers and of other choice systems being considered.

The free market economist's theory that competition among for-profit enterprises will produce the best products and services at the lowest costs was supported by the observed performance levels of for-profit K-12 schools. In Chapter 17 we saw *that in spades* with respect to Challenger School and Basis Schools, Inc. This for-profit category of K-12 education, for the numbers we have seen, was superior to all of the other formats: Public, charter, non-profit private, and homeschooling.

What was learned from Asora's research efforts. Much of the analysis done by the author and his small education consulting firm, Asora Education Enterprises, has been described in Chapter 16. This work has been based primarily on the *Nation's Report Card* (or NAEP testing) and its reporting of percentages of students performing at or above the proficient level, typically for mathematics and reading. We extended the *reach* of these NAEP proficiencies by developing a mapping technique that allows us to report estimates of NAEP proficiencies at the local levels: For the school and the district.

Much of our analysis has been based on NAEP proficiencies for the demographic of economically disadvantaged students (the FRL group) because we believe those measures accord well with the intrinsic performance of a school in which case the effects of family affluence are small. Some of our results included these:

- Contrary to the very negative public perceptions of public schools in Washington, D.C. we found that they are no worse than those in their neighboring states of Maryland and Virginia when the 8th grade performance of the FRL demographic is tested, and the comparison is done equitably. It's not that the DC schools are just as good: No, it is that the MD and VA schools are just as bad.

- When we made five quintile subgroups or tranches of schools according to percentages of students in the FRL category we found amazing consistency in 8th grade student performance among 17 East Coast states. This, sadly, fits with the slur that, *Demography is Destiny*. All these states seem to be in the same rut?

- Applying a similar tranche analysis to Florida's 4th grade students we found an unlikely result that their public education system had actually cured social promotion from 3rd grade. That gave its former governor, Jeb Bush, something to brag about as he was the one who pushed for and helped direct its elimination.

- For the disadvantaged demographic, our review of national NAEP proficiencies of 8th grade students, over recent decades, shows that public schools reached a tie with private schools in the subject of mathematics though were still somewhat behind in reading. This has been an encouraging trend.

- In more recent NAEP testing, after 2011, we have observed a significant decline in national mathematics and reading proficiencies that correlate with the imposition of *Common Core State Standards* in most states. Some would say quite plausibly, "they are caused by the imposition of *Common Core*."

Many of our encouraging findings are attributed to various forms of competition, and most of our disappointing findings we attribute to the bureaucratic sclerosis engineered by the progressive educationists. The competition comes from *parental choices* and the sclerosis from *educrat choices*.

Maintain an open mind. In research it is important to seek new knowledge and it is important to scrutinize earlier work to ensure its ongoing value and validity. This is why we believe *economic incentives* are just as important as the *methods and technologies* used in K-12 education. We see it this way:

> The better of the *former* will help school operators choose the better of the *latter*.

There are so many things to consider. We've discussed some of them, and hope that readers will benefit. We believe that analysts and other researchers in the field of K-12 education need to adopt a broader perspective. We particularly urge researchers and other analysts interested in the public education sector to keep abreast of, and acknowledge, the private side of education where there are many encouraging developments that should not be ignored.

We assume that they have access to a good research or university library. They could start there.

What else should they do? *They should read this book.*

RESPONSIBILITIES OF STATE LEGISLATURES

Within any state, its legislators typically number in the dozens and sometimes over one-hundred. There are, consequently, far fewer of these representatives than their elected counterparts serving on school boards.

Within each state, it is the legislature and the governor who have the ultimate responsibility for the legal framework of K-12 education. But there is a quasi-legal framework that is also imposed by the federal government and its Department of Education. We say quasi-legal because many constitutional scholars believe the federal Education Department and its operations are a violation of the Constitution's 10th Amendment. But as a practical policy, states still need to follow the federal laws until and unless they are willing to file lawsuits to have them properly nullified.

If a legislature and the governor are to maximally fulfill their legal obligations under the Constitution and their responsibilities to their state's citizens, then in the legislation about K-12 education they should consider the following proposals:

- File lawsuit(s) against the federal government to curtail or nullify U.S. Department of Education laws and regulations under which they operate. These would be based on the *10*[th] *Amendment* restrictions.

- Pass legislation that maximally empowers parents to have the rights guaranteed them by the *United Nations Declaration of Human Rights, Article 26.*

- Pass legislation that devolves power to the districts and schools.

- Retain powers at the state level that require centralization. These would include the establishment of minimum curricular standards and testing systems to measure student performance against those standards. The testing should include students in private schools and those who are homeschooled. State legislation could also include vehicles such as state funded vouchers and state funded consumer information about the schools.

Such new laws and regulations supporting parental rights would involve significant decentralization of the state's public school systems and would ideally create school boards at the school level: One board for each school. These laws would also provide means for parents to move their children to schools they deem better suited for them. Such means could include vouchers, education savings accounts or tax credit vehicles.

A state's department of education would become more of a research organization than one of central control. Its setting of minimal standards would be just that: minimal. Local school boards would set the remaining standards that we believe should comprise well over half of the total standards imposed on any school. In its setting of standards, each state should consider existing standards and testing systems such as those provided by the ACT or the ITBS. We would also steer away from the SAT based tests given their unfortunate association with the substandard *Common Core State Standards* (CCSS).

State legislators have much more on their plates than just education policies. But they need to have some kind of familiarity with what is at stake in K-12 education policies.

If they have access to a good research or university library, they could start there.

What else should they do? *They should read this book.*

RESPONSIBILITIES OF PHILANTHROPISTS

Unless their wealth was inherited, most individuals who are wealthy enough to be philanthropists were also enterprising people who earned their wealth because they understood the dynamics of the free-market system in which they labored and prospered.

As this former financial planner knows, people with wealth are advised to invest it in a variety of profit-making companies. That is often done by means of the stock market. The result of that is often increasing wealth for them. Some individuals simply continue to reinvest their earnings into new stock market holdings. Many wealthy people have a charitable inclination to donate some of their wealth into socially important causes. And, as they age there comes a time when they need to make decisions about estate planning. Where should their wealth go? Again, they may want to donate some of it to one or more charities.

A few pages back we discussed the *Responsibilities of Investors*, and made note of what we labelled *adventure investors*. They are the folks who very often have two motivations for their investment:

- Financial profit—because they like the income and the things those monies can purchase or benefit.

- Social betterment—because they engage in charitable activities in which they donate some of their income and wealth.

The *adventure investors* are obviously willing to risk their investment capital even if they lose their entire investment. They like the fact that a byproduct of their investment is socially beneficial even if it isn't financially profitable. And, they like the idea that the possible profits from their investment would help them have resources that they could also put to charitable purposes later. That sounds very much like a philanthropist. These investor donors have the twin motivations just listed. We suggest that philanthropists consider taking that route, and become high risk investors in commercial activities that have societal benefits.

How have traditional philanthropists looked at their societal investments? For the most part they have had this motivation for their monetary donations:

- Social Betterment—because they donate to non-profit charities and other socially beneficial NGO's.

Their philosophy seems to be this: Why not put one's wealth directly towards good social benefits as would be found in a non-profit organization? There is a cautious answer that Adam Smith would have immediately understood: He'd tell you that donating to a non-profit isn't good enough. He'd tell you to put some of in a for-profit enterprise. For-profit enterprises often produce considerable social benefits, even when that was not the intention of the entrepreneur. For-profit schools can be more efficient and more profitable than any other kind of schools. Their charitable aspect is tied up in their efficient operations. It translates to more education for the dollar. That can benefit the students in these schools irrespective of who paid their tuition.

We are suggesting that philanthropists recognize the social benefits that come from profit making enterprises, and then consider a pair of motivating factors for some of their philanthropy:

- Social Betterment—because their primary goal is societal.
- Financial profit—because there is a category of social benefits that result only from commerce.

It is this combination that we have been calling *adventure capitalism.*

Thus, these *adventurous philanthropists* should consider becoming *adventure capitalists.* And, they will still get a tax deduction if their enterprises lose money— the only difference being they'll deduct it as a loss rather than taking a charitable deduction.

As these wealthy individuals ponder such opportunities to gain social benefit from *adventure capitalism* they may want to have a better understanding of the K-12 education sector of our economy.

If they have access to a good research or university library, they could start there.

What else should they do? *They should read this book.*

RESPONSIBILITIES OF NEWS MEDIA

As most of us know, there are two kinds of presentations by the news media, whether print, radio, video or online. They are:

- Reporting in which the newsworthy relevant facts should be presented in some kind of balanced manner.

- Commentary in which the commentator argues for one or more perspectives on the news.

Many, if not most, media organs have education reporters and other education advocates in their employ or that work under contract. We shall focus here on the responsibilities of the reporters only while leaving those of commentators for others to consider. Generally, education reporters are not analysts or scholars of education, but bring an informal mix of knowledge about the field they are tasked to cover and explain.

These reporters frequently do not drill down for details of newsworthy developments in education, and as a result their coverage can be superficial. To become better prepared to cover education, these reporters need to have more knowledge about K-12 education than what they would learn, let's say, by taking courses in a school of education. Rather than that or in addition to that they need to have some background in K-12 education research that is conducted by outsiders. This is particularly important in the field of K-12 education because its in-house educationists are not serious scholars with a neutral scientific approach. Rather they are mostly biased towards supporting the public education system's government schools, and pay little attention to the successes of private education.

For them to be able to present news about K-12 education fairly they need to have some understanding of the various issues that are relevant to students and their families. They also need to have some understanding of the legal issues—particularly those giving parents certain rights in the decisions made in their children's education.

If they have access to a good research or university library, they could start there.

What else should they do? *They should read this book.*

SUMMARY OF PART IV: 1951—2030

In this Part IV of our book, we have discussed a variety of proposals for K-12 education reform. There are essentially four categories of ideas:

- New technologies enable more efficient and more thorough means to deliver instruction and content.

- New methodologies enable schools to more efficiently and effectively grow student knowledge and skills.

- New financial and informational vehicles enable parents to make better choices for their children. They also are the ingredients of a revitalized competitive economic marketplace for K-12 education.

- New laws are needed to enable parental rights and to end K-12 corruption by unions and others.

The new technologies are almost all based on video and computer developments. Video, and its constant companion audio, first in the form of synchronous broadcast television, later in the form of cable television, and more recently in the form of computer generated and interactive media, have together made the provision of academic content better. Most, but not all, computer generated instruction is accessed through the Internet while some of it comes from hard media such as flash drives, CDs, and DVD disks. The content from these newer technologies looks better in color video, and that content can be provided, on demand, much less expensively than before. It particularly allows on-demand asynchronous transmission of information that is quite valuable in efforts to provide students with self-paced instruction.

Many of the new methodologies are based on history's oldest instructional format, that of tutoring. Enabled, in part, by asynchronous delivery technologies, teachers no longer need to instruct age-based groups within a classroom. Instead, they can have the instruction delivered from the textbook and from the video devices while morphing themselves from teacher to tutor to enable one-on-one assistance to students seeking help. Sometimes, in what is called a blended environment, teachers can efficiently instruct smaller sub-groups of students while simultaneously having the remaining students work online, on computers, or simply read from old-fashioned textbooks. One of the most promising new instructional formats is that of flipped-blended. In that arrangement, students receive their instruction online when they are at home, and then interact with their tutor or teaching assistant to complete their assignments at school. Flipped blended means no homework! Students like that until they realize that it means doing that work at the school site.

The economic sector or marketplace of K-12 educational products and services, as we discussed in Chapter 9 of Part III, has shown many signs of distress and stagnation. We think that if the K-12 economic sector of American industries were operated similarly to the other sectors, the story would be much different. Then the evolving technologies and methodologies would have been used in improving the operations of K-12 schools. That would have led to steady progress that would have resulted in significant productivity increases. What is missing is the free market in which parents can choose schools wisely.

Government funded scholarships, also known as school vouchers, were eventually introduced some 35 years after famed economist Milton Friedman first proposed them in 1955. The education establishment's fear of vouchers led to the compromise choice mechanism found in charter schools. Research into these choice mechanisms has shown that school vouchers are popular with parents, but have produced only minor improvements in the skills of the children using them. Asora's own research has shown, and has been confirmed by the *Nation's Report Card*, that by 2013 public schools had improved enough in mathematics to then equal the performance levels of private schools when the comparison is done fairly using the economically disadvantaged FRL demographic. And, they were closing the reading gap. What has been missing is good consumer information for the K-12 marketplace. Without it, many parents with vouchers have used them for private schools that were arguably, on average, no better than their former public school. We, at Asora, have been offering guidebooks and other informational resources to give parents and other consumers this information. Sadly, we have had very little interest shown in this.

A new legal framework is required. Many current traditions and practices, usually with embedded conflicts of interest need to be outlawed. We would outlaw nonpartisan elections, for example, because they are really corrupt "one party" elections that allow the unions to control K-12 education.

We discussed how needed improvements to K-12 education have been frustrated, and how educators and other stakeholders seem reluctant to get busy reforming this sector. It's not so much not knowing what should be done if we are to achieve substantial reforms by the year 2030. Rather, we believe it's more a problem of motivating the key players to do something. To achieve that we identified 13 groups of stakeholders, including the parents, that can be challenged to do something. The basic message to each of them was the same. In essence we said,

> Get off the sofa. Learn how your expertise can help. Learn more by reading this book. And, then go to work.

To those who have already read this book, there must be things we advised that you can do to help. If you are uncertain about that, consider reading the book again.

PART V

A *Free to Choose* Reformation

This book began by describing how Gutenberg's printing press, and its enabling of the Protestant Reformation, ushered in a major revolution in the way children were schooled. That phase of reform was motivated, in part, by corruption in the Roman Catholic Church. Over the intervening centuries, that corruption has been overcome, but now there is a new corruption. This is no longer much of a problem for churches. Now the corruption is in the K-12 schools, specifically the public and private schools within the United States. By analogy it is now time for a new Reformation that we might call the Sick Schools Reformation. But that would confuse the object from the subject. Instead, we actually label this phase after school reforms' most important advocate and his most important theme: Free to Choose. His best-selling book had that title.[693] Yes, Milton Friedman knew and proposed remedies for American schools based on parents having the freedom to choose their children's schools. This gives us the *Free to Choose Reformation* or we can shorten the title and call it the *Choice Reformation*.

Nine treatments for nine diseases

Being metaphorical physicians of the diseased schools, we examined these patients to find an assortment of ailments as well as proposed courses of treatment for them. The treatments we found are mostly preventative measures designed to keep schools healthy and to improve their levels of academic health. What we found and what we propose is summarized in the following ranking, from most important to least important as follows:

- Of most concern is the lack of reliable consumer information about school characteristics, and particularly the academic performance of their students measured against standards for college admission.

- To solve this problem, schools need to provide reliable information that is publicly available while researchers and news media need to report their findings in consumer digestible formats. This will help restore a free market to the K-12 economic sector in which the ensuing competitive forces will push numerous reforms that its consumers, the parents, want.

- Nearly as important as the issue of consumer information is the lack of investment capital going to for-profit schools. Without that money, parents will rarely have any for-profit schools to consider for their children.

    - To solve this problem, wealthy investors need to take a philanthropic stance, and become what we have labelled adventure capitalists—like those currently putting their money into fusion energy.

- Thirdly, public schools suffer from the interference of teachers unions. Here, sensible administrative policies are replaced by union favored strategies that do not give priority to student interests.

    - To solve this problem, we would follow the advice of Franklin D. Roosevelt, and abolish these unions.

- Fourth, public schools suffer from the so-called non-partisan elections for electing school officials. This non-democratic policy gives the teachers union the status of a monopoly political party. That leads to corruption that is swept under the rug of tradition.

    - To solve this problem, candidates seeking election to school management positions should run under the banner of a political party or as an independent.

- Fifth, the management of public schools is centralized at the state level. That reduces local control, and makes it more difficult for parents to have an appreciable influence of school policies.

    - To solve this problem, schools need to be operated at the local community level. Only a few educational functions would remain centralized such as state testing. Then parents would have more influence.

- Sixth, the United States is in violation of its Treaty obligation under the United Nations Universal Declaration of Human Rights, Article 26 that provides, "Parents have a prior right to choose the kind of education that shall be given to their children."

    - To solve this problem, the governments at the federal, state, and local levels should be erecting educational frameworks that give parents that "prior right." Vouchers and other choice mechanisms will help this. As Friedman advocated, parents should be "free to choose" their children's schools.

- Seventh, nearly all schools perform their official testing in-house in formats that invite conflicts of interest. Look-good grading and social promotion are two of the bad policies stemming from this corruption.

  - To solve this problem, all official testing should be conducted off site by an independent testing organization. High school AP courses do this already.

- Eighth, attendance and truancy laws interfere with families seeking part-time schooling for their children.

  - To solve this problem, restructure truancy laws to accommodate more flexibility in this area.

- Ninth, standardized testing administered at the state level exaggerates student performance levels, and report results that are often difficult to interpret against reliable standards, such as those used in ACT testing.

  - To solve this problem, use the ACT tests or something else that is just as good.

Not adequately discussed in this list are vouchers and other financial mechanisms allowing parents to have the choices promised them in the UN treaty of which the United States is a ratifier and signatory. We need a much more robust means of giving them this financial support when they are unable to afford school tuitions. We have the Food Stamp program for nutritional needs that arguably works well enough that few Americans are starving. We seek a similar program in each state, call it an Education Stamp program, that would provide vouchers to fund the school choices made by parents.

For encouragement we repeat the old cliché that this is less difficult than *rocket science*, but then we bolster that claim with a brief discussion of the author's own involvement in that challenging field.

Abandoning socialist education: The slow trend towards capitalist schools

We close the book with two essays about the roles of socialism and capitalism in the provision of educational services.

The history of K-12 education, both in the United States and Europe, has been heavily dominated by advocates of socialist economics. This has resulted in government operated highly centralized systems of public education while some accommodation has been made for the existence of private schools. These systems tolerate their non-profit private counterparts, but generally take measures to harm and reduce the market share of for-profit schools.

On the capitalist side, it is interesting to observe that almost all of the physical objects used in K-12 education are provided by commercial for-profit enterprises—including most of the books. Providing the instructional services commercially has been difficult, but the market share of for-profit schools is slowly increasing. Though a very small sub-sector, there are very successful for-profit schools and for-profit opera-tors of charter schools who have demonstrated not only best in America schools, but in some instances the best in the world. They are not only best in academics, but are also best in terms of cost efficiencies.

Read on to learn more.

CHAPTER 20

Conclusions

ONE OF THE INFERENCES from our title *Sick Schools: Diagnosis, Cure, and Prevention of School Maladies,* is that this author is a *physician* of American K-12 education who will tell us

- What is wrong with these schools: The *diagnosis.*
- What can be done to fix them: The *cure.*
- What should we do to prevent a relapse into bad habits: The *prevention.*

Well, he's not a physician of anything. But he has *been around the block* of education a few times. Building on that metaphor of a physician let's consult the *Hippocratic Oath* to learn what we must promise. The actual translation of the relevant clause of the original Greek version is this

> I will use treatment to help the sick according to my ability and judgment, but never with a view to injury and wrong-doing.[694]

In modern parlance this is popularly translated as

> First, do no harm.

We believe the word *First* is not to be interpreted as the sentence order in the original, but rather as the instruction with the highest (and first) priority. With this digression aside, we now know how to proceed in this concluding chapter.

FIRST, DO NO HARM

A considerable portion of the content of this book has addressed various problems in K-12 education that have resulted from the detrimental actions of education authorities and other influential players. In particular, a number of these players have done harm, most often through negligence or incompetence, but sometimes through greed or misguided ideology, such as found in socialism.

The admonition that we *do no harm* applies to us—the reformers. We should not aggravate the problems of K-12 education with our remedies. A corollary of this suggestion is that we prioritize our steps of reform according to those problems that are currently the most in need of relief and correction. Or as an alternative to this we may wish to take those steps that are most easily accomplished?

WHAT ARE THE MALADIES?

Now, in order of their severity, the serious problems we seek to remedy and our corrective steps for them are covered in this section and the one following it, respectively. Surely, there is no harm in identifying the problems. It can be harmful if we propose remedies that further aggravate the issues. And, when we get to the remedies, we shall be careful to consider those solutions that seem harmless. In the introduction to Part V we already have identified many problems, with the most serious first, as follows:

1. Lack of reliable public information about school performance and other characteristics

2. Lack of investors and entrepreneurs who will establish more for-profit schools

3. Collective bargaining of public school teachers unions

4. Non-partisan elections for public school system officials

5. Overly centralized school administration, usually at state level

6. Neglecting obligations under UN treaty giving parents more control

7. School level in-house testing has major conflicts of interest

8. Overly rigid truancy laws forbid part-time enrollment, and some types of homeschooling.

9. State level minimum standards and testing systems are often unrelatable and unreliable

In what follows we expand on each of these items in separate sub-sections.

1. Lack of reliable public information about school characteristics

Most of the American public is confused about the schools around them and many of them are unaware of their ignorance in this area. The polite term for this is that they are misinformed. And, the reality of this is that in many cases others have deliberately misinformed them. Some of it is propaganda and some of it is misunderstanding properly presented information. The misinformation falls in several categories:

- Student performance levels on standardized tests, which are exaggerated in nearly every state

- Student performance levels on report cards, which are exaggerated in nearly every school

- Student behavior infractions, which go unpunished in many if not most schools

- Student indoctrination levels, which are difficult to measure and define

- School security enforcement mechanisms and school safety/health statistics

Generally, it is the first of these that concerns most parents who are seeking schools with capable instructional systems and formats.

We will discuss some possible remedies in the next major section.

2. Lack of investors and entrepreneurs establishing more for-profit schools

The dollars are there. Wealthy Americans who are either philanthropic or aggressive investors or both actually exist. Why aren't they at work making investments in for-profit schools? The answer? See preceding sub-section on the lack of information. They also appear to be misinformed and don't see the opportunities out there. How many of them know about the for-profit Basis Schools, Inc. and its successes?

3. Collective bargaining with public teachers' unions undermines student success.

A number of observers, including the twentieth century's longest serving President, Franklin Roosevelt, have argued that in each state where it is practiced, collective bargaining effectively forms a new legislative body, the union, which was not established in the state's constitution.[695] It would seem that this body is unconstitutional except in those states where their state constitution explicitly gives teachers unions some sort of legal status.

We found four states where collective bargaining by unionized government employees is protected by the state's constitution: Arizona, Kentucky, Louisiana, and Mississippi. It is explicitly illegal in the five states of Georgia, North Carolina, South Carolina, Texas, and Virginia. Do the math, and you'll see that on the surface it is considered legal in the remaining 43 states and the District of Columbia.[696] But is it legal when it violates those states' Constitutions?

A supporting view on this comes from Patrick Wright of the Mackinac Center who said,

> As the U.S. Supreme Court has observed, collective bargaining with government is not a fundamental right, but rather a statutory privilege—a privilege

that gives government unions systemic leverage that private unions do not have.[697]

One may wonder where the harm is in this? There are several concerns:

- Collective bargaining takes time away from K-12 administrators' education priorities.

- Collective bargaining leads to an inefficient teacher workforce.

- Collective bargaining can lead to interference with the curricula and other academic policies.

- Collective bargaining can lead to improper policies for student discipline.

- Collective bargaining can lead to strikes and other actions against employers.

- Collective bargaining can lead to seniority protections that can violate the civil rights of minority students.

We will discuss some possible remedies in the next major section.

4. Non-partisan elections are actually one-party elections of the NEA/AFT party.

In theory, the policy of restricting school board elections to non-partisan candidates and supporters was going to remove the corrupting influence of partisan elections involving Democrats and Republicans. That theory is erroneous because these non-partisan elections have another political organization that hides its true identity behind the professional sounding label of an education association or of a teachers union. The education association or union claims to be non-partisan when in fact it is not only partisan, but it is also the party, and is the only party.

Of course, we most often are talking about the National Education Association or the American Federation of Teachers that rival the major political parties in their members, in their fund raising, and in their clout lobbying. Were the two major political parties allowed to participate they would be able to balance the proposals of the NEA with alternatives for the voters to consider. But, no, they are forbidden to compete. Individual school board candidates who nevertheless used their party affiliations displayed in school board election campaign materials often found themselves prosecuted or otherwise hampered by law enforcement authorities and other regulators. Some of them had to file lawsuits to maintain their candidacies—usually filed on the basis that 1st *Amendment* free speech rights were abridged by the rules of non-partisan elections. They often lost in court.

Again, as before, we shall discuss remedies in the next major section.

5. Overly centralized school administration reduces parental choices and influence.

The structure of most states K-12 public education systems is based on the old social-ist idea that there can be *one best system* for the management and operation of public schools. An argument for such centralization was efficiency. Its advocates held that economies of scale would make their system less costly to operate and they also held that a system of uniform standards would be fairer to the students enrolled in their schools. In Chapter 6 we discussed some of the problems with such one size fits all systems of schools. They included these:

- A *one size fits all* curriculum is required statewide in all public schools. The re-cent attempt under the Obama administration to impose a national curriculum caused considerable harm as national testing has shown. It was the *Common Core State Standards* fiasco. Though no longer a mandate, several states continue to use this inferior set of academic standards.

- The ability of parents to influence public school policy is very limited when all decisions are made at the state level. Were the administration of schools more lo-cal then the voices of parents carry greater weight. In any case, the centralization of public school management is inconsistent with the treaty giving parents the right to direct their children's education.

- Likewise, when textbooks are selected at the state level it removes the possibility that a local selection process would give parents more choices, especially when combined with the parent's ability to move or transfer their children to different school.

- The imposition of statewide criteria for teachers' qualifications may also disap-point parents in various localities. For example, they may not want teachers with so-called credentials, and instead would favor instructors who have mastered the subjects they will teach. Think of it: *Teachers would actually know their stuff!*

Overcoming these highly centralized public education systems will help parents have more control, and move them closer to the choices they would have under the *Article 26* rights of the *United Nations Declaration of Human Rights.*

Remedies to these problems follow in the next major section.

6. Neglecting obligations under UN treaty that gives parents more control

This treaty's requirement that "Parents have a prior right to choose the kind of educa-tion that shall be given to their children," is generally ignored in nearly all public school systems in America. Under the education laws of most states, parents have very little say about the schools their children will attend, and have very little influence over public schools at the political level because the systems are so highly centralized under a "one size fits all" format.

More on this in the next major section.

7. School level in-house testing creates conflicts of interest and inaccurate results.

The testing practices in most public and private schools give teachers too much latitude in constructing tests that are used to evaluate their students and used indirectly to evaluate teachers. There is too much incentive to grade on the curve, and do so in such a way to make the students look better than a more objective testing system would reveal. This is an obvious conflict of interest. It leads to corruption when they yield to the incentives.

We mentioned a counter example in Chapter 7 where a public charter high school in Massachusetts used an external testing service. It had the best performance in the state on the state's own standardized test, the MCAS.

We would not impose such testing for all tests taken by the students. Rather it would be required for all testing in which the test results contributed to official records, transcripts, graduation requirements and/or decisions about passing to the next grade level or not.

We shall have more to say about the reformed testing systems in the next major section.

8. Overly rigid attendance laws are often illegal and restrict part-time enrollment

The joke here is that our public schools and most private schools, have attendance schedules from the *Stone Age*. There is no longer any real need to match school attendance to the needs of an agrarian society. There is surely no need in the towns, and cities where there are no farms. And, where there are farms, the need for child labor during the summer season is quite minimal (and could probably be done by the youngsters after school on a part-time basis).

Referring back to a state's obligation to obey the law as set forth in the *United Nations Declaration of Human Rights, Article 26*, we note that it restricts compulsory attendance laws to the elementary years. We presume that means grades 1–8. Compulsory attendance does not mean full-time attendance in one school, but it means that the student is enrolled full-time in a combination of schools, which could also include some homeschooling.

See the next major section on how this can be improved.

9. State level minimum standards and testing systems use awkward metrics

Every state rightly wants to have a testing regime that can help education officials and the general public monitor the performance levels in its schools, districts, counties, and statewide. Most states use assessment systems that are difficult to relate to more reliable testing regimes.

We will discuss reform proposals in the next major section, soon to follow.

Then for the above: Consider Remedies

Producing the preceding list of the problems, or *diseases*, of American K-12 education was not an easy task. And, our list is likely incomplete based on our own lack of detailed knowledge about the field. But making those lists of what is wrong has been an easier assignment than pondering the remedies. Using our medical metaphors, we have provided a rather detailed array of various *diagnoses* of what the problems are. And, in some cases, we have elaborated on the future developments to be expected if these problems are not solved. That is to say, in medical terminology, we have a variety of *prognoses* concerning the health of K-12 education if we do nothing. They are bleak.

Alternatively, we could try to develop a variety of remedies addressing the various problems identified in our *diagnoses*. Or in our medical metaphorical vocabulary we can formulate plans of treatment to find *cures*. Once we have plans for each treatment, we can make new predictions or metaphorically new *prognoses* about the brighter future that awaits American K-12 education and its stakeholders. We can *cure* present problems and we can *prevent* future ones. Or can we? Do we have the expertise to succeed?

In the preceding chapters we have discussed a variety of *cures* and other measures that seem to have merit in addressing the diseases of K-12 education. We are on much less solid ground in developing these treatments than we were in making the *diagnoses*. Because we are much less confident about the solutions to these problems, it is left to others to push this forward.

If we are confident about any class of solutions, it is the proposal that we rely on a healthy for-profit marketplace of education enterprises to produce those better schools and systems for K-12 education. Part of any free-market capitalistic solution to our K-12 education problems requires that we escape the nostrums and constraints of our socialist peers. More on that in the next section.

A MENU OF REFORM PROPOSALS

Let us now go through the preceding diagnosed problems, and propose possible treatments for each. As in medicine we'll surely need specialists to actually make the treatment decisions, and then carry them out. We are not those specialists. But we will throw out some ideas for consideration.

As we go through these proposals, we will refer to some of the 13 stakeholder groups discussed in Chapter 19. We will not discuss the details of the many proposed solutions because we have been discussing them throughout this book. You can go back and review them! Look them up in the Index and go from there!

1. What to do about the lack of reliable public information about school characteristics

In this and each of the subsequent sub-sections we will begin the discussion by identifying the sub-set of stakeholders listed in Chapter 19 who have some expertise or specific responsibility for the topic at hand. Regarding those who have the backgrounds to help find solutions to this lack of *reliable public information,* we think that

- school administrators
- school boards
- researchers
- news media

have the best preparation to offer and implement solutions. The last two of these, in particular, should be able to develop the information, and then publicize it to the public. What can the other stakeholders do to help?

> They can *pester* the more adept stakeholders who have the expertise to do something.

2. What to do about the lack of investors and entrepreneurs developing for-profit schools

For this dearth of investment capital in the K-12 education sector for the creation of for-profit schools, we believe that

- researchers
- investors
- philanthropists

are best suited to formulate plans to increase the investments in this area.

The researchers, in particular, can study the demographics of investors and philanthropists to estimate which ones would be most likely to participate. In particular, they could target the ones they judge susceptible to becoming the *adventure capitalists* that we discussed in Chapter 19. And, as before, the other stakeholders can do this:

> They can *pester* the more adept stakeholders . . .

3, What to do about collective bargaining when it undermines the health of K-12 health.

As we have discussed above, collective bargaining is not only a bad idea and harmful to K-12 education, it is also often illegal or unconstitutional. Whether illegal, in violation of state constitutions or just plain harmful, who can work to end its involvement in public education? Of the stakeholder list we would ask

- employers
- teachers
- school administrators
- school boards
- researchers
- news media

to develop solutions and, where they have influence or control, take action to help end this practice. And, everyone else can do this:

> They can *pester* the more adept . . .

4. What to do about non-partisan elections that are actually one-party elections of the NEA or AFT.

These elections remind us that one-party elections are a staple of *communism*. Looking at the history of the NEA, they certainly come across as *socialists* given that they want the government to run almost everything in K-12 education. We don't see them so far gone to put the *communist* label on them. Not yet. Among the stakeholders we would persuade into action are

- voters
- employers
- teachers
- school boards
- civic and charitable organizations

- researchers
- state legislatures
- news media

They would almost certainly need to involve lawyers in this as well. And, all others can help a little:

> They can *pester . . .*

5. What to do about overly centralized systems that reduce parental choices and influence.

As we just mentioned some of the problems in K-12 public education result from its *socialist* structure. A key attribute of such systems is that of centralization. Getting rid of them will require the attention of

- teachers
- school administrators
- school boards
- researchers
- state legislatures
- news media

The others can do this:

> They can *pester . . .*

6. What to do about the neglect of obligations to parents under UN treaty.

In theory, the United States and its several states would enact legislation giving parents more control over their children's education. But the treaty obligation is generally ignored. Among the stakeholders we would persuade into action are

- voters
- employers
- teachers
- school boards
- civic and charitable organizations
- researchers

- state legislatures
- news media

They would almost certainly need to involve lawyers in this as well. They could file law suits demanding compliance. And, the others can help a little:

> They can *pester* . . .

7. What to do about school-level in-house testing and associated conflicts of interest.

To end the implied conflict of interest that exists in-house, plans need to be formulated to do the testing outside of that environment. We envisage

- teachers
- school administrators
- school boards
- researchers
- state legislatures

getting involved. As to those not mentioned:

> They can *pester* . . .

8. What to do about overly rigid attendance laws that are often illegal and harmful

We say these laws are illegal because they restrict parental rights in the direction of their children's education. We would discuss this issue with

- parents
- teachers
- school administrators
- school boards
- state legislatures
- news media

For the others not on this list:

> They can *pester* . . .

9. What to do about State level minimum standards and their awkward testing systems

Here is an area where the author has sufficient expertise to give an answer: Use the ACT organization's various tests covering the entire K-12 grade range. We'd do that because the ACT has the most defensible testing system that's comparable with the NAEP testing of the *Nation's Report Card*, and which has a solid longitudinal statistical analytical method for determining cut scores and other parameters of their testing environment. We would also test all K-12 students in each state—public and private. We see roles in this for

- researchers
- teachers
- school administrators
- school boards
- state legislatures
- news media

And, for the other stakeholders, as we've said repeatedly:

> They can *pester* the more adept stakeholders who have the expertise to do something.

ECONOMIC REFORM: SAY "NO" TO THE SOCIALISTS

Surely, reform will work better if there are incentives in place to motivate the needed changes.

Perhaps the first concept to understand before seeking free market solutions to K-12 education problems is to acknowledge that the present systems of public education are not working. Over 25 years ago in the Fall of 1993, at a debate between the Proposition 174 advocates of school vouchers and their public education opponents we heard the Executive Director of the NEA affiliate California Teachers Association (CTA) say something revealing. It was Ralph Flynn defending the public education system in California in front of the Commonwealth Club of San Francisco. In his rebuttal, this is what Flynn, in his words, acknowledged:

> It has taken us a hundred years to screw up the public schools, and it will probably take us another hundred to fix them.[698]

That produced an outburst of laughter from nearly everyone in the room, including the voucher opponents. This author, in my role as a coordinator of the local Prop 174

Speakers Bureau, was present that day, and remember the comment well. It was one of the funniest remarks made during the entire campaign.

But that comment from Flynn implicitly acknowledged a lack of know-how within the public education establishment. A more optimistic leader of public education would have an idea or two about needed improvements, and it would surely be accomplished in well short of one hundred years. It was a confession of sorts. He was almost neutral in the voucher debate for if you can't offer a solution to a problem when your opponents have one spelled out, you're in trouble. And, all he could answer was that wisecrack.

We are more optimistic than Flynn was. We think K-12 education can be made cost-effective. To put our proposals in the simplest terms, we could simply mimic the food industry, and make it almost entirely commercial with government paid subsidies to those unable to afford their children's education. Maybe call that program,

Education stamps?

Now, you the reader:

Go do something about this!

THIS ISN'T ROCKET SCIENCE AND I SHOULD KNOW

We so often hear remarks about something being simple enough that "it doesn't take a rocket scientist" to understand or deal with a problem that is simpler than so-called rocket science. As author, I know something about *rocket science*. I can make three points:

1. Rocket science is obviously in a different field than K-12 education. After all, it deals with rocket engines and with the power sources of those engines. That is quite different from education where there are other subjects beyond science, and there are many other fields of science beyond rockets and their power sources.

2. Rocket science is arguably a much more difficult pursuit than K-12 education reform in terms of how many years might be required to reach its goals. We believe that the proposals for reform discussed in this book could be brought on line within a decade. In rocket science the key difficulty is not so much the rocket engines. Rather it is the power source. For a spaceship to leave the solar system and possibly reach the nearest stars will require an extremely lightweight combination of fuel, power source and rocket engines. That's because our current best estimates of how long it would take a contemporary generation vehicle to reach the nearest stars is a very disappointing 10,000 years. That's what physicists (aka rocket scientists) Ralph Moir and William Barr have estimated.[699] It is no accident that these two physicists earlier had worked in the field of *controlled*

thermonuclear fusion in efforts to eventually create fusion reactors for the future. Spaceships of the future will need them. Such power sources would almost certainly be needed on better spacecraft that could cut the time for a voyage down to something more manageable than 10,000 years.

3. During the 1980s as a part of my assigned research work at Livermore I acted as a liaison physicist with NASA physicist and astronaut Franklin Chang-Diaz. He was interested in using fusion reactors as a direct or indirect power source for spaceship propulsion. His work in rocket engineering continues even now in his retirement from NASA. In 1977 he invented the *Variable Specific Impulse Magnetoplasma Rocket* (VASIMIR) that generates its thrust using ion acceleration.[700] He continues to work in that area at his enterprise in Houston, the *Ad Astra Rocket Company*. Now, get out your Latin books. *Ad Astra* translates to this: *To the stars.* To close this circle, Chang-Diaz also collaborates with the aforementioned Ralph Moir on proposals for integrating fusion reactors into spacecraft that could use the VASIMIR propulsion systems or other novel rocket engines.

> During the 1970s and 1980s this author was a physicist colleague of Drs. Moir and Barr at the Lawrence Livermore National Laboratory where we and others were working on the physics of thermonuclear fusion reactor designs.

So, there you have it. Fixing K-12 education shouldn't be that difficult. It's *not rocket science.*

We can do it.

AFTERWORD

Relevance of Socialism and Capitalism

WE CLOSE OUR BOOK with comments on the political and economic philosophies contributing to and subtracting from the good schools we seek for our children. It is interesting to see the combination of politics and economics here. They are a natural combination. In fact, many universities have combined departments sometimes called the department of *political economy* instead of, let's say, *political science* and another one *economics*. Their association is natural because the political system of any state is the environment in which economics occurs. Sometimes, the political system actually has an economic label. A number of countries call themselves communist or socialist, but interestingly none we know of call themselves capitalist?

None of the countries described in this book had any of these labels. Almost all of them were nominally capitalistic yet almost all of them had varying levels of government control over schools. Now, here in the United States, that level of control has become excessive and overwhelming.

As we compare Socialism and Capitalism, as they relate to K-12 education, we want to make clear that socialism, or government ownership and/or control of certain services, is sometimes the better format for providing those services. Public highways, the postal services, and public libraries come to mind. In many cases a public-private combination works well as we saw in the management of public libraries by for-profit enterprises. Ditto for public charter schools managed by for-profit EMO's. That said, there are many kinds of services that are best provided by capitalistic for-profit enterprises. K-12 schooling, we believe, would be best provided by for-profit enterprises. As we showed in Chapter 17, in the section, *Astounding Successes of Some For-Profits*, the best high school in the U.S. is for-profit while being 40% less expensive than the best non-profit school, which was not quite as good on the SAT. This does not mean that non-profit and government owned and operated schools should be closed, but it does mean that for-profit schools should be considered fairly. Given the impressive track record of for-profit schools we wonder why they are not more prevalent among American K-12 schools?

SOCIALISM AND SCHOOLS

Without getting too deeply immersed in technicalities, we shall use the term *socialism* to mean centralized government control of an industry at the state and/or federal levels. For the K-12 economic sector, most of our narratives in this book have tacitly assumed it to be government control of K-12 schools. They are the regular public schools. The centralized control is mostly at the state and district levels. As to public charter schools, we see them as a hybrid because the government has some control. How much control depends on the details, which can and do vary.

Who brought socialism to K-12 education?

Before we discuss the individuals, who worked to bring centralized government control over schools, we should make clear that we do not regard local government control of schools to be socialistic. Thus, individual community level schools operated by a town or village school board do not fall under our definition of socialistic. When a school district operates more than one school it is on the road to a centralized system, and as that district's schools become more numerous then that district is on the road to socialism, according to our definition given above. Small districts, in the author's opinion, are acceptable. But as they grow larger, the *camel's nose* of socialism comes under the tent.

We are not historians of education, and as such may not have a complete list of those education leaders who brought socialism to the K-12 education sector. We have identified four historic individuals and two enormous organizations of educators that were quite influential in the development of public education within the United States. They are:

- Horace Mann—He *imported* the Prussian system of centralized public education into Massachusetts.

- Horace Greeley—His socialist and communist friends affected his advocacy of public education.

- John Dewey—He pushed for *organized social planning* (aka socialism) in the operation of public schools.

- Jessie Newlon—This father of *social studies* hated financial profits and loved socialists.

- American Federation of Teachers—This second largest teachers union was led by Albert Shanker.

- National Education Association—This once professional organization morphed into a behemoth union.

Let us now look at each of these influential entities, in turn.

Mann: Effectively a socialist before the word socialist entered the vocabulary. Limiting our narrative to K-12 schools in the United States, we begin with the first consequential advocate for public education, Horace Mann. As we discussed in Chapter 5, in the mid-nineteenth century, Mann visited and studied Prussian schools in Europe. He used their model of central government-controlled schools to propose his version of public schools, but he called them common schools. Then, in rather short order, he led to their establishment in Massachusetts. Mann was not interested in the schools having much of a Christian orientation or curriculum, which is understandable given his Unitarian background. He preferred a more secular approach. On this he said,

> The common school is the greatest discovery ever made by man . . . Let the common school be expanded to its capabilities, let it be worked with efficiency of which it is susceptible, and nine-tenths of the crimes in the penal code would become obsolete; the long catalogue of human ills would be abridged . . .

He didn't use the word *socialism*, but the concept is in those words—particularly his reference to "it" being "worked with efficiency . . ." that suggests a centrally controlled government run system.[701]

Greeley: He hired Marx and Engels to write columns. Horace Greeley is a very interesting political player in nineteenth century American history. We already had a brief introduction to Greeley in Chapter 5. He not only helped establish the Republican Party, but he also hired Karl Marx to write opinion pieces for his newspaper: *The New York Tribune*. The cognitive dissonance of that combination aside, Greeley had a similar outlook to Horace Mann:

- They were both Unitarians, consistent with their almost secular Christian beliefs.
- They were both socialist in word and deed. Some would say Utopian Socialists?

According to a Unitarian source, he was characterized this way:

> Greeley was a social reformer, a romantic idealist who set his sights high. He demanded more and better teacher-training and a free, tax-supported public school system with practical instruction.[702]

He was also a political reformer, with a preference for socialism. A reviewer of a biography of Greeley said this about his newspaper's editorial side:

During its Greeley era, the [New York] *Tribune* was simultaneously an influential voice in the Whig and Republican parties and a vigorous advocate of socialism. Historians and biographers have struggled to reconcile these seemingly contradictory tendencies.[703]

To show Greeley's inexperience, and poor judgement in politics, we note that he ran against war hero Ulysses S. Grant in the 1872 presidential election on the Liberal Republican ticket. His side lost in a landslide. In an odd twist of history, the Democrat Party, at its quadrennial convention that year, seeing no hope for victory under its own banner, had actually nominated Liberal Republicans to replace its own slate of candidates! After his loss, Greeley soon took ill and died in late November 1872.[704]

Dewey: Progressive here and socialist there. We have discussed a number of issues involving John Dewey in Chapters 6 and 11. We noted how early formulations of progressive education were child-centered in the sense that children would control many aspects of the curriculum, and the learning process. In the last decades of the nineteenth century and in the early decades of the twentieth century there was a gradual transition away from that format to one in which progressive educators became advocates of centralized systems of public education. Dewey was there for that transition, and became an advocate for central control in education. It didn't take long for him to enter the political sphere and propose new government structures that were socialistic.[705] On this he said,

> Organized social planning, put into effect for the creation of an order in which industry and finance are socially directed in behalf of institutions that provide the material basis for the cultural liberation and growth of individuals, is now the sole method of social action.[706]

If you unwind those words, it is evident that Dewey is discussing the centralized and controlling organizations of government. The key phrase, *industry and finance are socially directed*, seems inconsistent with multiple points of control. That leaves the inference that there is one control point at the center of government. In turn, that is a definition of socialism in which government (the center) controls and owns the industries and the financial institutions.

Jessie Newlon: He hated the profit system. We encountered Newlon in Chapter 11 where his work in Denver, Colorado establishing a *social studies* curriculum in 1922 was noted. Within a decade, he was a professor at the Teachers College of Columbia University in New York City. By 1933, he was an active member of an anti-capitalist group of professors who gave themselves the moniker Frontier Thinkers. Most of them, including Newlon, were also members of the Progressive Education Association, as was the just mentioned John Dewey. The group believed it was time to advance a socialist agenda. Newlon was comfortable working with not just socialists, but their more strident cousins—the communists. According to a Mises Institute report, he told his colleagues,

> I believe we can work with the Communists, and at other times with the socialists . . .[707]

That same report said that within the Frontier Thinkers group,

> Plans for a new curriculum and a new policy of indoctrination in the classroom were evolved. Social studies were to be the propaganda vehicle, the medium for the new short cut to implant *social consciousness* in pupils. Instead of the disciplines of biology, physics and chemistry, a mongrel subject called *general science* took its place in the curriculum. Civics, economics, and history also fell before the onslaught.[708]

We draw two conclusions from the developments concerning social studies:

- Largely hidden from public view was a progressive agenda that the new curricula would help establish a socialist system in the United States.

- Despite these proposals, public education systems generally did not replace the traditional curricula with the progressive social studies proposals. Instead, they compromised: They augmented the traditional curricula with the social studies and general science additions. While most of the traditional subjects were retained, the time allocated to them was often reduced.

> The reader may recall that the author already mentioned his Chicago high school, Lane Technical High School, as an example of a school following one of John Dewey's proposals—that of including vocational training in a high school program. But unlike Dewey's wish that the traditional subjects should be replaced by the vocational ones, these vocational classes were simply added to augment the traditional curriculum. A similar compromise was reached in science instruction: General science was taught in 9th grade, but it did not replace the other sciences. Thus, biology, physics, and chemistry were still taught in 10th, 11th, and 12th grades, respectively. And, I took all four of these science courses.

American Federation of Teachers (AFT). This organization was formed as a union in 1915. It eventually came under the umbrella of the AFL-CIO, and for many years (1974–1997) was led by the maverick educator Albert Shanker. Once when asked why his union was not more supportive of students' needs he responded,

> When school children start paying union dues, that's when I'll start representing the interests of school children.

Some friends of the AFT found his quote offensive, and even went so far to deny it was ever said.[709] We find it as an *it goes without saying* comment that is not offensive. It's cute.

The AFT has an interesting history. In its early decades some of its union locals were organized by USSR friendly American Communists. In the late 1940s these unhelpful locals were expelled from the union. That was probably no coincidence given that the Cold War was just getting underway at that time.[710]

Our focus, in what follows, will not be on the AFT, but on its larger rival, the NEA.

National Education Association (NEA): Socialistic, subversive, and secular. This 169 year-old association of public school teachers eventually morphed into the largest labor union in the United States. Let's now look at aspects of these three *s-words*, each in turn, to better understand this union's characteristics and behavior. Each of these three characteristics are so important that we give each one its own sub-section in the following:

Socialism and the National Education Association (NEA)

The NEA is socialistic in both word and deed.

In "word?" So, says a former teachers union leader. K-12 education analyst Myron Lieberman said this about their *words* advocating socialism, as they came from the mouths of its members and friends:

> The NEA and AFT conventions feature attacks on *profits* and *corporate greed* that could easily pass for a series of speeches at a Communist party convention. Hunger, child labor, inadequate health care, malnutrition—whatever the problem, *corporate profits* and *greed* are either responsible for it or stand in the way of ameliorating it. It would be surprising if NEA/AFT rhetoric did not affect attitudes toward market-oriented reforms generally, as they are obviously intended to do.[711]

From the NEA website we find more of their words that spell out their opinions on their advocacy of government solutions (socialism) and their disdain for private or for-profit solutions (capitalism). We learned a number of things. Quoting and paraphrasing from their website the NEA says a number of things that we follow with commentary in [square] brackets, as follows:

1. NEA strongly supports access to quality, affordable, and comprehensive *health care* coverage for all residents of the United States. [Sorry, health care, though important, is not a K-12 issue.]

2. As for charter schools the NEA is mostly in opposition. They want the charter schools to be under public school management—which is socialistic. For example, they say this about charter schools:

- None adequately prevent for-profit management and operations of its charter schools. [This contradicts our findings that for-profit EMO's often do a superior job of operating charter schools.]

- Many do not require charter school teachers to meet the same certification requirements as public school teachers. [This requirement is detrimental when research shows that teachers need to know their subjects.]

- Charter schools must be authorized and held accountable by the local school board as only a local, democratically accountable authorizing entity can ensure. . . [They want charter schools to be managed by the local district's school board and other administrators, and they want them unionized if the district operates under a collective bargaining agreement. This robs charter schools of their independence and freedom to innovate away from the heavy socialistic hand of a public school district.]

3. Favors *Common Core State Standards*. [This one-size-fits-all regime of standards was imposed nationally during the Obama administration. Some states still use it. Some gullible private schools use it. The standards are incompetent. It has a socialist *one-size fits all* format.]

4. Through collective bargaining and advocacy at both the state and local level, NEA members fight for more than their own economic security. They also make demands to improve student learning and the educational environment by making proposals for smaller class sizes, fewer standardized tests, more recess, more art and music classes, and additional counselors. [Their efforts here suggest that they would like to have significant control over the government units operating the schools. This is how socialists run their schools. In many jurisdictions, the NEA has de-facto control of the schools.]

5. Privatization, or *contracting out*, is part of a broad campaign that seeks to transfer many parts of our community life, including the delivery of education services, into the hands of private, for-profit corporations. In many ways, the pushes for school vouchers and charter schools are parts of this same movement. . . .Privatization is a threat to public education, and more broadly, to our democracy itself. [Or put it this way: Privatization fits the capitalistic format which is opposed by the socialists. In this case it is the NEA socialists fighting capitalism.]

6. NEA opposes school vouchers because they divert essential resources from public schools to private and religious schools, while offering no real *choice* for the overwhelming majority of students. [This kind of privatization, whether involving non-profit schools or for profit schools, is not under the control of

the government, and therefore is not as socialistic as the NEA would apparently prefer.][712]

After reading these NEA claims, and comments, one might ask, why is the NEA socialistic? Why do they prefer public schools over private schools?

One NEA report claims that private schools are no better than public schools when the comparisons are controlled for the students' families' economic circumstances. That claim is roughly true, as we have already discussed, but the private schools are better for black children. For other economically disadvantaged children there was a slight advantage attending a private school, but it wasn't large enough to be statistically significant.[713] There are two problems with the NEA analysis:

- Parents don't have reliable information about local schools, and therefore have difficulties making informed choices.

- The studies done by the NEA and our own earlier studies did not consider for-profit private schools. We have already discussed them briefly and noted that they are very often stellar performers.

In the preceding paragraphs we have found that the NEA does not like for-profit firms playing any kind of role in public education management or operations. They don't see any advantage for students who attend non-profit private or for-profit private schools. They not only want the government operating the schools, but they also want to play a central role in choosing the curriculum, instructional methods, and getting themselves involved in political issues outside of the schools. At a minimum, this paints them as socialists regarding the operation of K-12 schools. But it goes beyond that. It is almost as if they first want to control K-12 education, and then later take over the entire government? We'll have more on this latter concern in the next sub-section on subversion.

Subversion and the National Education Association (NEA)

The NEA is subversive in a number of different ways. By subversion we mean the inappropriate or illegal interference with accepted practices in various fields of work. One way to evaluate any subversive activities of the NEA is to consider what resolutions have been approved by the NEA's Representative Assembly that also match this definition of subversion.

On a White Supremacy Culture. At its 2018 convention, one of the approved proposals was New Business Item #90 (of 122 resolutions that were proposed), addressing one of their continuing concerns: The problems of a *White Supremacy Culture* that they imply is responsible for many of the problems being experienced within the United

States. I hate to waste space on this topic, but it is too important to skip without some commentary that will give readers a flavor of the subversive character of the NEA. Here is its text:

> Given NEA's policy of fighting racism and the current state of racial affairs within this great nation, it is imperative that NEA actively support, and promote, using existing resources, such as *Teaching Tolerance, Facing History and Ourselves, and Rethinking Schools*, that describe and deconstruct the systemic proliferation of a White supremacy culture, and its constituent elements of White privilege and institutional racism, in order to create equitable outcomes for people of all colors, languages, and ethnic backgrounds. Additionally, the NEA will encourage its affiliates to do the same.[714]

We weren't quite sure how to interpret this attack on the so-called white racial group. So, we looked to see what others were saying about *White Supremacy Culture*. Perhaps most detailed was an article or essay by Kenneth Jones and Tema Okun that was entitled, *Dismantling Racism: A Workbook for Social Change Groups*. They present 13 traits or characteristics of the *White Supremacy Culture*. These items are essentially the characteristics of almost any well-organized nation—not just of a white or European ethnic group. You can read them for yourselves.[715] They then go on to make the very critical self-rebuttal that this author would also make:

> Organizations that are people of color led or a majority people of color can also demonstrate many *damaging* characteristics of white supremacy culture. [italics added]

They are saying that a well-organized society would have traits that, in the author's opinion, almost any successful human endeavor would exhibit. They see these traits as harmful when in reality they are mostly ethical and supportive of a healthy society. I said "almost" because the italicized word *damaging* contradicts the actual constructive aspects in most of the traits they described. I would change the word *damaging* to the word *positive*.

But here is the rub: They couch this perfectly reasonable discussion in a supposedly *racist white society*. With its implicit presumption that white people are bad, it is difficult to not see it as a case of the *pot calling the kettle black* except here the kitchenware is white. The result of this resolution is cognitive dissonance for anyone reading it carefully.

These fearmongers, who see racism in every corner, and particularly as a sin of the so-called white race, show their ignorance of human biology and genetics when they rave about their concerns. Don't they know, as this author knows, that most Americans have multi-racial genetic composition? This author has 3% or so from India. The average American black has about 25% European (white) DNA. Even Senator Elizabeth Warren has a small amount of indigenous American Indian ancestry—quite small though significant. How can a simple racial characteristic, like skin color, relate to one's more detailed ethnicity, nationality, religion, culture, and integrity? They don't. Go figure!

For those just doing a quick read, they will likely conclude that this NEA resolution is *labeling white people as racist*. They will wonder which *white people* are actually exhibiting white supremacy in their behavior. How many will agree with this author that, yes, there are *racist white* people, but their numbers are not that large?

But we have not said how this is resolution is *subversive*. The racial animus towards whites soon becomes one against the European immigrants who founded and populated the United States. It then turns to dislike for the founding documents of the United States.

Subversion in the NEA. Why respect the U.S. Constitution when it was the product of a bunch of dead white guys, who, by the way, were acknowledged racists in their time? This is where the *subversion* comes in. And, if enough Americans wanted to replace our founding documents there is a way to do it through a new Constitutional convention. Outside of the NEA organization there seems to be little appetite for such a change. But that's not the course these subversive thinkers are following. Instead, they are supporting a breakdown of law and order, supporting illegal immigration, and sometimes even supporting higher levels of crime (as happens when they criticize police officers, others working in law enforcement—such as ICE).

We have other indicators of subversive tendencies in the NEA. Among the resolutions that were passed in 2018 there were several that could or will subvert the laws, customs and/or the rights of American citizens. Consider this list:

- New Business Item 4. This was directing NEA affiliates to support *Black Lives Matter* Week.

- New Business Item 18. This was to support a local Seattle affiliate's moratorium on standardized testing.

- New Business Item 22. This was to advise affiliates to boycott private companies involved in privatization efforts affecting public schools.

- New Business Item 28. This was to support a moratorium on new charter schools not to their liking.

- New Business Item 29. This was to support the abolition of standardized testing for teacher qualification criteria.

- New Business Item 33. This was to urge police unions to advocate for newfangled and untested enforcement tactics including *restorative justice*.

- New Business Item 60. This was to help local affiliates interfere with ICE agency enforcement activities. I think this paints the NEA as an *outlaw* syndicate of teachers. Do their members see themselves as *outlaws*?

Some of these have a rather obvious disruptive effect on effective law enforcement while others are somewhat more subtle in their consequences.

Three of these resolutions, 4, 33, and 60, will have adverse effects on law enforcement policies. All three of these are not directly relevant to education policies, and as such amount to an off-topic excursion into policy areas that are not generally the business of educators. To the extent these proposals would lead to interference with legitimate law enforcement practices there would be an element of *subversion* of lawful policies in these areas.

Two of these resolutions, 18 and 29, seek to reduce or end the use of standardized tests. In one case these were tests taken by students and in the other case they were the tests used to hire teachers. Expert educators know the value of standardized tests. They are particularly valuable for making comparisons with other schools and districts. They provide reliable metrics for judging student performance as well as teacher competency. To the extent the proposals in these resolutions are put into operation there will be an adverse effect on academic performance levels. In other words, they will *subvert* these assessment system's proper operation and roles in supporting high academic standards.

The remaining two resolutions, 22 and 28, oppose any changes that move in the direction of privatization. Free market economists recognize the superior performance of privatized organizations in the provision of education services. Both of these resolutions undermine and subvert any improvements stemming from privatization. Moreover, they work to *subvert* the United States' capitalistic system by chipping away at its component parts.

Secularism and the National Education Association (NEA)

The NEA has an history of being influenced by the twentieth century religion of *Humanism* or *Secular Humanism*. Its most famous member in the twentieth century was John Dewey, who was also famous for helping found the First Humanist Society of New York under the leadership of Rev. Charles Francis Potter. As we discussed in Chapter 10, Potter had an interesting background: Evolving from a Baptist pastor to a Unitarian pastor and then to a pastor of Humanism.[716]

> We use upper case letters here to begin the words *Secular*, and *Humanism*, and do so according to the custom that the formal names of religions use that practice. This anticipates our opinion, and that of many others, that *Secular Humanism* is a religion.

Potter was not alone in his claim that Humanism or Secular Humanism is a religion. As we learned in Chapter 10, court rulings have also held the latter version of it to be a religion. Humanism seems to be what we would call agnostic as to belief in God, while Secular Humanism is more on the atheistic side.

Despite the NEA's historical association with Humanism, the members of the NEA are followers of many religious persuasions. But as we saw in Chapter 11, *K-12 Education Is Flunking History*, Dewey was also very much an advocate of socialism as were many others in the NEA of the twentieth century. While the modern NEA does not label itself socialistic, its policies of opposing private sector alternatives in education makes this organization de-facto socialist.

Finally, as we discussed in Chapter 10, the court rulings on religious instruction have put public schools into a very awkward position. How can they teach what parents want taught about religion without violating the court rulings? Sometimes they can. But at other times they cannot. It is inescapable that parents need access to private schools and other instructional providers if their rights of choice are to be respected. It is the government's responsibility to finance that access when the parents have no other recourse.

Who will push the government to honor that duty? You will. You the reader will? You the reader should do it.

Do it now!

CAPITALISM AND SCHOOLS

Before considering the roles of capitalism in different types of K-12 schools, we need to look at the big picture. Consider this: what do you see when you look inside of a typical school, after hours? You'll see the building, its furniture, various appliances, computers, and books among the physical items in view. And, so what? Every one of these items or things was made by a capitalist. Would you hire an educator to construct the school building, to make its furnishings or print its books? It is even unlikely that you'd use a government paid educator to author the textbooks although there are a small number of cases where that does happen.

Would you hire a geometry teacher to design and organize the construction of your high school building? That teacher would have some of the skills needed—such as getting the angles right in the blueprints. But that teacher would not have the practical experience and know-how to complete the project. Would other teachers run the printing presses to produce the textbooks? Can they make the school desks? The audio-visual systems? What about the pens and pencils? Who will make them?

There are certain areas of support services where commercial firms often provide help. This could include custodial staff, kitchen workers, security guards, and school bus drivers who would be employees of a contractor firm that the school would out-source from a for-profit enterprise.

So, there are many ways in which the capitalists, who make things and provide services, can profit from K-12 schools, independent of their ownership types. When we look at some of the intangible things in K-12 education, such as instruction, man-agement, and curriculum, we arrive in a much different environment for the capitalist. It is a very difficult one for the entrepreneur to navigate. We can blame the socialist minded public educators for some of that. And, we can even blame non-profit private school educators for that too. In the next three sub-sections we shall consider how for-profit enterprises can adapt to three different configurations of K-12 education.

Capitalism helps non-profit and charter K-12 schools

On the instructional side there is not much done by capitalists in non-profit schools, or for that matter in public charter schools. However, there is one area where capital-ists and their for-profit cousins do participate: Commercial temporary employment agencies often provide substitute teachers to the non-profit schools as well as charter schools. In the past, this author has worked through more than one such commercial agency to do substitute teaching in non-profit schools and charter schools. I was paid and the capitalists were paid too.

Capitalism and for-profit operators of K-12 schools

Another kind of commercial enterprise that works in K-12 education is the Educa-tion Management Organization (EMO). We discussed them in Chapter 17. In that arrangement the owner of the school, a for-profit, non-profit, charter or public dis-trict, contracts with a commercial management organization to provide management services. Such services include teaching, human resources, and purchasing.

Capitalism and for-profit privately owned K-12 schools

Lastly, and potentially the most important category of capitalism in K-12 education are the firms that own schools as well as operate them. Unlike their non-profit and public education counterparts, here the risk of loss is greater than in the other ar-rangements while the outlook for profits is also higher than in the alternative formats. In this format, the competition is more intense, and that usually leads to more cost-efficient delivery of the instructional services. That kind of cost-efficiency has two benefits:

- Profits for the capitalists, in the sense that they attract paying customers when they provide a good service.

- Profits for the students, in the sense that they get good instruction for less tuition than for the alternatives.

It has been opined that vouchers and other means of school choice will not really work all that well until some of the available schools are for-profit.[717] Why should that be true? Well, as we have seen in the foregoing, for-profit schools, on average, perform considerably better than non-profit schools, and even better than homeschooled children. Given their just mentioned cost-efficiency many parents will be attracted to these schools, even without government funded school vouchers. As we saw in Chapter 17, the for-profit schools seem to be roughly 40% less expensive than their non-profit competitors. That attracts parents, for sure.

It's at this point that the state governments can help. The analogy is food stamps. Humans need food even more than education and yet they prefer purchasing that food from for-profit supermarkets. Those who can't afford food are given food stamps. Hardly anyone in the United States is starving so this system must be working fairly well.

Do something similar for education. Provide parents vouchers and the consumer information they need to make an informed choice. Just like food stamps, the vouchers would be preferentially provided to economically disadvantaged children. Sounds easy? Right? No, there are many impediments, and most stem from the socialist public education establishment.

To help reconfigure the marketplace for K-12 education it will be necessary to clean up the public school systems. We can think of several types of legislative actions that can be taken. For the nine diseases and treatments discussed earlier we have these nine proposals for:

1. New legislation to require honest reporting of testing results and other school characteristics.

2. New legislation to ensure equitable treatment of for-profit schools and other education providers.

3. New legislation to abolish government employee unions and their associated collective bargaining.

4. New legislation to abolish non-partisan elections.

5. New legislation to devolve most K-12 public education functions to the district and school levels.

6. New legislation requiring adherence to the *United Nations Declaration of Human Rights, Article 26.*

7. New legislation requiring official testing to be done by objective and external third parties.

8. New legislation to establish and allow part-time enrollment in public schools.

9. New legislation to reconfigure the setting of minimum standards and the testing thereon.

Though not included in the previous list, we also propose,

- New legislation to establish year around mathematics instruction.
- New legislation to replace teaching credentials with subject matter certifications.

How to start this? See your local state legislators and school board members, and push them to act on these things.

Who will push the government to honor that duty? You will. You the reader will? You the reader should do it.

Do it now!

Endnotes

1. Heinrich, Meyer, and Whitten, "Supplemental Education Services Under No Child Left Behind . . . 273–298.
2. Ballotpedia staff, "California_Proposition_174,_School_Vouchers_(1993)."
3. Ballotpedia staff, "California_Proposition 38,_School_Vouchers_(2000)."
4. Friedman, "The Role of Government in Education," in *Economics and the Public Interest*, 123–44.
5. Friedman, "The Role of Government in Education," in *Capitalism, and Freedom*, 85–98.
6. Anderson, "Business plan . . ."
7. Finn, "The Case for Saturday School."
8. Anderson, *Replacing Common Core—With Proven Standards of Excellence*, 1–16.
9. Anderson, "Are R. I. Test Results Misleading?"
10. Anderson, *Guidebook & Resources for Parents in Maryland, Virginia & Washington D.C. . . .* , 1–51.
11. Anderson, "Four prototypical guidebooks produced by Asora Education."
12. Shearer, *The Grading of Schools,* 19.
13. Anderson, *Parents' Guide . . .* , 22.
14. Anderson, *Parents' Guide . . .* , 20.
15. Website Editor, ClassicalConversations.
16. Challenger School, "Challenger School: Positive Results."
17. Niche Analyst, "Obtaining the SAT scores of Basis Independent Schools . . . "
18. Private communication with Robert Coli, MD, 2019.
19. Cubberley, *The History of Education,* 312.
20. Vollmer, *John Calvin, Theologian, Preacher, Statesman,* 131–35.
21. Westminster John Knox Press, "Zwingli, and Bullinger," 102–118.
22. Harran, "Reflections on Martin Luther, and Childhood Education," 2.
23. Shearer, *The Grading of Schools,* 19.
24. Barnard, *Pestalozzi, and His Educational System,* 1–762.
25. Klencke, *Lives of Brothers Humboldt, Alexander, and William,* 1–444.
26. Kaestle, *Joseph Lancaster, and the Monitorial School Movement: A Documentary History,* 46–99.
27. Salmon, *The Practical Parts of Lancaster's Improvements, and Bell's Experiment,* 1–102.
28. UN Treaty, "United Nations Declaration of Human Rights, Article 26."
29. SE Mom [pseud.], "FDR warned against collective bargaining for government unions"
30. Wikipedia contributors, "Hippocratic Oath—Earliest surviving copy."
31. Coulson, *Market Education—The Unknown History,* 1–471.
32. Ho, "Johannes Gutenberg: Renaissance Inventor of the Printing Press."
33. Bauer, and Wise, *The Well-Trained Mind,* 1–848.
34. Ho, "Johannes Gutenberg: Renaissance Inventor of the Printing Press."
35. Durant, *The Story of Civilization: Part VI—The Reformation. . . ,* 159.
36. Eisenstein, *The Printing Revolution In Early Modern Europe, 2nd Edition,* 259.
37. Durant, *The Story of Civilization: Part VI—The Reformation. . . ,* 160.
38. Faber, "Martin Luther on Reformed Education," 376–87.
39. Durant, *The Story of Civilization: Part VI—The Reformation. . . ,* 786.

40. Howard, *Protestant Theology, and the Making of the Modern German University,* 62.
41. Cubberley, *The History of Education,* 307.
42. Cubberley, *The History of Education,* 312.
43. Cubberley, *The History of Education,* 312.
44. Strauss, "Success, and Failure in the German Reformation," 230–231.
45. Rothbard, *Education: Free, and Compulsory*, 20.
46. Saint Paul, *II Timothy 2:16*, 701.
47. Rothbard, *Education: Free, and Compulsory*, 20, 22.
48. Strauss, "Success, and Failure in the German Reformation," 238.
49. Howard, *Protestant Theology, and the Making of the Modern German University,* 60, 330.
50. Eklund, Hébert, and Tollson, "An Economic Analysis of the Protestant Reformation," 646–71.
51. Wikipedia contributors, "Pope Adrian IV."
52. Tuchman, *The March of Folly: From Troy to Vietnam,* 118.
53. Tuchman, *The March of Folly: From Troy to Vietnam,* 118.
54. Wikipedia contributors, "Johannes Sturm
55. Arnold, "John Calvin—The Strasbourg Years (1538–1541)."
56. Staff Writer, "Sturm, Johannes," 613–14.
57. Shearer, *The Grading of Schools,* 19–20.
58. Staff Writer, "Sturm, Johannes," 613–14.
59. Shearer, *The Grading of Schools,* 21.
60. Wikipedia contributors, "Peace of Augsburg."
61. Cubberley, *The History of Education,* 318.
62. Rothbard, *Education: Free, and Compulsory*, 24.
63. Rothbard, *Education: Free, and Compulsory*, 25.
64. Cubberley, *The History of Education,* 558–559.
65. Cubberley, *The History of Education,* 560.
66. Cubberley, *The History of Education,* 561.
67. Rothbard, *Education: Free, and Compulsory*, 25–28.
68. Cubberley, *The History of Education,* 540–541.
69. Cubberley, *The History of Education,* 299.
70. Perrin, "The History of Compulsory Education in New England."
71. Cubberley, *The History of Education,* 333–334.
72. Cousin, *On the State of Education in Holland . . . ,* xxxi.
73. Cousin, *On the State of Education in Holland . . . ,* 172–178.
74. Buringh, and Van Zanden, "Charting the 'Rise of the West'. . . ," 405–445.
75. Cameron, *The First Book Of Discipline,* 1–236.
76. Rothbard, *Education: Free, and Compulsory*, 24.
77. Wikipedia contributors, "Education Act of 1646."
78. Devine, *The Scottish Nation: A History, 1700–2000,* 409–445.
79. Cubberley, *The History of Education,* 644.
80. Cubberley, *The History of Education,* 359.
81. Buringh, and Van Zanden, "Charting the 'Rise of the West'. . . ," 409–445.
82. Cubberley, *The History of Education,* 615.
83. Cubberley, *The History of Education,* 616.
84. Cubberley, *The History of Education,* 617.
85. Full Wiki Writer, "Samuel Slater."
86. Appold, *The Reformation- A Brief History,* 187.
87. Loach, "Revolutionary Pedagogues? How Jesuits Used . . . ," 66.
88. Hufton, "Every Tub on its Own Bottom . . .," 7.
89. Wright, *God's Soldiers: History of Jesuits,* 53.
90. Wright, *God's Soldiers: History of Jesuits,* 54.
91. Wright, *God's Soldiers: History of Jesuits,* 216–217.
92. Hayes, *A Political, and Social History of Modern Europe—Volume I, 1500–1815,* 530.

93. Wikipedia contributors, "Compulsory education."

94. Kaestle, *Joseph Lancaster, and the Monitorial School Movement: A Documentary History*, 46–99.

95. Balfour, *The Educational Systems of Great Britain, and Ireland*, 1–352.

96. Salmon, *The Practical Parts of Lancaster's Improvements, and Bell's Experiment*, 1–102.

97. Lancaster, *Improvements in Education as it Respects the Industrial Classes of the Community*, 1–102.

98. Wikipedia contributors, "Monitorial System."

99. Cubberley, *The History of Education*, 624–630, 662–664.

100. Cousin, *On the State of Education in Holland . . .* , 18–21, 32–35, 171.

101. Kaestle, *Pillars of the Republic: Common Schools, and American Society*, 1–57.

102. Buringh, and Van Zanden, "Charting the 'Rise of the West'. . . ," 409–445.

103. Quora Website, "Literacy in medieval England."

104. Woodbury, "Literacy in the Middle Ages."

105. Yahoo Answers service, "European literacy rates."

106. LaBerge, "Literacy in Renaissance Europe," paras. 3–6.

107. Maddison, *Contours of the World Economy 1–2030*, 379.

108. Weber, *The Protestant Ethic, and the 'Spirit of Capitalism*,' 115.

109. Cantoni, "The Economic Effects of the Protestant Reformation . . . ," 561–598.

110. Wikipedia contributors, "Pedagogy."

111. Hirsch, *The Schools We Need, and Why We Don't Have Them*, 100.

112. Webb, Metha, and Jordan, *Foundations of American Education—5th Edition*, 74–95.

113. Isaacson, *Einstein: His Life, and Universe*, 65.

114. Bruner, *The Process of Education*, 1–97.

115. Rakic, "Article about Rakic's brain research," 68.

116. Hirsch, *The Schools We Need, and Why We Don't Have Them*, 100.

117. Hirsch, *The Schools We Need, and Why We Don't Have Them*, 100.

118. Glenn, *Contrasting Models of State, and School*, 1–288.

119. Cubberley, *The History of Education*, 190.

120. McClusky, "Introduction of Grading Into the Public Schools of New England—Part I," 34–38.

121. Cubberley, *The History of Education*, 361.

122. Cubberley, *The History of Education*, 364–365.

123. Cubberley, *The History of Education*, 366.

124. Cubberley, *The History of Education*, 362.

125. Cubberley, *The History of Education*, 663–664.

126. Angus, Mirel, and Vinovskis, "Historical Development of Age-Stratification in Schooling," 212.

127. Angus, Mirel, and Vinovskis, "Historical Development of Age-Stratification in Schooling," 213.

128. Angus, Mirel, and Vinovskis, "Historical Development of Age-Stratification in Schooling," 213.

129. Angus, Mirel, and Vinovskis, "Historical Development of Age-Stratification in Schooling," 213.

130. McClusky, "Introduction of Grading Into the Public Schools of New England—Part I," 34–38.

131. Cubberley, *The History of Education*, 756–758.

132. Cousin, *Report on the State of Public Instruction in Prussia*, 1–333.

133. McClusky, "Introduction of Grading Into the Public Schools of New England—Part I," 45–46.

134. Wikipedia contributors, "William Channing Woodbridge."

135. Albree, *Charles Brooks, and His Work for Normal Schools*, 12–16.

136. Albree, *Charles Brooks, and His Work for Normal Schools*, 17.

137. McClusky, "Introduction of Grading Into the Public Schools of New England—Part I.," 43.

138. Stowe, "Report on Elementary Public Instruction in Europe," 19–22.

139. Mann, "Seventh Annual Report for 1843." 240–418.

140. McClusky, "Introduction of Grading Into the Public Schools of New England—Part I.," 39–40.

141. McClusky, "Introduction of Grading Into the Public Schools of New England—Part II." 137.

142. Mann, "Seventh Annual Report for 1843," 240–43.

143. Shearer, *The Grading of Schools*, 21.

144. Shearer, *The Grading of Schools*, 21.

145. Wikipedia contributors, "History of education in the United States."
146. Angus, Mirel, and Vinovskis, "Historical Development of Age-Stratification in Schooling," 218.
147. Coulson, *Market Education—The Unknown History*, 81.
148. Pallardy, *Horace Greeley, American Journalist*, paras. 1–5.
149. Wikipedia contributors, "School Prayer."
150. Webb, Metha, and Jordan, *Foundations of American Education—5th Edition,* 283–289.
151. Howley, A., and C. Howley, "Rural School Busing."
152. Angus, Mirel, and Vinovskis, "Historical Development of Age-Stratification in Schooling," 219.
153. Staff Reporter, "William J. Shearer, Obituary."
154. Shearer, *The Grading of Schools,* 1–220.
155. Shearer, *The Grading of Schools,* 28.
156. Shearer, *The Grading of Schools,* 203–208.
157. Shearer, *The Grading of Schools,* 7.
158. Angus, Mirel, and Vinovskis, "Historical Development of Age-Stratification in Schooling," 219.
159. DeFalco, "Dewey, and Vocational Education: Still Timely?" 54–64.
160. Tyack, *The One Best System—A History of American Urban Education,* 1–368.
161. Tyack, *The One Best System—A History of American Urban Education,* 43
162. Lastra-Anadón, Xabel, and Peterson, "Learning from the International Experience . . . ," 52–59.
163. UN Treaty, "United Nations Declaration of Human Rights, Article 26."
164. Bell, "My Long Recovery From Kindergarten."
165. Wikipedia contributors, "Progressive education."
166. Hanushek, "How Much Is A Good Teacher Worth," 41.
167. Jimerson et al., "Beyond Grade Retention, and Social Promotion: Interventions . . . ," 15–16.
168. Walberg, *Advancing Student Achievement,* 56–57.
169. Walberg, and Bast, *Rewards: How to use rewards to help children learn –, and why teachers don't use them well,* 84–85.
170. Anderson, "Parents' Guide To Schools & Services In Rhode Island & Massachusetts," 8–9.
171. ITBS Staff, "Iowa Test of Basic Skills."
172. ACT Representative, "ACT tests used in K-12 years."
173. NCES Staff, "Description of the 'National Assessment of Educational Progress', and the 'Nation's Report Card.'"
174. Akerlof, *The Market for 'Lemons'. . . ,* 488–500.
175. Gold, *School's in: The History of Summer Education in American Public Schools,* 208.
176. Cooper, et al., "Making the Most of Summer School: A Meta-Analytic . . . ," 89–94.
177. Franco, "The Relationship Between Double Dosing, and Middle School Math Student Achievement," ii–24.
178. Johnson, *Basic Remedial Mathematics,* 1–186.
179. Chicago Board of Education, *Chicago Public Schools Policy Manual—Elementary School Promotion.*
180. Cooper, et al., "Making the Most of Summer School: A Meta-Analytic . . . ," 89–94.
181. Cooper, et al., "Making the Most of Summer School: A Meta-Analytic . . . ," 94.
182. Cooper, et al., "Making the Most of Summer School: A Meta-Analytic . . . ," 94.
183. Cooper, et al., "Making the Most of Summer School: A Meta-Analytic . . . ," 94.
184. NCES Staff, "Description of the 'National Assessment of Educational Progress', and the 'Nation's Report Card.'"
185. McKown, and Roberts, *Audio-Visual Aids to Instruction,* 1–385.
186. McKown, and Roberts, *Audio-Visual Aids to Instruction,* 7–8.
187. McKown, and Roberts, *Audio-Visual Aids to Instruction,* 152.
188. McKown, and Roberts, *Audio-Visual Aids to Instruction,* 154.
189. McKown, and Roberts, *Audio-Visual Aids to Instruction,* 155.
190. Dale, *Audio-Visual Methods in Teaching,* 38–41.
191. Dunn, and Schneider, *Teaching With The Motion Picture, and Other Visual Aids,* 237–238.
192. Wikipedia contributors, "National Education Association."

193. Wikipedia contributors, "SAT."
194. CBO Staff, "Trends in Educational Achievement."
195. ACT Representative, "ACT College Readiness Benchmarks?"
196. National Center for Education Statistics, NAEP Data Explorer
197. Anderson, "Mapping NAEP Proficiencies to ACT's POT."
198. ACT Representative, "ACT College Readiness Benchmarks?"
199. Anderson, "Generating Local NAEP Proficiency Estimates . . ."
200. Anderson, "Mapping NAEP Proficiencies to ACT's POT."
201. Anderson, "Integrity is Remedy for Harms Caused by Social Promotion . . . ,"
202. Advisory Panel, "Foundations for Success: The Final Report of the National Mathematics Advisory Panel."
203. Clough, and Montgomery, "How ACT Assessments Align with State College, and Career Readiness Standards."
204. Phelps, and Milgram, "The Revenge of K-12 . . . ," 16–17.
205. Tienken, "The Common Core State Standards: The Emperor Is Still Looking . . . ," 152–55.
206. Gass, and Stergios, "The Beginning of Common Core's Trouble."
207. Strauss, "Common Core's odd approach to teaching Gettysburg Address," paras. 1–18.
208. Stotsky, and Wurman, "Common Core's Standards Still Don't Make the Grade: Why . . . ," 27.
209. Milgram, and Stotsky, "Lowering the Bar: How Common Core Math Fails . . . ," 7.
210. Advisory Panel, "Foundations for Success: The Final Report of the National Mathematics Advisory Panel."
211. Anderson, *Replacing Common Core—With Proven Standards of Excellence*, 6.
212. Bauerlein, and Stotsky, "How Common Core's ELA Standards Place College Readiness at Risk," 2.
213. Anderson, *Replacing Common Core—With Proven Standards of Excellence,* 1–16.
214. BLS Report. "Historical Consumer Price Index for All Urban Consumers."
215. Benedict, "No Prior Art: A Dedication," para. 30.
216. Litten, "Which Came First, the Apple or the Cray?" paras. 1–2.
217. Sprague, "What can labor productivity tell us about the U.S. economy?" 3.
218. Powers and Flint, "Labor productivity growth in . . . school services: 1989–2012," 10.
219. Lieberman, *Public Education—An Autopsy,* 109.
220. Private communication with Carl Brodt of Berkeley, California, 1993.
221. Anderson, "Signs of Competition in Private & Public K-12 Schools," 37.
222. Ruthhart, and Chase, "Rauner email: Half of CPS teachers 'virtually illiterate.'"
223. Miller, "Rauner's Janus victory may ring hollow—at least in Illinois."
224. Sweet, "Janus v. AFSCME: Rauner, Lisa Madigan, and the Illinois case at the Supreme Court."
225. Burnett, "Supreme Court hands Illinois governor a rare win over unions."
226. Coulson, *Market Education—The Unknown History*, 388.
227. Sewall, "Religion, and the Textbooks," 81.
228. Sewall, "Religion, and the Textbooks," 81.
229. Nord, *Does God Make a Difference: Taking Religion Seriously in our Schools, and Universities,* 156.
230. Nord, *Does God Make a Difference: Taking Religion Seriously in our Schools, and Universities,* 156.
231. Nord, *Does God Make a Difference: Taking Religion Seriously in our Schools, and Universities,* 157.
232. Wikipedia contributors, "Treaty of Tripoli," para 3.
233. Nord, *Does God Make a Difference: Taking Religion Seriously in our Schools, and Universities,* 105–106.
234. Stewart, *Georges Lemaître.*
235. Deprit, "Monsignor Georges Lemaître," 370.
236. Kragh, *Cosmology, and Controversy—The Historical Development of Two Theories of the Universe,* 55.

237. Pious XII, Pope, "To the eminent Cardinals . . . to the members of the Pontifical Academy of Sciences . . ."

238. McKenna, "Pope says evolution, Big Bang are real."

239. Wikipedia contributors, "Charles Francis Potter."

240. Potter, *Humanism: A New Religion,* 1–133.

241. Hand, "Smith v. Board of School Commissioners of Mobile County."

242. Nord, *Does God Make a Difference: Taking Religion Seriously in our Schools, and Universities,* 286–288.

243. Feinberg, and Layton, *For the Civic Good—The Liberal Case for Teaching Religion in the Public Schools,* 64.

244. Feinberg, and Layton, *For the Civic Good—The Liberal Case for Teaching Religion in the Public Schools,* 64–65.

245. UN Treaty, "United Nations Declaration of Human Rights—Article 26."

246. Santayana, *The Life of Reason: Reason in Common Sense,* 284.

247. NAEP Reporting, "Civics—Grade 12 National Results."

248. NAEP Reporting, "U. S. History—Grade 12 National Results."

249. NAEP Reporting, "U. S. History—Grade 8 National Results."

250. Farlex, Inc. "The Free Dictionary by Farlex, s.v. "educationist."

251. Collins English Dictionary, 13th Edition, s.v. "educationist."

252. Sykes, *Dumbing Down Our Kids—Why American Children . . . Can't Read, Write or Add,* 34.

253. Pondiscio, "Meta-Analysis Confirms Effectiveness of . . . Direct Instruction. . . ," paras. 1–16.

254. Harris, "How the School Strengthens the Individuality of the Pupils," 118–125.

255. Curti, *The Social Ideas of American Educators,* 310–347.

256. Jefferson, "Notes on Virginia 1782," 265.

257. Ravitch, *Left Back—A Century of Battles Over School Reform,* 43.

258. Hall, *Adolescence: Its Psychology, and its Relations to . . . ,* Vol. 2, 510.

259. Eliot, "The Fundamental Assumptions in the Report of the Committee of Ten," 330–332.

260. Dewey, *My Pedagogic Creed,* 19–32.

261. This bulleted item, and the next two such items are from: Diane Ravitch, *Left Back . . . ,* 57.

262. Sykes, *Dumbing Down Our Kids—Why American Children . . . Can't Read, Write or Add,* 203.

263. This bulleted item, and the next such item is from: Diane Ravitch, *Left Back . . . ,* 59.

264. Dewey, *Democracy, and Education,* 1–196.

265. Ravitch, *Left Back—A Century of Battles Over School Reform,* 199.

266. Dewey, "The Need for a New Party."

267. Dewey, "Education, and Social Change," 472–474.

268. Ravitch, *Left Back—A Century of Battles Over School Reform,* 303–304.

269. Ravitch, *Left Back—A Century of Battles Over School Reform,* 235.

270. Thayer, Zachry, and Kotinsky, *Reorganizing Secondary Education,* 7–11, 19, 34–37, 57.

271. The next five bulleted items are from: Ravitch, *Left Back . . . ,* 274–275.

272. Ravitch, *Left Back—A Century of Battles Over School Reform,* 77.

273. Ravitch, *Left Back—A Century of Battles Over School Reform,* 77.

274. Fitzgerald, *America Revised—History Schoolbooks in the Twentieth Century,* 214.

275. Fitzgerald, *America Revised—History Schoolbooks in the Twentieth Century,* 191.

276. Fitzgerald, *America Revised—History Schoolbooks in the Twentieth Century,* 197.

277. Fitzgerald, *America Revised—History Schoolbooks in the Twentieth Century,* 274–275.

278. Fitzgerald, *America Revised—History Schoolbooks in the Twentieth Century,* 274–275.

279. Fitzgerald, *America Revised—History Schoolbooks in the Twentieth Century,* 280.

280. Fitzgerald, *America Revised—History Schoolbooks in the Twentieth Century,* 341–342.

281. Fitzgerald, *America Revised—History Schoolbooks in the Twentieth Century,* 391–392.

282. Sewall, *Necessary Lessons—Decline, and Renewal in American Schools,* 6—7.

283. Sewall, *Necessary Lessons—Decline, and Renewal in American Schools,* 4.

284. Anderson, "Signs of Competition in Private & Public K-12 Schools," 37.

285. Ravitch, taken from *A Glossary of Banned Words*, in her book, *The Language Police . . .* , 183–218.

286. Ravitch, *The Language Police: How Pressure Groups Restrict What Students Learn,* 138.

287. Sykes, *Dumbing Down Our Kids—Why American Children . . . Can't Read, Write or Add*, 205.

288. Sykes, *Dumbing Down Our Kids—Why American Children . . . Can't Read, Write or Add*, 206.

289. Ravitch, *Left Back—A Century of Battles Over School Reform,* 127–128.

290. Farkas, and Johnson, *A Lot To Be Thankful For: What Parents Want Children To Learn,* 16.

291. Stotsky, *Changing the Course of Failure—How Schools, and Parents Can Help Low-Achieving Students,* 97.

292. Am, "Progressives Rule By Words, Not Laws—First they steal your words, then they steal . . . ,"

293. United States Code, Title 20. "Sections 1232a, 3403b, and 7907a, respectively."

294. Hudson, "Ending Common Core extortion."

295. Wikipedia contributors, "Student Success Act."

296. Harrington, "Understanding the Common Core State Standards in California: A quick guide."

297. Miller, "Common Core Disaster," paras. 1–13.

298. Sewall, "Religion, and the Textbooks," 81.

299. Sewall, "Religion, and the Textbooks," 82.

300. Ravitch, *The Language Police: How Pressure Groups Restrict What Students Learn,* 148–149.

301. Fitzgerald, *America Revised—History Schoolbooks in the Twentieth Century,* 8.

302. Zinn, *A People's History of the United States,* 1–14.

303. *Webster's Third New International Dictionary . . .* , s.v. "murder." 1488.

304. Zinn, *A People's History of the United States,* The four quotes, respectively, are from 3, 6, 5, and 5.

305. OMRF Analyst, "Columbus brought more than ships to the New World."

306. Morrison, *Christopher Columbus: Mariner,* 129.

307. Strayer, Gatzke, and Harbison, *The Course of Civilization—Volume One: To 1660,* 547.

308. Strayer, Gatzke, and Harbison, *The Course of Civilization—Volume One: To 1660,* 547.

309. Wikipedia contributors, "Gonçalo Coelho."

310. Durant, *The Story of Civilization: Part V—The Renaissance . . .* , 530.

311. Wikipedia contributors. "John F. Kennedy."

312. Yardley, "The complex Thomas Jefferson in his place, and time."

313. Trump, and Schwartz, *The Art of the Deal,* 1–384.

314. Wikipedia contributors, "Thomas Jefferson

315. Holowchak, "Did Jefferson Really Write the Declaration of Independence?"

316. Maier, *American Scripture: Making the Declaration of Independence,* 99.

317. Boyd, "The Changes Made to Jefferson's Original Rough Draught," paras. 1–39.

318. Fitzgerald, *America Revised—History Schoolbooks in the Twentieth Century,* 9.

319. Ravitch, *The Language Police: How Pressure Groups Restrict What Students Learn,* 133.

320. Ravitch, *The Language Police: How Pressure Groups Restrict What Students Learn,* 134.

321. Ravitch, *The Language Police: How Pressure Groups Restrict What Students Learn,* 135.

322. Ravitch, *The Language Police: How Pressure Groups Restrict What Students Learn,* 135.

323. *English Oxford Living Dictionaries*, 2018 s.v. "multiculturalism."

324. Hawley, "Against Tide, Some Seek Mexican Citizenship."

325. Wikipedia contributors, "In Afroyim v. Rusk the Supreme Court voided a federal law on dual citizenship."

326. Colson, "Why Multiculturalism Can't Work."

327. Rayne, "Poll shows high levels of support for sharia law, and violence among American Muslims."

328. Carcamo, "San Francisco will allow noncitizens to vote . . ."

329. Wikipedia contributors, "1996 California Proposition 209."

330. Ovando, and McLaren, "Cultural recognition, and civil discourse . . . ," xix.

331. Scott, "The 50 greatest Yogi Berra quotes."

332. Roy-Davis, "Can Multiculturalism Work? Part I: Nationalism, and Its Critics."

333. Eaton, "Resentment, Multiculturalism, and Identity Politics," paras. 1–20.

334. Wikipedia contributors, "Howard Zinn."

335. Fisher, "Disparate-Impact Theory Finally Gets Its Test At Supreme Court."

336. Statista Analyst, "Percentage of U.S. population as of 2016, and 2060, by race, and Hispanic origin."

337. Wade, "Genetic study reveals surprising ancestry of many Americans," para. 5.

338. Census Report, "Population—Census.gov."

339. Ravitch, *The Language Police: How Pressure Groups Restrict What Students Learn*, 137.

340. Associated Press, "Multicultural History Standards Rejected by Senate in 99–1 Vote."

341. Ravitch, *The Language Police: How Pressure Groups Restrict What Students Learn*, 137–138.

342. Ravitch, *The Language Police: How Pressure Groups Restrict What Students Learn*, 138.

343. Ravitch, *The Language Police: How Pressure Groups Restrict What Students Learn*, 138.

344. Ravitch, *The Language Police: How Pressure Groups Restrict What Students Learn*, 140.

345. Ravitch, *The Language Police: How Pressure Groups Restrict What Students Learn*, 149.

346. Ravitch, *The Language Police: How Pressure Groups Restrict What Students Learn*, 149.

347. Ravitch, *The Language Police: How Pressure Groups Restrict What Students Learn*, 150.

348. Schweikart, *48 Liberal Lies About American History*, 1–13.

349. Schweikart, *48 Liberal Lies About American History*, 150–151.

350. Ravitch, *The Language Police: How Pressure Groups Restrict What Students Learn*, 152.

351. Ravitch, *The Language Police: How Pressure Groups Restrict What Students Learn*, 152–154.

352. Ravitch, *The Language Police: How Pressure Groups Restrict What Students Learn*, 152.

353. Hanes, *World History: Continuity, and Change*, 441–446.

354. Nash, *American Odyssey: The United States in the Twentieth Century*, 23–24.

355. Gray, "When Spain Reigned on Central Park South."

356. Britannica Editors, "Apartment house—Architecture."

357. Ravitch, *The Language Police: How Pressure Groups Restrict What Students Learn*, 153–154.

358. Ellis, and Esler, *World History: Connections to Today*, 1–1066.

359. C. Turner, and J. Turner, *Man Corn: Cannibalism, and Violence in the Prehistoric American Southwest*, 1–552.

360. Bennetta, *A Book of Far-Left Propaganda That Fosters Anti-Intellectualism*.

361. Ravitch, *The Language Police: How Pressure Groups Restrict What Students Learn*, 154–155.

362. *English Oxford Living Dictionaries*, 2019 s.v. "intersectionality."

363. Keiler, "Intersectional Nonsense."

364. Dershowitz, "The Bigotry of 'Intersectionality'," para. 15.

365. Wikipedia contributors, "Intersectionality."

366. Morningside Center Article, "Intersectionality: What is it? How can it help us?"

367. Ravitch, *The Language Police: How Pressure Groups Restrict What Students Learn*, 155.

368. C. Carson, and D. Carson, "Black Panther Party," paras. 1–7.

369. Wikipedia contributors, "Eldridge Cleaver."

370. Ravitch, *The Language Police: How Pressure Groups Restrict What Students Learn*, 156.

371. Sewall, "The Postmodern Schoolhouse," 59.

372. Wikipedia contributors, "History of the United States."

373. Johnson, *A History of the American People*, 3–6.

374. Wikipedia contributors, "Henry I Sinclair, Earl of Orkney."

375. Goudsward, *The Westford Knight, and Henry Sinclair*, 1–260.

376. Cheatle, "Medieval cross found on The Curse of Oak Island 'could end up rewriting history'."

377. Prometheus Entertainment. "The Curse of Oak Island: Season 6, Episode 6- Precious Metal."

378. Ravitch, *The Language Police: How Pressure Groups Restrict What Students Learn*, 156.

379. Ravitch, *A Consumer's Guide to High School History Textbooks*, 16–41.

380. American Textbook Council, "Widely Adopted History Textbooks."

381. Friedman, "The Role of Government in Education," in *Capitalism, and Freedom*, 89.

382. Walberg, *Tests, Testing, and Genuine School Reform*, 59–62.

383. Walberg, *Tests, Testing, and Genuine School Reform*, 63–64

384. Gay, "An Idiot's Guide to Bribing, and Cheating Your Way Into College."
385. Korn, Levitz, and Ailworth, "Federal Prosecutors Charge Dozens in College Admissions Cheating Scheme."
386. Korn, Levitz, and Ailworth, "Federal Prosecutors Charge Dozens in College Admissions Cheating Scheme."
387. Walberg, *Tests, Testing, and Genuine School Reform*, 63–66.
388. Coulson, *Market Education—The Unknown History*, 212.
389. Sykes, *Dumbing Down Our Kids—Why American Children . . . Can't Read, Write or Add*, 230–231.
390. Bonsteel, and Bonilla, *A Choice For Our Children—Curing The Crisis In America's Schools*, 10, 219.
391. Lieberman, *Public Education—An Autopsy*, 337.
392. Lieberman, *Public Education—An Autopsy*, 337–338.
393. Walberg, and Bast, *Education, and Capitalism . . .* , 39.
394. Walberg, and Bast, *Education, and Capitalism . . .* , 39.
395. Bockelman and Overton, ". . . MEA's Money Machine, Executive Summary."

396. Brimelow and Spencer, "The National Extortion Association."
397. Sykes, *Dumbing Down Our Kids—Why American Children . . . Can't Read, Write or Add*, 233.
398. Stern, *Breaking free—Public School Lessons, and the Imperative of School Choice*, 119.
399. Walberg, *Tests, Testing, and Genuine School Reform*, 63–64.
400. Avenoso, "Suspected tampering on test answers embroils Connecticut school in scandal."
401. Times Reporting Staff, "Principal Blamed in Test-Score Altering."
402. Dave, "5 educators charged with fostering cheating in Philadelphia schools."
403. Woodall, "Former Cayuga Elementary principal sentenced to 10 years' probation . . ."
404. Coulson, *Market Education—The Unknown History*, 193–195.
405. Feynman, *"Surely You're Joking Mr. Feynman!"—Adventures of a Curious Character*, 290–291.
406. Staff Reporters, "A timeline of how the Atlanta school cheating scandal unfolded."
407. Staff Reporters, "8 of 10 Atlanta educators in cheating scandal sentenced to prison."
408. Schemo, "As Testing Rises, 9th Grade Becomes Pivotal."
409. Eltagouri, "10 years for board member . . . for pocketing $566,000 in kickbacks."
410. Owen, "Former North Chicago school board member gets 30 months for taking kickbacks."
411. Horowitz, "NYC School Bus Inspectors Sentenced, Union Officials Indicted in Bribery Scam."
412. Coulson, *Market Education—The Unknown History*, 210–211.
413. Staff Writer, "Richardson Indicted."
414. Staff Reporter, "Fourteen indicted in alleged thefts from Floyd school system."
415. Williams, *Cheating Our Kids—How Politics, and Greed Ruin Education*, 71–72.
416. Williams, *Cheating Our Kids—How Politics, and Greed Ruin Education*, 16–17.
417. Anzia, and Moe, "Collective Bargaining, Transfer Rights, and Disadvantaged Schools," 83–111.
418. Twain, *Following the Equator: A Journey around the World*, 561.
419. Coulson, *Market Education—The Unknown History*, 212.
420. Taylor, *Reds at the Blackboard—Communism, Civil Rights, and the New York City Teachers Union*, 34–60.
421. Perez, "San Francisco allows non-citizens to vote in school elections."
422. Anzia, "Election Timing, and the Electoral Influence of Interest Groups," 412–27.
423. Office of Inspector General, "Investigative Report: Maine Department of Education to Pay United States . . ."
424. Office of Inspector General, "Investigation Report: Puerto Rico Department of Education Pays . . ."
425. Office of Inspector General, "Former State School Superintendent Linda Schrenko Sentenced to Eight Years . . ."
426. Feynman, *"Surely You're Joking Mr. Feynman!"—Adventures of a Curious Character*, 294–295.
427. Feynman, *"Surely You're Joking Mr. Feynman!"—Adventures of a Curious Character*, 301–302.

428. Ravitch, *The Language Police: How Pressure Groups Restrict What Students Learn,* 148–149.

429. Ravitch, *The Language Police: How Pressure Groups Restrict What Students Learn,* 24.

430. Ravitch, *The Language Police: How Pressure Groups Restrict What Students Learn,* 25.

431. Ravitch, *The Language Police: How Pressure Groups Restrict What Students Learn,* 25–26.

432. Ansary, "A Textbook Example of What's Wrong with Education."

433. Anderson, "Common Core's double whammy—The Nation's Report Card shows a turn for the worse."

434. Bidwell, "Common Core: A Divisive Issue for Catholic School Parents Too."

435. Brown, "Common Core, Fresno Christian Schools. "

436. School Administrator, "Curriculum of Trinity Lutheran School, Hawthorne, California."

437. Wikipedia contributors, "The road to Hell is paved with good intentions."

438. Gordon, "Common Core State Standards—Message from the Superintendent."

439. Healey, "For Profit School Advisory."

440. Crawford, "Why Nonpartisan– Versus Partisan– School Board Elections Do Not Tell The Whole Story."

441. Wolfson, "Judge candidate sues to run openly as a Republican."

442. Norton, "Partisan School Board Election Arguments."

443. Truth In American Education Representative, "No Child Left Behind Waivers."

444. UN Treaty, "United Nations Declaration of Human Rights, Article 26."

445. Ravitch, *The Language Police: How Pressure Groups Restrict What Students Learn,* 150.

446. Nazworth, "Homeschool Advocate Responds to Sex Scandals of Homeschool Leaders . . ."

447. Bauer, and Wise, *The Well-Trained Mind,* 1–848.

448. McCluskey, "Corruption in the Public Schools—The Market Is the Answer . . . ," 1–20.

449. McCluskey, "Corruption in the Public Schools—The Market Is the Answer . . . ," 2.

450. McCluskey, "Corruption in the Public Schools—The Market Is the Answer . . . ," 3.

451. UN Treaty, "United Nations Declaration of Human Rights, Article 26."

452. Boyd, Plank, and Sykes, "Teachers' Unions In Hard Times, in Conflicting Missions?" 178–180.

453. Radosh, "Is Socialism Part of the American Tradition?" paras. 12–13.

454. SE Mom [pseud.], "FDR warned against collective bargaining for government unions"

455. Walsh, and Jacobs, *Alternative Certification Isn't Alternative,* 1–38.

456. Walsh, and Jacobs, *Alternative Certification Isn't Alternative,* 8.

457. Stone, "Direct Instruction: What the Research Says," 9.

458. Stone, "Aligning Teacher Training with Public Policy," 34–38.

459. Smith, *An Inquiry into the Nature, and Causes of the Wealth of Nations—A Selected Edition,* 291–292.

460. Tooley, "From Village School to Global Brand– Changing the World Through Education," x.

461. Isenberg, "SABIS—A Global Education Venture from Lebanon," 6.

462. Tooley, "From Village School to Global Brand– Changing the World Through Education," 302–303.

463. Tooley, "From Village School to Global Brand– Changing the World Through Education," 304.

464. Wikipedia contributors, "Distance Education."

465. Keairns, "History of Distance Education," paras. 1–2.

466. Miller, "History of Distance Learning," para. 3.

467. White, "Physics Course on TV."

468. Wikipedia contributors, "Harvey Elliott White."

469. Twyford, "The national program in the use of television in the public schools. A report . . . ," 156.

470. Wikipedia contributors, "Jones International University."

471. Kirkpatrick, "Teachers Unions, and Educational Reform," paras. 24–27.

472. Moore, *Handbook of Distance Education,* 1–606.

473. Staff Reporter, "China's new-gen supercomputer expected to be 10-times faster than current champion."

474. Chen, "How Stanley Kubrick's HAL 9000 laid the blueprint for AI in film."

475. Brown, "AI Is on the Upswing in Optimizing K–12 Education."

476. Wikipedia contributors, "Luddite."

477. Economist staff reporter, "Difference Engine: Luddite legacy . . ."

478. Mack, "Elon Musk called out by creepy artificial intelligence robot."

479. Glowatz, "Robot Granted Citizenship In Saudi Arabia Immediately Trolls Elon Musk."

480. Private communication: Dominic Nuccio, Geometry Teacher, Lane Technical High School, Chicago, 1957.

481. Zolfagharifard, "Artificial intelligence 'could be the worst thing to happen to humanity' . . ."

482. Stockard, et al., "The Effectiveness of Direct Instruction Curricula: A Meta-Analysis . . . ," 479–507.

483. Anderson, *Business Plan for Asora Education Enterprises' Stellar Schools Franchising Company.*

484. Amplifire Representative, "Amplifire instructional/assessment system—how it works."

485. Anderson, *Business Plan for Asora Education Enterprises' Stellar Schools Franchising Company.*

486. Friedman, "The Role of Government in Education," in *Economics, and the Public Interest,* 123–144.

487. Friedman, "The Role of Government in Education," in *Capitalism, and Freedom,* 85–98.

488. Friedman, "The Role of Government in Education," in *Capitalism, and Freedom,* 89.

489. Sewall, *Necessary Lessons—Decline, and Renewal in American Schools,* 4.

490. Sewall, *Necessary Lessons—Decline, and Renewal in American Schools,* 4.

491. Hirsch, *The Schools We Need, and Why We Don't Have Them,* 2–3.

492. Gross, *The Conspiracy of Ignorance—The Failure of American Public Schools,* 5.

493. Walberg, and Bast, *Rewards: How to use rewards to help children learn . . . why teachers don't use them well,* 153.

494. Moe, *Schools, Vouchers, and the American Public,* 43.

495. Anderson, "Signs of Competition in Private & Public K-12 Schools," 9.

496. Borgson, "Free Schooling for the Poor," 128–134.

497. Cutler, "Public Education: The School District of Philadelphia.," paras. 1–22.

498. West, "The Future of Tax Credits," 161–164.

499. Annette Polly Williams, private communication during her visit in San Francisco to the Prop 174 campaign in October 1993.

500. Peterson, and Howell, "Efficiency, Bias, and Classification Schemes . . . ," 699–717.

501. Martinez, Godwin, and Kemerer, "Private Vouchers in San Antonio: The CEO Program," 74–96.

502. Greene, and Forster, *Rising to the Challenge: The effects of School Choice in Milwaukee, and San Antonio,* 1–8.

503. Burke, "Expanding Education Choices: From Vouchers, and Tax Credits to Savings Accounts."

504. Moe, *Private Vouchers,* 1–35.

505. Ballotpedia staff, "Charter schools, and vouchers on the ballot."

506. Gallaher, "The Original Pink Ladies—Grease's girl gang . . ."

507. Henig, and Sugarman, "The Nature, and Extent of School Choice," 14–16.

508. Henig, and Sugarman, "The Nature, and Extent of School Choice," 19.

509. Henig, and Sugarman, "The Nature, and Extent of School Choice," 21.

510. Junge, *Zero Chance of Passage—The Pioneering Charter School Story,* 30–31.

511. Brownstein, "Implementing No Child Left Behind," 216.

512. Brownstein, "Implementing No Child Left Behind," 218.

513. Webb, Metha, and Jordan, *Foundations of American Education—5th Edition,* 183.

514. Derthick, and Rotherham, "Obama's NCLB Waivers: Are they necessary or illegal?" 56–61.

515. *Merriam-Webster.com,* s.v. "charter school."

516. Wikipedia contributors, "Grant-maintained schools."

517. Budde, *Education by Charter: Restructuring School Districts,* 23–101.

518. Vinovskis, "Teachers Unions, and Educational Research," 222, 225.

519. Shanker, "Where We Stand."

520. Budde, "The Evolution of the Charter Concept," 72–3.

521. Kolderie, "How the idea of 'chartering' schools came about—What role did the Citizens League play?" 5–6.
522. Rollwagen, and McLellan, "Chartered Schools = Choices for Educators + Quality for All Students."
523. Kolderie, "How the idea of 'chartering' schools came about—What role did the Citizens League play?" 6.
524. Junge, *Zero Chance of Passage—The Pioneering Charter School Story*, 75–76.
525. Butrymowicz, "As charter schools come of age, measuring their success is tricky."
526. Edwards, and Perry, "Charter Schools in California—An Experiment Coming of Age," 2.
527. Hart, and Burr, "The Story of California's Charter School Legislation," 37–40.
528. NCES Reporting, "Charter school numbers of schools and students."
529. Staff Reporter, "Kingsburg Public Schools."
530. Harrington-Lueker, "Reform by Charter: Superintendents Discover How Charter Schools Fit . . ."
531. Gross, *The Conspiracy of Ignorance—The Failure of American Public Schools*, 172.
532. Stockard, et al., "The Effectiveness of Direct Instruction Curricula: A Meta-Analysis . . . ," 479–507.
533. Walberg, and Bast, *. . . How to use rewards to help children learn . . . why teachers don't use them well*, 134–138.
534. Hirsch, *The Making of Americans—Democracy, and our Schools*, 56.
535. Hillsdale Academy, "Hillsdale Academy curriculum."
536. Hirsch, *The Making of Americans—Democracy, and our Schools*, 147.
537. Bauer, and Wise, *The Well-Trained Mind*, 1–848.
538. Staff Reporter, "Oakland Military Institute Preparatory Academy Test Scores."
539. Anderson, *Guidebook & Resources for Parents in Maryland, Virginia & Washington D.C. . . .* , 2
540. Anderson, "Generating Local NAEP Proficiency Estimates . . ."
541. NAEP Reporting, "NAEP Data Tools and Applications."
542. Chen, "Knowledge is Power Program . . ," paras. 1–14.
543. Anderson, "Generating Local NAEP Proficiency Estimates . . ."
544. Anderson, "Tranche related spreadsheets."
545. Anderson, "Signs of Competition in Private & Public K-12 Schools," 37.
546. Anderson, "Signs of Competition in Private & Public K-12 Schools," in Competition-TchApnd-01.pdf.
547. Wattenberg, and Scammon, *The Real Majority*, 45.
548. Bush, "Accountability is Working in Florida's Schools."
549. Walberg, and Bast, *Rewards: How to use rewards to help children learn –, and why teachers don't use them well*, 137.
550. Hassel, and Terrell, *Charter School Achievement: What We Know*, 1–52.
551. NAEP Reporting, "NAEP Data Tools, and Applications."
552. Wikipedia contributors, "A rising tide lifts all boats."
553. Anderson, "Signs of Competition in Private & Public K-12 Schools," 29–31.
554. Moe, *Schools, Vouchers, and the American Public*, 40.
555. NAEP Reporting, "Mathematics, and reading proficiencies of 8th grade demographic groups."
556. Anderson, "Signs of Competition in Private & Public K-12 Schools," 37.
557. Anderson, "Signs of Competition in Private & Public K-12 Schools," 36.
558. Coleman, Hofer, and Kilgore, *High School Achievement: Public, Catholic, and Private Schools Compared*, 1–289.
559. NAEP Reporting, "Long Term Trend studies performance statistics."
560. NAEP Reporting, "Mathematics and reading proficiencies of 8th grade demographic groups."
561. Moses Brown School, "Moses Brown School of Providence."
562. Strauss, "Gates Foundation chief admits Common Core mistakes."
563. Rose, and Gallup, "The . . . Poll of the Public's Attitudes toward the Public Schools," 41–56.
564. Institute for Justice Writer, "Public Opinion Data: Americans Want School Choice."

565. Peterson, "Secret Finding from PDK Poll: Support for Vouchers is Rising."

566. Bonsteel, and Bonilla, *A Choice For Our Children—Curing The Crisis In America's Schools*, 168.

567. Hill, *Learning as We Go—Why School Choice is Worth the Wait*, 90.

568. Hill, *Learning as We Go—Why School Choice is Worth the Wait*, 9.

569. Greene, *Education Myths*, 150–156.

570. Peterson, and Howell, "Efficiency, Bias, and Classification Schemes . . . ," 699–717.

571. Anzia, and Moe, "Collective Bargaining, Transfer Rights, and Disadvantaged Schools," 83–111.

572. Skandera, and Souza, *School Figures: The Data behind the Debate*, 251.

573. Mills, and Wolfe, *How Has the Louisiana Scholarship Program Affected Students? . . .*

574. Anderson, "Honest school information crucial for school choice."

575. Anderson, "Spurring Competition In K-12 Education—Inducing Stakeholders to Want . . ."

576. Hill, "Private Vouchers in New York City: The Student-Sponsor Partnership Program 120–124.

577. Gallup, "How the Nation Views the Public Schools: A Study of the Public Schools . . . ," 12, 19.

578. Gallup, "How the Nation Views the Public Schools: A Study of the Public Schools . . . ," 20, 27.

579. Cunningham, *Accountability in Private School Choice Programs*, 1–6.

580. Anderson, "Parents' Guide To Schools & Services In Rhode Island & Massachusetts."

581. Glenn, and de Groof, "Freedom, and Accountability—An International Overview," 228–234.

582. McMurray, "Converting Nonprofit to For-Profit Status—The due diligence process . . ."

583. Smith, *An Inquiry into the Nature, and Causes of the Wealth of Nations—A Selected Edition*, 291–292.

584. Fullerton, "What Happened to the Berkeley Coop—A Collection of Opinions."

585. Wikipedia contributors, "Publishing—Publishing as a business."

586. Peterson, "Education in Colonial America."

587. Smith, *An Inquiry into the Nature, and Causes of the Wealth of Nations—A Selected Edition*, 906.

588. West, "Tom Paine's Voucher Scheme for Public Education . . . ," 378–82.

589. Wikipedia contributors, "Thomas Paine- Criticism of George Washington."

590. Lieberman, *Public Education—An Autopsy*, 14.

591. Lieberman, *Public Education—An Autopsy*, 310.

592. Lieberman, *Public Education—An Autopsy*, 6–7.

593. Lieberman, *Public Education—An Autopsy*, 297.

594. Lieberman, *Public Education—An Autopsy*, 9.

595. Challenger School, "Challenger School: By the strength of their own thinking."

596. Basis Schools, "Basis Schools, Inc., for-profit independent schools."

597. Niche Analyst. "Obtaining the SAT scores of Basis Independent schools."

598. Kronholz, "High Scores at BASIS Charter Schools—Arizona students outperform . . . ," 30–36.

599. Cano, "Report: America's top 5 high schools are all Basis charter schools in Arizona."

600. SABIS Website, "SABIS: Education for a changing world."

601. Fairmont Schools, "Fairmont Private Schools, Orange County, CA."

602. Niche Analyst, "Futures Academy, San Diego."

603. Futures Academies, "Futures Academies: Accelerate, and advance."

604. Fast Facts, "Regarding 2018 national count of private, and public schools."

605. Challenger School. "Challenger School: Positive Results."

606. Rudner, "Scholastic Achievement, and Demographic Characteristics of Home School Students . . ," 2–37.

607. Leisey, and Lavaroni, *The Educational Entrepreneur—Making A Difference*, 31–36.

608. Kronholz, "High Scores at BASIS Charter Schools—Arizona students outperform . . . ," 31–36.

609. Rubin, Interview with Basis founder Michael Block, "The Global Search for Education: Block Building."

610. Niche Analyst, "Obtaining the SAT scores of Basis Independent schools . . ."

611. Linzey, and Lewis, "BOT Report."

612. Niche Analyst, "2019 Best Charter High Schools in America."

613. Abrams, *Education, and the Commercial Mindset*, 18.

614. Friedman, "Selling School Like Groceries: The Voucher Idea."

615. Byron, "A Lesson in Corporate Values for Edison Schools."
616. Abrams, *Education, and the Commercial Mindset,* 19.
617. Abrams, *Education, and the Commercial Mindset,* 17–18.
618. Glassman, "An Entrepreneur Goes to School," 1.
619. Glassman, "An Entrepreneur Goes to School," 35.
620. Bonsteel, and Bonilla, *A Choice For Our Children—Curing The Crisis In America's Schools*, 168.
621. Bonsteel, and Bonilla, *A Choice For Our Children—Curing The Crisis In America's Schools*, 7.
622. Hill, *Learning as We Go—Why School Choice is Worth the Wait,* 98.
623. Peterson, and Chingos, "For-Profit, and Nonprofit Management in Philadelphia Schools . . . ," 69.
624. Peterson, and Chingos, "For-Profit, and Nonprofit Management in Philadelphia Schools . . . ," 66.
625. Wikipedia contributors, "EdisonLearning."
626. Glassman, "An Entrepreneur Goes to School," 3.
627. Smith, "Many Muskegon Heights students dig the charter company's curriculum: 'It's fun.'"
628. G. Eidelman, and D. Eidelman, "Mosaica—History, and Milestones."
629. Leagle Reporter, "Tatonka Capital Corporation v. Mosaica Education, Inc."
630. National Heritage Academies, "National Heritage Academies—Who we are."
631. Clowes, "Bringing the Profit Motive, and Moral Values to Education."
632. Jacobs, "Counting on Character: National Heritage Academies, and Civic Education."
633. Loew, "BASIS schools fight criticism, work to increase student retention."
634. Website Editor, "Achievement First."
635. KIPP Representative, "KIPP: Knowledge is power program."
636. Success Academy, "Success Academy Charter Schools."
637. Uncommon Schools Website, "Uncommon Schools."
638. Broad Foundation, "Broad Prize for Public Charter Schools, 2012–2018, Winners."
639. Stone, "School Performance Nationally."
640. Niche Analyst, "2019 Best Charter Middle Schools in America."
641. Joan Loverro, private communication, 1998.
642. Anderson, "Jersey City Library Privatization."
643. David V. Anderson, in private email to Frank Pezzanite, then CEO of Library Systems & Service, Inc., . . .
644. Murray, "National Independent Private Schools Association (NIPSA)."
645. Anderson, "K-P Education: Superior For-Profit Schools through Franchising."
646. Anderson, "K-P Education: Superior For-Profit Schools through Franchising."
647. Richard Woodbridge, Esq., private communication, 2006
648. Anderson, *Business Plan for Asora Education Enterprises' Stellar Schools Franchising Company.* 1–128.
649. Anderson, *Business Plan for Asora Education Enterprises' Stellar Schools Franchising Company.* 93–100.
650. Anderson, *Business Plan for Asora Education Enterprises' Stellar Schools Franchising Company*, 107–22.
651. Anderson, *Business Plan for Asora Education Enterprises' Stellar Schools Franchising Company.* 113–19.
652. Kaestle, *Joseph Lancaster, and the Monitorial School Movement: A Documentary History.*
653. Anderson, *Business Plan for Asora Education Enterprises' Stellar Schools Franchising Company*, 107 –22.
654. Geddes, *Competing with the Government: Anticompetitive Behavior, and Public Enterprises*, xii–xiii.
655. Sappington, and Sidak, "Anticompetitive Behavior by State-Owned Enterprises . . . ," 11–12.
656. NCES Staff, "Total undergraduate fall enrollment in degree-granting postsecondary institutions . . ."
657. Knee, *Class Clowns: How the Smartest Investors Lost Billions in Education,* 182–183.

658. Lewin, "Facing Cuts in Federal Aid, For-Profit Colleges Are in a Fight."
659. Anderson, "GAO revises its report critical of practices at for-profit schools . . . ,"
660. Review & Outlook, "Obama's For-Profit Execution."
661. Knee, *Class Clowns: How the Smartest Investors Lost Billions in Education,* 11–12, 34.
662. Mitchell, "Trump Administration Scraps Obama-Era Rules on For-Profit Colleges . . ."
663. Anderson, "Parents' Guide To Schools & Services In Rhode Island & Massachusetts," 24.
664. Vedder, *Can Teachers Own Their Own Schools?* 1–44.
665. Anderson, *Business Plan for Asora Education Enterprises' Stellar Schools Franchising Company.*
666. Milton Friedman, in letter to David V. Anderson, July 23, 2003. See Anderson, "K-P Education . . ."
667. Wan, "When Edtech Networks Combine: SIIA's Education Division Absorbs Education Industry Association."
668. Tuchman, *The March of Folly: From Troy to Vietnam,* 118
669. Private communication with Steven Drake, public relations consultant, circa 2012. . . .
670. Anderson, "Guidebook & Resources for Parents in . . ."
671. Anderson, "Four prototypical guidebooks . . ."
672. Anderson, "Parents' Guide to Schools & Services In Rhode Island & Massachusetts."
673. Niche Analyst, "2019 Best Schools in the Providence Area."
674. UN Treaty, "United Nations Declaration of Human Rights, Article 26."
675. Bizapedia Writer, "Parents, and Students United Of The San Fernando Valley."
676. Warnick, *Understanding Student Rights in Schools—Speech, Religion, and Privacy in Educational Settings,* 43.
677. Krejcir, *Statistics, and Reasons for Church Decline,* paras. 1–19.
678. Staff Writer, "Employed Persons."
679. DMDatabases.com, "USA Business List—Employee Size Profile."
680. Martinez, Godwin, and Kemerer, "Private Vouchers in San Antonio: The CEO Program," 74–96.
681. Phillips, Yuan, and Tharp-Gilliam, "Evaluation of the Regional Choice Initiative," 58.
682. NCES Reporting. "Number of public school districts, and public, and private elementary, and secondary schools . . ."
683. Whaley, "Douglas County school voucher program now officially dead . . ."
684. Cary, "New Era Schools."
685. Rathi, "A piece of the sun. . . investments in nuclear-fusion startups are heating up."
686. Herman, *An Educators' Guide to Schoolwide Reform,* 1.
687. Hinchey, *Student Rights—A Reference Handbook,* 167.
688. Hinchey, *Student Rights—A Reference Handbook,* 101.
689. Lauglo, "Forms of decentralization, and their Implications for Education," 36—37.
690. Institute Writer, "The Annenberg Institute for School Reform at Brown University, Interim Report," 6.
691. Institute Writer, "The Annenberg Institute for School Reform at Brown University, Interim Report," 13.
692. Greenhut, "Democrats Rig Rules to Boost Unions Against Janus Decision."
693. Friedman, M., and Friedman R., *Free to Choose: A Personal Statement,* 148–65.
694. Wikipedia contributors, "Hippocratic Oath—Earliest surviving copy."
695. SE Mom [pseud.], "FDR warned against collective bargaining for government unions"
696. Sanes, and Schmitt, *Regulation of Public Sector Collective Bargaining in the States,* 1–11.
697. Wright, "Public-Sector Bargaining Privileges Are Not Inalienable Rights."
698. Bonsteel, and Bonilla, *A Choice For Our Children—Curing The Crisis In America's Schools,* 170.
699. Moir, and Barr, "Analysis of Interstellar Spacecraft Cycling Between the Sun, and the Near Stars," 332–41
700. Longmier, et al., "Improved Efficiency, and Throttling Range of the VX-200 Magnetoplasma Thruster. . . ," 123–32.
701. Bascom, "A Brief History of 'Progressive' Education," paras. 1–47.

702. *Unitarians, and Universalists on Stamps*, By the Quincy, Illinois Unitarian Church . . .

703. Tuchinsky, *Horace Greeley's 'New-York Tribune'- Civil War-Era Socialism, and the Crisis of Free Labor,* 139.

704. Wikipedia contributors, "1872 United States presidential election."

705. Dewey, "The Need for a New Party."

706. Dewey, *Liberalism, and Social Action,* 54–55.

707. DeArmond, *Democracy in the Schoolroom,* 1–4.

708. DeArmond, *Democracy in the Schoolroom,* 1–4.

709. Di Carlo, "Quote—Unquote," lines 3–4.

710. Wikipedia contributors, "American Federation of Teachers—History."

711. Lieberman, *The Teachers Unions,* 123.

712. NEA Representative, "Issues & Advocacy."

713. Walker, "Study Upends Conventional Wisdom About Private School Advantages."

714. NEA Adopted Actions, " . . . on deconstructing 'the systemic proliferation of a White supremacy culture.'"

715. Jones and Okun, *White Supremacy Culture -From Dismantling Racism: A Workbook for Social Change Groups.*

716. Wikipedia contributors, "Charles Francis Potter."

717. Lieberman, *Public Education—An Autopsy,* 32

Bibliography

Abrams. Samuel E. *Education and the Commercial Mindset.* Cambridge, MA: Harvard University Press, 2016.

ACT Representative. "(What Are the) ACT College Readiness Benchmarks?" *ACT, Inc.,* Iowa City, IA, September 2013. http://www.act.org/content/dam/act/unsecured/documents/benchmarks.pdf.

Advisory Panel. "Foundations for Success: The Final Report of the National Mathematics Advisory Panel." *National Mathematics Advisory Panel,* U.S. Department of Education, Washington, D.C., 2008. http://www2.ed.gov/about/bdscomm/list/mathpanel/report/final-report.pdf.

Akerlof, George A. "The Market for 'Lemons': Quality Uncertainty and the Market Mechanism." *Quarterly Journal of Economics* 84 (Summer 1970) 488–500.

Albree, John. *Charles Brooks and His Work for Normal Schools.* Medford, MA: Miller, 1907.

Am, Onar. "Progressives Rule By Words, Not Laws—First they steal your words, then they steal your country." *Liberty Nation,* December 2, 2018. https://www.libertynation.com/progressives-rule-by-words-not-laws/.

American Textbook Council. "Widely Adopted History Textbooks." *HistoryTextBooks.net,* 2018. http://historytextbooks.net/adopted.htm.

Amplifire Representative. "Amplifire instructional/assessment system—how it works." *Amplifire,* Boulder, CO. Accessed July 27, 2018. https://amplifire.com/how-it-works/.

Anderson, David. "Are R. I. Test Results Misleading?" *Providence Journal,* February 18, 2009.

Anderson, David V. *Business Plan for Asora® Education Enterprises' Stellar Schools Franchising Company.* Attleboro, MA: Asora Education Enterprises, March 2, 2008. http://asoraeducation.com/page41/page36/page36.html.

Anderson, David V. "Common Core's double whammy—The Nation's Report Card shows a turn for the worse." Op-Ed, in *Washington Times,* November 11, 2015. Also accessible at https://www.washingtontimes.com/news/2015/nov/11/david-anderson-common-cores-double-whammy/.

Anderson, David V. "Four prototypical guidebooks produced by Asora Education." *Asora Education Enterprises,* Attleboro, MA, 2018. In files at http://asoraeducation.com/page59/page60/page60.html.

Anderson, David V. "Generating Local NAEP Proficiency Estimates By The Ellipse-Quartic (ELQ) Mapping Methods." *Asora Education Enterprises,* Attleboro, MA, 2009. In ELQ-Mappings.docx and its associated spreadsheet workbook ELQ-Derivation.xlsx are both downloadable (after some scrolling down) from http://www.asoraeducation.com/page35/page40/page40.html.

Anderson, David V. "Guidebook & Resources for Parents in Maryland, Virginia & Washington D.C.—It Takes More Than A Village to educate your child, when the schools aren't up to the task." *Asora Education Enterprises,* Attleboro, MA, 2010. In the file MTAVillage_06. pdf at http://asoraeducation.com/page59/page60/page60.html.

Anderson, David V. "Honest school information crucial for school choice." *The Hill,* February 9, 2016.

Anderson, David V. "Integrity is Remedy for Harms Caused by Social Promotion." *School Reform News,* April 2007. https://www.heartland.org/news-opinion/news/analysis-integrity-is-remedy-for-harms-caused-by-social-promotion.

Anderson, David V. "Jersey City Library Privatization." *Privatization Watch- Reason Public Policy Institute,* August 1999.

Anderson, David V. "K-P Education: Superior For-Profit Schools through Franchising." *Asora Education Enterprises,* Attleboro, MA, June 9, 2014. In file FriedmanCorrespondence. pdf on Asora website. http://www.asoraeducation.com/page35/page40/page40.html.

Anderson, David V. "Mapping NAEP Proficiencies to ACT's POT." *Asora Education Enterprises,* Attleboro, MA, June 9, 2014. http://www.asoraeducation.com/page35/page40/page40.html.

Anderson, David V. "Parents' Guide To Schools & Services In Rhode Island & Massachusetts." *New England Parents' Club* (envisioned for the future), *Asora Education Enterprises,* Attleboro, MA, February 2017, in a pdf file RIMA-Guide-01.pdf, can be downloaded from http://asoraeducation.com/page59/page60/page60.html.

Anderson, David V. *Replacing Common Core—With Proven Standards of Excellence.* Arlington Heights, IL: The Heartland Institute, 2014. http://asoraeducation.com/page35/page40/files/Replacing Common Core.pdf.

Anderson, David V. "Signs of Competition in Private & Public K-12 Schools—Causes and Correlations Revealed by NAEP Trend Studies." *Asora Education Enterprises,* Attleboro, MA, 2015. In pdf files Competition-K-12-02.pdf and Competition-TchApnd-01.pdf. http://asoraeducation.com/page35/page40/page40.html.

Anderson, David V. "Spurring Competition In K-12 Education—Inducing Stakeholders to Want the Consumer Information They Need." *Asora Education Enterprises,* Attleboro, MA, 2016. In pdf file Spurring-Competition-03.pdf. http://asoraeducation.com/page35/page40/page40.html.

Anderson, David V. "Tranche related spreadsheets." TranchDemogs.xlsx, TranchMathDemogs. xlsx and TranchReadingDemogs.xlsx are available by request from david.anderson@asoraeducation.com.

Anderson, Nick. "GAO revises its report critical of practices at for-profit schools." *Washington Post,* December 8, 2010.

Angus, David L., Jeffrey E. Mirel, and Maris A. Vinovskis. "Historical Development of Age-Stratification in Schooling." *Teachers College Record* 90 no. 2 (1988) 208–15.

Ansary, Tamin. "A Textbook Example of What's Wrong with Education." *Edutopia,* November 9, 2004. Accessed February 15, 2019. https://www.edutopia.org/textbook-publishing-controversy.

Anzia, Sarah F. "Election Timing and the Electoral Influence of Interest Groups." *The Journal of Politics* 73 no. 2 (March 2010) 412–27.

Anzia, Sarah F. and Terry M. Moe. "Collective Bargaining, Transfer Rights, and Disadvantaged Schools." *Educational Evaluation and Policy Analysis* 36 no. 1 (2014) 83–111. https://gspp.berkeley.edu/assets/uploads/research/pdf/Anzia_Moe_Seniority_9_2011.pdf.

Appold, Kenneth G. *The Reformation- A Brief History*, Hoboken: Wiley-Blackwell, 2011.

Arnold, Matthieu, ed. *John Calvin—The Strasbourg Years (1538–1541).* Eugene, OR: Wipf & Stock, 2016. http://readingreligion.org/books/john-calvin.

Associated Press. "Multicultural History Standards Rejected by Senate in 99 1 Vote." *Los Angeles Times,* Jan 19, 1995. http://articles.latimes.com/1995–01-19/news/mn-21834_1_ history-standards.

Avenoso, Karen. "Suspected tampering on test answers embroils Connecticut school in scandal." *Baltimore Sun,* July 21, 1996.

Balfour, Graham. *The Educational Systems of Great Britain and Ireland.* Oxford: Clarendon, 1904. Boston: Reprinted by Adamant Media Corporation, 2004.

Ballotpedia staff. "California Proposition 174, School Vouchers (1993)." *Ballotpedia.* https:// ballotpedia.org/California_Proposition_174,_School_Vouchers_(1993).

Ballotpedia staff. "California Proposition 38, School Vouchers (2000)." *Ballotpedia.* https:// ballotpedia.org/California_Proposition_38,_School_Vouchers_(2000).

Ballotpedia staff. "Charter schools and vouchers on the ballot." *Ballotpedia.* Accessed February 15, 2019. https://ballotpedia.org/Charter_schools_and_vouchers_on_the_ballot.

Barnard, Henry. *Pestalozzi and His Educational System.* Syracuse, NY: C. W. Bardeen, 1906.

Bascom, James. "A Brief History of 'Progressive' Education." *TFP Student Action* (blog). July 12, 2015. https://www.tfpstudentaction.org/blog/a-brief-history-of-progressive-education.

Basis Schools Representative. "Basis Schools, Inc., for-profit independent schools." *Basis Independent Schools,* Accessed February 15, 2019. https://info.basisindependent.com/.

Bauer, Susan Wise and Jessie Wise. *The Well-Trained Mind: A Guide to Classical Education at Home, Third Edition.* New York: W. W. Norton, Inc., 2009. This book has a good description of the popular Trivium curriculum used in homeschooling.

Bauerlein, Mark, and Sandra Stotsky. "How Common Core's ELA Standards Place College Readiness at Risk." *White Paper* no. 89, Pioneer Institute, Boston, MA, September 2012. http://pioneerinstitute.org/download/how-common-cores-elastandards-place-college-readiness-at-risk/.

Bell, Pamela Jane. "My Long Recovery From Kindergarten," Opinion Section. *Wall Street Journal,* May 14, 2018,

Benedict, J. K. "No Prior Art: A Dedication." Includes legend about Seymour Cray stating that his supercomputer design group numbered 30 "including the janitor." *Wordpress. com* (blog), January 25, 2017. https://xenfomation.wordpress.com/tag/seymour-cray/.

Bennetta, William J. "A Book of Far-Left Propaganda That Fosters Anti-Intellectualism." *Textbook Letter,* Jan—Feb 1997, It was accessible at http://textbookleague.org/76west. htm, but when we attempted to access it again in July 2019, we were not able to connect.

Bidwell, Allie. "Common Core: A Divisive Issue for Catholic School Parents Too." *U. S. News & World Report,* January 13, 2014. https://www.usnews.com/news/special-reports/a-guide-to-common-core/2014/01/13/common-core-a-divisive-issue-for-catholic-school-parents-too.

Bizapedia Writer. "Parents And Students United Of The San Fernando Valley." *Bizapedia.* In the mid 1990's the author once met the leader of one such organization in Los Angeles County, Eadie Gieb. Her organization, since disbanded, attempted to lobby the public school system- but without much effect. Accessed April 29, 2019. https://www.bizapedia. com/ca/parents-and-students-united-of-the-san-fernando-valley.html.

BLS Report. "Historical Consumer Price Index for All Urban Consumers." *Bureau of Labor Statistics,* United States Department of Labor, Washington, DC, May 2018. https://www.bls.gov/cpi/tables/supplemental-files/historical-cpi-u-201805.pdf.

Bockelman, Andrew and Joseph P. Overton. "Michigan Education Special Services Association: The MEA's Money Machine. Executive Summary." *Mackinac Center Studies,* November 1, 1993. https://www.mackinac.org/S1993-10.

Bonsteel, Alan and Carlos A. Bonilla. *A Choice For Our Children—Curing The Crisis In America's Schools.* San Francisco: Institute for Contemporary Studies, 1997.

Borgson, Hob. "Free Schooling for the Poor." *Tredyffrin Easttown Historical Society Quarterly Digital Archives* 25 no. 4 (October 1987) 128–34. https://tehistory.org/hqda/html/v25/v25n4p128.html.

Boyd, Julian P. "The Changes Made to Jefferson's Original Rough Draught." Edited by Alex Peak. *AlexPeak.com* (blog). 2009. http://alexpeak.com/twr/doi/change/ and http://alexpeak.com/twr/doi/draft/.

Boyd, William Lowe, David N. Plank and Gary Sykes. "Teachers' Unions In Hard Times, in Conflicting Missions?" in *Teachers Unions and Educational Reform,* edited by Tom Loveless, 174–210. Washington DC: The Brookings Institution, 2000. http://education.msu.edu/epc/forms/union.pdf.

Brimelow, Peter and Leslie Spencer. "The National Extortion Association." *Forbes,* June 7, 1993.

Britannica Editors. "Apartment house—Architecture." *Encyclopedia Britannica.* Accessed April 22, 2019. Print editions no longer produced since 2012. https://www.britannica.com/technology/apartment-house.

Broad Foundation. "Broad Prize for Public Charter Schools, 2012–2018, Winners." Accessed June 1, 2019. https://broadfoundation.org/the-broad-prize-for-public-charter-schools/.

Brown, Amy. "AI Is on the Upswing in Optimizing K–12 Education." *EdTech Magazine,* November 2017. https://edtechmagazine.com/k12/article/2017/10/ai-upswing-optimizing-k-12-education.

Brown, Jeremy L. "Common Core." *Fresno Christian Schools,* Fresno, CA, March 25, 2015. http://www.fresnochristian.com/cc/.

Brownstein, Ronald. "Implementing No Child Left Behind." In *The Future of School Choice,* edited by Paul E. Peterson, 213–26. Stanford: Hoover Institution, 2003.

Bruner, Jerome. *The Process of Education.* Cambridge: Harvard University Press, 1977.

Budde, Ray. *Education by Charter: Restructuring School Districts.* Andover, MA: Regional Laboratory for Educational Improvement of the Northeast and Islands, 1988.

Budde, Ray. "The Evolution of the Charter Concept," *Phi Delta Kappan* 78 no. 1 (September 1996) 72–3.

Buringh, E. and J. L. Van Zanden. "Charting the 'Rise of the West': Manuscripts and Printed Books in Europe, A long-term perspective from the sixth through the eighteenth centuries." *The Journal of Economic History* 69 no. 2 (2009) 405–45. Some of their data can be found at www.ourworldindata.org/data/education-knowledge-literacy

Burke, Lindsey. *Expanding Education Choices: From Vouchers and Tax Credits to Savings Accounts.* Washington DC: The Heritage Foundation, 2013. https://www.heritage.org/education/report/expanding-education-choices-vouchers-and-tax-credits-savings-accounts.

Burnett, Sara, AP. "Supreme Court hands Illinois governor a rare win over unions." *Washington Post,* June 27, 2018. https://www.washingtonpost.com/national/supreme-court-hands-illinois-governor-a-rare-win-over-unions/2018/06/27/8b84beb0–7a21–11e8-ac4e-421ef7165923_story.html?utm_term=.1275d7be8bc2.

Bush, Jeb. "Accountability is Working in Florida's Schools." *Wall Street Journal,* January 3, 2011. https://www.wsj.com/articles/SB10001424052748703860104575508141083798802.

Butrymowicz, Sarah. "As charter schools come of age, measuring their success is tricky." *Hechinger Report,* August 22, 2013. http://hechingerreport.org/as-charter-schools-come-of-age-measuring-their-success-is-tricky-2/.

Byron, Christopher. "A Lesson in Corporate Values for Edison Schools." *New York Observer,* August 18, 1999.

Cameron, James K. *The First Book Of Discipline.* Edinburgh: Zeticula Publishers, 2004.

Cano, Ricardo. "Report: America's top 5 high schools are all Basis charter schools in Arizona." *The Republic, AZ Central,* May 10, 2019. https://www.azcentral.com/story/news/local/arizona-education/2018/05/09/arizona-basis-charter-schools-sweep-national-ranking-top-high-schools-us-news-world-report/595588002/.

Cantoni, Davide. "The Economic Effects of the Protestant Reformation: Testing the Weber Hypothesis in the German Lands." *Journal of the European Economic Association* 13 no. 4 (2015) 561–98.

Carcamo, Cindy. "San Francisco will allow noncitizens to vote in a local election, creating a new immigration flashpoint." *Los Angeles Times,* Oct 26, 2018. http://www.latimes.com/local/california/la-me-san-francisco-election-immigration-20181026-story.html.

Carson, Clayborne and David Malcolm Carson. "Black Panther Party." *Encyclopedia of the American Left,* edited by Mari Jo Buhle et al., 58–96. New York: Garland Publishing, 1990. Related article at: https://web.stanford.edu/~ccarson/articles/am_left.htm.

Cary, Dave. "New Era Schools." *New Era Schools,* Vallejo, CA. 2018. https://www.neweraschools.org.

CBO Staff. "Trends in Educational Achievement." *The Congressional Budget Office,* Washington, DC, 1986.

Census Report. "Population—Census.gov." *U.S. Census Bureau.* Accessed February 23, 2019. https://www.census.gov/library/publications/2011/compendia/statab/131ed/population.html.

Challenger School. "Challenger School: By the strength of their own thinking." Accessed May 24, 2019. https://www.challengerschool.com/.

Challenger School. "Challenger School: Positive Results." Accessed May 27, 2019. https://www.challengerschool.com/positive-results.

Cheatle, Julian. "Medieval cross found on The Curse of Oak Island 'could end up rewriting history'." *Monsters & Critics,* January 17, 2018. https://www.monstersandcritics.com/smallscreen/medieval-cross-found-on-the-curse-of-oak-island-could-end-up-rewriting-history/.

Chen, Grace. "Knowledge is Power Program: A Strong Model for Public Schools." *Public School Review* (blog). 2018. https://www.publicschoolreview.com/blog/knowledge-is-power-program-a-strong-model-for-public-schools.

Chen, Nick. "How Stanley Kubrick's HAL 9000 laid the blueprint for AI in film." *Dazed Digital Newsletter,* April 3, 2018. http://www.dazeddigital.com/film-tv/article/39557/1/space-odyssey-stanley-kubrick-hal-9000-ai-in-film.

Chicago Board of Education. *Chicago Public Schools Policy Manual—Elementary School Promotion.* Chicago: Chicago Board of Education, October 28, 2009. http://policy.cps.edu/documents/605.2.pdf/documents/605.2.pdf.

Clough, Sara and Scott Montgomery. "How ACT Assessments Align with State College and Career Readiness Standards." *ACT White Paper,* Iowa City, IA, 2015. Accessed November 14, 2018. http://www.act.org/content/dam/act/unsecured/documents/Alignment-White-Paper.pdf.

Clowes, George A. "Bringing the Profit Motive and Moral Values to Education." *Heartlander,* April 1, 2005. http://news.heartland.org/newspaper-article/2005/04/01/bringing-profit-motive-and-moral-values-education-exclusive-interview-j.

Coleman, James S., Ernest Q. Campbell, Carol J. Hobson, James McPartland, Alexander M. Mood, Frederic D. Weinfeld and Robert L. York. *Equality of Educational Opportunity,* Washington, DC: A publication of the National Center for Educational Statistics, 1966. http://eric.ed.gov/?id=ED012275.

Coleman, James S., Thomas Hofer and Sally Kilgore. *High School Achievement: Public, Catholic and Private Schools Compared.* New York: Basic Books, 1982.

Collins English Dictionary, 13th Edition. Glasgow: Harper Collins, 2018. s. v. "educationist." https://www.collinsdictionary.com/dictionary/english/educationist.

Colson, Chuck. "Why Multiculturalism Can't Work." *Christian Post,* Feb 18, 2011. https://www.christianpost.com/news/why-multiculturalism-cant-work-49052/.

Cooper, Harris, Kelly Charlton, Jeff C. Valentine and Laura Muhlenbruck. "Making the Most of Summer School: A Meta–Analytic and Narrative Review." *Monographs of the Society for Research in Child Development* 65 no. 1 (2000) 1–109.

Cornell University Press. Review of Adam Tuchinsky book: *Horace Greeley's "New-York Tribune—Civil War-Era Socialism and the Crisis of Free Labor.* http://www.cornellpress.cornell.edu/book/?GCOI=80140100930150.

Coulson, Andrew J. *Market Education—The Unknown History.* New Brunswick, NJ: Transaction Publishers, 1999.

Cousin, M. Victor. *On the State of Education in Holland as Regards Schools for the Working Classes and for the Poor.* Translated by Leonard Horner. London: John Murray Publishers, 1838. https://babel.hathitrust.org/cgi/pt?id=nyp.33433081630323;view=1up;seq=79;size=75.

Cousin, M. Victor. *Report on the State of Public Instruction in Prussia.* Translated by Sarah Austin. London: Effingham Wilson, 1834. London: Reprinted by Forgotten Books, 2019.

Crawford, Evan. "Why Nonpartisan—Versus Partisan– School Board Elections Do Not Tell The Whole Story." *Scholars Strategy Network,* April 12, 2017. https://scholars.org/brief/why-nonpartisan---versus-partisan---school-board-elections-do-not-tell-whole-story.

Cubberley, Ellwood P. *The History of Education: Educational Practice and Progress Considered as a Phase of the Development and Spread of Western Civilization.* Boston: Houghton Mifflin, 1920.

Cunningham, Josh. *Accountability in Private School Choice Programs.* Denver: National Conference of State Legislatures, February 18, 2015.

Curti, Merle. *The Social Ideas of American Educators.* New York: Pageant Publishers, 1959.

Cutler III, William W. "Public Education: The School District of Philadelphia." *Encyclopedia of Greater Philadelphia,* Camden, NJ: Mid-Atlantic Regional Center for the Humanities (MARCH) at Rutgers-Camden, 2016. https://philadelphiaencyclopedia.org/archive/public-educationthe-school-district-of-philadelphia/.

Dale, Edgar. *Audio-Visual Methods in Teaching*. New York: Dryden, 1946.

Dave, Paresh. "5 educators charged with fostering cheating in Philadelphia schools." *Los Angeles Times*, May 8, 2014. https://www.latimes.com/nation/nationnow/la-na-philadelphia-schools-alleged-cheating-indictment-20140508-story.html.

David L. Angus, Jeffrey E. Mirel and Maris A. Vinovskis. "Historical Development of Age-Stratification in Schooling." *Teachers College Record* 90 no. 2 (November 2, 1988) 211–36.

DeArmond, Fred. *Democracy in the Schoolroom*. Auburn, AL: Mises Institute, August 12, 2009. https://mises.org/library/democracy-schoolroom.

DeFalco, Anthony. "Dewey and Vocational Education: Still Timely?" *The Journal of School and Society* 3 no. 1 (2016) 54–64.

Deprit, Andre. "Monsignor Georges Lemaître." In *The Big Bang and Georges Lemaître*, edited by A. Barger, 363–92. Dordrecht: D. Reidel, 1984.

Dershowitz, Alan M. "The Bigotry of 'Intersectionality.'" *Gatestone Institute*, March 29, 2017. https://www.gatestoneinstitute.org/10131/the-bigotry-of-intersectionality.

Derthick, Martha, and Andy Rotherham. "Obama's NCLB Waivers: Are they necessary or illegal?" *EducationNext* (Spring 2012): 56–61. https://www.educationnext.org/obamas-nclb-waivers-are-they-necessary-or-illegal/.

Devine, T. M. *The Scottish Nation, a History, 1700–2000*. London: Penguin Books, 2001.

Dewey, John. *Democracy and Education*. New York: The Free Press, 1915. Republished, New York: Simon & Shuster, 1966.

Dewey, John. "Education and Social Change." *Bulletin of the American Association of University Professors* 23 (October 1937): 472–74.

Dewey, John. *Liberalism and Social Action*. New York: G. P. Putnam's Sons, 1935.

Dewey, John. "My Pedagogic Creed." *School Journal* 54 (January 1897) 77–80.

Dewey, John. "The Need for a New Party." *New Republic*, 1931. https://newrepublic.com/article/104638/the-need-new-party March 18.

Di Carlo, Matthew. "Quote—Unquote." *The Albert Shanker Institute* (blog). May 13, 2011. http://www.shankerinstitute.org/blog/quote-unquote.

DMDatabases.com. "USA Business List—Employee Size Profile." *Dirmark Media, Inc.* Accessed March 3, 2019. https://dmdatabases.com/databases/business-mailing-lists/how-many-businesses.

Dunn, Fannie W. and Etta Schneider. "Teaching With The Motion Picture and Other Visual Aids." In *Motion Pictures in Education*, edited by Edgar Dale, 113–246. New York: H. W. Wilson Company, 1937.

Durant, Will. *The Story of Civilization: Part 5—The Renaissance—A History of Civilization in Italy from 1304–1576 A.D.* New York: Simon and Shuster, 1957.

Durant, Will. *The Story of Civilization: Part 6—The Reformation—A History of European Civilization from Wycliffe to Calvin: 1300–1564*. New York: Simon and Shuster, 1957.

Eaton, David. "Resentment, Multiculturalism and Identity Politics." *Applied Unificationism: A Blog of Unification Theological Seminary* (blog). February 27, 2017. https://appliedunificationism.com/2017/02/27/resentment-multiculturalism-and-identity-politics/comment-page-1/.

Economist staff reporter. "Difference Engine: Luddite legacy—Is smart technology now destroying more jobs than it creates?" *Economist Blog* (blog). London: The Economist Newspaper Limited, 2011. http://www.economist.com/blogs/babbage/2011/11/artificial-intelligence?fsrc=scn/tw/te/bl/ludditelegacy.

Edwards, Brian and Mary Perry. "Charter Schools in California—An Experiment Coming of Age." *EdSource Report,* June 2004. https://edsource.org/wp-content/publications/CharterSchools04.pdf.

Eidelman, Gene and Dawn Eidelman. "Mosaica—History and Milestones." *Mosaica Education,* Atlanta, GA. Accessed February 15, 2019. http://mosaicaeducation.com/about-mosaica/history-and-milestones.

Eisenstein, Elizabeth L. *The Printing Revolution In Early Modern Europe, 2nd Edition.* Cambridge: Cambridge University Press, 2005.

Eklund, Jr., Robert B., Robert F. Hébert and Robert D. Tollson. "An Economic Analysis of the Protestant Reformation." *Journal of Political Economy* 110 no. 3 (2002) 646–71.

Eliot, Charles W. "The Fundamental Assumptions in the Report of the Committee of Ten." *Educational Review* 30 (November 1905) 325–43.

Ellis, Elisabeth Gaynor and Anthony Esler. *World History: Connections to Today.* Upper Saddle River, NJ: Prentice Hall, 2003.

Eltagouri, Marwa. "10 years for board member from impoverished school for pocketing $566,000 in kickbacks." *Chicago Tribune,* July 16, 2014.

English Oxford Living Dictionaries. Oxford: Oxford University Press, 2018, s.v. "multiculturalism." https://en.oxforddictionaries.com/definition/multiculturalism.

English Oxford Living Dictionaries. Oxford: Oxford University Press, 2019, s.v. "intersectionality." https://en.oxforddictionaries.com/definition/intersectionality.

Everpedia Editor. "Mosaica Education." *Everpedia.* June 4, 2019. https://everipedia.org/wiki/Mosaica_Education/.

Faber, Riemer. "Martin Luther on Reformed Education." *Clarion* 47 no. 16, (1998) 376–87. http://spindleworks.com/library/rfaber/luther_edu.htm.

Fairmont Schools. "Fairmont Private Schools, Orange County, CA." Accessed November 6, 2018. https://www.fairmontschools.com.

Farkas, Steve and Jean Johnson. *A Lot To Be Thankful For: What Parents Want Children To Learn About America.* New York: Public Agenda, 1998.

Farlex, Inc. The Free Dictionary by Farlex, s.v. "educationist." https://www.thefreedictionary.com/educationist.

Fast Facts (regarding 2018 national count of private and public schools). *National Center for Education Statistics, (NCES).* https://nces.ed.gov/fastfacts/display.asp?id=372.

Feinberg, Walter and Richard A. Layton. *For the Civic Good—The Liberal Case for Teaching Religion in the Public Schools.* Ann Arbor: The University of Michigan Press, 2014.

Feynman, Richard P. *"Surely You're Joking Mr. Feynman!"—Adventures of a Curious Character.* New York: W. W. Norton & Company, 1985.

Finn, Chester E. "The Case for Saturday School." *Wall Street Journal,* March 20, 2010.

Fisher, Daniel. "Disparate-Impact Theory Finally Gets Its Test At Supreme Court." *Forbes,* January 21, 2015. https://www.forbes.com/sites/danielfisher/2015/01/21/disparate-impact-at-supreme-court/#3bae8fcc6331.

Fitzgerald, Frances. *America Revised—History Schoolbooks in the Twentieth Century.* Boston: Little, Brown and Company, 1979.

Franco, Jon. "The Relationship Between Double Dosing and Middle School Math Student Achievement." E.D. diss., *George Fox University School of Education,* Newberg, Oregon, 2013. ii–24. http://digitalcommons.georgefox.edu/cgi/viewcontent.cgi?article=1025&context=edd.

Friedman, Milton and Rose D. Friedman. *Free to Choose: A Personal Statement.* New York: Avon Books, 1979.

Friedman, Milton. "The Role of Government in Education." In *Capitalism and Freedom,* 85–107. Chicago: The University of Chicago Press, 1962:

Friedman, Milton. "The Role of Government in Education." In *Economics and the Public Interest,* edited by Robert Solo, 123–44. New Brunswick, NJ: Rutgers University Press, 1955:

Friedman, Milton. "Selling School Like Groceries: The Voucher Idea." *New York Times Magazine,* September 23, 1975.

Full Wiki Writer. "Samuel Slater." *The Full Wiki,* Woolwich NSW 2110, Australia. www.thefullwiki.org/Samuel_Slater

Fullerton, Michael. "What Happened to the Berkeley Coop?—A Collection of Opinions." *Center for Cooperatives,* University of California, Berkeley, CA, 1992. http://www.megacz.com/otherpeople/what.happened.to.the.berkeley.co-op.pdf.

Futures Academies. "Futures Academies: Accelerate and advance." (formerly the Halstrom Academies until 2018). https://www.futures.edu.

Gallaher, Cynthia. "The Original Pink Ladies—Grease's girl gang had a real-life model on the northwest side." *ChicagoReader.com,* April 2011. https://www.chicagoreader.com/chicago/grease-pink-ladies-chicago/Content?oid=3682406.

Gallup, George. "How the Nation Views the Public Schools: A Study of the Public Schools of the United States." *IDEA Information and Services Division,* Melbourne, FL, Fall, 1969. https://files.eric.ed.gov/fulltext/ED046097.pdf.

Gass, Jamie and Jim Stergios. "The Beginning of Common Core's Trouble." Weekly Standard, May 29, 2013. http://www.weeklystandard.com/print/blogs/beginning-common-cores-trouble_731923.html?page=1.

Gay, Jason. "An Idiot's Guide to Bribing and Cheating Your Way into College." *Wall Street Journal,* March 13, 2019. Accessible with subscription at https://www.wsj.com/articles/an-idiots-guide-to-bribing-and-cheating-your-way-into-college-11552479762?mod=searchresults&page=1&pos=16.

Geddes, R. Richard. *Competing with the Government: Anticompetitive Behavior and Public Enterprises.* Stanford: Hoover Institution, 2004.

Glassman, James K. Review entitled "An Entrepreneur Goes to School." Book review of *Crash Course,* by Chris Whittle. *Wall Street Journal,* September 7, 2005.

Glenn, Charles L. and Jan de Groof. "Freedom and Accountability—An International Overview." In *The Future of School Choice,* edited by Paul E. Peterson, 227–60. Stanford: Hoover Institution, 2003.

Glenn, Charles L. *Contrasting Models of State and School.* New York: Bloomsbury Academic, 2011.

Glowatz, Elana. "Robot Granted Citizenship In Saudi Arabia Immediately Trolls Elon Musk." *International Business Times,* October 26, 2017.

Gold, Kenneth M. *School's in: The History of Summer Education in American Public Schools.* New York: Peter Lang, 2002.

Gordon, Samuel. "Common Core State Standards—Message from the Superintendent." *Capital Christian School,* Sacramento, CA, 2018. https://www.ccscougars.org/about-us/common-core-state-standards.

Goudsward, David. *The Westford Knight and Henry Sinclair: Evidence of a 14th Century Scottish Voyage to North America.* Jefferson, NC: McFarland & Co., 2010.

Gray, Christopher. "When Spain Reigned on Central Park South." *New York Times,* June 17, 2007. https://www.nytimes.com/2007/06/17/realestate/17scap.html.

Greene, Jay P. and Greg Forster. *Rising to the Challenge: The effects of School Choice in Milwaukee and San Antonio.* New York: The Manhattan Institute Center for Civic Innovation, October 2002. https://www.manhattan-institute.org/pdf/cb_27.pdf.

Greene, Jay P. *Education Myths.* Lanham, MD: Roman & Littlefield, 2005.

Greenhut, Steven. "Democrats Rig Rules to Boost Unions Against Janus Decision." *American Spectator,* January 31, 2019. https://spectator.org/democrats-rig-rules-to-boost-unions-against-janus-decision/.

Gross, Martin L. *The Conspiracy of Ignorance—The Failure of American Public Schools.* New York: HarperCollins, 1999.

Hall, G. Stanley. *Adolescence: its Psychology and its Relations to Physiology, Anthropology, Sociology, Sex, Crime, Religion and Education. Vol. 2.* New York: Appleton, 1904.

Hand, William B. "Smith v. Board of School Commissioners of Mobile County." *Belcher Foundation,* Belcher, KY, 1987. http://belcherfoundation.org/smith_v_board.htm.

Hanes, William Travis. *World History: Continuity and Change.* Austin, TX: Holt Rinehart & Winston, 1997.

Hanushek, Eric A. "How Much Is A Good Teacher Worth." *Education Next,* Summer 2011. 40–45.

Harran, Marilyn J. "Reflections on Martin Luther and Childhood Education." *Journal of Lutheran Ethics* 4 no. 1 (2004) 1–4. https://elca.org/JLE/Articles/797.

Harrington-Lueker, Donna. "Reform by Charter: Superintendents Discover How Charter Schools Fit (or Don't) Their Districts' Agendas." *American Association of School Administrators,* Alexandria, VA, August 1997. http://www.aasa.org/SchoolAdministratorArticle.aspx?id=15460.

Harrington, Theresa. "Understanding the Common Core State Standards in California: A quick guide." *EdSource,* August 25, 2017. https://edsource.org/2017/understanding-the-common-core-state-standards-in-california-a-quick-guide/585006.

Harris, William T. "How the School Strengthens the Individuality of the Pupils." *Educational Review* 24 (June 1902) 228–37. https://archive.org/details/educationalrevie24newyuoft/page/228?q=How+the+School+Strengthens+the+Individuality+of+the+Pupils.

Hart, Gary K. and Sue Burr. "The Story of California's Charter School Legislation." *Phi Delta Kappan* 78 no. 1 (September 1996) 37–40. https://www.questia.com/library/journal/1G1-18751786/the-story-of-california-s-charter-school-legislation.

Hassel, Bryan C. and Michelle Godard Terrell. *Charter School Achievement: What We Know, 3rd Edition.* Chapel Hill, NC: Public Impact, October 2006. http://publicimpact.com/publications/Charter_School_Achievement_update_Oct06.pdf.

Hawley, Chris. "Against Tide, Some Seek Mexican Citizenship." *Arizona Republic,* May 25, 2006.

Hayes, Carleton J. H. *A Political and Social History of Modern Europe—Volume I, 1500–1815.* London: Macmillan, 1917.

Healey, Maura. "For Profit School Advisory." *Office of the Attorney General,* Boston, MA, September 2017. https://www.mass.gov/service-details/for-profit-school-advisory.

Heinrich, Carolyn J., Robert H. Meyer, and Greg Whitten. "Supplemental Education Services Under No Child Left Behind: Who Signs Up, and What Do They Gain?" *Educational Evaluation and Policy Analysis* 32 no. 2 (2010) 273–98. https://doi.org/10.3102/0162373710361640.

Henig, Jeffrey R. and Stephen D. Sugarman. "The Nature and Extent of School Choice." In *School Choice and Social Controversy*, edited by Sugarman and Kemerer, 13–35. Washington DC: The Brookings Institution, 1999.

Herman, Rebecca. *An Educators' Guide to Schoolwide Reform*. Arlington, VA: American Institutes for Research 1999.

Hill, Paul T. *Learning As We Go—Why School Choice Is Worth The Wait*. Stanford, CA: EducationNext Books, 2010.

Hill, Paul T. "Private Vouchers in New York City: The Student-Sponsor Partnership Program." In *Private Vouchers*, edited by Terry Moe, 120–35. Stanford: Hoover Institution, 1995.

Hillsdale Academy Representative. "Hillsdale Academy curriculum." *Hillsdale Academy*, Hillsdale, MI. Accessed June 11, 2018. https://academy.hillsdale.edu/academics/curriculum.

Hinchey, Patricia H. *Student Rights—A Reference Handbook*. Santa Barbara, CA: ABC-CLIO, 2001.

Hirsch, E. D. Jr. *The Making of Americans—Democracy and our Schools*. New Haven: Yale University Press, 2009.

Hirsch, E. D. Jr. *The Schools We Need and Why We Don't Have Them*. New York: Anchor Books, 1996.

Ho, Michelle. "Johannes Gutenberg: Renaissance Inventor of the Printing Press." *A Haiku Deck PowerPoint presentation*. Accessed November 14, 2018. https://www.haikudeck.com/johannes-gutenberg-first-version-events-presentation-RehzF6HJw3#slide4.

Holowchak, M. Andrew. "Did Jefferson Really Write the Declaration of Independence?" *Washington Post*, July 4, 2018.

Horowitz, Carl. "NYC School Bus Inspectors Sentenced, Union Officials Indicted in Bribery Scam." *National Legal and Policy Center*, Falls Church, VA, July 15, 2009. https://nlpc.org/2009/07/15/nyc-school-bus-inspectors-sentenced-union-officials-indicted-bribery-scam/.

Howard, Thomas Albert. *Protestant Theology and the Making of the Modern German University*. Oxford: Oxford University Press, 2006.

Howell, William G. and Paul E. Peterson. *The Education Gap—Vouchers and Urban Schools*. Washington DC: The Brookings Institution, 2002.

Howley, Aimee and Craig Howley. "Rural School Busing." *ERIC Digest*, 2001, ERIC Identifier: ED459969. https://www.ericdigests.org/2002–3/busing.htm.

Hudson, Richard, Contributing Columnist. "Ending Common Core extortion." *Richmond County Daily Journal*, July 13, 2015. https://www.yourdailyjournal.com/opinion/columns/1906/ending-common-core-extortion.

Hufton, Olwen. "Every Tub on its Own Bottom: Funding a Jesuit College in Early Modern Europe—1500–1760." In *The Jesuits II—Culture, Sciences, and the Arts*, edited by John W. O'Malley, S. J., Gauvin Alexander Bailey, Steven J. Harris and T. Frank Kennedy, S. J., 5–23. Toronto: University of Toronto Press, 2006.

Institute for Justice Writer. "Public Opinion Data: Americans Want School Choice." *Institute for Justice*, Arlington, VA, 2004. https://www.ij.org/images/pdf_folder/school_choice/public_opinion_data.pdf.

Institute Writer. "The Annenberg Institute for School Reform at Brown University, Interim Report." *Brown University*, Providence, RI, 1995.

Isaacson, Walter. *Einstein: His Life and Universe*. New York: Simon & Schuster, 2007.

Isenberg, Daniel. "SABIS—A Global Education Venture from Lebanon." In *Harvard Business School Case Study*, N9—809—167. Boston: Harvard Business School, June 2009.

ITBS Staff. "Iowa Test of Basic Skills." *University of Iowa*, Iowa City, IA. Description at: http://itp.education.uiowa.edu.

Jacobs, Joanne. "Counting on Character: National Heritage Academies and Civic Education." *Policy Brief*, 5, AEI Program on American Citizenship, January 2013. http://citizenship-aei.org/wp-content/uploads/American-Citizenship_Counting-on-Character-05_Jacobs.pdf.

Jefferson, Thomas. "Notes on Virginia 1782." In *The Life and Selected Writings of Thomas Jefferson*, edited by William Peden, 185–288. New York: Modern Library Edition, 1972.

Jimerson, Shane R., Amber M. Kaufman, Gabrielle E. Anderson, Angela D. Whipple, Lisa R. Figueroa, Francisco Rocco and Kathyrn M. O'Brien. "Beyond Grade Retention and Social Promotion: Interventions to Promote Social and Cognitive Competence." *Pre-publication draft* of Gevirtz Graduate School of Education, University of California, Santa Barbara, 2002. https://www.researchgate.net/publication/228505162_Beyond_Grade_Retention_and_Social_Promotion_Interventions_to_Promote_Social_Cognitive_Competence.

Johnson, James, Jr. *Basic Remedial Mathematics*. Bloomington, IN: Xlibris, 2006. Reviewed on the Amazon.com website at https://www.amazon.com/BASIC-REMEDIAL-MATHEMATICS-Mastering-Mathematical/dp/1599266520.

Johnson, Paul. *A History of the American People*. New York: HarperPerennial, 1999.

Jones, Kenneth and Tema Okun. *White Supremacy Culture -From Dismantling Racism: A Workbook for Social Change Groups*. Cambridge, MA: ChangeWork, 2001. http://chna17.org/wp-content/uploads/2016/11/White-Supremacy-Culture.pdf.

Junge, Ember Reichgott. *Zero Chance of Passage—The Pioneering Charter School Story*. Edina, MN: Beaver's Pond, 2012.

Kaestle, Carl, ed. *Joseph Lancaster and the Monitorial School Movement: A Documentary History*. New York: Teachers' College Press, 1973.

Kaestle, Carl. *Pillars of the Republic: Common Schools and American Society. 1780–1860*. New York: Hill and Wang, 1983.

Keairns, Kathy. "History of Distance Education." *University of Denver*, Denver, CO, May 31, 2001. http://mysite.du.edu/~kkeairns/doc/history.html.

Keiler, Jonathan F. "Intersectional Nonsense." *AmericanThinker.com*, April 11, 2017. https://www.americanthinker.com/articles/2017/04/intersectional_nonsense.html.

KIPP Representative. "KIPP: Knowledge is power program." Accessed February 27, 2017. https://www.kipp.org.

Kirkpatrick, David W. "Teachers Unions and Educational Reform." *Government Union Review* 19 no. 2 (2016) paras. 1–135. https://psrf.org/government-union-review-1/2016/11/13/teacher-unions-and-educational-reform-the-view-from-inside-by-david-w-kirkpatrick.

Klencke, Hermann. *Lives of Brothers Humboldt, Alexander and William*. London: Ingram, Cooke & Co., 1852.

Knee, Jonathan A. *Class Clowns: How the Smartest Investors Lost Billions in Education*. New York: Columbia University Press, 2017.

Kolderie, Ted. "How the idea of 'chartering' schools came about—What role did the Citizens League play?" *Minnesota Journal of the Citizens League*, St. Paul, MN, June 2008. https://www.educationevolving.org/pdf/Origins-of-Chartering-Citizens-League-Role.pdf.

Korn, Melissa, Jennifer Levitz and Erin Ailworth. "Federal Prosecutors Charge Dozens in College Admissions Cheating Scheme." *Wall Street Journal,* March 12, 2019. https://www.wsj.com/articles/federal-prosecutors-charge-dozens-in-broad-college-admissions-fraud-scheme-11552403149?mod=searchresults&page=1&pos–2.

Kragh, Helge. *Cosmology and Controversy—The Historical Development of Two Theories of the Universe.* Princeton: Princeton University Press, 1996.

Krejcir, Richard J. *Statistics and Reasons for Church Decline.* Pasadena, CA: Francis A. Schaeffer Institute of Church Leadership Development, 2007. http://www.churchleadership.org/apps/articles/default.asp?articleid=42346.

Kronholz, June. "High Scores at BASIS Charter Schools—Arizona students outperform Shanghai," *EducationNext* (Winter 2014): 30–36. https://www.educationnext.org/high-scores-at-basis-charter-schools/.

LaBerge, Philip. "Literacy in Renaissance Europe." Developed for Charles Scribner's Sons by Visual Education Corporation, Princeton, N.J. New York: Charles Scribner's Sons, 2004. http://www.philiplaberge.com/FamilyHistory/LaBergeInfo/Literacy.pdf.

Lancaster, Joseph. *Improvements in Education as it Respects the Industrial Classes of the Community.* Cambridge: Cambridge University Press, 2014.

Lastra-Anadón, Carlos Xabel and Paul E. Peterson. "Learning from the International Experience—What U.S. schools can and cannot learn from other countries." *EducationNext* (Winter 2012): 52–9. http://educationnext.org/the-international-experience/.

Lauglo, Jon. "Forms of decentralization and their implications for Education." In *The Reconstruction of Education—Quality, Equality and Control,* edited by Judith D. Chapman, William L. Boyd, Rolf Lander, and David Reynolds. 18–46. London: Cassell, 1996.

Leagle Reporter. "Tatonka Capital Corporation v. Mosaica Education, Inc." *Leagle,* October 31, 2014. https://www.leagle.com/decision/infdco20141218950.

Leisey, Donald E. and Charles Lavaroni. *The Educational Entrepreneur—Making A Difference.* San Rafael, CA: Edupreneur, 2000.

Lewin, Tamar. "Facing Cuts in Federal Aid, For-Profit Colleges Are in a Fight." *New York Times,* June 5, 2010.

Lieberman, Myron. *Public Education—An Autopsy.* Cambridge, MA: Harvard University Press, 1999.

Lieberman, Myron. *The Teachers Unions.* New York: The Free Press, 1997.

Linzey, E. and A. Lewis. "BOT Report." *AMSA Eagle,* October 26, 2018. https://www.amsacs.org/pdf/bot/10–25-18%20October%202018%20ED%20BOT%20Report%20.pdf.

Litten, Nick. "Which Came First, the Apple or the Cray?" *A Nick Litten blogpost* (blog). Circa 1997. https://www.nicklitten.com/which-came-first-the-apple-or-the-cray/.

Loach, Judi. "Revolutionary Pedagogues? How Jesuits Used Education to Change Society." In *The Jesuits II—Culture, Sciences, and the Arts,* edited by John W. O'Malley, S. J., Gauvin Alexander Bailey, Steven J. Harris and T. Frank Kennedy, S. J., 66–85. Toronto: University of Toronto Press, 2006.

Loew, Morgan. "BASIS schools fight criticism, work to increase student retention." *AzFamily.com,* August 6, 2015. https://www.azfamily.com/basis-schools-fight-criticism-work-to-increase-student-retention/article_462085ee-f5ce-5514-b3c2-b0cfc48169a7.html.

Longmier, B.W., J.P. Squire, L.D. Cassady, M.G. Ballenger, M.D. Carter, F.R. Chang-Díaz, T.G. Glover, A.V. Ilin, G.E. McCaskill, and C.S. Olsen. "Improved Efficiency and Throttling

Range of the VX-200 Magnetoplasma Thruster." *AIAA Journal of Propulsion and Power* 30, no. 1 (January 2014) 123–32. https://doi.org/10.2514/1.B34801.

Mack, Eric. "Elon Musk called out by creepy artificial intelligence robot." *CNET News,* October 26, 2017. https://www.cnet.com/news/elon-musk-artificial-intelligence-ai-robot-sophia-hanson-robotics/?ftag=COS-05-10aaa0g.

Maddison, Angus. *Contours of the World Economy 1–2030.* Oxford: University Press, 2007. Also at: Wikipedia contributors, "List of regions by past GDP (PPP) per capita," Wikipedia, The Free Encyclopedia, https://en.wikipedia.org/w/index.php?title=List_of_regions_by_past_GDP_(PPP)_per_capita&oldid=906408886 (accessed August 27, 2019).

Maier, Pauline. *American Scripture: Making the Declaration of Independence.* New York: Random House, 1997.

Mann, Horace. "Seventh Annual Report for 1843." In *Annual Reports of the Secretary of the Board of Education of Massachusetts for the Years 1839–1844.* New York: Lee and Shepard Publishers, 1844. https://babel.hathitrust.org/cgi/pt?id=hvd.hxq9wu;view=1up;seq=1.

Martinez, Valerie, Kenneth Godwin and Frank R. Kemerer. "Private Vouchers in San Antonio: The CEO Program." In *Private Vouchers,* edited by Terry M. Moe, 74–99. Stanford CA: Hoover Institution, 1995.

McCluskey, Neal. "Corruption in the Public Schools—The Market Is the Answer." *Policy Analysis* no. 542 (April 20, 2005) 1–20. https://object.cato.org/sites/cato.org/files/pubs/pdf/pa542.pdf.

McClusky, Frederick D. "Introduction of Grading Into the Public Schools of New England—Part 1." *Elementary School Journal* 21 no. 1 (September 1920) 34–46. https://ia801905.us.archive.org/29/items/jstor-993768/993768.pdf.

McClusky, Frederick D. "Introduction of Grading Into the Public Schools of New England—Part 2." *Elementary School Journal* 21 no. 2 (October 1920) 132–45. https://www.journals.uchicago.edu/doi/pdfplus/10.1086/454893.

McKenna, Josephine. "Pope says evolution, Big Bang are real." *USA Today,* October 28, 2014.

McKown, Harry C. and Alvin B. Roberts. *Audio-Visual Aids to Instruction.* New York: McGraw Hill, 1940.

McMurray, Daniel T. "Converting Nonprofit to For-Profit Status—The due diligence process for implementing a change of status for hospital entities." *Trustee Magazine,* February 2012. We found this to be a good article on this process that despite its use in the medical field, and is probably a good model to follow in bringing a non-profit school into for-profit status. http://www.focusmg.com/wordpress/wp-content/uploads/2012/02/Change-of-Status-Trustee-Publication-2-2012.pdf.

Merriam-Webster Dictionary, s.v. "charter school." https://www.merriam-webster.com/dictionary/charter%20school.

Milgram, R. James and Sandra Stotsky. "Lowering the Bar: How Common Core Math Fails to Prepare High School Students for STEM." *Pioneer Institute White Paper,* no. 103, Boston, MA, September 2013. Accessed August 16, 2018. http://pioneerinstitute.org/download/lowering-the-bar-how-common-core-math-fails-to-prepare-highschool-students-for-stem/.

Miller, Darren. "Common Core Disaster." *Right on the Left Coast Blogspot* (blog). May 9, 2018. http://rightontheleftcoast.blogspot.com/2018/05/common-core-disaster.html.

Miller, Georgie. "History of Distance Learning." *WorldWideLearn,* Foster City, CA, November 10, 2014. https://www.worldwidelearn.com/education-articles/history-of-distance-learning.html.

Miller, Rich. "Rauner's Janus victory may ring hollow—at least in Illinois." *Crain's Chicago Business,* June 29, 2018. http://www.chicagobusiness.com/article/20180629/ISSUE11/180629827/rauners-janus-v-afscme-victory-may-ring-hollow-in-illinois.

Mills, Jonathan N. and Patrick J. Wolfe. *How Has the Louisiana Scholarship Program Affected Students?—A Comprehensive Summary of the Effects after Three Years.* New Orleans, LA: EducationResearchAllianceNOLA.org, June 26, 2017. https://educationresearchalliancenola.org/files/publications/ERA-Policy-Brief-Public-Private-School-Choice-160218.pdf.

Mitchell, Josh. "Trump Administration Scraps Obama-Era Rules on For-Profit Colleges—Education Department to rewrite rules, intended to combat fraud and high student-debt burdens." *Wall Street Journal*, June 14, 2017.

Moe, Terry M. "Private Vouchers." In *Private Vouchers,* edited by Terry Moe, 1–40. Stanford: Hoover Institution, 1995.

Moe, Terry M. *Schools, Vouchers, and the American Public.* Washington DC: The Brookings Institution, 2001.

Moir, Ralph W. and W. L. Barr. "Analysis Of Interstellar Spacecraft Cycling Between The Sun and the Near Stars." *Journal of the British Interplanetary Society* 58 (2005) 332–41.

Moore, Michael G., ed. *Handbook of Distance Education.* New York: Routledge, 2013.

Morningside Center Article. "On intersectionality: What is it? How can it help us?" *Morningside Center for Teaching Social Responsibility,* New York, NY. Accessed February 15, 2019. https://sharemylesson.com/teaching-resource/intersectionality-what-it-how-can-it-help-us-299212.

Morrison, Samuel Eliot. *Christopher Columbus—Mariner.* New York: Meridian, 1983.

Moses Brown School. "Moses Brown School of Providence." Accessed June 15, 2019. https://www.mosesbrown.org.

Murray, Karyn E. "National Independent Private Schools Association (NIPSA)." *NIPSA.* For 2019, we obtained a count of 125 member schools within the United States. 16 years earlier, in the year 2003, they reported that count to be 100 schools, but unfortunately that number no longer seems accessible from their website. Accessed February 11, 2019. http://www.nipsa.org/schools/.

NAEP Reporting. "Civics—Grade 12 National Results." *The Nation's Report Card.* https://www.nationsreportcard.gov/civics_2010/g12_national.aspx?tab_id=tab2&subtab_id=Tab_1#chart.

NAEP Reporting. "Long Term Trend performance statistics." *NAEP Data Explorer.* Last accessed March 27, 2019. http://nces.ed.gov/nationsreportcard/lttdata/report.aspx.

NAEP Reporting. "Mathematics and reading proficiencies of 8th grade demographic groups." *NAEP Data Explorer.* http://nces.ed.gov/nationsreportcard/naepdata/dataset.aspx.

NAEP Reporting. "NAEP Data Tools and Applications." *National Center for Education Statistics.* Accessed May 13, 2018. https://nces.ed.gov/nationsreportcard/about/naeptools.aspx.

NAEP Reporting. "U. S. History—Grade 8 National Results." *The Nation's Report Card.* https://www.nationsreportcard.gov/ushistory_2010/g8_nat.aspx?tab_id=tab2&subtab_id=Tab_4#chart.

NAEP Reporting. "U. S. History—Grade 12 National Results." *The Nation's Report Card.* https://www.nationsreportcard.gov/ushistory_2010/about_ushistory.aspx.

Nash, Gary B. *American Odyssey: The United States in the Twentieth Century.* St. Louis, MO: Glencoe/McGraw Hill, 1999.

National Center for Education Statistics, *NAEP Data Explorer.* https://nces.ed.gov/nationsreportcard/tdw/database/data_tool.asp.

National Heritage Academies. "National Heritage Academies—Who we are." *National Heritage Academies*, Grand Rapids, MI. Accessed March 22, 2019. https://www.nhaschools.com/en/who-we-are.

Nazworth, Napp. "Homeschool Advocate Michael Farris Responds to Sex Scandals of Homeschool Leaders Bill Gothard, Doug Phillips." *The Christian Post,* August 29, 2014. https://www.christianpost.com/news/homeschool-advocate-michael-farris-responds-to-sex-scandals-of-homeschool-leaders-bill-gothard-doug-phillips-125549/.

NCES Reporting, "Charter school numbers of schools and students." *National Center for Education Statistics*, Common Core of Data (CCD), "Public Elementary/Secondary School Universe Survey," 2000–01 through 2015–16. (This table was prepared August 2017.)

NCES Reporting. "Number of public school districts and public and private elementary and secondary schools: Selected years, 1869–70 through 2012–13." *National Center for Education Statistics,* Washington, DC, 2014. https://nces.ed.gov/programs/digest/d14/tables/dt14_214.10.asp?current=yes.

NCES Staff. "Description of the 'National Assessment of Educational Progress' and the 'Nation's Report Card.'" *National Center for Educational Statistics (NCES).* https://www.nationsreportcard.gov.

NCES Staff. "Total undergraduate fall enrollment in degree-granting postsecondary institutions, by attendance status, sex of student, and control and level of institution: Selected years, 1970 through 2027." *In Table 303.70: Digest of Education Statistics,* National Center of Education Statistics, Washington, DC, 2017. https://nces.ed.gov/programs/digest/d17/tables/dt17_303.70.asp.

NEA Adopted Actions. "New Business Item 90—on deconstructing 'the systemic proliferation of a White supremacy culture." *2018 Annual Meeting and Representative Assembly,* National Education Association. https://ra.nea.org/business-item/2018-nbi-090/.

NEA Representative. "Issues & Advocacy." *NEA National Education Association,* Washington, DC. Accessed February 15, 2019. http://www.nea.org/home/35330.htm.

New England Parents' Club [David V. Anderson]. *Gadzooks! Parents' Guide To Schools & Services In Rhode Island & Massachusetts,* Attleboro, MA: Asora Education Enterprises, 2017. This unpublished, prototypical guidebook is available in the file RIMA-Guide-01.pdf at: http://asoraeducation.com/page59/page60/page60.html.

Niche Analyst. "2019 Best Charter High Schools in America." *Niche.com.* https://www.niche.com/k12/search/best-charter-high-schools/.

Niche Analyst. "2019 Best Charter Middle Schools in America." *Niche.com.* 2019. https://www.niche.com/k12/search/best-charter-middle-schools/.

Niche Analyst. "2019 Best Schools in the Providence Area." *Niche.com*, 2019. https://www.niche.com/k12/search/best-schools/m/providence-metro-area/.

Niche Analyst. "Futures Academy, San Diego." *Niche.com.* Accessed January 4, 2019. https://www.niche.com/k12/futures-academy—-san-diego-san-diego-ca/.

Niche Analyst. "Obtaining the SAT scores of Basis Independent schools." *This was accomplished on Niche.com.* Accessed February 15, 2019. For example, its Silicon Valley school's scores were found at: https://www.niche.com/k12/basis-independent-silicon-valley-san-jose-ca/.

Nord, Warren A. *Does God Make a Difference—Taking Religion Seriously in Our Schools and Universities.* Oxford: Oxford University Press, 2010.

Norton, Oak, "Partisan School Board Election Arguments." *Utahns Against Common Core,* Salt Lake City, UT, May 7, 2014. https://www.utahnsagainstcommoncore.com/partisan-school-board-election-arguments/.

Office of Inspector General. "Former State School Superintendent Linda Schrenko Sentenced to Eight Years in Federal Prison." U. S. Department of Education, Washington, DC, July 12, 2006. https://www2.ed.gov/about/offices/list/oig/invtreports/dc072006.html.

Office of Inspector General. "Investigative Report: Maine Department of Education to Pay United States $1.5 Million to Settle False Claims Involving Migrant Education Program." U. S. Department of Education, Washington, DC, May 21, 2009. https://www2.ed.gov/about/offices/list/oig/invtreports/dc052009.html.

Office of Inspector General. "Investigation Report: Puerto Rico Department of Education Pays U. S. over $19 Million to Settle False Claims Involving Migrant Education Program." U. S. Department of Education, Washington, DC, February 15, 2008. https://www2.ed.gov/about/offices/list/oig/invtreports/dc022008.html.

OMRF Analyst. "Columbus brought more than ships to the New World." *Oklahoma Medical Research Foundation,* Oklahoma City, OK, October 10, 2013. https://omrf.org/2013/10/10/columbus-brought-more-than-ships-to-the-new-world/.

Ovando, C. and P. McLaren. "Cultural recognition and civil discourse in a democracy." In the Preface of *The politics of multiculturalism and bilingual education: Students and teachers caught in the cross fire,* edited by C. Ovando and P. McLaren, xvii–xxiii. Boston: McGraw-Hill, 2000.

Owen, Jordan. "Former North Chicago school board member gets 30 months for taking kickbacks." *Chicago Sun Times,* April 21, 2015.

Pallardy, Richard. "Horace Greeley, American Journalist.*" Encyclopedia Britannica*. Chicago: Encyclopedia Britannica, 2019. Accessed April 3, 2019. Print editions no longer produced since 2012. https://www.britannica.com/biography/Horace-Greeley.

Perez, Chris. "San Francisco allows non-citizens to vote in school elections." *New York Post,* July 18, 2018.

Perrin, John William. "The History of Compulsory Education in New England." *PhD diss.,* University of Chicago, 1896). https://ia800302.us.archive.org/29/items/historyofcompuls00perr/historyofcompuls00perr.pdf.

Peterson, Paul E. and Matthew M. Chingos. "For-Profit and Nonprofit Management in Philadelphia Schools." *EducationNext* (Spring 2009) 65–70.

Peterson, Paul E. and William G. Howell. "Efficiency, Bias, and Classification Schemes—A Response to Alan B. Krueger and Pei Zhu." *American Behavioral Scientist* 47 no. 5 (January 5, 2004) 699–717.

Peterson, Paul E. "Secret Finding from PDK Poll: Support for Vouchers is Rising." *EducationNext* (blog), Summer 2017. https://www.educationnext.org/secret-finding-pdk-poll-support-vouchers-rising/.

Peterson, Robert A. "Education in Colonial America." *Freeman Online.* Accessed December 10, 2018. http://www.pilgrimacademy.org/raplibrary/thefreemanonline.org-Education_in_Colonial_America__The_Freeman.pdf.

Phelps, Richard P. and R. James Milgram. "The Revenge of K-12: How Common Core and the New SAT Lower College Standards in the U.S." *Pioneer Institute White Paper* no. 122, Boston, September 2014.

Phillips, Andrea, Kun Yuan and Shannah Tharp-Gilliam. "Evaluation of the Regional Choice Initiative." *Rand Corporation,* Santa Monica, CA, 2016.

Pious XII, Pope. "To the eminent Cardinals present, to the very excellent delegates of the Foreign Nations, and to the members of the Pontifical Academy of Sciences." *Vatican Library.* November 22, 1951. Accessed December 9 2018. http://w2.vatican.va/content/pius-xii/it/speeches/1951/documents/hf_p-xii_spe_19511122_di-serena.html.

Pondiscio, Robert. "Meta-Analysis Confirms Effectiveness of an Old School Approach: Direct Instruction." *EducationNext* (blog), February 8, 2018. https://www.educationnext.org/meta-analysis-confirms-effectiveness-old-school-approach-direct-instruction/.

Potter, Charles F. *Humanism: A New Religion.* New York: Simon & Shuster, 1930.

Powers, Susan G. and Steven Flint. "Labor productivity growth in elementary and secondary school services: 1989–2012." *Monthly Labor Review*, U. S. Bureau of Labor Statistics, Washington, DC, June 2016, https://doi.org/10.21916/mlr. 2016.29.

Prometheus Entertainment. "The Curse of Oak Island: Season 6, Episode 6- Precious Metal." *History Channel.* https://www.mysteriesofcanada.com/nova-scotia/the-curse-of-oak-island-season-6-episode-6-precious-metal/.

Quora website. "Here queried on European literacy rates." https://www.quora.com/What-were-literacy-rates-in-Medieval-Europe-How-did-they-compare-to-literacy-rates-in-the-Roman-Empire.

Quora website. "Literacy in medieval England." The Quora website says that England had 6% literate in the year 1300. Assuming a fairly flat temporal profile in the years before and shortly after Gutenberg this fits well with our 5% literacy estimate for the year 1475. Access this at https://www.quora.com/What-were-literacy-rates-in-Medieval-Europe-How-did-they-compare-to-literacy-rates-in-the-Roman-Empire.

Radosh, Ronald. *Is Socialism Part of the American Tradition?* Washington DC: Hudson Institute, April 8 2011. https://www.hudson.org/research/7937-is-socialism-part-of-the-american-tradition-.

Rakic, Pasko. "Article about Rakic's brain research." *Life Magazine,* July 1994.

Rathi, Akshat. "A Piece of the Sun—In search of clean energy, investments in nuclear-fusion startups are heating up." *Quartz,* September 26, 2018. https://qz.com/1402282/in-search-of-clean-energy-investments-in-nuclear-fusion-startups-are-heating-up/.

Ravitch, Diane. *A Consumer's Guide to High School History Textbooks.* Washington DC: Thomas B. Fordham Institute, 2004. https://eric.ed.gov/?id=ED485529.

Ravitch, Diane. *The Language Police—How Pressure Groups Restrict What Students Learn.* New York: Vintage Books, 2004.

Ravitch, Diane. *Left Back—A Century of Battles Over School Reform.* New York: A Touchstone Book Published by Simon & Schuster, 2000.

Rayne, Sierra. "Poll shows high levels of support for sharia law and violence among American Muslims." *American Thinker,* June 25, 2015. https://www.americanthinker.com/blog/2015/06/poll_shows_high_levels_of_support_for_shariah_law_and_violence_among_american_muslims.html#ixzz5kVVfVtts.

Review & Outlook. "Obama's For-Profit Execution." *Wall Street Journal,* August 29, 2016.

Rollwagen, John and Donn McLellan. "Chartered Schools = Choices for Educators + Quality for All Students." *School Structure Committee of the Citizens League,* St. Paul, MN, November 1988. https://citizensleague.org/wp-content/uploads/2017/07/PolicyReportEducationNov-1988.pdf.

Rose, Lowell C. and Alec M. Gallup. "The 36th Annual Phi Delta Kappa/Gallup Poll of the Public's Attitudes toward the Public Schools." *Phi Delta Kappan* 86 no. 1 (September 2004) 41–56. https://doi.org/10.1177/003172170408600108.

Rothbard, Murray N. *Education: Free and Compulsory.* Auburn, AL: Ludwig von Mises Institute, 1999.

Roy-Davis, Julius. "Can Multiculturalism Work? Part I: Nationalism and Its Critics." *Republic Standard—Conservative Thought & Culture Magazine,* May 17, 2018. https://republicstandard.com/can-multiculturalism-work-part-1-nationalism-critics/.

Rubin, C. M. Interview with Michael Block. "The Global Search for Education: Block Building." *Education News,* December 6, 2011. https://www.educationnews.org/education-policy-and-politics/the-global-search-for-education-block-building/.

Rudner, Lawrence M. "Scholastic Achievement and Demographic Characteristics of Home School Students in 1998." *Educational Policy Analysis Archives* 7 no. 8 (March 23, 1999) 2–37.

Ruthhart, Bill and John Chase. "Rauner email: Half of CPS teachers 'virtually illiterate.'" *Chicago Tribune,* July 22, 2016. http://www.chicagotribune.com/news/local/politics/ct-bruce-rauner-cps-teachers-met-0722-20160721-story.html.

SABIS Website. "SABIS: Education for a changing world." Accessed April 4, 2019. https://www.sabis.net.

Saint Paul. "II Timothy 2:16." *King James Version of the Holy Bible,* American Bible Company, Nashville, TN, 1995, 701.

Salmon, David, ed. *The Practical Parts of Lancaster's Improvements and Bell's Experiment.* Cambridge: Cambridge University Press, 1932.

Sanes, Milla, and John Schmitt. *Regulation of Public Sector Collective Bargaining in the States.* Washington, D C: Center for Economic and Policy Research, March 2014. http://cepr.net/documents/state-public-cb-2014–03.pdf.

Santayana, George. *The Life of Reason: Reason in Common Sense.* Mineola, NY: Dover Books, 1980.

Sappington, David E. M. and J. Gregory Sidak. "Anticompetitive Behavior by State-Owned Enterprises: Incentives and Capabilities." In *Competing with the Government: Anticompetitive Behavior and Public Enterprises,* edited by R. Richard Geddes, 1–17. Stanford: Hoover Institution, 2004.

Schemo, Diana Jean. "As Testing Rises, 9th Grade Becomes Pivotal." *New York Times,* January 18, 2004.

School Administrator. "Curriculum of Trinity Lutheran School, Hawthorne, California." *Trinity Lutheran School,* Accessed March 2, 2019. http://tlchurch-hawthorne.org/generalinfo1.html.

Schweikart, Larry. *48 Liberal Lies About American History (that you probably learned in school).* London: Penguin Books, 2008.

Scott, Nate. "The 50 greatest Yogi Berra quotes." *USA Today,* September 23, 2015. https://ftw.usatoday.com/2015/09/the-50-greatest-yogi-berra-quotes.

SE Mom [pseud.]. "FDR warned against collective bargaining for government unions." *The American Presidency Project,* UC Santa Barbara, Santa Barbara, CA, February 18, 2011. http://www.freerepublic.com/focus/f-chat/2675825/posts.

Sewall, Gilbert T. *Necessary Lessons—Decline and Renewal in American Schools.* New York: The Free Press, 1983.

Sewall, Gilbert T. "The Postmodern Schoolhouse." In *Dumbing Down—Essays on the Strip Mining of American Culture,* edited by Katharine Washburn and John F. Thornton, 57–67. New York: W. W. Norton & Company, 1996.

Sewall, Gilbert T. "Religion and the Textbooks." In *Curriculum, Religion, and Public Education—Conversations for an Enlarging Public Square,* edited by James T. Sears, 73–84. New York: Teachers College Press, 1998.

Shanker, Albert. "Where We Stand." *The New York Times,* July 10, 1988.

Shearer, William J. *The Grading of Schools.* New York: H. P. Smith Publishing Co., 1899. Early editions are out of print, but book is available at Palala, 2016. https://www.bookdepository.com/Grading-Schools-William-John-Shearer/9781355177265.

Skandera, Hanna and Richard Souza. *School Figures: The Data behind the Debate.* Stanford: Hoover Institution, 2003.

Smith, Adam. *An Inquiry into the Nature and Causes of the Wealth of Nations—A Selected Edition.* Edited with an Introduction and Notes by Kathryn Sutherland. Oxford: Oxford University Press, (World's Classics Paperback), Oxford, 1993.

Smith, Lindsey. "Many Muskegon Heights students dig the charter company's curriculum: 'It's fun.'" *Michigan Radio,* January 4, 2013. http://www.michiganradio.org/post/many-muskegon-heights-students-dig-charter-company-s-curriculum-it-s-fun.

Sprague, Shawn. "What can labor productivity tell us about the U.S. economy?" *Beyond the Numbers,* Bureau of Labor Statistics, US Department of Labor, Washington, May 2014. https://www.bls.gov/opub/btn/volume-3/what-can-labor-productivity-tell-us-about-the-us-economy.htm.

Staff Reporter. "8 of 10 Atlanta educators in cheating scandal sentenced to prison." *Atlanta Journal & Constitution,* April 14, 2015. https://www.ajc.com/news/education/atlanta-educators-cheating-scandal-sentenced-prison/1gL2add42XwXgsOCPtAkFM/.

Staff Reporter. "China's new-gen supercomputer expected to be 10 times faster than current champion." *Indian Express,* March 28, 2019. https://indianexpress.com/article/technology/science/chinas-new-gen-supercomputer-expected-to-be-10-times-faster-than-current-champion-4534497/.

Staff Reporter. "Fourteen indicted in alleged thefts from Floyd school system." *WRGA Local News Now,* October 1, 2018. http://wrganews.com/common/page.php?feed=1&id=132891&is_corp=1.

Staff Reporter. "Kingsburg Public Schools." *Public School Review,* New York, 2018. https://www.publicschoolreview.com/california/kingsburg.

Staff Reporter. "Oakland Military Institute Preparatory Academy Test Scores." *U. S. News & World Report,* June 2018. https://www.usnews.com/education/best-high-schools/california/districts/oakland-unified/oakland-military-institute-preparatory-academy-2928/test-scores.

Staff Reporter. "A timeline of how the Atlanta school cheating scandal unfolded." *Atlanta Journal & Constitution,* April 2, 2015. https://www.ajc.com/news/timeline-how-the-atlanta-school-cheating-scandal-unfolded/jn4vTk7GZUQoQRJTVR7UHK/.

Staff Reporter. "William J. Shearer, Obituary." *Evening Sentinel,* Carlisle, PA, January 1, 1925. http://www.pa-roots.org/data/read.php?894,386273.

Staff Writer. "Employed Persons." *Trading Economics,* 2019. https://tradingeconomics.com/united-states/employed-persons.

Staff Writer. "Richardson Indicted." *AllOnGeorgia,* October 2, 2018.

Staff Writer. "Sturm, Johannes." In *New International Encyclopedia* 21, 613–614. New York: Dodd, Mead and Company, 1914. https://en.wikisource.org/wiki/The_New_International_Encyclopædia/Sturm,_Johannes.

Statista Analyst. "Percentage of U.S. population as of 2016 and 2060, by race and Hispanic origin." *Statista—The Statistics Portal,* Hamburg, Germany. Accessed February 16, 2019. https://www.statista.com/statistics/270272/percentage-of-us-population-by-ethnicities/.

Stern, Sol. *Breaking free—Public School Lessons and the Imperative of School Choice.* San Francisco: Encounter Books, 2003.

Stewart, Doug. "Georges Lemaître." In *Famous Scientists—The Art of Genius,* website, 2017. https://www.famousscientists.org/georges-lemaitre/.

Stockard, Jean, Timothy W. Wood, Cristy Coughlin and Caitlin Rasplica Khoury. "The Effectiveness of Direct Instruction Curricula: A Meta-Analysis of a Half Century of Research." *Review of Educational Research* 88 no. 4 (August 2018) 479–507. http://journals.sagepub.com/doi/abs/10.3102/0034654317751919.

Stone, J. E. "Aligning Teacher Training with Public Policy." *The State Education Standard* (Winter 2000): 34–38. http://education-consumers.org/issues-public-education-research-analysis/aligning-teacher-training-public-policy/.

Stone, J. E. *Direct Instruction: What the Research Says.* Arlington, VA: Education Consumers Foundation, November 28, 2011. http://education-consumers.org/pdf/DI_Research.pdf.

Stone, J. E. "School Performance Nationally." *Education Consumers Foundation,* Arlington, VA. Accessed March 4, 2019. http://education-consumers.org/school-performance-nationally/.

Stotsky, Sandra and Ze'ev Wurman. "Common Core's Standards Still Don't Make the Grade: Why Massachusetts and California Must Regain Control Over Their Academic Destinies." *Pioneer Institute White Paper* no. 65, Boston, MA, July 2010. http://pioneerinstitute.org/download/common-cores-standards-still-dontmake-the-grade/.

Stotsky, Sandra. *Changing the Course of Failure—How Schools and Parents Can Help Low-Achieving Students.* New York: Rowman & Littlefield, 2018.

Stowe, Calvin E. "Report on Elementary Public Instruction in Europe." *36th General Assembly of the State of Ohio,* 1837, reprinted by order of the House of Representatives of the Legislature of Massachusetts, Boston, March 1838. https://ia802705.us.archive.org/24/items/reportonelementa00stowiala/reportonelementa00stowiala.pdf.

Strauss, Gerald. "Success and Failure in the German Reformation." in *The German Reformation- The Essential Readings,* edited by C. Scott Dixon, 221–57. Oxford: Blackwell, 1999.

Strauss, Valerie. "Common Core's odd approach to teaching Gettysburg Address." *Washington Post Blogs* (blog), November 19, 2013. https://www.washingtonpost.com/news/answer-sheet/wp/2013/11/19/common-cores-odd-approach-to-teaching-gettysburg-address/.

Strauss, Valerie. "Gates Foundation chief admits Common Core mistakes." *Washington Post,* June 2, 2016.

Strayer, Joseph R, Hans W. Gatzke and E. Harris Harbison. *The Course of Civilization—Volume One: To 1660.* New York: Harcourt, Brace & World, Inc. 1961.

Success Academy. "Success Academy Charter Schools." Accessed April 29, 2019. https://www.successacademies.org/schools/.

Sweet, Lynn. "Janus v. AFSCME: Rauner, Lisa Madigan and the Illinois case at the Supreme Court," *Chicago Sun Times,* June 28, 2018.

Sykes, Charles J. *Dumbing Down Our Kids—Why American Children Feel Good About Themselves But Can't Read, Write or Add.* New York: St. Martin's Griffin, 1995.

Taylor, Clarence. *Reds at the Blackboard—Communism, Civil Rights, and the New York City Teachers Union.* New York: Columbia University Press, 2011.

Thayer, V. T., Caroline B. Zachry and Ruth Kotinsky. *Reorganizing Secondary Education.* New York: Appleton-Century, 1939.

Tienken, Christopher H. "The Common Core State Standards: The Emperor Is Still Looking For His Clothes." *Kappa Delta Pi Record* 48 (October 31, 2012) 152–55. http://christienken.com/wp-content/uploads/2013/01/CCSS_Emperor_Still_Naked.pdf.

Times Reporting Staff. "Principal Blamed in Test-Score Altering." *Los Angeles Times*, March 15, 1997.

Tooley, James. *From Village School to Global Brand– Changing the World Through Education.* London: Profile Books Ltd, 2012.

Trump, Donald J. and Tony Schwartz. *The Art of the Deal.* New York: Random House, 1987.

Truth In American Education Representative. "No Child Left Behind Waivers." *Truth In American Education,* 4:15 Communications, Des Moines, IA. Accessed February 15, 2019. https://truthinamericaneducation.com/elementary-and-secondary-education-act/child-left-waivers/.

Tuchinsky, Adam-Max. *Horace Greeley's 'New-York Tribune'—Civil War-Era Socialism and the Crisis of Free Labor.* Ithaca, NY: Cornell University Press, November 2009. https://www.cornellpress.cornell.edu/book/9780801446672/horace-greeleys-new-york-tribune/.

Tuchman, Barbara W. *The March of Folly: From Troy to Vietnam.* New York: Random House, 1985.

Turner II, Christy G. and Jacqueline A. Turner. *Man Corn: Cannibalism and Violence in the Prehistoric American Southwest.* Salt Lake City, UT: University of Utah Press, 2011.

Twain, Mark. *Following the Equator: A Journey around the World.* New York: Ecco, reissue edition, 1996.

Twyford, L. "The national program in the use of television in the public schools. A report on the first year 1957–58." In *Audiovisual Communication Review* 8 no. 3 (1960) 156–160. https://doi.org/10.1007/BF02713419.

Tyack, David. *The One Best System—A History of American Urban Education.* Cambridge, MA: Harvard University Press, 1974.

UN Treaty. "United Nations Declaration of Human Rights—Article 26." The linked site includes the Article 26 provision on parental rights in education. http://www.un.org/en/universal-declaration-human-rights/index.html.

Uncommon Schools Website. Accessed March 22, 2019. https://uncommonschools.org.

Unitarians and Universalists on Stamps. By Quincy, Illinois Unitarian Church, http://www.uuquincy.org/projects/stamps/11horacegreeley.htm.

United States Code, Title 20, Sections 1232a, 3403b and 7907a.

Vedder, Richard K. *Can Teachers Own Their Own Schools?* Oakland, CA: The Independent Institute, 2000.

Vinovskis, Maris A. "Teachers Unions and Educational Research," in *Conflicting Missions?—Teachers Unions And Educational Reform,* edited by Tom Loveless, 211–39. Washington DC: Brookings Institution, 2000.

Vollmer, Phillip. *John Calvin, Theologian, Preacher, Statesman.* Philadephia: Heidelberg, 1909.

Wade, Lizzie. "Genetic study reveals surprising ancestry of many Americans." *Science,* December 18, 2014.

Walberg, Herbert J. *Advancing Student Achievement.* Stanford: Hoover Institution, 2010.

Walberg, Herbert J. and Joseph L. Bast. *Education and Capitalism—How Overcoming Our Fear of Markets and Economics Can Improve America's Schools.* Stanford: Hoover Institution, 2003.

Walberg, Herbert J. and Joseph L. Bast. *Rewards—How to use rewards to help children learn—and why teachers don't use them well.* Arlington Heights, IL: The Heartland Institute, 2014.

Walberg, Herbert J. *Tests, Testing, and Genuine School Reform.* Stanford: Hoover Institution, 2011.

Walker, Tim. "Study Upends Conventional Wisdom About Private School Advantages." *NEA Today,* September 24, 2018. http://neatoday.org/2018/09/24/are-private-school-better-than-public-schools/.

Walsh, Kate and Sandi Jacobs. *Alternative Certification Isn't Alternative.* Washington, DC: Thomas B. Fordham Institute National Council on Teacher Quality, September 2007. https://www.nctq.org/nctq/images/Alternative_Certification_Isnt_Alternative.pdf.

Wan, Tony. "When Edtech Networks Combine: SIIA's Education Division Absorbs Education Industry Association." *EdSurge,* April 2016. https://www.edsurge.com/news/2016-04-07-when-edtech-networks-combine-siia-s-education-division-absorbs-education-industry-association.

Warnick, Bryan R. *Understanding Student Rights in Schools—Speech, Religion, and Privacy in Educational Settings.* New York: Teachers College Press, 2013.

Wattenberg, Ben and Richard M. Scammon. *The Real Majority: An Extraordinary Examination of the American Electorate.* New York: Coward-McCann, Inc., 1970.

Webb, L. Dean. Arlene Metha, and K. Forbis Jordan. *Foundations of American Education—5th Edition.* London: Pearson Education, 2007.

Weber, Max. *The Protestant Ethic and the "Spirit of Capitalism.* London: Penguin Books, 2002.

Website Editor. "Achievement First." https://www.achievementfirst.org.

Website Editor. "ClassicalConversations." https://www.classicalconversations.com.

Webster's Third New International Dictionary—Of the English Language Unabridged. s.v. " murder." Edited by Phillip Babcok Gove. Springfield, MA: G. C. Merriam Co., 1981.

West, Edwin G. "Tom Paine's Voucher Scheme for Public Education." *Southern Economic Journal* 33 no. 3 (January 1967) 378–82.

West, Martin R. "The Future of Tax Credits." in *The Future of School Choice,* edited by Paul E. Peterson, 157–86. Stanford: Hoover Institution, 2003.

Westminster John Knox Press. "Zwingli and Bullinger" Edited and translated by G. W. Bromley. In *Library of Christian Classics,* Book 24, Philadelphia: Westminster, 1953.

Whaley, Monte. "Douglas County school voucher program now officially dead after case dismissed by Colorado Supreme Court, officials say," *Denver Post,* January 27, 2018, https://www.denverpost.com/2018/01/27/douglas-county-school-vouchers-end/.

White, Harvey E. "Physics Course on TV." *Physics Today,* January 1957.

Wikipedia contributors. "1872 United States presidential election." *Wikipedia*. June 20, 2019. https://en.wikipedia.org/wiki/1872_United_States_presidential_election.

Wikipedia contributors. "1996 California Proposition 209." *Wikipedia*. September 9, 2019. https://en.wikipedia.org/wiki/1996_California_Proposition_209.

Wikipedia contributors. "Afroyim v. Rusk." In Afroyim v. Rusk The Supreme Court voided a federal law on dual citizenship. *Wikipedia*. July 28,2018. https://en.wtkipedia.org/wiki/Afroyim_v._Rusk.

Wikipedia contributors. "American Federation of Teachers—History." *Wikipedia*. December 28, 2018. https://en.wikipedia.org/wiki/American_Federation_of_Teachers#History.

Wikipedia contributors. "Charles Francis Potter." *Wikipedia*. May 10, 2019. https://en.wikipedia.org/wiki/Charles_Francis_Potter.

Wikipedia contributors. "Compulsory education." *Wikipedia*. June 13, 2018. https://en.wikipedia.org/wiki/Compulsory_education.

Wikipedia contributors. "Distance Education." *Wikipedia*. Includes a discussion about broadcast instructional television. December 30, 2018. https://en.wikipedia.org/wiki/Distance_education.

Wikipedia contributors. "EdisonLearning." *Wikipedia*. November 29, 2018. https://en.wikipedia.org/wiki/EdisonLearning.

Wikipedia contributors. "Education Act of 1646." *Wikipedia*. September 29, 2018. https://en.wikipedia.org/wiki/Education_Act_1646.

Wikipedia contributors. "Eldridge Cleaver." *Wikipedia*. February 13, 2019. https://en.wikipedia.org/wiki/Eldridge_Cleaver.

Wikipedia contributors. "Gonçalo Coelho." *Wikipedia*. March 5, 2019. https://en.wikipedia.org/wiki/Gonçalo_Coelho.

Wikipedia contributors. "Grant-maintained school." *Wikipedia*. July 25, 2018. https://en.wikipedia.org/wiki/Grant-maintained_school.

Wikipedia contributors. "Harvey Elliott White." *Wikipedia*. July 18, 2019. https://en.wikipedia.org/wiki/Harvey_Elliott_White.

Wikipedia contributors. "Henry I Sinclair, Earl of Orkney." *Wikipedia*. May 3, 2019. https://en.wikipedia.org/wiki/Henry_I_Sinclair,_Earl_of_Orkney.

Wikipedia contributors. "Hippocratic Oath—Earliest surviving copy." *Wikipedia*. May 10, 2019. https://en.wikipedia.org/wiki/Hippocratic_Oath#Earliest_surviving_copy.

Wikipedia contributors. "History of education in the United States." *Wikipedia*. August 16, 2018. https://en.wikipedia.org/wiki/History_of_education_in_the_United_States.

Wikipedia contributors. "History of the United States." *Wikipedia*. Here, its pre-history begins 15,000 years ago. March 14, 2018. https://en.wikipedia.org/wiki/History_of_the_United_States.

Wikipedia contributors. "Howard Zinn." *Wikipedia*. May 2, 2019. https://en.wikipedia.org/wiki/Howard_Zinn.

Wikipedia contributors. "Intersectionality." *Wikipedia*. April 30, 2019. https://en.wikipedia.org/wiki/Intersectionality.

Wikipedia contributors. "Johannes Sturm." *Wikipedia*. July 30, 2018. https://en.wikipedia.org/wiki/Johannes_Sturm.

Wikipedia contributors. "John F. Kennedy." *Wikipedia*. https://en.wikipedia.org/wiki/John_F._Kennedy.

Wikipedia contributors. "Jones International University." *Wikipedia*. June 4, 2019. https://en.wikipedia.org/wiki/Jones_International_University.

Wikipedia contributors. "Luddite." *Wikipedia*. May 12, 2019. https://en.wikipedia.org/wiki/Luddite.

Wikipedia contributors. "Monitorial System." *Wikipedia*. April 19, 2019. https://en.wikipedia.org/w/index.php?title=Monitorial_System&oldid=895762282..

Wikipedia contributors. "National Education Association." *Wikipedia*. March 28, 2019. https://en.wikipedia.org/wiki/National_Education_Association.

Wikipedia contributors. "Peace of Augsburg." *Wikipedia*. May 3, 2018. https://en.wikipedia.org/wiki/Peace_of_Augsburg.

Wikipedia contributors. "Pedagogy." *Wikipedia*. October 14, 2018. https://en.wikipedia.org/wiki/Pedagogy.

Wikipedia contributors. "Pope Adrian IV." *Wikipedia*. October 11, 2018. https://en.wikipedia.org/wiki/Pope_Adrian_IV.

Wikipedia contributors. "Progressive education." *Wikipedia*. February 19, 2019. https://en.wikipedia.org/wiki/Progressive_education.

Wikipedia contributors. "Publishing—Publishing as a business." *Wikipedia*. March 21, 2019. https://en.wikipedia.org/wiki/Publishing#Publishing_as_a_business.

Wikipedia contributors. "A rising tide lifts all boats." *Wikipedia*. August 31, 2018. Usually attributed to President John F. Kennedy, it was actually found earlier in a report of a regional chamber of commerce, The New England Council, from which a Kennedy speechwriter found the quote. Kennedy liked it and used it frequently. https://en.wikipedia.org/wiki/A_rising_tide_lifts_all_boats.

Wikipedia contributors. "The Road to Hell is Paved with Good Intentions." *Wikipedia*. February 2, 2019. https://en.wikipedia.org/wiki/The_road_to_hell_is_paved_with_good_intentions.

Wikipedia contributors. "SAT." *Wikipedia*, https://en.wikipedia.org/wiki/SAT#/media/File:Historical_Average_SAT_Scores_(Vector).svg. This graph was originally obtained under a Creative Commons Agreement from https://www.erikthered.com/tutor/historical-average-SAT-scores-plot.pdf.

Wikipedia contributors. "School Prayer." *Wikipedia*. November 20, 2018. https://en.wikipedia.org/wiki/School_prayer.

Wikipedia contributors. "Student Success Act." *Wikipedia*. April 3, 2019. https://en.wikipedia.org/wiki/Student_Success_Act.

Wikipedia contributors. "Thomas Jefferson." *Wikipedia*. February 16, 2019. https://en.wikipedia.org/wiki/Thomas_Jefferson.

Wikipedia contributors. "Thomas Paine—Criticism of George Washington." *Wikipedia*. May 3, 2019. https://en.wikipedia.org/wiki/Thomas_Paine#Criticism_of_George_Washington.

Wikipedia contributors. "Treaty of Tripoli." *Wikipedia*. November 24, 2019. https://en.wikipedia.org/wiki/Treaty_of_Tripoli.

Wikipedia contributors. "William Channing Woodbridge." *Wikipedia*. February 22, 2019. https://en.wikipedia.org/wiki/William_Channing_Woodbridge.

Williams, Joe. *Cheating Our Kids—How Politics and Greed Ruin Education*. New York: Palgrave Macmillan, 2005.

Wolfson, Andrew. "Judge candidate sues to run openly as a Republican." *Courier-Journal*, July 11, 2014. https://www.courier-journal.com/story/news/local/2014/07/11/lawsuit-challenges-non-partisan-judicial-races/12546173/.

Woodall, Martha. "Former Cayuga Elementary principal sentenced to 10 years' probation in test cheating scandal." *Philadelphia Inquirer,* July 11, 2016.

Woodbury, Sarah. "Literacy in the Middle Ages." *Sarah Woodbury website.* Accessed June 3, 2019. http://www.sarahwoodbury.com/literacy-in-the-middle-ages/.

Wright, Jonathan. *God's Soldiers: History of Jesuits.* New York: Doubleday, 2004.

Wright, Patrick J., "Public-Sector Bargaining Privileges Are Not Inalienable Rights." *Mackinac Center for Public Policy,* Midland, MI, March 11, 2011. https://www.mackinac.org/14734.

Yahoo Answers service. "European literacy rates." https://answers.yahoo.com/question/.

Yardley, Jonathan. "The complex Thomas Jefferson in his place and time." *Washington Post,* May 12, 2017, Opinion Section.

Zinn, Howard. *A People's History of the United States.* New York: HarperPerennial, 2015.

Zolfagharifard, Ellie. "Artificial intelligence 'could be the worst thing to happen to humanity': Stephen Hawking warns that rise of robots may be disastrous for mankind." *Daily Mail,* May 2, 2014. https://www.dailymail.co.uk/sciencetech/article-2618434/Artificial-intelligence-worst-thing-happen-humanity-Stephen-Hawking-warns-rise-robots-disastrous-mankind.html.

Index

www.ingramcontent.com/pod-product-compliance
Lightning Source LLC
Chambersburg PA
CBHW081105050426
R18088400001B/R180884PG42334CBX00002B/1